Regional Economy of India

Regional Economy of India

Growth and Finance

Editor
Deepak Mohanty

ACADEMIC FOUNDATION
NEW DELHI

www.academicfoundation.com

भारतीय रिज़र्व बैंक
RESERVE BANK OF INDIA
www.rbi.org.in

First published in 2012
by

ACADEMIC FOUNDATION
4772-73 / 23 Bharat Ram Road, (23 Ansari Road),
Darya Ganj, New Delhi - 110 002 (India).
Phones : 23245001 / 02 / 03 / 04.
Fax : +91-11-23245005.
E-mail : books@academicfoundation.com
www. academicfoundation.com

in association with:

Reserve Bank of India
Central Office Building,
Shahid Bhagat Singh Marg, Mumbai - 400 001.
Tel: 022 - 2260 1000
Fax: 022 - 2266 0358
E-mail: helpdoc@rbi.org.in
www.rbi.org.in

Cataloging in Publication Data--DK
Courtesy: D.K. Agencies (P) Ltd. <docinfo@dkagencies.com>

Regional economy of India : growth and finance / editor, Deepak Mohanty.
p. Cm.
ISBN 13: 9788171889235
ISBN 10: 8171889239

1. Regional economics--India. 2. India--Economic conditions--Regional disparities. 3. Banks and banking--India. 4. Finance--India. 5. Monetary policy--India. I. Mohanty, Deepak. II. Reserve Bank of India.

DDC 338.954 23

Typeset by Italics India, New Delhi.
Printed and bound in India.

Contents

Section I

Growth and Inflation

Section II

Banking and Finance

Section III

Financial Inclusion

Section IV

Structural Issues

List of Tables and Figures

Tables

Figures

Foreword

An unexamined life is not worth living, said the famous Greek philosopher, Socrates. I think writing a research paper is also an examination, *albeit*, of issues that touch the lives of individuals and shapes institutions. In the developmental context, an important dimension of inclusive growth is regional economic development. Viewed from this perspective, research on regional issues is critical.

In the context of the recent global economic crisis, regional growth strategies and issues have gained prominence on the macroeconomic policy agenda not only in emerging market economies but also in several developed economies. Renewed interest in regional economies arises due to three possible reasons. First, disparities both across and within regions in the country have widened over the years. Second, economic growth is increasingly being driven by the higher productivity of firms and workers concentrated around a small number of regional clusters. Third, closer integration of regions driven by technology has shrunk human as well as geographical distances, but economic distance is widening.

The Reserve Bank of India has a long history of carrying out policy oriented research in the spheres of macroeconomics and financial systems. For sustained inclusive economic growth at the national level, understanding regional dimensions is very important. Going by the need to 'think global but act local', economists in regional offices of the Reserve Bank have taken this initiative to disseminate their research to a larger audience through this book *Regional Economy of India: Growth and Finance*.

My compliments to all the authors, who under the guidance of Regional Economy Monitoring Division (REMD), DEPR have put in hard work to bring out this publication. In particular, I appreciate efforts of

K.U.B. Rao, Adviser, R. Kausaliya, Director and P.K. Nayak, Assistant Adviser.

My compliments also to Subir Gokarn, Deputy Governor for his leadership in promoting research on regional issues. I commend Deepak Mohanty, Executive Director for editing the volume. I hope and believe this book will provoke further research on regional economy.

Duvvuri Subbarao
Governor
Reserve Bank of India

Preface

Ultimately, the performance of the Indian economy depends on how each of its regions is doing. Understanding the drivers of growth at a regional level is, therefore, crucial for effective policy formulation. Differences in income levels across regions, if sustained over time, may have significant implications for the economy and politics of the country.

From this perspective, the collection of research articles being presented in this volume reflects the priority that the Department of Economic and Policy Research places on regional economic forces in India. Using a multidisciplinary approach, this book encompasses a wide range of topics such as, growth and inflation, banking and finance, financial inclusion, and structural issues. Based on specific characteristics of various regions, it provides rich insights into the regional development experiences, which help deepen the Reserve Bank's understanding of them both from analytical and operational viewpoints.

I commend all the authors who worked hard under the guidance of K.U.B. Rao, Adviser and the overall supervision of R.Kausaliya,Director to bring out this book. The painstaking efforts of P.K. Nayak, Assistant Adviser, who coordinated the project of bringing out this volume, need special mention. I also appreciate the editing of this volume by Deepak Mohanty, Executive Director.

This volume is an important research initiative on regional issues and also makes useful contributions from the perspective of financial development. I hope that it will be a significant contribution to understanding regional economic dynamics in India. It is really the first step in an important long-term research agenda for the Reserve Bank.

Subir Gokarn
Deputy Governor
Reserve Bank of India

Regional Economy of India

Growth and Finance

DEEPAK MOHANTY

Introduction

Macroeconomic management and policy formulation in a vast country like India requires sound knowledge of the micro-regional dimensions of the economy. Diversities among regions are significant in terms of topography, climatic conditions, natural resources and demographic characteristics. More importantly, there are also differences in terms of infrastructure, configuration of industry, presence of financial institutions, structure of governance and policies of sub-national governments. The need for regional perspective, therefore, becomes important in economic policy formulation.

Regional economic input constitutes an important information base for the central banks in various countries. For example, the Federal Reserve Bank in its 'Beige Book' collects anecdotal information on current economic conditions in the regions covering developments in agriculture, manufacturing, transportation, real estate, banking and finance, employment, wages, prices and consumer spending. This is prepared based on reports from banks, interviews with key business contacts, economists, market experts and other sources. The Reserve Bank of India (RBI) captures information on developments in the regional economy through a number of surveys, which are largely based on the perceptions of the respondents. While these have their own utility in providing quick assessment of the economic conditions, analytical studies are required for effective policy formulation.

Given the regional divergence in financial developments and inflation, studies on regional economies become particularly relevant for the RBI. While the RBI conducts specific studies on regional economy, the process has largely been internal. This volume makes an attempt to place in public domain select papers by economists working in the regional offices of the economic research department of the RBI on various aspects of the regional economy. The papers have been grouped under four major themes taking into account the broad similarity of the issues covered, although some of the papers delve into a variety of issues cutting across the themes. The themes are: (i) growth and inflation; (ii) banking and finance; (iii) financial inclusion and (iv) structural issues.

Growth and Inflation

The growth rate of India's GDP improved significantly in the post-1991 reform period. However, there are wide variations in the growth performance across regions and across sectors. This has raised questions about the sustainability and inclusiveness of economic growth. Further, in the recent period, following the global economic crisis of 2008, the balance between growth and inflation has been central to the discourse on macroeconomic management. The supply-side factors affecting the output of agricultural commodities have assumed greater significance in the analytics of inflation. States are important stakeholders in inflation management as their contribution is important in addressing the supply-side constraints. They could, for instance, help better management of public distribution system (PDS), improve productivity in agriculture and allied activities, reform the Agriculture Produce Marketing Committee (APMC) Acts and improve the infrastructure, such as, storage facilities.[1]

There are five papers centring around this theme, which contain detailed analyses on the rate and pattern of regional economic growth. The paper *Inclusive Growth and its Regional Dimension* by P.K. Nayak, Sadhan Kumar Chattopadhyay, Arun Vishnu Kumar and V. Dhanya (NCKD) focusses on the inclusiveness of macroeconomic growth. Apart from the analyses on the sectoral and regional pattern of economic growth, this paper also looks into other parameters of inclusiveness, such as, male-female literacy gap and infant mortality rates across the states/UTs. The paper also presents comparative analyses on the rural-urban population,

1. Dr D. Subbarao, Governor, Reserve Bank of India, Speech at the State Finance Secretaries conference held on May 24, 2011, Mumbai.

rural health care, gender disparity and poverty and unemployment in India relative to other countries.

The analysis of sectoral growth using all-India data for the past six decades in the NCKD paper reveals that the growth rate in agriculture has been the lowest and the most volatile; the growth in industry exhibited less variability and the growth in services improved sharply. Given the continued dependence of a large section of the population on agriculture, this pattern of growth, has adverse implications for inclusive growth. The analysis of financial penetration presented in the paper also shows that the distribution of bank credit has been uneven across the sectors and regions. For making the growth more inclusive, the paper emphasises on the need for faster growth of agriculture and greater absorption of labour in the manufacturing sector. NCKD emphasise on innovations in products and services to improve their affordability for the common man. The paper also highlights the need for expansion in social security scheme for unorganised workers and greater devolution of power to Panchayati Raj Institutions (PRIs) and urban local bodies (ULBs).

The decadal analysis of growth in the paper reveals that the disparity in the rate of NSDP growth across the states as measured by the coefficient of variation (CV), which increased to 32.4 per cent during the 1990s from 27.2 per cent in the 1980s, has declined to 21.1 per cent during 2000s. The analyses on per capita income revealed similar pattern: the CV, which increased from 48.0 per cent in the 1980s to 53.5 per cent in the 1990s declined to 26.3 per cent during the 2000s. These findings are in line with the assessment of the Planning Commission, which suggests that interstate disparity in income growth has declined in recent years. The Draft Approach Paper to the Twelfth Plan observed: 'several of the economically weaker states have demonstrated improvement in their growth rates...no state has averaged GSDP growth of less than 6 per cent during the Eleventh Plan period'. Notwithstanding these favourable developments, the NCKD paper finds increase in inequality over time based on the computed Gini coefficient: in terms of the actual per capita income of 22 states, the Gini coefficient has increased over the years from 0.164 in 1980-81 to 0.245 in 2007-08. The paper also provides evidence on increase in inequality based on Gini coefficients for the per capita consumption expenditure in urban areas.

It is generally believed that financial development contributes to economic growth by creating the enabling conditions, although the direction of causality between the two remains a debatable proposition. The econometric results of NCKD paper show evidence on the existence of long-term relation between per capita GDP, investment ratio and financial development in the Indian economy. The results also support the hypothesis that institutional finance leads to economic growth in India. This underscores the importance of bank credit in financing private investment in India.

The econometric analysis of V. Dhanya in the paper *Impact of Bank Credit on Growth Dynamics of Kerala* shows positive relationship between bank credit and economic growth in Kerala at the aggregate level, both in the long run as well as in the short run. However, the paper does not find significant relationship between output and bank credit at the sectoral level, even though the pattern of credit deployment in Kerala across the sectors compares well with the sectoral pattern of growth in the state. The study indicates that Kerala has witnessed significant structural changes recently with sectors like construction, real estate, transport, storage and communication playing an important role. Overall, the economy continues to be in consumption mode as the demand for most of the producer services were met from neighbouring state. The analysis of credit deployment also revealed similar trend with personal loan occupying nearly 40 per cent of total advances.

The recent acceleration of growth has also given rise to concerns regarding the increase in the inflationary pressure. An analysis of regional inflation in the paper *Determinants of Inflation in Tamil Nadu* by K. Jayanthi Anand shows that the average inflation during second half of the 2000s for the southern states *viz.*, Tamil Nadu, Andhra Pradesh, Karnataka and Kerala was higher as compared with the first half reflecting a combination of both structural and temporary factors. The study found that the moderation of inflation in Tamil Nadu is the reason for the divergence in movement of inflation in the state *vis-à-vis* all-India. Sustained rapid growth in incomes has changed the consumption patterns both in the rural as well as urban areas and is one of the main structural factors behind the food inflation in India. Higher incomes have led to greater demand for conventional and new goods, of either a better quality or of a different nature.

Development of northeastern states (NES) has been high on the agenda of the Centre and the state governments. To accelerate the pace of growth in NES, Deepak Mohanty in his paper on *Economic and Financial Developments in Northeastern States* has emphasised the need to scale up investment in infrastructure through public-private partnership (PPP) model, encourage agro-based industries, improve market access for agriculture and industrial products and increase the penetration of the formal financial sector.

Rajiv Lochan in his paper *Inter-District Growth Performance in Madhya Pradesh* finds that the differences in the growth rates across districts within Madhya Pradesh have widened over the years. Lochan attributes this disparity to excessive dependence of some districts on the primary sector. The study also shows strong correlation between agricultural output and net credit outstanding in most districts. This is an issue which has been recognised in the Draft Approach Paper to the Twelfth Plan which observes that 'while the economically weaker states are catching up in growth rates, there is growing concern about the backwardness of individual districts...'. Lochan emphasises the importance of increasing agricultural output through better access to bank credit.

Banking and Finance

The expansion of banking services, particularly, in the rural and unbanked areas of the country remains a policy priority. The outreach of banking services to every household in India requires concerted and coordinated effort by all stakeholders of the society facilitated by technological developments. The paper on *Microfinance in India: Progress and Problems* by J.S. Moses, Raj Rajesh, Gopal Prasad, Neeraj Kumar and Naveen Kumar (MRPKK) addresses various issues relating to microfinance. The microfinance sector has demonstrated that it is possible to provide cost-effective and tailor-made financial services to the poor. The paper observes that the pattern of development of the microfinance sector in the country has been highly skewed as poorer regions remain underserved. The paper concludes that despite the significant progress of microfinance in

India, it still has a long way to go in furthering its social objective of fostering financial inclusion among the deprived and poorer sections of the society. In this context, the paper emphasises the need for policy intervention to provide both demand and supply-side impetus to the microfinance sector in the country.

The paper on *Regional Dimensions of Banking Services* by V.K. Srivastava, A.K. Shukla, Rajiv Lochan and John Guria (SSLG) judges financial inclusion using a single parameter of availability of savings bank account. The paper finds huge disparity in this regard in terms of indicators, such as, population per branch and number of savings and credit account as per cent to population. The paper observes that the southern region has the best banking facilities. However, banking outreach is highly inadequate in northeastern, central and eastern regions of the country. The paper finds that the regional disparity in the outreach of banking services has increased during the period 1996-2008. This has affected the growth of unorganised manufacturing enterprises and services enterprises which are facing capital shortage as their biggest challenge. The paper, however, notes that the measures taken by the Government of India and the RBI have helped in accelerating the process of financial inclusion. The paper reports the results of a survey conducted in four cities (*viz.*, Ahmedabad, Bhopal, Jammu and Lucknow) which showed that the dependence on informal sources of finance is generally low, except in Ahmedabad.

The paper titled *Bank Finance in the Development of Real Estate Sector in Bihar* by Raj Rajesh looks into the developments in real estate sector in Bihar and examines its linkage with bank credit. Rajesh finds that prices of commercial as well as residential properties in Bihar in the recent years exhibited an upswing following improvement in law and order and governance in the state that has given a big push to the pent-up demand for real estate. The paper also finds that in the recent years, there has been a substantial growth in housing loans extended by the commercial banks in the state reflecting the fact that bank finance played a facilitating role in propping up the real estate market in the state.

The paper on *A Disaggregated Analysis of Monetary Transmission Mechanism: Evidence from the Dispersion of Bank Credit to Indian States* by Sarat Dhal evaluates the impact of monetary policy on the dispersion of credit to the states in the presence of some state-specific explanatory variables and the level of lendable resources of the banking sector, taking into account the role of key demand and supply-side factors affecting the loan market. Empirical exercises, based on pooled cross-section regression analysis, support asymmetry in the credit and bank lending channel of transmission mechanism. The study finds that monetary policy induced impact on credit dispersion could be different across rich and poor states. At the same time, economic progress, infrastructure development and scope for commercial activities could significantly influence the dispersion of bank credit across the states.

Financial Inclusion

Lack of access to formal financial services of a vast majority of the households is a matter of serious concern. The Government and the RBI have taken a series of measures to remedy the situation. Assessment of the impact of such measures and quantification of the extent of financial inclusion in various states and union territories (UTs) is crucial for the appropriate design of future policies concerning the financial sector.

There are three papers on this topic. Of these, two papers—one by John V. Guria and the other by Sadhan Kumar Chattopadhyay—have used composite indices to quantify the extent of financial inclusion across regions (states/UTs and districts). The other paper by Dhanya uses a number of indicators to provide a comparative assessment of the extent of financial inclusion in Kerala.

Guria in his paper on *Financial Inclusion in Jammu and Kashmir* analyses the status and progress of financial inclusion in India with special reference to Jammu and Kashmir. This paper has also constructed a financial inclusion index (FII) covering various dimensions of financial inclusion for all states/UTs in India and then for all the districts of Jammu and Kashmir. This exercise places Chandigarh, Delhi and Goa in the category of high/medium financial inclusion. Jammu and Kashmir is classified in the category of very low financial inclusion. Within the state, however, three districts (*viz.*, Srinagar, Jammu and Leh) are in the high/medium categories while the remaining presently existing 19 districts are grouped under low or very low financial inclusion categories.

Chattopadhyay in his paper on *Financial Inclusion in West Bengal* measured the extent of financial inclusion across states, using an index of financial inclusion (IFI). He observes that although there has been improvement in outreach activity in the banking sector, heterogeneity across states has been widespread. While significant improvement has taken place in credit/loan account in the urban households, the situation has become worse for the rural households. The paper finds that Kerala leads with the highest value of IFI followed by Maharashtra and Karnataka. As regards West Bengal, the survey results revealed that the moneylenders accounted for two-thirds of the rural finance, despite the wide presence of banks. The paper argues that only the supply side factors cannot achieve financial inclusion; the demand-side factors are equally important.

Kerala's success in financial inclusion, according to Dhanya's paper on *Financial Inclusion in Kerala*, has to be viewed as a natural extension of the social and cultural inclusion. Kerala traditionally had a system of health and educational institutions, which were made accessible even to the lower strata of the society. Further, Kerala had high physical access to banking in terms of bank branches. This was facilitated historically by its trade relations with external world which fostered banking in the state. Later on, outmigration of the Keralites also played a role in facilitating financial inclusion in the state. The cooperative sector with the large nucleus of cooperative banks and primary agricultural credit societies (PACSs) facilitated the provision of banking services to the poor. The institutional interventions made by the Government in the form of *Kudumbashree*, the state run poverty eradication programme, and the payments of National Rural Employment Guarantee Act (NREGA) wages through banks also helped improving the financial inclusion in the state. The results of a survey conducted in four districts of Kerala reveal the importance of SHGs, NREGA, cooperative structure and general awareness as the determining factors of financial inclusion in the state. The high awareness among the people made it possible to better appreciate and assimilate the various financial inclusion initiatives.

Structural Issues

There are five papers examining structural drivers of growth across states. Naveen Kumar in the paper on *Structural Transformation in Punjab*

Economy discusses about the unique features of the economy of Punjab with a relatively high share of agriculture, which is double than that of the national average. The study highlighted structural transformation of the Punjab economy in the last three decades, especially in response to the forces of liberalisation and globalisation during post-reform era. The key concern emerging in the agriculture sector has been the fact that yield levels of principal crops in Punjab have reached a plateau. According to the study, diversification could be the answer to make agriculture more productive and value-rich but would require fundamental changes in incentives, institutions and investments in the state. The paper finds that services sector is steadily gaining ground providing some stimulus to the growth of the state economy. The study argues that Punjab needs to reposition itself in line with the requirements of the new economy to strengthen its economic structure.

The budgetary operations of the state governments, in particular, the structure and composition of the expenditure, have significant implications for the rate and pattern of economic growth in various ways. The differences in the pattern of social sector expenditure, the factors affecting the spending capacity of the states and the impact of such spending on the well-being of the people have been the subject matter of intense debate amongst research scholars and policymakers. The paper on *Social Sector Expenditure across States* by Avdhesh Kumar Shukla analyses the pattern of social sector expenditure of the governments of 16 major states. His paper makes a distinction between the 'developed' and the 'underdeveloped' states and observes that the social sector expenditure as percentage of the aggregate expenditure (SSE-AE) of the developed states displayed convergence during the second half of 2000s. On the other hand, in the case of the underdeveloped states, the divergence in the SSE-AE increased.

The paper, however, observes that the underdeveloped states are spending more in terms of social sector expenditure as percentage of aggregate expenditure as well as GSDP. However, the underdeveloped states are constrained by the low level of revenue resources and their spending capacity on social sector is significantly less *vis-à-vis* the developed states. Though the successive Finance Commissions have given special emphasis to fill the gap in availability of various social services in different states by recommending grant-in-aid of revenue to backward states, these resources were not sufficient to fill this gap. The study underscores the need for reprioritisation of the expenditure by the states giving preference to various public and merit goods for bring about improvement in the human resources.

Jayanta Kumar Mallik and Monika Kathuria in their paper on *Issues in Services Sector: A Case Study of Delhi* address the issue of sustainability of growth drawing on a case study of Delhi where the rate of economic growth has been relatively faster and the services sector has been the main contributor. The paper finds that the share of services in employment in Delhi is fairly close to its share in output unlike the gap between the relative shares in output and employment of this sector observed at the all-India level.

The paper on *Regional Dimensions of Realty Sector in India* by R. Kausaliya and Suraj S. captures regional dimensions of the trends in the realty sector across the major states of India during the period 1999-2009, as this phase was marked by strong growth ever experienced by the Indian economy. The study observed that the change in the structural composition of growth witnessed across the states was characterised by the decline of the primary sector and increase of the service sector with a greater convergence in the growth in per capita income. Increasing per capita income raised demand for housing credit, which in turn accelerated the real estate business activity across the states. This was reflected in the increased share of states' revenue from registration and stamp duties. Concomitantly, the share of realty sector to GSDP also showed a rise in the regional economic growth. The empirical results show the increased role of credit availability in determining the demand for housing credit across the states.

The decade of 1990s witnessed the transition towards market orientation and transparent practices of domestic debt both at the Central and state levels. In this direction, state governments have generally put in place institutional mechanisms to contain the level of debt, also to bring it to a sustainable level by way of the enactment of fiscal responsibility legislations (FRLs), setting up of consolidated sinking funds (CSFs), guarantee redemption funds (GRFs) and placing ceiling on guarantees. In this context, the paper on *Debt Management Strategies in Uttar Pradesh and Uttarakhand* by Vineet Kumar Srivastava reviews fiscal reform and debt management strategies in Uttar Pradesh and Uttarakhand. These two states have moved towards achieving the target fixed under their Fiscal Responsibility Acts of containing fiscal deficit to 3.0 per cent of GSDP as also revenue deficit to zero. The excessive payouts under the Sixth Pay Commission put pressure on the fiscal deficits of these states. However, deficits and debts of these states have started showing signs of improvement. Both the states need to further continue with the reform processes and improve debt management strategies to enhance their fiscal sustainability.

Conclusion

The collection of the papers in the volume focuses on both macro- and micro-regional dimensions of development in India. While a number of papers included in this volume bring out the specific nature of economic activity in some of the states, there are some common threads from which broad lessons can be drawn.

First, the growth acceleration of the 2000s was accompanied by a significant shrinkage of the share of the agricultural sector with a corresponding increase in the share of the services sector. Even in agriculturally leading states such as Punjab, agricultural growth and productivity stagnated. Therefore, there is a need for focused attention on agriculture so that it does not become a serious constraint on growth through reduced food supplies and high food inflation.

Second, industrial development has been uneven and industrial growth more volatile across states. Policies at the state level have played no less an important role in location of industries. This calls for special attention on industrial climate at the state level with greater thrust on improving infrastructural developments.

Third, growth impulses were broad-based across states. However, urban-rural inequality has worsened and the gap between developed and underdeveloped districts within the states has widened. Therefore, there is a need for special attention both at national level and state level as also at the level of underdeveloped districts.

Fourth, prioritisation of expenditure at the state level towards social sector could play a major role in developing the quality of the labour force thereby contributing significantly to overall growth and well-being.

Fifth, organised finance has played a lead role in economic development. It has been quite pronounced in the development of the housing sector. However, financial penetration shows wide disparity in the outreach of banking services across regions underscoring the need for further efforts to bring about substantial improvements.

Sixth, the Draft Approach Paper to the Twelfth Plan (2012-2017) envisages 'faster, sustainable and more inclusive growth' of 9 per cent per annum. The attainment of the higher growth would necessitate greater focus on sectoral composition and regional dimension of growth.

I commend the authors for their research which enhances our understanding of regional dimensions of development and finance. I appreciate the efforts of K.U.B. Rao, Adviser, R. Kausaliya, Director and P.K. Nayak, Assistant Adviser, in coordinating the publication of this book.

I thank the Governor, Dr Duvvuri Subbarao and Deputy Governor, Dr Subir Gokarn for their encouragement in bringing out this volume. Thanks are due to Sona Kapila, Academic Foundation for evincing keen interest in the publication of this book.

I trust this volume will stimulate debate and further research on regional issues and draw the attention of policymakers both at sub-national and national level to focus on multifarious developmental challenges raised by the authors.

Section I

Growth and Inflation

1

Inclusive Growth and its Regional Dimension

P.K. NAYAK, S.K. CHATTOPADHYAY, ARUN VISHNU KUMAR and V. DHANYA[1]

I

Introduction

Indian economy has registered an impressive growth in the post-1991 reform period. However, there are wide variations in the growth performance across regions, sectors and sections of population. This has raised serious questions about the sustainability and inclusiveness of economic growth. The less effective the growth process in creating jobs, both in terms of numbers and quality, the greater is the political threat and, consequently, the less sustainable the growth process itself (Gokarn, 2010).While some level of growth is obviously a necessary condition for sustained poverty reduction, there is an increasingly unanimous view that growth by itself is not a sufficient condition for eradicating poverty (Ali and Son, 2007). It is argued that growth could marginalise the poorer sections and increase inequality. High and rising levels of inequality can hinder poverty reduction, which in turn, can slow down the growth process. One important indication of inadequate inclusion in India is that poverty reduction has been muted in the last decade even with rising growth. The poverty rate has declined by less than 1 per cent per annum over the past decade, markedly below trends in neighbouring countries such as Nepal and Bangladesh where both average income levels and growth are lower (World Bank, 2007).

1. The views expressed in this paper are of the authors and not of the organisation they are working with.

The concept of inclusive growth has gained wide importance in several countries including India. The Approach Paper of the Eleventh Five Year Plan provides 'an opportunity to restructure policies to achieve a new vision based on faster, more broad-based and inclusive growth. It is designed to reduce poverty and focuses on bringing down the various divides that continue to fragment our society' [GoI, 2006: 1]. While the Indian economy has come a long way from the 'Hindu rate of growth', achieving broad-based improvement in living standards continues to be the ultimate goal. It is argued that 'rapid, sustained and inclusive growth will take place when large numbers of people move from low-productivity jobs to high-productivity ones' (Gokarn, 2010). For this to happen, the growth must be inclusive in the broadest sense. And it must be spread across all states and not just limited to some. It must generate sufficient volumes of high quality employment to provide the means for uplifting large numbers of our population from the low income-low quality occupations in which too many of them have been traditionally locked. While the need for inclusive growth is stressed, it is to be seen, whether it is the inadequate growth of certain sectors like agriculture or the inability of certain groups like SC/STs to form part of the growth process or the lack of both physical and financial infrastructure that pull back the particular regions/sections from enjoying the economic growth. It is possible that a combination of all these factors is preventing certain sections/areas to be out of the growth process. The inter-linkages between different development indicators and growth in the context of various regions and sections need to be analysed to understand the nuances of India's growth process. In this context, a study on regional perspectives of inclusive growth is of utmost importance.

With this backdrop, the paper is organised as follows. Section II analyses the interstate growth performance. Here we look into the growth of net state domestic product and per capita income from 1950-51 onwards. We also examine the sectoral contributions of economic growth across different states. Section III discusses the socioeconomic factors which are important from the perspective of inclusive growth. Section IV deals with relationship between finance and growth. It also highlights state-wise, sector-wise allocation of credit over the years. Section V concludes the paper.

II

Economic Growth: Spatial and Temporal Analysis

During the three decades 1950s to 1980s, the Indian economy was witnessing so-called 'Hindu' rate of growth and the major concern was accelerated growth apart from ensuring equity.

While the growth rate of the Indian economy has been increasing in recent times, one phenomenon which was observed was that the growth performance of the three major sectors of the economy, namely, agriculture, industry and services, has been diverse. The growth in the agriculture sector has been the most volatile and also the least among the three sectors most of the times. While the growth in the industrial sector has remained more or less constant, growth rate in the services sector has risen sharply (Figure 1.1).

Figure 1.1

Annual Growth Rate of the Major Sectors

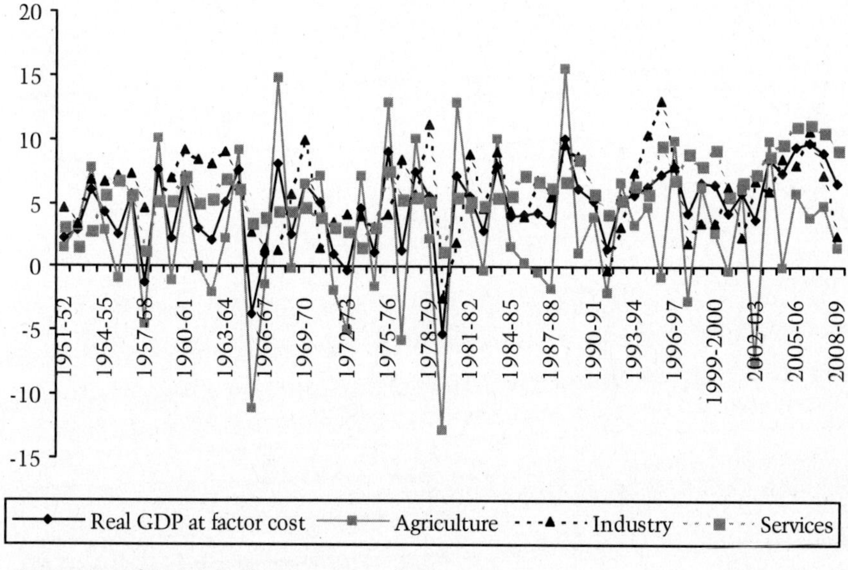

Source: Central Statistical Office, Government of India.

The diverse growth rate in the three sectors has resulted in structural change in the contribution of the sectors in the total GDP. The share of the agriculture sector in the overall GDP has declined more or less consistently since Independence from 55.3 per cent in 1950-51 to 17 per cent in 2008-2009. The share of the industrial sector has increased from 10.6 per cent in 1950-51 to about 19 per cent in 2008-09. The share of the services sector has nearly doubled from 34.1 per cent in 1950-51 to 64.5 per cent in 2008-2009 (Figure 1.2).

Figure 1.2

Share of Sectors in the Real GDP

Source: Central Statistical Office, Government of India.

Since a large section of the population continues to be dependent on the agriculture sector, directly or indirectly, this has serious implications for 'inclusiveness'. One major factor that has contributed to the decline in share of agriculture is the decline in public investment. In fact, the public investment in agriculture in real terms has witnessed steady decline from the Sixth Five Year Plan (1980-1985) to the Tenth Five Year Plan (2002-2007). It has consistently declined in real terms (at 1999-2000 prices) from Rs 64,012 crore in Sixth Plan to Rs 42,226 crore during the Ninth Five Year Plan (1997-2002). However, during the Tenth Plan, this has increased in absolute terms to Rs 67,260 crore. It can also be observed that the public investment has gone down over the year, while private investment remained stagnant.

Declining investment in the agriculture sector had a direct bearing on the productivity of food grains in the country. Although average yield/hectare (productivity) of food grains in India has increased over the years, the productivity is low compared to many other developing countries.

As per the World Bank database, in respect of cereal productivity, India remained far below China, Indonesia, Sri Lanka and Thailand (Table 1.1).

Table 1.1

Cereal Productivity

(Kg/hectare)

Country	*1980*	*1985*	*1990*	*1995*	*2000*	*2005*	*2006*	*2007*	*2008*
Brazil	1575.7	1827.7	1755	2513.1	2660.6	2882.5	3210.5	3553.1	3828.8
China	2948.7	3827.7	4322.7	4663.7	4756.3	5225.5	5313.3	5315.3	5535.3
Egypt	4094.4	4539.1	5702.9	5903.7	7280	7569.2	7541	7562.2	7506.4
Indonesia	2865.6	3513.3	3800.2	3842.7	4026.3	4311.3	4365.8	4464.7	4694.2
Poland	2336.8	2893.5	3283.7	3022.3	2534.7	3233	2598.2	3249.5	3217.2
Russia	NA	NA	NA	1223.5	1563.3	1860.1	1894.4	1994.9	2388.1
Sri Lanka	2501	2960.5	2965	3052.6	3338.1	3467.1	3619.4	3821.6	3659.8
Thailand	1911	2125.4	2009	2507.4	2719.1	3001.5	2963	3043.7	3013.7
Turkey	1855.1	1931	2214.1	2037.8	2311	2624.2	2661.9	2381.4	2601.2
Vietnam	2016.1	2691.7	3072.9	3569.9	4112.3	4726.1	4749.7	4833.6	5064.2
India	1350	1592.2	1891.2	2111.7	2293.5	2411.5	2455.6	2618.6	2647.2

Note : NA: Not Available.
Source : *http://data.worldbank.org/indicator/AG.YLD.CREL.KG*

Interstate Comparisons of Growth Performance

In regard to interstate comparison of growth performance, it can be observed from the Table 1.2 that there is a wide disparity in growth performance in the three time periods (*viz.*, 1980-81 to 1989-90, 1990-91 to 1999-2000 and 2000-01 to 2009-10), though the disparity has come down in the last period. However, during the nineties, disparity was high as revealed from the coefficient of variation (CV) at 32.4 per cent. The CV has increased from 27.2 per cent during the eighties to 32.4 per cent in the nineties. However, there was a decline in disparity during the last period where the CV came down to 21.1 per cent.

Table 1.2

State-wise, Period-wise Compound Growth Rate of NSDP

(Estimated Compounded Growth Rate of NSDP of Each State at Different Time Periods)

States	1980-81 to 1989-90		1990-91 to 1999-2000		2000-01 to 2009-10	
	Growth Rate	Rank	Growth Rate	Rank	Growth Rate	Rank
Gujarat	4.8	12	8.0	2	10.5	1
Chhattisgarh	—	—	2.5	25	10.0	2
Uttarakhand	—	—	2.6	24	9.9	3
Maharashtra	5.6	5	6.9	5	9.5	4
Orissa	4.8	14	4.0	22	9.3	5
Haryana	6.3	3	4.7	17	9.3	6
Kerala	2.6	22	5.9	12	8.6	7
Goa	5.2	9	8.4	1	8.4	8
Nagaland	7.5	2	5.6	13	8.4	9
Bihar	4.7	16	2.0	27	8.3	10
Andhra Pradesh	5.3	7	5.3	16	8.0	11
Jharkhand	—	—	6.5	8	8.0	12
Tamil Nadu	5.0	11	6.4	9	7.9	13
Sikkim	NA	NA	6.3	10	7.8	14
Arunachal Pradesh	8.1	1	4.6	20	7.7	15
Karnataka	5.3	8	7.1	4	7.6	16
Rajasthan	5.9	4	6.5	7	7.6	17
Tripura	5.0	10	7.3	3	7.5	18
Himachal Pradesh	4.5	18	6.2	11	6.8	19
West Bengal	4.6	17	6.9	6	6.6	20
Meghalaya	4.4	19	5.5	15	6.6	21
Manipur	4.8	13	4.7	18	5.8	22
Uttar Pradesh	4.8	15	3.6	23	5.6	23
Jammu & Kashmir	2.0	23	4.7	19	5.5	24
Punjab	5.4	6	4.4	21	5.4	25
Assam	3.3	21	2.2	26	5.1	26
Madhya Pradesh	3.6	20	5.6	14	4.5	27

Note : NA: Not Available. — Not Applicable.

Source: Authors' own calculation by using semi-logarithmic trend.

The period (i.e., 2000-01 to 2009-10) also witnessed high growth rates across the states where all states, with the exception of Madhya Pradesh, recorded growth of more than 5.0 per cent and 12 states recorded growth of above 8.0 per cent. This is further revealed from the average growth rate of 7.6 per cent registered during 2000-01 to 2009-10 compared to 4.9 per cent and 5.3 per cent, recorded during the first two periods, respectively. Further, certain states like Kerala, Uttarakhand, Orissa and Nagaland showed significant improvement during 2000-2009.

Thus, the NSDP figures show that the years since 2000 witnessed better inclusive growth than the previous periods. However, it is quite premature to presume that the latter years indicate inclusive growth. To probe further into the details, we look into the per capita NSDP figures which give a better indicator of standard of living compared to the states' average growth. Here again, it is noted that per capita income also has limited value in examining inclusive growth as it gives little revelation on the distribution of income across the population.

Figure 1.3 gives the distribution of per capita income across states. It shows that there is a wide disparity in per capita income across states with Bihar at the lowest and Goa at the top position. The CV is as high as 41.0 per cent.

Figure 1.3

Distribution of Per Capita NSDP in Rupees (Average of 2005-06 to 2009-10)

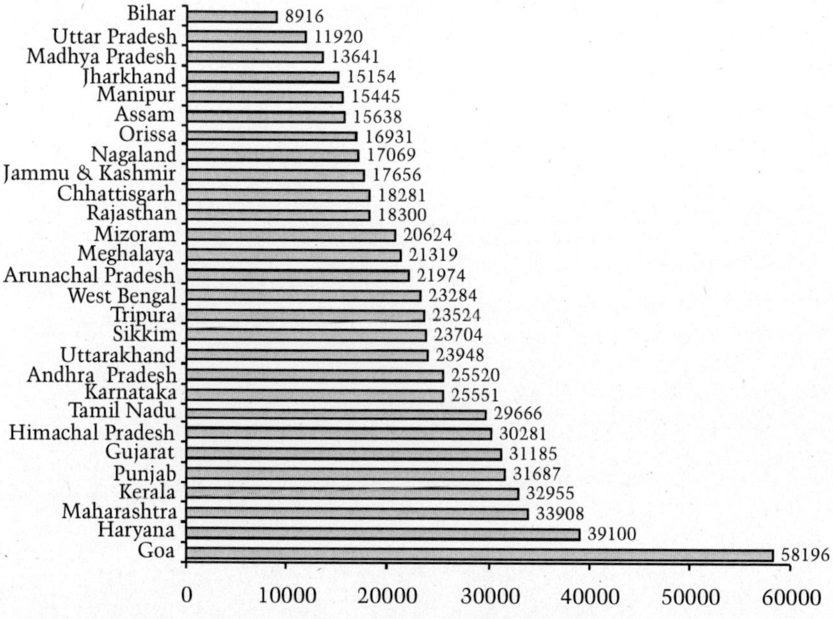

Source: Central Statistical Office, Government of India.

We further examine the inequality across the states in respect of per capita NSDP across the time periods. For Jammu & Kashmir (1980-81 to 1989-90), Bihar and Uttarakhand for 1990-91 to 1999-2000 and Nagaland for 1990-91 to 1999-2000 and 2000-01 to 2009-10, the figures came insignificant. The growth rates for the rest of the states are given in Table 1.3.

Table 1.3

State-wise, Period-wise Compound Growth Rate of Per Capita NSDP

States	*1980-81 to 1989-90*		*1990-91 to 1999-2000*		*2000-01 to 2009-10*	
	Growth Rate	*Rank*	*Growth Rate*	*Rank*	*Growth Rate*	*Rank*
Gujarat	2.8	12	6	2	9.0	1
Orissa	2.9	11	2.4	17	8.1	2
Kerala	1.1	21	4.8	7	7.9	3
Chhattisgarh	-	-	0.9	23	7.9	4
Uttarakhand	-	-	NS	-	7.5	5
Haryana	3.7	2	2.2	19	7.3	6
Maharashtra	3.2	8	4.7	8	7.1	7
Andhra Pradesh	3	10	3.8	12	6.9	8
Tamil Nadu	3.5	6	5.3	5	6.8	9
Sikkim	NA	-	3.4	14	6.6	10
Jharkhand	-	-	4.7	9	6.6	11
Bihar	2.5	14	NS	-	6.5	12
Karnataka	3.2	9	5.4	4	6.4	13
Goa	3.6	3	6.8	1	6.4	14
Tripura	2	18	5.4	3	6.1	15
Arunachal Pradesh	4.8	1	2.1	20	6.0	16
Rajasthan	3.2	7	4	11	5.6	17
West Bengal	2.3	16	5.1	6	5.5	18
Meghalaya	1.4	19	2.8	15	5.5	19
Himachal Pradesh	2.7	13	4.4	10	5.0	20
Jammu & Kashmir	NS	-	2	21	4.0	21
Manipur	2.1	17	2.3	18	4.0	22
Assam	1.1	22	0.3	25	3.6	23
Uttar Pradesh	2.4	15	1.3	22	3.6	24
Punjab	3.5	4	2.5	16	3.5	25
Madhya Pradesh	1.2	20	3.4	13	3.4	26
Nagaland	3.5	5	NS	-	NS	-

Notes: NA: Not Available. NS: Not Significant.

Source: Authors' own calculation by using semi-logarithmic trend.

Compared to NSDP, the disparity is higher in the case of per capita income. However, similar to NSDP, the 1990s witnessed higher disparity in per capita income which came down in 2000s. The CV increased from 48.0 per cent during the eighties to 53.5 per cent in the nineties before coming down to 26.3 per cent during the last period.

Though the inequality in terms of growth rates have come down in 2000s, inequality measured by Gini coefficient of the level variables, have shown an increase over the period. Gini coefficient has increased from 0.164 in 1980-81 to 0.245 in 2007-08 before reducing to 0.150 in 2009-10 (Figure 1.4). Gini coefficient has been calculated for 22 states omitting Chhattisgarh, Jharkhand, Uttarakhand, Mizoram, Sikkim and Nagaland due to non-availability of continuous data series.[2]

Figure 1.4

Gini Coefficient of State Per Capita NSDP

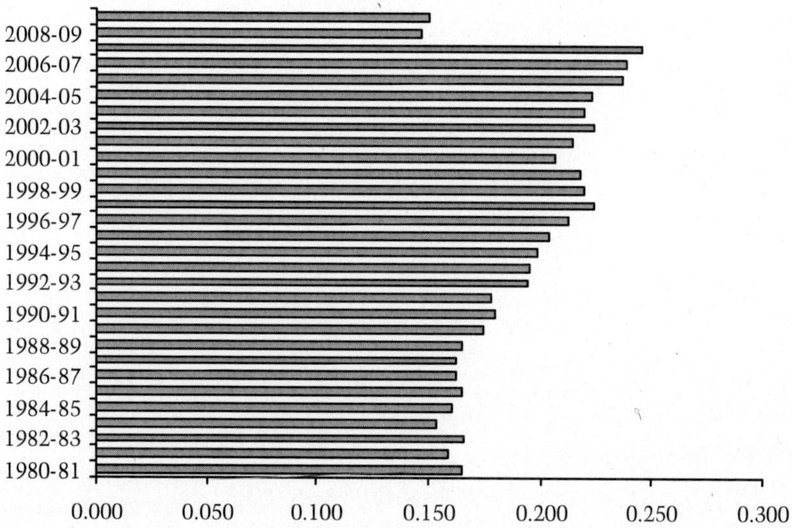

In general, growth rate of states has improved in the last time period with the exception of Madhya Pradesh and Punjab. Both the states showed dismal performance in case of growth in NSDP and per capita income. On the other hand, Kerala and Orissa showed significant improvement in the

2. The Gini coefficient is calculated using Deaton's formula:

$$G = \frac{N+1}{N-1} - \frac{2}{N(N-1)u}\left(\sum_{i=1}^{n} P_i X_i\right)$$

last decade, with Kerala registering tremendous improvement both in the growth and level of income. Orissa, which ranked 17 in terms of per capita income growth during the nineties, improved its position to the second in 2000-01 to 2009-10 (Table 1.3). However, in terms of the level of per capita income, it is still low at Rs 19,456.

Table 1.4 provides the share of each sector in NSDP across the three time periods. In most of the states, the share of primary sector has declined over the time period considered and tertiary sector showing an increase in share and secondary sector registering marginal or no increase.[3] However, Maharashtra which is often hailed as the industrial capital of India, witnessed a decline in the share of secondary sector and an increase in tertiary sector. In all the states, tertiary sector occupies the major share of NSDP which conforms to the earlier studies showing India's difference in development path with the general East Asian growth path (Bhattacharya and Mitra, 1990; Bhattacharya and Sakthivel, 2004).

Table 1.4

Sector-wise Share in NSDP across States

	Primary	*Secondary*	*Tertiary*	*Primary*	*Secondary*	*Tertiary*
	ANDHRA PRADESH			ARUNACHAL PRADESH		
1980-81 to 1989-90	48.7	13.3	38	50.9	16.7	32.4
1990-91 to 1999-2000	37.1	18	44.9	42.2	19.7	38.1
2000-01 to 2009-10	30.2	18.5	51.4	27.6	28.8	43.6
	ASSAM			BIHAR		
1980-81 to 1989-90	49.0	15.6	35.4	50.3	9.4	40.3
1990-91 to 1999-2000	44.3	13.7	42	41.6	9.6	48.8
2000-01 to 2009-10	33.8	14.5	51.7	31.3	13.3	55.4
	CHHATTISGARH			GOA		
1980-81 to 1989-90				32.9	22.5	44.6
1990-91 to 1999-2000	40.5	21.5	38	20.7	27.9	51.4
2000-01 to 2009-10	34.8	23.3	41.9	12.7	35.6	51.7
	GUJARAT			HARYANA		
1980-81 to 1989-90	40.4	25.8	33.8	46.1	24.3	29.6
1990-91 to 1999-2000	29.1	32	38.8	39.4	26.3	34.4
2000-01 to 2009-10	19.7	33.6	46.6	25.2	26.6	48.2

contd...

3. We have followed the CSO allocation of sectors and accordingly construction is included in the secondary sector.

...contd...

	Primary	*Secondary*	*Tertiary*	*Primary*	*Secondary*	*Tertiary*
	HIMACHAL PRADESH			JAMMU & KASHMIR		
1980-81 to 1989-90	47.1	21.6	31.3	38.7	25.6	35.8
1990-91 to 1999-2000	34.8	31.1	34.2	33.3	25.4	41.2
2000-01 to 2009-10	24.4	37.4	38.2	30.7	22.1	47.2
	JHARKHAND			KARNATAKA		
1980-81 to 1989-90	—	—	—	45.2	20.1	34.7
1990-91 to 1999-2000	29.8	31.1	39.1	36.1	22	41.9
2000-01 to 2009-10	26.9	29.4	43.7	21.7	24.2	54.1
	KERALA			MADHYA PRADESH		
1980-81 to 1989-90	31.0	20.1	48.9	45.9	12	42.2
1990-91 to 1999-2000	26.5	21.4	52.1	38.9	14.7	46.4
2000-01 to 2009-10	16.4	22.1	61.5	30.1	18.3	51.6
	MAHARASHTRA			MANIPUR		
1980-81 to 1989-90	25.7	30.4	43.9	39.6	19.9	40.5
1990-91 to 1999-2000	20.1	29.1	50.7	32.4	19.6	48.0
2000-01 to 2009-10	15.5	23.9	60.7	28.1	26.8	45.2
	MEGHALAYA			MIZORAM		
1980-81 to 1989-90	39.1	12.4	48.5			
1990-91 to 1999-2000	31.2	12.9	55.9	24.2	14.1	61.6
2000-01 to 2009-10	30.6	17.3	52.1	18.3	17.6	64.2
	NAGALAND			ORISSA		
1980-81 to 1989-90	24.6	6.8	68.5	52.5	15.6	32.0
1990-91 to 1999-2000	23.9	16.1	60.1	41.9	16.8	41.4
2000-01 to 2009-10	34.5	14.1	51.4	32.1	17.2	50.7
	PUNJAB			RAJASTHAN		
1980-81 to 1989-90	46.5	15.7	37.8	47.6	16.7	35.7
1990-91 to 1999-2000	43.6	19.6	36.8	41.0	19.2	39.8
2000-01 to 2009-10	35.5	21.8	42.7	31.9	22.8	45.3
	SIKKIM			TAMIL NADU		
1980-81 to 1989-90	NA	NA	NA	26.1	30.3	43.6
1990-91 to 1999-2000	31.3	18.5	50.2	22.2	28.6	49.2
2000-01 to 2009-10	20.7	26.2	53.1	13.9	26.2	59.9
	TRIPURA			UTTAR PRADESH		
1980-81 to 1989-90	51.2	9.7	39.1	44.2	17.8	38.0
1990-91 to 1999-2000	37.3	9.6	53.1	38.3	19.8	41.9
2000-01 to 2009-10	26.1	20.7	53.2	32.8	21.6	45.6
	UTTARAKHAND			WEST BENGAL		
1980-81 to 1989-90	-	-	-	40	15.6	44.4
1990-91 to 1999-2000	30.3	18.8	51	37.6	14.8	47.6
2000-01 to 2009-10	22.5	29.1	48.4	27.4	16.1	56.5

Note: NA : Not Applicable. -: Not Available.
Source: Central Statistical Office, Government of India.

III

Socioeconomic Inclusiveness

The ultimate objective of planned development is to ensure human well-being through sustained improvement in the quality of life of the people, particularly of the poor and the vulnerable segments of population. Development strategy, therefore, needs to continuously strive for broad-based improvement in standards of living.

As per the UNDP *Human Development Report 2009* (HDR, 2009), India ranked 134th out of 182 countries of the world placing it at the same rank as in 2006 despite the gradual increase in the Human Development Index (HDI) value from 0.427 in 1980 to 0.556 in 2000 and subsequently to 0.612 in 2007.[4] India continues to be in the Medium Human Development category while countries like China, Sri Lanka and Indonesia have better rankings.

Poverty

Poverty is a major issue in the emerging economies, though its intensity varies across countries as reflected in the World Bank's data on the poverty headcount ratio at $1.25 a day on purchasing power parity (PPP) basis. South Asia continues to have a significant amount of poor people, mainly on account of the high poverty ratios in India and Bangladesh.

As per the official estimates, the incidence of poverty has declined over the years though it still remains at a very high level. The percentage of the population below the official poverty line has come down from 36 per cent in 1993–94 to 27.5 per cent in 2004–05. However, not only is the rate still high, but also the rate of decline in poverty has not accelerated in line with the growth in GDP, and the incidence of poverty among certain marginalised groups, (for example the poverty rate among the scheduled tribes (STs)), has hardly declined. Moreover, the absolute number of poor people has declined only marginally from 320 million in 1993–94 to 302 million in 2004–05. If we take the World Bank measurement of poverty of

4. HDI is based on three indicators, *viz.*, GDP per capita (PPP US $), life expectancy at birth, and education as measured by adult literacy rate and gross enrollment ratio (combined for primary, secondary and tertiary education).

41.6 per cent (as per PPP) of population below poverty line, it is much higher than the official national poverty ratio of about 28 per cent.

It can further be stated that around 80.0 per cent of the poor are from rural areas. Poverty is mostly concentrated in few states, *viz.*, Bihar, Uttar Pradesh, Madhya Pradesh, Orissa, Chhattisgarh and Jharkhand. Poverty is concentrated among agricultural labourers, casual workers, scheduled castes (SCs) and scheduled tribes (STs).

While the poverty rates have declined over the years, even at a marginal level, there are increasing evidence of inequality as measured by Gini coefficient of per capita consumption expenditure. The inequality is higher in the case of urban areas and it has shown an increase in majority of states (Table 1.5).

Employment and Unemployment Situation

Nature and extent of employment is crucial for poverty reduction and inclusive growth. It may be mentioned that although employment in the industrial and services sector has increased in 2004 in comparison to 1961, agriculture still remains the major sector which continues to employ the largest segment of the population (Dev, 2007).

Employment growth in the organised sector, both public and private combined, has declined during the period 1994-2007. Employment in the organised sector grew at 1.20 per cent per annum during 1983-1994, but declined to (-) 0.03 per cent per annum during 1994-2007 (GoI, 2009). However, the decline in employment during the latter period was mainly due to a decline in employment in the public sector establishments from 1.53 per cent in the earlier period to (-) 0.57 per cent in the later period, whereas the private sector showed moderate growth of 1.30 per cent per annum.

According to NSSO, compared to 1999-2000, during 2004-05, the unemployment rate in terms of the usual status remained almost the same in rural and urban areas for males, though it has increased by around 2 percentage points for females. As can be observed from Table 1.6, overall unemployment rates are not too high. However, urban unemployment rates are higher than the rural rates. The unemployment rates according to 'current daily status' (CDS) approach are higher than the rates obtained

Table 1.5

Gini Coefficient for Per Capita Consumption Expenditure

	1973-74		*1977-78*		*1983*		*1993-94*		*1999-2000*		*2004-05 (URP)*		*2004-05 (MRP)*	
	Rural	*Urban*	*Rural*	*Urban*	*Rural*	*Urban*	*Rural*	*Urban*	*Rural*	*Urban*	*Rural*	*Urban*	*Rural*	*Urban*
India	0.28	0.30	0.34	0.34	0.30	0.33	0.28	0.34	0.26	0.34	0.30	0.37	0.25	0.35
Andhra Pradesh	0.29	0.29	0.30	0.32	0.29	0.31	0.29	0.32	0.24	0.31	0.29	0.37	0.24	0.34
Assam	0.20	0.30	0.18	0.32	0.19	0.25	0.18	0.29	0.20	0.31	0.19	0.32	0.17	0.30
Bihar	0.27	0.26	0.26	0.30	0.26	0.30	0.22	0.31	0.21	0.32	0.20	0.33	0.17	0.31
Jharkhand											0.22	0.35	0.20	0.33
Gujarat	0.23	0.25	0.29	0.31	0.25	0.26	0.24	0.29	0.23	0.29	0.27	0.31	0.25	0.32
Haryana	0.29	0.31	0.29	0.31	0.27	0.30	0.30	0.28	0.24	0.29	0.32	0.36	0.31	0.36
Himachal Pradesh	0.24	0.27	0.26	0.30	0.27	0.31	0.28	0.43	0.23	0.30	0.30	0.32	0.26	0.26
Jammu & Kashmir	0.22	0.22	0.22	0.33	0.22	0.24	0.23	0.28	0.17	0.22	0.24	0.24	0.20	0.24
Karnataka	0.28	0.29	0.32	0.34	0.30	0.33	0.27	0.32	0.24	0.32	0.26	0.36	0.23	0.36
Kerala	0.31	0.37	0.35	0.36	0.33	0.37	0.29	0.34	0.27	0.32	0.34	0.40	0.29	0.35
Madhya Pradesh	0.29	0.27	0.33	0.38	0.29	0.29	0.28	0.33	0.24	0.32	0.27	0.39	0.24	0.37
Chhattisgarh											0.29	0.43	0.24	0.35
Maharashtra	0.26	0.33	0.46	0.36	0.28	0.33	0.30	0.35	0.26	0.35	0.31	0.37	0.27	0.35
Orissa	0.26	0.34	0.30	0.32	0.27	0.29	0.24	0.30	0.24	0.29	0.28	0.35	0.25	0.33
Punjab	0.27	0.29	0.30	0.38	0.28	0.32	0.26	0.28	0.24	0.29	0.28	0.39	0.26	0.32
Rajasthan	0.28	0.29	0.46	0.30	0.34	0.30	0.26	0.29	0.21	0.28	0.25	0.37	0.20	0.30
Tamil Nadu	0.27	0.31	0.32	0.33	0.32	0.35	0.31	0.34	0.28	0.38	0.32	0.36	0.26	0.34
Uttar Pradesh	0.24	0.29	0.30	0.33	0.29	0.31	0.28	0.32	0.25	0.33	0.29	0.37	0.23	0.34
Uttarakhand											0.28	0.32	0.22	0.30
West Bengal	0.30	0.32	0.29	0.32	0.28	0.33	0.25	0.33	0.22	0.34	0.27	0.38	0.24	0.36
Delhi	0.15	0.35	0.29	0.33	0.29	0.33	0.24	0.21	0.29	0.34	0.26	0.33	0.24	0.32

Note: URP - Uniform Reference Period. MRP - Mixed Reference Period.

Source: Planning Commission, Government of India.

according to 'usual status' approach and 'weekly status' approach, thereby indicating a high degree of intermittent unemployment. The unemployment rate, measured through the usual status is very low in the rural areas.

Table 1.6

Unemployment Rates in India during 1972-73 to 2004-05

Year (Round)	*Male*			*Female*		
	Usual Status	*CWS*	*CDS*	*Usual Status*	*CWS*	*CDS*
			Rural			
1972-73 (27th round)	1.2	3.0	6.8	0.5	5.5	11.2
1977-78 (32nd round)	2.2	3.6	7.1	5.5	4.1	9.2
1983 (38th round)	2.1	3.7	7.5	1.4	4.3	9.0
1987-88 (43rd round)	2.8	4.2	4.6	3.5	4.4	6.7
1993-94 (50th round)	2.0	3.1	5.6	1.3	2.9	5.6
1999-2000 (55th round)	2.1	3.9	7.2	1.5	3.7	7.0
2004-05 (61st round)	2.1	3.8	8.0	3.1	4.2	8.7
			Urban			
1972-73 (27th round)	4.8	6.0	8.0	6.0	9.2	13.7
1977-78 (32nd round)	6.5	7.1	9.4	17.8	10.9	14.5
1983 (38th round)	5.9	6.7	9.2	6.9	7.5	11.0
1987-88 (43rd round)	6.1	6.6	8.8	8.5	9.2	12.0
1993-94 (50th round)	5.4	5.2	6.7	8.3	7.9	10.4
1999-2000 (55th round)	4.8	5.6	7.3	7.1	7.3	9.4
2004-05 (61st round)	4.4	5.2	7.5	9.1	9.0	11.6

Note: CWS: Current Weekly Status. CDS: Current Daily Status.

Source: NSSO, 61st Round.

Basic Amenities

Another aspect of looking into the development of the region is the provision of basic facilities. While there is significant improvement in the availability of electricity, there is huge difference in rural-urban divide (Table 1.7). While only 8 per cent of urban population is not having electricity, the share is 44 per cent in the case of rural areas.

Table 1.7

Percentage of Population Living with Housing Amenities (Lighting)

	1999-2000		2005-06	
	R	*U*	*R*	*U*
No lighting	0.5	0.3	0.5	0.2
Kerosene	50.6	10.3	42.2	7.2
Other oil	0.2	0.1	0.2	0.1
Gas	0.1	0.1	0.1	0.1
Candle	0.1	0	0.2	0.3
Electricity	48.4	89.1	56.3	92
Other	0.1	0.1	0.5	0.1
Not recorded	0	0	0	0
All	100	100	100	100

Note: R: Rural. U: Urban.

Source: *Selected Socio-Economic Statistics, India,* CSO.

As per the NSSO data, 49 per cent of ST households falls under the lowest five Monthly Per Capita Expenditure (MPCE) class (i.e., less than Rs 410) compared to 40 per cent of SC households, 30 per cent of OBC households and 20 per cent of 'other' category (Table 1.8). The proportion of households in the highest MPCE class (i.e., those who spent Rs 1,155 or more per month) was higher among 'others' category of households (12%) than among the OBCs (5%), SCs (3%) or STs (2%).

In urban India too, proportion of households in each of the five lower MPCE classes (i.e., less than Rs 675) was higher among SCs, STs and OBCs than among the other category of households. About 51 per cent of the SCs of urban India spent less than Rs 675 per month during 2004-05; the corresponding percentages being 43, 40 and 21 for the STs, OBCs and the others, respectively. The proportion of households in the lowest MPCE class (i.e., those spending less than Rs 335 per month) was higher among the STs (8%) than that among SCs (7%). The proportion of urban households spending Rs 2,540 or more per month was higher among others (13%) category of households than among the OBCs or STs (3% each) or SCs (1%).

Table 1.8

Per 1,000 Distribution of Households by Household Monthly Per Capita Consumer Expenditure for Each Social Group

Monthly Per Capita Consumer Expenditure (Rs)	*Rural*					*Monthly Per Capita Consumer Expenditure (Rs)*	*Urban*				
	ST	*SC*	*OBC*	*Others*	*All*		*ST*	*SC*	*OBC*	*Others*	*All*
Less than 235	91 (9.1)	35 (3.5)	20 (2.0)	12 (1.2)	29 (2.9)	Less than 335	81 (8.1)	70 (7.0)	34 (3.4)	16 (1.6)	33 (3.3)
235-270	62 (6.2)	43 (4.3)	24 (2.4)	16 (1.6)	30 (3.0)	335-395	54 (5.4)	58 (5.8)	42 (4.2)	15 (1.5)	32 (3.2)
270-320	113 (11.3)	94 (9.4)	70 (7.0)	37 (3.7)	71 (7.1)	395-485	84 (8.4)	120 (12.0)	88 (8.8)	46 (4.6)	73 (7.3)
320-365	117 (11.7)	115 (11.5)	89 (8.9)	60 (6.0)	90 (9.0)	485-580	122 (12.2)	131 (13.1)	116 (11.6)	63 (6.3)	93 (9.3)
365-410	108 (10.8)	113 (11.3)	95 (9.5)	71 (7.1)	94 (9.4)	580-675	84 (8.4)	131 (13.1)	120 (12.0)	69 (6.9)	97 (9.7)
410-455	92 (9.2)	108 (10.8)	95 (9.5)	73 (7.3)	92 (9.2)	675-790	75 (7.5)	110 (11.0)	107 (10.7)	78 (7.8)	93 (9.3)
455-510	94 (9.4)	112 (11.2)	113 (11.3)	92 (9.2)	106 (10.6)	790-930	85 (8.5)	109 (10.9)	109 (10.9)	90 (9.0)	99 (9.9)
510-580	93 (9.3)	114 (11.4)	121 (12.1)	122 (12.2)	117 (11.7)	930-1100	113 (11.3)	78 (7.8)	98 (9.8)	102 (10.2)	97 (9.7)
580-690	97 (9.7)	107 (10.7)	135 (13.5)	142 (14.2)	127 (12.7)	1100-1380	135 (13.5)	82 (8.2)	104 (10.4)	127 (12.7)	113 (11.3)
690-890	82 (8.2)	93 (9.3)	122 (12.2)	153 (15.3)	119 (11.9)	1380-1880	92 (9.2)	70 (7.0)	96 (9.6)	157 (15.7)	121 (12.1)
890-1155	30 (3.0)	37 (3.7)	63 (6.3)	108 (10.8)	65 (6.5)	1880-2540	43 (4.3)	28 (2.8)	49 (4.9)	112 (11.2)	75 (7.5)
1155 & above	19 (1.9)	27 (2.7)	53 (5.3)	115 (11.5)	60 (6.0)	2540 & above	33 (3.3)	14 (1.4)	34 (3.4)	126 (12.6)	74 (7.4)
All classes	1000	1000	1000	1000	1000	All classes	1000	1000	1000	1000	1000

Note: Figures in parenthesis refer to percentage share to total.

Source: *Employment and Unemployment Situation among Social Groups in India*, NSSO 61st Round.

IV

Institutional Finance and Growth

There is a general consensus among economists that financial development spurs economic growth. Theoretically, financial development creates enabling conditions for growth through either a supply-leading (financial development spurs growth) or a demand-following (growth generates demand for financial products) channel. A large body of empirical research supports the view that development of the financial system contributes to economic growth (Rajan and Zingales, 2003). Empirical evidence consistently emphasises the nexus between finance and growth, though the direction of causality is still debated. At the cross-country level, evidence indicates that various measures of financial development (including assets of the financial intermediaries, liquid liabilities of financial institutions, domestic credit to private sector, stock and bond market capitalisation) are robustly and positively related to economic growth (King and Levine, 1993a; Levine and Zervos, 1998). Other studies establish a positive relationship between financial development and industrial growth (Rajan and Zingales, 1998). Even the recent endogeneous growth literature, building on 'learning by doing' processes, assigns a special role to finance (Aghion and Howitt, 1998 and 2005).

For any productive activity, capital investment is vital and, it is possible only when finance is available. The endogeneous growth literature stresses the importance of financial development for economic growth as many important services are provided by a country's financial system. Thus, as part of our inclusive growth study, it is useful to examine if there is finance-growth nexus in our economy. After 60 years of Independence of our country, although banking sector has developed to a great extent, it is worth examining whether formal finance did play any role in our growth process. At this stage, it is important to examine the relationship between finance and growth at the aggregated level.[5]

---

5. Ideally, it should have been an analysis at the disaggregated level using panel data framework, but due to non-availability of data at the disaggregated level we have done the exercise at the aggregated level.

The Model

Empirical work on causality between financial development and economic growth is sparse, owing to a lack of sufficiently long time-series data for developing countries. Jung (1986) was among the first to test for causality by applying a Granger causality procedure. He used annual data on per capital GNP and two measures of financial development: the ratio of currency to M_1 and the ratio of M_2 to GDP, for 56 developed and developing countries. However, his results were inconclusive because they varied according to the financial development indicator used and the development level of the various countries. For example, using the currency ratio as a measure for financial development, Granger causality from financial development to economic growth in least developed countries (LDCs) was more frequently observed than the reverse and an opposite conclusion was obtained for the developed countries. However, when the M_2/GDP ratio was used, causality from financial development to economic growth was as frequently observed as causality from economic growth to financial development both in LDCs and developed countries. Jung's test was conducted in a levels vector autoregression (VAR) framework without testing for stationarity of the data. As data are very likely to be non-stationary, Jung's findings are debatable (Granger and Newbold, 1977). In a frequently-cited paper, Demetriades and Hussein (1996) tested for cointegration among variables and used an error correction model for 16 countries to test for a possible long-run causal relationship between financial development and economic growth. Their findings showed little evidence to support the view that finance leads to economic growth.

In the present paper, we examine the causal relationship between financial and economic development from a time-series perspective for India. For this, we apply cointegration tests and error correction models after pre-testing for unit roots in all variables and choosing the optimal lag order in our VAR system. We use three different measures of financial development and relatively long annual time-series data. We also include a third variable, namely the share of fixed investment in GDP, in the system. This allows us to test channels through which financial development and investment for explaining changes in the growth rate of per capita GDP beyond the sample period.

Measurement and Data Sources

Financial Development Indicators

Financial development is usually defined as a process that marks improvement in quantity and efficiency of financial intermediary services. This process involves the interaction of many activities and institutions. Consequently, it cannot be captured by a single measure. In this study we employ four commonly used measures of financial development for the sake of testing the robustness of our findings.

The first, M_3Y, represents the ratio of money stock, M_3, to nominal GDP. M_3Y has been used as a standard measure of financial development in numerous studies (Gelb, 1989; World Bank, 1989; King and Levine, 1993a and 1993b; Calderon and Liu, 2003). According to Demetriades and Hussein (1996), this indicator accords well with McKinnon's outside money model where the accumulation of lumpy money balances is necessary before self-financed investment can take place. However, it conflicts somewhat with the debt-intermediation approach developed by Gurley and Shaw (1955) and the endogeneous growth literature, because a large part of the broad money stock in developing countries is currency held outside banks. As such, an increase in the M_3/GDP ratio may reflect an extensive use of currency rather than an increase in bank deposits, and for this reason this measure is less indicative of the degree of financial intermediation by banking institutions. Financial intermediaries serve two main functions: to provide liquidity services and to provide saving opportunities, the latter being relevant for promoting investment and consequently growth. For this reason, Demetriades and Hussein (1996) proposed to subtract currency outside banks from M_3 and to take the ratio of M_3 minus currency to GDP as a proxy for financial development. On this basis, we chose QMY, the ratio of M_3 minus currency to GDP, to serve as our second measure of financial development.

Our third measure of financial development is the ratio of bank credit to the private sector to nominal GDP (PRIVY). This indicator is frequently used to provide direct information about the allocation of financial assets. A ratio of M_3 (including or excluding currency) to GDP may increase as a result of an increase in private financial saving. On the other hand, with high reserve requirements, credit to the private sector which eventually is responsible for the quantity and quality of investment and therefore to economic growth, may not increase. Therefore, an increase in this ratio does not necessarily mean an increase in productive investments. Rather, the private credit GDP ratio can be a better estimate of the proportion of domestic assets allocated to productive activity in the private sector. Figure 1.5 shows that M_3Y had increased tremendously starting 1979 to reach around 90 per cent in 2008. However, the high M_3Y rate does not necessarily imply a larger pool of resources for the private sector and therefore is not a good indicator of financial development, in contradiction, to PRIVY. Two explanations for this behaviour were given by Roe (1998). The first is the possibility that the dominating state-owned banks did not have a profit maximising goal. The second is that banks preferred to serve the interest of their non-private clients, and offered loans to public enterprises even at the expense of their profitability. The latter is most evidently related to the quantity and efficiency of investment and hence to economic growth (De Gregorio and Guidotti, 1995). PRIVY has been used extensively in numerous works (King and Levine, 1993a and 1993b; De Gregorio and Guidotti, 1995; Levine and Zervos, 1998; Demetriades and Hussein, 1996; Beck *et al.*, 2000 among others), with different definitions of the stock of private credit depending on the institutions supplying the credit.

Figure 1.5

Financial Development Indicators: India (1950-2008)

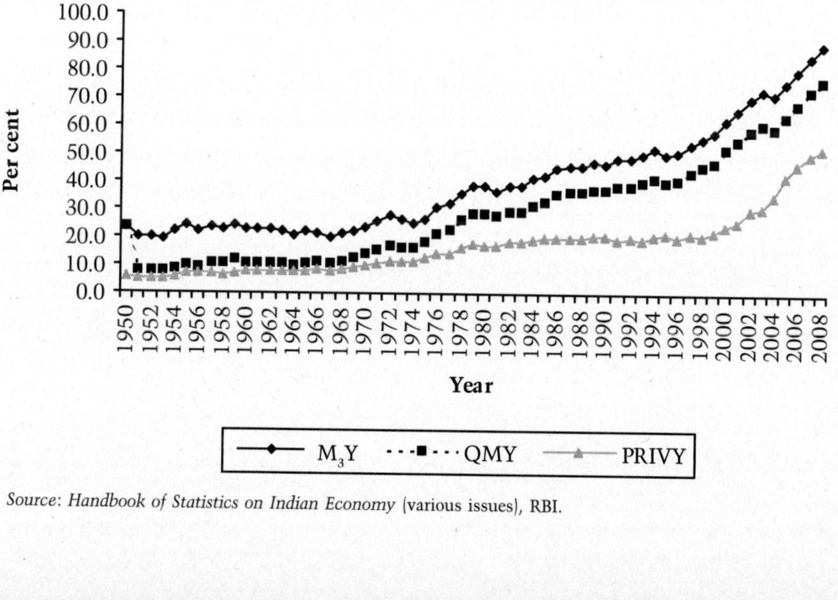

Source: *Handbook of Statistics on Indian Economy* (various issues), RBI.

Other Variables

Following standard practice, we use real GDP per capita, GDPPC, as our measure for economic development (see Gelb, 1989; Roubini and Sala-i-Martin, 1992; King and Levine, 1993a and 1993b; Demetriades and Hussein, 1996). In addition to the per capita real GDP and the financial development indicator, we introduced a third variable in our VAR system, the share of investment in GDP, IY. This variable is considered to be one of the few economic variables with a robust correlation of economic growth regardless of the information set (Levine and Renelt, 1992). Including the investment variable in our regressions enables us to identify the channels through which financial development causes economic growth. If financial development causes economic development, given the investment variable, then this causality supports the endogeneous growth theories that finance affects economic growth mainly through the enhancement of investment efficiency. Furthermore, we can then test if financial development causes economic growth through an increase of investment resources. We can examine this supposition indirectly by testing the causality between financial development indicators and investment on the one hand and between investment and economic growth on the other. All the variables in our data set are expressed in natural logarithms.

Data Sources

All the data have been obtained from the *Handbook of Statistics on Indian Economy* published by the Reserve Bank of India. Our sample covers the period 1950-2008; the choice of this period is governed by data availability. We have used the standard Granger Causality approach as suggested by Granger (1969) in order to test the causality between financial development and growth. We have also used Johansen's (1988) approach in order to test for the presence of multiple cointegrated relationships in a single-step procedure. The results of the models are discussed in the following paragraphs.

Empirical Results

Granger Causality Results

The first of our empirical works was to determine the degree of integration of each variable. The Augmented Dickey Fuller (ADF) test results for the levels and first differences are reported in Table 1.9. The results show that all the variables are non-stationary i.e., I(1) in their levels, but stationary in their first differences.[6]

Table 1.9

ADF Unit Root Test Results

Variable	*ADF with Trend and Intercept*			
	Levels		*First Differences*	
	ADF	*k**	*ADF*	*k**
LGDPPC	-3.403	0	-6.827***	0
LPRIVY	-1.183	0	-6.922***	0
LM3Y	-2.643	0	-7.976***	0
LQMY	-1.969	1	-19.601***	0
LIY	-3.836	0	-7.884***	0

Notes:

1) LGDPPC, LPRIVY, LM3Y, LQMY and LIY are the natural logarithms of real per capita GDP, share of credit to private sector in GDP, share of M3 in GDP, share of M3 minus currency outside of banking in GDP, and the share of gross fixed capital formation in GDP, respectively.
2) k* the optimal lag lengths chosen by Schwarz selection criterion with maximum of 9 lags.
3) *, **, and *** indicate significance at the 10 per cent, 5 per cent and 1 per cent levels, respectively.

The second step was to test for a cointegration relationship among the relevant variables. The results of Johansen's maximum eigenvalue test (λ_{max}) support the existence of a unique long-run relation between per capita GDP, the investment ratio and financial development under the various measures of the latter. In all cases, we reject the null hypothesis of a no-cointegration relationship at least at the 5 per cent level (Table 1.10). It is also observed from Granger causality test that the null hypothesis of finance does not lead to economic growth is rejected at 1 per cent level of significance (Table 1.11). It also confirms that financial development leads to capital formation (Table 1.12).

6. Using Phillips-Perron test we obtained similar results.

Table 1.10

Johansen Cointegration Test Results

Variables	λ_{max}			P^*	r^*
	$r = 0$	$r = 1$	$r = 2$		
LGDPPC, LIY, LPRIVY	29.809***	11.979	3.041	1	1
LGDPPC, LIY, LM3Y	37.175***	10.289	2.333	1	1
LGDPPC, LIY, LQMY	37.860***	10.606	1.927	1	1

Notes : *; **; *** indicate significance at the 10 per cent, 5 per cent and 1 per cent levels, respectively.

λ_{max} is the maximum eigenvalue statistic.

p* represents the optimal lag length based on AIC from the unrestricted VAR model.

r* is the number of cointegration vectors based on Johansen's method.

Table 1.11

Results of Granger Causality Tests (Direct)

Financial Development Indicator	*Null Hypothesis* Financial Development does not Granger Cause Income Growth	
	F-Statistic	*Prob*
LPRIVY	6.63	0.003***
LM3	9.69	.0003***
LMQ	7.89	0.001***

Panel B

Financial Development Indicator	*Null Hypothesis* Income Growth does not Granger Cause Financial Development	
	F-Statistic	*Prob*
LPRIVY	1.49	0.235
LM3	3.90	0.0264**
LMQ	1.49	0.236

Note: ***: Significant at 1 per cent level.

**: Significant at 5 per cent level.

Table 1.12

Results of Granger Causality Tests (Indirect)

Financial Development Indicator	*Null Hypothesis*	
	Financial Development does not Granger Cause Fixed Capital Formation Share in GDP	
	F-Statistic	*Prob*
LPRIVY	6.63	0.003***
LM3	9.69	0.003***
LMQ	7.89	0.001***

Panel B

Financial Development Indicator	*Null Hypothesis*	
	Fixed Capital Formation Share in GDP does not Granger Cause Income Growth given the Financial Indicator below	
	F-Statistic	*Prob*
LPRIVY	1.49	0.235
LM3	3.90	0.0264**
LMQ	1.49	0.236

Note: *, **, *** indicate significance at the 10 per cent, 5 per cent and 1 per cent levels, respectively.

In a nutshell, we have examined the causal relationship between measures of financial development and real GDP per capita in India over the past five decades. It is found that the null hypothesis of no causality from financial development to economic growth was significantly rejected in all the cases. The causality is mostly unidirectional since the other direction of causality from economic growth to financial development was not observed. Thus, our results support our hypothesis that institutional finance leads to economic growth in our economy. One of the leading proponents of this theory is Joseph Schumpeter (1912) who stated that well-functioning banks spur technological innovation by identifying and funding those entrepreneurs with the best chances of successfully implementing innovative products and production processes. Thus, the causality tests provide some evidence that financial development leads to growth.

Distribution of Credit across Sectors and Regions

In this section, we have discussed the distribution of formal credit across sectors and regions, given the importance of formal credit. It is necessary to examine now whether allocation of finance is equitable across regions and sectors. This is because nature of distribution of credit has a direct bearing on economic growth, which in turn can impact poverty and inequality.

As per the *Basic Statistical Returns*, Reserve Bank of India, there has been a gradual decrease in share of agriculture credit over the years. The share had gone down from 14.8 per cent in 1980 to 9.9 per cent in 2005, though it had gone up to 11.3 per cent in 2008. The share of industrial credit had also gone down from 48.0 per cent in 1980 to 38.4 per cent in 2008. However, the share of credit to services has gone up substantially from 37.2 per cent in 1980 to 50.4 per cent in 2005, although it has gone down marginally to 50.2 per cent in 2008.

Sector-wise/region-wise allocation of credit indicates that there has been a decline in credit to agriculture and industrial sectors across all the regions over the period 1980-2008. However, the share of credit to services sector has increased substantially in all the regions during the period 1980-2008. This change in the distribution of credit is in alignment with the growth pattern of the economy showing significant contributions from the services sector. But, if we consider from the point of sector-wise dependency of population, it means agriculture getting marginalised. The shares of agriculture in the northern region decreased marginally while in the southern region it decreased substantially by around 10 percentage points. The share of agriculture credit in the western region has remained below 10 per cent throughout the three-decade period. Further, the share of agriculture credit to the eastern region went down by around 3.0 percentage points.

It is worth mentioning that there is wide disparity in C-D ratio across the regions and states. The ratio remains above 80 per cent in the southern and western regions during 2009, which has increased from above 75 per cent. On the other hand, the situation is not encouraging in the northern region where the C-D ratio has become 68.5 per cent in 2009, going down from 76.1 per cent in 1980. The condition is much worse in the eastern, northeastern and central regions. While the C-D ratio in the northeastern region and central region remained constant at 36 per cent and 45 per cent, respectively during the three-decade period, it has gone down significantly from 56.1 per cent in 1980 to 48.9 per cent in 2009 in the eastern region.

Financial Inclusion

Financial inclusion can be defined as delivery of banking services at an affordable cost to the vast sections of disadvantaged and low income groups. In the case of credit, the proper definition of the financially excluded would include households who are denied credit in spite of their demand. Although credit is the major component, financial inclusion covers various other services such as savings, insurance, payments and remittance facilities by the formal financial system to those who tend to be excluded.

Credit to farmer households is one of the important elements of financial inclusion. As per the results of the *All-India Debt and Investment Survey* (AIDIS), the share of non-institutional sources of credit in total sources of credit for cultivator households had declined sharply from about 93 per cent in 1951 to about 31 per cent in 1991, with the share of moneylenders having declined from 69.7 per cent to 17.5 per cent. In 2002, however, the share of moneylenders had again increased to 27 per cent, while that of non-institutional sources rose to 39 per cent .

As per the *Basic Statistical Returns*, Reserve Bank of India (various issues) the share of direct accounts with a credit limit of less than Rs 25,000 (small loans) in total direct accounts declined from 93.4 per cent in 1980 to 35.8 per cent in 2008. The decline in share is observed across all the sectors.

It can also be observed from Table 1.13 that there is an inverse proportional relation between size-class distribution of land and non-indebtedness. In other words, minimum size-class had the lowest inclusion.

Table 1.13

Distribution of Size-Class-wise Indebtedness of Farmer Households: 2002

Size-Class	*Number*			*Per cent*		
	Included	*Excluded*	*Total*	*Included*	*Excluded*	*Total*
Upto 0.40 ha	135820	169641	305461	44.5	55.5	100.0
0.41 to 1.00 ha	129211	154399	283610	45.6	54.4	100.0
1.01 to 2.00 ha	81920	78680	160600	51.0	49.0	100.0
Upto 2.00	346951	402720	749671	46.3	53.7	100.0
2.01 to 4.00 ha	54409	39095	93504	58.2	41.8	100.0
4.01 and above	32882	17447	50329	65.3	34.7	100.0
Above 2.00 ha	37291	56542	93833	60.7	39.3	100.0
All sizes	434242	459262	893504	48.6	51.4	100.0

Source: *Situational Assessment Survey of Farmers* (59th Round NSSO).

V

Conclusion and Policy Prescriptions

Indian economy is on a high growth path triggered mainly by the expansion of economic activities across the sectors. However, there are some serious concerns about a number of imbalances in the growth scenario—intersectoral, interregional and interstate. The study reveals that the poverty ratio is still very high in the economy. There is no significant increase in employment in the unorganised sector of the economy. The study shows that while the contribution of the agriculture sector in the real GDP has declined fairly fast, the share of the employment in the agriculture sector has not declined to that extent. As a result, the average productivity in this sector has remained very low. Since a large section of the population continues to be dependent on the agriculture sector, directly or indirectly, this has serious implications for 'inclusiveness'. The study also found that bank finance has been playing a major role in our growth process. However, distribution of bank credit across sectors and regions is not equitable.

Indian economy is well poised to achieve an impressive growth in near future. The strength and resilience of the Indian economy were well tested while weathering the global turbulence of recent time. We need to harness this rising growth momentum to achieve inclusiveness. Rapid growth can promote the inclusiveness agenda if the growth is associated with faster growth in agriculture, rural infrastructure and greater absorption of labour in manufacturing.

In this context, innovations are needed in products and services which reduce costs, economise on energy and serve the needs of the common man in an affordable manner. Innovations are also needed in processes and delivery mechanisms, especially in government delivery mechanisms which need to be redesigned so that they can deliver outcomes in commensurate with the considerable resources they now absorb.

Further a much greater effort is needed to improve the implementation of social sector programmes in the field. These programmes receive assistance from the Central government, but they are implemented by state agencies. Much greater devolution of power to Panchayati Raj Institutions (PRIs) and urban local bodies (ULBs), together with effective participation by the local community is needed to achieve better oversight and accountability. Progress in governance agenda is critical to achieve the goal of inclusiveness and should be given high priority by state governments.

Financial institutions are required to play crucial role in the overall scheme of inclusive growth. Innovation of different financial products and processes that increase the accessibility of common man to the financial institutions can be considered as *sine qua non* of inclusive growth.

Infrastructure constraints have been considered as a binding constraint on growth. Promotion of infrastructure, especially in rural areas can be a catalyst of inclusive growth through better delivery of social services to the common man. Financial institutions should play a crucial role in infrastructure financing especially in rural areas.

In the globalised world order, there has been interplay among macroeconomic reforms, globalisation and technology, which can propel growth towards high trajectory. However, the synergetic links among the sectors can be reaped for achieving inclusive growth. Inclusive governance and inclusive growth go hand in hand. Empowerment and participation of people through further activation of PRIs and ULBs can enable to achieve inclusive governance and public accountability, thus ensuring demand-driven inclusive growth.

References

Aghion, P. and P. Howitt (1998). *Endogenous Growth Theory.* MIT Press.

———. (2005). "Appropriate Growth Policy: A Unifying Framework", *Joseph Schumpeter Lecture.* Amsterdam: European Economic Association.

Ali, Ifzai and Hyun Hwa Son (2007). "Measuring Inclusive Growth", *Asian Development Review* 24(1): 11-31.

Bhattacharya, B.B. and Arup Mitra (1990). "Excess Growth of Tertiary Sector in Indian Economy: Issues and Implications", *Economic and Political Weekly*, November 3.

Bhattacharya, B.B. and S. Sakthivel (2004). "Regional Growth and Disparity in India: Comparision of Pre-and Post-Reform Decades", *Economic and Political Weekly* 39(10): 1071-77.

Beck, Thorsten, Ross Levine and Narsan Loayzo (2000). "Finance and the Sources of Growth", *Journal of Financial Economics* 58 (1&2): 261-300.

Calderon, Cesar and Lin Liu (2003). "The Direction of Causality between Financial Development and Economic Growth", *Journal of Development Economics* 72(1): 321-34, October. Elsevier.

De Gregorio, Jose and Pablo E. Guidotti (1995). "Financial Development and Economic Growth", *World Development* 23(3): 433-448, Elsevier, March.

Demetriades, Panicos O. and Khaled A. Hussein (1996). "Does Financial Development Cause Economic Growth? Time-series Evidence from 16 Countries", *Journal of Development Economics* 51(2): 387-411, Elsevier, December.

Dev, Mahendra S. (2007). "Financial Inclusion: Issues and Challenges", *Economic and Political Weekly*, October 14.

Gelb, A.H. (1989). "Financial Policies, Growth and Efficiency, Policy, Planning and Research", *Working Paper 202.* World Bank.

Gokarn, Subir (2010). "People, Jobs and Productivity: The 'Simple' Dynamics of Inclusive Growth", Keynote Address at CII Western Region's Annual Regional Meeting and National Conference on *Achieving Double Digit Growth*, March 26.

Government of India (2006). *Towards Faster and More Inclusive Growth: An Approach to the 11th Five Year Plan.* New Delhi: Planning Commission.

———. (2009). *Economic Survey, 2009-10.* New Delhi: Ministry of Finance.

Granger, C. (1969). "Investigating Causal Relations by Econometric Models and Cross-spectral Methods", *Econometrica* 37: 424–38.

Granger, C.W.J and P. Newbold (1977). *Forecasting Economic Time-series.* New York: Academic Press.

Gurley, J.G. and E.S. Shaw (1955). "Financial Aspects of Economic Development", *The American Economic Review* 45: 515-38, September.

Johansen, S. (1988). "Statistical Analysis of Cointegration Vectors", *Journal of Economic Dynamics and Control* 12: 231-254.

Jung, W.S. (1986). "Financial Development and Economic Growth: International Evidence", *Economic Development and Cultural Change* 34: 336-46.

King, Robert G. and R. Levine (1993a). "Finance and Growth: Schumpeter Might Be Right", *The Quarterly Journal of Economics*: 717-737. August.

———. (1993b). "Finance, Entrepreneurship and Growth: Theory and Evidence", *Journal of Monetary Economics*: 513-542.

Levine, R. and Renelt D. (1992). "A Sensitivity Analysis of Cross-country Growth Regressions", *American Economic Review* 82(4): 942-63.

Levine, R. and S. Zervos (1998). "Stock Markets, Banks and Economic Growth", *American Economic Review* 88: 537-58.

Mishra, S. (2006). "Risks, Farmers' Suicide and Agrarian Crisis in India: Is there a Way Out?", *IGIDR Working Paper* No. WP-2007-014, September.

Rajan, R.G. and L. Zingales (1998). "Power in a Theory of the Firm", *Quarterly Journal of Economics* 113: 387-432.

———. (2003). *Saving Capitalism from Capitalists*. New York: Crown Business.

Roe, Alan (1998). "The Egyptian Banking System: Liberalisation, Competition, and Privatisation", in El-Erian and Mohieldin (eds.), *Financial Development in Emerging Markets: The Egyptian Experience*. Cairo: Egyptian Centre for Economic Studies.

Roubini and Sala-i-Martin (1992). "Financial Repression and Economic Growth", *Journal of Development Economics* 39 (1): 5-30.

Schumpeter, Joseph (1912). *The Theory of Economic Development*. Cambridge, MA: Harvard University Press.

World Bank (1989). *World Development Report*. New York: Oxford University Press.

———. (2007). *World Development Report*. New York: Oxford University Press.

2 Impact of Bank Credit on Growth Dynamics of Kerala

V. DHANYA

I

Introduction

Kerala which lies in the southwestern tip of India is known for its unique development experience. For a long time, economic backwardness has coexisted with high quality of life in Kerala, which usually is an uncommon existence. These two features were not normally expected to exist together as it is apprehended that either the development deficit might end up pulling down the quality of life or on the other hand, the high development indicators and quality of life will push up the economy onto higher trajectories of growth (Planning Commission, 2008). Therefore the discussion on the economy of Kerala, for a very long time, centred on the sustainability of Kerala model of development. However, Kerala economy witnessed a revival in economic growth since early 1990s which got strengthened in the present century. In fact, it was pointed out by many studies that the state had already moved on to a virtuous cycle of development path (Chakravarthy, 2005; Kannan 2005).

The economic growth in the recent period is spearheaded by the growth in the services sector which accounted for 62.5 per cent of state NSDP during 2008-09. Similarly in the banking sector also, services accounted for a major share of credit deployed. A lot has been written on the development experience of Kerala, similarly, Kerala's banking sector; particularly the low credit-deposit ratio has been analysed. While there is

---

The author is grateful to the comments given by E. Madhavan, former O-i-C, RBI Kochi. The views expressed in this paper are of the author herself and not of the organisation she is working with.

no dearth of studies independently on the two topics, very little analysis has been done on the role of bank credit in promoting economic growth in Kerala. The present study is an attempt to understand the role of deployment of credit on economic growth of Kerala.

The present study intends to trace the structural changes that have happened in the state economy. It also aims to understand whether the distribution of credit is in alignment with the developments in the economy. More specifically, it aims to examine the trends and structure of Kerala economy over time; what are the drivers of economic growth in Kerala, whether the economy has become more diversified overtime? On the banking aspect, trend and pattern of distribution of credit in Kerala and how far the deployment of credit is contributing to economic growth is studied.

Methodology and Data Set

The paper is organised as follows. Section II looks into the structural changes that have taken place in the economy of Kerala over the years. It examines the drivers of economic growth in Kerala during the recent period. Section III analyses the banking sector in Kerala with particular emphasis on the deployment of credit. Section IV examines the relation between credit and economic growth in Kerala. Section V sets out the conclusion of the paper.

The study is based on secondary data. The sector specific analysis of state income is based on the data from Department of Economics and Statistics, Government of Kerala. For credit deployment across different sectors, data from RBI's *Basic Statistical Returns of Scheduled Commercial Banks* in India is used. Due to data restrictions, the study confines itself to bank credit and hence, it may not capture the impact of long term finance from term lending institutions/DFIs and NBFCs on growth. Again, total credit disbursal could have been a better indicator than the credit outstanding, but again due to data limitations credit outstanding as the dependent variable is taken.

II

Structural Changes and Drivers of Growth in Kerala

Kerala economy for a very long time witnessed low levels of growth. During the 70s and 80s the growth rate of Kerala NSDP was lower than that registered at the All-India level (Table 2.1). In fact, Kerala was left out of the growth process witnessed during the 80s at the all-India level. However, during the last two decades, Kerala witnessed a turn around in growth registering a higher growth than the all-India level. High growth was witnessed both at the secondary as well as tertiary sector, while primary sector witnessed positive growth compared to the previous period. In terms of per capita income also Kerala registered stronger growth.

Table 2.1

Growth Performance of Kerala (Annual Average Growth Rate)

Sectors	*1970-71 to 1979-80*	*1980-81 to 1989-90*	*1990-91 to 1999-2000*	*2000-01 to 2008-09*
Kerala NSDP	1.4	2.3	5.8	7.8
Primary	-0.5	-0.7	3.5	0.6
Secondary	4.2	3.9	6.1	9.2
Tertiary	2.2	3.9	6.8	9.1
Per capita NSDP	-0.4	0.8	4.8	6.9
India	2.9	5.6	5.7	7.2
Primary	1.3	4.7	3.4	2.8
Secondary	3.7	5.7	5.7	8.1
Tertiary	4.4	6.5	7.3	8.5
Per capita NNP	0.5	3.2	3.6	5.4

Note: Figures for India corresponds to GDP at constant prices and for Kerala it is NSDP at constant prices.

Source: *Economic Survey 2010-11* and Central Statistical Organisation.

The services sector clearly spearheaded the economic growth in recent times. Figure 2.1 which shows the drivers of Kerala's economic growth during the last four decades clearly shows the increasing importance of services sector in Kerala's economy. During the current decade, 71 per cent of the economic growth in Kerala was attributed to the growth in services sector, a rise from 40 per cent in the 70s. There was a marginal increase in the contribution of industrial sector also. On the other hand, agriculture sector performed poorly.

Figure 2.1

Sector-wise Contribution to Kerala's Economic Growth[1]

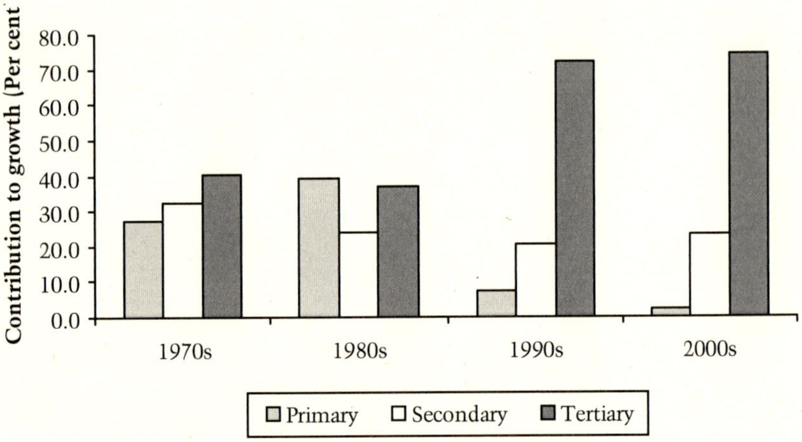

Source: Calculations based on Department of Economics, Government of Kerala data

Studies have shown that the service sector growth propelled the economic growth in Kerala since the 1980s (Pillai and Shanta, 2005). Balakrishnan (1999) and Harilal and Joseph (2003) opines that the migration-remittance phenomenon has lots to do with this pattern of growth in Kerala. The Dutch disease effect got manifested in Kerala following the resource movement and spending effects associated with migration and remittances (Harilal and Joseph, 2003). The huge and sustained flow of remittances kept the prices of non-tradables (services) high relative to the prices of tradables (agriculture and industrial products) (Planning Commission, 2008). With opening up of economy, the demand for tradables were easily met by imports and the less competitive sectors clearly lost in the international competition.

Subramanian (2006) showed that the low growth of industrial sector in the post-reform period was due mainly to the depressingly low growth rates in large number of capital goods and modern manufacturing industry.

1. Contribution to economic growth has been calculated by taking the differential share of output.

However, in recent years, there is a revival in the industrial sector (excluding construction) which registered a growth of 11.5 per cent during the period 2006-07 to 2009-10. Similarly, in the face of resource constraints, agriculture sector also witnessed significant structural change with cultivators moving away from labour intensive annual crops like rice and cassava to commercial crops like natural rubber. At present, food crops account for only 12.05 per cent of the gross cropped area of the state.

Growth in Sub-Sectors

Broad three-sector economic classification throws little light into the underlying structural changes. To get a more detailed picture sub-sector of the broad classification of sectors is studied. As per this, the entire economy is classified into eight broad sectors: (i) agriculture and allied, (ii) industry covering manufacturing, mining and quarrying and electricity, gas and water supply, (iii) construction, (iv) transport, storage and communication, (v) trade hotels and restaurants, (vi) real estate, business ownership services, (vii) banking and insurance and (viii) other services including public administration also.

Table 2.2

Trends in Growth (Annual Average Growth)

Sectors	*1970-1979*	*1980-1989*	*1990-1999*	*2000-2009*
Agriculture and allied	-0.5	-0.9	3.5	0.4
Industry	4.4	6.2	5.4	5.8
Construction	4.3	2.1	7.4	11.9
Transport, storage & comm.	5.5	6.7	14.1	14.2
Trade, hotel & restaurants	1.0	2.5	5.5	7.3
Banking & insurance	11.1	12.2	12.2	12.0
Real estate ownership, business, legal services	3.0	3.5	4.0	10.0
Other services	3.5	5.2	6.4	7.3
NSDP	1.4	2.3	5.8	7.7

Source: Department of Economics and Statistics data, Government of Kerala.

Table 2.2 provides the annual average growth of the sub-sectors across the years. All the sectors recorded strong growth since 1990 which is also reflected in the turn around in the overall NSDP. Among the sectors, banking and insurance have been showing consistent growth over the four time periods. Double digit growth has been registered by construction, transport, storage and communication, banking and insurance and real estate ownership business in the current decade. In fact, the economy has become more diversified with more sectors registering strong growth. The changes observed in the share of subsector to the total NSDP also reveals a more diversified Kerala economy (Figure 2.2).

Figure 2.2

Broad Sectoral Classification: 1970-71 to 2008-09

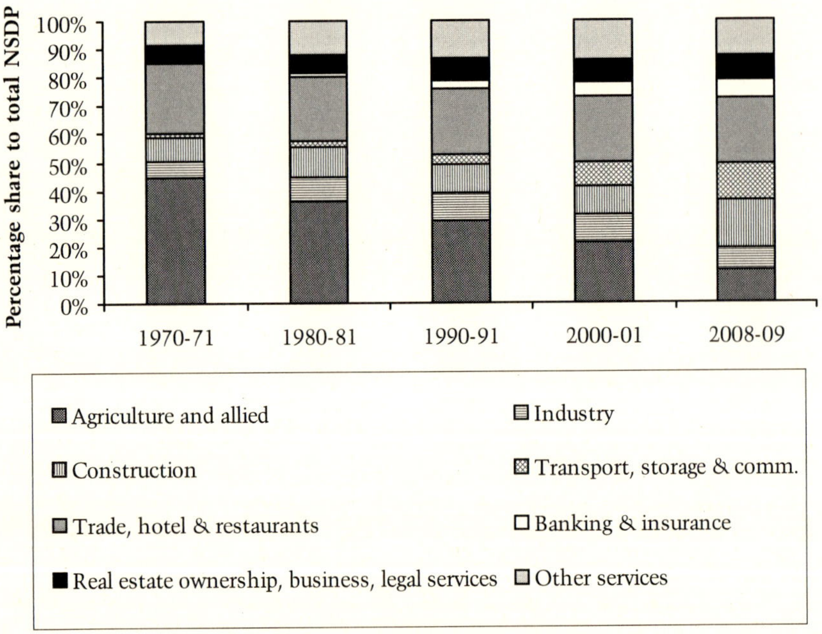

The share of agriculture and allied sector has come down significantly over the years. In the recent period, sectors like construction, real estate, banking services and transport and communication became the major players in the growth process of the economy. On the other hand, the share of trade, hotels and restaurant remained more or less same at 23 per cent signifying its continuous importance in the state economy.

The structural shift becomes clearer when the contributions to economic growth is examined. There is a remarkable shift in the sectors contributing to growth in the current decade (Figure 2.3). Transport, storage and communication (within it communication services), construction, trade, hotels and restaurants and real estate, ownership of business were the major contributing factor to the growth in NSDP during the period 2000-2009. Together, they contributed to 70 per cent of the growth recorded during the period 2000-2010, though trade, hotels and restaurants were traditionally a major contributor to economic growth in Kerala. However, communication services, real estate and construction are relatively new entrants as the major contributor to economic growth. Thus, apart from construction that falls under secondary sector all the other major contributors comes from services sector.

Figure 2.3

Sectoral Contribution to NSDP

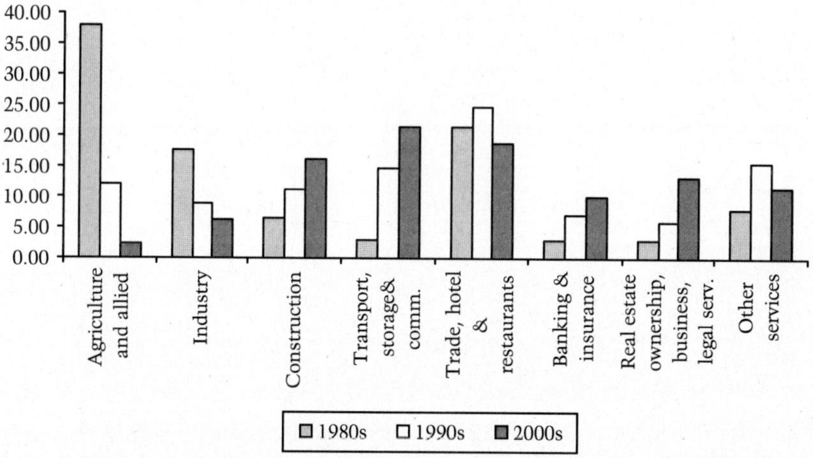

The structural shift reflected both in terms of growth rates as well as shares shows that the economy has become more diversified in recent years. To measure the extant of diversification we calculate the diversification ratio. The diversification ratio is the inverse of concentration ratio. Essentially, the lower the concentration ratio and the higher the diversification quotient, the more diversified a nation's economy.[2] Figure 2.4 provides the diversification index for Kerala and India over different time periods. Kerala economy was more diversified than the Indian economy up to the recent period. In the years 2007-08 and 2009-10 Kerala's diversification remained stagnant and was lower than that of India.

Figure 2.4

Diversification Index for Kerala and India

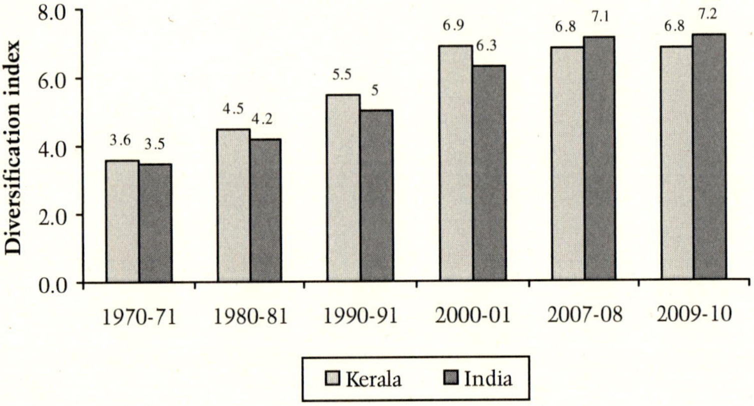

Linkages of Service Sector to the Productive Sector

The empirical literature has pointed out that the growth process in Kerala is spearheaded by the non-tradable sector, which is less exposed to international competition (Harilal and Joseph, 2003; Planning Commission, 2008). The services sector which produces mainly non-tradables thus became more and more prominent (Pillai and Shanta, 2005). To understand the production linkages of services sector we differentiate services into productive services and consumption services.

Following Reserve Bank of India (2002) and Pillai and Shanta (2005) the paper divides the services sector into consumer services, producer

2. We use the Herfindahl Index, used generally in industry studies, to measure the degree of concentration in the economy. It is computed as:

$$H = \sum_{i=1}^{N} S_i^2$$

where N is the number of sectors in the economy, S is the market share of ith sector. The Herfindahl Index ranges from 1/N to one. The inverse of Herfindahl Index is taken as the Diversification Index.

services, other services and government services. RBI study has put other services (which include those services offered by government and private agencies in various areas such as health care, education etc.) under consumer services. But considering the role of these services in the economic growth of Kerala, the paper follows Pillai and Shanta (2005) in classifying it as a separate category. Accordingly, producer services consists of 'transport and communication, banking and insurance, real estate and business services'; consumer services consists of 'trade, hotels and restaurants[3] and government services comprise 'public administration and defence'.

Figure 2.5

Classification of Services Sector

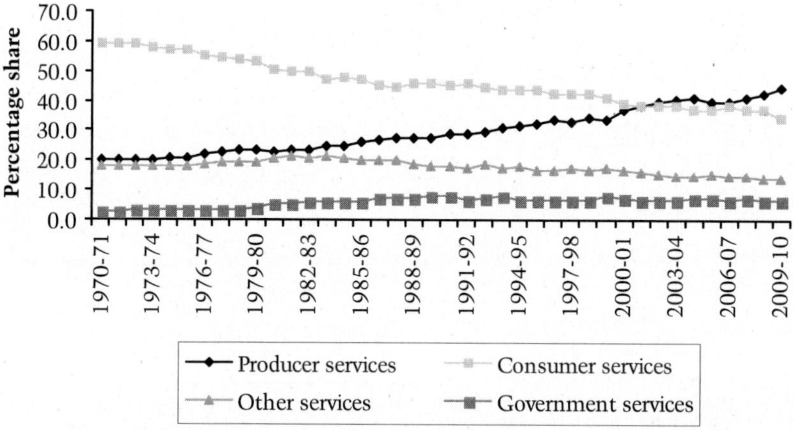

Figure 2.5 which shows the trend in the four groups over the years clearly shows an importance to productive services. During 2009-10, productive sector accounted for 44.7 per cent of total service sector. However, whether the productive services are contributing to the productive sectors is unclear as it is only the construction sector that has shown high growth in the current decade. Pillai and Shanta (2005) have opined that development of the service sector in Kerala and in particular the

3. RBI study has classified hotels and restaurants under consumer services and trade under producer services, but due to the non-availability of separate data we include all the three in consumer services.

producers's services is having strong linkages with the production sector in other regions while Kerala continues to remain a consumer/trading state.

Kerala Getting more Globalised?

The analysis so far revealed new sectors coming to prominence in the economy in recent years. At the same time, economy has become more diversified compared to the earlier years. However, the underlying growth mechanism associated with structural change reveals an increasing dependence on the external economy. The economy of Kerala traditionally was a highly globalised economy with commercial links with the outside world. The migration-remittance phenomenon further added its link with the outside world. Further, with the shift towards commercial agriculture, Kerala's agriculture sector became more globalised as the prices of most of the commodities were determined internationally (Planning Commission, 2008).

The importance of remittances in promoting economic growth in Kerala is well studied. While the amount of remittances is not included in the calculation of NSDP,[4] the impact of remittances can be felt in various facets of Kerala economy. According to Kannan and Hari (2002), Kerala's per capita income could have been 49 per cent above the national average by the end of the 90s if the remittances were included in the state income. Our analysis shows that the Kerala's linkages with the external economy, particularly, the role of remittance from abroad, has become more direct in recent years. This is evident from the developments in construction and real estate sector. From the 1970s onwards, a major share of remittances was allocated for housing purposes. However, the growth in real estate and construction sector in recent times, is attributed mostly to the investment in real estate by the NRIs. But little data is available on the extent of investment by NRIs in Kerala. However, the slowdown to near stagnation in the construction and real estate sector during the recent Dubai crisis, reveals the role of NRIs in the real estate sector in Kerala. Similarly, hotels and restaurants are also linked with the external economy by way of

4. Unfortunately, there is no data on state income including remittances. Remittances being part of the current account of BoP statisitics is not included in the calculation of NSDP. In fact, many have opined that while estimating state income, remittances has to be included to the NSDP.

tourism sector. The above factors along with the highly commercialised agricultural sector in Kerala have made the Kerala economy more globalised than the rest of the country.

III

Banking Sector and Deployment of Credit in Kerala

Kerala is one of the intensely banked states in India, ranking 7th at the all-India level and 1st among southern states in terms of density of bank branches. Kerala has one bank branch for every 8190 persons as against all India average of 14,555 as on March 2009. This is commendable achievement considering the high density of population in the state. The basic facts of Kerala banking sector is set out in Table 2.3.

As on March 2009, Kerala accounted from 5.2 per cent of total bank branches, 3.4 per cent of deposits and 2.8 per cent of credit in the country. Kerala has higher per capita deposits and per capita credit than the all-India level. However, Kerala's share in total deposits and total credit has come down over the years, reflecting the slower growth in deposits and credit compared to the all-India level (Table 2.4). During the entire period of the study, growth rate in deposit and advances in the state was lower than the all-India average. The only exceptions are higher growth in deposits during 1990-1994 and marginally higher growth in credit during the period 2000-2004.

An often discussed issue while examining the banking statistics is the low C-D ratio in Kerala compared to the all-India level. Quite a few studies have been done on the low C-D ratio in Kerala. The task force constituted by the Reserve Bank of India (1994) noted that banking system in Kerala was not able to cater to the developmental needs of the commodity producing sectors due to institutional and organisational constraints which are peculiar to the state. Further, it was pointed out that banks are not getting viable proposals to finance (Jeromi, 2003). Jeromi (2008) opined that it was not the movements in credit that determined the C-D ratio; rather it was the movement in NRI deposits. In fact, the C-D ratio in Kerala came down to 41.3 per cent in 2000 when the share of NRI deposits in total deposits increased to 48 per cent. In recent times, the C-D ratio in

Table 2.3

Major Indicators of Commercial Banking Development in Kerala

Major Indicators	*1996 March*			*2008 March*			*2009 March*		
	India	*Kerala*	*% Share*	*India*	*Kerala*	*% Share*	*India*	*Kerala*	*% Share*
No. of branches	63,026	3,161	4.9	76,050	4,007	5.3	80,547	4,170	5.2
Deposits (Rs crore)	433,819	20,105	4.7	3,196,939	109,919	3.4	3,834,110	135,119	3.4
Credits (Rs crore)	254,015	8,939	3.5	2,361,914	69,689	3.0	2,775,549	80,713	2.8
Per capita deposits	4,644	5,679	-	28,327	34,288	-	33,471	42,078	-
Per capita credits	2,719	2,527	-	20,928	21,738	-	24,230	25,143	-
Population per office (in '000)	15	11	-	15	8	-	15	8	-
C-D ratio	59	45	-	74	63	-	74	60	-

Source: *Basic Statistical Returns*, Reserve Bank of India, SLBC, Kerala.

Kerala has improved. Jeromi (2008) has pointed out that high growth in housing loans and rise in loans to agriculture and other priority sectors due to persuasion made by the government was the major reasons for the improvement in C-D ratio in recent years.

Table 2.4

Trends in Deposits and Advances

(% change)

	India		*Kerala*	
	Credit	*Deposits*	*Credit*	*Deposits*
1985-1989	15.3	17.3	13.0	13.1
1990-1994	14.9	17.1	11.7	21.4
1995-1999	16.9	16.6	16.3	16.1
2000-2004	18.2	16.7	18.7	16.0
2005-2009	26.6	18.9	19.8	15.4

Source: Calculations based on *Basic Statistical Returns* data, RBI.

Figure 2.6

Trend in C-D Ratio in Kerala

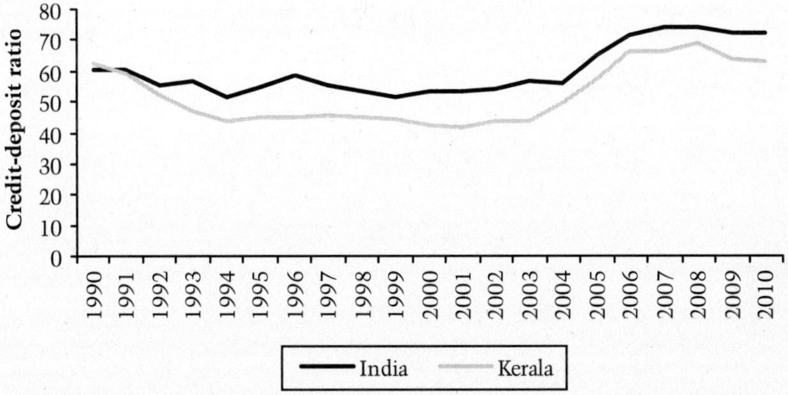

Irrespective of the fact that C-D ratio in Kerala is lower than that of the all-India level, the per capita availability of credit, which is a better indicator of financial development, is higher in Kerala than at the all-India level. Further, a more detailed analysis of credit deployment is needed to elaborate on the linkages with economic development. In the next section we look into the trends in credit deployment in detail.

Credit Deployment in Kerala

Traditionally, a major share of credit deployed in the state is in the tertiary sector. The growth of credit deployed in the services sector was also higher than the other two sectors. Largely, this confirmed with the development in the state economy where tertiary sector plays the major role. However, a more detailed examination of the data shows that there is a shift in the deployment of credit from productive purpose to consumption purpose (Table 2.5). During the period 1980-1989, industry accounted for 34.9 per cent of total credit deployed in the state. Its share came down to 20.3 per cent during 2000-2009 and in 2009 the share of industrial sector was only 14.6 per cent. On the other hand, personal loan which accounted for only 7.2 per cent during the period 1980-1989 increased its share to 41.4 per cent in 2009, reflecting the increased importance of consumption in Kerala. Between the time points 2000 and 2009, industrial credit increased by 174 per cent while the increase in personal loans was 876 per cent. Along with the productive sectors like industry and agriculture, productive services like transport operators and trade also witnessed a reduction in share.

Table 2.5

Trend and Structure of Credit Deployment in Kerala

Sector/period	*Growth (%)*				*Share (%)*			
	1980-1989	*1990-1999*	*2000-2009*	*2009*	*1980-1989*	*1990-1999*	*2000-2009*	*2009*
Agriculture	16.3	10.7	21.9	1.9	18.0	15.2	13.1	14.7
Industry	14.1	11.9	12.3	5.6	34.9	31.9	20.3	14.6
Services	18.2	16.3	22.1	18.4	47.1	52.9	66.6	70.6
Transport operators	18.6	11.1	10.8	15.3	5.7	4.1	1.5	1.2
Professional & other services	23.4	9.4	24.4	28.1	5.7	4.2	5.5	6.2
Personal loans	22.1	24.8	29.0	22.5	7.2	16.3	32.5	41.4
Trade	15.0	17.0	16.0	8.5	15.5	17.2	16.1	13.3
Others including finance	19.6	13.4	19.6	17.6	13.1	11.1	11.0	8.5
Total credit	16.3	14.0	19.8	14.3	100.0	100.0	100.0	100.0

Source: Calculations based on *Basic Statistical Returns*, Reserve Bank of India.

The increasing importance of personal loans is witnessed in the case of other states also. However, Kerala's share in personal loan is a relatively higher figure when compared with other South Indian states as well as at the all-India level (Table 2.6). Within the personal loan, housing loan accounted for a major share. During the period 2007-2009, housing loan accounted for 22 per cent of total advances in the state.

Table 2.6

Sectoral Deployment of Credit: Average of 2007-2009

(% share)

	Kerala	*Tamil Nadu*	*Karnataka*	*Andhra Pradesh*	*India*
Agriculture	15	12	12	17	11
Industry	16	37	35	33	39
Transport operators	1	1	2	1	2
Professional and other services	6	8	10	6	8
Personal loans	40	24	26	26	21
Trade	14	8	7	7	10
Finance	3	5	4	3	7
All others	6	5	4	6	4

Source: *Basic Statistical Returns*, Reserve Bank of India.

While the deployment in credit has witnessed a structural shift, the diversification index has remained more or less the same (Figure 2.7). This is because, the relative importance of sectors have changed with only a limited change in the distribution of shares. On the other hand, the diversification index at the all-India level has clearly improved over the years.

Figure 2.7

Diversification Index of Credit

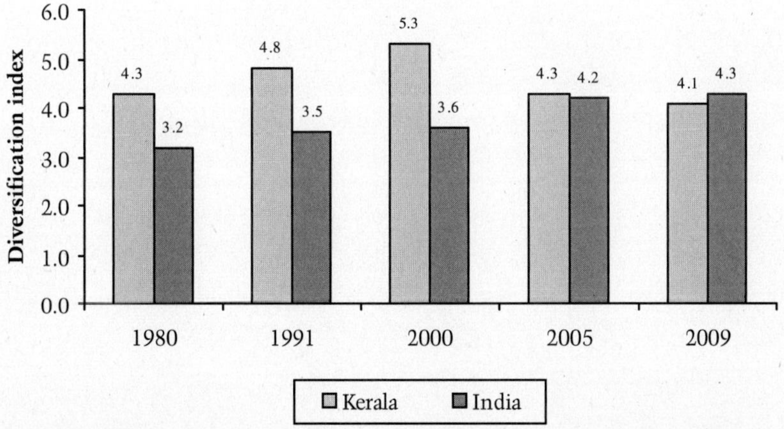

The analysis of the banking sector revealed that Kerala performed better than the all-India level in terms of per capita availability of credit. However, there is a structural shift in the deployment of credit from productive purpose to consumption purpose as revealed by the increasing share of personal loan segment. The share of most of the productive services also has come down over the period reflecting the move towards a consumption oriented economy.

IV

Credit-Output Linkages in Kerala

The analysis in the last two sections has shown that the economy has become more diversified in recent years while the credit deployment has witnessed significant structural shift. In this section we examine whether, the deployment of credit is catering to economic growth, particularly, the impact of sector-wise deployment of credit on economic growth. There exist vast number of studies at the cross-country level looking into the linkages between economic growth and financial sector development, though the direction of causality often differs in different studies. In the Indian context, Misra (2003) looked into the state-wise credit–output nexus in India using Granger Causality. He has found unidirectional relation between output and credit in the case of Kerala. On the other hand, Das *et al.* (2009) using district level data for 2007 found no significant correlation between agricultural credit and agricultural output in Kerala. In this study, we use the Autoregressive Distributed Lag (ARDL) Model (also called Bound Test Method) for examining whether credit deployment is contributing to economic growth in Kerala.

The Model

The ARDL had the advantage of being applicable irrespective of whether the underlying regressors were purely I(0), purely I(1) or even mutually cointegrated. It differs from the other methods of examining long run relation like the Engle and Granger two-step residual-based procedure and Johansen's system-based approach, in that potentially no pre-testing of the variables is necessary in the ARDL model. A problem with pre-testing is that it invariably introduces a further degree of uncertainty. Given the doubt surrounding the order of integration of some variables and the traditional criticisms of ADF tests (Maddala and Kim, 1998; Perron, 1988; Rappoport and Reichlin, 1989), the applicability of this approach seemed particularly relevant. Further, the ARDL model avoids the large number of specification to be made in the standard cointegration test. These include decisions regarding the number of endogenous and exogenous variables (if any) to be included, the treatment of deterministic elements as well as the optimal number of lags to be specified (Duasa, 2007). The empirical results are generally very sensitive to the method and various alternative choices available in the estimation procedure (Persaran and Smith, 1998). Further the model could be used with limited sample data.

The ARDL approach to cointegration (Pesaran *et al.*, 2001) involves estimating the conditional error correction version of the ARDL model for the dependent and independent variables. In our analysis, per capita income is the dependent variable and per capita credit is the independent variable. The data spans for the period 1980-81 to 2009-10. The Conditional Error Correction Model (ECM) is specified as below.

$$\Delta ln\, PY = \alpha + \alpha_1 t + \beta_1 ln\, PY_{t-1} + \beta_2 ln\, PC_{t-1} + \sum_{i=1}^{\rho-1} \gamma_1 \Delta ln\, PY_{t-i} + \sum_{i=o}^{\rho-1} \gamma_2 \Delta ln\, PC_{t-i} + \varepsilon_t \qquad (1)$$

where lnPY is log of per capita income, lnPC is the per capita credit, ρ is the order of the lag and Δ the first difference operator.

We then 'bound test' the above equation for the presence of a long-run relationship using equation (1). The first involves an F-test or Wald test on the null hypothesis that the coefficients of variables are jointly equal to zero irrespective of the order of integration. Two sets of critical values are provided for the two polar case which assume that all the regressors are, on the one hand, purely I(1) and on the other, purely I(0). If the computed F statistic falls beyond the critical bounds, then we reject the null hypothesis that there is no level relationship between these variables. If the statistic falls inside the critical bounds, then, inference is inconclusive and knowledge of the integration of variables is needed before conclusive evidence can be made. The second is a t-test on the lagged level dependent variable in an unrestricted conditional Error Correction Model (ECM). The statistics have a non-standard distribution and depend on whether the variables are individually I(0) or I(1). In the light of consistency Pesaran and Shin (1999) suggests the following procedure. Test H0 based on F statistic: (a). if H0 is not rejected, proceed no further; (b) if H0 is rejected test H0: β_1 using t statistic. If this is rejected, a large value of t should result confirming the existence of level relationship.

Results

Evidence of Cointegration

We bound test the eq (1) to look for long run relation. We select lag order of 2 based on SBC criterion to determine the optimum lag order. Since the data set was annual, 2 was also selected as the maximum lag order as suggested by Pesaran and Shin (1999) and Narayan (2004). The results are given in Table 2.7.

Table 2.7

Test of Cointegration: ARDL Model

Test Statistic	*Value*		*Bound Values*	
	With Trend	*Without Trend*	*With Trend (5% Level)*	*Without Trend (5% Level)*
F-statistic	5.4596	7.5223**	6.56; 7.30	4.94; 5.73
t-statistic	-2.9507	-2.9273*	-3.41; -3.69	-2.57;-2.91(10%)

Note: ** Significant at 5 per cent level; * significant at 10 per cent level.

The results show that there exists long run relation only when trend is not included in the model. When trend is included the F statistics is below the lower bound and hence we accept the null hypothesis of no cointegration. When the trend is excluded, both F and t statistic became significant and we reject the null hypothesis of no cointegration.

Long Run Relationship

Once the existence of long run relation is confirmed we proceeded to estimate the long run relation through the ARDL model

$$\Delta ln\, PY = \alpha + \beta_1 ln\, PC + \mu \qquad (2)$$

The coefficients of long run relation are given in Table 2.8.

Table 2.8

ARDL Long Run Coefficients

Repressor	*Coefficient*	*t-statistic*
LPC	0.43379**	7.7622
Constant	6.4628**	17.9425

Note: ** significant at 5 per cent level.

As seen from the table, per capita credit is having a positive relation with per capita income in Kerala. For a 1 per cent increase in per capita credit, the per capita income increases by 0.43 per cent, i.e. by almost half per cent.

Short Run Relation

For determining the short run relationship between the variables, the error correction model based upon ARDL approach is estimated through eq(3).

$$\Delta ln\ PY = \alpha + \beta_1 \Delta ln\ PC + \beta_2 EC_{t-1} + \mu \quad (3)$$

The results are given in Table 2.9.

Table 2.9

ECM based on ARDL (1,0) Model

Regressor	*Coefficient*	*t-Ratio*
dlnPC	.080567 **	2.9585
Constant	1.2005 **	2.0226
ecm(-1)	-.18573**	-2.2337

The significant error correction term confirms the existence of long run relation. The coefficient of ECM shows the speed of adjustment of the short run to the long run equilibrium. In the short run, the elasticity of per capita credit to per capita income is lower compared to the long run. A 1 per cent increase in the credit will result in only 0.08 per cent increase in per capita income.

Thus, the ARDL model shows that there exist significant relation between per capita credit and per capita output. At the next step we examine how the sector wise credit deployment is contributing to per capita income. i.e. the elasticity of sector wise credit in relation to per capita output.

$$\Delta \ln PY = \alpha + \alpha_1 t + \beta_1 \ln PY_{t-1} + \beta_2 \ln PAC_{t-1} + \beta_3 \ln PIC_{t-1} + \beta_4 \ln PTC_{t-1} + \sum_{i=1}^{\rho-1} \gamma_1 \Delta \ln PY_{t-1} + \sum_{i=0}^{\rho-1} \gamma_2 \Delta 1$$

The equation 3 is then bound test for co-integration.

where lnPY is per capita income, lnPAC per capita agricultural credit, lnPIC per capita industrial credit and ln PTC per capita tertiary sector credit. All the variables are in log form. Based on the SBC criterion, we selected the model of lag 2. Results of conditional Error Correction Model are given in Table 2.10.

Table 2.10

Results of Conditional ECM

Test Statistic	*Value*		*Bound Values*	
	With Trend	*Without Trend*	*With Trend (5% Level)*	*Without Trend (5% Level)*
F-statistic	2.5691	4.1105*	4.01; 5.07	3.23; 4.35 (5%) 2.72; 3.77 (10 %)
t-statistic	-1.4503	-1.4521	-3.41; 4.16	-2.86; -3.78

Note: * Significant at 10 per cent.

The F-statistic came significant only at 10 per cent when trend is excluded from the model. T-statistic came non-significant in both cases showing evidence for no cointegration. However, since the F-statistic showed significant relation at 10 per cent level we proceeded to examine the long run estimates and the ECM associated with it. The error correction term came insignificant further strengthening our earlier finding of no significant relation between the variables.

V

Conclusion

The paper tries to examine the structural changes that have taken place in the state of Kerela economy and further, looks into the relation between deployment of credit and economic growth. The analysis on the state economy reveals that the economy has become more diversified over the years. At the same time, the dependence of external economy has increased with more externally oriented sectors coming into prominence. Further, the economy continues to be consumption oriented economy with demand for producer services being met from other states.

An analysis of credit deployment in the state also reveals the state to be consumer oriented with the share of credit for productive purposes coming down drastically over time. In line with the trends in the state economy of the increasing importance of construction and real estate, credit is mostly used for housing purpose. The regression analysis also revealed positive relation between credit and growth. However, no significant relation is found between output growth and sector wise deployment of credit.

References

Balakrishnan, Pulapre (1999). "Trends in Agricultural Wages in Kerala", *Economic and Political Weekly*, May 22.

Chakravarty, Achin (2005). "Kerala's Changing Development Narratives", *Economic and Political Weekly,* May 22.

Das, Abhiman, M. Senapati and J. John (2009). "Impact of Agricultural Credit on Agriculture Production: An Empirical Analysis in India", *Reserve Bank of India Occasional Papers* 30(2), Monsoon.

Duasa, Jarita (2007). "Determinants of Malaysian Trade Balance: An ARDL Bound Testing Approach", *Journal of Economic Cooperation* 28 (3).

Harilal, K.N. and K.J. Joseph (2003). "Stagnation and Revival of Kerala Economy: An Open Economy Perspective", *Economic and Political Weekly*, June 7.

———. (2005). "India-SriLanka Free Trade Accord", *Economic and Political Weekly* 34, March 27.

Jeromi, P.D. (2003). "Bank Credit in Kerala: An Analysis of Trends and Issues", *RBI Staff Studies*, SS DEAP 7/2003.

———. (2008). "Credit Deposit Ratio in Kerala: Myth and Reality", in B.A. Prakash and V.R. Prabhakaran Nair (eds.), *Kerala's Development Issues in the New Millennium.* New Delhi: Serials Publications.

Kannan, K.P. (2005). "Kerala's Turnaround in Growth: The Role of Social Development Remittances and Reform", *Economic and Political Weekly, February* 5.

Kannan, K.P. and K.S. Hari (2002). "Kerala's Gulf Connection: Emigration, Remittances and their Macroeconomic Impact 1972-2000", *Working Paper* No. 328. Thiruvananthapuram: Centre for Development Studies.

Maddala, G.S. and I.M. Kim (1998). *Unit Roots, Cointegration and Structural Change.* Cambridge: Cambridge University Press.

Misra, B.S. (2003). "Analytics of Credit—Output Nexus in India", *Reserve Bank of India Occasional Papers* 24 (1,2), Summer and Monsoon.

Narayan, P.K. (2004). "Reformulating Critical Values for the bounds F Statistics Approach to Cointegration: An application to the Tourism Demand Model for Fiji", *Discussion Papers*. Australia: Department of Economics, Monash University.

Perron, P. (1988). "The Great Crash, the Oil Shock and the Unit Root Hypothesis", *Econometrica* 57: 1361-402.

Pesaran, M.H. and Y. Shin (1999). "An Autoregressive Distributed Lag Modelling Approach to Cointegration Analysis", in S. Strom (ed.), *Econometrics and Economic Theory in the 20th Century: The Ragner Frisch Centennial Symposium*. Cambridge: Cambridge University Press.

Pesaran, M.H., Y. Shin and R.J. Smith (2001). "Bounds Testing Approaches to the Analysis of Level Relationships", *Journal of Applied Econometrics* 16: 289-326.

Pesaran, M. Hashem and Ron P. Smith (1998). "Structural Analysis of Cointegrating VARs", *Journal of Economic Surveys* 12(5): 471-505, December. Blackwell Publishing

Pillai, Mohanan P. and N. Shanta (2005). "Long Term Trends in the Growth and Structure of the Net State Domestic Product in Kerala", *Working Paper* 376. Thiruvananthapuram: Centre for Development Studies.

Planning Commission (2008). *Kerala Development Report*. New Delhi: Academic Foundation.

Rappoport, P. and L. Reichlin (1989). "Segmented Trends and Non-Stationary Time Series", *Economic Journal* 99: 168-77.

Reserve Bank of India (1994). *Report of the Committee on Credit-Deposit Ratio in Kerala*.

———. (2002). *Report on Currency and Finance, 2001-02*.

Subrahmanian, K.K. (2006). "Economic Growth in the Regime of Reforms: Kerala's Experience", *Economic and Political Weekly* XLI(10): 885-90.

3 Determinants of Inflation in Tamil Nadu

K. JAYANTHI ANAND[1]

I

Introduction

All over the world, inflation generally connotes a purely macroeconomic episode and hence its micro-regional aspects have remained in the background. The persistence of current inflation in general and food inflation in particular has led to a renewed interest in identifying the determinants of inflation at the micro-regional level in the recent decade. Inflation at the national level, emerging due to supply shocks, is closely associated with the mismatches in the demand and supply of goods and services at the regional level. This has posed new challenges for the monetary policy in managing inflation and anchoring inflationary expectations.

Along with globalisation, changing trade dynamics and higher income growth have led to changes in the lifestyles and consumption pattern both in the rural and urban areas, especially in the emerging economies. The recent commodity price spirals in the international markets have also had its impact at the regional level. In the domestic markets, there are differences in the price levels across states and across districts within a state. Further, removal of restrictions on free mobility of goods and services across states tends to reduce regional price variations. Given that supply is inelastic in the short run, differences in the production and productivity in the regions due to its unique structural factors, impact the aggregate price

1. The views expressed in this paper are of the author herself and not of the organisation she is working with.

level at the national level. Further, state level policies have played a crucial role in managing inflationary pressures within the state.

Studying regional inflation in a region with a common regional characteristic is important as it may throw some rich insights on the possible existence and characteristics of inflation differentials. Price indices across and within regions vary because of different weights in the representative basket of consumption. This can be eliminated by including homogeneous product categories within the consumption basket. Large and persistent differences in regional inflation rates might lead to contradicting policy environment for monetary policy. Therefore, it is essential for policy-makers to understand how and to what extent differences between inflation rates across different regions arise within and across national borders. Thus, an assessment of underlying factors in inflation at the disaggregated regional level becomes important to understand and identify factors that might not be revealed by the aggregate national level information. Analysis of regional level policies would help in emulating in other homogeneous regions for managing inflationary pressures at the country level.

While understanding the factors in regional inflation is necessary as aggregate national inflation is nothing but an aggregation of regional inflation. National inflation, whether measured by Wholesale Price Index (WPI) or Consumer Price Index (CPI), is a weighted average of centres surveyed by National Sample Survey Organisation (NSSO). An analysis of regional inflation reveals that regions differ in terms of commodity consumption basket, quality of commodities and its price. At the regional level, this is on account of several factors such as variations in transportation cost, tax rates, and wage rate. Apart from differences in the sectoral level and incomes, the cost of living too differs. However, studies on regional inflation are rare and very few.

Therefore, the study aims to make a comparative analysis of inflation and inflationary expectations at the regional level and thereby to identify the determinants of regional inflation. In India, inflation is measured in terms of WPI. However, given the limitations of data and their availability at the state level, the study focuses on Tamil Nadu as it is one of the few states which compiles monthly data on WPI. Besides, Tamil Nadu being the 11th largest state in terms of area, 7th largest in terms of population

(2011 Census), 3rd largest in terms of size of net state domestic product (NSDP), and with inflation expectations lower than the other states in the southern region, it would serve as a benchmark for other states in the country.

The organisation of the paper is as follows: Section II surveys the literature. Section III analyses regional inflation. Section IV deals with factors underlying regional inflation. Section V discusses the empirical findings of regional inflation in Tamil Nadu. Lastly, Section VI concludes with some policy implications.

II

Survey of Literature

The economic literature reveals that demand-side factors and supply-side factors are two major sources of inflation whether in the national level or regional level.

Regional Inflation

While there are several studies on inflation at the national level, only few papers investigate the inflation process at the regional and national levels and particularly during the last decade. Earlier, Parsley and Wei (1996) found that distance, proxying for arbitrage costs, does affect the size of price differences and its convergence rate. A similar role for distance was found by Engel and Rogers (1996). Parsley and Wei (1996) also show that prices of tradable goods converge faster than non-tradable ones. Alberola and Marqués (2001) found that inflation differentials in Spain were small (less than half point per year in the long-run). Relative price shifts were found to be determined by characteristics which are intrinsic to very deep economic integration, in particular, price and wage mechanisms which operate at the national level. The existence of tariffs, nominal exchange rates (between countries) or transportation costs set a wedge between the price of the same products in different areas.

Oft quoted study by Cecchetti *et al.* (2002) find that relative price adjustment has a half-life of 8.5 years in the US. The reasons for slow convergence were: i) distance between two cities; ii) different adjustment costs for small and large deviations and iii) prices of non-traded goods converge faster than tradable goods. Altissimo *et al.* (2005) show that at the consumer level, movements in the prices of non-traded goods that enter in the production or transportation of traded goods can be an important source of price dispersion for traded goods.

Das and Bhattacharya (2004) using monthly data on consumer price indices for industrial workers (CPI-IW) in India indicate significant presence of cross-sectional dependence in prices in India, rendering some of the standard panel unit root tests inapplicable. It is found that relative price levels among various regions in India mean-revert and idiosyncratic price shocks are found to be more persistent as compared to the common factor. The results also indicate that transportation costs proxied by distance can explain a part of the variation in prices between two locations in India.

Brodjonegoro *et al.* (2005) postulate that regional inflation in Indonesia is mainly due to non-monetary factors, i.e., local government revenues, routine expenditure, and local transportation cost. Local government routine expenditures had the largest elasticity on inflation. Cointegration tests proved that purchasing power parity does not hold for all regions. It is found from the cross-tabulation that regional inflation is significantly affected by the infrastructure conditions. Furthermore, the logistic analysis concludes that regional inflation is also affected by local regulations. Different regions have different inflation threshold and this is conducive for regional economic growth. It was demonstrated that as long as inflation is below the threshold, the inflation would not harm the economy and the contrary is true.

Beck and Weber (2005a and 2005b) study inflation rate dispersion and convergence across the US, Japan, Canada and EMU regions using distribution dynamics methodology. They find that: i) there is no smooth sigma convergence of regional inflation; ii) substantial internal volatility—regions with a high inflation ranking in the present could have a low inflation in the future; iii) a positive relationship between regional inflation dispersion and mean permitting central banks to reduce the average inflation by 1 per cent without pushing a sizeable percentage of regions into deflation; iv) inflation half-life can be rather long, ranging from 0.5 to 75.1 years for different sub-samples as mean-reversion takes place at a slow pace. Beck *et al.* (2006) find that there is a substantial common area-wide component that is related to the common monetary policy in the Euro area and to external developments, in particular exchange rate movements and changes in oil prices. The effects of the area-wide factors differ across regions, and also they find a substantial national component. Busetti *et al.* (2006) using a dataset of 19 Italian cities find evidence of convergence in both the level of prices and inflation rates. Rogoff (2007) warns that the turbulence of recent years (such as the bursting of the tech stock and housing bubbles, the 9/11 terrorist attacks, wars, and volatile energy prices) may raise inflation uncertainty and thus global inflation in coming years. Mehrotra *et al.* (2007) model provincial inflation in China under the New Keynesian Phillips Curve (NKPC) framework. The study finds that the forward-looking inflation component is statistically significant in 22 of the 29 provinces. A probit analysis suggests that the forward looking inflation component and the output gap are important inflation drivers in advanced provinces (degree of development of the market system, share of state-controlled sector in total output, openness to trade, financial deepening and the relative exposure to excess demand pressures Gross Domestic Product (GDP) growth rates, labour productivity, level of industrialisation, migration).

Vaona (2007) found that inflation appeared to be characterised by a low degree of persistence and by conditional convergence across provinces. Vaona (2008) showed that statistically significant variability can exist in the local long-run inflation in the 71 Italian regions. On the one hand they are negatively correlated with productivity growth and on the other, the less competitive the local retail sector, the higher is the long-run inflation. Vaona and Ascari (2010), show that economically backward regions display greater inflation persistence. Higher persistence is linked to a lower degree of competitiveness in the retail sector. Finally, they find that inflation persistence at the national level does not present any geographical aggregation bias, because it equals the mean of inflation persistence of provincial data. While, Cecchetti and Debelle (2006) and Altissimo *et al.* (2007) underline the existence of an across sectors aggregation bias, because aggregate series inherit the properties of their most persistent component, thus justifying the importance to look at different sectoral prices. Altissimo *et al.* (2007) stressed that cross-country heterogeneity is less pronounced than cross-sector heterogeneity in the Euro area.

Marques *et al.* (2009) indicate that spatial allocation together with transport costs are important determinants of regional inflation while macroeconomic common factors do not play an important role in this process. In their model, exchange rates are fixed and do not adjust to fulfill the law of one price. Nagayasu (2009) confirm a long-run relationship between price, money and output in China. Second, provide evidence that inflation can be explained by economic fundamentals such as money, credits, productivity, and exchange rate growth. Lastly, in the context of increased concern about regional discrepancies in recent years, the relationship is found to be more sensitive to the sample period than to the region type than it is. More interestingly, it is found that money does not seem to be closely associated with inflation during the recent years. Nagayasu (2010) verifies the conventional belief that members in monetary union experience a similar level of inflation in Japan. It is found that not only does the average inflation differ significantly across regions, but regional inflation responds differently to common economic and monetary factors. The results show that even a country with heterogeneous inflation can maintain monetary union and thus rethink the importance of homogeneous prices and/or inflation (or more generally convergence criteria) when forming a monetary union. Thus, findings suggest that countries and regions which lack an intergovernmental fiscal transfer system may need to consider more seriously inflation/price heterogeneity.

Valdovinos and Gerling (2011) show evidence of the two major channels for real effects of inflation: inflation uncertainty and relative price variability for eight member countries of the West African Economic and Monetary Union (WAEMU). The study finds that higher inflation increases inflation uncertainty and relative price variability (RPV) in all WAEMU countries. However, the pattern, magnitude and timing of these two channels vary considerably by country. Overall, the study finds a strong statistical evidence for both transmission channels of inflation in WAEMU countries. However, inflation raises not only inflation uncertainty, but also RPV.

Food Inflation

According to the Asian Development Bank Report (2008), there are various structural and cyclical factors determining the food prices in developing Asian countries. The report states that the structural forces augmented by adverse cyclical events have put food prices on an upward trajectory that will not end soon unless trade is kept open and relative prices are allowed to reflect market scarcity. Loening *et al.* (2009) in Ethiopia found that international food commodity prices and producer prices determine the domestic food and non-food prices in Ethiopia. Inflation expectations (inertia) affected food price inflation more than non-food inflation. In the short and medium run, agriculture supply shocks and inertia affect the inflation. They found no evidence of direct impact of excess money supply and world energy price inflation on both food and non-food inflation.

Abdullah and Kalim (2010) found that all the determinants affect food price inflation positively and significantly except money supply which is insignificant with correct positive sign. In the short run, only inflation expectations, support prices and food exports affect the food price inflation in Pakistan. Yanliang *et al.* (2011) make a case for a competitive storage model by taking a holistic approach to food commodity prices by incorporating a more comprehensive and realistic supply and demand factors, viz., output and demand trends, shocks to the yield, and time-varying interest rates.

Dasgupta *et al.* (2011) found that wholesale domestic wheat markets and price formation in India are only moderately affected by international price movements and instead significantly intermediated by other domestic factors. For other factors, the study finds that a higher level of physical wheat stocks in the Public Distribution System (PDS) lowers wholesale prices, *albeit*, effect is statistically quite weak and insignificant. With respect to drought and wholesale wheat prices, the relationship is not statistically significant. The study finds that the wheat export ban variable is related positively with domestic wheat prices. On commodity futures trading ban on wheat, the study finds a statistically significant and very strong effect on domestic wholesale prices, independent of the effects of other factors or controlling for them.

In sum, regional inflation studies in the US, India, Japan, China, Canada, Spain, Italy etc., found that non-monetary factors like distance, transportation cost, wage mechanisms, agro-climatic conditions, and federal structure to be affecting prices. Further, factors such as local government revenues and routine expenditures determined regional inflation. External developments like exchange rate fluctuations, oil prices also tend to influence the prices. It was also found that inflation responded differently among regions. The studies also demonstrated that as the growth in production was below the growth in consumption for several years, the food prices were on an upward trajectory. While money supply had limited impact on food inflation, agricultural supply shock was a major determinant of food inflation. Higher the buffer stocks in PDS, lower the prices.

III

Analysis of Regional Inflation

Measurement of Regional Inflation

Broadly, inflation can be measured in two ways: (i) GDP/Gross State Domestic Product (GSDP) deflator and (ii) price indices. The GDP deflator is derived from the national accounts as a ratio of GDP at current prices to GDP at constant prices. This is available on an annual basis and the quarterly series of GDP have become available in the recent years. However, quarterly revisions in the data make it difficult for using them in inflation-related price interventions as it does not provide any new or additional information beyond those contained in the WPI and CPI as demonstrated by Nadhanael and Pattnaik (2010). At the state level, while such quarterly data is not available, there are time lags in the revision of the base year period across states and all-India. Inflation measurement through the GDP/GSDP deflator method at the state level, have the advantage in terms of having a common methodology and coverage of similar items at the all-India and state level.

Among the several price indices, the WPI is used extensively as a measure of inflation for the purposes of monetary and fiscal policies. The weekly index numbers of wholesale prices have acquired considerable significance over time for short-term policy interventions, since this is the only index which gives an idea of the week-to-week fluctuations in the prices among three major sub-groups, *viz.*, primary articles, fuel, power, light and lubricants and manufactured products. Most recently, the base year for construction of WPI at the all-India is changed to 2004-05 with total number of 676 commodities comprising 102 primary articles, 19 fuel and power items and 555 manufactured products. The weights of the goods are based on the value of quantities traded in the domestic market. In Tamil Nadu, the WPI is compiled on a monthly basis and covers only 177 commodities (both agricultural and industrial) with 1970-71 as the base year, comprising 510 quotations from 41 centres. At the state level, the WPI indices are also used for the purpose of escalation clauses in the supply of raw materials, machinery and construction work.

CPI measures the increase in retail prices that a consumer has to pay for the designated commodity basket. In India, there is no single aggregate CPI to measure the trend and so, sectional CPIs for different consumer categories like industrial workers (CPI-IW), agricultural labourer (CPI-AL), urban non-manual employees (CPI-UNME) and rural labourers (CPI-RL)[2] are compiled on a monthly basis by the Labour Bureau, Government of India. The CPI-IW measures changes in the retail prices of fixed baskets of goods and services being consumed by the target group (namely the average working class family) and is based on the Income and Expenditure surveys. The CPI-IW captures to some extent the price increase in the service sector and is also used for determining the dearness allowances to be paid to Central and state government employees and to industrial workers besides fixation and revision of minimum wages to scheduled employments. The coverage of CPI-IW is broader than that for CPI-AL and CPI-UNME. The CPI-AL and CPI-UNME are designed for specific groups of population with the main objective of measuring the impact of increase in prices on rural and urban poverty. The CPI reflects the cost of living for a homogeneous group of consumers. There is a lag in the availability of CPI data in a disaggregated manner.

Following noticeable difference between WPI and CPI inflation, the question of appropriate index to track inflation came to surface. The IMF data shows that 24 countries use WPI while 157 countries use CPI as a measure of inflation. Internationally, major economies like the US, the UK, Japan, France, Singapore and also China use CPI as its official indicator to

2. The compilation of CPI-UNME and CPI-RL have been discontinued since 2008 and recently a new CPI with base 2010 which combines data from rural and urban areas has been introduced since January 2011.

measure inflation. India is amongst few countries of the world, which use WPI, compiled by the Government of India,[3] as their official measure of headline inflation. The preference of WPI over the CPI is often explained in terms of three criteria—national coverage, timeliness of release (now only limited to food products) and its availability in a disaggregate format (Mohanty, 2010). Moreover, the revisions in the base year for WPI makes it better aligned with the changing production and consumption patterns.

The existence of multiple indicators of inflation in India has posed dilemmas in inflation-related policy interventions. The headline inflation is measured by WPI and that does not, by definition, reflect the consumer price situation (Subbarao, 2010a). Besides, four types of CPI are compiled at the regional and all-India level taking into account the different segments of population employed in the industrial and agricultural sectors. These indices apart from differing in terms of coverage, weighting diagram and base year, still do not give a single representative inflation rate (Subbarao, 2010b).

Moreover, WPI is not available at the disaggregated level for the states. Consequently, some of the states compile their own wholesale price indices (mostly with monthly frequency) which differ in their scope, coverage and base years.[4] Therefore, in order to get a better understanding of the inflationary process at the regional level, for the purpose of analysis, inflation measured in terms of: (i) GDP/GSDP deflator and (ii) price indices such as WPI, CPI-IW and CPI-AL is considered and analysed.

Features of Regional Inflation

Features of regional inflation can be evaluated from statistical properties such as average, coefficient of variation (CV) and correlation analysis. For comparison purposes, periodisation is as follows: (i) pre-crisis

3. The Office of the Economic Adviser in the Department of Industrial Policy and Promotion, Ministry of Commerce and Industry, Government of India, is the official body for compilation, construction and publication of WPI on weekly basis.

4. In the southern region, Tamil Nadu compiles a monthly WPI covering 177 commodities (both agricultural and industrial) with 1970-71 as the base year, comprising 510 quotations from 41 centres. Andhra Pradesh and Karnataka compile a WPI only for agricultural commodities with 1981-82 as base year and the data is available with a time lag. Kerala compiles a WPI of food and non-food crops which again is available after a considerable time lag.

period (2001-2005) and (ii) crisis period (2006-2010). As the sub-prime mortgage crisis in the US came into limelight during the second and third quarters of 2006, and the cumulative drag on GDP growth due to falling residential investment was 1.8 percentage points (an average of 0.9 percentage points per quarter), making it the most intense two-quarter drag since 1981, the year 2006 is included under the crisis period.

GDP/GSDP Deflator

For the purpose of regional inflation calculation, the GSDP at constant 1999-2000 prices was used for the period from 2001 to 2005 and at constant 2004-05 prices for the period from 2006 to 2010. Measured in terms of GSDP deflator, the average inflation during 2001-2010 was higher than all-India (5.1%), for Andhra Pradesh and Karnataka both at 5.3 per cent, while it was lower at 4.8 per cent for Tamil Nadu and Kerala (4.0 %). The average inflation during the crisis period (2006-2010) was higher for all the states as compared with the pre-crisis period (2001-2005) (Figure 3.1).

Figure 3.1

Inflation based on GSDP Deflator

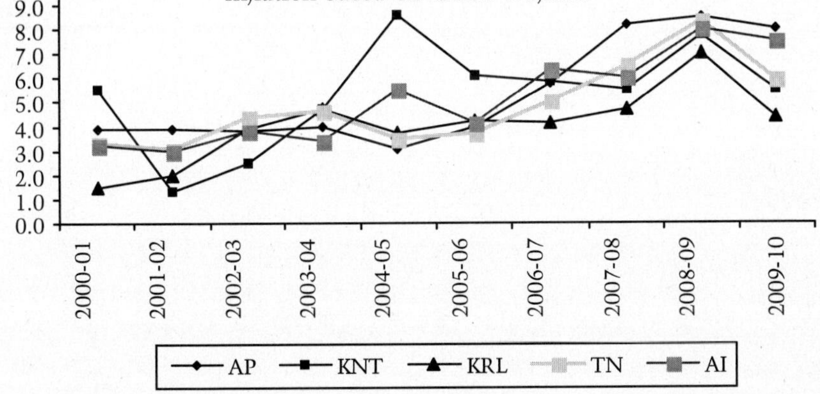

Source: Central Statistical Organisation, Government of India and respective state governments.

The coefficient of variation (CV) topped for Karnataka (0.41), followed by Andhra Pradesh (0.40), Kerala (0.38) and Tamil Nadu (0.35), while it stood at 0.36 for all-India during 2001-2010. It is observed that the CV was very high for Karnataka (0.63) and Kerala (0.44) during 2001-2005 and was above all-India (0.26) indicating higher volatility in inflation in these two states. On the contrary, the CV was higher for Andhra Pradesh and Tamil Nadu (0.29) and above all-India (0.23) during the period 2001-2010 as compared with the period 2001-2005.

The correlation matrix revealed that inflation in the four states was highly correlated with all-India during 2006-2010. During 2001-2005, there was no correlation between Tamil Nadu and all-India, while it was negative for Andhra Pradesh. Among the states, the correlation was higher in the case of Andhra Pradesh and Kerala with respect to Tamil Nadu, while it was lower for Karnataka (Table 3.1).

Table 3.1

Correlation Matrix: GSDP Deflator Inflation

	APGSDP	KNTGSDP	KRLGSDP	TNGSDP	AIGSDP
2001-2005					
APGSDP	1.0	-0.7	-0.2	0.2	-1.0
KNTGSDP	-0.7	1.0	0.2	0.0	0.8
KRLGSDP	-0.2	0.2	1.0	0.9	0.4
TNGSDP	0.2	0.0	0.9	1.0	0.0
AIGSDP	-1.0	0.8	0.4	0.0	1.0
2006-2010					
APGSDP	1.0	0.2	0.6	0.9	0.8
KNTGSDP	0.2	1.0	0.9	0.6	0.4
KRLGSDP	0.6	0.9	1.0	0.9	0.6
TNGSDP	0.9	0.6	0.9	1.0	0.8
AIGSDP	0.8	0.4	0.6	0.8	1.0

Note: AP: Andhra Pradesh; KNT: Karnataka; KRL: Kerala; TN: Tamil Nadu; AI: All-India.

WPI Inflation

For the purpose of this analysis, the WPI for Tamil Nadu and all-India is compared as similar data for other three states are not available. The monthly average WPI inflation for Tamil Nadu (2.7%) for all commodities during 2001-2005 (financial year basis) was higher than that of all-India (1.7%). The average inflation for Tamil Nadu significantly rose to 3.3 per cent during the 2006-2010 as against a marginal increase in all-India (1.8%) indicating more volatility in Tamil Nadu inflation. The average WPI food inflation for Tamil Nadu witnessed three major spikes during 2002-03, 2005-06 and 2007-08 to 2008-09 and was higher than that of all-India (Figure 3.2). The years 2002-03, 2004-05 and 2008-09 were drought years. The agricultural sector in the southern region, which is largely dependent on the monsoon, was significantly affected. During the 2009-10, food inflation in Tamil Nadu had significantly come down and was below all-India. Government policy measures played a crucial role in reducing the inflationary pressures in the recent years.

Figure 3.2

WPI Inflation: All Commodities and Food—
Tamil Nadu and All-India

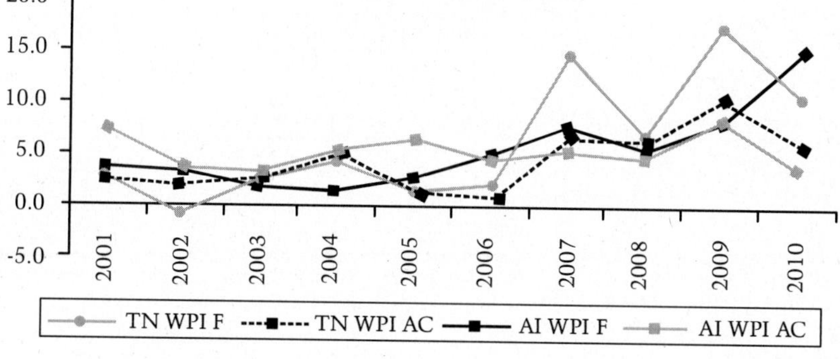

Source: Office of the Economic Adviser to the Government of India, Ministry of Commerce and Industry and WPI of Tamil Nadu is from Department of Economics and Statistics, Government of Tamil Nadu.

The main drivers of inflation in Tamil Nadu were the manufacturing and non-food sectors (Figure 3.3). The average WPI for manufacturing and non-food closely followed the respective all-India inflation. The manufacturing sector inflation was at its peak in 2003-04 in Tamil Nadu and which was much below food inflation, rose to above 5 per cent in 2008-09. The non-food inflation was above 8 per cent and higher than food inflation in 2003-04 steeply fell in 2005-06 and rose sharply to above 10 per cent in 2007-08.

Figure 3.3

Non-Food and Manufactured Products Inflation: Tamil Nadu and All-India

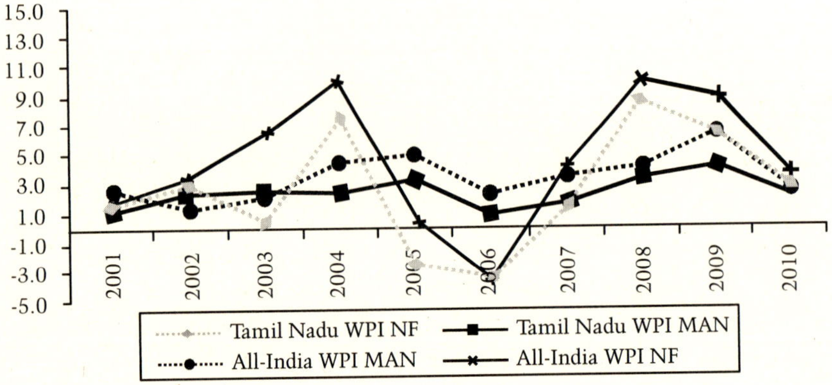

Source: Office of the Economic Adviser to the Government of India, Ministry of Commerce and Industry and WPI of Tamil Nadu is from Department of Economics and Statistics, Government of Tamil Nadu.

The CV for Tamil Nadu was high for WPI all commodities at 0.7 as against 0.3 for all-India (AI) during 2001-2010 reflecting higher volatility in inflation in Tamil Nadu. The CV for food (1.0) and non-food (1.5) for Tamil Nadu was higher than all-India (0.8 and 1.0, respectively during 2001-2010) except manufacturing (0.4 each for Tamil Nadu and all-India).

The correlation matrix revealed that WPI inflation (all commodities), non-food and manufacturing sector inflation in Tamil Nadu was highly correlated with all-India during the crisis period (2006-2010) unlike the period in 2001-2005. Food inflation in Tamil Nadu was negatively correlated with that of all-India during 2001-2005 and there was almost no correlation between WPI for all commodities in Tamil Nadu and that of manufacturing (Table 3.2).

Table 3.2

Correlation Matrix: Tamil Nadu WPI and All-India WPI

	AC	*FOOD*	*MANU*	*NF*
2001-2010	0.43	0.68	0.69	0.90
2001-2005	0.04	-0.69	0.45	0.78
2006-2010	0.96	0.04	0.83	0.95

CPI Inflation

Consumer Price Index for Industrial Workers (CPI-IW)

The Consumer Price Index for Industrial Workers (CPI-IW) brought out by the Labour Bureau, Government of India, for various centres[5] in the southern states and all-India is used. The average inflation measured by CPI-IW during the crisis period (2006-2010) doubled for all the states except Kerala as compared with the pre-crisis period (2001-2005), see Figure 3.4. The average inflation in Andhra Pradesh and Karnataka was highest at 9.1 per cent and 8.7 per cent, respectively. Inflation in Tamil Nadu (7.6%) was closer to all-India (7.9%) in the crisis period. Only Kerala (5.9%) had a lower average inflation than that of all-India during the crisis and pre-crisis period. Tamil Nadu's average inflation which was above than that of other states and all-India during 2002-03 slided sharply and was lower in 2004-05. Thereafter, it rose higher and converged with those of other states in 2008-09 but was above all-India and had remained stable in 2009-10. Inflation in the other states and all-India reached their maximum (over 11%).

The coefficient of variation (CV) of CPI-IW topped for Kerala (0.65) followed by Andhra Pradesh (0.64), Tamil Nadu (0.58) and Karnataka (0.55) as compared with 0.44 for all-India during 2001-2010. It is observed that the CV was very high for Tamil Nadu (0.55), Kerala (0.49) and Andhra Pradesh (0.42), during the 2001-2005 pre-crisis period and much above that of all-India (0.26). The CV of Karnataka (0.26) was closer to all-India. The period 2006-2010 (crisis period) witnessed a higher CV for Kerala (0.63), Andhra Pradesh (0.47) and Karnataka (0.37) indicating higher volatility in inflation in these three states. On the contrary, the CV was lower for Tamil Nadu (0.42) but remained above all-India (0.29) during the crisis period.

---

5. The CPI-IW (Base=1982), is compiled for six centres in Andhra Pradesh (Godavarikhani, Guntur, Hyderabad, Vijayawada, Visakhapatnam and Warangal), five centres in Karnataka (Bangalore, Belgaum, Hubli-Dharwad, Mercara and Mysore), three centres in Kerala (Ernakulam, Mundakayam and Kollam), one centre in Puducherry (Puducherry) and six centres in Tamil Nadu (Chennai, Coimbatore, Coonoor, Madurai, Salem and Tiruchirapalli).

Figure 3.4

CPI Industrial Workers: States and All-India

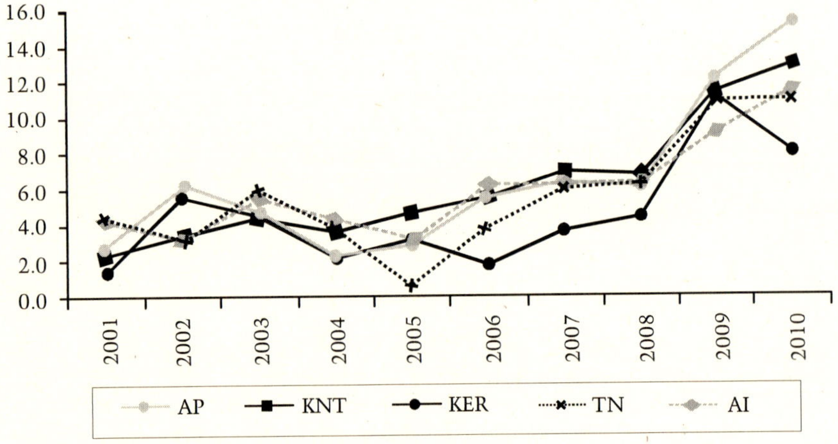

Source: Labour Bureau, Ministry of Labour & Employment, Government of India.

The correlation matrix revealed that CPI-IW inflation in all the four states were highly correlated with all-India as well as with other states during the crisis period (2006-2010). During the period 2001-2005, there was no or low correlation between Tamil Nadu, Andhra Pradesh and all-India. Correlation was negative for Karnataka and highest for Kerala with Tamil Nadu (Table 3.3).

Consumer Price Index for Agricultural Labourers (CPI-AL)

The Consumer Price Index for Agricultural Labourers (CPI-AL) brought out by the Labour Bureau, Government of India for various centres[6] in the southern states and all-India, is used. The average inflation CPI-AL during the crisis period (2006-2010) more than doubled for all the states except for Kerala as compared with the pre-crisis period (2001-2005). The average inflation in Karnataka and Andhra Pradesh was highest at 8.7 per cent and 8.6 per cent, respectively. The average inflation in Kerala

6. The CPI-AL, with 1986-87 as the base year, is compiled for six centres in Andhra Pradesh (Godavarikhani, Guntur, Hyderabad, Vijayawada, Visakhapatnam and Warangal), five centres in Karnataka (Bangalore, Belgaum, Hubli-Dharwad, Mercara and Mysore), three centres in Kerala (Ernakulam, Mundakayam and Kollam), one centre in Puducherry (Puducherry) and six centres in Tamil Nadu (Chennai, Coimbatore, Coonoor, Madurai, Salem and Tiruchirapalli).

(6.8%) and Tamil Nadu (7.6%) was below that of all-India (8.7%) in the crisis period (Figure 3.5).

Table 3.3

Correlation Matrix: CPI-IW Inflation

	CPIIWAP	CPIIWKNT	CPIIWKER	CPIIWTN	CPIIWAI
2001-2005					
CPIIWAP	1.0	0.4	-0.3	0.0	0.8
CPIIWKNT	0.4	1.0	0.0	-0.1	0.5
CPIIWKER	-0.3	0.0	1.0	0.9	0.2
CPIIWTN	0.0	-0.1	0.9	1.0	0.5
CPIIWAI	0.8	0.5	0.2	0.5	1.0
2006-2010					
CPIIWAP	1.0	0.9	1.0	1.0	1.0
CPIIWKNT	0.9	1.0	1.0	0.8	0.9
CPIIWKER	1.0	1.0	1.0	0.9	1.0
CPIIWTN	1.0	0.8	0.9	1.0	0.9
CPIIWAI	1.0	0.9	1.0	0.9	1.0

Note: AP=Andhra Pradesh; KNT=Karnataka; KER=Kerala; TN=Tamil Nadu and AI= All-India.

Figure 3.5

CPI Agricultural Labourers: States and All-India

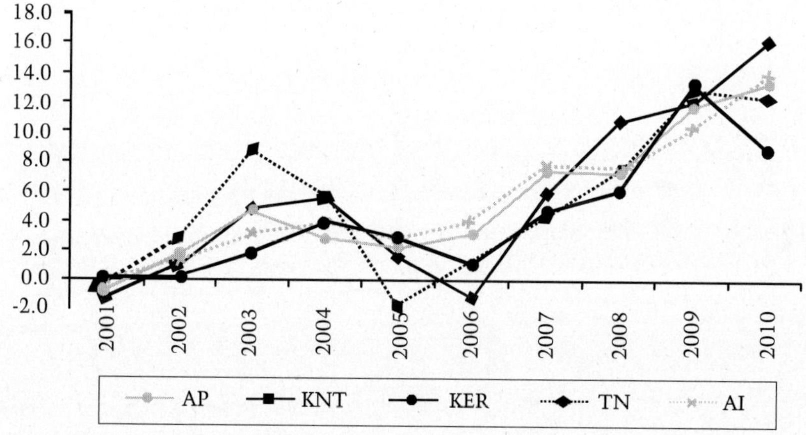

Source: Labour Bureau, Ministry of Labour & Employment, Government of India.

The coefficient of variation (CV) of CPI-AL topped for Karnataka (1.1), followed by Kerala (1.0), Tamil Nadu (1.0) and Andhra Pradesh (0.9), while it stood at 0.8 for all-India during 2001-2010. It is observed that the CV was very high for Karnataka (0.8), Kerala (0.7), Tamil Nadu (0.7) and Andhra Pradesh (0.5) during 2006-2010 and above all-India (0.4). On the contrary, the CV was higher for Tamil Nadu (1.4), Karnataka (1.2), Andhra Pradesh and Kerala (1.0) and was above all-India (0.8) during the 2001-2005. The coefficient of variation (CV) of CPI-AL (food) for Tamil Nadu (2.4) was higher than that of all-India (2.0) during 2001-2005 and was significantly lower (0.9 and 0.5, respectively) during 2006-2010.

The correlation matrix revealed that CPI-AL inflation in all the four states were negatively correlated with that of all-India during the crisis period (2006-2010) implying that regional factors played a dominant role in the regional inflation. The correlation of CPI-AL food inflation between Tamil Nadu and all-India was higher (0.8) during 2006-2010 as compared with (0.6) during 2001-2005 (Table 3.4). During the period 2001-2005, barring Kerala, other states were positively correlated with all-India.

Table 3.4

Correlation Matrix: CPI-AL Inflation

	CPIALAP	CPIALKNT	CPIALKER	CPIALTN	CPIALAI
2001-2005					
CPIALAP	1.0	0.8	0.8	0.9	0.3
CPIALKNT	0.8	1.0	0.3	0.9	0.8
CPIALKER	0.8	0.3	1.0	0.6	-0.3
CPIALTN	0.9	0.9	0.6	1.0	0.6
CPIALAI	0.3	0.8	-0.3	0.6	1.0
2006-2010					
CPIALAP	1.0	0.8	0.9	0.9	-0.1
CPIALKNT	0.8	1.0	1.0	0.8	-0.2
CPIALKER	0.9	1.0	1.0	0.9	-0.3
CPIALTN	0.9	0.8	0.9	1.0	-0.4
CPIALAI	-0.1	-0.2	-0.3	-0.4	1.0

Note: AP = Andhra Pradesh; KNT = Karnataka; KER = Kerala; TN = Tamil Nadu and AI = All-India.

Weighted Contribution

The magnitude of influence of the major sub-groups in the overall price index depends upon their weights assigned in the commodity basket. The divergence in the weighted contributions by the sub-groups for all-India and Tamil Nadu in the WPI inflation is evident from Table 3.5. It is pertinent to note that similar to the trend in all-India, the weighted contribution in Tamil Nadu during 2001 was negative for food and positive for non-food and significantly higher than all-India in 2010 and 2011. While the contribution of minerals was negligible, those of fuel, power, light and lubricants and manufacturing were significantly lower than all-India. The above analysis clearly indicates the need for aligning the price indices in Tamil Nadu with all-India in terms of base year, coverage of commodities and its structure.

Table 3.5

Weighted Contribution

All-India	*(Base 1993-94=100)*			*(Base 2004-05=100)*		
WPI	*2001*	*2006*	*2010*	*2006*	*2010*	*2011*
All commodities	100.0	100.0	100.0	100.0	100.0	100.0
I. Primary articles	4.4	23.8	39.3	29.0	47.3	34.0
1. Food	-1.3	20.4	25.3	23.7	31.4	16.7
2. Non-food	4.9	-3.2	13.9	2.7	8.5	13.3
II. Minerals	0.7	6.5	0.2	2.5	7.6	4.1
III. Fuel, power, light etc.	59.3	49.4	24.9	37.8	19.8	19.8
IV. Manufactured products	37.2	25.0	36.1	33.2	32.5	46.3

Tamil Nadu	*(Base 1970-71=100)*			
WPI	*2001*	*2006*	*2010*	*2011*
All commodities	100.0	100.0	100.0	100.0
I. Primary articles	20	80.1	82.2	74.7
1. Food	-27.6	88.3	67.0	59.2
2. Non-food	47.7	-8.2	15.2	15.4
II. Minerals	0.0	0.0	0.0	0.0
III. Fuel, power, light etc.	27.6	11.7	1.0	0.3
IV. Manufactured products	52.4	8.3	16.8	25.2

Source: Office of the Economic Advisor, Ministry of Industry, Government of India and Department of Economics and Statistics, Government of Tamil Nadu.

IV

Regional Factors underlying the Inflation

Regional inflation, similar to the aggregate national inflation, can be explained both by demand-side and supply-side factors.

Supply-Side Factors

Supply-side factors are more structural in nature emanating from the limited production capacity of the region. The average total area under food grains (*kharif* and *rabi*) as well as share in all-India area under food grains increased for all the states during the five-year period between 2006-2010 as compared with the previous five-year period between 2001-2005. In terms of area size during the period 2006-2010, the largest coverage under food grains was for Karnataka with a 6.2 per cent share in all-India, and it was followed by Andhra Pradesh (5.9 per cent), Tamil Nadu (2.6 per cent) and Kerala (0.2 per cent). The average area under food grains for all-India grew by 2.1 per cent during 2006-2010 as against a decline by 0.4 per cent during 2001-2005.

The average total food grains production (*kharif* and *rabi*) as well as share in all-India area increased during 2006-2010 over the period 2001-2005. The largest producer of food grains was Andhra Pradesh (175.7 lakh tonnes or 28.1 per cent and 7.9 per cent share in all-India food grain production) followed by Karnataka (114.4 lakh tonnes or 31.8 per cent and 5.2 per cent share), Tamil Nadu (73.0 lakh tonnes or 16.4 per cent and 3.3 per cent share) and Kerala (6.1 lakh tonnes or decline by (-)11.2 per cent and 0.3 per cent share). The all-India average food grain production at 2218.6 lakh tonnes grew by 11.4 per cent as against decline by 1.0 per cent during 2001-2005.

The annual average yield of food grains increased and was highest in the case of Andhra Pradesh (2,465 kg per hectare or 21.9 per cent) followed by Kerala (2,387 kg per hectare or 8.4 per cent), Tamil Nadu (2,077 kg per Hectare or 22.0 per cent), Karnataka (1,443 kg per hectare or 8.4 per cent) and all-India (1,848 kg per hectare or 7.5 per cent).

Supply Elasticity

Supply elasticity with respect to CPI-IW showed that supply was highly elastic during the period 2001-2005 and inelastic during 2006-2010 in the three states, while supply was inelastic throughout the period for Kerala and all-India. If we take CPI-AL, the supply was inelastic for all the four states and all-India during 2001-2005, while it was elastic in the case of Andhra Pradesh and Tamil Nadu during the period 2006-2010. This indicates that supply depends upon other local regional factors like rainfall, availability of inputs, state government policies as well as trade policy. The supply elasticity of food grains with respect to WPI food inflation for Tamil Nadu and all-India showed that it was highly elastic during the period 2001-2005 and was inelastic during the period 2006-2010. This shows that supply is influenced by factors such as change in tastes and preferences (outcome of increased incomes), availability of substitutes, etc.

In sum, the above analysis shows that the area and production of food grains in the four states have increased except for Kerala and inflation in Kerala was relatively higher than other states in the region during 2006-2010. However, the rate of growth in food grain production has been significantly lower as compared with the rate of growth in income (NSDP) for all the southern states except Tamil Nadu where the growth in food production at 8.1 per cent was closer to income (NSDP) growth at 9.8 per cent during 2006-2010. At the same time the average growth in population has marginally declined in Andhra Pradesh and Karnataka, while it has more or less stagnated in Kerala and Tamil Nadu. The food grains' yield has increased in all the states and is much above the all-India average yield. It shows that there is potential to increase overall food grain output as well as increasing the area under those crops on which there is a competitive advantage for the states. Production of commercial crops are largely influenced by movements in global commodity prices, rather than by domestic policies as nearly 40 per cent of the edible oil demand is met through imports.

Other Factors in Supply

There are several other factors such as crop cycle, identification of cropping zones, post-harvest losses, weather and rainfall, water management and other infrastructure facilities which influence the supply-side. As the southern region is largely dependent on rainfall, changes in the crop cycles are capable of influencing the supply. Droughts, irregular and unseasonal monsoon disrupts the crop cycle and the production processes. It is observed that due to this factor and also due to higher prices of certain commodities like pulses, crop substitution was undertaken. Identification of the potential zones for cultivation of various food (Poornima *et al.*, 2008) as well as horticulture crops (Thavaprakaash *et al.*, 2008) is essential for increasing productivity and yield. This is important for managing supply shocks particularly in food. Most often, farmers tend to grow crops in an area which is either unremunerative or uneconomical due to lack of knowledge or experience. Growing efficient crops as per the area-specific potentials will not only enhance production but also save the costs involved in transportation, marketing and sales. Progress in scientific agricultural research can be utilised in assessing the potential cropping zones for different crops.

High post-harvest losses reduce food supplies. Farmers lose their share of income while consumers lose in terms of quantity. Losses of food crops occur due to a number of factors such as weight loss, loss of food values (price), loss in terms of increasing cost of production, loss of quality or acceptability and loss of seeds itself. On the export front too, superior methods of processing, storage, packaging, transport and marketing are essential to avoid post-harvest losses. As per a World Bank study (1999), post-harvest losses of food grains in India are 7-10 per cent of the total production from farm to market level and 4-5 per cent at market and distribution levels. Post-harvest losses in food grains is influenced by weather, rainfall, crop disease (Basavaraja *et al.*, 2007) and level of technological practices adopted during threshing and milling, and knowledge of post-harvest technology for storage, preservation, processing and handling (Basappa *et al.*, 2007). Post-harvest losses in perishables (fruits and vegetables) occur due to reasons like damages by birds, pest and disease attack (Kumar *et al.*, 2005), malformation, crushing and rotting. While at market level, the reasons are poor handling and packing, lack of scientific knowledge on post-harvest technology, poor transportation and storage facilities (Prabakar *et al.*, 2005). Thus, the post-harvest losses have impact at both the micro and macro levels of the economy.

Furthermore, in Tamil Nadu, the weather and rainfall sets in motion for favourable or unfavourable factors which considerably influence the harvest. Factors such as fertility of land, monsoon behaviour, rainfall, irrigation, application of fertilisers, climatic conditions, marketing facilities, prices, availability of agricultural labourers etc., determine the area and productivity of any crop. Due to the variability of northeast monsoon rainfall, floods and droughts are common in most parts of Tamil Nadu (Parasuraman *et al.*, 2008). Studies showed that water management and cultural practices had significant influence on rice yields (Ahamed et al., 2008). The System of Rice Intensification (SRI) has led to significant increase in productivity and substantial reduction in the quantum of use of water in Tamil Nadu. Furthermore, under the World Bank funded Irrigated Agriculture Modernisation and Water-Bodies Restoration and Management (IAMWARM) project works are underway benefitting 16 lakh acres of agricultural land. Schemes like National Agricultural Development Programme, National Food Security Mission, Pulses and Oilseeds Production Programme are being implemented intensively in Tamil Nadu. Steps are being taken to increase the production of vegetables by adopting new cultivation methods like precision farming, greenhouse cultivation, etc.

Demand-Side Factors

Among the demand-side factors, income and population growth are important causal factors in the regional inflationary process. Per capita income reflects the purchasing power and standard of living of the people of each state. Rising population directly affects the demand for essential commodities like food, which has a significant weightage in the price indices. In terms of size, the average per capita NSDP was highest in Kerala during 2001-2005 and its position was taken by Tamil Nadu during 2006-2010. It can be observed that the absolute amount of per capita income has almost doubled for the states as compared with that of all-India (Table 3.6).

Table 3.6

Average Growth in Per Capita NSDP

	Andhra Pradesh	*Karnataka*	*Kerala*	*Tamil Nadu*	*All-India*
2001-2005	5.3	2.6	5.3	3.5	4.1
2006-2010	7.5	7.0	7.9	9.3	6.9
		Average Amount of Per Capita NSDP			
2001-2005	17556	18075	21703	20474	17262
2006-2010	32380	34088	40313	40776	29999
		Average Growth in NSDP			
2001-2005	6.4	4.0	6.1	4.4	5.8
2006-2010	8.6	2.4	8.7	10.1	8.4

Source: CSO and the respective state governments.

It is pertinent to note that there is a perceptible decline in the share of agriculture in the total NDP both at the all-India level as well as state level, while the level of employment continue to be stable. Ramamurti and Radhai (2005) emphasise that any poverty reduction policy measure in the rural sector need to pay attention to non-farming sector activities as alternative avenues of employment. On the other hand, Kalirajan and Shand (2004), found farmers use advanced rice production technology and it has the capacity to absorb a considerable amount of hired labour. If such technologies are adopted, labour shortages in agriculture in Tamil Nadu could be minimised. There is an imperative need to focus policy reforms in non-farming sector.

It is also observed that among the southern states, while in terms of geographical area, Andhra Pradesh ranks 4th, followed by Karnataka in the 8th place, Tamil Nadu in the 11th place and Kerala in the 21st place, the decadal growth in population as per the 2011 Census was highest for Karnataka at 15.7 per cent (ranks 9th in terms of population), followed by Tamil Nadu at 15.6 per cent (ranks 7th in terms of population), Andhra Pradesh at 11.1 per cent (ranks 5th in terms of population) and Kerala at 4.9 per cent (ranks 12th in terms of population). The data from NSSO show that the household monthly per capita consumer expenditure (MPCE) has considerably increased both in the rural and urban areas in the states as compared with for all-India (Table 3.7). The percentage of expenditure on food to total consumption expenditure also showed deceleration in the rural and urban areas reflecting the change in food preferences.

Table 3.7

NSSO Rounds: Monthly Per Capita Consumption Expenditure

States	Monthly Per Capita Consumption Expenditure (Rs)						Percentage of Food to Consumption Expenditure			
	Rural			Urban			Rural		Urban	
	2007-08	2004-05	% Var	2007-08	2004-05	% Var	2004-05	2007-08	2004-05	2007-08
Andhra Pradesh	816	586	39.2	1550	1019	52.1	55.2	52.0	41.6	37.0
Karnataka	819	508	61.2	1668	1033	61.5	55.7	51.0	43.2	37.0
Kerala	1383	1013	36.5	1948	1291	50.9	45.0	41.0	40.0	36.0
Tamil Nadu	834	602	38.5	1410	1080	30.6	52.4	50.0	42.7	39.0
All-India	772	559	38.1	1472	1052	39.9	55.0	52.0	42.5	40.0

As pulses are considered an important dietary food, special efforts have been taken both by the Central and state governments in the recent years to enhance production. The dominant source of protein in Indian diet is pulses, which vary quite significantly across regions and, to some extent, between income groups (Gokarn, 2010). The Tamil Nadu Integrated Nutrition Project (TINP) for instance, particularly has been termed as successful and other states could learn mutually beneficial lessons. There has been a perceptible change in the consumption pattern characterised by declining share of food grains and the increasing share of non-food grain items in the consumption baskets particularly fruits and vegetables. Tamil Nadu with seven agro-climatic conditions and varied soil types is better placed for production of fruits, vegetables, spices, plantation crops, flower, medicinal and aromatic plants. In Tamil Nadu the co-operative stores, public distribution system outlets, and the Uzhavar Sandhais (farmers' shanties) have ensured fair price for agricultural produces like pulses and vegetables.

Fiscal Measures

In order to step up procurement, the Tamil Nadu government has provided an incentive of Rs 70 per quintal for Grade-A variety and Rs 50 per quintal for common variety of rice. In the same manner, higher procurement price for sugarcane, *tur dal*, green gram and black gram has incentivised farmers to cultivate these crops. The Tamil Nadu government has initiated several measures to reduce prices through a modified tax regime. Sales tax on pulses and grams have been completely abolished while on wheat, it has been reduced to 2 per cent. Sales tax on groundnut oil, gingelly (sesame) oil and coconut oil has been removed. Sales tax on sunflower oil was reduced to 1 per cent. Tamil Nadu is one of the few states which is not levying any sales tax on rice.

V

Empirical Evidence from Tamil Nadu

As the main aim was to identify factors determining inflation in Tamil Nadu, a testing for unit roots in all the variables was undertaken. Using ADF method, it was found that except rainfall (RAINPC), average call money rates (CALLAV), Index of Industrial Production (General Index and Manufacturing) in Tamil Nadu (TNIIPG and TNIIPM) were stationary only in the trend and intercept. All other variables were non-stationary at level (0) (Annexure Table A-3.1). Therefore, cointegration regression procedures were adopted for estimation. The Dynamic Ordinary Least Square (DOLS) procedure (Saikonnen, 1991 and Stock and Watson, 1993) was used as it has several advantages. The endogeneity of any of the regressors has no effect asymptotically on the robustness of the estimates. The statistical inference on the parameters of cointegrating vector is facilitated as statistics of the estimated coefficient have asymptotic normal distribution even with endogeneous regressors. It enables direct estimation of I(0) and I(1) variables. It is asymptotically equivalent to the maximum likelihood estimator of Johansen (1988) and is known to perform well in infinite samples. It also incorporates lags and leads of the first differences of the variables which are useful to estimate expectations.

In order to explore the determinants of inflation in Tamil Nadu, three models were adopted, *viz*.: (1) demand-supply factors, (2) external shocks and (3) inflationary expectations. Monthly data covering the period April 2001 to December 2010 are sourced from various publications of Government of Tamil Nadu, Labour Bureau, GoI, Simla and Reserve Bank of India. The DOLS equations were separately run at the sectoral levels viz.: (i) all commodities (ii) food and (iii) manufacturing. The following variables were used: (1) Wholesale Price Index (WPI) of Tamil Nadu (TNWPI) (Base 1970-71=100) including all commodities (TNWPIAC) and Manufacturing (TNWPIM), (2) As Tax collections in Tamil Nadu (TAXCOLL) are based on actual production and since monthly real sector data at the state level is not available, tax collections were used as a proxy for production, (3) Index of Industrial Production for Tamil Nadu (TNIIP) bifurcated into General Index (TNIIPG) and Manufacturing Index (TNIIPM), (4) Agricultural Wage Index for Tamil Nadu (TNAGWG), (5) monthly deviation of actual rainfall from the normal in per cent (RAINPC), (6) for external factors, monthly average Rupee *vs* Dollar Exchange Rate (REUSD), monthly average of International Fertiliser Prices (UREA and AMMONIA) and (7) monthly average of International Crude Oil Prices (DUBAIOIL) were used.

Results

The demand-supply factors are imputed in Model I and it was found that headline inflation in Tamil Nadu is significantly influenced by domestic demand and supply factors. It is interesting to note that the rainfall had limited impact on inflation implying that receipt of rainfall *per se* is not a sufficient condition, but its storage, timely availability and distribution is a necessary condition. Second, the coefficients of IIPG and TAXCOLL are negative and significant. The TNAGWG is positive and also significant. (Annexure Table A-3.2). Model 2 showed that oil shock and exchange rate have a very significant impact on WPI inflation in Tamil Nadu. Finally, in Model 3 expectations have been imputed by specifying variables such as rice stock, call money and WPI lag as consumers are backward looking, when it comes to inflation. It is been observed that rice stock and call money rates do have some augmenting inflation expectation in Tamil Nadu, while lag of WPI is highly significant in influencing inflationary expectations.

At the sectoral level, food inflation in Tamil Nadu is largely determined by agricultural wage index, while rainfall has no significant impact (Annexure Table A-3.3). The IIPG and tax collections negatively influence food inflation. Among external factors, FAO Food Index and exchange rate is highly significant at 1 per cent level, while international prices of Dubai Oil and Urea are significant at 5 per cent level. With regard to non-food inflation (Annexure Table A-3.4), the same factors holds good except for Urea which is not significant. Inflation originating in the manufacturing sector in Tamil Nadu is significantly influenced by agricultural wages, tax collections and international prices of ammonia (Annexure Table A-3.5). External factors like International Dubai Oil and exchange rates do have a positive and significant impact. While own lag and exchange rate have a significant influence on inflationary expectations. Inflation originating in the manufacturing sector is not influenced by rice stocks and call money rates.

Food articles, and to some extent non-food articles, appears to be the prime drivers of WPI inflation in Tamil Nadu. Due to poor agriculture growth and continuing high food inflation at all-India level, the inflation based on WPI food articles remained relatively lower in Tamil Nadu only in the recent years. In fact inflation in Tamil Nadu was higher than all-India during 2005-2007 and 2008-09. One possible reason could be the regional bias and prominence of regional factors in the inflation process. Second, the number of commodities covered in the WPI basket is only 177 in Tamil Nadu and it is also possible that the other commodities that are largely consumed by a wider segment of population may not find a place in the WPI basket. Partly, lower inflation in Tamil Nadu in the recent years is due to the recent supply-side measures taken by the state government to arrest inflationary pressures along with improvements in market infrastructural facilities.

Apart from moderation in inflation based on WPI food articles, non-food component has also witnessed a significant downward movements in Tamil Nadu relative to all-India. It may be noted that this is contrary to the trend of WPI (all-India), where the manufacturing component witnessed a sharp rise in tandem with the consolidation of recovery in GDP growth. Thus, it implies that the moderation of inflation in Tamil Nadu is the reason for the divergence in movement of inflation in TN *vis-à-vis* all-India. Very low correlation of rainfall with TNWPIAC (0.09), TNWPIFD (0.08) and TNWPIM (0.12) suggests that the deviation from normal rainfall do not have positive impact on inflation in Tamil Nadu. It also suggests that the manufacturing sector is not dependent on rainfall and points towards the non-dependence of manufacturing sector on agriculture-based industries. Overall, WPI inflation in Tamil Nadu is more defined by a combination of supply, demand factors and external shocks. Different model specifications suggest that the policy measures have stronger role in anchoring inflation and inflationary expectations in Tamil Nadu.

VI

Conclusion and Policy Implications

High inflation persists in any economy either due to supply shortages or higher demand or a combination of both. However, what matters is the identification of structural and temporary factors to aid policy decisions. In Tamil Nadu several factors like supply bottlenecks, inefficient intermediation between producers and consumers, frequent occurrence of natural calamities and floods have damaged the standing crops and have exerted pressure on the primary articles. Moreover, the hike in fuel charges also contributed to the inflation process as hike in transportation charges get reflected in the price increase. Lower inflation scenario in Tamil Nadu can be attributed to supply management strategies adopted by the state government and the normal to excess rainfall received in the state have recharged the irrigation reservoirs. Contrary to the general perception that inflation in Tamil Nadu is lower than all-India inflation, the data shows that inflation in Tamil Nadu has been higher than that of all-India during the decade (2001-2010).

On the supply side, minimisation of quantitative losses is a greater priority than qualitative losses. The Government has already introduced central scheme *viz.*, Post Harvest Technology and Management to reduce the post-harvest losses and promote value addition of the produce through creation of adequate infrastructure in the production areas. Education and training on post-harvest operations, along with creation of awareness among the farmers as well as other associated agencies would greatly help in reducing the post-harvest losses in food grains. Improvements in cold storage facilities require immediate attention of the policymakers for reducing post-harvest loss in maize and in fruits and vegetables. Towards this end, adoption of the zero energy cool chambers technology developed by the Indian Council of Agricultural Research (ICAR) needs to be encouraged among the stakeholders. Solving the post-harvest food distribution problems requires cooperation and effective communication among all the research, extension, and industry personnel involved.

Among the temporary factors, poor harvests due to natural phenomena, hike in global food prices during the period between 2006 and 2008, transient cuts in domestic investments in agriculture, depreciation of the United States dollar during 2006 and 2008 are the major factors responsible for the surge in domestic food prices in Tamil Nadu. Although speculations and hoarding of essential food items were to an extent responsible for regional inflation, timely actions by the Central and state governments have played a greater role in minimising the effects. Notwithstanding the fact that trading in commodity also had a role, there has been no empirical evidence on this. In the event of short supply of food grains, the prices of food articles are bound to remain at higher level. Measures like, banning exports of wheat flour (September 2007), introduction of a minimum export price for non-*basmati* rice (October 2007), banning exports of non-*basmati* rice (March 2008), increase of the minimum price on exports of *basmati* rice (March 2008) and lastly, banning exports and facilitating imports of onions and potatoes (November 2010) have had a dampening effect on domestic inflation. However, fall in export incomes may affect overall growth. High food prices across globe may affect India in the long term as overseas Indian remittances may fall as high cost of living may spare less for remitting home. Further weakening of the dollar may also encourage imports from the non-dollar countries. However, comfortable forex reserves enable imports and provide a cushion against food insecurity in the short term.

On the whole, both regional and national inflation have been impacted by a combination of structural and temporary factors. Among the structural factors, increase in production costs due to international fuel and fertiliser prices has exhibited a major influence from early 2002 until the middle of 2008, when prices peaked and then dropped as a direct consequence of the global financial and economic crisis. Second, sustained rapid growth in incomes have changed the consumption patterns both in the rural as well as urban areas and is one of the main structural factors behind the food inflation in India. Although per capita expenditure as well as consumption of food has decelerated, the higher incomes have led to higher demand for conventional and new goods, of either a better quality or of a different nature. Managing supply shocks involves not only quantitative factors like area, production and productivity but also involves attention to a host of immediate factors. Besides, it is also essential to expand the inventories in other food items other than rice and wheat. Expansion of inventories also should be made applicable to seeds, fertilisers and water resources. More importantly for a better understanding of the regional inflation, there is a need for aligning the price indices at the regional level with those of all-India in terms of base year, coverage of commodities and its structure.

References

Abdullah, Muhammad and Rukhsana Kalim (2010). *Determinants of Food Price Inflation in Pakistan.* (Online).

Ahamed, S. Nazeer, A. Arokiaraj, B. Chandrasekaran and V. Muralidharan (2008). "Influence of Water Management and Cultural Practices on the Yield Attributes and Yield of Rice", *Madras Agricultural Journal* 95 (7-12): 472-474, July-December.

Alberola, Enrique and José Manuel Marqués (2001). "On the Relavance and Nature of Regional Inflation Differentials: The case of Spain", *Banco de España—Servicio de Estudios Documento de Trabajo* 9913.

Altissimo, F., B. Mojon and P. Zaffaroni (2007). *"Fast Micro and Slow Macro: Can Aggregation Explain the Persistence of Inflation?"*, *ECB Working Paper* No. 729, Frankfurt: ECB.

Altissimo, F., P. Benigno and D.R. Palenzuela (2005). "Long-run Determinants of Inflation Differentials in a Monetary Union", *Working Paper* No. 11473, National Bureau of Economic Research.

Asian Development Bank Report (2008). "Special Report: Food Prices and Inflation in Developing Asia: Is Poverty Reduction Coming to an End", Economics and Research Department, April.

Basappa, G., J.B. Deshmanya and B.L Patil (2007). "Post- Harvest Losses of Maize Crop in Karnataka: An Economic Analysis", *Karnataka Journal of Agricultural Sciences* 20(1): (69-71).

Basavaraja, H., S.B. Mahajanashetti and Naveen C. Udagatti (2007). "Economic Analysis of Post-harvest Losses in Food Grains in India: A Case Study of Karnataka", *Agricultural Economics Research Review* 20: 117-126, January-June.

Beck, G.W. and A.A. Weber (2005a). "Price Stability, Inflation Convergence and Diversity in EMU: Does One Size Fit All?", *CFS Working Paper* No. 2005/30.

———. (2005b). "Inflation Dispersion and Convergence in Monetary and Economic Unions: Lessons for the ECB", *CFS Working Paper* No. 2005/31.

Beck, G.W., K. Hubrich and M. Marcellino (2006). "Regional Inflation Dynamics within and across Euro Area Countries and a Comparison with the US", *Working Paper Series* 681, European Central Bank.

Brodjonegoro, Bambang P.S., Telissa Falianty and Beta Y. Gitaharie (2005). "Determinant Factors of Regional Inflation in Decentralised Indonesia", *Economic and Finance in Indonesia* 53(1): 1-31.

Busetti, F., S. Fabiani and A. Harvey (2006). "Convergence of Prices and Rates of Inflation", *Oxford Bulletin of Economics and Statistics* 68: 863-877.

Cecchetti, S.G. and G. Debelle (2006). "Inflation Persistence", *Economic Policy* 21: 311-352.

Cecchetti, S.G., N.C. Mark and R. Sonora (2002). "Price Level Convergence among United States Cities: Lessons for the European Central Bank", *International Economic Review* 43: 1081-1099.

Das, Samarjit and Kaushik Bhattacharya (2004). "Price Convergence across Regions in India", *Bonn Econ Discussion Papers, Discussion Paper* 1/2005, December.

Dasgupta, Dipak, R.N. Dubey and R. Sathish (2011). "Domestic Wheat Price Formation and Food Inflation in India: International Prices, Domestic Drivers (Stocks, Weather, Public Policy), and the Efficacy of Public Policy Interventions in Wheat Markets",

Working Paper No.2/2011-DEA, Department of Economic Affairs, Ministry of Finance, Government of India, May.

Engel, C., and J.H. Rogers (1996). "Regional Patterns in the Law of One Price: The Roles of Geography vs. Currencies", *International Finance Discussion Paper* No. 533. Board of Governors of the Federal Reserve System.

Gokarn, Subir (2010). "The Price of Protein", Inaugural Address at Special Conference in Honour of Dr. Kirit Parikh, Mumbai: IGIDR, October 26.

Johansen, S. (1988). "Statistical Analysis of Co-integrating Vectors", *Journal of Economic Dynamics and Control* 12: 231-54.

Kalirajan, K. and R.T. Shand (2004). *Labour Absorption in Tamil Nadu: A Micro Analysis*. (Online).

Kumar, G.M. Sunil, J.G. Angadi, L.V. Hirevenkanagoudar and Sadaqath Syed (*2005*). "Knowledge of Farmers Regarding Production and Post-Harvest Technology of Tomato", *Karnataka Journal of Agricultural Sciences* 19(1): 177-179.

Loening, L.J., D. Durevall and Y.A. Birru (2009). "Inflation Dynamics and Food Prices in an Agricultural Economy: The Case of Ethiopia", *Working Paper* No. 347. Gothenburg, Sweden: University of Gothenburg.

Marques, Helena, Gabriel Pino and J.D. Tena (2009). *Regional Inflation Dynamics using Space-time Models*. (Online).

Mehrotra, Aaron, Peltonen Tuomas and Alvaro Santos Rivera (2007). "Modelling Inflation in China: A Regional Perspective", *Working Paper Series* No. 829/2007. European Central Bank, November.

Mohanty, D. (2010). "Measures of Inflation: Issues and Perspectives", Speech at the Conference of Indian Association for Research in National Income and Wealth, Thiruvananthapuram: CDS. January 09.

Nadhanael, G.V. and S. Pattnaik (2010). "Measurement of Inflation in India: Issues and Associated Challenges for the Conduct of Monetary Policy", in *RBI Staff Papers*, Reserve Bank of India.

Nagayasu, Jun (2009). *Regional Inflation in China*. Japan: University of Tsukuba, Department of Social Systems and Management, 1-1-1 Tennodai, Ibaraki 305-8573 Japan, December.

———. (2010),"Regional Inflation (Price) Behaviors: Heterogeneity and Convergence", *MPRA Paper No*. 25430. Online at *http://mpra.ub.uni-muenchen.de/25430/*posted 25. September 2010/01:59

Parasuraman, P., R. Prakash, S.D. Sivakumar, G. Sudhakar, A. Arokiaraj and B. Chandrasekaran (2008). "Assessment of Drought and Flood in Cauvery Delta Zone with a Special Reference to Tamil Nadu Rice Research Institute, Aduthurai", *Madras Agricultural Journal* 95 (7-12): 457-461, July-December.

Parsley, D.C and S.J. Wei (1996). "Convergence to the Law of One Price without Trade Barriers or Currency Fluctuations", *Quarterly Journal of Economics* 111: 1211-36.

Poornima, S., S. Kokilavani, N. Thavaprakaash, C. Babu, V. Geethalakshmi and R. Jagannathan (2008). "Examining the Prospective Cropping Zone of Important Field Crops of Tamil Nadu", *Madras Agricultural Journal* 95 (7-12): 364-370 July-December.

Prabakar, K., T. Raguchander, V.K. Parthiban, P. Muthulakshmi and V. Prakasam (2005). "Post Harvest Fungal Spoilage in Mango at Different Levels Marketing", *Madras Agricultural Journal* 92(1-3): 42-48, January-March.

Ramamurti, Shantha and Radhai (2005). "The Impact of the Non Farming Sources of Income On the Socio Economic Conditions of the Village Economy of Tamilnadu, India", *Economic Studies : Research Study* No.1, Center for Asia Studies.

Rogoff, K. (2007). "The Impact of Globalisation on Monetary Policy", in *The New Economic Geography: Effects and Policy Implications.* Kansas City: Federal Reserve Bank.

Saikkonen, Pentti (1991). "Asymptotically Efficient Estimation of Cointegration Regressions", *Econometric Theory* 7(1): 1-21.

Stock, J.H. and M.W. Watson (1993). "A Simple Estimator of Cointegrating Vectors in Higher-order Integrated Systems", *Econometrica* 61: 783-820.

Subbarao, D (2010a). "Financial Crisis: Some Old Questions and Maybe Some New Answers", *Tenth CD Deshmukh Memorial Lecture.* Hyderabad: Council for Social Development, Southern Regional Centre.

———. (2010b). *India and the Global Financial Crisis Transcending from Recovery to Growth.* Washington DC: Peterson Institute for International Economics, April 26.

Thavaprakaash, N., Babu N.C. and R. Jagannathan (2008). "Identifying Potential Cropping Zones for Important Horticultural Crops of Tamil Nadu", *Madras Agricultural Journal* 95 (7-12): 418-424 July-December.

Valdovinos, Carlos G. Fernández and Kerstin Gerling (2011). "Inflation Uncertainty and Relative Price Variability in WAEMU Countries", *IMF Working Paper* No. *WP/11/59*, March.

Vaona, A. (2007). "Merging the Purchasing Power Parity and the Phillips Curve Literatures: Regional Panel Data Evidence from Italy", *International Regional Science Review* 30: 152-172.

———. (2008). "A Cross-sectional Approach to Regional Long-run Inflation in Italy", *Institute for Economic Research, University of Lugano, Via Maderno 24, CH-6904 Lugano, Switzerland.*

Vaona, Andrea and Guido Ascari (2010). "Regional Inflation Persistence: Evidence from Italy", *Working Paper Series, WP* No. 4, February, ISSN: 2036-2919 (paper), 2036-4679 (Online). Department of Economics, University of Verona.

World Bank (1999). *India Food grain Marketing Policies: Reforming to Meet Food Security Needs, Vols. I and II.* Report No. 18329. Washington, D.C.: The World Bank.

Yanliang, Miao, Weifeng Wu and Norbert Funke (2011). "Reviving the Competitive Storage Model: A Holistic Approach to Food Commodity Prices", *IMF Working Paper*, March.

Annexure Table A-3.1

Test of the Unit Root Hypothesis

Level	ADF Statistic				PP Statistic			
Variables	*Coefficient*	*Std. Error*	*t-Statistic*	*Prob.*	*Coefficient*	*Std. Error*	*t-Statistic*	*Prob.*
TNWPIAC (-1)	0.0080	0.0039	2.0634	0.0400	-0.0084	0.0129	-0.6467	0.5191
TNWPIFD (-1)	0.0086	0.0056	1.5472	0.1247	-0.0148	0.0150	-0.9870	0.3257
TNWPINF (-1)	0.0130	0.0114	1.1462	0.2541	0.0138	0.0106	1.3020	0.1956
TNWPIM (-1)	0.0219	0.0243	0.8994	0.3709	-0.6199	0.0870	-7.1282	0.0000
TNIIPG (-1)	0.0165	0.0247	0.6655	0.5100	-0.6990	0.0893	-7.8255	0.0000
TNIIPM (-1)	0.0033	0.0044	0.7695	0.4432	-0.6199	0.0869	-7.1282	0.0000
TAXCOLL (-1)	0.0375	0.0246	1.5285	0.1299	-0.0174	0.0222	-0.7865	0.4332
TNAGWG (-1)	0.0741	0.0266	2.7875	0.0065	-0.0018	0.0178	-0.0996	0.9208
RAINPC (-1)	-.9188	0.0932	-9.8519	0.0000	-0.9188	0.0933	-9.8519	0.0000
DUBAIOIL (-1)	-0.0293	0.01745	-1.6771	0.0964	-0.0683	0.0339	-2.0088	0.0469
REUSD (-1)	-0.0532	0.0251	-2.1231	0.0360	-0.0401	0.0259	-1.5426	0.1257
TNRICEST (-1)	-0.2076	0.4230	-4.9087	0.0000	-0.1478	0.0464	-3.1837	0.0019
CALLAV (-1)	-0.2378	0.0605	-3.9310	0.0001	-0.2333	0.0613	-3.8052	0.0002
FAOFOOD (-1)	-0.0075	0.0101	-0.7399	0.4609	-0.0262	0.0225	-1.0392	0.3009
UREA (-1)	-0.0870	0.0276	-3.1500	0.0021	-0.0885	0.0388	-2.2836	0.0243
AMMONIA (-1)	-0.0811	0.0373	-2.1745	0.3180	-0.0870	0.0382	-2.2774	0.0246

Annexure Table A-3.2

Tamil Nadu Inflation: Method—Dynamic Least Squares (DOLS)

Model I: Demand-supply factors affecting TN WPI (All Commodities)

Fixed leads and lags specification (lead=0, lag=4)

(a) Dependent variable: TNWPIAC

Variable	*Coefficient*	*Std. Error*	*t-Statistic*	*Prob.*
IIPG	-1.939729	0.876409	-2.213269	0.0295
TAXCOLL	-0.197028	0.05322	-3.702158	0.0004
TNAGWG	1.518625	0.106412	14.2712	0.000
RAINPC	0.129303	0.089552	1.443887	0.1524
C	1182.2	79.77446	14.81928	0.000
@TREND	6.240876	0.71032	8.786008	0.000
R-squared	0.993299	Mean dependent var		1518.721
Adjusted R-squared	0.991351	S.D. dependent var		216.6428
S.E. of regression	20.14789	Sum squared resid		34910.63
Durbin-Watson stat	0.380314	Long-run variance		1399.16

Model II: External shocks affecting TN WPI (All Commodities)

Fixed leads and lags specification (lead=0, lag=0)

Dependent variable: TNWPIAC

Variable	*Coefficient*	*Std. Error*	*t-Statistic*	*Prob.*
DUBAIOIL	8.731205	1.015926	8.59433	0.0000
REUSD	36.96071	10.19452	3.625546	0.0004
C	-631.4515	495.8252	-1.273536	0.2055
R-squared	0.72453	Mean dependent var		1509.698
Adjusted R-squared	0.714603	S.D. dependent var		218.1797
S.E. of regression	116.5573	Sum squared resid		1508001
Durbin-Watson stat	0.246656	Long-run variance		52679.29

Model III: Inflation expectations and TN WPI (All Commodities)

Fixed leads and lags specification (lead=0, lag=0)

Dependent variable: TNWPIAC

Variable	*Coefficient*	*Std. Error*	*t-Statistic*	*Prob.*
TNRICEST	6.42E-19	3.50E-19	1.834032	0.0694
CALLAV	-1.26E-13	4.77E-14	-2.644072	0.0094
TNWPIAC(1)	1.00	4.38E-16	2.28E+15	0.0000
C	3.25E-12	7.77E-13	4.177777	0.0001
R-squared	1.000	Mean dependent var		1505.815
Adjusted R-squared	1.000	S.D. dependent var		215.0718
S.E. of regression	5.01E-13	Sum squared resid		2.710E-23
Durbin-Watson stat	0.428245	Long-run variance		8.800E-25

Annexure Table A-3.3

Tamil Nadu Inflation: Method—Dynamic Least Squares (DOLS)

Model I (i): Demand-supply factors affecting TN WPI (Food)

Fixed leads and lags specification (lead=4, lag=0)
Dependent variable: TNWPIFD

Variable	*Coefficient*	*Std. Error*	*t-Statistic*	*Prob.*
IIPG	-1.896237	1.726724	-1.09817	0.2752
TAXCOLL	-0.260643	0.104855	-2.485747	0.0149
TNAGWG	3.625974	0.209655	17.29491	0.000
RAINPC	-0.195294	0.176437	-1.106874	0.2714
C	845.9878	161.2857	5.245274	0.000
@TREND	6.694622	1.399491	4.783613	0.000
R-squared	0.992122	Mean dependent var		1783.635
Adjusted R-squared	0.989832	S.D. dependent var		393.7153
S.E. of regression	39.70138	Sum squared resid		135553.2
Durbin-Watson stat	0.405307	Long-run variance		5431.245

Model II (i): External shocks affecting TN WPI (Food)

Fixed leads and lags specification (lead=0, lag=0)
Dependent variable: TNWPIFD

Variable	*Coefficient*	*Std. Error*	*t-Statistic*	*Prob.*
FAOFOOD	11.63505	1.658117	7.017027	0.000
DUBAIOIL	7.739152	2.733584	2.831137	0.0055
REUSD	73.68034	10.75881	6.848375	0.000
UREA	-1.492302	0.391638	-3.810407	0.0002
C	-3139.366	522.5838	-6.007393	0.000
R-squared	0.925512	Mean dependent var		1813.765
Adjusted R-squared	0.919943	S.D. dependent var		418.6434
S.E. of regression	118.4522	Sum squared resid		1501309
Durbin-Watson stat	0.41023	Long-run variance		47950.82

Model III (i): Inflation expectations and TN WPI (Food)

Fixed leads and lags specification (lead=6, lag=0)
Dependent variable: TNWPIFD

Variable	*Coefficient*	*Std. Error*	*t-Statistic*	*Prob.*
TNWPIFD(-1)	1	7.26E-14	1.38E+13	0.000
CALLAV	-8.38E-12	4.76E-12	-1.758786	0.0827
REUSD	-1.65E-11	3.76E-12	-4.394714	0.000
TNRICEST	1.04E-17	3.92E-17	0.265358	0.7915
C	5.02E-10	1.33E-10	3.7663	0.0003
@TREND	-4.11E-12	1.02E-12	-4.008887	0.0001
R-squared	1.00	Mean dependent var		1771.178
Adjusted R-squared	1.00	S.D. dependent var		378.779
S.E. of regression	2.76E-11	Sum squared resid		5.70E-20
Durbin-Watson stat	0.37877	Long-run variance		2.66E-21

Annexure Table A-3.4

Tamil Nadu Inflation: Method—Dynamic Least Squares (DOLS)

Model I (ii): Demand-supply factors affecting TN WPI (Non-food)

Fixed leads and lags specification (lead=0, lag=0)
Dependent variable: TNWPINF

Variable	*Coefficient*	*Std. Error*	*t-Statistic*	*Prob.*
IIPG	-2.55922	1.149879	-2.225646	0.0282
TAXCOLL	-0.13828	0.07659	-1.805485	0.0738
TNAGWG	1.342626	0.193067	6.954182	0.000
RAINPC	0.090992	0.099717	0.912498	0.3636
C	1064.449	113.1519	9.407254	0.000
@TREND	3.471101	1.111205	3.123728	0.0023
R-squared	0.912613	Mean dependent var		1152.136
Adjusted R-squared	0.905193	S.D. dependent var		128.6641
S.E. of regression	39.61663	Sum squared resid		166364.6
Durbin-Watson stat	0.365341	Long-run variance		5961.51

Model II (ii): External shocks affecting TN WPI (Non-food)

Fixed leads and lags specification (lead=6, lag=0)
Dependent variable: TNWPINF

Variable	*Coefficient*	*Std. Error*	*t-Statistic*	*Prob.*
DUBAIOIL	-6.36926	2.205802	-2.887503	0.0049
REUSD	4.284901	7.564419	0.566455	0.5726
UREA	0.280161	0.286852	0.976674	0.3315
C	850.3203	378.0484	2.249237	0.0271
@TREND	6.542599	1.138244	5.747975	0
R-squared	0.843464	Mean dependent var		1137.085
Adjusted R-squared	0.796876	S.D. dependent var		114.1491
S.E. of regression	51.44613	Sum squared resid		222323.2
Durbin-Watson stat	0.277983	Long-run variance		10023.18

Model III (ii): Inflation expectations and TN WPI (Non-food)

Fixed leads and lags specification (lead=6, lag=0)
Dependent variable: TNWPINF

Variable	*Coefficient*	*Std. Error*	*t-Statistic*	*Prob.*
TNWPINF(-1)	1.00000	3.54E-14	2.82E+13	0
CALLAV	6.43E-13	1.51E-12	0.426241	0.6712
REUSD	-2.59E-12	1.07E-12	-2.42598	0.0177
TNRICEST	4.55E-18	1.37E-17	0.330896	0.7416
C	1.81E-10	4.37E-11	4.153393	0.0001
@TREND	2.05E-13	1.42E-13	1.442071	0.1534
R-squared	1.0000	Mean dependent var		1138.066
Adjusted R-squared	1.0000	S.D. dependent var		114.2097
S.E. of regression	8.70E-12	Sum squared resid		5.67E-21
Durbin-Watson stat	0.245294	Long-run variance		3.11E-22

Annexure Table A-3.5

Tamil Nadu Inflation: Method—Dynamic Least Squares (DOLS)

Model I (iii): Demand-supply factors affecting TN WPI (Manufacturing)

Fixed leads and lags specification (lead=0, lag=0)
Dependent variable: TNWPIM

Variable	*Coefficient*	*Std. Error*	*t-Statistic*	*Prob.*
IIPM	1.228861	0.653176	1.881362	0.0626
TAXCOLL	0.097891	0.045281	2.161843	0.0329
TNAGWG	0.288065	0.146247	1.96972	0.0515
AMMONIA	0.106169	0.052766	2.012085	0.0467
C	943.8309	47.01944	20.07321	0.0000
R-squared	0.953336	Mean dependent var		1384.305
Adjusted R-squared	0.949847	S.D. dependent var		124.5615
S.E. of regression	27.8953	Sum squared resid		83261.79
Durbin-Watson stat	0.224255	Long-run variance		3113.034

Model II (iii): External shocks affecting TN WPI (Manufacturing)

Fixed leads and lags specification (lead=0, lag=0)
Dependent variable: TNWPIM

Variable	*Coefficient*	*Std. Error*	*t-Statistic*	*Prob.*
DUBAIOIL	6.308631	0.994946	6.340674	0.000
REUSD	12.35004	5.77168	2.139766	0.0346
UREA	-0.35512	0.206599	-1.718894	0.0885
C	572.3107	280.4129	2.040957	0.0437
R-squared	0.757725	Mean dependent var		1384.305
Adjusted R-squared	0.744388	S.D. dependent var		124.5615
S.E. of regression	62.97586	Sum squared resid		432289.5
Durbin-Watson stat	0.219732	Long-run variance		15608.69

Model III (iii): Inflation expectations and TN WPI (Manufacturing)

Fixed leads and lags specification (lead=6, lag=0)
Dependent variable: TNWPIM

Variable	*Coefficient*	*Std. Error*	*t-Statistic*	*Prob.*
TNWPIM(-1)	1	3.26E-13	3.07E+12	0.0000
CALLAV	2.25E-12	3.49E-12	0.643733	0.5217
REUSD	-8.31E-12	2.76E-12	-3.012033	0.0035
TNRICEST	2.99E-17	3.30E-17	0.904409	0.3687
C	7.65E-10	3.31E-10	2.307748	0.0238
@TREND	1.16E-12	1.23E-12	0.94996	0.3452
R-squared	1.000	Mean dependent var		1373.986
Adjusted R-squared	1.000	S.D. dependent var		115.6004
S.E. of regression	2.12E-11	Sum squared resid		3.37E-20
Durbin-Watson stat	0.31049	Long-run variance		1.75E-21

4

Economic and Financial Developments in the North-Eastern States*

DEEPAK MOHANTY

The northeastern states (NES),[1] also known as land of seven sisters, are very richly endowed. The northeastern region covers 5.5 per cent of the total geographical area of the country and accounts for 3.9 per cent of the national population and 2.7 per cent of all-India net domestic product (NDP). The lushness of its landscape, geographical and ecological diversity and range of communities residing make NES one of the most ethnically and linguistically diverse regions in Asia. Each state in the region has its own distinct culture and tradition.

A well-functioning financial system is the key to sustainable economic development of a country. Although the Reserve Bank has been actively engaged in the development of the financial sector in the country for a long time, it has stepped up its efforts in recent years to enhance the penetration of the formal financial sector and promote financial inclusion with a view to improving the well-being of our society. Given the special difficulties faced by the northeastern region, the Reserve Bank has been undertaking special initiatives for extending the outreach of banking facilities in the region. Against this background, I propose to briefly delineate the economic and financial structure of the region. I shall then highlight various financial inclusion initiatives taken by the Reserve Bank, especially for NES. In conclusion, I shall present some thoughts on policy challenges that lie ahead.

---

* Speech delivered at Gauhati University on March 24, 2011. The assistance provided by Dr P.K. Nayak is acknowledged.

1. Northeastern states comprise Arunachal Pradesh, Assam, Manipur, Meghalaya, Mizoram, Nagaland and Tripura.

I

Macroeconomic Trends

Let me begin with some macroeconomic trends. The last decade was characterised by high economic growth at the all-India level. Where do NES stand in this process? They contributed in varying degrees to this uptick in growth. The data on net state domestic product (NSDP) is available on a comparable basis up to 2007-08. Over the 8-year period, 2001-2008, the weighted average NSDP growth in NES was lower at 5.2 per cent as compared with 7.1 per cent at the all-India level. There were, however, significant inter-state variations within NES with the growth performances of three states, *viz.*, Nagaland, Arunachal Pradesh and Tripura being better than the all-India average (Table 4.1). The low growth in Assam and Manipur was mainly due to the poor performance of agriculture and industry. While the growth rate in agriculture has been particularly low in Assam and Mizoram, the growth rate of agriculture in Nagaland was high. An important lesson from this is that if the states replicate the best sectoral growth pattern within the region, growth in NES could easily surpass the all-India level.

Table 4.1

Average Growth Rates: 2000-01 to 2007-08

State	*Agriculture*	*Industry*	*Services (NSDP)*	*Total*
Assam	0.1	5.2	7.0	4.5
Arunachal Pradesh	3.6	13.7	9.1	7.3
Manipur	2.6	3.1	5.4	4.3
Mizoram	0.7	9.1	6.8	5.6
Meghalaya	4.3	12.7	6.6	6.8
Tripura	4.5	10.3	8.4	7.2
Nagaland	11.0	9.2	6.8	8.2
NES (simple average)	3.8	9.0	7.2	6.3
NES (weighted average)	1.5	5.9	7.0	5.2
All-India (NDP)	2.8	6.5	9.0	7.1

Note: Figures for Nagaland are up to the year 2006-07.

Sectoral analysis reveals that the economic structure of the NES more or less mirrors that of the Indian economy as a whole with the services sector dominating the economic activity. However, the share of industry in GDP was half of that of the Indian economy as a whole (Table 4.2). The need, therefore, is to place a greater emphasis on promoting the growth of the industrial sector in the region.

Table 4.2

Average Sectoral Shares: 2000-01 to 2007-08

State	*Agriculture*	*Industry*	*Services*
Assam	31	13	56
Arunachal Pradesh	28	7	65
Manipur	29	8	63
Mizoram	20	4	77
Meghalaya	22	14	64
Tripura	25	5	70
Nagaland	34	3	63
NES	27	8	65
All-India (NDP)	22	16	62

Note: Figures for Nagaland are up to the year 2006-07.

Notwithstanding significant differences in growth rates, the growth in per capita real income during the period 2000-01 to 2007-08 in NES was almost twice as the all-India level, with significant inter-state differences (Table 4.3).

Table 4.3

Real Per Capita Income$

State	*Amount in Rupees*		*Growth Rate (%)**
	2000-01	*2007-08*	
Assam	12,447	15,526	25.7
Arunachal Pradesh	14,726	21,582	46.6
Manipur	12,157	15,667	28.9
Meghalaya	14,910	21,597	44.8
Mizoram	16,635	20,688	24.4
Nagaland	15,699	17,129#	9.1
Tripura	14,933	22,493	50.6
NES	13,129	20,655	57.3
All-India (1999-2000 Base)	17,537	22,581	28.8

Note: $ At 1999-2000 Prices.
the figure pertains to the year 2006-07.
* 2007-08 over 2000-01.

Income distribution in NES has been more equitable than the all-India level as reflected in the much lower Gini coefficient of the per capita income in NES as compared with the all-India level (Table 4.4).

Table 4.4

Gini Coefficient: All-India and NES

Year	*All-India*	*NE States*	*All-India (excluding NE)*
2000-01	0.2178	0.0662	0.2359
2007-08	0.2454	0.0845	0.2556

II

Fiscal Trends

Following a move towards rule-based fiscal consolidation at the Centre in the early 2000s, many fiscal reform measures were also undertaken by the states, including NES. Consequently, NES began to improve their revenue accounts in 2003-04 when most of the states achieved revenue surplus. By 2005-06, all NES had achieved revenue surplus which persisted till 2008-09. Improvement was mainly on account of growth in revenue receipts outstripping growth in revenue expenditure. It may be noted that within revenue receipts, current transfers from the Centre in the form of grants and tax devolution were the key components behind the correction in revenue account achieved by most of the NES. During 2004-2009, current transfers accounted for over 80 per cent of total collection, while NES' own efforts towards better revenue collections contributed to a limited extent. Consequently, the consolidated GFD-GSDP ratio of NES declined significantly during 2005-2009 (Table 4.5).

State finances witnessed considerable deterioration in 2009-10 as is evident from key deficit indicators. Even though there was a moderate impact on States' own tax revenue and tax devolution from the Centre (as ratio to GSDP) due to overall macroeconomic slowdown observed in the Indian economy in 2009-10, revenue expenditure increased due to higher administrative expenditures arising out of revised pay structure. However, capital outlays also increased with a greater focus on transport, water supply and sanitation, irrigation and flood control, education, sports, art and culture. The fiscal consolidation process, however, was resumed by NES in their 2010-11 budgets. It is important for NES to improve the quality of their expenditure with greater emphasis on capital expenditure for sustaining the fiscal consolidation process. There is also a need for NES to improve their own tax revenue.

Table 4.5

Fiscal Indicators for NES

(As per cent to GSDP)

Year	*Gross Fiscal Deficit*	*Revenue Deficit*	*Primary Deficit*	*Outstanding Debt*
2001-02	6.0	2.0	2.5	37.3
2002-03	4.2	0.8	0.6	37.9
2003-04	3.6	-0.4	-0.1	42.2
2004-05	4.8	-0.5	1.4	43.1
2005-06	1.3	-3.4	-1.9	43.4
2006-07	-0.1	-5.2	-3.1	40.1
2007-08	0.1	-5.6	-2.6	38.8
2008-09	0.2	-6.5	-2.4	41.1
2009-10 (RE)	10.5	0.7	7.5	40.3
2010-11 (BE)	7.5	0.3	4.6	37.8

Note: RE: Revised Estimates. BE: Budget Estimates.
Minus (-) sign indicates surplus.

Source: Budget documents of the state governments.

III

Financial Indicators

The formal financial system in India is dominated by banks. NES, however, lag behind other parts of India in terms of development of banking. This is evident from the low banking penetration (higher average population per branch) in NES as compared with the all-India average, though there were significant variations across states in the region with Mizoram and Meghalaya having much better ratios. The credit-deposit (C-D) ratio in NES is much lower at 34 per cent at the end of March 2010 than that of 73 per cent at the all-India level (Table 4.6). Even as credit expanded at a faster pace than deposits in the last decade, the gap remained very wide.

Table 4.6

Banking Development Indicators in NES

State	Population per Branch (As on June 2010)	C-D Ratio (Per Cent)		Average Growth (2000-01 to 2009-10)	
		End-March 2001	End-March 2001	Credit	Deposits
Assam	21,000	32.8	36.1	21.7	19.7
Arunachal Pradesh	15,000	12.7	25.3	34.5	24.4
Manipur	34,000	38.9	40.7	23.1	20.7
Meghalaya	13,000	23.5	47.3	31.5	22.6
Mizoram	10,000	16.0	24.4	27.2	19.1
Nagaland	25,000	13.8	29.9	27.7	19.4
Tripura	16,000	20.0	25.3	21.1	20.0
NES	20,000	27.8	33.5	22.5	19.8
All-India	14,000	59.2	73.2	21.9	18.9

The credit penetration, as measured by the ratio of bank credit to the NSDP, in NES also remained significantly lower than the all-India level (Figure 4.1).

Figure 4.1

Credit Penetration

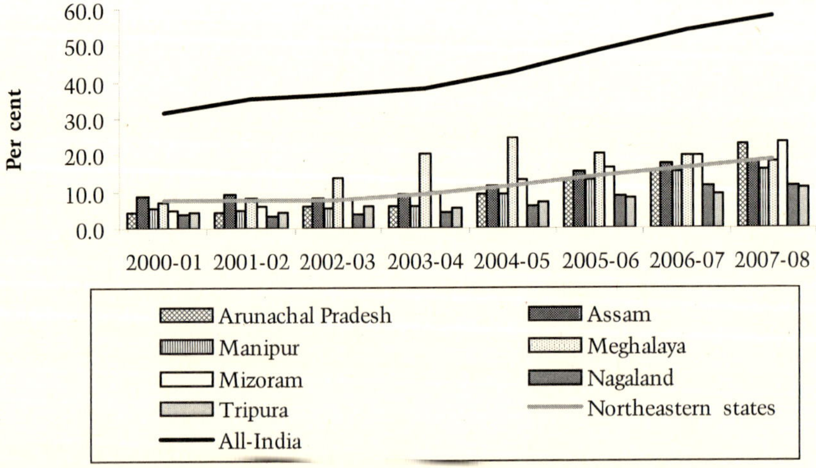

This raises the question as to whether low credit penetration in NES was due to lack of absorptive capacity in the region. However, this does not seem to be the case as non-formal sources of finance in the region dominate the financing activity in the rural sector. As per the 59th round of National Sample Survey (NSS) data on indebtedness of farmer household in NES, 45 per cent of the finance availed of by the farmers was from the formal financial sector, while the remaining 55 per cent was from the non-formal sector. This was significantly higher than the all-India level with the share of the informal sector at 42 per cent (Figure 4.2). This shows that there is absorptive capacity and that there is considerable scope for improving banking penetration in NES.

Figure 4.2

Sources of Finance

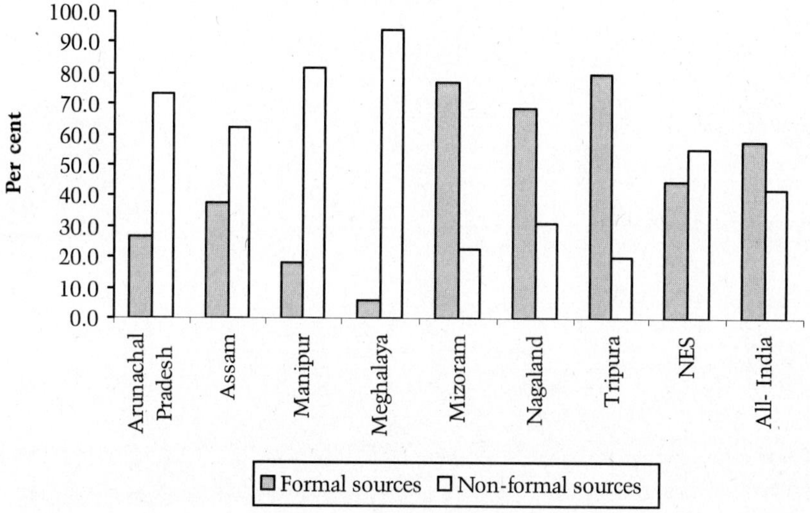

IV

Financial Inclusion Measures

Financial inclusion is important for bringing the poor and under-privileged sections of society within the banking fold and thereby generating and sustaining equitable growth. Let me now turn to the various measures initiated by the Reserve Bank for promoting financial inclusion.

First, the Reserve Bank for long has instituted a mechanism called 'priority sector lending' through which credit is channelled to certain preferred sectors, which, *inter alia*, include small-scale industry, small businesses and agriculture. In the post-reform period, the priority sector has been expanded to include advances to retail trade, educational loans, micro-finance and low-cost housing. This has helped in furthering the cause of financial inclusion.

Second, the Union Finance Minister announced in the Budget 2010-2011 that every village in the country with over 2000 population must have access to banking services by March 2012. In order to operationalise this process, commercial banks have prepared financial inclusion plans which have been submitted to the Reserve Bank. As brick-and-mortar branches will not be viable in very small centres, the approach is to meet this challenge through the business correspondent (BC) model and by leveraging communication technology. Under this model, banks appoint agents who provide basic banking services at the door-step of a client on behalf of banks.

Third, the Reserve Bank has asked banks to open no-frills accounts. These accounts have no or very low minimum balance requirement and have provisions for small loans by way of overdrafts. This is a very convenient account for small depositors, especially in rural areas.

Fourth, a major impediment for a common person to open bank account is the 'Know Your Customer' (KYC) norm. The norm has been relaxed for small accounts, *viz.*, deposits up to Rs 50,000 and credit up to Rs 1 lakh. A simple introduction by an existing account holder in a bank should be adequate to open an account. In this regard, Aadhar, the Unique Identification Number (UID) Project of the Central Government, which aims at providing a unique ID number for everyone in the country, will help the poor to establish their identity to meet the banks' KYC norms.

Fifth, farmers can get credit from banks conveniently through Kisan Credit Cards (KCCs) and General Purpose Credit Cards (GCCs).

Sixth, while several banking facilities are available, a common person may not be aware of them. Hence, financial literacy becomes critically important. Accordingly, the Reserve Bank has initiated a 'Project Financial

Literacy' with the objective of disseminating information regarding the central bank and general banking concepts to various target groups. Our 'Financial Education' website link offers basics of banking, finance and central banking for children of all ages. Our website is also available in 13 languages, including Assamese.

Finally, there is also a learning process for the Reserve Bank. We recognise that being responsible for banking, we must be sensitive to the needs of a common person. Accordingly, our Governor, Dr. Subbarao initiated the outreach programme last year as a part of our Platinum Jubilee celebrations. Under the outreach programme, the top management of the Reserve Bank visits at least one village in every state and union territory with state government officials and commercial banks to give focussed attention on financial inclusion. This has been highly enriching experience for us to understand the ground realities. Accordingly, we have decided to continue these programmes. I am glad to indicate that we have already conducted outreach camps in Assam and Arunachal Pradesh. During my current visit, outreach camps have been organised in Manipur, Nagaland and Tripura.

V

Special Financial Inclusion Measures for NES

While financial inclusion measures are expected to improve the banking facilities in general throughout the country, including NES, I would also like to highlight some of the special financial inclusion measures initiated for NES.

First, in December 2009, the Reserve Bank relaxed the branch authorisation policy and permitted domestic scheduled commercial banks (other than RRBs) to open branches in rural, semi-urban and urban centres in NES and Sikkim without having the need to take permission from the Reserve Bank in each case, subject to reporting.

Second, to improve banking penetration in the NES, the Reserve Bank requested the state governments and banks to identify centres where there is a need for setting up either full-fledged branches or those offering forex facilities, handling government business or for meeting currency requirements. We have also offered to fund the capital and running costs for five years provided the state government concerned is willing to make available the premises and put in place appropriate security arrangements. Meghalaya was the first State to take advantage of this facility: eight centres were allotted to three public sector banks, following a bidding process in the state. However, the progress towards opening branches has been slow because of lack of proper infrastructure in the identified centres. In Tripura, five centres were allocated to Tripura Gramin Bank in December 2010. I understand that branches are expected to open shortly in two of these centres. Similarly, the work for identification of centres for opening up branches has been completed for Arunachal Pradesh, Nagaland and Manipur.

VI

Policy Challenges

Let me now turn to broader macroeconomic policy challenges. Development of NES has been high on the agenda of the Central and the respective state governments. Recognising the special requirements of the region and the need for significant levels of government investment, NES have been recognised as Special Category States and Central Plan assistance to these states is significant. As I indicated, the Reserve Bank has also initiated special measures for spread of banking and promotion of financial inclusion. Nevertheless, to accelerate the pace of growth in NES, I may highlight a few challenges that lie ahead.

First, weak market linkages are a major constraint in the development of the region. For this reason, urgent attention needs to be paid to developing roads, air links, telecommunications and other components of transport and communications. Investment in infrastructure could be scaled up through the Public-Private Partnership (PPP) model.

Second, initiatives need to be taken to promote sustainable industrial development compatible with the unique bio-diversity of the region. Agro-based industries, food processing, wood products, traditional textiles and light manufacturing industries can be encouraged to come up in the region.

Third, there is a need to increase agricultural productivity and promote diversification into horticulture and floriculture for which the agro-climatic conditions in the region are well-suited.

Fourth, a sustainable growth paradigm will not only help further acceleration in growth but will also improve fiscal sustainability by helping to lower the debt-GSDP ratio.

Fifth, the high level of literacy and human development levels coupled with bio-diversity provides ample opportunity for development of tourism and exports.

Sixth, a deterrent for bank lending is the high level of non-performing assets (NPAs) in the region. This has been, in part, due to unviability of some of the activities financed by banks and lack of adequate engagement with the borrowers. There is, therefore, a need to improve credit culture in which financial education could play a vital role. In addition, banks will have to augment the staff strength in their branches with an emphasis on staff with knowledge of local customs and practices. Given the preponderance of community-based society in NES, group lending could be a successful mode of credit delivery. Hence, there is a need for promotion of self-help groups (SHGs) with greater linkage with banks. In this regard, NABARD has an important role to play, not only in promotion of SHGs, but also in capacity building, along with SIDBI and concerned state government agencies. Another area where there is substantial scope for expansion is low-cost housing. Expansion of housing loan remains poor as mortgages cannot be created in many parts of NES. However, banks can explore innovative structures for housing loans with a greater emphasis on group lending.

Seventh, in any plan for financial sector development, the physical presence of a bank branch is important. But the topography of the region, the dispersal of population, transport bottlenecks and law and order conditions in some areas inhibit branch expansion other than in certain commercial centres. Hence, all the stakeholders—banks, state governments and the Reserve Bank—need to work in close co-ordination for increasing banking penetration and promoting financial inclusion in the region.

VII

Conclusion

To conclude, the northeastern region has immense potential. The need, therefore, is to identify the opportunities and recognise the challenges to work towards a sustainable and inclusive growth of the region with greater penetration of the formal financial sector.

5 Inter-District Growth Performance in Madhya Pradesh

RAJIV LOCHAN[1]

I

Introduction

This study is concerned with the performance of districts in Madhya Pradesh in terms of both net domestic product and per capita income at constant prices and the reasons for the persistence of disparity among the districts in terms of both these parameters. This study is relevant because it highlights lack of balanced development in Madhya Pradesh. Balanced regional development is important because of many reasons. First, it is desirable that everyone should receive the fruits of development. Second, every district, indeed every place has some resources, some skill and if we do not use them for the growth of these districts/places, we are not using valuable resources. Third, growth based on a few districts will hit an upper limit, at least in sectors like agriculture and therefore growth beyond a point demands that it should be broad based. Finally, growth based on a few locations causes various problems like air pollution, congestion, shortage of water, etc., to avoid these problems, growth should be as broad based as possible. All these factors underline importance of balanced development.

Methodology and Data Set

This study is divided into six sections. Following introduction, Section II sets out studies that have researched on this topic. Section III discusses

1. The views expressed in this paper are of the author himself and not of the organisation he is working with.

inter-district disparity both in net domestic product as well as per capita income at constant prices during the period, 1999-2000 to 2007-08. In Section IV, factors responsible for this disparity and its persistence are set out. In Section V, the relationship between agriculture output and net credit outstanding in real terms in different districts is studied. Policy implications and conclusions are set out in Section VI.

In this paper, districts of Madhya Pradesh have been ranked in descending order in terms of per capita income and net domestic product at constant prices and total agricultural output. The trend rate of growth of net domestic product and total agriculture output of various districts are calculated and presented in the paper. We have mainly used correlation-coefficient as a statistical tool, e.g. correlation-coefficient between per capita income at constant prices and net domestic product at constant prices, correlation-coefficient between net domestic product and share of employment in primary sector' employment to total employment, correlation-coefficient between level of net domestic product at constant prices and trend growth rates of the same in different districts, correlation-coefficient between trend rate of growth of net domestic product at constant prices and total agriculture output in different districts and correlation-coefficient between total agriculture output and net credit outstanding at constant prices in various districts.

II

Review of Literature

There are many studies on inter-district disparity in India and for other states, however, not many studies for the state of Madhya Pradesh. A study on Madhya Pradesh by Chaurasia (2010) briefly touches this topic. He does not make detailed analysis of net domestic product as well as per capita income at constant prices at district levels. The study notes that 'another feature of the State economy that is of serious concern is a strong and persistent distribution inequality.' By 'distribution inequality' he means 'inter-district inequality'. He also notes, 'At the same time, economic growth and its associated economic development have largely been confined to a few districts of the State, thus resulting in an increase in the inter-district inequality in the distribution of resources.' Though these assertions are not based on detailed analysis of data, it is consistent with our conclusions. However, there are differences in approach and certain conclusions. He tries to investigate reasons for inter-district inequality in per capita income at constant prices while we prefer to investigate the reasons for inter-district inequality in net domestic product at district level at constant prices as we feel that per capita income also depends on population and growth of population depends on factors including sociological ones. More importantly, he notes that, 'The regression analysis suggests a very strong relationship of the real per capita income with the degree of urbanisation across the districts'. But this is not very helpful as urbanisation is more of an effect than a cause. Unlike him, we find strong negative correlation between net domestic product at 1999-2000 prices and share of employment in primary sector in total employment at district level. Our result has greater explanatory power since labour productivity is known to be higher in non-primary sectors compared to primary sectors. But it has to be explained how urbanisation *per se* will lead to higher per capita income. He also finds that regression coefficient of registered industries per 100,000 population and per capita income is not significant. This may be because number of industries *per se* does not mean much unless we know the value of industrial output and number of employees in the industry. He also does not assign any role to growth of agricultural output in persistence of inter-district inequality (in fact there is no analysis of agricultural output in his article) while we find it to be an important factor.

Regional inequality is also high in other states. Shaban (2006) noted in case of Maharashtra that during the 10-year period 1993-94–2002-2003 'notwithstanding its overall high economic development, Maharashtra suffers from acute regional inequality.' He also noted that Konkan region, consisting of Greater Mumbai, Thane, Raigad, Sindhudurg and Ratnagiri alone received about half of the total income of the state. He also found that Konkan was more developed than western Maharashtra. Vidharbha was even less developed than western Maharashtra and Marathwada was the least developed. He also significantly noted that, 'There has been marked stability in the ranking of regions in economic development over the years in almost all the sectors. The Konkan region has been the highest developed region, followed by western Maharashtra, Vidharbha and Marathwada.'

Chelliah and Shanmugam (2002) found evidence of inter-district inequality in Tamil Nadu. They noted that 'the per capita income of the top ranked district is about 2.85 times larger than that of the poorest district (i.e. the latter is only 35 per cent of the former).' Their reasons for inter-district inequality are also broadly similar to that of Madhya Pradesh. They found that 'the relatively high income-districts are associated with a larger share of non-primary sector in district income.' They also found that 'low productivity in agriculture is another reason for low per capita income' at district level.

III

Inter-District Disparity both in Net Domestic Product as well as Per Capita Income

Inter-district disparity in Madhya Pradesh is very large and persisting. In Table 5.1, we have ranked districts of Madhya Pradesh in descending order of per capita income at 1999-2000 prices in two years: 1999-2000 and 2007-08. In 1999-2000, while Indore had per capita income of Rs 27,571 and Bhopal had per capita income of Rs 21,717, per capita income of Dindori was only Rs 6,993 and that of Umaria only Rs 8,657. The situation has not changed much in 2007-08. Per capita income of Indore at 1999-2000 prices in 2007-08 was Rs 29,364 and that of Bhopal Rs 27,515. On the other hand per capita income of Dindori was Rs 8,799. Thus, regional disparity is not only huge but persisting. However, per capita income depends on two variables—net domestic product and population. Since growth of population or lack of it depends on many factors including sociological ones, we will concentrate on net domestic product in different districts. Two series are also highly correlated. Therefore, we have another reason for analysing net domestic product instead of per capita income. In 1999-2000, correlation-coefficient between net domestic products of different districts and per capita income of the same districts at 1999-2000 prices was 0.87. In 2007-08, correlation-coefficient between net domestic products of different districts and per capita income of the same districts at

Table 5.1

Per Capita Income at 1999-2000 Prices in Descending Order

(in Rupees)

Districts	*Per Capita Income in 1999-2000*	*Districts*	*Per Capita Income in 2007-08*
Indore	27,571	Indore	29,364
Bhopal	21,717	Bhopal	27,515
Ujjain	17,546	Jabalpur	18,654
Gwalior	17,447	Gwalior	18,293
Ratlam	16,209	Hoshangabad	17,847
Mandsaur	15,659	Sidhi	17,163
Jabalpur	15,613	Ujjain	17,017
Sidhi	15,168	Ratlam	15,952
Hoshangabad	14,677	Chhaindwara	14,704
Neemuch	14,373	Harda	14,346
Chhindwara	13,168	Shahdol	14,069
Katni	12,781	Neemuch	13,978
Shajapur	12,250	Mandsaur	13,769
Shahdol	12,053	Katni	13,365
Dewas	11,938	Betul	13,231
Harda	11,811	Khandwa	13,166
Vidisha	11,721	Balaghat	12,706
Narasimhapur	11,488	Narasimhapur	12,278
Datia	11,207	Dhar	11,994
Sehore	11,056	Dewas	11,821
Raisen	10,951	Vidisha	11,291
Betul	10,868	Seoni	11,022
Dhar	10,815	Datia	10,993
Satna	10,748	Damoh	10,986
Khndwa	10,609	Sagar	10,906
Rajgarh	10,606	Shajapur	10,883
Balaghat	10,283	Satna	10,665
Damoh	10,223	Guna	10,592
Sagar	10,140	Raisen	10,519
Guna	10,015	Sehore	10,404
Chhatarpur	9,837	Rajgarh	10,.400
Seoni	9,515	Khargone	10,264
Shivpuri	9,351	Umaria	10,020
Morena	9,316	Morena	9,346
Tikamgarh	9,270	Chhatarpur	9,107
Sheopur	9,194	Panna	9,086
Khargone	9,137	Rewa	9,067
Rewa	9,003	Dindori	8,799
Umaria	8,657	Sheopur	8,569
Panna	8,625	Jhabua	8,541
Bhind	8,577	Mandla	8,525
Mandla	8,401	Bhind	8,383
Jhabua	7,292	Shivpuri	8,199
Barwani	7,267	Barwani	8,119
Dindori	6,993	Tikamgarh	7,933

Source: Economic Survey, 2009-10, Government of Madhya Pradesh.

1999-2000 prices was 0.89. In Table 5.2, we have listed districts of Madhya Pradesh in the descending order of net domestic product at 1999-2000 prices for two years—1999-2000, first year of our period and 2007-08, terminal year of our period. Comparison of the two lists reveals the following: first 7 districts and last 8 districts in both the lists are the same though Ujjain has moved from 4th position in 1999-2000 to 6th position in 2007-08 and Sidhi has moved from sixth position in 1999-2000 to 4th position in 2007-08 and Datia has moved from 41st position in 1999-2000 to 42nd position in 2007-08 and Harda has moved from 42nd position in 1999-2000 to 41st position in 2007-08. All the districts except Mandsaur in the group of districts occupying position between 8th and 15th in 1999-2000 are also in the group of districts occupying position between 8th and 15th in 2007-08. Only Hoshangabad has jumped from 17th position in 1999-2000 to 14th position in 2007-08 and Mandsaur has fallen from 13th position in 1999-2000 to 19th position in 2007-08. All the districts except Hoshangabad and Chhatarpur in the group of districts occupying position between 16th and 25th in 1999-2000 are also in the group of districts occupying position between 16th and 25th in 2007-08. Only Hoshangabad has jumped from 17th position in 1999-2000 to 14th position in 2007-08 and Chhatarpur has fallen from 23th position in 1999-2000 to 26th position in 2007-08. All the districts except Katni in the group of districts occupying position between 26th and 37th in 1999-2000 are also in the group of districts occupying position between 26th and 37th in 2007-08. The last 8 districts are the same in both the list. Therefore, disparity among different districts has not reduced during this period. In fact, the disparity has increased as is apparent when we compare the minimum and maximum in both the periods—while net domestic product of Indore at 1999-2000 prices has gone up from Rs 6,559 crore in 1999-2000 prices to Rs 8,633 crore in 2007-08, the net domestic product of Dindori at 1999-2000 prices has only marginally changed from RS 409 crore in 1999-2000 to Rs 454 crore in 2007-08. Coefficient of variation has increased from 65.30 per cent in 1999-2000 to 72.70 per cent in 2007-08. There are two questions: i) why is there regional inequality, ii) why does it persist.

Table 5.2

Net Domestic Product at 1999-2000 Prices in Descending Order

(in Rs 100 crore)

Districts	*Net Domestic Product in 1999-2000*	*Districts*	*Net Domestic Product in 2007-08*
Indore	65.59	Indore	86.33
Bhopal	38.57	Bhopal	61.13
Jabalpur	32.72	Jabalpur	44.64
Ujjain	29.20	Sidhi	37.28
Gwalior	27.65	Gwalior	34.07
Sidhi	26.82	Ujjain	32.77
Chhindwara	23.80	Chhindwara	29.59
Sagar	19.96	Khandwa	24.80
Satna	19.49	Sagar	24.68
Ratlam	19.14	Shahdol	24.29
Shahdol	18.54	Dhar	23.97
Dhar	18.26	Satna	22.94
Mandsaur	18.03	Ratlam	21.99
Khandwa	17.74	Hoshangabad	21.61
Rewa	17.24	Rewa	20.50
Guna	16.19	Guna	20.26
Hoshangabad	15.50	Betul	20.11
Shajapur	15.37	Balaghat	19.69
Balaghat	15.17	Mandsaur	18.34
Dewas	15.16	Khargone	18.09
Betul	14.82	Dewas	17.68
Morena	14.42	Morena	16.83
Chhatarpur	14.07	Shajapur	15.92
Vidisha	13.83	Katni	15.73
Khargone	13.55	Vidisha	15.57
Katni	13.26	Chhatarpur	15.43
Shivpuri	13.08	Rajgarh	14.90
Rajgarh	12.91	Seoni	13.88
Bhind	11.98	Raisen	13.67
Raisen	11.94	Shivpuri	13.57
Sehore	11.56	Jhabua	13.38
Seoni	10.86	Damoh	13.17
Tikamgarh	10.81	Narasimhpur	13.10
Damoh	10.81	Bhind	12.98
Narsimhapur	10.72	Sehore	12.96
Neemuch	10.17	Neemuch	11.27
Jhabua	9.89	Tikamgarh	10.99
Barwani	7.61	Barwani	10.23
Mandla	7.21	Mandla	9.42
Panna	7.18	Panna	8.80
Datia	6.86	Harda	7.70
Harda	5.45	Datia	7.69
Sheopur	4.98	Umaria	5.78
Umaria	4.35	Sheopur	5.58
Dindori	4.09	Dindori	4.54

Source: Economic Survey, 2009-10, Government of Madhya Pradesh.

IV

Explanation for Inter-Districts Inequality and its Persistence

One answer to the first question is different share of primary sector in the economy of different districts. Since this is not available, we take share of employment in primary sector in total employment in these districts (Table 5.3). Data for share of employment in total employment is available for all districts except 7 districts *viz.*, Katni, Neemuch, Barwani, Harda, Sheopur, Umaria and Dindori (*Second Human Development Report of Madhya Pradesh*, 1998). The correlation-coefficient between net domestic

Table 5.3

Share of Primary Sector Employment in Total Employment

(in Percentage)

Districts	*Share of Primary Sector in Total Employment*	*Districts*	*Share of Primary Sector in Total Employment*
Indore	34.3	Bhopal	24.9
Jabalpur	56.2	Ujjain	65.9
Gwalior	47.2	Sidhi	87.5
Chhindwara	81.3	Sagar	57.4
Satna	47.2	Ratlam	74.2
Shahdol	85.0	Dhar	84.1
Mandsaur	80.3	Khandwa	76.7
Rewa	79.7	Guna	79.1
Hoshangawad	71.4	Shajapur	82.9
Balaghat	83.5	Dewas	76.6
Betul	84.8	Morena	81.7
Chhatarpur	82.6	Vidisha	79.3
Khargone	84.8	Shivpuri	84.6
Rajgarh	82.4	Bhind	79.9
Raisen	78.6	Sehore	81.4
Seoni	87.3	Tikamgarh	86.4
Damoh	63.8	Narasimhapur	79.8
Jhabua	90.6	Mandla	90.4
Panna	86.3	Datia	77.1

Source: *Madhya Pradesh' Second Human Development Report, 1998.*

product at 1999-2000 prices in districts (excluding 7 districts mentioned above) in 1999-2000 and the share of employment in primary sector in total employment in the same districts is negative (as we should expect) and reasonably high (-)0.75. The share of primary sector in total employment in top 5 districts (in terms of net domestic product at 1999-2000 prices in 1999-2000) is as follows: Indore (34.3%), Bhopal (24.9%), Jabalpur (56.2%), Ujjain (65.9%), and Gwalior (47.2%). On the other hand, share of employment in primary sector in total employment in bottom 5 districts (in terms of net domestic product at 1999-2000 prices in 1999-2000) is as follows: Datia (77.1%), Panna (86.3%), Mandla (90.4%), Jhabua (90.6%), and Narsimhapur (79.8%). The range of share of primary sector in total employment in top 10 districts (in terms of net domestic product at 1999-2000 prices in 1999-2000) is (24.3% to 74.2%) except in Sidhi (87.5%) and Chhindwara (81.3%). High net domestic product of Sidhi is mainly due to existence of Vindhyachal Super Thermal Power Plant in the district. Chhindwara produced second highest amount of agriculture output in 1999-2000 (1,214.6 thousand metric tonnes, first position being occupied by Ujjain, producing 1275.5 thousand metric tonnes). On the other hand, share of primary sector in total employment in bottom 10 districts (in terms of net domestic product at 1999-2000 prices in 1999-2000) is (63.8% to 90.6%). The answer to the question of persistence of inequality is simply that poorer districts have not grown much faster than the richer ones to catch up with them. On the contrary, correlation-coefficient between net domestic product at 1999-2000 prices in 1999-2000 and trend rate of growth of net domestic product of different districts during 1999-2000 to 2007-08 is positive, though not very high at 0.30. While the average of trend growth rates of top 10 districts (arranged in terms of net domestic product at 1999-2000 prices) for the period 1999-2000 to 2007-08 was 3.81 per cent, average of trend growth rates of bottom 10 districts (arranged in terms of net domestic product at 1999-2000 prices) for the period 1999-2000 to 2007-08 was 3.45 per cent. Average of trend growth rates of middle 25 districts (arranged in terms of net domestic product at 1999-2000 prices) for the period 1999-2000 to 2007-08 was 3.0 per cent (Table 5.4). This means that top 10 districts have further improved their position in comparison to both the middle 25 districts and the bottom 10 districts. It also means that the position of the middle 25 districts has

Table 5.4

Net Domestic Product in Descending Order and its Trend Growth Rate

District	*Net Domestic Product (at 1999-2000 Prices) in 1999-2000 (in Rs 100 crore)*	*Trend Growth Rate of Net Domestic Product (at 1999-2000 Prices) during 1999-2000 to 2007-08 (in per cent)*
Indore	65.59	3.73
Bhopal	38.57	6.03
Jabalpur	32.72	4.35
Ujjain	29.20	3.26
Gwalior	27.65	3.00
Sidhi	26.82	4.60
Chhindwara	23.80	3.89
Sagar	19.96	3.00
Satna	19.49	2.56
Ratlam	19.14	3.63
Shahdol	18.54	3.80
Dhar	18.26	4.28
Mandsaur	18.03	2.70
Khandwa	17.74	3.87
Rewa	17.24	2.45
Guna	16.19	3.35
Hoshangabad	15.50	3.83
Shajapur	15.37	2.78
Balaghat	15.17	3.35
Dewas	15.16	2.98
Betul	14.82	4.32
Morena	14.42	2.74
Chhatarpur	14.07	1.89
Vidisha	13.83	2.52
Khargone	13.55	4.33
Katni	13.26	2.59
Shivpuri	13.08	1.78
Rajgarh	12.91	3.59
Bhind	11.98	2.00
Raisen	11.94	2.45
Sehore	11.56	2.93
Seoni	10.86	3.81
Tikamgarh	10.81	0.76
Damoh	10.81	3.16
Narsimhapur	10.72	2.62
Neemuch	10.17	2.87
Jhabua	9.89	4.38
Barwani	7.61	4.19
Mandla	7.21	3.75
Panna	7.18	3.49
Datia	6.86	1.99
Harda	5.45	4.91
Sheopur	4.98	2.66
Umaria	4.35	3.99
Dindori	4.09	2.28

Source: Economic Survey, 2009-10, Government of Madhya Pradesh.

fallen *vis-à-vis* the group of first 10 districts. One reason for the low growth rate of net domestic product of the middle 25 districts is low trend rate of growth of agriculture in these districts during this period. The correlation-coefficient between trend growth rate of net domestic product of these 25 districts and trend growth rate of agricultural output of these districts during the period 1999-2000 to 2007-08 is 0.62 (see Table 5.5). One reason for strong correlation coefficient in these districts is importance of agriculture in these districts' economy as indicated by high share of primary sector' employment in total employment in these districts. On the other hand correlation-coefficient between trend growth rate of net domestic product and that of agricultural output during this period is not high for the top 10 districts (0.12) and bottom 10 districts (0.28). For top 10 districts, low correlation-coefficient may be due to relatively less dependence on agriculture as indicated by lower share of primary sector' employment in total employment in these districts. Most of the bottom 10 districts are also districts with low agriculture output; that means that rate of growth of agriculture is less important.

Table 5.5

Net Domestic Product in Descending Order, its Trend Growth Rate and Trend Growth Rate of Agriculture Output

District	*Net Domestic Product (at 1999-2000 Prices) in 1999-2000 (in Rs 100 crore)*	*Trend Growth Rate of Net Domestic Product at 1999-2000 Prices during 1999-2000 to 2007-08 (in per cent)*	*Trend Growth Rate of Agriculture Output* during 1999-2000 to 2007-08 (in per cent)*
1	*2*	*3*	*4*
Indore	65.59	3.73	3.75
Bhopal	38.57	6.03	1.15
Jabalpur	32.72	4.35	1.05
Ujjain	29.20	3.26	7.31
Gwalior	27.65	3.00	-7.04
Sidhi	26.82	4.60	-0.08
Chhindwara	23.80	3.89	-3.89
Sagar	19.96	3.00	2.28
Satna	19.49	2.56	-2.91

contd...

...contd..

1	2	3	4.
Ratlam	19.14	3.63	5.75
Shahdol	18.54	3.80	-11.76
Dhar	18.26	4.28	7.88
Mandsaur	18.03	2.70	0.28
Khandwa	17.74	3.87	-1.46
Rewa	17.24	2.45	-3.88
Guna	16.19	3.35	-6.29
Hoshangabad	15.50	3.83	4.08
Shajapur	15.37	2.78	0.49
Balaghat	15.17	3.35	0.79
Dewas	15.16	2.98	2.78
Betul	14.82	4.32	0.86
Morena	14.42	2.74	-4.20
Chhatarpur	14.07	1.89	-9.76
Vidisha	13.83	2.52	-0.19
Khargone	13.55	4.33	4.32
Katni	13.26	2.59	-5.92
Shivpuri	13.08	1.78	-3.37
Rajgarh	12.91	3.59	5.60
Bhind	11.98	2.00	-1.87
Raisen	11.94	2.45	2.28
Sehore	11.56	2.93	0.77
Seoni	10.86	3.81	4.23
Tikamgarh	10.81	0.76	-17.59
Damoh	10.81	3.16	3.18
Narsimhapur	10.72	2.62	-7.74
Neemuch	10.17	2.87	-0.05
Jhabua	9.89	4.38	4.21
Barwani	7.61	4.19	-3.28
Mandla	7.21	3.75	-0.31
Panna	7.18	3.49	-0.49
Datia	6.86	1.99	5.86
Harda	5.45	4.91	8.81
Sheopur	4.98	2.66	1.24
Umaria	4.35	3.99	17.58
Dindori	4.09	2.28	-0.97

Note: * Includes output of paddy, wheat, gram, rapeseed, mustard, soyabean, cotton, *jowar* and maize.

Source: *Economic Survey* (various issues), *Summary Statistics, 2003* and *Agriculture Statistics, 2009*, Government of Madhya Pradesh and *Area, Production and Yield of Major Crops in Madhya Pradesh 1999-2000 to 2003-04*, Directorate of Agriculture, Government of Madhya Pradesh.

V

Relation between Agriculture Output and Net Credit Outstanding to Agriculture

To find out the relation between these two variables, we have worked out correlation-coefficient between average of annual agriculture production during the period 1999-2000 to 2007-08 and simple average of net credit outstanding to agriculture at March-end in different years during 1999-2000 to 2007-08 at 1993-94 prices in all districts except developed districts: Indore, Jabalpur, Bhopal and Gwalior (these districts have unusually high net credit outstanding; this may be due to availability of much better banking services in these districts). The correlation-coefficient between the two is reasonably high at 0.74 (Table 5.6). In the top 10 districts, minimum agriculture production in each district in a year is 548 thousand metric tonnes and net credit outstanding in real terms in each district (except Chhindwara (Rs 56.4 crore), Narsimhapur (Rs 73.7 crore), Betul (Rs 46.4 crore), is more than Rs 100 crore. On the other hand, in the bottom 10 districts, maximum agriculture production in a district is 251 thousand metric tonnes and the maximum net credit outstanding in real terms is Rs 37.8 crore. In the middle 21 districts, output range is (278.8-530.2 thousand metric tonnes) and the range of net credit outstanding in real terms (except Guna (Rs 129.3 crore), Raisen (Rs 105.8 crore), Sagar (Rs 111.4 crore), and Morena (Rs 109.5 crore) is (Rs 21.7 crore-Rs 93.7 crore).

VI

Policy Implications and Conclusion

This study underlines importance of promoting non-primary sector activities in underdeveloped districts. At the same time, agriculture output too has to be increased in poorer districts. Strong correlation between agriculture output and net credit outstanding in real terms indicates the possibility of increasing agriculture output with availability of higher credit, provided other factors do not worsen.

Table 5.6

Average of Annual Agriculture Production and Average of Net Credit Outstanding to Agriculture at Constant Prices

Districts	*Average of Annual Agriculture Production during 1999-2000 to 2007-08 ('000 metric tonnes)*	*Average of Net Credit Outstanding to Agriculture at March-End in Different Years during 1999-2000 to 2007-08 at 1993-94 Prices (in Rs crore)*
1	*2*	*3*
Chhindwara	810.8	56.4
Hoshangabad	762.4	104.6
Ujjain	747.2	163.9
Sehore	711.0	124.4
Narasimhapur	710.9	73.7
Dhar	691.8	126.4
Dewas	666.2	110.7
Vidisha	645.7	103.9
Shajapur	608.7	104.4
Betul	548.3	46.4
Balaghat	530.2	21.7
Guna	527.2	129.3
Raisen	499.2	105.8
Ratlam	497.9	76.0
Sagar	463.2	111.4
Rajgarh	462.5	89.6
Morena	457.1	109.5
Harda	441.4	47.1
Mandsaur	437.7	79.0
Shivpuri	423.8	67.5
Rewa	411.8	60.0
Seoni	408.2	31.7
Datia	393.9	77.8
Khandwa	382.6	93.7
Satna	348.9	82.1
Bhind	340.6	66.4
Chhatarpur	330.3	47.4
Khargone	311.8	78.0
Damoh	304.6	57.4
Tikamgarh	279.7	29.4

contd...

...contd..

1	2	3
Sidhi	278.8	28.0
Neemuch	251.0	32.5
Shahdol	248.5	22.0
Jhabua	246.7	29.1
Sheopur	221.2	26.0
Katni	196.0	33.0
Mandla	189.3	18.0
Barwani	183.0	37.8
Panna	181.4	29.3
Dindori	148.9	8.7
Umaria	129.0	15.1

Note: Excluding Indore, Jabalpur, Bhopal and Gwalior.

Source: *Economic Survey* (various issues), *Summary Statistics, 2003*, and *Agriculture Statistics, 2009*, Government of Madhya Pradesh; *Area, Production and Yield of major crops in Madhya Pradesh 1999-2000 to 2003-04*, Directorate of Agriculture, Government of Madhya Pradesh; *Basic Statistical Returns of Scheduled Commercial Banks in India* (various issues), RBI.

Whether we rank districts in terms of net domestic product at constant prices or per capita income at constant prices, disparity is large and persistent, even increasing. There is strong negative correlation between net domestic product of districts at constant prices and the share of employment in primary sector in total employment in same districts. Disparity has widened because richer districts have grown faster than the poorer districts. A large number of poor districts have done badly because of low trend rate of growth of agriculture output in these districts. There is strong correlation between agriculture output and net credit outstanding in real terms in all districts (except Indore, Bhopal, Jabalpur and Gwalior).

References

Chaurasia, Alok Ranjan (2010). "Madhya Pradesh: A Tale of Poverty Versus Growth", in Shovan Ray (ed.), *Backwaters of Development: Six Deprived States of India*. New Delhi: Oxford University Press.

Chelliah R.J. and K.R. Shanmugam (2002). "Some Aspects of Inter-District Disparities in Tamil Nadu", *Annual Indian Econometric Conference*. Chennai.

Government of Madhya Pradesh (n.d.). *Economic Survey, 2005-06*.

———. (n.d.). *Economic Survey, 2009-10*.

———. (n.d.). *Area, Production and Yield of Major Crops in Madhya Pradesh, 1999-2000 to 2003-04*, Directorate of Agriculture.

———. (n.d.). *Agriculture Statistics, 2009*. Directorate of Farmer' Welfare and Agriculture Development.

———. (n.d.). *Basic Statistics, 2003*. Directorate of Economics and Statistics.

———. (n.d.). *Basic Statistics, 2008*. Directorate of Economics and Statistics.

Madhya Pradesh Second Human Development Report, 1998.

Reserve Bank of India (n.d.). *Basic Statistical Returns* (various issues).

Shaban, Abdul (2006). "Regional Structures, Growth and Convergence of Income in Maharashtra", *Economic and Political Weekly*, May 6.

Section II

Banking and Finance

6 Microfinance in India

Progress and Problems

J.S. MOSES, RAJ RAJESH,
GOPAL PRASAD, NEERAJ KUMAR and
NAVEEN KUMAR[1]

I

Introduction

The world over, the poor have lacked access to formal/institutional financial services as most of the formal financial institutions found banking with them unviable, owing to high cost involved in small transactions, perceived lower profitability, high risk of default and inability of the poor to provide physical collateral for raising loans. In the last four decades or so, attempts have been made to extend formal financial services to the poor across various economies and in this endeavour, microfinance[2] has emerged as a vital tool in expanding the outreach of the formal financial sector to the deprived sections. The rise and success of microfinance has been a remarkable accomplishment and it has been demonstrated that the poor also are creditworthy and financial services can be provided to (and accessed by them) on a profitable basis and at lower transaction costs, without relying on physical collateral, if it is done with

---

1. The authors are thankful to Ratan Kumar Ghosh, WPA, DEPR, RBI, Patna, for rendering typing assistance. Views and errors/omissions in this paper are those of the authors alone and do not in any way represent the views of their affiliated institution.

2. Microfinance is an activity of provision of financial services such as credit, thrift, insurance, remittance services, etc., to poor households. The Asian Development Bank (2000) defines microfinance as the provision of a broad range of financial services such as deposits, loans, payment services, money transfers and insurance to poor and low-income households and their microenterprises. As such, microcredit, being a sub-set of microfinance, is a narrower term, which refers to provision of small quantum of credit to poor households to enable them to begin income generating activities.

appropriate financial technology and a commitment to achieve efficiency (ADB, 2000).

As the microfinance business mainly caters to poor clients, it has a number of distinctive features that differentiates it from the commercial banking business. First, unlike banks, the microfinance institutions (MFIs) usually cater to low-income clients and as such, microcredit loans are tiny amount, usually short-term and unsecured loans with more frequent repayments (e.g. weekly or bi-weekly) and such loans entail higher interest rates than traditional bank loans. MFIs, in general, charge higher interest rates to offset higher operational costs as the microfinance activity is labour-intensive. Second, unlike banks, microlending tends to be a highly decentralised process as microcredit borrowers often lack formal financial statements and, therefore, loan documentation is generated largely by the loan officer through visits to the borrower's place of business or home. Third, unlike the lending of bank funds, some microlenders use group lending methods, where loans are made to small groups of people who cross-guarantee other members of the group. In such a framework, peer pressure helps to ensure high repayment levels, as the default of one group member could adversely affect the availability of credit to others. Fourth, the product design, client profile and underwriting methods of the MFIs differ significantly from the banks. Finally, the dynamics of assets and liabilities of MFIs and their risk profile differ from those of a commercial bank. On the asset side, loan repayment in case of MFIs is often driven by expectations of repeat loans over time, transforming short-term loan portfolios into long-term fixed-rate assets. Further, unlike the commercial banks, the MFIs may lack a cushion of unencumbered, high-quality liquid assets to enable them to withstand a range of stress events, since most funds are designated to support loan growth. On the liability side, the MFIs remain vulnerable to disruptions in commercial borrowings due to delays or changes in policies of public (Government) and private (donors and lenders) funders.

In India, over the years, microfinance has made significant progress. In view of its potential for large outreach, it seems apposite to review the progress and regional outreach of the microfinance sector in the country. Against this backdrop, the scheme of the paper is as follows. Section II analyses the development of microfinance in India, covering therein policy initiatives, microfinance delivery models in India and its recent progress in the country. Section III discusses the issue of regional spread of microfinance activity in the country. Section IV analyses select issues and problems of microfinance in India. Section V marks the concluding observations.

II

Development of Microfinance in India

Policy Initiatives

Microcredit has a long history in India, which dates back to pre-modern times. Even in the ancient times, various rulers in India used to respond to the needs of poor peasants in the times of distress of drought/famines by extending concessionary credit to them for buying seeds, digging wells, enhancing the productivity of farms, etc. In medieval times of the Mughal rulers, Muhammad-bin-Tughluq became the first Indian ruler in recorded history to advance *taccavi* loans to the villagers for carrying out rehabilitation activities in the aftermath of a disastrous famine. In the early modern period in India also, various rulers used to extend concessionary finance to poor peasants. Tipu Sultan of Mysore used to provide to resourceless farmers *taccavi* loans to enable them to undertake cultivation.

In post-independent India, expanding access to the poor has remained a core issue for policymakers. Accordingly, both the Government of India and the RBI have taken several initiatives from time to time such as nationalisation of banks, prescription of priority sector lending, differential interest rate scheme for weaker sections of the society, etc. (RBI, 2008). Following the report of the *All-India Rural Credit Survey* in mid-1950s, the Government took crucial steps in reviewing the cooperative structure including the partnership of the state in cooperatives. Also, the policy initiative of the social banking concept, which led to the nationalisation of commercial banks in 1969 and 1980, the adoption of direct lending programmes in rural areas, and the development of credit institutions such as regional rural banks (RRBs) led to the extension of formal credit channels to the deprived sections. The Government initiatives for extending credit facilities during the seventies and during the Fourth Five

Year Plan (1969-74) focused on small and marginal farmers and agricultural labourers.

Non-achievement of the desired results led to realisation that further directed efforts were required to address the credit needs of the poor. Further, inadequacies inherent in running programmes focused on individual households called for shift from individual-based approach to a group-based approach. In 1991-92, National Bank for Agriculture and Rural Development (NABARD) launched the SHG-Bank Linkage Programme (SBLP) on a pilot basis to finance the self-help groups (SHGs)[3] across the country through the formal banking system. High repayment rates by the SHGs encouraged banks to finance them. Under this system, the banks lend to the SHGs who, in turn, are free to disburse loan to their members in their best judgment, whether for production or for consumption purposes. The introduction of SBLP in the 1990s has in some ways addressed the need for consumption credit by the poor. In 1996, the RBI included financing of SHGs by the banks under the SBLP as advances to 'weaker sections' in the priority sector lending.

With the objective of facilitating and supporting the orderly growth of the microfinance sector, by especially assisting the women and vulnerable sections of the society and also by supporting their capacity building, the Government of India started a dedicated fund called as the 'Micro-finance Development Fund (MDF) with an initial corpus of Rs 100 crore. Later, the MDF was re-designated as the Micro Finance Development and Equity Fund in 2005-06 and the size of the fund was enhanced from Rs 100 crore to Rs 200 crore. The additional amount to the fund was contributed by the RBI, NABARD and the commercial banks in 40:20:20 proportion. The Union Budget (2011-12) had proposed to create a dedicated fund, called the microfinance equity fund of Rs 100 crore with SIDBI, which would provide equity to smaller MFIs and help them maintain growth and achieve scale and efficiency in operations. Besides, it has also proposed to create a 'Women's SHGs Development Fund' with a corpus of Rs 500 crore, which would seek to empower women and promote the SHGs run by them.

---

3. A SHG is a small, informal and homogeneous (registered or unregistered) group of micro entrepreneurs, with similar social and economic background who voluntarily come together to save small amounts regularly in a common fund and meet their emergency needs on a mutual help basis. The group members employ peer pressure to ensure proper end-use of credit and timely repayment thereof, and this has been found to be an effective substitute for collaterals.

Delivery Models

In India, a variety of agencies, *viz.*, commercial banks, non-bank financial companies (NBFCs), MFIs, non-governmental organisations (NGOs), SHGs, societies, cooperatives, trusts, etc., are involved in the provision of microfinance services. These institutions, nevertheless, have different institutional goals and together they provide both complementary and competitive models of microfinance delivery models in India. At present, there are two main models of microfinance delivery in India, *viz.*:(i) SBLP and (ii) MFI model. The SBLP has not only emerged as a very successful programme, but has become the force behind the microfinance movement in India. In terms of coverage, SHG-bank linkage model is considered to be the largest microfinance programme in the world (RBI, 2008). This model involves the SHGs being financed directly by the banks, *viz.*, commercial banks (public and private sector), RRBs and cooperative banks. The important advantages to banks for financing through the SHGs include lower transaction costs and ease of handling a single SHG account instead of a large number of small-sized individual accounts, while borrowers benefit in terms of improved creditworthiness of the economically poor persons in the SHG and reduced transaction costs. Commercial banks, cooperative banks and RRBs have actively contributed to the advancement of this model.

While the SBLP model remains the dominant model of microfinance in India, the MFI model has also gained momentum in recent years. MFIs in India exist in a variety of forms, *viz.*, trusts (registered under the Indian Trust Act, 1882/Public Trust Act, 1920); societies (registered under the Societies Registration Act, 1860); Co-operatives (registered under the Mutually Aided Cooperative Societies Act of the states); and NBFCs, which are registered under Section 25 of the Companies Act, 1956 or NBFCs registered with the Reserve Bank (RBI, 2008). These MFIs are scattered across the country and due to the multiplicity of registering authorities, there is no reliable estimate on the number of MFIs. The most frequently used reliable estimates for the number of MFIs operating in India is estimated to be around 800 (RBI, 2008).

As per the comparative performance of the two models, it is found that in recent years, the performance of SBLP *vis-à-vis* MFI model has taken a beating in terms of share of customer base, outstanding loans and incremental loans

(Table 6.1). The spurt in the average size of loan per borrower in the case of MFIs suggests that either there has been an increase in the size of the average individual loan given to borrower or there has been multiple lending/over borrowing resulting from more than one loan being given to the same borrower (RBI, 2011b). In their quest for higher profitability, MFIs often use existing SHGs as the target for attracting new customers (RBI, 2011b). As compared to the SBLP, MFIs are found to attract customers more easily because of their deeper, aggressive, flexible and informal approach to business, and simpler and hassle-free loan procedures. Thus, it appears that the recent growth of the MFI model is at the cost of the SBLP.

Table 6.1

Comparative Position of SBLP and MFIs in Terms of Customer Base and Loans

Particulars	*Absolute*			*Share (%)*		
	2007-08	*2008-09*	*2009-10*	*2007-08*	*2008-09*	*2009-10*
No. of customers (million)						
SBLP	50.8	59.1	64.5	78.3	72.3	70.7
MFI	14.1	22.6	26.7	21.7	27.7	29.3
Total	64.9	81.7	91.2	100.0	100.0	100.0
Portfolio outstanding (Rs billion)						
SBLP	167.0	226.8	272.7	73.7	65.9	59.8
MFI	59.5	117.3	183.4	26.3	34.1	40.2
Total	226.5	344.1	456.1	100.0	100.0	100.0
Incremental loans outstanding (Rs billion)						
SBLP	46.3	56.8	45.9	64.9	49.6	41.0
MFI	25.0	57.8	66.1	35.1	50.4	59.0
Total	71.3	114.6	112.0	100.0	100.0	100.0
Loan amount per borrower (Rs)						
SBLP	3287.4	3837.6	4227.9	-	-	-
MFI	4220.0	5190.0	6869.0	-	-	-
Total	3490.0	4211.8	5001.0	-	-	-

Source: RBI (2011b).

Recent Progress of Microfinance in India

Bank financing to the microfinance sector, to the SHGs and the MFIs, has increased significantly in the recent period (Table 6.2). Microcredit deployed by the banks increased in the Indian economy even in the aftermath of the global financial crisis, which had a minimal impact on the microfinance activity in the country (Figure 6.1). This is primarily attributable to three factors. First, India's domestic sector experienced less economic dislocations and remained, by and large, insulated from the onslaught of the global financial crisis as India had been a relatively less open economy and it pursued prudent policies in the financial sector characterised by gradual and sequenced reforms. This prevented the Indian economy from facing a sharp economic slowdown, which could have otherwise severely impacted the MFIs in India. Second, the Indian MFIs fared better than other countries' MFIs, given the fact that they were relatively isolated from adverse developments in foreign financial markets, as the Reserve Bank of India restricts the MFIs from borrowing from international markets. Third, as per the Government's stipulations, banks' advances to the MFIs are treated as 'priority sector' lending, which prevented banks from completely pulling out of the sector.

Figure 6.1

Trends in Deployment of Microcredit by Banks

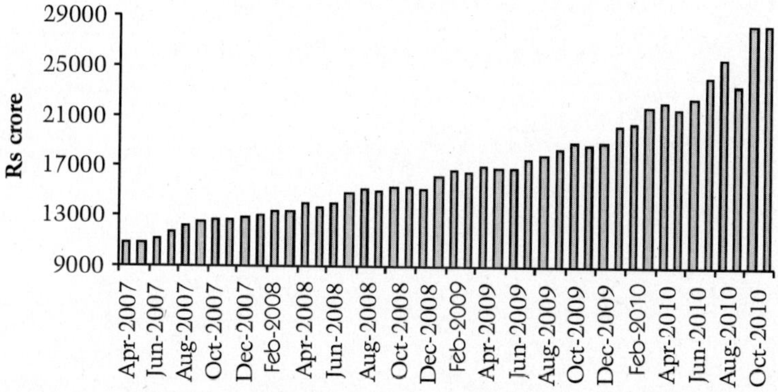

Source: RBI.

III

Regional Spread of the Microfinance Sector

There are regional imbalances in the spread of microfinance activities across the country. The spread of microfinance movement has been skewed in favour of the Southern Region owing to positive intervention by the respective state governments, presence of well-performing NGOs and keen participation

Table 6.2

Overall Progress under Microfinance during the Recent Period

(Amount in Rs crore)

Particulars	2007-08		2008-09		2009-10		Growth (%) (2008-09)		Growth (%) (2009-10)	
	No.of SHGs	Amount	No. of SHGs	Amount	No. of SHGs	Amount	No.of SHGs	Amount	No.of SHGs	Amount
A. SHG-Bank Linkage										
Savings of SHGs with banks as on 31st March	50,09,794	3785.39	61,21,147	5545.62	69,53,250	6198.71	22.2	46.5	13.6	11.8
Bank loans disbursed to SHGs during the year	12,27,770	8849.26	16,09,586	12253.51	15,86,822	14453.30	31.1	38.5	-1.4	17.9
Bank loans outstanding with SHGs as on 31st March	36,25,941	16999.91	42,24,338	22679.84	48,51,356	28038.28	16.5	33.4	14.8	23.6
B. MFI-Bank Linkage										
Bank loans disbursed to MFIs during the year	518	1970.15	581	3732.33	691	8062.74	12.2	89.4	18.9	116.0
Bank loans outstanding with MFIs as on 31st March	1109	2748.84	1915	5009.09	1513	10147.54	72.7	82.2	21.0	102.6

Note: Actual number of MFIs provided with bank loans would be less as several MFIs could have availed loans from more than one bank.

Source: *Status of Microfinance in India, 2009-10*, NABARD.

of the banking sector in microfinance activity in these states. The Andhra Pradesh government has played a proactive role in promoting SHG movement in the state as it routed several of its poverty reduction schemes (such as *Velugu* progamme) via the SHG route. Besides, various NGOs and international development agencies have also contributed to the growth of SHGs in the state. The Tamil Nadu government also extended help to the SHG movement in the state through the support to Tamil Nadu's development programme and the International Fund for Agriculture Development (IFAD). In Karnataka, the banking system had a significant role in promotion of microfinance as many of the commercial banks have their headquarters in the state and these banks with their positive outlook on the rural markets have been constructively engaged with the SHGs. Besides the efforts of these agencies, the supporting environment rendered by prevalence of higher level of education, vibrant economy, a natural environment where microfinance is well understood, etc., has also helped the higher growth of microfinance in the Southern Region as compared to other regions in the country.

In terms of the region's share in the number of SHGs formed and loans extended to them, the Southern Region states scored over the other regions of the country. The Southern Region had the largest share of SHGs accounting for 62.7 per cent share at all-India level, while the loans disbursed accounted for a share of 76.4 per cent (Table 6.3). As per the bank loans outstanding against SHGs as on 31st March 2010, it is found that the total number of SHGs having loans outstanding with banks was

Table 6.3

Region-wise Disbursements of Bank Loans to SHGs: Share (2009-10)

(Per cent)

Region	*Commercial Banks*		*Regional Rural Banks*		*Cooperative Banks*		*Total*	
	No. of SHGs	*Bank Loan*	*No. of SHGs*	*Bank Loan*	*No. of SHGs*	*Bank Loan*	*No. of SHGs*	*Bank Loan*
Northern Region	1.5	1.6	2.9	2.4	4.8	5.4	2.4	2.1
North Eastern Region	1.7	1.3	5.7	3.4	4.9	3.7	3.1	2.0
Eastern Region	16.1	8.7	20.6	16.2	18.5	11.1	17.5	10.7
Central Region	3.5	2.9	10.0	9.1	2.6	3.3	4.9	4.4
Western Region	6.9	3.8	5.3	1.4	26.6	17.4	9.4	4.5
Southern Region	70.3	81.7	55.5	67.6	42.6	59.1	62.7	76.4
All-India	100.0	100.0	100.0	100.0	100.0	100.0	100.0	100.0

Source: Status of Microfinance in India, 2009-10, NABARD.

Table 6.4

Progress under Microfinance: Bank Loans Outstanding against SHGs
Region-wise/State-wise/Agency-wise Position (as on March 31, 2010)

(Amount in Rs crore)

Sl. No.	Region/State	Commercial Banks		Regional Rural Banks		Cooperative Banks		Total	
		No. of SHGs	Bank Loan	No. of SHGs	Bank Loan	No. of SHGs	Bank Loan	No. of SHGs	Bank Loan
A	**Northern Region**	**65759**	**497.48**	**41415**	**178.52**	**45317**	**139.13**	**152491**	**815.13**
	1. Haryana	11407	105.00	3951	44.62	444	5.46	15802	155.07
	2. Himachal Pradesh	7459	55.56	4667	17.67	15083	32.74	27209	105.97
	3. Punjab	6112	47.60	1914	12.53	2019	6.95	10045	67.08
	4. Jammu & Kashmir	976	6.55	344	2.24	345	1.54	1665	10.33
	5. Rajasthan	38241	269.38	30539	101.47	27426	92.43	96206	463.29
	6. New Delhi	1564	13.39	NA	NA	NA	NA	1564	13.39
B	**North Eastern Region**	**69571**	**388.26**	**50297**	**228.54**	**13917**	**56.68**	**133785**	**673.48**
	1. Assam	49925	302.16	38656	145.34	11841	43.73	100422	491.23
	2. Meghalaya	2267	8.46	812	3.47	112	1.47	3191	13.40
	3. Nagaland	4236	14.50	NA	NA	NA	NA	4236	14.50
	4. Tripura	5404	27.55	7467	60.09	1709	9.23	14580	96.87
	5. Arunachal Pradesh	2889	7.98	122	0.92	192	1.79	3203	10.68
	6. Mizoram	636	7.99	1455	15.22	6	0.04	2097	23.26
	7. Manipur	2667	15.28	1785	3.50	NA	NA	4452	18.79
	8. Sikkim	1547	4.33	NA	NA	57	0.42	1604	4.74

contd...

...contd...

Sl. No.	Region/State	Commercial Banks		Regional Rural Banks		Cooperative Banks		Total	
		No. of SHGs	Bank Loan	No. of SHGs	Bank Loan	No. of SHGs	Bank Loan	No. of SHGs	Bank Loan
C	**Eastern Region**	**561579**	**2365.56**	**313118**	**1086.46**	**152873**	**242.89**	**1027570**	**3694.91**
	1. Bihar	56630	376.42	25585	181.35	NA	NA	82215	557.77
	2. Jharkhand	45513	245.54	18228	45.21	NA	NA	63741	290.75
	3. Orissa	208898	1013.54	135055	406.75	28693	95.80	372646	1516.08
	4. West Bengal	250108	728.97	134250	453.14	123424	144.81	507782	1326.93
	5. A & N Islands (UT)	430	1.09	NA	NA	756	2.28	1186	3.37
D	**Central Region**	**317021**	**1577.26**	**153582**	**772.76**	**27319**	**112.37**	**497922**	**2462.40**
	1. Chhattisgarh	28804	131.17	19332	64.63	4452	3.26	52588	199.06
	2. Madhya Pradesh	45557	318.40	18102	76.65	13269	50.08	76928	445.13
	3. Uttarakhand	19238	122.65	5878	30.87	4933	28.81	30049	182.33
	4. Uttar Pradesh	223422	1005.04	110270	600.61	4665	30.22	338357	1635.88
E	**Western Region**	**331693**	**1045.92**	**38064**	**133.66**	**87719**	**189.91**	**457476**	**1369.48**
	1. Goa	2277	13.31	NA	NA	1148	11.24	3425	24.56
	2. Gujarat	57406	107.00	8582	20.36	3298	14.26	69286	141.62
	3. Maharashtra	272010	925.61	29482	113.30	83273	164.40	384765	1203.31
F	**Southern Region**	**1891640**	**14290.23**	**507504**	**3744.64**	**182968**	**988.01**	**2582112**	**19022.88**
	1. Andhra Pradesh	1062726	8686.46	390122	2900.10	18436	152.98	1471284	11739.54
	2. Karnataka	168624	1376.17	75418	505.27	56696	173.86	300738	2055.30
	3. Kerala	223741	805.92	12042	86.75	21977	122.64	257760	1015.31
	4. Tamil Nadu	424763	3292.92	29582	249.11	84522	517.39	538867	4059.42
	5. Puducherry	11786	128.76	340	3.41	1337	21.14	13463	153.31
	Total	**3237263**	**20164.71**	**1103980**	**6144.58**	**510113**	**1728.99**	**4851356**	**28038.28**

Notes: NA – Not Available/Not Reported.

Source: *Status of Microfinance in India 2009-10*, NABARD.

48,51,356 and the total amount of loans outstanding stood at Rs 28038.28 crore (Table 6.4). Similarly, in respect of the number of MFI clients and amount of loans extended by the MFIs to their clients, the Southern Region dominated other regions of the country (Table 6.5).

Table 6.5

Regional Spread of MFI Clients and Loan Outreach

(Per cent)

Sl. No	Region	No. of Clients	Loan Amount
1.	Northern Region	2.1	4.3
2.	North Eastern Region	1.9	1.8
3.	Eastern Region	21.3	22.5
4.	Central Region	9.5	9.9
5.	Western Region	14.2	6.8
6.	Southern Region	51.1	54.8

Source: Srinivasan (2010).

Furthermore, poorer states in India such as Bihar, Jharkhand, Madhya Pradesh, Chhattisgarh, Uttar Pradesh and Uttarakhand seem to be underserved by the SHGs (Figure 6.2). In general, it is also found that as compared to regions with higher poverty levels (Eastern and Central Region), lower poverty level regions (Southern, North Eastern and Western

Figure 6.2

Scatter-Plot of Number of SHGs per '000 Persons and Poverty Ratio across States

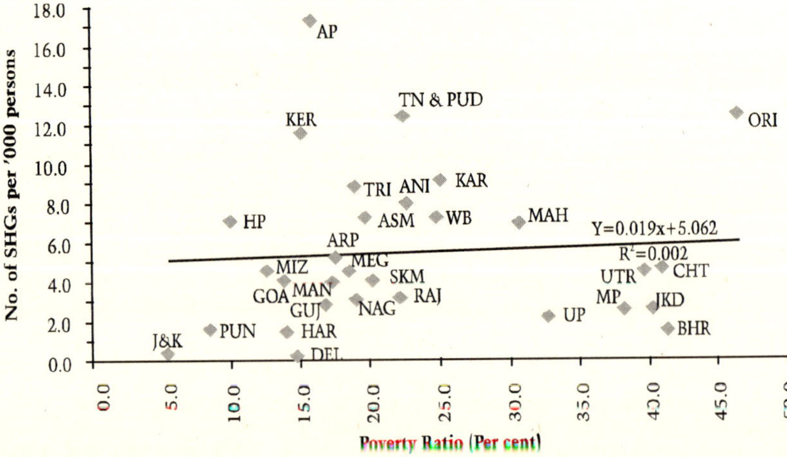

Source: NABARD, RBI and CSO.

Table 6.6

Pattern of SHGs' Spread and Poverty across the States/UTs in India

Sl. No.	*States*	*Position as on 31st March 2010*		*Poverty % (based on URP Consumption, 2004-05)*
		No. of SHGs per '000 Persons	*Per Capita Bank Loans Outstanding against SHGs (Rupees)*	
1.	Haryana	1.5	62.4	14.0
2.	Himachal Pradesh	7.1	150.0	10.0
3.	Punjab	1.6	23.5	8.4
4.	Jammu & Kashmir	0.4	9.0	5.4
5.	Rajasthan	3.2	69.9	22.1
6.	New Delhi	0.1	7.6	14.7
7.	Assam	7.3	163.5	19.7
8.	Meghalaya	4.6	52.0	18.5
9.	Nagaland*	3.1	76.3	19.0
10.	Tripura	8.8	272.3	18.9
11.	Arunachal Pradesh	5.3	87.5	17.6
12.	Mizoram	4.6	210.6	12.6
13.	Manipur	4.0	69.0	17.3
14.	Sikkim	4.0	78.6	20.1
15.	Bihar	1.5	58.2	41.4
16.	Jharkhand	2.6	94.2	40.3
17.	Orissa	12.5	375.2	46.4
18.	West Bengal	7.3	150.2	24.7
19.	A & N Islands (UT)	7.9	71.1	22.6
20.	Chhattisgarh	4.7	81.2	40.9
21.	Madhya Pradesh	2.5	63.1	38.3
22.	Uttarakhand	4.5	187.2	39.6
23.	Uttar Pradesh	2.2	83.5	32.8
24.	Goa	4.0	146.3	13.8
25.	Gujarat	2.9	24.5	16.8
26.	Maharashtra	7.0	108.9	30.7
27.	Andhra Pradesh	17.3	1403.4	15.8
28.	Karnataka	9.1	351.0	25.0
29.	Kerala	11.5	296.7	15.0
30.	Tamil Nadu & Puducherry (UT)	12.5	619.7	22.5**

Note: *: Population figures for Nagaland are for 2008-09

**: Figure for Tamil Nadu alone. URP: Uniform Recall Period.

Source: NABARD, CSO and *Handbook of Statistics on the Indian Economy, 2009-10*, RBI.

Region) have a relatively larger presence of SHGs per thousand persons and a higher per capita outstanding bank loan (Table 6.6). *Ipso facto*, moderately poor states seem to have a larger concentration of the SHGs, which may be attributable to the fact that SHGs have penetrated more in those states where the banking system (SHG-led model has been driven by banks themselves) had been relatively well-developed, while the states with more underbanked areas have lesser penetration by the SHGs.

In terms of microfinance activity, the Eastern, Northern, North Eastern and Western states are lagging behind on account of conducive socioeconomic and political setup required for such interventions (GoI, 2007b). The absence of local institutions to start, manage and upscale credit programmes, lack of focus on the part of FIs/banks, lack of social services providers, etc., have been some of possible impediments that have hindered the growth of MFIs in these parts of the country. In the Eastern and North Eastern parts of the country, poor law and order, which escalates administrative costs of microcredit operations as it involves physical movement of cash, has put a brake on the growth of microfinance activity.

IV

Issues and Problems of Microfinance in India

Despite the phenomenal growth of microfinance in the country, certain undesired developments in the sector have led to policy concerns. Some of the issues facing the microfinance sector in India are discussed as below.

Multiple Borrowing

In recent years, competition has intensified amongst the MFIs in India as they have tended to concentrate around the same towns and peripheries (Srinivasan, 2010). This has led to a situation wherein the same set of households is being offered loans from several institutions leading to the problem of multiple borrowing (i.e., the same borrower taking loans from more than one MFI or the borrower becoming member of more than one SHG) and sometimes excessive debt. This has resulted in rise in defaults on loans raised from the MFIs as the aggregate loans made to these households exceed their repayment capacity. The dynamics of such multiple lending can be understood from the fact that when the newer

MFIs enter the market, in their quest for an early break–even in a short period of time, they hunt for 'ring leaders' who have a clout in the local microfinance market and help these new MFIs to register customers. The ring leader sometimes charges registration fees from the borrowers. In some instances, it has been found that these ring leaders use the relative unfamiliarity of the new field staff and new MFIs to their advantage by obtaining loans in *benami* names, which result in fictitious loans being made to 'Ghost' borrowers. Such loans with serious processing deficiencies and poor customer appraisal have a tendency to default.

Johnson and Meka (2010) in their survey on access to finance in Andhra Pradesh found that 93 per cent of all households in Andhra Pradesh had access to loans and 82 per cent of such loans were being availed from informal sources. They observed that 83 per cent of these families had two or more loans and the median number of loans per household was four. They also found that apart from consumption needs, loans from joint liability groups (JLGs) and SHGs were primarily being raised for repaying the old loans rather than for making newer investments for which loans were made (Table 6.7).

Table 6.7

Usage of Loan Money by Lender Type in Andhra Pradesh (Per cent)

Sl. No.	*Usage of Loan Money*	*Banks*	*JLG*	*SHG*	*Informal Sector*
1.	Start new business	2	3	2	1
2.	Buy agricultural inputs	58	13	19	20
3.	Purchase stock	3	10	4	3
4.	Repay old debt	15	25	20	7
5.	Health	11	11	19	25
6.	Marriage	4	5	2	12
7.	Funeral	0.1	0	0.5	2
8.	Other festival	1	4	4	5
9.	Home improvement	10	22	13	14
10.	Unemployment	0	0	0.1	0.8
11.	Purchase land	1	1	1	1
12.	Education	4	4	6	5
13.	Purchase jewellery	1	1	2	0.4
14.	Consumption	27	32	50	25
15.	Buy livestock	3	6	6	2

Note: Totals may be greater than 100 per cent as loans may be used for more than one purpose.

Source: Johnson and Meka (2010).

On this issue, RBI (2011b)[4] observed that multiple lending and over borrowing have been rising in the Indian economy possibly because of two reasons. First, MFIs in their quest for higher profitability and lower transaction costs have been found to be using existing SHGs as the target for obtaining new borrowers. Second, borrowers may be raising loans from other MFIs to repay their old debts as they may not be getting adequate time to generate income to repay their old debts. The Malegam Committee took serious note of this and had made several recommendations to reduce such incidences of multiple lending (RBI *op.cit.*).

Further, the Committee examined various other issues in the microfinance sector ranging from regulation, ceiling on interest rate charged by the MFIs, priority sector status for bank lending to MFIs, etc., and made several recommendations. After a thorough discussion on the recommendations of the Committee with other agencies, the RBI accepted the broad framework of regulations recommended by the Malegam Committee. The RBI has stipulated that bank loans to all MFIs, including NBFCs working as MFIs, on or after April 1, 2011, would be eligible for classification as priority sector loans under respective category of indirect finance only if the prescribed percentage of such loans are in the nature of 'qualifying assets' and they ensure that the MFIs adhere to the 'pricing of interest' guidelines. As per the guidelines, a 'qualifying asset' is required to satisfy the criteria of: (i) loan disbursed by an MFI to a borrower with a rural household annual income not exceeding Rs 60,000 or urban and semi-urban household income not exceeding Rs 1,20,000; (ii) loan amount not to exceed Rs 35,000 in the first cycle and Rs 50,000 in subsequent cycles; (iii) total indebtedness of a borrower not to exceed Rs 50,000; (iv) tenure of loan not to be less than 24 months for loan amount in excess of Rs 15,000 without prepayment penalty; (v) loan to be extended without collateral; (vi) aggregate amount of loan, given for income generation, not to be less than 75 per cent of the total loans given by the MFIs and (vii) loan to be repayable by weekly, fortnightly or monthly instalments at the choice of the borrower. It also laid down that banks would be able to get their loans to the MFIs classified as priority sector loan only if they ensure

4. As indicated in its Second Quarter Review of November 2010, the RBI had constituted a Sub-Committee of the Central Board of the Reserve Bank (Chairman: Y.H. Malegam) to study issues and concerns in the MFI sector. It submitted its report in January 2011.

that the MFIs to whom the bank lends imposes a margin cap of 12 per cent and overall an interest rate cap of 26 per cent for its lending to microfinance clients. Further, it stipulated that loans by MFIs can also be extended to individuals outside the SHG/JLG.

Regulatory Issues

Regulation increases the cost of operation of the regulated entity. Regulatory costs attached with the MFIs are higher than that of the banks. This is primarily because of the fact that regulatory costs exhibit economies of scale and thus smaller financial entities face higher average costs than larger institutions in complying with regulations (Elliehausen and Kurtz, 1988).

Further, concern has been expressed that while regulation may increase costs, it may also affect outreach adversely. Hartarska and Nadolnyak (2007) found that regulation of the MFIs has no impact on their financial performance either in terms of operational self-sustainability or outreach *per se*. They found weak evidence that regulated MFIs serve less poor borrowers. On the contrary, Cull *et al.* (2009) found that supervision of the MFIs is negatively associated with their profitability as also those profit-oriented MFIs absorb the cost of supervision by curtailing their outreach to market segments where operational costs are high.

Most of the MFIs across the world face some form of non-prudential regulation. These regulations can include rules governing MFI formation and operations, consumer protection, fraud prevention, establishing credit information services, secured transactions, interest rate limits, foreign ownership limitations, and tax and accounting issues (Christen *et al.*, 2003). Prudential regulations are less common and are imposed when system-wide concerns are justified or protecting small depositors is an issue.

The Indian microfinance industry is characterised by a multiplicity of microfinance providers dispersed across the country. These players belong to diverse institutional forms—NBFC-MFIs, cooperative societies, not-for-profit companies (under Section 25 of the Companies Act, 1956), trusts and as such are subject to different laws and regulations. India has a unique status when it comes to microfinance regulation and supervision. Most of the large MFIs in India today operate as NBFCs and fall under RBI regulation. With the involvement of the formal banking sector, mainly by way of linkages with

SHGs under different models and large MFIs being registered as NBFCs, a major part of the microfinance sector is regulated. Insofar as SHGs are concerned, in view of the limited size of their membership, small volumes of funds involved and collective decision-making process, which ensure strong internal control, they pose a low systemic risk in India. In addition, the microfinance industry has taken some significant steps towards systemic regulation. However, a view has been expressed that when there is growth in a sector, self-regulation is important, otherwise the organisations in the sector are susceptible to risk. Recognising the need for better governance practices, several MFIs came together in 2009 to create a self-regulatory organisation called the Microfinance Institutions Network (MFIN). The MFIN consist of 46 NBFC-MFIs in India. MFIN has taken some steps such as building a credit bureau, creating task forces for transparency and establishing a code of conduct. This code of conduct underlines the commitment of the institutions to good governance and customer protection. It emphasises transparency in interest rates, limits a borrower's loans through group lending to a total of less than Rs 50,000 from three MFIs. It also includes a 'whistle blower' policy on code of conduct violations.

Notwithstanding these initiatives of the MFIs, there have been several complaints of coercive recovery practices of the MFIs across the country. Also, unhealthy competition amongst the MFIs has added to the problem of multiple borrowings and over-indebtedness of microfinance clients. This had led some states like Andhra Pradesh to frame their own legislation for regulating the activities of the MFIs in the state. If the states frame their own legislations for regulating the activities of microfinance within their own jurisdiction, then this would create a situation of regulatory arbitrage. In this regard, RBI (2011b) has observed that a comprehensive set of regulatory guidelines may be laid down by the Government of India[5] for regulating the activities of microfinance in the country.

---

5. To promote a healthy growth of the sector, a need has always been felt for providing a formal statutory framework for microfinance sector. In this connection, the Government had drawn up the Micro Financial Sector (Development and Regulation) Bill in 2007. This Bill was originally introduced in the Lok Sabha on March 20, 2007, but it lapsed. It was again introduced in subsequent years, but it lapsed again.

Rate of Interest

In most of the countries, concerns have been expressed over the high rate of interest charged by the MFIs. Even in the countries, where the MFIs receive concessional funding, interest rate charged by them remains high. Fernando (2006) underlines four key factors that result in higher microcredit rates, *viz.*, higher cost of funds, higher operating expenses of the MFIs, loan losses and profits needed to expand their capital base and funds, and expected future growth. The operating costs of the MFIs are very high as microlending is a labour-intensive operation and making and recovering small loans is costly on a per unit basis. Inadequate law and order and poor physical infrastructure in a country/region in which a MFI operates also contribute to higher administrative costs and thereby higher microcredit interest rates. Fernando *op. cit.*, opines that comparison of interest rates charged by the MFIs and those by the commercial banks is inappropriate as the latter most often deal with large loans and their transaction costs (on a per unit basis) are lower than those of the MFIs. Further, the interest rates necessary to cover all costs (including costs of funds and loan losses) are much higher for MFI loans than for conventional bank loans. Collins *et al.* (2009) observe that interest rates charged by the MFIs may often be better understood as 'fees' for a service rather than a rate for the use of money for a specified period.

Theoretically, any ceiling on interest rate would lead to a sub-optimal situation (Figure 6.3). Fernando *op. cit.*, argues that rate ceilings would create an artificially high demand for microcredit relative to supply and encourage credit officers and others to adopt rationing devices that, in turn, create rent-seeking opportunities. Collins *op. cit.*, opines that legislation restricting interest rates would be counter-productive for provision of pro-poor financial services as rendered by the MFIs.

Other countries have formally or informally sought to put a control on the rate of interest charged by the MFIs. In Bangladesh, there is an official ceiling on the interest rate that can be charged by the MFIs. The Microcredit Regulatory Authority (MRA) in Bangladesh has put a ceiling on the interest rate that can be charged from the microfinance clients at 27 per cent per annum. In Ethiopia, though there is no official interest rate ceiling, the central bank, being the regulator of microfinance, controls the larger MFIs in the country and tries to keep the interest rates charged by

Figure 6.3

Situation of Excess Demand for Loan in Event of Ceiling on Interest on Loan

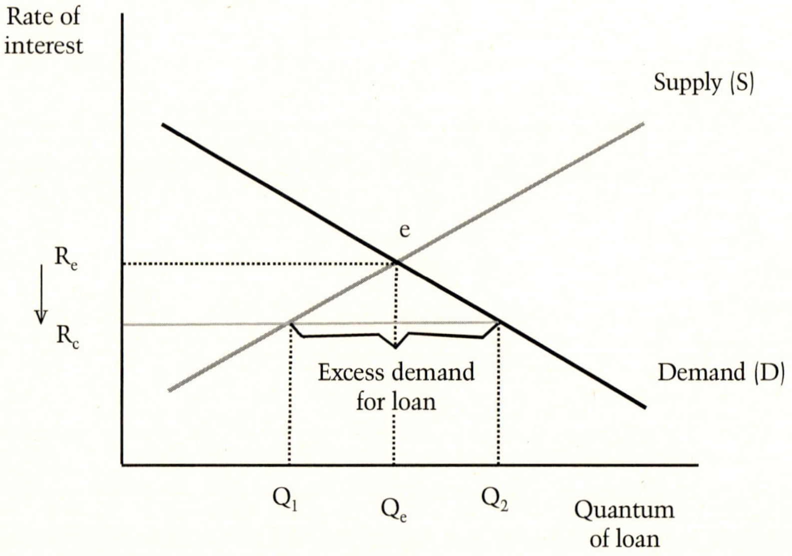

them low. The RBI in its *Monetary Policy Statement 2011* has exhorted the commercial banks, which lend their funds to the MFIs, that they should ensure that the MFIs impose an interest rate cap of 26 per cent per annum while lending to the microfinance clients. It is only then that the bank loans to the MFIs would qualify as priority sector loans.

V

Concluding Observations

Microfinance has made significant progress in the country over the last two decades or so and this gradual and evolutionary growth process has led to economic, social and cultural empowerment of rural households in the country. However, given the high incidence of poverty and the level of financial exclusion, providing microfinance services to this excluded segment continues to remain a major challenge in the country. In the rural areas of the country where institutional finance had not been adequately available, microfinance has delivered, but its outreach has been too meagre.

While the SHG-bank linkage programme has emerged as the most popular model of microfinance in the country; its spread has been skewed in favour of the Southern States. There is a dire need for innovative projects for further developing the SHG-Bank linkage, particularly in areas which are lagging behind, in order to increase financial inclusion. Furthermore, for expanding the outreach of microfinance business, the MFIs in India should redraw their business models and introduce a newer set of services.

In this regard, policy efforts are needed to help further develop the microfinance industry, while tackling the trade-off between outreach and sustainability. Further, serious efforts need to be made to strengthen the linkage between microfinance and the formal financial system as it has the potential for bringing down the cost of capital and operating costs of the MFIs, which can give a renewed impetus to the growth of microfinance industry in India. To improve the viability and sustainability of MFIs in rural areas, it is important that policy measures be taken that give a boost to rural infrastructure as this would provide both demand and supply-side impetus to microfinance in India.

Further, despite the fact that microfinance activities in the country have increased significantly, the sector has not yet been brought under a comprehensive regulation. The Government has attempted to bring in legislation for regulating the microfinance sector since 2007, but it has not succeeded so far on account of significant differences of opinion on the proposed legislation. While it is argued that a major part of the microfinance sector, comprising the NBFCs that account for around 89 per cent of the microfinance loan portfolio, is regulated by the RBI; regulation of these institutions needs to be further fine-tuned and made more comprehensive. Further, the MFIs, which were formed as societies/ trusts, etc., have so far been not brought under a comprehensive regulation, which has led some states like Kerala and Andhra Pradesh to devise their own regulatory norms for the sector. This is an undesirable development, which may lead to regulatory arbitrage. Since the microfinance sector in India is large, with a vast number of poor clients, a comprehensive set of regulations by the Government of India needs to be instituted.

References

Asian Development Bank (2000). *Finance for the Poor: Microfinance Development Strategy*. Manila: ADB.

Christen, Robert P., Timothy R. Lyman and Richard Rosenberg (2003). *Microfinance Consensus Guidelines: Guiding Principles on Regulation and Supervision of Microfinance*. Washington : CGAP/The World Bank Group. June. Available at: *http://www.cgap.org/gm/document-1.9.2787/Guideline_RegSup.pdf*

Collins, Daryl, Jonathan Murdoch, Stuart Rutherford and Orlanda Ruthven (2009). *Portfolios of the Poor: How the World's Poor Live on $2 a Day*. Princeton University Press.

Cull, Robert, Asli Demirgüç-Kunt and Jonathan Morduch (2009). "Does Regulatory Supervision Curtail Microfinance Profitability and Outreach?", *World Bank Policy Research Working Paper* WPS4948, June.

Elliehausen, Gregory (1998). "The Cost of Bank Regulation: A Review of the Evidence", *United States Federal Reserve System, Staff Studies Series* Number 171, Washington, DC: Board of Governors of the Federal Reserve System.

Elliehausen, Gregory E. and Robert D. Kurtz (1988). "Scale Economies in Compliance Costs for Federal Consumer Credit Regulations", *Journal of Financial Service Research* 1: 147–59, January.

Fernando, Nimal A. (2006). *Understanding and Dealing with High Interest Rates on Microcredit—A Note to Policy Makers in the Asia and Pacific Region*. Asian Development Bank, May.

Government of India (1991). *All India Debt and Investment Survey, 1991*.

———. (1951). *All India Rural Credit Survey, 1951*.

———. (2007a). *Report of the Sub-Group on Innovative Finance and Microfinance*. Planning Commission, January.

———. (2007b). *Report of the Steering Committee on Microfinance and Poverty Alleviation*. Planning Commission, May.

Hartarska, V. and D. Nadolnyak (2007). "Do Regulated MFIs Achieve Better Sustainability and Outreach? Cross-country Evidence", *Applied Economics* 39(10): 1207-22.

International Monetary Fund (2009). *The Implications of the Global Financial Crisis for Low-Income Countries*, March. Available at *http://www.imf.org/external/pubs/ft/books/2009/globalfin/globalfin.pdf*

Johnson, Doug and Sushmita Meka (2010). *Access to Finance in Rural Andhra Pradesh 2010*. Centre for Microfinance, IFMR Research, October.

NABARD (2010). *Status of Microfinance in India-2009-10*.

RBI (2008). *Report on Trend and Progress of Banking in India 2007-08*.

———. (2010). *Annual Policy Statement for the Year 2009-10*, April.

———. (2011a). *Monetary Policy Statement 2011-12*, May.

———. (2011b). *Report of the Sub-Committee of the Central Board of Directors of Reserve Bank of India to Study Issues and Concerns in the MFI Sector*. January.

Srinivasan, N. (2010). *Microfinance India: State of the Sector Report, 2010*. New Delhi: Sage Publications India Pvt. Ltd.

7 Regional Dimensions of Banking Services

VINEET KUMAR SRIVASTAVA,
A.K. SHUKLA, RAJIV LOCHAN,
JOHN V. GURIA[1]

I

Introduction

The banking industry has shown tremendous growth in volume and outreach during the last few decades. Significant strides have been made in terms of financial viability, profitability and competitiveness by the banking sector as a whole. However, a vast segment of the population, especially the underprivileged sections of the society are yet to be brought into the fold of basic banking services. The broad-based delivery of banking and other financial services at affordable cost to the marginalised sections of society is the socioeconomic responsibility of banking sector as they enjoy several privileges over other economic entities *viz.*, collecting public deposits on a highly leveraged basis. The objective of financial inclusion is to provide access to minimum financial services, *viz.*, deposit, credit, insurance, remittance facilities, etc., to the masses at affordable cost within reasonable distance from their habitat. It is now a well established fact that the access to the formal banking system leads to significant improvement in the lives of the masses by enhancing savings and saving habits, smoothening consumption expenditure, fostering entrepreneurial talent, creating resilience against various social and natural shocks, etc. In empirical studies, it has been proved that financial inclusion helps in confidence building, enhances decision-making capacity as also helps the banking

1. Paper was presented in DEPR's Regional Offices Conference held in December 2010 in Mumbai. Views expressed in paper are personal of authors and in no way represent the views of the Reserve Bank of India.

system to reach to the unbanked areas so as to increase their business opportunity (Beck and Peria, 2007; Planning Commission, 2008). The concept of financial inclusion is not new to the Indian banking system. The nationalisation of banks may be deemed as first major step towards the process of financial inclusion followed by opening of regional rural banks (RRBs), extension of lead bank scheme, etc. In the *Annual Policy Statement for 2005-06*, for the first time the term financial inclusion was used and a broad approach to the financial inclusion was formulated by the Reserve Bank. Since then, the Bank has undertaken various policy measures for attracting the financially excluded population into the structured financial system such as asking banks to open no-frills accounts with relaxed KYC norms, offering of modest overdraft facility/General Credit Card, use of intermediaries to act as agents (BC/BF) for enhancing banks' outreach, adoption of districts for 100 per cent financial inclusion, promotion of financial literacy and credit counselling, special policy package for northeastern states, etc.

In India, the financially excluded sections comprise largely marginal farmers, landless labourers, oral lessees, self-employed and unorganised sector enterprises, urban slum dwellers, migrants, ethnic minorities and socially excluded groups, senior citizens and women. Some of the important causes of relatively low extension of institutional credit in the rural areas are risk perception, cost of its assessment and management, lack of rural infrastructure and vast geographical spread of the rural areas with more than half a million villages, some sparsely populated (Mohan, 2006). The spread of banking facilities along with other financial institutions leads to reduction of poverty, increase in entrepreneurial skill, reduction in the cost of family maintenance among poorer people, improvement in social relationship, etc. The banking outreach has salutary impact on the women empowerment (Mahajan and Bansal, 2008).

The present study attempts to analyse the extent of outreach of banking services in India at regional level. The study is also supplemented by a sample survey conducted in the capital cities of Gujarat, Jammu & Kashmir, Madhya Pradesh and Uttar Pradesh, to assess the various facets of availability of the financial services to the marginalised section of metropolitan areas of these states. The samples for the survey have been taken out of marginalised class of the society such as slum dwellers, roadside vendors/shop owners, migratory labourers living on pavements, etc., and data/information were collected on uses of banking/ financial services by them. Besides this introductory section, the study is divided into six sections. The definition and theoretical underpinnings along with brief literature survey related to financial inclusion are presented in Section II. An overview of outreach of banking in India is presented in Section III. This section has analysed the banking outreach of individuals as well as of enterprises. An analysis of banking penetration at regional level is presented in Section IV. The findings of sample survey conducted in the capital cities of Gujarat, Jammu & Kashmir, Madhya Pradesh and Uttar Pradesh are discussed in Section V. Finally, the concluding observations and certain recommendations to pace up the process of achieving the goal of outreach of banking services are presented in Section VI.

II

Brief Literature Survey

Outreach is an act of extending services, benefits, etc., to a wider section of the population, as in community work. Hence, banking outreach can be defined as an attempt by the system, including policymaking authorities, banks, non-government organisations, etc., to provide banking services in a calibrated manner to that section of citizenry to whom it has not reached hitherto. In India, due to the dominant share of banking in the financial system, financial inclusion has become synonymous for banking outreach. However, in a broader perspective, banking outreach is considered as a necessary pre-condition in order to achieve holistic financial inclusion. It may be defined in two ways, viz., in narrow manner and broader manner. In India, it has been defined in a narrower sense as to ensuring a bare minimum access to a savings bank account without frills, to all (Leeladhar, 2005). According to the narrow definition those who have even a bank account (current or saving) may be treated as financially included. However, internationally it has been seen in much broader perspective. In a broader sense, financial inclusion is defined as 'availability of saving, credit, remittance, insurance and financial counselling services at affordable cost, and within a reasonable distance from their habitat'.

In literature of financial economics most of the time inclusion has been explained in opposite way, i.e., by defining financial exclusion, as it is easier to recognise. Mohan (2006) defines it as lack of access by certain segments of the society to appropriate, low-cost, fair and safe financial products and services from mainstream providers. Over the years, several definitions of financial inclusion/exclusion have evolved. The review of literature suggests that the most operational definitions are context-specific, originating from country-specific problems of financial exclusion and socioeconomic conditions. Thus, the context-specific dimensions of financial exclusion assume importance from the public policy perspective. Furthermore, the definitions have witnessed a shift in emphasis from defining financial inclusion/exclusion in terms of physical access to a broader definition covering access to and use and understanding of products and services. Definitions of financial exclusion in the literature vary depending on the dimensions such as 'breadth', 'focus' and 'degree' of exclusion. The 'breadth' dimension is the broadest of all definitions linking financial exclusion to social exclusion. Leyshon and Thrift (1995) define financial exclusion as referring to 'those processes that serve to prevent certain social groups and individuals from gaining access to the formal financial system'. Further, Carbo *et al.* (2005) defined financial exclusion as 'broadly the inability (however occasioned) of some societal groups to access the financial system'. According to Conroy (2005), financial exclusion is a process that prevents poor and disadvantaged social groups from gaining access to the formal financial systems of their countries. The 'focus' dimension is in the middle of the spectrum that links financial exclusion to other dimensions of exclusion. It defines financial exclusion as the potential difficulties faced by some segments of population in accessing mainstream financial services such as bank accounts/home insurance (Meadows *et al.*, 2004). The definitions laying emphasis on the 'focus' also vary significantly to include various segments of population such as individuals, households, communities and businesses. The 'degree' dimension, which is the narrowest of all definitions of financial exclusion, defines financial exclusion as exclusion from particular sources of credit and other financial services including insurance, bill-payment services and accessible and appropriate deposit accounts (Rogaly *et al.*, 1999).

A Committee on Financial Inclusion set up by NABARD (Rangarajan Committee, 2008) defines financial inclusion as the process of ensuring access to financial services and timely and adequate credit where needed by vulnerable groups such as the weaker sections and low income groups at an affordable cost (NABARD, Rangarajan Committee, 2008). Present study also accepts financial inclusion as process rather than an event. This process begins with opening of a savings bank account with bank and expands towards greater integration with banking system.

III

Overview of Outreach of Banking in India

This section has attempted to make an assessment of the outreach of banking services in India among individuals and enterprises. In case of enterprises, the study has used data of 62nd and 63rd round of National Sample Survey (NSS) available with National Sample Survey Organisation (NSSO). In case of individuals, study has analysed banking statistics available with the Reserve Bank of India. This section has analysed population group-wise outreach of banking services in India.

Population Group-wise Banking Services

The availability of commercial banking services is skewed towards metropolitan centres. In recent years it seems that bias towards metropolitan areas has been increasing. This phenomenon of increase in the concentration of banking services in metropolitan areas is due to faster economic growth in metropolitan areas *vis-à-vis* peers. Also the banking and financial sector reforms initiated in early nineties led to rationalisation of branches according to their economic sustainability and viability. During earlier years, in order to meet plan targets, banks had opened many branches in rural areas which were not sustainable due to high cost involved in their operations. During the period 2000-2009, scheduled commercial banks (SCBs) witnessed an increase of about 22.4 per cent in its branch network whereas it declined by 3.5 per cent in rural areas mainly due to the closure of unviable branches[2] (Figure 7.1). During the same period, metropolitan, urban and semi-urban areas witnessed an increase in number of branches by 69.0 per cent, 54 per cent and 32.3 per cent, respectively. Even after adjusting the impact of change in classification of population groups, branches of SCBs in rural areas witnessed decline till end-March 2006. However, there has been a turnaround from 2006-07 onwards in regard to the increase in the branches particularly in the rural areas mainly on account of the initiatives taken by the Reserve Bank and the Government of India (Table 7.1). As at end-March 2009, 589 branches were opened in rural areas as compared to 523 branches at end-March 2008.

The share of different population groups in deposits and credit in terms of accounts as well as outstandings reveal that except in metropolitan areas, the share of all population groups in deposits and credit at all-India level has declined during 1991-2009 period (Figure 7.2). In case of deposit accounts share of different population groups remained almost same during 1991-2009 period but during the same period share of metropolitan areas in deposit outstandings increased considerably.

Pattern of growth in number of credit accounts and amount of credit outstandings during the period 1991-2009 was also tilted towards metropolitan areas. Concentration of banking services is increasing in metropolitan centres. The growth pattern of credit outstanding and accounts also indicates that although banks are increasing their business in rural areas, they are not expanding their customer base proportionately to

2. Change in classification of population groups according to the census 2001 also led to a decline in number of rural branches mainly due to upgradation of population group of banked centres from lower population group to higher population group consequent upon growth in the population of centres as per 2001 Census compared to that based on 1991 Census (Table A).

Table A

Change in Share of Offices of Commercial Banks in 2005

	As per 1991 Census	As per 2001 Census	Change in Sharc
Rural	45.7	43.8	-1.9
Semi-urban	22.3	21.8	-0.5
Urban	17.6	17.6	0
Metropolitan	14.4	16.7	2.3

Source: Basic Statistical Return 2006.

Figure 7.1

Population Group-wise Distribution of SCB Branches

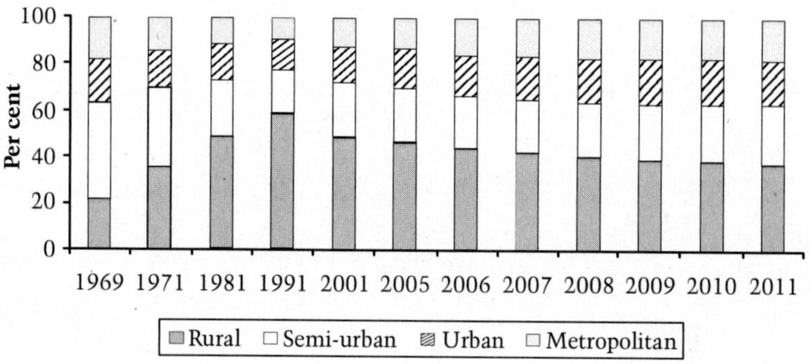

Source: *Handbook of Statistics on Indian Economy, 2009-10.*

Table 7.1

Year-wise Increase/Decrease in the Number of SCB Branches

End-March	*Rural*	*Semi-Urban*	*Urban*	*Metropolitan*	*Total*
1995	-76	212	157	187	480
1996	-8	227	228	245	692
1997	-44	183	243	224	606
1998	-39	229	292	262	744
1999	4	182	261	288	735
2000	-67	133	139	170	375
2001	-150	60	92	67	69
2002	-82	119	135	86	258
2003	-84	124	214	96	350
2004	-56	153	240	234	571
2005	10	228	494	461	1193
2006	-15	179	323	317	804
2007	176	745	931	619	2471
2008	523	1224	1350	952	4049
2009	589	1172	1091	877	3729
2010	852	1558	1478	1086	4974

Source: *Statistical Tables Relating to Banks in India*, various issues.

Figure 7.2

Population Group-wise Share of Deposits and Credit

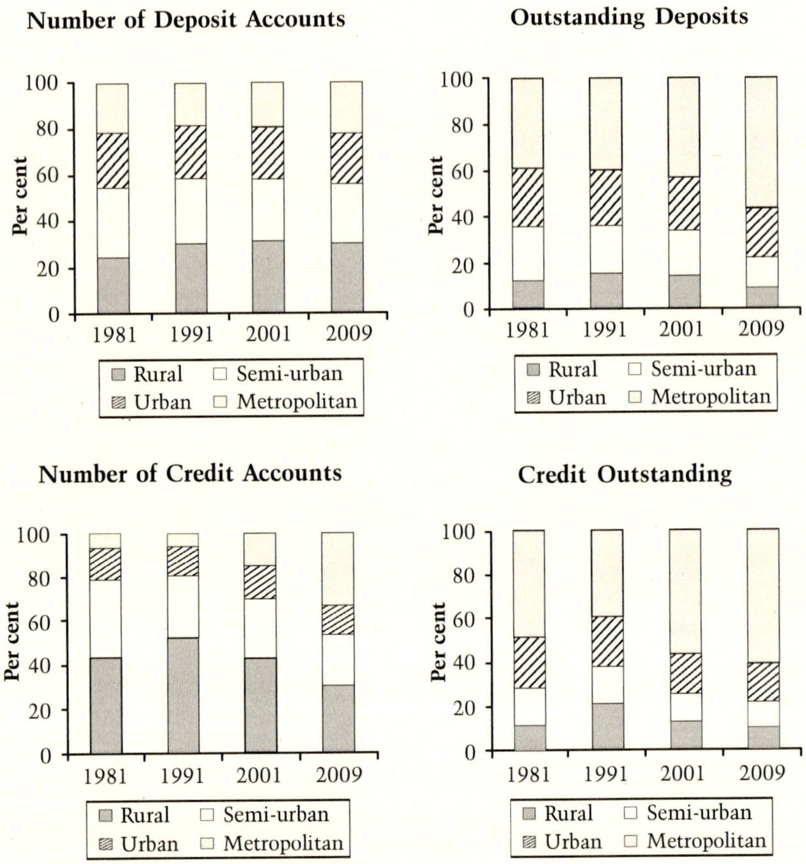

Source: *Handbook of Statistics on Indian Economy, 2009-10.*

metropolitan areas. Emergence of personal loans segment in metropolitan areas could be one possible explanation for this pattern of credit accounts growth. As at end-March 2009 share of metropolitan areas in toal personal loan accounts was around 60 per cent. Share of personal loans in total outstanding credit has increased sharply over the years. Besides this, due to increasing urbanisation of country, share of metropolitan centres is also increasing. Some centres which earlier were counted as urban centres, due to this have changed as metropolitan centres. This also would have led to increase in share of metropolitan centres in bank deposits and credit.

Shift in the concentration pattern of banking services in metropolitan areas can be observed in terms of share of five major banking centres *viz.*, Mumbai, Delhi, Kolkata, Chennai and Bengaluru, in respect of number of branches, amount of deposits and credit (Table 7.2). During studied period, the share of five major banking centres in deposits and credit increased significantly. Share of top five banking centres in total deposits increased from 33.9 per cent as at end-March 1999 to 43.6 per cent at end-March 2009. Interestingly, the share of deposit as at end-March 2008 stands almost at the same level as at end-December 1969. The concentration is also observed in the share of credit of the five major banking centres as it increased from 49.1 per cent as at end-March 1999 to 53.5 per cent as at end-March 2009. Increase in concentration of banking services in five major centres confirms the increase in concentration of banking services in metropolitan areas.

Table 7.2

Share of Top Five Banking Centres in Deposits, Credit and Branches

End March	*Deposits (Rs crore)*	*Share in Total Deposits (per cent)*	*Credit (Rs crore)*	*Share in Total Credit (Rs crore)*	*Number of Branches*	*Share in Total Branches (per cent)*
1969*	2,287	44.2	2,235	59.9	1,307	14.5
1999	2,37,733	33.9	1,91,093	49.1	5,093	7.8
2000	2,75,682	33.5	2,39,656	51.1	5,181	7.9
2001	3,17,403	33.4	2,84,715	51.2	5,283	8.0
2002	3,61,510	33.0	2,86,487	41.9	5,358	8.1
2003	4,51,760	35.3	4,00,375	52.7	5,380	8.1
2004	5,80,147	38.2	4,56,513	51.2	5,532	8.3
2005	6,97,595	39.8	6,13,099	53.0	5,789	8.5
2006	8,68,864	41.5	8,08,528	53.3	5,896	8.6
2007	11,35,604	43.7	10,49,662	53.8	6,176	8.7
2008	14,35,456	44.5	12,83,930	53.6	6,583	8.9
2009	17,17,423	43.6	15,28,668	53.5	7,082	9.0
2010	20,17,232	43.8	17,32,515	51.8	7695	9.2

Note: *: End-December.

Top Five banking centres include Mumbai, Delhi, Kolkata, Chennai and Bengaluru.

Source: *Quarterly Statistics on Deposits and Credit of Scheduled Commercial Banks*, various issues.

Firm-Level Analysis of Banking Penetration in India

In order to assess the firm level access of financial and banking services at regional level in India, we have analysed the data of National Sample Survey (NSS) 62nd and 63rd rounds relating to unorganised manufacturing sector and services sector in India. According to NSS 62nd round estimates, there were 1,70,70,820 unorganised manufacturing enterprises in India during 2005-06 employing 3,64,42,799 persons. About 71 per cent of manufacturing enterprises were working in rural areas while 29 per cent were based in urban areas. During the same period, there were 1.65 crore enterprises in services sector with 3.35 crore employees. Of which, 60 per cent of the total enterprises were located in rural areas. Stipulation of priority sector lending norms were adopted to enhance the bank credit to the productive sectors with immense employment potential and historically starved from the institutional credit. Underlying assumption was that if credit need of productive sector is fulfilled, it may lead to huge expansion of economic activities. Unorganised micro and small enterprises are at the bottom of industrial pyramid. In a developing economy, they provide first window of structural transformation of economy, they also nurture future entrepreneurs of the economy and therefore, the access of institutional finance is vital for them. In the following sections we have analysed the outreach of banking services at regional level for unorganised manufacturing and service enterprises.

Unorganised Manufacturing Enterprises

The NSS 62nd round gives information related to outreach of institutional finance to unorganised manufacturing sector in two ways—one in terms of assistance received and second in terms of problems faced by the enterprises. It is observed that only about 6 per cent of all enterprises received any kind of external finance at all-India level, while only 3.6 per cent received institutional finance. In rural areas only 3.0 per cent enterprises received institutional finance as against 5.30 per cent in urban areas. At regional level, access to the institutional finance has varied widely (Table 7.3 and Annexure Table A-7.1). In western region, maximum 7.35 per cent enterprises have access to institutional finance, whereas in northeastern region only 0.73 per cent enterprises have access to institutional finance. In southern region highest number of enterprises relied on non-institutional finance (moneylender, relatives, etc.) followed by western region. An interesting phenomenon about the access to finance is the existence of positive correlation between institutional and non-institutional finance at regional level. One possible explanation of this positive correlation is that non-institutional sources are meeting the demand of finance unmet by institutional sources particularly banks as they have dominant position in the system.

Table 7.3

Access to Finance to Unorganised Manufacturing Enterprises

(Percentage of total enterprises)

Region	*Rural*		*Urban*		*Combined*	
	Institutional	*Non-Institutional*	*Institutional*	*Non-Institutional*	*Institutional*	*Non-Institutional*
Northern region	3.34	0.78	6.32	1.94	4.53	1.22
Northeastern region	0.52	0.57	2.16	1.60	0.73	0.72
Eastern region	1.27	1.36	2.88	3.23	1.50	1.63
Central region	1.60	0.76	2.68	1.45	1.87	0.93
Western region	6.94	3.43	7.77	3.09	7.35	3.22
Southern region	5.56	3.86	6.48	7.43	5.86	5.06
All-India	3.00	1.90	5.30	4.00	3.60	2.50

Source: National Sample Survey Organisation, 62nd round.

At state level, in Kerala, 13.7 per cent enterprises received assistance in the form of loan from institutional sources as at end-March 2008 (highest in India) as against only 0.5 per cent enterprises in Bihar (lowest). In majority of states, access to institutional and non-institutional finance in urban areas was better than rural areas, however, in some states/UTs, *viz*., Delhi, Chandigarh, etc., it was lower than rural areas. Across the states and regions, access to finance to directory enterprises was better than non-directory enterprises and own account enterprises. This indicates existence of positive relationship between availability of quantitative information, size of the enterprise and access to institutional finance. The shortage of capital is the most critical problem faced by unorganised manufacturing enterprises in India. At all-India level during 2005-06, around 42 per cent unorganised enterprises faced shortage of capital. Like other financial indicators, there are wide variations across the states in shortage of capital. It was highest in Tripura where more than 93 per cent enterprises are facing capital shortage, while it was lowest in Daman & Diu, where only 0.9 per cent enterprises reported capital shortage. Shortage of capital has a positive and significant correlation with other problems, *viz.*, non-availability of electricity connection, power cut, non-availability of raw materials, marketing of products, non-recovery of dues of services rendered, lack of infrastructure and competition from larger enterprises.

Outstanding loan per enterprise, indicating assistance received by the firm from external sources, vary significantly across the states (Figure 7.3). Although banks are biggest creditors in all states to unorganised enterprises, they are not meeting a substantial part of credit demand. Consequently, enterprises are forced to borrow at a very high interest rate from moneylenders. During 2005-06, firms' interest burden as percentage of their loan outstanding was highest for moneylenders at 27 per cent as against 15 per cent for banks. Debt to asset ratio is an important indicator, which may be used to assess the extent of external support unorganised enterprises are receiving. In case of unorganised manufacturing sector, debt to asset ratio was about 22 per cent. This ratio cannot be accepted as sufficient. It indicates that unorganised manufacturing sector is starved of institutional finance. This also indicates that a huge latent opportunity is lying in this sector that needs to be utilised.

Service Sector Enterprises

NSS 63rd round covered the operational characteristics of service sector enterprises in India during the period 2006-07. According to the survey, about 12 per cent of enterprises received assistance in form of loan, which is better than unorganised manufacturing enterprises. However, lesser percentage of service sector enterprises received loan assistance in urban areas (11%) than in rural areas (16%). As in unorganised manufacturing sector, establishment enterprises have better access to external finance than own account enterprises.

Like unorganised manufacturing sector, access to external finance to services sector enterprises varies significantly across the states and regions (Table 7.4). In southern region at highest level 19.8 per cent enterprises

Figure 7.3

State-wise per Enterprise Outstanding Loan

A. Outstanding Aggregate Loan

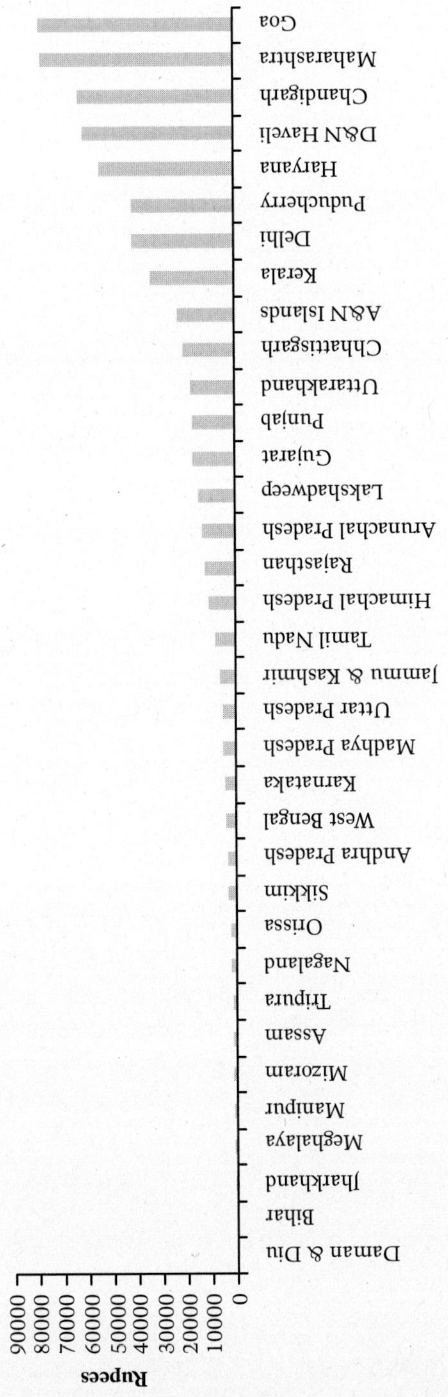

B. Outstanding Bank Loan

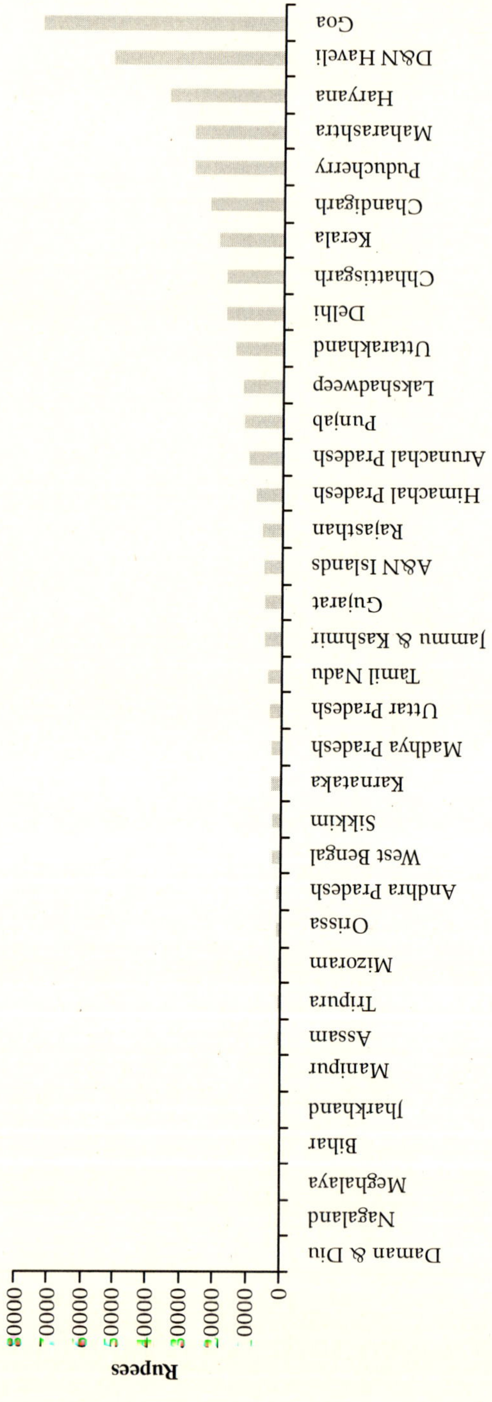

C. Outstanding Loan from Moneylender

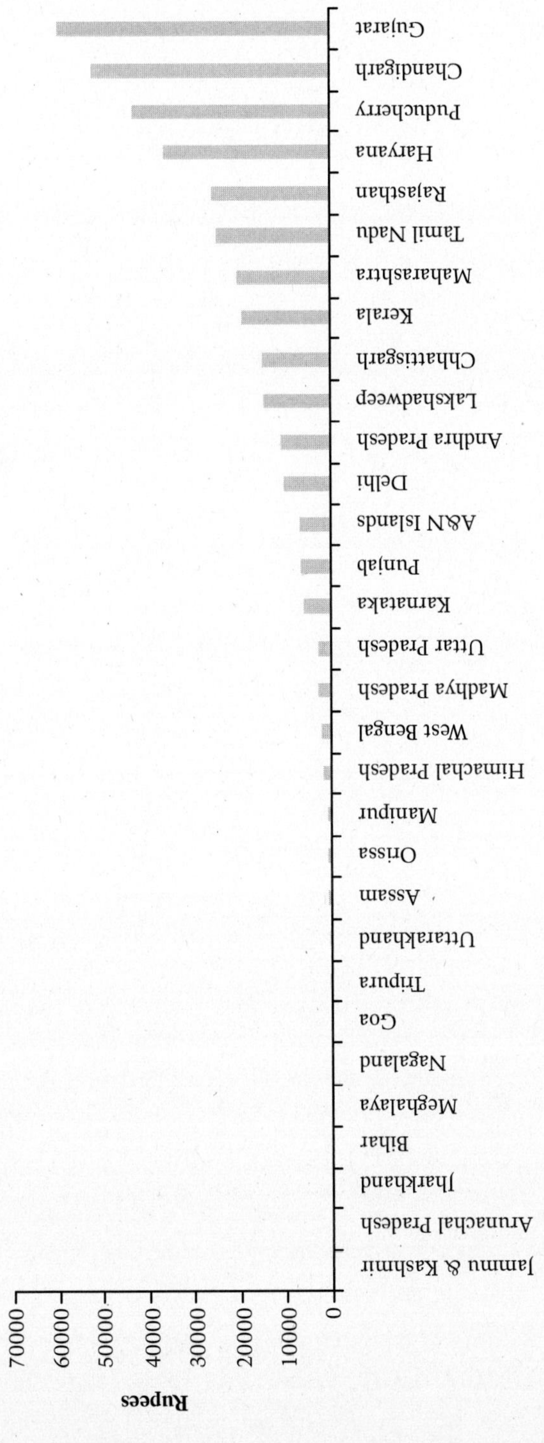

Source: National Sample Survey, 62nd Round, Government of India.

received loan from external agencies[3] as against only 2.4 per cent enterprises in northeastern region. Among all states and UTs, in Delhi only 1.2 per cent service enterprises received loan as against 27.7 per cent enterprises in Chandigarh. In Bihar only 2.4 per cent of enterprises received loan assistance as against 27.5 per cent in Kerala. In terms of problems faced by the service sector enterprises, shortage of capital along with competition from others is on the top. In those states where access to external finance is comparatively better, share of enterprises facing capital shortage is lower. In fact, there is a negative correlation of 0.38 between share of enterprises receiving loan and share of enterprises facing problem of capital shortage.

IV

Outreach of Banking Services at Regional Level

Alongwith outreach of SCBs, this section covers the outreach of cooperative banks (perticularly urban cooperative banks), RRBs and self-help groups (SHGs) based microfinance institutions (MFIs). Besides this, section also covers region-wise distribution of priority sector advances.

Scheduled Commerical Banks (SCBs)

The availability of banking services at regional level can be compared from a variety of indiactors, *viz.*, population per branch, area per branch, per capita deposit and credit amount, percentage of population with deposit and credit account, credit deposit ratio and ratio of credit and deposits with net state doemstic product, etc. In following paras, an attempt has been made to analyse outreach of banking services at region and state level based on these broad indicators.

Outreach of banking services in India is dependent on a number of factors, *viz.*, general economic development of the state/region, topography, development of physical infrastructure and financial litracy of general populace, etc. It is evident that there are huge disparities in terms of

---

3. External agencies include Central and state level term-lending institutions, Government (Central, state, local bodies), banks and societies, moneylenders, business partner, supplier/contractor, friends and relatives and others.

Table 7.4

State-wise Position of Access to External Finance and Problem of Capital Shortage faced by Service Sector Enterprises

Northern Region	*Loan (%)*	*Problems* (%)*	*Total Enterprises (No.)*	*Northeastern Region*	*Loan (%)*	*Problems* (%)*	*Total Enterprises (No.)*
Delhi	1.2	19.7	1,47,171	Sikkim	1.3	4.8	9,847
Haryana	4.8	14.6	3,27,958	Assam	2.0	28.3	5,96,102
Punjab	5.5	29.8	4,51,127	Meghalaya	2.7	14.8	52,132
Rajasthan	8.7	18.2	6,00,292	Manipur	3.9	13.3	27,253
Jammu & Kashmir	11.6	13.7	1,38,831	Tripura	4.3	67.8	62,486
Himachal Pradesh	25.3	21.1	1,14,654	Mizoram	7.4	15.0	6,306
Chandigarh	27.7	8.9	24,672	Nagaland	8.1	14.2	8,284
Sub Total	**8.1**	**20.3**	**18,04,705**	Arunachal Pradesh	10.0	8.7	2,591
				Sub Total	**2.4**	**29.4**	**7,65,001**
Eastern Region	*Loan (%)*	*Problems* (%)*	*Total Enterprises (No.)*	*Central Region*	*Loan (%)*	*Problems* (%)*	*Total Enterprises (No.)*
Jharkhand	1.4	31.4	4,34,794	Uttar Pradesh	3.7	35.3	22,46,240
Bihar	2.4	37.5	8,71,656	Madhya Pradesh	3.9	29.1	4,68,498
West Bengal	7.4	20.5	20,91,732	Uttarakhand	6.6	20.8	1,49,003
Orissa	15.4	27.8	6,21,970	Chhattisgarh	7.7	17.4	1,77,116
A&N Islands	21.3	5.6	2,695	**Sub Total**	**4.1**	**32.6**	**30,40,857**
Sub Total	**6.9**	**26.5**	**40,22,847**				

contd...

...contd...

Western Region	*Loan (%)*	*Problems* (%)*	*Total Enterprises (No.)*	*Southern Region*	*Loan (%)*	*Problems* (%)*	*Total Enterprises (No.)*
D&N Haveli	6.9	14.9	1,578	Andhra Pradesh	10.0	9.5	17,22,633
Daman & Diu	9.8	12.3	1,907	Lakshadweep	13.4	5.8	844
Gujarat	10.5	12.6	6,43,540	Puducherry	14.4	6.0	33,121
Goa	11.8	5.6	27,979	Karnataka	22.2	7.5	8,05,344
Maharashtra	17	21.4	14,89,371	Tamil Nadu	26.2	14.0	11,93,060
Sub Total	**15.0**	**18.6**	**21,64,375**	Kerala	27.5	13.2	9,59,663
				Sub Total	**19.8**	**11.0**	**47,14,665**
All-India	**12.4**	**21.6**	**16512450**				

Note: * Enterprises facing problem of capital shortage as percentage of total enterprises in state.

Source: National Sample Survey Organisation, 63rd round.

availability of banking services across the country (Table 7.5 and Annexure Table A-7.2). In terms of branch expansion, population per branch, percentage of population with credit and deposit accounts, it can be concluded that southern region has the best banking facilities in India. Banking outreach in northeastern region, eastern region and central region, in particular, is inadequate. Unfortunately, these regions are habitat to majority of poor in India. At all-India level, the average population per branch declined from 15,583 at end-March 2001 to 14,503 as at end-March 2010. During 2001 to 2010, there has not been significant changes in terms of population per branch except in Dadra & Nagar Haveli, Sikkim, Puducherry, Haryana and Punjab. Average population per branch in north-east region was 17,333 persons as against only 8,182 persons in southern India. In fact at state level this variation is even bigger. As against only 4,133 persons per branch in Chandigarh, in Manipur population per branch was 33,235. In fact, in certain districts of Manipur and Nagaland one branch serves more than 45,000 population. Although it does not seem possible to increase branch penetration in the central, eastern and north-eastern region at par with advance regions in a short span of time, but on priority basis it may be ensured that those districts and blocks where population per branch is more than 25,000, banks may be encouraged to open branches within one year. In northeast region there are still some blocks where no brick and mortar branch is opened.

Even though at policy level a number of decisions have been taken by the authorities to increase the penetration of banking system in areas with less banking presence, it appears that banks are giving preference to higher per capita income level over other factors. Figure 7.4 shows a scatter plot which indicates that there is a good positive relationship between banking penetration as measured in terms of number of people per bank branch and per capita income of the states.

During 1996-2009 period, at regional level disparity of outreach of banking services increased considerably (Table 7.6). Cofficient of variation of both amount outstanding and number of accounts of deposits and credit increased substantially. During the period 1996-2009, the share of western region in amount outstanding and number of accounts increased while in that of eastern region it showed decline. There was a decline in the amount of deposit in the southern region though the number of accounts increased

Table 7.5

Region-wise Indicators of Banking Outreach 2009

State/Region	*Share in All-India Population (%)*	*Share in Total Branches (%)*	*Population per Branch (No.)*	*Per Capita Deposits (Rs)*	*Per Capita Credit (Rs)*	*Percentage of Population with Deposit Accounts (%)*	*Percentage of Population with Credit Account (%)*	*Deposit per Account (Rs)*	*Credit per Account (Rs) (%)*	*Credit NSDP Ratio (%)*	*Deposit -NSDP Ratio (%)*
Northern region	13.25	17.20	11003	57811	39820	71.33	7.23	81042	550503	91.41	132.71
Northeastern region	3.74	2.67	19983	14473	5212	36.53	4.59	39621	113492	22.24	61.77
Eastern region	22.01	16.71	18720	17375	8475	40.67	4.76	42722	177885	38.06	78.04
Central region	25.56	19.86	18379	14985	6878	45.22	4.75	33140	139746	34.61	78.15
Western region	14.41	15.48	13233	72240	62752	65.88	18.67	109662	331162	137.29	160.41
Southern region	21.03	28.08	10607	35344	31586	76.52	16.09	46188	193228	78.90	89.72
All-India	100.00	100.00	14231	33690	24462	56.89	9.45	59217	258751	65.41	90.09

Source: *Banking Statistical Returns*, various issues.

Figure 7.4

Population per Branch and Per Capita Income

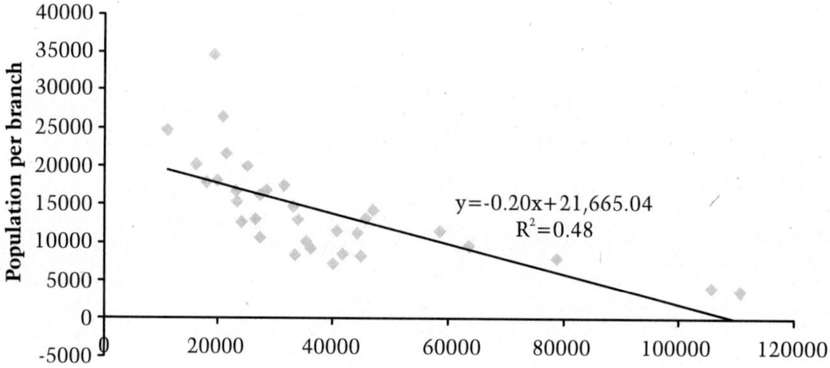

marginally during 1996-2009. This shift in pattern of credit disbursement and deposit mobilisation is disconcerting as it may lead to uneven economic development of the country.

Cooperative Banking in India

Most important attribute of the cooperative system is that unlike commercial banks, cooperative institutions are based on the relationship of the members and due to that they enjoy advantage of qualitative information over them. Due to their relationship based lending methodology they can overcome the problems of assets and collateral based lending of commercial banks where small net worth borrowers are at disadvantage. Cooperative credit structure in India is very heterogeneous and varies from rural to urban areas as well as among states and tenure. The urban areas are served by urban cooperative banks (UCBs). As at end-March 2009, credit to priority sector by UCBs was Rs 55,248 crore which accounted for 56.4 per cent of total advances of UCBs. Similarly, in case of primary agriculture cooperative societies (PACSs), size of outstanding loan per borrower as at end-March 2008 was only Rs 5,912/- as against Rs 71,020/- for direct agriculture loans by SCBs. They have an advantage of regional spread also over the commercial banks. As at end-March 2008, on

Table 7.6

Regional Share of Deposit and Credit of SCBs

(Per cent)

	Account						Amount					
	Northern	North-eastern	Eastern	Central	Western	Southern	Northern	North-eastern	Eastern	Central	Western	Southern
						Deposits						
1996	17.27	2.74	17.30	20.23	15.94	26.52	22.22	1.61	13.05	13.52	27.18	22.42
1997	17.41	2.80	17.67	20.40	15.87	25.86	22.44	1.63	13.05	13.58	27.19	22.11
1998	17.43	2.70	17.41	20.86	15.84	25.77	22.51	1.59	13.26	13.78	26.64	22.23
1999	17.45	2.71	17.26	20.83	15.82	25.93	22.90	1.60	13.39	13.85	25.79	22.48
2000	17.58	2.52	17.17	20.64	15.92	26.17	23.18	1.61	13.48	13.83	25.03	22.88
2001	17.36	2.46	17.09	20.89	16.06	26.14	23.49	1.62	13.30	13.83	24.78	22.97
2002	17.37	2.32	16.77	20.24	17.51	25.78	22.85	1.63	12.95	13.59	26.40	22.58
2003	17.49	2.30	16.49	20.12	17.54	26.07	23.02	1.60	12.70	13.61	25.99	23.08
2004	17.53	2.20	16.01	19.86	17.43	26.97	23.17	1.56	11.94	12.98	27.42	22.93
2005	17.29	2.22	15.84	19.78	17.07	27.81	23.49	1.59	11.97	12.57	28.20	22.18
2006	17.17	2.35	16.06	19.69	17.39	27.34	23.56	1.58	11.38	12.07	29.09	22.33
2007	16.69	2.35	15.63	19.79	17.32	28.22	23.08	1.54	11.10	11.59	30.56	22.13
2008	17.11	2.31	15.64	19.76	17.14	28.03	22.87	1.49	11.05	11.20	31.80	21.59
2009	16.67	2.40	15.71	20.38	16.67	28.15	22.82	1.61	11.34	11.41	30.87	21.96

contd...

...contd...

(Per cent)

	Account						Amount					
	Northern	*North-eastern*	*Eastern*	*Central*	*Western*	*Southern*	*Northern*	*North-eastern*	*Eastern*	*Central*	*Western*	*Southern*
							Credit					
1996	10.26	2.88	22.23	17.51	11.09	36.02	19.09	0.96	10.25	9.04	32.84	27.82
1997	10.75	2.88	20.40	17.68	11.37	36.93	19.13	0.92	9.83	8.97	32.14	29.01
1998	10.37	2.87	20.99	17.31	11.14	37.33	19.84	0.87	9.80	8.91	32.02	28.55
1999	11.48	2.49	18.05	16.84	13.08	38.06	21.35	0.85	9.33	8.51	31.99	27.97
2000	11.91	2.39	18.05	16.42	12.76	38.46	21.17	0.81	8.91	8.36	33.70	27.05
2001	14.18	2.02	16.04	17.45	12.51	37.79	22.66	0.79	8.61	7.97	32.99	26.98
2002	12.60	2.08	16.50	16.38	12.86	39.58	22.00	0.76	8.34	7.90	36.03	24.98
2003	11.32	1.99	16.08	16.34	12.68	41.60	21.76	0.74	8.48	7.66	35.53	25.83
2004	10.53	1.83	13.78	15.22	13.74	44.90	21.82	0.80	8.57	7.94	33.90	26.97
2005	10.38	1.78	13.18	15.17	15.41	44.08	21.19	0.84	8.25	7.77	35.69	26.26
2006	10.82	1.92	12.84	14.36	14.42	45.64	21.03	0.89	7.73	7.37	36.95	26.03
2007	10.90	1.90	12.34	13.48	18.92	42.46	21.43	0.84	8.01	7.32	36.72	25.68
2008	10.02	1.84	11.04	12.57	27.28	37.25	20.83	0.82	7.66	6.94	37.90	25.86
2009	10.17	1.82	11.08	12.88	28.43	35.62	21.65	0.80	7.62	6.96	36.38	26.60

Source: *Basic Statistical Returns*, various issues.

an average there was one PACS for every seven villages at all-India level as against one branch about 20 villages in case of commercial banks.[4]

Urban Cooperative Banks (ULCBs)

The regional distribution of the UCBs is highly skewed (Table 7.7). As at end-March 2010, more than 82 per cent of total UCB branches in India are located in four states, *viz.*, Maharashtra, Gujarat, Karnataka and Kerala. In fact, in case of number of ATMs installed by the UCBs, share of Maharashtra, Gujarat and Karnataka is 97.5 per cent as at end-March 2010. During the period 1999-2010, number of UCBs declined considerably, due to policy led consolidation of the sector. As at end-March 2010, there were only 1,674 UCBs as compared to 1,936 UCBs as at end-March 1999. Similarly, many states also witnessed decline in number of branches of UCBs. However, at all-India level number of branches along with extension branches increased marginally by 268 during the period from 1999 to 2010.

Regional Rural Banks (RRBs)

RRBs have a special role to play in overall development of the underdeveloped areas. The main objective of RRBs is to act as conduit for providing credit and mobilising deposits to hitherto neglected areas with local feel and familiarity without losing professionalism of bigger banks. As at end-March 2009, there were 15,265 branches of RRBs at all-India level. However, due to some structural problems these banks faced severe challenge towards their sustainability. Due to their strategic importance for financial inclusion several measures were taken by the Government of India, the Reserve Bank and National Bank for Agriculture and Rural Development (NABARD) to make use of their wide presence in the rural areas. Consequent to these efforts, the number of total RRBs declined to 86 as at end-March 2009 as against 196 in 2005. These included 45 amalgamated banks, 40 stand alone banks and one new bank. The network of RRBs has increased significantly over the years and at the end of March 2009, RRBs covered 585 out of the 622 districts of the country. The

---

4. Calculated on basis of data published in *Report on Trend and Progress of Banking in India 2008-09.*

Table 7.7

State-wise Distribution of Urban Cooperative Banks

(As at end-March)

State	Number of UCBs		Number of Branches		Number of Extension Counters	Number of ATMs
	1999	2010	1999	2010	2010	2010
1	2	3	4	5	6	7
Andhra Pradesh	137	111	257	245	5	2
Tamil Nadu/Puducherry	138	130	290	313	0	4
Kerala	63	60	302	339	2	0
Karnataka	299	270	723	848	9	19
Gujarat	341	249	958	874	10	69
Maharashtra/Goa	623	557	3408	3407	122	731
Other states	335	297	678	858	52	15
All-India	1,936	1,674	6,616	6,884	200	840

Source: Report on Trend and Progress of Banking in India, 2009-10.

majority of RRB branches are situated in rural areas. In total branch network, the combined share of rural and semi-urban areas is more than 95 per cent. From financial inclusion perspective, the role of RRBs is very significant. In total credit disbursement, share of small borrower accounts is about 79 per cent of outstanding while 98 per cent of total number of accounts. In terms of spatial distribution of branch network and operations, RRBs have better presence in relatively underdeveloped parts of country (Table 7.8).

Despite their better presence in the rural and semi-urban areas of the country, there are some disconcerting realities relating to operations of RRBs. Although number of deposit accounts of the RRBs increased by around 86.0 per cent during 1996-2009, growth of credit accounts remained stunted. RRBs have better presence in central and eastern regions though their credit-deposit (C-D) ratio is lower than C-D ratio at all-India level. At regional level, there are huge disparities in C-D ratio. It was only 41.2 per cent in eastern region as against about 90.4 per cent in southern region. The C-D ratio of RRBs in Arunachal Pradesh worked out to a lower level at 25.0 per cent as at end-March 2009.

Table 7.8

Some Regional Indicators of RRBs

(Percentage share in total)

Region	Number of Branches	Deposits		Credit		C-D Ratio
		Account	Amount	Account	Amount	
Northern region	13.42	9.79	13.72	7.71	14.16	58.18
Northeastern region	4.48	4.84	4.66	3.36	3.71	44.85
Eastern region	24.07	21.36	23.19	23.39	16.96	41.23
Central region	30.81	37.36	31.87	26.26	26.21	46.36
Western region	6.56	5.16	5.72	4.97	5.52	54.40
Southern region	20.66	21.49	20.84	34.30	33.43	90.41
All-India	100.00	100.00	100.00	100.00	100.00	56.36

Note: Data pertains to end-March 2009.

Source: *Basic Statistical Return*, 2009.

Regional-Level Distribution of Priority Sector Advances

During late sixties, it was emphasised that a large part of productive sector of economy was not receiving sufficient institutional credit and as a result their growth was affected adversely. In view of this, it was emphasised by the National Credit Council that there should be a priority sector, comprising agriculture, small scale industries, etc. Since then, priority sector lending has undergone massive change. It includes agriculture, small and micro enterprises, weaker section, loan to SC/ST and minorities, etc. Many flagship government programmes relating to poverty eradication are part of priority sector lending. Although lending to priority sector is expected to be more equitable at regional level due to its emphasis on equity, poverty eradication, directed nature of lending, etc., but in reality, it is skewed (Table 7.9). Share of southern region in priority sector advances is comparetively higher *vis-à-vis* other regions. Not only that, share of eastern and northeastern region has witnessed decline.

Table 7.9

Regional Distribution of Priority Sector Advances

(Per cent to total)

Region	*1996-97*		*2007-08*	
	Number of Accounts	*Amount Outstanding*	*Number of Accounts*	*Amount Outstanding*
Northern	9.16	18.25	11.19	20.36
Northeastern	2.60	1.57	1.68	0.93
Eastern	21.57	10.99	13.12	8.98
Central	16.55	12.81	18.06	11.76
Western	11.46	22.89	11.66	26.31
Southern	38.65	33.49	44.29	31.67

Source: *Statistical Tables Relating to Banks in India* (various issues).

Self-Help Group (SHG) Model

Microfinance in India has traversed a great journey from micro-savings to microcredit and now in the form of microinsurance, micro remittances, micro pension, etc. In India microcredit is based on two models: (a) SHG led bank linkage model and (b) MFI led model. The SHG led model has been accorded preference over MFI led model as along with credit facility it also inculcate thrift habits among its members whereas MFIs perform only lending. Since its launch as a pilot project in 1992, self-help group (SHG) model has evolved as a supplement to banking system in India. Growth of SHG model has generated very huge debate about its outreach and limitations. Due to its democratic and community based character, SHGs have been accorded priority over other models for financing of poor. The number of SHGs and credit disbursement to them recorded a sharp increase after 2001-02 (Figure 7.5). This model has been applauded for its women centric approach as it empowers them and gives greater say in financial decision-making. In academic literature it has been acclaimed for its impact on poverty reduction, increasing additional income for households, generating thrift habits among members. This model has been praised for high repayments of loans also. For banks, SHG based model of lending is beneficial over individual based lending models as it reduces the cost of bank relating to appraisal of borrower at individual level.

Figure 7.5

Self-Help Group-Bank Linkage Programme

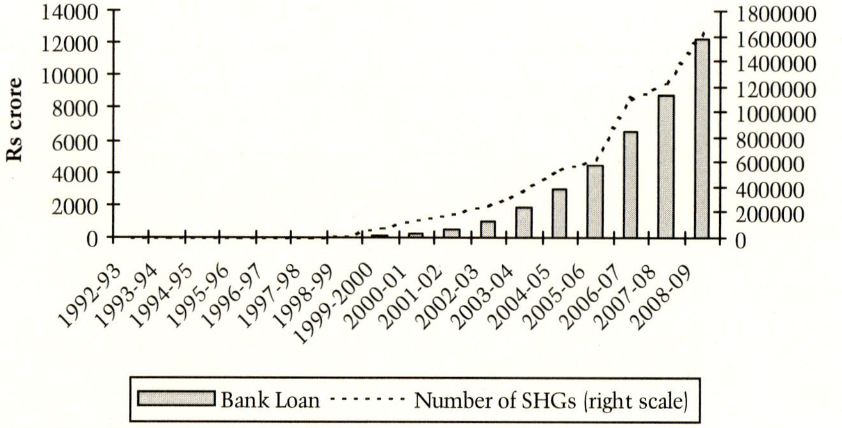

Source: *Handbook of Statistics on Indian Economy, 2009-10.*

Regional Distribution of SHG led Bank Linkage

Region-wise distribution of SHGs is very much skewed. Southern region has maximum presence of SHGs both in terms of numbers as well as in savings and advances. Combined share of southern region and eastern region in all-India was more than 76 per cent in numbers and 79.08 per cent in terms of amount outstanding whereas northeastern region has a meagre share of 2.79 per cent in numbers and 2.07 per cent in amount outstanding (Table 7.10). Evolution of SHGs led credit growth is even more skewed at the state level. Majority of the SHGs are based in those states which are traditionally well penetrated by the banking system.

The skewed development of SHGs in India is attributed to social-economic factors, level of poverty and efforts of local government (Kumar and Golait, 2009). It was emphasised that development of SHGs in states has great impact on the existing financial infrastructure. SHGs have penetrated more in those states where banking system was comparatively better developed.

Though theoretically it is assumed that in order to fill the gap of banking outreach SHGs should have relatively better presence in the underdeveloped states, the reality is in contrast to it. The states with more

Table 7.10

Regional Distribution of SHGs in India (End-March 2009)

(Amount in Rs crore)

Region	Number of SHGs	Amount of Savings	Amount of Lending	Share in All-India (per cent)		
				Number	Saving	Lending
Northern region	1,66,511	67,882	40,767	3.94	2.99	14.59
Northeastern region	1,17,812	46,931	39,835	2.79	2.07	14.28
Eastern region	9,33,489	3,02,300	32,384	22.10	13.33	11.59
Central region	3,32,116	2,04,533	61,585	7.86	9.02	22.04
Western region	3,93,499	1,55,115	39,419	9.32	6.84	14.11
Southern region	22,80,911	1,49,1214	65,378	53.99	65.75	23.40
Total	42,24,338	22,69,975	2,79,368	100.00	100.00	100.00

Source: *Status of Microfinance in India 2008-09*, NABARD.

underbanked areas are having lesser penetration by the SHGs. In India, growth of the SHG led model is driven by banks themselves. In states where presence of banking services is robust, penetration of the microfinance is more. The constitution, day to day management and record maintenance, etc., of a SHG requires better understanding and managerial skill.

V

Survey to Assess the Causes of Exclusion among Marginalised Classes of Urban and Metropolitan India

A sample survey, to assess the outreach of banking sector among the marginalised sections of the population, was conducted in Lucknow, Bhopal, Ahmedabad and Jammu district. The samples were selected from the marginalised sections of the society, i.e., daily wage earners, roadside vendors, rural people involved in agriculture and small businesses, etc. The survey was an attempt to identify the reasons of exclusion of certain classes of the society from banking services network. The total number of sample respondents was 393, which include 100 respondents each in Lucknow and Bhopal, 104 respondents in Ahmedabad and 89 in Jammu. Of the total respondents 49.4 per cent were self-employed and 30.5 per cent were daily wage earners (Table 7.11).

Table 7.11

Occupation-wise Details of Respondents

City	*Daily Wage Labourer*	*Self-Employed*	*Others*	*Total*
Ahmedabad	52	26	26	104
Bhopal	31	45	24	100
Jammu	9	64	16	89
Lucknow	28	59	13	100
Total	120	194	79	393

Source: Based on information collected through survey.

Out of 393 respondents, 160 respondents had savings bank accounts. However, only one respondent had a loan account with a bank. At regional level, Jammu had the highest percentage of population with savings bank accounts (78.65%), followed by Bhopal (34.0%), Ahmedabad (27.9%), and Lucknow (27.0%) (Figure 7.6). Besides bank accounts, one respondent in Ahmedabad, seven in Bhopal and two in Jammu and Lucknow each admitted that they have deposit accounts with post office. Variation in share of respondents with bank accounts in different cities is mainly due to variation in income level of surveyed population in different cities. In Jammu, majority of respondents were comparatively well-off *vis-à-vis* respondents of other cities. In the sample taken from Jammu, maximum 64 respondents were self-employed, whereas in Lucknow, Bhopal and Ahmedabad their numbers were 59, 45 and 26, respectively.

Data relating uses of accounts indicate that in Ahmedabad highest percentage of account holders are active users followed by Jammu, Bhopal and Lucknow, respectively (Table 7.12). Lower frequency of account is mainly due to lack of financial literacy, dependence on informal channel and use of bank accounts as instruments of savings only.

Figure 7.6

Percentage Share of Bank Accounts

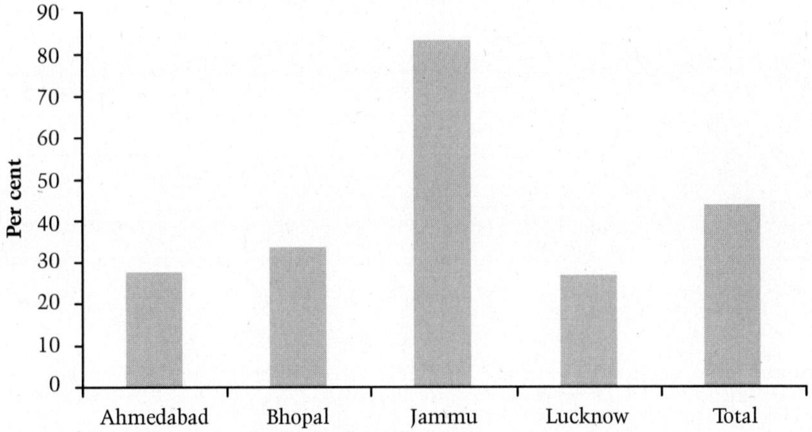

Source: Based on information collected through survey.

Table 7.12

Activity-wise Distribution of Account Holders

(In per cent)

Activity of Account	*Ahmedabad*	*Bhopal*	*Jammu*	*Lucknow*	*Total*
Active	84.2	47.1	67.0	44.4	63.8
Semi-active	0.0	14.7	29.0	14.8	19.1
Others	15.8	38.2	4.0	40.7	17.1

Note: In this study an account has been defined as active if frequency of use is monthly, whereas it has been defined as semi-active if frequency is quarterly. Any longer frequency has been defined as others.

Source: Based on information collected through survey.

Even though bank accounts are the fastest and most efficient way of remitting money, among poor they are not popular as means of remittances. Post offices are still a popular institution for sending remittances by the marginal workers. However, the share of non-institutional sources of remittances is very high. Sending money through these sources is very costly and inefficient.

In order to meet their financial needs, 36.4 per cent of the total respondents, who do not have any bank accounts, said that they borrow money from informal sources (such as moneylenders), and 64.9 per cent of these borrowers pay interest from 5 per cent to 10 per cent per month on loans taken from moneylenders, which is abnormally high. The survey indicates that some of these people have to pay around 15 per cent per month for their borrowing requirements from these moneylenders (more than 180 per cent per annum). Among four cities, a maximum of 78.8 per cent of the total respondents borrow money from informal sources at Ahmedabad, while lower reliance on non-institutional sources for meeting the financial requirements are reported at Jammu. Mostly the financial requirements of these people are consumption based and also the frequency of such borrowings is high, which in result often put them through financial hardships. If these marginal workers/daily wage earners are provided banking facilities with some minimal financial knowledge they would be able to reduce their dependence on moneylenders. It may be mentioned that majority of respondents in our survey felt that they should be provided basic financial education.

The survey brought out some interesting facts relating to causes of exclusion, which are very important from the perspective of policy formulation. In fact the results of this survey are in consonance with findings of another survey conducted in slums in Mumbai (Bhatia and Chatterjee, 2010). In all the cities, majority of respondents cited no savings (44.4%) and lack of proper knowledge about finance and banking (36.8%) as primary reasons for their exclusion. Overall, only 10.3 per cent of the total respondents, who do not have bank accounts, cited lack of necessary documents as reason for exclusion (Table 7.13). However, in Bhopal comparatively higher percentage of respondents cited lack of proper documents as the main reason for exclusion (27.3%). In Ahmedabad, maximum of 48.0 per cent respondents said that they do not have sufficient savings to open and maintain bank accounts. In Jammu, maximum 54.5 per cent respondents said that lack of knowledge and understanding about financial products is the major reason for their exclusion.[5]

5. Calculated on the basis of first reason of exclusion given by the respondents. In this case, more than two reasons were given.

Table 7.13

Causes of Exclusion

(Per cent)

Causes of Exclusion	*Ahmedabad*	*Bhopal*	*Jammu*	*Lucknow*	*Total*
No savings/meagre income	48.0	40.9	40.9	45.1	44.4
Lack of knowledge	38.7	24.2	54.5	40.8	36.8
Lack of necessary documents	5.3	27.3	0.0	2.8	10.3
Others	8.0	7.6	4.5	11.3	8.5

Source: Based on information collected through survey.

VI

Concluding Observations and the Way Forward

Conclusion

From analysis of above sections following broad conclusions can be made: (i) concentration of banking institutions in metropolitan area in comparison to rural and semi-urban areas have increased during studied period (i.e., 1999-2009), (ii) during studied period expansion of banking services was faster in southern region *vis-à-vis* other regions. Northeastern region has minimal outreach of banking services, (iii) presence of UCBs is limited to a few states but in those states they can play a major role if their financial health can be improved, (iv) outreach of banking services is dependent on income level of the state and development of overall infrastructure, (v) small and medium enterprises are highly starved for institutional finance in almost all states. But scarcity of institutional finance among small enterprises is more severe in north-eastern states and central states.

Policy Suggestions

The transition from brick and mortar banking to the ICT based banking services has already making its mark visible even in the rural areas. However, according to the findings of survey conducted in the capital cities of Gujarat, Jammu, Madhya Pradesh and Uttar Pradesh, lack of savings and awareness about the banking services are the major causes of exclusion in the marginalised class. The development of microfinance can supplement the traditional financial institutions in achieving the goal of financial inclusion and ultimate goal of poverty eradication. The expansion of SHGs may be taken up by the banking sector in a big way, particularly in those states where these are yet to make their presence felt *viz.*, Uttar Pradesh, Bihar, Chhattisgarh, Madhya Pradesh, etc. It is observed that lack of involvement on part of bankers in activities of SHGs has come in the way of their growth. Commercial banks' involvement at the formation level of SHGs will help in developing strong relationship between banks and the SHG members. The involvement of banks from the initial stages of formation of SHGs would help in developing necessary managerial skills among the members. Banks should be sensitised to equip their rural branches for making proactive initiatives in the formation of SHGs.

Banks should undertake in-house performance appraisal to ensure the viability of unorganised manufacturing enterprises and services enterprises. Further, lack of registration details and account books lead to opaqueness and information asymmetry. Entrepreneur also faces difficulty in proving that the assistance sought by him is for business expansion rather than for personal consumption. It ultimately leads to rejection of loan applications for want of necessary documents. State governments and local bodies should launch a special drive for registration of unregistered firms.

Along with supply-side issues, banking outreach is a function of actual demand, infrastructure development and governance. Role of state and local governments is very crucial as states with better infrastructure and effective governance are doing well in the outreach of banking services. Arrangements should be made at local government level to provide necessary documents for opening of bank accounts such as identity and residence proof. In empirical studies, it has been proved that contract enforcement and speedy recovery of loan increases availability of institutional finance. State government machinery should coordinate with banks for speedy recovery and contract enforcement at local level.

In the recent past, the combined efforts of the Government of India, the Reserve Bank and commercial banks have certainly made a remarkable progress towards outreach of banking services. There has been a turnaround in the branch expansion network after 2006-07. Since 2005, more than 39 million no-frills accounts have been opened so far. The technological advances in banking services has reduced the cost of transactions. A study conducted by National Council of Applied Economic Research (NCAER) estimated that a cash withdrawal at a branch costs a bank Rs 10, an ATM costs Rs 4 and a debit card costs just Re 1. The implementation of BCs/ BFs concept in banking sector has been quite commendable. However, there have been some operational/technical issues which need to be handled carefully to provide safe and secure branch network in the unbanked areas. The outreach of banking services could be achieved only if concerted and coordinated efforts are put in place by all the stakeholders of the society with the help of technological developments in the banking sector, innovative financial products and macro-policy initiatives.

References

Asian Development Bank (ADB) (2000). *Finance for the Poor: Microfinance Development Strategy.*

Beck, Demirgüç-Kunt and Martinez Peria (2007). "Reaching Out: Access to and Use of Banking Services across Countries", *Journal of Financial Economics* 8.

Bhatia, N. and A. Chatterjee (2010). "Financial Inclusion in Slums of Mumbai", *Economic & Political Weekly* XLV(42), October 16.

Carbo, S., E.P. Gardener and P. Molyneux (2005). *Financial Exclusion*. Palgrave MacMillan.

Chakravarty, Satya R. and Rupayan Pal (2010). *Measuring Financial Inclusion: An Axiomatic Approach*. Indira Gandhi Institute of Development Research (IGIDR). March.

Chant Link and Associates (2004). *A Report on Financial Exclusion in Australia*.

Conroy, J. (2005). "APEC and Financial Exclusion: Missed Opportunities for Collective Action?", *Asia-Pacific Development Journal*. June.

European Commission (2008). *Financial Services Provision and Prevention of Financial Exclusion*. March.

Kempson, E. *et al.* (2000). *In or Out? Financial Exclusion: A Literature and Research Review*. London: Financial Services Authority.

Kumar, Pankaj and Ramesh Golait (2009). "Bank Penetration and SHG-Bank Linkage Programme: A Critique", *Reserve Bank of India Occasional Papers* (29)3.

Leeladhar, V. (2005). *Tanking Banking Services to the Common Man: Financial Inclusion*. December. Available on *www.rbi.org.in*.

Leyshon, Andrew and Nigel Thrift (1995). *Geographies of Financial Exclusion: Financial Abandonment in Britain and the United States*. Royal Geographical Society (with the Institute of British Geographies).

Mahajan, R.K. and Deepty Bansal (2008). "Microfinance and Women Empowerment: A Case Study of Punjab", *The Microfinance Review, Journal of the Microfinance Research*. Lucknow, India: Bankers Institute of Rural Development.

Meadows, P., P. Ormerod and W. Cook (2004). *Social Networks: Their Role in Access to Financial Services in Britain*. National Institute Economic Review.

"Measuring Banking Sector Outreach". Available on *http://siteresources.worldbank.org*.

Mohan, Rakesh (2006). *Economic Growth, Financial Deepening and Financial Inclusion*. November. Available on *www.rbi.org.in*

National Bank for Agriculture and Rural Development (NABARD) (2008). *Report of the Committee on Financial Inclusion*. (Chairman: Dr C. Rangarajan). January.

———. (2008-09). *Status of Microfinance in India, 2008-09*.

Pal, Rupayan (2009). *Outreach of Banking Services, Infrastructure Penetration, Labour Regulation and Industrial Growth: Evidence from Indian States*. Indira Gandhi Institute of Development Research (IGIDR). January.

Planning Commission (2008). *Report of the Committee on Financial Sector Reforms*. (Chairman: Raghuram Rajan). Government of India.

Reserve Bank of India (2008). "Financial Inclusion", *Report on Currency and Finance 2006-08*.

———. (n.d.). *Basic Statistical Returns of Scheduled Commercial Banks in India*.

———. (n.d.). *Handbook of Statistics on Indian Economy, 2008-09*.

Rogaly, B., T. Fisher and E. Mayo (1999). *Poverty, Social Exclusion and Microfinance in Britain*. Oxford: Oxfam and New Economics Foundation.

Sarma, Mandira (2008). *Index of Financial Inclusion*. Indian Council for Research on International Economic Relations (ICRIER). June.

Sarma, Mandira and Jesim Pais (2008). *Financial Inclusion and Development: A Cross Country Analysis*. Indian Council for Research on International Economic Relations (ICRIER). September.

Scottish Executive, Edinburgh (2005). *Financial Inclusion Action Plan*. January.

Sinclair, Stephen P. (2001). *Financial Exclusion: An Introductory Survey*. Centre for Research into Socially Inclusive Services (CRSIS), Edinburgh College of Art, Heriot Watt University.

United Nations (2006). *Building Inclusive Financial Sectors for Development*. May.

World Bank (2008). *Finance for All? Policies and Pitfalls in Expanding Access*.

Annexure Table A-7.1

Share of Unorganised Manufacturing Enterprises Received Financial Assistance: 2005-06

State/Region	Rural		Urban		Combined	
	Institutional	Non-Institutional	Institutional	Non-Institutional	Institutional	Non-Institutional
Northern region	**3.34**	**0.78**	**6.32**	**1.94**	**4.53**	**1.22**
Haryana	5.4	1.1	11.4	3.4	8.3	2.2
Himachal Pradesh	7.5	1.1	14.6	1.6	8	1.1
Jammu & Kashmir	0.7	0.2	3.4	0.2	1.2	0.2
Punjab	2.7	0.5	7.7	1.4	5.1	0.9
Rajasthan	2.8	0.9	4.2	0.7	3.3	0.8
Delhi	6.7	1.8	4	4.8	4.1	4.6
Chandigarh	9.5	0	1.8	0.6	6	0.3
Northeastern region	**0.52**	**0.57**	**2.16**	**1.60**	**0.73**	**0.72**
Arunachal Pradesh	0.4	0.2	0.3	2	0.3	0.9
Assam	0.4	0.5	2.7	0.2	0.6	0.5
Manipur	1.1	0.8	0.6	3.4	1	1.6
Meghalaya	0	0	2.8	0.1	0.2	0
Mizoram	1.7	0	2	0	1.8	0
Nagaland	1.7	3.4	2.5	10.9	1.9	5.5
Sikkim	1.5	0	3.1	0	1.7	0
Tripura	1.1	1	2.7	2.3	1.4	1.2
Eastern region	**1.27**	**1.36**	**2.88**	**3.23**	**1.50**	**1.63**
Bihar	0.6	0.4	0.5	0.9	0.5	0.5
Jharkhand	1.3	0.3	2	1.2	1.4	0.4
Orissa	1.4	1.1	5.6	1.3	1.8	1.1

contd...

...contd...

State/Region	*Rural*		*Urban*		*Combined*	
	Institutional	*Non-Institutional*	*Institutional*	*Non-Institutional*	*Institutional*	*Non-Institutional*
West Bengal	1.4	2	3	4.2	1.7	2.4
A&N Islands	8.2	3.7	4.2	2.1	7.4	3.4
Central region	**1.60**	**0.76**	**2.68**	**1.45**	**1.87**	**0.93**
Chhattisgarh	1.5	0.7	7.6	3.9	2.5	1.2
Madhya Pradesh	1.5	0.7	2.4	1.5	1.8	1
Uttarakhand	6	0.3	9.1	1.4	6.7	0.5
Uttar Pradesh	1.5	0.8	2.4	1.3	1.7	0.9
Western region	6.94	3.43	7.77	3.09	7.35	3.22
Goa	16.7	1.9	11.8	2.5	14	2.8
Gujarat	2.6	0.4	3.8	1	3.2	0.7
Maharashtra	9.2	5.1	10.2	4.4	9.7	4.7
D&N Haveli	23	0	14.8	0	21.6	0
Daman & Diu	0.3	0	0.8	0	0.5	0
Southern region	**5.56**	**3.86**	**6.48**	**7.43**	**5.86**	**5.06**
Andhra Pradesh	5.1	3.7	4.7	7.3	5	4.8
Karnataka	4.6	2.5	8.6	4.2	5.8	3
Kerala	13.3	4.9	15.1	4.4	13.7	4.8
Tamil Nadu	2.4	4.5	4.5	9.7	3.3	6.7
Lakshadweep	1.8	4.7	7.2	1.8	3.7	3.7
Paducherry	11.8	7.3	4.3	16.7	6.5	13.8
All-India	**3.00**	**1.90**	**5.30**	**4.00**	**3.60**	**2.50**

Source: NSS 62nd round.

Annexure Table A-7.2

Metrics of Banking Outreach in India

(As at end-March 2009)

State/Region	Share in All-India Population (%)	Population per Branch (No.)	Per Capita Deposits (in Rs)	Per Capita Credit (in Rs)	Percentage of Population with Deposit Accounts	Percentage of Population with Credit Account	Deposit per Account (in Rs)	Credit per Account (in Rs)	Credit Intensity (%)	Deposit -NSDP Ratio (%)
Northern region	**13.25**	**11003**	**57811**	**39820**	**71.33**	**7.23**	**81042**	**550503**	**91.41**	**132.71**
Chandigarh	0.09	3547	255372	293613	206.46	17.48	123693	1679303	241.35	209.92
Delhi	1.49	7748	292582	201729	140.74	15.13	207890	1333188	269.25	390.52
Haryana	2.07	11007	36043	22119	71.71	6.77	50263	326583	32.18	52.44
Himachal Pradesh	0.57	6907	35937	13861	82.59	8.42	43511	164618	33.27	86.25
Jammu and Kashmir	1.08	12987	22906	10801	55.62	4.59	41183	235331	50.93	108.01
Punjab	2.32	8088	44755	29396	96.83	7.78	46220	377672	55.85	85.03
Rajasthan	5.63	16293	13967	11260	41.86	5.29	33368	212996	44.24	54.87
Northeastern region	**3.74**	**19983**	**14473**	**5212**	**36.53**	**4.59**	**39621**	**113492**	**22.24**	**61.77**
Arunachal Pradesh	0.10	15779	29423	7507	42.89	4.68	68603	160494	27.93	109.46
Assam	2.61	21381	12924	4977	37.81	4.28	34179	116247	21.88	56.80
Manipur	0.23	32827	9490	3419	18.55	2.78	51163	122863	18.02	50.03
Meghalaya	0.22	12522	24171	6830	35.67	4.49	67764	152159	26.14	92.51
Mizoram	0.09	10553	17849	10330	32.61	6.07	54730	170093	32.18	55.61
Nagaland	0.19	26047	15551	4790	21.71	4.13	71620	116122	20.18	65.52
Tripura	0.31	16298	17714	5440	47.77	8.53	37080	63798	20.27	66.02

contd...

...contd...

State/Region	*Share in All-India Population (%)*	*Population per Branch (No.)*	*Per Capita Deposits (in Rs)*	*Per Capita Credit (in Rs)*	*Percentage of Population with Deposit Accounts*	*Percentage of Population with Credit Account*	*Deposit per Account (in Rs)*	*Credit per Account (in Rs)*	*Credit Intensity (%)*	*Deposit -NSDP Ratio (%)*
Eastern region	**22.01**	**18720**	**17375**	**8475**	**40.67**	**4.76**	**42722**	**177885**	**38.06**	**78.04**
A &N Islands	0.04	11351	33699	10686	62.86	5.85	53608	182707	22.45	70.80
Bihar	8.18	24406	9131	2446	28.38	3.98	32178	61404	19.51	72.84
Jharkhand	2.61	17409	18119	5806	41.59	4.36	43569	133107	27.03	84.35
Orissa	3.48	14747	17396	8844	42.71	7.63	40726	115858	33.60	66.09
Sikkim	0.05	8465	41969	17455	47.91	6.05	87598	288539	52.72	126.75
West Bengal	7.66	17166	25705	15612	52.45	4.42	49006	352922	50.48	83.12
Central region	**25.56**	**18379**	**14985**	**6878**	**45.22**	**4.75**	**33140**	**139746**	**34.61**	**78.15**
Chhattisgarh	2.06	19333	16293	8889	33.76	3.95	48269	191297	25.73	55.54
Madhya Pradesh	6.04	17398	14224	8366	36.88	4.98	38567	164002	46.68	81.38
Uttar Pradesh	16.63	19747	13533	5825	48.32	4.63	28010	123431	31.72	75.10
Uttarakhand	0.83	8719	46576	12188	72.26	7.47	64455	157660	39.89	157.71
Western region	**14.41**	**13233**	**72240**	**62752**	**65.88**	**18.67**	**109662**	**331162**	**137.29**	**160.41**
Dadra & Nagar Haveli	0.02	11292	28649	6107	83.25	1.87	34412	277405		0.00
Daman & Diu	0.02	10667	65396	12872	118.41	2.30	55230	548709		0.00
Goa	0.14	3990	141242	38962	198.05	11.07	71318	340365	38.13	142.99
Gujarat	4.91	12894	32680	21040	65.15	5.64	50160	369018	51.03	80.14
Maharashtra	9.31	13938	92189	85353	64.07	25.74	143878	326696	180.29	197.65

contd...

...contd...

State/Region	*Share in All-India Population (%)*	*Population per Branch (No.)*	*Per Capita Deposits (in Rs)*	*Per Capita Credit (in Rs)*	*Percentage of Population with Deposit Accounts*	*Percentage of Population with Credit Account*	*Deposit per Account (in Rs)*	*Credit per Account (in Rs)*	*Credit Intensity (%)*	*Deposit -NSDP Ratio (%)*
Southern region	**21.03**	**10607**	**35344**	**31586**	**76.52**	**16.09**	**46188**	**193228**	**78.90**	**89.72**
Andhra Pradesh	7.16	12514	26298	25819	72.52	14.47	36264	175117	75.28	78.13
Karnataka	5.00	9750	44208	34272	75.65	14.60	58439	234025	84.89	109.83
Kerala	2.98	8287	39100	23841	83.79	16.50	46663	141529	57.29	95.90
Lakshadweep	0.01	6455	67541	3768	61.17	6.54	110417	55656		0.00
Puducherry	0.09	8531	50004	26443	108.66	18.82	46021	136563	40.08	77.98
Tamil Nadu	5.79	11009	36670	40509	77.98	19.13	47023	207222	88.70	82.06
All-India	**100.00**	**14231**	**33690**	**24462**	**56.89**	**9.45**	**59217**	**258751**	65.41	**90.09**

8 Bank Finance in the Development of Real Estate Sector in Bihar

RAJ RAJESH[1]

I

Introduction

In the last couple of years (preceding the global financial crisis), there had been a phenomenal rise in real estate prices across a large number of economies. Boom in real estate prices in these economies was fuelled by spectacular growth of global economy and the prevailing low interest rate regime. The global financial crisis, which initially originated in the housing market of the USA, put a brake on the real estate prices in most of the countries including India. In the aftermath of global financial crisis, real estate prices, which were in the last couple of years advancing at a frenetic pace, in India had stagnated in most parts of the country. In the capital city of Bihar, Patna, prices of commercial as well as residential properties witnessed upswing even in the aftermath of global financial crisis during 2008 and 2009. This is all the more surprising as none of the major cities (such as Patna, Muzaffarpur, Bhagalpur, Gaya, etc.) in the state of Bihar were ever known as prime destination(s) to settle or invest largely owing to lack of basic infrastructural facilities and absence of industrial clusters in and around these cities. Real estate prices in the capital city of Bihar, Patna, have appreciated very sharply in last couple of years as a result of

---

1. Author is thankful to G. Mahalingam, CGM, FMD, RBI, Mumbai; V.S. Damodar, DGM, DBS and Q.F. Ahmed, Manager, DBS, RBI, Patna for their comments on an earlier draft of the paper. Author is also thankful to all the regional offices of DEPR for making available some data inputs. Views and errors or omissions are those of the author's alone and not of the institution he works with.

improvement in law & order and governance As such Bihar makes an interesting case for studying the recent trends in real estate market.

Against this backdrop, the present study apart from studying the trends in real estate would also explore how the bank finance has helped the growth of real estate in the state. For the same, the study relies on data gathered both from banks and real estate developers in the state. The scheme of the study is as follows. Section II lays down the objectives of the study and methodology used therein. Reforms undertaken by the Government of Bihar in respect of real estate market in Bihar are underlined in Section III, while Section IV brings out trends in development of real estate in the state. Section V analyses the role of bank finance in development of real estate in the state. Prospects in development of real estate in the state are covered in Section VI. Finally concluding observations are covered in Section VII.

II

Objective of the Study and Methodology Used

The study was undertaken with the overall objective of understanding the trends in real estate sector in Bihar. The study also seeks to probe into the issue whether bank finance has helped the growth of the real estate in the state. Further, the study also explores whether global slowdown had any adverse impact on real estate sector in Bihar.

The study relies on the data gathered both from banks and real estate developers. Information on the number of accounts and the amount financed to commercial and non-commercial real estate in the state for three years (2007-08 to 2009-10) was collected from the banks. Information from the real estate developers was gathered by interviewing some major builders through a questionnaire, which sought information on the real estate price trends in the state, impact of global slowdown on real estate sector, sources of finance for the real estate projects, etc.

III

Reforms undertaken by the Government of Bihar

Some of the reform measures undertaken by the Government of Bihar that has facilitated growth in real estate market in Bihar are as follows:

- Computerised registration of land and property, and property title certification.
- Government of Bihar enacted Bihar Apartment Ownership Act, 2006 under which registration of property has been made compulsory.
- To facilitate an easy and hassle-free administration, amendment has been made in the Bihar Regional Development Rule, 1982, which empowers listed registered architects to sanction the building plan up to 500 square metre area.
- Government of Bihar has encouraged public-private partnership (PPP) in providing basic amenities and services in town areas. Many ULBs have taken up street lighting, garbage disposal, construction of bus stands, etc., involving the private sector.
- Building bye-laws have been amended to facilitate construction of shopping malls and multiplexes.
- One of the most remarkable reforms to make the real estate transactions smoother has been the rationalisation of stamp duty and registration charges, which have been brought down from a high of 18.7 per cent in 2002 to 10 per cent in May 2006 (Table 8.1).
- Urban Land (Ceiling and Regulation) Act was repealed in August 2006.
- Building bye-laws have been amended in April 2006 to incorporate structural safety norms, rainwater harvesting and provision for disabled persons, etc. Further, amendment of building bye-laws has facilitated construction of shopping malls & multiplexes.
- The Government has also brought reforms in property tax.

- The Government has put emphasis on creating and augmenting basic infrastructure facilities in water supply, sewerage, storm water drainage, solid waste management, roads and bridges in all the 122 urban local bodies (ULBs) in the state.

Table 8.1

Stamp Duty and Registration Rates for Registration of Flats in Bihar

(Per cent)

Period	*Basic Stamp Duty*	*Additional Stamp Duty for Regional Authority*	*Additional Stamp Duty for Municipal Areas*	*Total Stamp Duty*	*Registration Charges*	*Total (Stamp and Registration Charges) in Regional Authority Areas*	*Total for Municipal Areas*	*Total for Rural Areas*
1	2	3	4	5 (=2+3+4)	6	7	8	9
Before July 2002	14.7	5	2	21.7	2	23.7	18.7	16.7
July 2002 to November 2005	8.4	5	2	15.4	2	17.4	12.4	10.4
December 2005 to April 2006	8.4	0	2	10.4	2	12.4	12.4	10.4
May 2006 - till date	6	0	2	8	2	10	10	8

Note: From December 2005 onwards additional stamp duty of 5 per cent has been scrapped.
Source: *Annual Report 2010-11*, Registration & Excise Prohibition Department, Government of Bihar.

IV

Trends in Development of Real Estate in Bihar

In the last few years, there has been a phenomenal growth in 'construction'[2] sector in Bihar (Figure 8.1). After a slide in 2003-04,

2. The estimates of gross value added (GVA) from construction are derived from the estimates of value of output from *pucca* construction and labour intensive *kutcha* construction. The value of all *pucca* construction undertaken is determined from the expenditure on the use of construction materials such as cement, steel, bricks, timber, fixtures, etc., while the estimates of labour intensive *kutcha* construction is determined with the help of expenses on the freely available materials like leaves, reeds, mud, etc.

construction sector in Bihar has consistently posted double-digit growth. High growth in construction sector was supported by substantial reconstruction of roads and bridges funded by multilateral development agencies and Central government sponsored road projects. The boom in this sector has also generated some employment opportunities in the state.

Figure 8.1

Trend in Growth in Construction Sector in Bihar

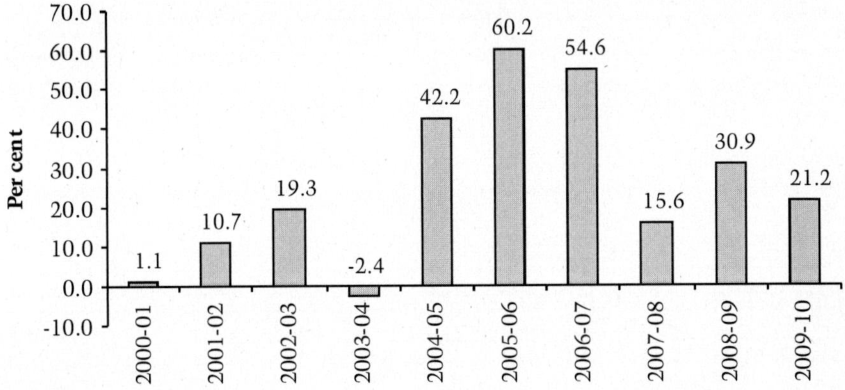

Source: CSO, Government of India.

On the contrary, one does not find a corresponding high growth in 'real estate, ownership of dwellings, and business services' (REOBS)[3] in Bihar in the last couple of years. It is found that the activity in REOBS in Bihar peaked in 2007-08, and thereafter growth slowed down both in 2008-2009 and 2009-10 (Table 8.2). Further, growth in REOBS in the state has been lower than the growth at all-India level.

3. As per the National Account Statistics (NAS), the economic activities covered in the real estate, ownership of dwellings, and business services (REOBS) sector include: (i) ownership of dwellings (occupied residential houses), (ii) real estate services (activities of all types of dealers such as operators, developers and agents connected with real estate) and (iii) business services. Ownership of dwellings also includes the imputed value of owner occupied dwellings.

Table 8.2

Growth in Real Estate, Ownership of Dwellings and Business Services (REOBS)

(Per cent)

	Bihar	*All-India*
2004-05	5.1	8.6
2005-06	5.5	9.2
2006-07	5.5	8.6
2007-08	6.2	8.5
2008-09	5.8	—
2009-10	5.6	—

Source: CSO, Government of India.

As per Census (2001), urbanisation rate of Bihar is 10.5 per cent, which implies that around 90 per cent of population of the state lives in rural areas. Bihar is one of the least urbanised amongst all the major states in India as more than 90 per cent of the population in 25 out of 38 districts in the state live in rural areas. Patna, the capital city, is the only important city in the state that has a relatively high urban population of 41.6 per cent followed by Bhagalpur, which has 18.7 per cent urban population. Patna is also the most densely populated city in the state with a density of 1,471 persons per square kilometre and is the hub of regional trade and business in the state and is also an important centre for education and health facilities. Besides, it is also a gateway to the world famous Buddhist and Jain pilgrimage centres *viz*., Vaishali, Rajgir, Nalanda, Bodhgaya and Pawapuri. Since Patna remains the only biggest urban centre in the state, wherein real estate market has picked up substantially, our study would primarily focus, by and large, on Patna alone.

In Patna urban agglomeration area, 60 per cent of the land is used for residential purpose, while the use of land for industrial and commercial purposes is 4 per cent (Figure 8.2). Since Patna lies in the gangetic belt, land is very fertile and relatively costly here. In recent times, with the boom in housing and property market, there has been a diversion in the use of land from agriculture to real estate development, though we do not have concrete data to corroborate.

Figure 8.2

Land Use Distribution of Patna Urban Agglomeration Area

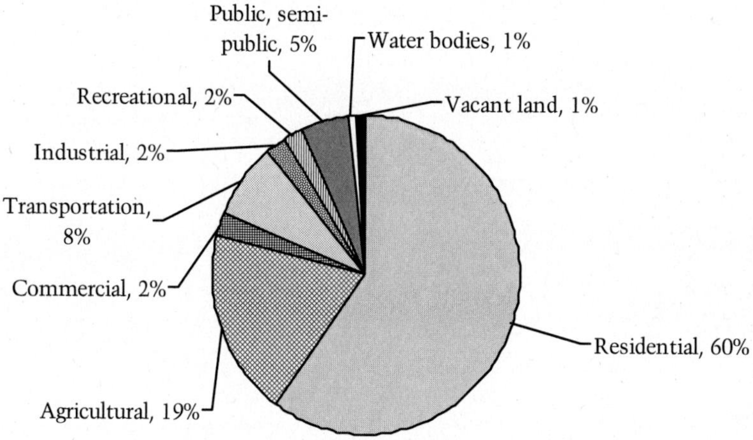

Source: DCL (2006). *Interim Report of Master Plan 2021*.

As per our interaction with the builders, it is found that the prices of real estate (both residential and commercial) in Bihar have appreciated very sharply in the last couple of years. Nevertheless, as per the National Housing Bank's NHB (RESIDEX) data, other cities (except metros) in India, *viz.*, Faridabad, Lucknow, Bhopal, etc., have witnessed much sharper appreciation in real estate prices than Patna (Table 8.3).

Though we do not have concrete time-series information on the number of apartments being built/developed, we have last few years' data available on registration of flats in Patna. In 2006, Government of Bihar enacted Bihar Apartment Ownership Act, 2006, which made the registration of flats mandatory. Subsequently, with the effort of the registration department many flats built earlier got registered in 2007-08 and 2008-09 (Table 8.4). Though trend in registration of flats does not clearly depict the demand- and supply-side dynamics of residential flats, nevertheless fact remains that real estate prices in Patna have recorded a sharp appreciation, which *inter alia* may be attributable to the pent-up demand for the real estate in the state capital.

Table 8.3

Trends in City-wise Housing Price Index in Select Cities of India
(Base Year: 2007=100)

Cities	Jan-June 2008	July-Dec 2008	Jan-June 2009	July-Dec 2009	Jan-Mar 2010	Apr-Jun 2010	Jul-Sep 2010	Oct-Dec 2010	Jan-Mar 2011	Apr-June 2011
Hyderabad	96	92	65	81	81	82	87	87	83	91
Faridabad	100	121	139	145	154	152	170	176	165	220
Patna	103	100	107	119	127	124	148	146	146	146
Ahmedabad	106	100	127	128	113	131	141	164	165	169
Chennai	104	95	120	143	164	183	210	214	218	248
Jaipur	119	115	71	63	66	61	63	69	67	64
Lucknow	103	102	104	119	112	133	148	152	157	160
Pune	101	97	103	117	124	135	140	141	148	150
Surat	101	98	111	123	109	136	128	133	128	149
Kochi	106	95	90	83	79	83	97	101	86	107
Bhopal	139	151	139	162	158	153	166	173	167	224
Kolkata	114	140	162	185	165	176	191	213	211	194
Mumbai	112	117	124	126	134	160	167	173	175	181
Bengaluru	73	76	58	59	64	68	74	101	88	92
Delhi	124	130	121	113	106	110	115	123	126	147

Source: National Housing Bank.

Table 8.4

Trends in Registration of Flats in Patna

Year	*No. of Flats Registered*	*Revenue from Registration of Flats (Rs crore)*
2007-08	11349	95.03
2008-09	3212	38.64
2009-10	3732	55.58
2010-11 (April-January)	1974	34.96

Source: *Annual Report 2010-11*, Registration & Excise Prohibition Department, Government of Bihar.

Improvement in law & order in the state in the last couple of years has caused larger influx of people from other districts to Patna and reverse migration of people from other parts of the country. As Patna is the only big urban centre in Bihar, there has been a sharp rise in demand for residential plots and apartments. On the supply side, however, landscape of the city, which is surrounded on three sides by different rivers[4] puts a binding constraint on its physical expansion, while the availability of non-agricultural space for development of residential and commercial use remains very limited. The situation of demand outstripping the supply of land that can be deployed for real estate development has led to a sharp rise in land prices in the state. This, in turn, has pushed up the real estate prices. Some of the instrumental factors that led to realisation of pent-up demand for real estate in Bihar are as follows:

Governance

In the last couple of years, the state government has made efforts on strengthening transparency and accountability in administration, which has helped improve governance and law & order in the state. Introduction of the Right to Information Act has brought transparency and accountability in administration. Besides, the Bihar government has taken a novel step in introducing a platform for dissemination of information to general public called as 'Jankari'—call centre for citizens for seeking information over phone—which was conferred the first prize for e-

4. On the northern side by River Ganga, southern side by River Punpun and eastern side by River Sone.

governance. To augment the existing police force, the state government has constituted Special Auxiliary Police (SAP) by recruiting ex-servicemen. Further, to improve the situation of law & order in Bihar, the state government has introduced 'speedy trials' for effecting quicker convictions so as to deter hardened criminals and reduce the incidence of crime in the state. This has resulted in sharp rise in the number of convicted criminals in the state, while the number of cases booked under Arms Act has seen a sharp decline (Table 8.5). This has led to a positive change and restoration of faith in the Government machinery, which has created a favourable environment for investors and tourists, etc.

Table 8.5

Trend in Conviction of Criminals in Bihar

Year	*No. of Cases*		*No. of Convicted Criminals*
	IPC	*Arms Act*	
2006	2178	1156	6839
2007	3695	800	9928
2008	4461	706	12012
2009	5333	482	13163
2010 (January-November)	5556	391	12941

Source: Department of Home, Government of Bihar.

Sharp Rise in Bihar's Per Capita Income in the Last Couple of Years

Being a poor state, Bihar has one of the lowest per capita income. Nevertheless, with the improvement in law & order in the state and the engagement of the state government with developmental activities, per capita income of the state has increased faster, which has been more than the rise in all-India per capita NSDP (Figure 8.3). Sharp expansion in income has also resulted in putting up the demand pressure on the real estate in the state.

Improvement in Urban Infrastructure

The Government of Bihar has undertaken various developmental activities to augment the physical, social and economic infrastructure of the state. In order to augment urban infrastructure, the Central government launched a progamme called as Jawaharlal Nehru Urban Renewal Mission (JNNURM) in 2005 and Bihar government has also made substantial allocation of funds for improving urban infrastructure in the state (Table 8.6).

Figure 8.3

Growth in Per Capita NSDP at Current Prices

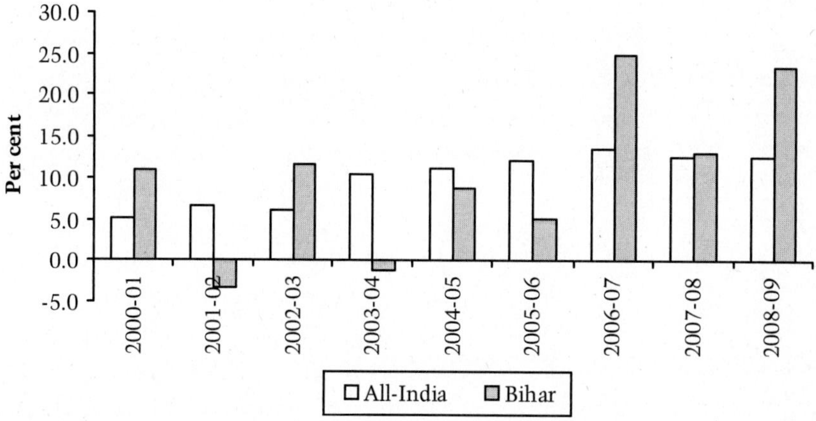

Source: CSO, Government of India.

V

Bank Finance and Real Estate Development in Bihar

For understanding the trends in real estate and the role of bank finance in propping it, we compiled last three years' data from 12 banks[5] having major presence in Bihar. On perusal of data regarding bank finance, it is observed that bank finance to real estate sector in Bihar increased by 45.9 per cent as at end-March 2010. It is also found that as at end-March 2010, 97.7 per cent of real estate bank loans were available to individuals in the form of housing loans followed by commercial real estate loans to builders with a share of 1.9 per cent, while the share of residential complexes loans to builders was a meagre 0.4 per cent (Table 8.7).

5. These banks include: Bank of India, Central Bank of India, Allahabad Bank, Indian Bank, Bank of Baroda, Canara Bank, Punjab & Sind Bank, Punjab National Bank, Federal Bank, Corporation Bank, Bank of Maharashtra and the State Bank of India.

Table 8.6

Status of Allocations and Sanctions under JNNURM

(Rs crore)

Scheme	Allocation (Central Share)	Additional Central Share Allocation	Allocation (Central+ State)	Total Sanctioned Projects	Central and State Share		Fund Released by GoI	
					GoI Share	GoB Share	GoI Share	GoB Share
Urban Infrastructure & Governance	592.41	150.00	1094.82	758.41	420.10	338.35	111.26	103.67
Basic Services for Urban Poor	496.54	35.00	993.08	709.98	312.75	391.40	78.19	70.93
Urban Infrastructure Development for Small and Medium Town	254.78	-	318.48	261.13	208.90	52.22	107.16	26.90
Integrated Housing & Slum Development Programme	140.06	28.00	175.08	235.86	123.97	70.13	61.98	20.41
Total	1483.79	213.00	2581.46	1965.38	1065.72	852.10	358.59	221.91

Note: GoI: Government of India; GoB: Government of Bihar.

Source: Department of Urban Development and Housing, Government of Bihar.

Table 8.7

Trend in Bank Loan to Real Estate Sector in Bihar (As on 31st March)

	Amount (Rs in crore)			Share in Total (%)		
Loans and Advances to	*2008*	*2009*	*2010*	*2008*	*2009*	*2010*
Builders dealing in commercial real estate	2432	4975	2574	2.7	5.4	1.9
Companies/builders dealing in residential complexes	736	367	583	0.8	0.4	0.4
Housing loans to individuals	85453	87164	134810	96.4	94.2	97.7
Total	88621	92506	137967	100.0	100.0	100.0

Source: Data based on information received from banks.

As per the growth trend, it is found that while there has been a phenomenal growth in residential/housing loans to individuals and builders, bank loans to builders dealing in commercial real estate declined substantially as at end-March 2010 (Figure 8.4). Bank-wise analysis of their real estate portfolio suggests that almost all the major banks had more than three-fourth of their real estate loans extended to individuals (housing loans) (Table 8.8).

Figure 8.4

Trends in Growth in Real Estate Loans by Banks in Bihar

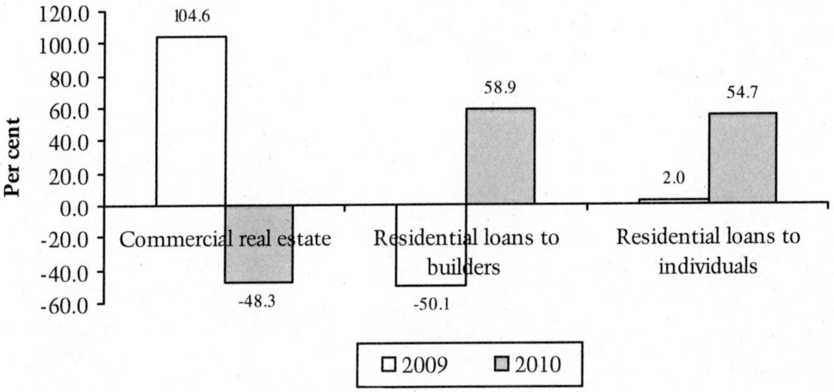

Source: Based on information received from banks.

Further among the banks, it is found that the State Bank of India was the major financier of real estate projects in Bihar (Table 8.9). Of the total loans and advances to real estate sector of major banks in the state as on March 31, 2010, the SBI alone commanded a share of 70 per cent, followed by Bank of Baroda (7.4%), Punjab National Bank (6.9%), Bank of India (6.11%), Central Bank of India (5.04%), etc.

To further probe the issue, we interviewed some real estate developers based in Patna to gather some information on the price trends, impact of global slowdown on real estate sector in the state, sources of finance for the real estate projects, etc. It was observed that recent global slowdown had no major impact on the real estate sector in the state as there had been a huge

Table 8.8

Real Estate Portfolio of Some Banks in Bihar (March 31, 2008 to March 31, 2010)

		Amount (Rs lakh)			Share (Per cent)		
S.No.	Banks	Commercial Real Estate Loans	Residential Loans to Builders	Housing Loans to Individuals	Commercial Real Estate Loans	Residential Loans to Builders	Housing Loans to Individuals
1.	Bank of India	1679	195	6557	19.9	2.3	77.8
2.	Central Bank of India	127	0	6821	1.8	0.0	98.2
3.	Allahabad Bank	0	0	1860	0.0	0.0	100.0
4.	Indian Bank	27	0	1356	2.0	0.0	98.0
5.	Bank of Baroda	478	378	9349	4.7	3.7	91.6
6.	Canara Bank	0	0	2154	0.0	0.0	100.0
7.	Punjab & Sind Bank	0	0	67	0.0	0.0	100.0
8.	Punjab National Bank	263	0	9250	2.8	0.0	97.2
9.	Federal Bank	0	0	110	0.0	0.0	100.0
10.	Corporation Bank	0	0	270	0.0	0.0	100.0
11.	Bank of Maharashtra	0	0	454	0.0	0.0	100.0
12.	State Bank of India	0	10	96562	0.0	0.0	100.0

Source: Data based on information received from select banks.

pent-up demand for residential flats, which was the result of improved law & order and governance. In respect of prices of lands and constructed flats, it was found that prices had nearly doubled in the last three years in Bihar. In respect of raising finances, it was observed that the builders were either using own resources or entering into partnership with landowners and other investors for the development of residential projects. The builders viewed that they desperately wanted project loans from banks but it had not been easy for them to procure such loans. Nevertheless, prospective buyers of flats had more access to housing loans from banks, which is validated by the available data in Table 8.7.

Table 8.9

Bank's Share in Real Estate Loans in Bihar (As on March 31, 2010)

(Per cent)

Bank	*Share in Real Estate Loans (%)*
State Bank of India	70.00
Bank of Baroda	7.40
Punjab National Bank	6.90
Bank of India	6.11
Central Bank of India	5.04
Canara Bank	1.56
Allahabad Bank	1.35
Indian Bank*	1.00
Bank of Maharashtra*	0.33
Corporation Bank	0.20
Federal Bank*	0.08
Punjab & Sind Bank	0.05

Note: * Data for both Bihar and Jharkhand.
Source: Data based on information received from banks.

VI

Prospects for Real Estate Development in Bihar

The population of the Patna urban agglomeration area is expected to grow up to 28.01 lakh by 2021. Besides, the floating population who commute from other districts to the Patna urban agglomeration area each day is expected to be 3.0 lakh by 2021 against the present figure of around 2.0 lakh. This dynamic pattern of population growth offers a big potential market for the real estate in Patna. Nevertheless, this would require substantial augmentation and improvement of urban infrastructure and environment.

The topography of Patna is like a saucer and it is surrounded on its three sides by different rivers and the city is also prone to flooding in the monsoons. Drainage is the most crucial problem of Patna and it is the root cause of many other physical and environment problems. Further, growth in Patna has, by and large, been unplanned. The old part of the city, Patna city, which is in the eastern part of Patna urban area is congested, with narrow lanes, and has crucial traffic congestion problems. Due to rapid urbanisation and the consequent build-up of population pressure, civic facilities have come under strain in the city. Following efforts are needed on various fronts to further improve the prospects of real estate market in Patna.

a. There is a great potential for tourism in the state as there are a large number of ancient heritage sites in and around Patna. Once it is fully exploited, this would further provide a great fillip to development of real estate in the state.

b. The peculiar topography has given a saucer like shape to Patna. Even though separate sewerage system has been adopted in the city, the same does not function well. There is a need to further improve the drainage system of the city through construction of new drains, upgradation of open and *kutcha* drains to closed drainage systems and de-silting of drains.

c. There is a need to improve the economic and physical infrastructure for the rapidly increasing urban population and also to provide essential facilities and services using public-private partnership. Such essential facilities and services include sub-sectors of water supply, sewerage and sanitation, drainage, solid waste management, roads and street lighting, energy, housing, urban transit systems and urban expressways.

d. The real estate market in India is narrow and extremely cumbersome and one of the many barriers to the efficient functioning of the real estate market has been, and continues to be, the high rates of stamp duty on conveyance transactions. Although a few states have taken steps to bring down the stamp duty rates, in several states, the rates are in excess of 10 per cent, deterring individuals, businesses and industry from registering properties at actual, or market values. Bihar needs to rationalise the stamp duty and registration charges levied on residential and commercial property prices. Like most other state governments, Bihar government also derives a major portion of its revenues from the stamp and registration charges (Table 8.10). Given its high dependence on stamp and registration charges as an important source of revenue, the Government of Bihar has not further

Table 8.10

Trends in Revenue Realisation from Stamp and Registration Charges

Year	*Revenue from Stamp & Registration Fees (Rs crore)*	*Growth (%)*	*Share in Total Revenues (%)*
2002-03	348.2	..	12.5
2003-04	417.6	19.9	14.3
2004-05	429.1	2.8	12.8
2005-06	505	17.7	14.2
2006-07	455	-9.9	11.3
2007-08	654	43.7	12.9
2008-09	716	9.5	11.6
2009-10	998	39.4	12.3
2010-11	1215	21.7	11.4

Note: Data in respect of 2010-11 is budgeted estimate.
Source: *Economic Survey*, various issues, Government of Bihar.

rationalised its stamp duty and registration charges since May 2006, when it was revised down to 10 per cent (Table 8.11). This does not compare favourably with other states like West Bengal, Jharkhand, Orissa, etc., wherein such rates are on the lower side (Annexure Table A-8.1).

VII

Concluding Observations

From the foregoing analysis, it is found that while real estate prices stagnated in most parts of India in the aftermath of global downturn, prices of commercial as well as residential properties in Patna witnessed upward swing even during 2008 and 2009. Improvement in governance and law & order situation has given a big push to the real estate sector in the state. In respect of real estate loans, banks in the state extended a large share of their loans in the form of housing loans to individuals. The State Bank of India is the major financier of real estate sector as it accounts for 70 per cent share in total real estate loans in Bihar. It is found that given the lower level of urbanisation and lack of basic infrastructure, the state needs to further improve the economic and physical infrastructure so as to facilitate the current growth momentum of the real estate sector.

Table 8.11

Revenue from Stamp Duty and Registration Fees

(Rs crore)

Source of Revenue	2006-07	2007-08	2008-09	2009-10	2010-11 (Upto Oct 2010)
Stamp duty					
(i) From printed non-judicial stamps	185	177	333	457	130
(ii) From non-judicial stamp duty deposited through bank challan	196	309	200	309	260
(iii) Non-judicial adhesive stamps	11	11	22	-	-
(iv) Non-judicial special adhesive stamp through franking machines	0	1	1	13	2
(v) Revenue stamps	0	2	2	4	1
(vi) Judicial stamps	19	22	24	24	16
Sub-total	411	522	582	807	409
Registration fee & other fees					
(i) Fees on registration of instruments	112	150	170	195	145
(ii) Landlord's registration fee	10	13	12	15	9
(iii) Landlord's process fee	5	7	3	13	2
(iv) Fee from searches of records & non-encumbrances	1	2	2	2	1
(v) Fee from certified copies	2	2	1	2	1
Sub-total	130	174	188	227	158
Total	541	696	770	1034	567

Source: *Economic Survey 2010-11*, Government of Bihar.

References

Government of Andhra Pradesh (n.d.). *http://www.ap.gov.in*

Government of Bihar (2011). *Economic Survey 2010-11*. February.

———. (2006). *City Development Plan For Patna under JNNURM*. Urban Development Department, Bihar Urban Development Agency. July,

———. (2010). *Draft Urban Sanitation Strategy*. December.

———. (2011). *Annual Report 2010-11*. Registration & Excise Prohibition Department.

———. (n.d.). Urban Development & Housing Department. *http://urban.bih.nic.in*

———. (n.d.). Registration & Excise Prohibition Department. *http://registration.bih.nic.in*

National Housing Bank website, *http://www.nhb.org.in*

National Housing Bank (n.d.). *Report on Trend & Progress of Housing in India 2008*.

Patna Municipal Corporation (n.d.). *http://pmc.bih.nic.in*

Annexure Table A-8.1

Stamp Duty and Registration Rates for Properties in Some States in India

State	*Rate of Stamp Duty*	*Registration Rate*
Andhra Pradesh	5%	N.A.
Bihar	8% + 2% additional stamp duty (for municipal areas)	2%
Gujarat	3.5% stamp duty + 1.5% additional as consideration charges	1%
Haryana	5% (rural area); 7% (urban area), where 2% is municipal duty	Various slabs: Rs 1-60,000: Rs 100 Above Rs 60,000-One lakh: Rs 500 Rs 1-5 lakh: Rs 1,000 Rs 5-10 lakh: Rs 5,000 Rs 10-20 lakh: Rs 10,000 Rs 20-25 lakh: Rs 12,500 Above Rs 25 lakh: Rs 15,000
Himachal Pradesh	5%	2%.
Jharkhand	4%	1%.
Karnataka	6.72% (for corporation area) and 6.78% (for other than corporation area) of market value or consideration value, whichever is higher	1% of market value or consideration value, whichever is higher
Kerala	Corporation areas: 9%; Municipality/township/ cantonment areas: 8%; and in *gram panchayats*: 7%.	2%
Orissa	5%	2%
Punjab	8%	1%
Tamil Nadu	8%	1%
Uttar Pradesh	Stamp duty: 8% + 2% under U.P. Town Improvement Act, 1919.	N.A.
West Bengal	6% in municipal areas; 5% in *panchayat* areas. For properties worth Rs 25 lakh and above—stamp duty of 1% more. For gift of property—0.5% of assessed value of the property & participation of property—0.5% of assessed value of the property.	Registration fees 1.1% for both

Note: N.A.: Not Available.

Source: Information collected from various state governments.

9

A Disaggregated Analysis of Monetary Transmission Mechanism

Evidence from the Dispersion of Bank Credit to Indian States

SARAT DHAL

I

Introduction

In a national context, the two major components of macroeconomic policy, namely, the fiscal policy and the monetary policy could be characterised with an important distinguishing feature. Fiscal policy across many countries encompasses the devolution of power between federal, state and local governments due to constitutional provisions for different types of taxes, expenditures and governance responsibilities. On the other hand, central banks serve as the sole authority in their area of operations. Accordingly, monetary policy actions through changes in monetary variables such as money supply, bank credit, interest rate and exchange rate are expected to have broad based implications for all sections of the society within a nation. This distinction between monetary and fiscal policies notwithstanding, there is a growing body of literature focussed on disaggregated analysis of monetary policy. According to this literature, though monetary policy can have national implications, it could be associated with differential implications for different sections of the society pertaining to households, firms, sectors, industries and regions within nations. The growth of disaggregated monetary transmission mechanism literature is attributable, *inter alia*, to the predictive failure of aggregative macroeconomic models, the 'black box' view on aggregate monetary transmission mechanism and the existence of bank credit and lending channels due to asymmetric information and moral hazard problems (Bernanke and Gertler, 1995). From policy perspective, disaggregate transmission mechanism studies are useful for indentifying sectors and regions which respond first to a policy innovation and whether the effects could be more pronounced in some sectors and regions than in others. A comparative analysis of monetary transmission mechanism across different sectors and regions may therefore provide valuable information for optimising welfare of the society at large, which is the ultimate policy objective (Ganley and Salmon, 1997).

There has been intensive empirical analysis across countries in the area of disaggregated monetary transmission mechanism. In the Indian context, although there have been some studies in this tradition including Nachne *et al.* (2002), Misra (2003) and Narayana (2000) but the literature is generally scarce. Thus, this study is motivated for an analysis of monetary transmission mechanism at regional level in India. At the outset, it is to be noted that monetary policy transmission mechanism can work in two stages: in the first stage, policy actions could percolate to the financial markets affecting deposit and lending rates and dispersion of bank lending to productive sectors across the regions. In the second stage, changes in cost of funds such as lending rate and availability of credit could affect private consumption and investment, and thus, real activity. This study is about the first stage of transmission mechanism, and thus, different from the previous studies. The study uses pooled cross-section regression methodology for analysing the dispersion of bank credit across 20 major states, excluding some smaller states for which data were not readily available. The empirical analysis demonstrates how monetary policy affects dispersion of credit to the states in the presence of state-specific variables such as states' real income, infrastructure development and commercialisation of economic activities and the level of funds available to the banking sector for lending purposes. At a time when there is national focus on inclusive growth and financial inclusion objectives, the findings of the study could provide some crucial perspectives for development policy purposes, apart from monetary policy implications. The remainder of the study is presented in four sections. Section II provides a review of the literature. Section III provides some stylised facts relating to states' share in bank credit in India. Section IV dwells on the empirical analysis and results in the Indian context. Section V concludes with some policy implications of the study.

II

The Literature

Until the 1980s, economists generally adhered to aggregative macroeconomic model *a la* the standard IS-LM model for analysing monetary transmission mechanism. Policy induced changes in monetary variables such as monetary aggregates, bank credit, interest rate, and exchange rate were postulated to affect aggregate demand and consequently, the growth rate of the economy-wide output such as real gross domestic product and the inflation in the aggregate price index. However, the predictive failure of macro models and the incongruent relationship between monetary variables, real activity and prices inspired economists to look for micro perspectives. Departing from the tradition, several studies including Bernanke and Gertler (1995) found the inadequacy of the aggregate transmission mechanism. They viewed the aggregative approach to monetary transmission mechanism as a 'black box' because 'it did not tell us what happens in the interim in the transmission of policy shocks to the real economy.' Thus, the more recent literature on monetary transmission mechanism has witnessed a paradigm shift in embracing disaggregated analyses for better understanding of how monetary variables affect various components of aggregate demand such as consumption, investment, trade and economic activities across firms, industries, sectors and regions within and across the countries. Studies in this tradition are inspired by the seminal works on asymmetric information, market imperfection and moral hazard (Stiglitz and Weiss, 1994), the bank credit channel comprising the balance sheet channel and the bank lending channel (Bernake and Gertler, 1997; Kashyap *et al.*, 1993 and Kashyap and Stein, 1995). Several other studies emphasising on the heterogeneous characteristics of producing sectors pertaining to different products, technologies, intensity of labour and capital inputs, financial structure, openness to trade, wage contracts and flexibility in product prices have contributed to disaggregate analysis of monetary transmission mechanism (Ahmed, 1987; Kretzmer, 1989; Kandil, 1991; Hayo and Uhlenbrock,

1999; Ahmed and Miller, 1997; Ganley and Salmon,1997; Guiso *et al.*, 1999 among several others).

According to the literature, the use of disaggregated data allows for a better identification of factors which are deemed important in the process of monetary transmission. The literature on disaggregated transmission mechanism has grown in various dimensions, reflecting the increased coverage and the use of alternative methodological approaches.

First, some early studies including Craig (1981), Enders and Falk (1984), Ahmed (1987), Gauger (1988), Gauger and Enders (1989), Kretzmer (1989) Kandil (1991) deliberated on the neutrality of money hypothesis, whether anticipated or unanticipated money growth matters across countries and industries, deriving from the studies which favoured disaggregate analysis for a better understanding of how aggregate demand shock in general affected different countries and producing industries at different points of time differently (Barro, 1977, 1978, 1981; Barro and Rush, 1980; Schultze, 1984; Ball *et al.*, 1988; Craig, 1981; Edwards, 1989; Lilien, 1982; Duca, 1987). These studies asserted that aggregate models by overlooking the composition of and changes in the different sectors cannot capture important aspects of the economy. Sectoral shifts in employment shares from durable manufacturing into service-related industries could induce general downturns in the economy. Models which consider sectoral differences and international factors better position themselves to explain the different effects of monetary and exchange rate policies on different economic variables, both at the sectoral and aggregate levels (Lilien, 1982). Schultze (1984) demonstrated that demand shocks affect variables in different countries, and even the same country, during different time periods differently. Similarly, Ball *et al.* (1988) found that shocks in nominal GNP affected real output and price levels differently in various countries. Craig (1981) showed that the real money supply affected the real trade balance of different countries with different intensities. Duca (1987), building on the work of Blinder and Mankiew (1984), developed a closed-economy two-sector model and suggested that wage stickiness in one sector allowed monetary policy to have real effects in the other sector, even if it had perfectly flexible wages and prices. Enders and Falk (1984) argued that taking a microeconomic perspective enables assessing how monetary shocks are vertically transmitted from the retail level to the wholesale level and ultimately to the production level. The approach also avoids some potential aggregation and measurement problems which can make the empirical analysis more difficult. Ahmed and Miller (1997) developed a two-sector economy where each sector was classified as classical/Keynesian (contract/noncontract) in the labour market and traded/non-traded in the product market. They considered the effects of changes in monetary and exchange rate policy on sectoral and aggregate prices and outputs for different sectoral characterisations to find that trade price rigidity provided a similar path for the effectiveness of monetary policy, even when both sectors are classical.

Second, as part of the more recent literature, Gertler and Gilchrist (1994) compared the response of small and large US manufacturing firms to monetary shocks in the US. Bernanke and Gertler (1995) used vector autoregressive (VAR) model to show the different impacts of monetary policy on spending components such as consumer durables, non-durable consumption, residential investment, and business fixed investment. Barth and Ramey (2001) explored a similar attempt in the US. Haimowitz (1996) used annual data across 450 standard industrial classification (SIC) 4-digit manufacturing industries in the US to examine how industry prices and output responded to monetary shocks, and how those responses were affected by certain industry characteristics. He found that durable-goods industries exhibited substantially larger output and marginally larger price responses to monetary shocks than non-durable-goods industries; industries producing goods for producers exhibited substantially larger output and price responses to monetary shocks than industries producing goods for consumers; high-concentration industries exhibited relatively smaller price responses and larger output responses; and industries with a high inventory-to-sales ratio exhibited relatively smaller price responses. Berument *et.al* (2004) suggested a number of channels through which monetary policy could affect various sectors differently. The degree to which firms are dependent on banks for credit (Bernanke and Blinder, 1988; Kashyap *et al.*, 1993) and the ease with which banks are able to adjust their balance sheets (Kashyap and Stein, 1995) might lead to a monetary policy action affecting the sectors differently. The principal reasons could be different levels of capital intensity, input/output demand patterns and production planning strategies. All these suggested that their patterns of bank credit usage might differ. In addition to this, banks' flexibility in adjusting their balance sheets determines the extent of the credit volume available to a specific sector. Firms forming their working capital by extensive use of bank credit and concentrated in a given sector might be influenced differently than another sector with less dependence on bank credit when the interest rates change temporarily. The employment composition of productive inputs is an important factor, as well. In any economy, not all sectors necessarily use the same composition of inputs; that is, some sectors might be more capital-intensive whereas others are more labour-intensive. Thus, an increase in interest rates may affect the capital-intensive sectors more than labour-intensive ones. Similarly, the composition of the manufactured input and raw material needs of different sectors might be differently allocated between domestic and import sources; not all sectors use the same combination of imported and domestically produced intermediate products. Therefore, the exchange rate movements may affect these sectors differently. For instance, a firm that imports more of its input can be affected to a larger extent by the depreciation of the local currency than a firm that imports less of its input. Another similar argument can be developed based on the trade orientation of the sectors. Importing sectors can be affected by currency depreciation differently from exporting ones, owing to their different operational natures. Practices of informal economy (i.e., officially unrecorded economic activity) should also be considered while accounting for the reasons behind the degree or extent of the same policy shock on different sectors. Under loose monetary policy, firms in the formal part of the economy can get credit from banks more easily compared to those in the informal part since the former has better book-keeping practices. If the firms of the formal economy are concentrated more in a specific sector, then that sector can be influenced more by negative shocks to the overall economy, compared to the less formalised sectors. Thus, the effect of monetary policy on each sector of economy will be different.

In the UK, Dale and Haldane (1995) compared the response of the UK personal and corporate sectors to unexpected changes in monetary policy. Ganley and Salmon (1997) compared the response of output to a monetary shock in 9 major sectors and 24 sub-sectors of the UK economy. They used a separate vector error-correction model involving the interest rate, aggregate GDP, the GDP deflator, and the sectoral output of each industrial sector and found that construction, distribution and transportation, and manufacturing exhibited the largest output responses to a monetary shock. Government services, financial services and utilities responded relatively little to the shock. The mining sector's response was somewhat erratic and ambiguous, and the agricultural sector's response was insignificant. Over all the subsectors, those industries closely linked to the construction sector, reacted substantially and fairly quickly (within a year), those linked to consumer durable and semi-durable goods, such as motor vehicles, reacted substantially with a lag (within 2 years) and those linked to food showed only a modest response. Sectors closely linked to industrial demand, such as machinery and chemicals, reacted substantially to monetary policy. Similarly, Hayo and Uhlenbrock (1999) used VAR model comprising seven variables, the exchange rate, a world commodity price index, a short- and a long-term interest rate, a monetary aggregate, a production index, and a producer price index using monthly data over the period 1978–1994, and analysed the impulse responses of 28 industries in the manufacturing and mining sector in Germany to monetary shocks. At the industry level, they found a wide difference in terms of the period of the effect, its length, and its magnitude, with more than half the total output accounted for by industries that behaved differently from the average. They found differential response of capital intensive and export orientation industries to monetary shocks.

Farès and Gabriel (2001) investigated the monetary transmission mechanism in broad sectors of the Canadian economy. They considered two types of disaggregation: one at the level of final expenditures and one at the level of production. At the level of final expenditures, they found that a monetary contraction affected exports relatively quickly, and investment much more substantially than the consumption of goods, while services were not much affected. Not surprisingly, durables responded much more substantially than semi-durables to a monetary contraction, while non-durables did not respond significantly. At the level of production, following a monetary contraction, construction reached the trough of the cycle first, although, cumulatively, manufacturing reacted twice as strongly.

Caruso (2004) in a study of Italy evaluated the effects of unanticipated monetary policy shocks on output of local industries using VAR methodology. The impact of unexpected changes in the money market interest rate on the pattern of industrial production—based on qualitative business opinion survey data—was computed for 164 local industries. The perceived output effects of monetary impulses increased for local industries with higher investment expenditures, less liquid firms and for industrial sectors that had a higher correlation with the aggregate business cycle. However, the hypothesis that small firms bear a disproportionate burden of monetary policy did not find support in this sample. On the contrary, Gertler and Gilchrist (1994), Dedola and Lippi (2000) noticed that a smaller firm size was associated with a stronger impact of monetary policy on manufacturing output, respectively in the US and in a sample of 5 main industrialised countries. Gaiotti and Generale (2001) used a panel data of Italian firms and found an impact of monetary policy on investment unfavourable to small firms, but to a very limited extent. They argued that the contribution of firm size can also be country-specific and influenced by institutional characteristics. Angeloni *et al.* (1995) provided evidence that in Italy large banks tightened credit conditions more than small banks following a monetary restriction; they also noted that bank size and borrower were positively correlated, implying a lower impact of monetary policy on small firms. Arnold and Vrugt (2002) suggested that firms differ with regard to their sensitivity to interest rate shocks, depending on their type of product and their leverage. A tightening of monetary policy may reduce demand for investment goods and (durable) consumer goods by increasing the real costs of capital of firms and consumers. Regional differences in Tobin's 'q' or in the distribution of wealth may lead to regional effects.

Loo and Lastrapes (1998) examined the dynamic responses of industry-level output to money supply shocks in the US. They too used the vector autoregression of four aggregate variables (interest rate, output, real money, nominal money), and found substantial variation in the response of industries to monetary shocks. Cross-industry regressions showed that these responses were positively related to the variance of industry-specific shocks, which provided support for Lucas hypothesis. Ehrmann and Ellison (2002) argued that advances such as just-in-time production, lean manufacturing and improved inventory management enabled firms to adjust their production levels more quickly, easily and at lower cost.

Dedola and Lippi (2000) estimated the effect of interest rate shocks on 21 manufacturing industries in five OECD countries. Relating their estimated interest rate elasticity to a set of industry characteristics, they found that credit channel variables (firm size, borrowing capacity, and interest payment burden) are as significant as interest rate channel variables (durability and investment intensity). Taking a regional perspective, Carlino and DeFina (1998) applied a two-stage procedure to measure and explain the differential regional effects of monetary policy in the United States. First, they used a VAR model to estimate cumulative impulse responses of state real personal income to a shock in the federal funds rate. Second, they tried to link these impulse responses to a variety of interest channel and credit channel variables in a cross-section of states. They found that the regional share of manufacturing industry was the most important explanatory variable. Credit channel variables such as firm size are insignificant. Interest rate shocks had a strong impact on the state of Michigan, which holds a large concentration of the car industry.

David *et al.*(2000) suggested that disaggregated data (at the sector or industry-level) could be much more useful to detect the distributional effects of monetary policy. Apart from product durability, the industry degree of exposure to credit market frictions can contribute to explain its sensitivity to monetary policy shocks. Heterogeneous effects of monetary policy could then be originated by a differential credit channel. This thesis lies on a link between the industry production technology and its financial characteristics. In an influential paper, Rajan and Zingales (1998) showed that industrial sectors that were relatively more in need of external finance developed faster in countries with more developed financial markets. Similarly, for the Euro area, Krugman (1993), Fujita, Krugman and Venables (1999) contended that the convergence process in progress in Europe, banking and financial markets integration and the increase of competition ensured a progressive harmonisation in financial structures and behaviours. But the effects still remained uncertain concerning the European economies' productive structure. A regional sectoral specialisation was not excluded. Hence, it seemed useful to assess the cross-country and cross-sector asymmetry of the output response to unanticipated monetary policy and determine the main source of this asymmetry either due to a country or a sectoral effect. The heterogeneity of the output response to monetary shocks was explored not only between the manufacturing industries (like previous studies already mentioned), but also between all sectors of activity, including services. This strategy allowed taking into account larger mechanisms than those lying on product durability. Especially, the monopolistically competitive services, the source of price stickiness was worth to study.

Shelley and Wallace (1998) argued that there are at least two reasons to test the link between money and output at the industry level. First, the question of causality is less likely to arise when the data are sufficiently disaggregated. At the aggregate level, feedback from output to money can make it difficult to isolate the effect of money on output. Indeed, real business cycle theorists interpret the observed link between money and aggregate output as one of reverse causality. At the disaggregated level reverse causality seems implausible as it is unlikely that output in, say, electrical machinery manufacturing causes money. Second, it is conceivable that money is neutral with respect to aggregate output but non-neutral at some level of disaggregation. A change in the money supply or its growth rate may alter the composition of output without changing the total.

Third, of particular importance to regional effects of monetary policy, a fairly large literature has evolved across the nations drawing on the studies focussed on firms and industries. Carlino and DeFina (1998) and de Lucio and Izquierdo (2002) provided evidence on differential geographical effects of monetary policy, respectively across the US states and the Spanish regions. Carlino and DeFina (1998) ascertained on US regional data and found that firm size variable was insignificantly different from zero. Peersman and Smets (2002) found that in the Euro area firm-size indicators did not explain the average impact of monetary policy, while industries with a higher share of small firms showed larger responses in recessions than in expansions. Mihov (2001) reported empirical results on the presence of regional heterogeneity in output responses to monetary policy shocks for France, Germany and Italy. Dedola and Lippi (2000) showed on the basis of numerous estimated VAR systems (with reference to 5 OECD countries and 21 manufacturing industries) that there was significant cross-industry heterogeneity of policy effects, while heterogeneity across countries was limited. Peersman and Smets (2002) examined the cross-industry differences in output responses to monetary policy changes in seven Euro area countries. These contributions also tried to identify the sources of the observed heterogeneity, by ascertaining whether the policy effects on output are related to structural differences (such as industry composition, firm size and financial characteristics) that can proxy the asymmetries suggested by the large theoretical literature on the channels of monetary policy.

III

Some Stylised Facts

For facilitating the empirical analysis, it is useful to consider some stylised facts about the credit dispersion across the states in India.[1] First, the trends in the share of credit for the states are shown in Table 9.1. Over the full sample period, on average, one industrial state accounted for almost a fourth of total bank credit. Six major states accounted for three-fifth share of total bank credit. The four southern states accounted for about a third of total bank credit. Thus, the distribution of bank credit across states is highly skewed and asymmetric.

Second, the volatility in credit share of states is another important indicator. During the sample period 1982-2009, the coefficient of variation in the credit share of states showed significant diversity (Figure 9.1). Relatively advanced states witnessed less volatility whereas underdeveloped poorer states witnessed greater volatility. The north-eastern states showed sharp volatility in credit share. Southern states witnessed lowest volatility as compared with other states. Industrially advanced states witnessed a more or less similar variability in their credit share.

Third, reflecting the diversity in credit shares of the states, the Herfindahl index[2] of concentration showed a rising trend over the years

1. Data source for this study is the RBI's annual publications *Banking Statistical Returns* and the *Statistical Tables Relating to Banks*. The sample covers the period 1980-2009. The cross-section sample includes 20 major states.

2. The Herfindahl Index (also known as Herfindahl–Hirschman Index or HHI) is a measure of the size of firms in relation to the industry and an indicator of the amount of competition among them. It is defined as: $H = \sum_{j=1}^{N} s_j^2$ where s_i is the market share of firm i in the market and N is the number of firms. The Herfindahl Index (H) ranges from $1/N$ to one, where N is the number of firms in the market. Equivalently, if percents are used as whole numbers, as in 75 instead of 0.75, the index can range up to 1002, or 10,000. A HHI index below 0.01 (or 100) indicates a highly competitive index. A HHI index below 0.15 (or 1,500) indicates an unconcentrated index. A HHI index between 0.15 to 0.25 (or 1,500 to 2,500) indicates moderate concentration. A HHI index above 0.25 (above 2,500) indicates high concentration [1]. A small index indicates a competitive industry with no dominant players.

(Figure 9.2). The concentration index during the 1980s, which had shown some moderation during the late 1980s and again in the late 1990s, accentuated in the 2000s and almost doubled for the more recent years since 2000-01. This period includes the period of high growth phase in the Indian economy. For the more recent period 2008-09, the concentration index showed some slightly declining trend.

Table 9.1

Trends in States' Share of Bank Credit

(Per cent)

States	*Full*	*1980s(I)*	*1980s(II)*	*1990s(I)*	*1990s(II)*	*2000s(I)*	*2000s(II)*
S1	6.724	6.319	7.270	6.870	6.841	6.238	6.828
S2	0.019	0.012	0.020	0.017	0.017	0.020	0.029
S3	0.715	0.772	0.985	0.784	0.616	0.538	0.564
S4	2.314	2.745	2.968	2.623	2.111	1.740	1.546
S5	5.004	5.485	5.572	5.152	5.191	4.349	4.094
S6	1.784	1.997	1.962	1.707	1.581	1.597	1.880
S7	0.363	0.399	0.413	0.363	0.304	0.339	0.354
S8	0.638	0.643	0.634	0.668	0.681	0.653	0.528
S9	6.534	6.308	7.094	6.173	6.437	6.331	6.941
S10	3.648	4.030	4.028	3.511	3.641	3.481	3.086
S11	3.327	3.058	3.898	3.627	3.446	3.013	2.818
S12	26.603	24.287	22.632	24.253	26.218	30.446	33.078
S13	0.041	0.032	0.051	0.052	0.047	0.028	0.038
S14	0.061	0.051	0.065	0.050	0.046	0.083	0.069
S15	1.416	1.455	1.749	1.457	1.200	1.282	1.337
S16	3.343	3.737	3.690	3.376	3.270	3.086	2.785
S17	2.485	2.565	2.642	2.372	2.338	2.449	2.560
S18	10.063	9.232	9.891	10.398	11.323	9.898	9.526
S19	5.993	7.120	7.406	6.551	5.216	4.840	4.535
S20	7.049	9.334	8.408	7.520	6.303	5.412	4.881
Six major states	61.977	60.966	60.867	60.365	62.314	62.674	65.350
Skewness measure of cross-state shares	2.965	2.594	2.298	2.657	2.886	3.431	3.579

Figure 9.1

Coefficient of Variation in Credit Share

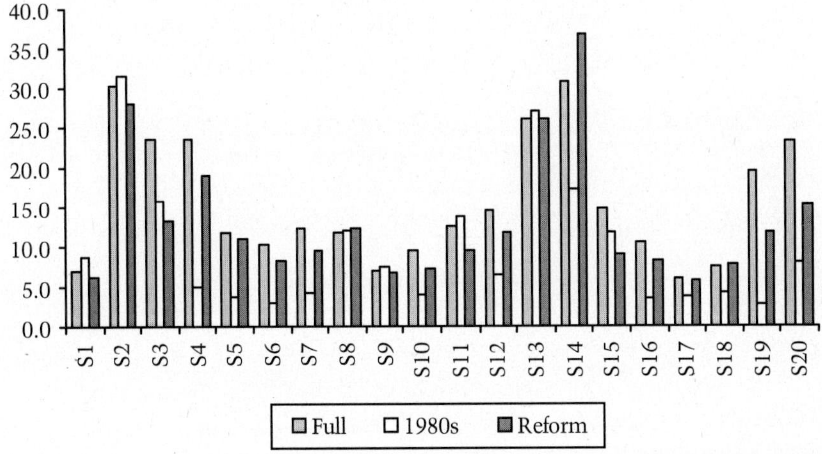

Figure 9.2

Herfindahl Index

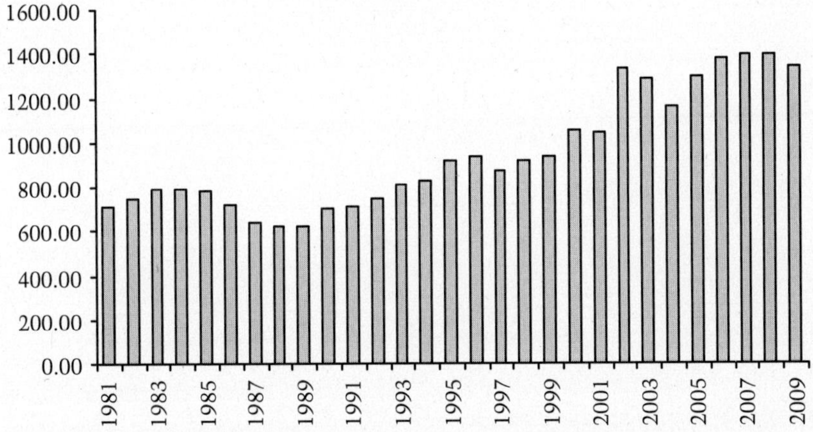

IV

Empirical Analysis and Evidence

For the empirical analysis, this study uses standard pooled cross-section least square regression technique. This approach has the advantage of allowing some variables to have cross-section specific effects, apart from the fixed effects. For our study, this is important for assessing whether the changes in policy variables such as interest rate could have differential state-specific effects. From a theoretical perspective, the empirical approach derives from the standard loan market hypothesis. In reduced form, bank loans (c) could be driven by demand and supply side factors, along with the policy variable (r). In our analysis, the dispersion of bank credit to various Indian states ($BC_{j,t}$) is explained by three types of factors: (i) state-specific variables, (ii) bank specific variables and (ii) an indicator of monetary policy (r):

$$BC_{j,t} = \alpha + \alpha_j + \beta Y_{j,t} + \gamma Z_{j,t} + \phi S_{j,t} + \theta F_t + \mu r_t + \lambda BC_{j,t-1}$$

The state-specific explanatory variables are real gross state domestic product (GSDP) denoted by $Y_{j,t}$, an indicator of infrastructure development as measured by the share of transport and power sectors in a state's gross domestic product ($Z_{j,t}$) and an indicator of commercialisation of economic activities (s) defined as the share of output originating from sectors other than agriculture, infrastructure and public administration, community and social services. The GSDP variable is expected to capture the overall economic progress and the aggregate demand condition for stimulating credit flow to economic activities. For productive activities, infrastructure holds the key. Moreover, due to the tradition of social and development banking, commercial banks cannot be passive intermediaries and therefore, they may provide credit to productive activities supported by infrastructure development. From the supply side of loan market, the major factor could relate to the aggregate level of funds (F) available for the banking sector for lending purposes. This variable is defined as total deposits less bank reserve balances held with central bank and the investment in government and other approved securities. For the indicator of monetary policy, we use the weighted average call money rate as provided by the Reserve Bank of India in its *Handbook of Statistics on the Indian Economy*. The call money rate (r) could capture both liquidity and interest rate effects, consistent with the use of both quantity of money and price (interest rate) channels of transmission mechanism in the Indian context. The one-period lag of dependent credit variable is used to capture the persistence in credit allocation as well as the transaction cost that banks could face in the adjustment of credit portfolio.

In the above equation, monetary policy effect (μ) is assumed to be similar across states. For the differential impact of monetary policy across the states (μ_j), we also estimate the above equation allowing cross-section specific monetary effects as follows:

$$BC_{j,t} = \alpha + \alpha_j + \beta Y_{j,t} + \gamma Z_{j,t} + \theta F_t + \mu_j r_t + \lambda BC_{j,t-1}$$

In both equations, we allow fixed effects, if validated by data.

Empirical Findings

For the empirical evidence, a structured analysis is adopted. First, to substantiate the importance of cross-section analysis and the disaggregate aspects of monetary transmission mechanism, aggregate bank credit of all scheduled commercial banks at national level was analysed as a function of real GDP and an indicator of monetary policy, i.e., call money interest rate and the lag dependent variable. The estimated equation is shown in Table 9.2. It was evident that real GDP had significant positive impact on bank credit. The estimated short-run elasticity of bank credit with respect to real GDP was positive 1.27 but the long-run elasticity was 2.86, twice larger than the short-run elasticity. A notable finding was that the interest rate had statistically insignificant and positive but close to zero impact on bank credit.

Table 9.2

All-India Bank Credit

Method: Least Square; Sample (adjusted): 1982 2009; HAC standard errors & covariance Bartlett kernel, Newey-West fixed; Dependent variable: Log of Bank credit (LBC)

Explanatory Variables	*Coefficient*	*Std. Error*	*t-Statistic*	*Prob.*
C	-12.39033	5.539135	-2.236871	0.0348
All-India: Log Real GDP	1.272248	0.562503	2.261763	0.0330
ZCALL	0.001636	0.002679	0.006105	0.9952
1-Lag Dependent variable	0.554679	0.198602	2.792914	0.0101
R-squared	0.998890	Mean dependent variable		12.39321
Adjusted R-squared	0.998751	S.D. dependent variable		1.337227
S.E. of regression	0.047257	Akaike info criterion		-3.134884
Sum squared residual	0.053597	Schwarz criterion		-2.944569
Log likelihood	47.88838	Hannan-Quinn criterion		-3.076703
F-statistic	7198.549	Durbin-Watson statistic		1.671146

For a comparative analysis, we replicated the equation in Table 9.2 using pooled regression technique (with fixed effect)[3] for state level bank credit regressed upon real state domestic products along with the interest rate variable as shown in Table 9.3. The short-run income elasticity of bank credit estimated at 0.18 was statistically significant but much lower than the national level estimate (1.27). However, due to the high persistence in state credit, the long run income elasticity of credit at the state level was estimated at 3.2, almost closer to the national level estimate (2.86). The critical finding here relates to the role of monetary policy in terms of the interest rate variable. The latter had significant negative impact on bank credit to states. In terms of the coefficient size, the short run impact of interest rate was estimated at 0.55 and the long run impact as high as 9.6, as compared with near zero interest elasticity of credit estimated at all India level in Table 9.2.

Table 9.3

State-wise Bank Credit
Dependent Variable: LBC

Variable	*Coefficient*	*Std. Error*	*t-Statistic*	*Prob.*
C	-1.230240	0.226231	-5.437980	0.0000
LY	0.184559	0.030114	6.128612	0.0000
LBC(-1)	0.942266	0.011154	84.47629	0.0000
ZCALL	-0.546421	0.081956	-6.667273	0.0000
	Weighted Statistics			
R-squared	0.998631	Mean dependent variable		10.71480
Adjusted R-squared	0.998573	S.D. dependent variable		4.719041
S.E. of regression	0.081565	Sum squared residual		3.426199
F-statistic (probability)	17076.71 (0.00)	Durbin-Watson statistic		1.744932

Redundant fixed effects test: F stat (degrees of freedom-df) (probability): 3.32 (19,515), (0.00)

In Table 9.3, all states were allowed to have similar interest elasticity of bank credit. After allowing interest rates to have cross-section state-specific effects, the estimated equation is shown in Table 9.4. It is evident

3. For all regressions in this paper, we investigated whether the random effect model could be appropriate. The Hausman Test rejected the random effect in terms of near zero chi-square test statistic, reflecting upon zero cross section random effects variance. On the other hand, the fixed effect model was validated by significant F statistic arising from the redundant fixed test. Thus, the empirical analysis in the study is based on fixed effect model.

from Table 9.4 that the income elasticity of state credit in the short run and long run could be positive, statistically significant and similar to Table 9.3. However, Table 9.4 shows different interest elasticity of credit for individual states. For all but one of the 20 states in the sample, the interest rate had negative coefficients. However, 13 states, mostly comprising

Table 9.4

State-wise Bank Credit Dispersion
(Cross-Section Interest Rate Effects)
Dependent Variable: LBC

Variable	*Coefficient*	*Std. Error*	*t-Statistic*	*Prob.*
C	-1.4430	0.2369	-6.0910	0.0000
LY	0.2151	0.0316	6.7980	0.0000
LBC(-1)	0.9309	0.0117	79.4441	0.0000
r1	-0.6227	0.3260	-1.9101	0.0567
r2	-1.9574	0.7590	-2.5789	0.0102
r3	-1.0132	0.4579	-2.2127	0.0274
r4	-0.6105	0.2716	-2.2476	0.0250
r5	0.1253	0.2906	0.4313	0.6665
r6	-0.6667	0.3058	-2.1800	0.0297
r7	-0.7255	0.3188	-2.2757	0.0233
r8	-0.6993	0.8085	-0.8650	0.3875
r9	-0.6719	0.3346	-2.0082	0.0452
r10	-0.3817	0.2046	-1.8656	0.0627
r11	-0.4068	0.3520	-1.1555	0.2484
r12	-0.4891	0.4411	-1.1090	0.2680
r13	-0.4043	0.7027	-0.5754	0.5653
r14	-1.7626	0.6241	-2.8241	0.0049
r15	-0.9866	0.3593	-2.7463	0.0062
r16	-0.6904	0.3239	-2.1317	0.0335
r17	-0.6879	0.2827	-2.4329	0.0153
r18	-0.0609	0.2834	-0.2148	0.8300
r19	-0.6817	0.3072	-2.2195	0.0269
r20	-0.0964	0.3013	-0.3201	0.7490
Weighted Statistics				
R-squared	0.9987	Mean dependent variable		10.7271
Adjusted R-squared	0.9986	S.D. dependent variable		4.8000
S.E. of regression	0.0814	Sum squared residual		3.2841
F-statistic	9285(0.00)	Durbin-Watson statistic		1.7854

Redundant fixed effects test: F stat (df) (probability): 3.98 (14,496)(0.00)

relatively less developed states, had statistically significant inverse relation of the interest rate with bank credit. On the other hand, for the remaining 7 states, which included the major advanced states, the coefficient of interest rate was not only statistically insignificant but also much lower in size than some of the poorer states. For one major industrially advanced state, the interest rate had a positive but statistically insignificant association with bank credit.

In order to capture the impact of supply side factors in the loan market, Table 9.5 extends the analysis with the inclusion of the availability funds of the banking sector for lending purpose. This variable had statistically significant positive impact on bank credit to the states. As a scale variable, the size of the coefficient of banks' fund was much lower than states income and interest rate variables. But the inclusion of this variable made some notable impact on the coefficients of other variables. Illustratively, the long-run income elasticity of credit turned out to be 1.4, closer to the all India level (Table 9.2) but lower than the earlier estimates for states in Table 9.3 and Table 9.4. However, it did not have significant impact on the coefficients of interest rate and infrastructure variables.

Table 9.5

State-wise Bank Credit Dispersion (Role of Banks' Lendable Resources)
Dependent Variable: LBC

Variable	*Coefficient*	*Std. Error*	*t-Statistic*	*Prob.*
C	-1.196343	0.226843	-5.273876	0.0000
LY	0.167124	0.031161	5.363207	0.0000
LBC(-1)	0.911425	0.018992	47.99086	0.0000
ZCALL	-0.525612	0.082355	-6.382273	0.0000
ZLFUND	0.032349	0.015880	2.037114	0.0422
	Weighted Statistics			
R-squared	0.998630	Mean dependent variable		10.61627
Adjusted R-squared	0.998569	S.D. dependent variable		4.699378
S.E. of regression	0.080734	Sum squared residual		3.350210
F-statistic	16292.68	Durbin-Watson statistic		1.689880

Redundant fixed effects test: F stat (df) (probability):2.83 (19,514)(0.00)

In the above analysis, the state GDP was used as a single variable for capturing economic condition of the states. For further insights, Table 9.6

provides empirical estimates with the inclusion of two other variables; state-level infrastructure development and commercial activity (the share of SDP excluding agriculture and infrastructure sectors in a state's total SDP). Table 9.6 confirms that infrastructure could play a significant role in dispersion of credit to various states. A comparison of Table 9.6 with Table 9.3 showed that the infrastructure variable did not have a significant weakening effect on the coefficients of state income, the interest rate and the lag-dependent variables. The variable commercialisation of economic activities was found with a significant positive impact on state credit. However, such impact was found to be significant at higher level, i.e., at about 10 per cent level of significance. Moreover, in terms of coefficient size, the impact of commercialisation was not as much as the impact of infrastructure development. In order to strengthen the empirical analysis, this variable was further refined with the exclusion of public administration and services. As expected, the modified commercial activity variable showed an improvement in terms of statistical significance and the coefficient size, thereby, validating its impact on state credit.

Table 9.6

State-wise Bank Credit Dispersion
(Role of Infrastructure and Commercial Activity)
Dependent Variable: LBC

Variable	*Coefficient*	*Std. Error*	*t-Statistic*	*Prob.*
C	-0.987987	0.238687	-4.139252	0.0000
LY	0.135666	0.033063	4.103278	0.0000
LBC(-1)	0.905689	0.019425	46.62404	0.0000
ZCALL	-0.494815	0.083036	-5.959022	0.0000
XINFR(-1)	0.429783	0.213772	2.010477	0.0449
XCOMM2(-1)	0.185615	0.097431	1.905084	0.0573
ZLFUND	0.036560	0.016106	2.269981	0.0236
	Weighted Statistics			
R-squared	0.998639	Mean dependent variable		10.59900
Adjusted R-squared	0.998573	S.D. dependent variable		4.710865
S.E. of regression	0.080375	Sum squared residual		3.307605
F-statistic	15029.34	Durbin-Watson stat		1.690550

Redundant fixed effects test: F stat (df) (probability): 2.60 (19,514)(0.00)

Table 9.6a

State-wise Bank Credit Dispersion
(State-Specific Interest Rate Effect)
Dependent Variable: LBC

Variable	*Coefficient*	*Std. Error*	*t-Statistic*	*Prob.*
C	-1.123072	0.249074	-4.508987	0.0000
LY	0.153152	0.034740	4.408572	0.0000
LBC(-1)	0.887224	0.020211	43.89915	0.0000
XINFR(-1)	0.557231	0.233145	2.390065	0.0172
XCOMM2(-1)	0.220207	0.101906	2.160876	0.0312
ZLFUND	0.044328	0.017034	2.602259	0.0095
r1	-0.619712	0.335830	-1.845314	0.0656
r2	-1.885671	0.686190	-2.748030	0.0062
r3	-0.963961	0.459122	-2.099573	0.0363
r4	-0.371208	0.260386	-1.425607	0.1546
r5	0.122877	0.306525	0.400872	0.6887
r6	-0.581637	0.305046	-1.906718	0.0571
r7	-0.664623	0.350421	-1.896643	0.0585
r8	-0.873400	0.798086	-1.094369	0.2743
r9	-0.600868	0.321898	-1.866641	0.0625
r10	-0.293624	0.214139	-1.371187	0.1709
r11	-0.292390	0.352418	-0.829667	0.4071
r12	-0.723202	0.464962	-1.555400	0.1205
r13	-0.437405	0.692925	-0.631245	0.5282
r14	-2.120058	0.641376	-3.305485	0.0010
r15	-0.862956	0.374651	-2.303361	0.0217
r16	-0.538267	0.305949	-1.759335	0.0791
r17	-0.663949	0.290183	-2.288034	0.0226
r18	-0.050431	0.284380	-0.177337	0.8593
r19	-0.645720	0.309152	-2.088685	0.0372
r20	0.002940	0.298868	0.009838	0.9922
	Weighted Statistics			
R-squared	0.998714	Mean dependent variable		10.54201
Adjusted R-squared	0.998599	S.D. dependent variable		4.763279
S.E. of regression	0.079618	Sum squared residual		3.125114
F-statistic	8702.152	Durbin-Watson statistic		1.725589

Redundant fixed effects test: F stat (df) (probability):1.85 (19,514)(0.02)

In line with the estimation in Table 9.4, the state-specific effects of monetary policy was captured through cross-section state-specific effects of the interest rate, along with the presence of other variables as in Table 9.6. The results are shown in Table 9.6a. It was evident that interest rate had negative association with bank credit for all states. However, not all states had statistically significant impact of interest rate on bank credit. Most of the major advanced states had insignificant interest rate effect on credit. Most of the relatively underdeveloped states had significant inverse relation of interest rate with the credit variable. Thus, on the whole, the empirical findings were in line with the literature on the role of disaggregate transmission mechanism. Also, the empirical findings suggest the asymmetric information and credit rationing hypothesis.

For robustness of the above empirical findings, we estimated the equation in Table 9.5 replacing the state GDP variable with its one-period lag and also two other definitions of the lendable resources, i.e., banks deposits with/without borrowing from the central bank and interbank market less investment in government securities. Empirical estimates showed a strengthening of the effects of infrastructure, commercial activity and interest rate variables but a weakening of the income effect on bank credit (Table 9.7a and Table 9.7b).

Table 9.7a

State Credit Dispersion (With a Lag of State Income)
Dependent Variable: LBC

Variable	*Coefficient*	*Std. Error*	*t-Statistic*	*Prob.*
C	-0.495320	0.228415	-2.168507	0.0306
LY(-1)	0.065909	0.031564	2.088095	0.0373
LBC(-1)	0.913199	0.018802	48.56861	0.0000
ZCALL	-0.507176	0.083727	-6.057511	0.0000
XINFR(-1)	0.547875	0.204827	2.674815	0.0077
XCOMM2(-1)	0.253970	0.092300	2.751569	0.0061
ZLFUND	0.047680	0.015519	3.072366	0.0022
	Weighted Statistics			
R-squared	0.998703	Mean dependent variable		10.60043
Adjusted R-squared	0.998642	S.D. dependent variable		4.713600
S.E. of regression	0.079993	Sum squared residual		3.404234
F-statistic	16385.50	Durbin-Watson statistic		1.709195

Fixed effects test: 2.07 (19,514), (0.001)

Table 9.7b

State Credit Dispersion
(With Availability of Funds including Borrowing)
Dependent Variable: LBC

Variable	*Coefficient*	*Std. Error*	*t-Statistic*	*Prob.*
C	-0.502464	0.228443	-2.199515	0.0283
LY(-1)	0.066741	0.031611	2.111361	0.0352
LBC(-1)	0.917139	0.018281	50.16855	0.0000
XINFR(-1)	0.546355	0.205269	2.661658	0.0080
XCOMM2(-1)	0.258787	0.092240	2.805597	0.0052
ZLFUND1	0.044420	0.015137	2.934569	0.0035
ZCALL	-0.506072	0.083890	-6.032543	0.0000
	Weighted Statistics			
R-squared	0.998701	Mean dependent variable		10.60739
Adjusted R-squared	0.998640	S.D. dependent variable		4.720974
S.E. of regression	0.080082	Sum squared residual		3.411770
F-statistic	16361.83	Durbin-Watson statistic		1.702532

Fixed effects test: 2.03 (19,514), (0.001)

Furthermore, it was evident from Table 9.3 through Table 9.7 that the one period lag of the dependent variable was highly significant. The presence of lag dependent variable could be subjected to non-stationary variables and endogeniety problem. In this regard, as alternative to the equations in Table 9.7, we estimated the state credit in its first difference form explained by the first difference of the two scale variables, i.e., state income and banks' funds. As regards the infrastructure and commercial activity variables, we used the difference between state variable and national average of the states, implying for the importance of relative development of the states in terms of infrastructure and commercial activity. The call money rate being a stationary variable was kept unchanged. The estimated equation is presented in Table 9.8. It was evident that all variables excepting the infrastructure variable were statistically significant with correct sign. The interest rate variable had significant inverse relation with state credit. However, when the cross-section specific effect of the interest rate was allowed, only seven states, mostly underdeveloped ones, showed significant negative interest rate cffcct. For thc rcmaining states, the interest rate had negative but insignificant coefficients. This was in contrast to the findings in Table 9.3

through 9.7. The reason was that the equation in Table 9.8 as compared with earlier equations pertained to short-term variation in credit as compared with both short-run and long-run effects.

Table 9.8

State Credit Dispersion (First Difference Data)
Dependent Variable: LBC

Variable	*Coefficient*	*Std. Error*	*t-Statistic*	*Prob.*
C	0.144974	0.011088	13.07540	0.0000
XINFR(-1)-ZINFR(-1)	-0.120078	0.308444	-0.389301	0.6973
XCOMM2(-1)-ZCOMM2(-1)	0.256626	0.126770	2.024346	0.0438
D(LY(-1))	0.198690	0.070741	2.808696	0.0053
D(ZLFUND)	0.343980	0.040569	8.478846	0.0000
ZCALL/100	-0.598140	0.108932	-5.490960	0.0000
	Weighted Statistics			
R-squared	0.316112	Mean dependent variable		0.219699
Adjusted R-squared	0.260094	S.D. dependent variable		0.112387
S.E. of regression	0.077278	Sum squared residual		1.749747
F-statistic	5.643030	Durbin-Watson statistic		1.735258

Dependent Variable: D(LBC)

Variable	*Coefficient*	*Std. Error*	*t-Statistic*	*Prob.*
C	0.152638	0.011095	13.75795	0.0000
XINFR(-1)-ZINFR(-1)	-0.070706	0.312138	-0.226522	0.8210
XCOMM2(-1)-ZCOMM2(-1)	0.266704	0.128677	2.072655	0.0391
D(LY(-1))	0.195831	0.072426	2.703866	0.0073
D(ZLFUND1)	0.302513	0.039487	7.661112	0.0000
ZCALL	-0.587259	0.110888	-5.295954	0.0000
	Weighted Statistics			
R-squared	0.290130	Mean dependent variable		0.217849
Adjusted R-squared	0.231984	S.D. dependent variable		0.111029
S.E. of regression	0.078041	Sum squared residual		1.784500
F-statistic	4.989654	Durbin-Watson stat		1.670939

In order to examine the effect of anticipated or unanticipated money, we re-estimated the equation in Table 9.7 with one period lag and current interest rate as shown in Table 9.9. It was evident that both current and lag value of interest rate had negative coefficient but the latter was only statistically significant. This result was contrary to standard hypothesis about the effectiveness of monetary policy. With cross-section specific effects of current and lag interest rate, the current interest rate had negative but insignificant coefficient for all states but lag interest rate had significant negative coefficients for all states excluding a few developed states (Annexure Table A-9.1); the latter finding was in line with Table 9.4.

Table 9.9

State Credit Dispersion
(With Current and One Period Lag of Interest Rate)
Dependent Variable: LBC

Variable	*Coefficient*	*Std. Error*	*t-Statistic*	*Prob.*
C	-0.398274	0.207203	-1.922142	0.0551
LY(-1)	0.067610	0.028660	2.359024	0.0187
LBC(-1)	0.928462	0.016686	55.64331	0.0000
XINFR(-1)	0.406192	0.197773	2.053829	0.0405
XCOMM2(-1)	0.190589	0.084648	2.251550	0.0248
ZLFUND1	0.034579	0.013781	2.509139	0.0124
ZCALL	-0.090096	0.086507	-1.041488	0.2981
ZCALL(-1)	-0.892540	0.083173	-10.73111	0.0000
	Weighted Statistics			
R-squared	0.998905	Mean dependent variable		10.90105
Adjusted R-squared	0.998851	S.D. dependent variable		4.675729
S.E. of regression	0.075147	Sum squared residual		2.998585
F-statistic	18631.53	Durbin-Watson statistic		1.853020

Fixed effects test: 1.88 (19,514), (0.01)

V

Conclusion

This study provided a disaggregated analysis of the first stage of monetary transmission mechanism in the Indian context. In line with the literature on bank credit channel, the study used pooled cross-section regression analysis based on data for 20 states over the period 1982 to 2009. The impact of monetary policy through the interest rate on the dispersion of credit to the states was assessed in the presence of other state-specific explanatory variables such as state's income, infrastructure development and commercial activity and also the level of lendable resources of the banking sector, taking into account the role of key demand and supply-side factors affecting the loan market. Empirical results broadly supported asymmetry in the credit and bank lending channel of transmission mechanism as monetary policy induced interest rate impact on credit dispersion was different across the states. The interest rate variable showed inverse relationship with credit allocation to all states. However, the effect was statistically significant for relatively poor states rather than the advanced states. This finding suggests that the poor states are likely to be more affected when a tight money policy occurs. Apart from the monetary policy effect, the study found that economic progress, infrastructure development and the scope for commercial activities had significant influence on bank credit dispersion across the states. These findings have crucial implications for development policy and reform.

References

Ahmed, H. and S.M. Miller (1997). "Monetary and Exchange Rate Policy in Multisectoral Economies", *Journal of Economics and Business* 49.

Ahmed, S. (1987). "Wage Stickiness and the Non-Neutrality of Money: A Cross-Industry Analysis", *Journal of Monetary Economics* 20.

Altissimo, Filippo, Benoit Mojon and Paolo Zaffaroni (2004). "Fast Micro and Slow Macro: Can Aggregation Explain the Persistence of Inflation?". Manuscript. European Central Bank.

Angeloni, I., A. Kashyap and B. Mojon (2003). *Monetary Policy Transmission in the Euro Area*. Cambridge University Press.

Angeloni, I., A. Kashyap, B. Mojon and D. Terlizzese (2002). "Monetary Transmission in the Euro Area: Where do we Stand?", *European Central Bank Working Paper* No. 114.

Angeloni, I., L. Buttiglione, G. Ferri and E. Gaiotti (1995). "The Credit Channel of Monetary Policy across Heterogeneous Banks: the Case of Italy", *Bank of Italy, Temi di discussione* No. 256.

Arnold, I.J.M. and Evert B. Vrugt (2002). "Regional Effects of Monetary Policy in the Netherlands", *International Journal of Business and Economics* 1(2).

Ball, L.N., N.G. Mankiw and D. Romer (1988). "The New Keynesian Economics and the Output-inflation Tradeoff", *Brookings Papers on Economic Activity* (1).

Ball, Laurence and David Romer (1990). "Real Rigidities and the Non-Neutrality of Money", *Review of Economic Studies* 57.

Balke, Nathan S. and Mark A. Wynne (2003). "The Relative Price Effects of Monetary Shocks", *FRB Dallas Working Paper* No. 0306.

Barro, R.J. (1977). "Unanticipated Money Growth and Unemployment in the United States", *American Economic Review* 67(2).

———. (1981). "Unanticipated Money, Output, and the Price Level in the United States", in R. Barro (ed.), *Money, Expectations and Business Cycles*. New York: Academic Press.

Barro, R.J. and M. Rush (1980). "Unanticipated Money and Economic Activity", in Stanley Fischer (ed.), *Rational Expectations and Economic Policy*. Chicago: University of Chicago Press.

Barth, M.J. and V.A. Ramey (2001). "The Cost Channel of Monetary Transmission", in B. Bernanke and K. Rogoff (eds.), *NBER Macroeconomic Annuals* 2001. Cambridge, MA: MIT Press.

Bernanke, B. and M. Gertler (1995). "Inside the Black Box: The Credit Channel of Monetary Policy Transmission", *Journal of Economic Perspectives* 9.

Bernanke, B.S. and A.S. Blinder (1988). "Credit, Money and Aggregate Demand", *American Economic Review Papers and Proceedings* 78.

Bernanke, Ben S. and Alan S. Blinder (1992). "The Federal Funds Rate and the Channels of Monetary Transmission", *American Economic Review* 82(4).

Bernanke, B.S. and M. Gertler (1995). "Inside the Black Box: The Credit Channel of Monetary Policy Transmission", *Journal of Economic Perspectives* 9.

Berument, H., N.B. Ceylan and E.M. Yucel (2004). "The Differential Sectoral Effects of Policy Shocks: Evidence from Turkey", *Working Paper* No. 0703, *Bilkent University, Department of Economics*.

Blinder, A. and Mankiw, N.G. Jan. (1984), "Aggregation and Stabilization Policy in a Multi-contract Economy", *Journal of Monetary Economics* 13(1).

Bodenborn, H. (1995). "A More Perfect Union: Regional Interest Rates in the United States, 1880-1960", in M.D. Bordo, R. Sylla (eds.), *Anglo-American Financial Systems*. New York, NY: Irwin Publishing. pp.415-55.

Brunner, K. and A.H. Meltzer (1963). "The Place of Financial Intermediaries in the Transmission of Monetary Policy", *American Economic Review* 53 (2).

Carlino, G. and R. deFina (1998). "The Differential Regional Effects of Monetary Policy", *Review of Economics and Statistics* 89(4).

————. (1999). "The Differential Regional Effects of Monetary Policy: Evidence from the U.S. states", *Journal of Regional Science* 39.

Caruso, M. (2004). "Monetary Policy Impulses, Local Output and the Transmission Mechanism", *Temi di discussion, del Servizio Studi* 537. Banca D'Italia.

Christiano, Lawrence, Martin Eichenbaum and Charles Evans (1994). "The Effects of Monetary Policy Shocks: Evidence from the Flow of Funds". Northwestern University. March. *mimeo*.

Clarida, R., J. Gali, M. Gertler (1998). "Monetary Policy Rule in Practice: Some International Evidence", *European Economic Review* 42.

Clark, Todd E. (2003). "Disaggregate Evidence on the Persistence of Consumer Price Inflation". Manuscript. Federal Reserve Bank of Kansas City.

Craig, G.A. (1981). "A Monetary Approach to the Balance of Trade", *American Economic Review* 71(3).

Cyrnak, A.W. and T.H. Hannan (1999). "Is the Cluster Still Valid in Defining Banking Markets? Evidence from a New Data Source", *The Antitrust Bulletin* 44(2).

Dale, S. and A.G. Haldane (1995). "Interest Rates and the Channels of Monetary Transmission: Some Sectoral Estimates", *European Economic Review* 39.

Dasgupta, D.P Maiti, R. Mukherjee, S. Sarkar and S. Chakrabarti (2000). "Growth and Inter-state Disparities in India', *Economic and Political Weekly*, July.

David, I.C., J.J. Durand and N. Payelle (2000). *The Heterogeneous Effects of Monetary Policy in the Euro Area : A Sectoral Approach*. France: University of Rennes.

Dedola, L. and F. Lippi (2000). "The Monetary Transmission Mechanism: Evidence from the Industries of five OECD Countries", *Bank of Italy, Temi di discussione* 389.

de Lucio, J.J. and M. Izquierdo (2002). "Local Responses to a Global Monetary Policy: The Regional Structure of Financial Systems", *Journal of Economic Studies* 29: 205-21.

Duca, J.V. (1987). "The Spillover Effects of Nominal Wage Rigidity in a Multisector Economy", *Journal of Money, Credit and Banking* 19(1).

Duca, J.V. and D.D. VanHoose (1990). "Optimal Monetary Policy in a Multisectoral Economy with An economy-wide Money Market", *Journal of Economics and Business* 42(4).

Edgren, G., K.O. Faxen and C. Odhner (1969). "Wages, Growth and the Distribution of Income", *Swedish Journal of Economics* 71(3).

Edwards, S. (1989). "Openness, Outward Orientation, Trade Liberalization and Economic Performance in Developing Countries", *National Bureau of Economic Research (NBER) Working Paper* No. 2908. US.

———. (1989). "Exchange Controls, Devaluations and Real Exchange Rates: the Latin American Experience", *Economic Development and Cultural Change* 37(3).

Ehrmann, M. and M. Ellison (2002). "The Changing Response of US Industry to Monetary Policy", *CEPR Papers*. UK.

Elbourne, A. and J. de Haan (2006). "Financial Structure and Monetary Policy Transmission in Transition Countries", *Journal of Comparative Economics*: 1-23.

Enders, W. and B. Falk (1984). "A Microeconomic Test of Money Neutrality", *The Review of Economics and Statistics* 66(4).

Erceg, C. and A. Levin (2002). "Optimal Monetary Policy with Durable and Non-Durable Goods", *ECB Working Paper* No. 179.

Farès, J. and S. Gabriel (2001). "The Monetary Transmission Mechanism at the Sectoral Level", *Bank of Canada Working Paper* 2001-27.

Fiorentini, R. and R. Tamborini (2001). "The Monetary Transmission Mechanism in Italy: the Credit Channel and a Missing Ring", *Giornale degli Economisti e Annali di Economia* 60(1).

Franco, Francesco and Thomas Philippon (2004). "Firms and Aggregate Dynamics". Manuscript. New York University.

Fuerst T. (1992). "Liquidity, Loanable Funds and Real Activity", *Journal of Monetary Economics* 29(1): 3-24.

Gaiotti, E.G. and A. Generale (2001). "Does Monetary Policy have Asymmetric Effects? A Look at the Investment Decisions of Italian Firms", *European Central Bank (ECB) Working Paper Series* 110.

———. (2003). "Does Monetary Policy have Asymmetric Effects? A Look at the Investment Decisions of Italian Firms", *Giornale degli Economisti e Annali di Economia* 61(1).

Gambacorta, L. (2001). "Bank-specific Characteristics and Monetary Policy Transmission: The Case of Italy", *Bank of Italy, Temi di discussione* 430.

Ganev, G., K. Molnar, K. Rybinski and P. Wozniak (2002). "Transmission Mechanism of Monetary Policy in Central and Eastern Europe", *CASE Reports* No.52.

Ganley, J. and C. Salmon (1997). "The Industrial Impact of Monetary Policy Transmission: the Case of Italy", *Bank of Italy, Temi di discussione* 430.

Garrison, C.B and J.R. Kort (1983). "Regional Impact of Monetary and Fiscal Policy: A Comment", *Journal of Regional Science* 23.

Gauger, J. (1988). "Disaggregate Level Evidence on Monetary Neutrality", *The Review of Economics and Statistics* 70(4).

Gauger, J. and W. Enders (1989). "Money Neutrality at Aggregate and Sectoral Levels," *Southern. Economic Journal* 55, January.

Gerlach, S. and F. Smets (1995). "The Monetary Transmission Mechanism: Evidence from the G-7 Countries", *CEPR Discussion Paper* 1219.

Gertler, M. and S. Gilchrist (1993). "The Role of Credit Market Imperfections in the Monetary Transmission Mechanism Argument and Review", *Scandinavian Journal of Economics* 95(1).

———. (1994). "Monetary Policy, Business Cycles and the Behavior of Small Manufacturing Firms", *Quarterly Journal of Economics* 109(2).

Guiso, L., A. Kashyap, F. Panetta and D. Terlizzese (1999). "Will a Common European Monetary Policy have Asymmetric Effects?", *Economic Perspectives*. Federal Reserve Bank of Chicago.

Hall, B. J. (1993). "Bank Lending and Income Growth: Evidence from Panel Data". Manuscript. Harvard University.

Hayo, B. and B. Uhlenbrock (1999). "Industry Effects of Monetary Policy in Germany", *Center for European Integration Studies Working Paper* No. B 14. Center for European Integration Studies.

Jaroeinski, M. (2006). "Responses to Monetary Policy Shocks to East and West of Europe: A Comparison", *Austrian National Bank, Working Paper* No.124.

Kackmeister, Alan (2001). "Has Retail Price Behavior Changed Since 1889? Evidence from Micro Data". Manuscript. University of California, Berkeley.

Kandil, M. (1991). "Variations in the Response of Real Output to Aggregate Demand Shocks: A Cross Industry Analysis", *Review of Economics and Statistics* 73.

Kashyap, A.K. and J. Stein (1994). "Monetary Policy and Bank Lending", in N.G. Mankiew (ed.), *Monetary Policy*. Chicago: University of Chicago Press.

————. (1995). "The Impact of Monetary Policy on Bank Balance Sheets", *Carnegie-Rochester Conference Series on Public Policy* 42.

————. (2000). "What do a Million Observations on Banks say about the Transmission of Monetary Policy?", *American Economic Review* 90(3).

Kashyap, A.K., J. Stein and D.W. Wilcox (1993). "Monetary Policy and Credit Conditions: Evidence from the Composition of External Finance", *American Economic Review* 83(1).

Kashyap, Anil and Jeremy Stein. "The Impact of Monetary Policy on Bank Balance Sheets", Carnegie Rochester Conference Series on Public Policy. (forthcoming).

Kim, S. (1999). "Do Monetary Policy Shocks Matter in the G-7 Countries? Using Common Identifying Assumptions about Monetary Policy Across Countries", *Journal of International Economics* 48(2).

Kretzmer, P.E. (1989). "The Cross-Industry Effects of Unanticipated Money in an Equilibrium Business Cycle Model", *Journal of Monetary Economics* 23.

Kuppers, M. (2001). "Curtailing the Black Box: German Banking Groups in the Transmission of Monetary Policy", *European Economic Review* 45(10).

Kurian, N.J. (2000). "Widening Regional Disparities in India: Some Indicators", *Economic and Political Weekly*, February.

Lastrapes, William D. (2006). "Inflation and the Distribution of Relative Prices: The Role of Productivity and Money Supply Shocks", *Journal of Money, Credit and Banking* 38(8).

Lilien, D.M. (1982). "Sectoral Shifts and Cyclical Unemployment", *Journal of Political Economy* 90(4).

Linde, J. (2003). "Comment on the Output Composition Puzzle: A Difference in the Monetary Transmission Mechanism in the Euro Area and U.S.", *Journal of Money, Credit, and Banking* 35.

Loo, C.M. and W.D. Lastrapes (1998). "Identifying the Effects of Money Supply Shocks on Industry-Level Output", *Journal of Macroeconomics* 20(3).

Mihov, I. (2001). "Monetary Policy Implementation and Transmission in the European Monetary Union", *Economic Policy* 33.

Misra, B.S. (2003). "Allocative Efficiency of the Indian Banking System in the Post-Reform Period: A State Level Analysis", *Reserve Bank of India Occasional Papers* 24(3), Winter.

Mojon, B. and G. Peersman (2003). "A VAR Description of the Effects of Monetary Policy in the Individual Countries of the Euro Area", in I. Angeloni, A. Kashyap and B. Mojon (ed.), *Monetary Policy Transmission in the Euro Area*. Cambridge, UK: Cambridge University Press.

Morgan, D.P. (1992). "Bank Loan Commitments and the Lending View of Monetary Policy". Manuscript.

Nachane, D.M., P. Ray and S. Ghosh (2002). "Does Monetary Policy Have Differential State-Level Effects? An Empirical Evaluation", *Economic and Political Weekly* 37(47), November.

Narayana, D. (2000). "Banking Sector Reforms and the Emerging Inequalities in Commercial Credit Deployment in India", *Center for Development Studies Working Paper* No. 300. Thiruvananthapuram.

Ostergard, C. (2000). "External Financing Constraints and Bank Loan Supply: Does the Structure of the Banking Sector Matter?". Manuscript. Norwegian School of Management.

Owyang, M. and H.J Wall (2005). "Structural Breaks and Regional Disparities in the Transmission of Monetary Policy", *Federal Reserve Bank of St. Louis Working Paper* 2003-008C.

Peersman, G. and F. Smets (2001). "The Monetary Transmission Mechanism in the Euro Area: More Evidence from VAR Analysis", *ECB Working Paper* No.91.

———. (2002). "The Industry Effects of Monetary Policy in the Euro Area, *European Central Bank, Working Paper*, no.165.

———. (2003). "The Monetary Transmission Mechanism in the Euro Area: More Evidence from VAR Analysis", in I. Angeloni, A. Kashyap and B. Mojon (ed.), *Monetary Policy Transmission in the Euro Area*, Cambridge, UK: Cambridge University Press. pp.36-55.

———. (2005). "The Industry Effects of Monetary Policy in Euro Area", *Economic Journal*.

Pratantoni, M. and S. Schuh (2003). "Monetary Policy, Housing and Heterogeneous Regional Markets", *Journal of Money, Credit and Banking* 35(4).

Rajan, R. and L. Zingales (1998). "Financial Dependence and Growth", *American Economic Review* 88.

Ramaswamy, R. and T. Sloek (1997). "The Real Effects of Monetary Policy in the European Union: What Are the Differences", *IMF Working Paper* No.160. Washington: IMF.

Rudebusch, G. (1998). "Do Measures of Monetary Policy in a VAR Make Sense?", *International Economic Review* 39.

Samolyk, K. (1989). "The Role of Banks in Influencing the Regional Flow of Funds", *Federal Reserve Bank of Cleveland Working Paper* No. 89/14, November.

———. (1994). "Banking Conditions of Regional Economic Performance: Evidence of a Regional Credit Channel", *Journal of Monetary Economics* 34(3).

Schultze, C.L. May (1984). "Cross-country and Cross-temporal Differences in Inflation Responsiveness", *American Economic Review* 74(2).

Shand, R. and S. Bhide (2000). "Sources of Economic Growth: Regional Dimensions of Reforms", *Economic and Political Weekly*, October.

Shelley, G.L. and F. H. Wallace (1998). "Tests of the Money-Output Relation Using Disaggregated Data", *The Quarterly Review of Economics and Finance* 38(4).

Stiglitz, J. and A. Weiss (1981). "Credit Rationing in Markets with Imperfect Information", *American Economic Review* 71: 393-410

Taylor, L.L. and M.K. Yucel (1996). "The Policy Sensitivity of Industries and Regions", *Working Paper* No.12. Federal Reserve Bank of Dallas.

Waller, C.J. (1992). "The Choice of Conservative Central Banker in a Multisectoral Economy", *American Economic Review* 82(4).

Annexure Table A-9.1

Dependent Variable: LBC

Method: Pooled EGLS (Cross-section weights); Sample (adjusted): 1982 2009; Total pool (unbalanced) observations: 558; Linear estimation after one-step weighting matrix; Cross-section weights (PCSE) standard errors & covariance (d.f. corrected)

Variable	*Coefficient*	*Std. Error*	*t-Statistic*	*Prob.*
C	-0.506065	0.223616	-2.263101	0.0241
LY(-1)	0.080387	0.031259	2.571680	0.0104
LBC(-1)	0.909581	0.017595	51.69665	0.0000
XINFR(-1)	0.638231	0.220116	2.899515	0.0039
XCOMM2(-1)	0.266095	0.092251	2.884452	0.0041
ZLFUND1	0.042152	0.014773	2.853224	0.0045
S1—ZCALL	-0.282634	0.380207	-0.743370	0.4576
S2—ZCALL	-1.001682	0.755599	-1.325680	0.1856
S3—ZCALL	-0.114523	0.453120	-0.252744	0.8006
S4—ZCALL	-0.162421	0.299057	-0.543111	0.5873
S5—ZCALL	0.368221	0.361483	1.018638	0.3089
S6—ZCALL	-0.122465	0.321040	-0.381464	0.7030
S7—ZCALL	-0.159242	0.385068	-0.413544	0.6794
S8—ZCALL	-0.785289	0.970919	-0.808809	0.4190
S9—ZCALL	-0.235972	0.337807	-0.698539	0.4852
S10—ZCALL	-0.343036	0.252660	-1.357699	0.1752
S11—ZCALL	0.375012	0.333540	1.124340	0.2614
S12—ZCALL	-0.024228	0.514069	-0.047129	0.9624
S13—ZCALL	0.039586	0.828697	0.047769	0.9619
S14—ZCALL	-1.624168	0.743214	-2.185331	0.0293
S15—ZCALL	-0.131421	0.390946	-0.336161	0.7369
S16—ZCALL	-0.215165	0.342862	-0.627556	0.5306
S17—ZCALL	-0.226062	0.318624	-0.709495	0.4784
S18—ZCALL	0.443735	0.303975	1.459774	0.1450
S19—ZCALL	-0.070432	0.283785	-0.248186	0.8041
S20—ZCALL	0.264170	0.307313	0.859611	0.3904
S1—ZCALL	-0.890093	0.380204	-2.341092	0.0196
S2—ZCALL	-1.382873	0.756577	-1.827803	0.0682
S3—ZCALL	-1.513683	0.449814	-3.365130	0.0008
S4—ZCALL	-0.468317	0.296074	-1.581755	0.1143

contd...

...contd...

Variable	*Coefficient*	*Std. Error*	*t-Statistic*	*Prob.*
S5—ZCALL	-0.975496	0.365407	-2.669617	0.0078
S6—ZCALL	-0.993655	0.319533	-3.109714	0.0020
S7—ZCALL	-1.021074	0.383653	-2.661452	0.0080
S8—ZCALL	-0.164862	0.969239	-0.170094	0.8650
S9—ZCALL	-0.761758	0.337573	-2.256572	0.0245
S10—ZCALL	-0.020533	0.248007	-0.082790	0.9341
S11—ZCALL	-1.292537	0.332157	-3.891345	0.0001
S12—ZCALL	-1.342114	0.512955	-2.616434	0.0092
S13—ZCALL	-0.917299	0.821157	-1.117081	0.2645
S14—ZCALL	-0.897899	0.750215	-1.196857	0.2319
S15-ZCALL	-1.348918	0.387806	-3.478335	0.0005
S16-ZCALL	-0.541691	0.342705	-1.580634	0.1146
S17—ZCALL	-0.906436	0.318302	-2.847725	0.0046
S18—ZCALL	-1.015612	0.302771	-3.354385	0.0009
S19—ZCALL	-1.125477	0.282137	-3.989114	0.0001
S20—ZCALL	-0.756731	0.304726	-2.483312	0.0133

Weighted Statistics

R-squared	0.998997	Mean dependent variable	10.93572
Adjusted R-squared	0.998867	S.D. dependent variable	4.855600
S.E. of regression	0.074842	Sum squared residual	2.761446
F-statistic	7673.807	Durbin-Watson stat	1.895615

Note: Fixed effect for intercept not reported.

Section III

Financial Inclusion

10 Financial Inclusion in Jammu and Kashmir

JOHN V. GURIA[1]

I

Introduction

Financial inclusion is a necessary condition for sustaining equitable growth. Lack of access to finance for small/marginal farmers and weaker sections of the society has been recognised as a serious threat to economic progress especially developing countries. Moreover, prolonged and persistent deprivation of financial services to a large segment of the population has the potential to fuel social tensions causing social exclusion. Financial inclusion is an explicit strategy for accelerated economic growth and is considered to be critical for achieving inclusive growth in the country.

Financial inclusion has been defined in opposite way, i.e., financial exclusion. Broadly defined, financial exclusion signifies the lack of access by certain segments of the society to appropriate, low-cost, fair and safe financial products and services from mainstream providers (Mohan, 2006). Financial exclusion leads to higher cost for operating a household, or a micro/small enterprise. It complicates day-to-day cash flow management—being financially excluded means households, and micro and small enterprises deal entirely in cash and are susceptible to irregular cash flows. The lack of financial planning and security in the absence of access to bank accounts and other saving opportunities for people in the unorganised sector limit their options for providing for themselves for their old age.

1. The views expressed in this paper are of the author himself and not of the organisation he is working with. Author thanks Shri B.M. Misra, Officer-in-Charge and Shri K.U.B. Rao, Adviser, for their encouragement and support.

The Committee on Financial Inclusion, 2008 (Chairman: C Rangarajan) defines financial inclusion as 'the process of ensuring access to financial services and timely and adequate credit where needed by vulnerable groups such as weaker sections and low income groups at an affordable cost.'

Access to financial services is especially powerful for the poor as it provides them opportunities to build savings, make investments and avail credit. Importantly, access to financial services also helps the poor insure themselves against income shocks and equips them to meet emergencies. Financial inclusion also protects the poor from the clutches of the usurious moneylenders.

Furthermore, financial inclusion provides an avenue for bringing the savings of the poor into the formal financial intermediation system and channel them into investment. Second, the large number of low cost deposits will offer banks an opportunity to reduce their dependence on bulk deposits and help them to better manage both liquidity risks and asset-liability mismatches.

The present study is an attempt to analyse the status and progress of financial inclusion in India with special reference to Jammu and Kashmir state. In this direction, the status and progress of financial inclusion in Jammu and Kashmir has been analysed with various parameters and cross states/UTs and district-wise comparison. There has been an attempt to construct a Financial Inclusion Index (FII) to capture various dimensions of financial inclusion for all states/UTs and all districts of Jammu and Kashmir. The various initiatives towards achieving 100 per cent financial inclusion in the state have also been analysed in the study.

The study has been divided into seven sections. The present section is an introduction. The basic characteristics of Jammu and Kashmir have been presented in Section II. The status and progress on financial inclusion in Jammu and Kashmir has been analysed in Section III. Section IV analyses the status of financial inclusion in Jammu and Kashmir with cross states/UTs comparison with various parameters. An attempt has been made to construct a Financial Inclusion Index (FII) for all states/UTs and all districts of Jammu and Kashmir in Section V. The various initiatives towards achieving 100 per cent financial inclusion in the state by the

Reserve Bank and banking sector have been presented in Section VI. Section VII makes concluding observations and policy recommendations for further intensifying the steps towards achieving 100 per cent financial inclusion in Jammu and Kashmir.

II

Basic Characteristics of Jammu and Kashmir

Jammu and Kashmir is the northernmost state of India. The total area of the state is 2,22,236 sq km including 78,114 sq km under the illegal occupation of Pakistan and 42,735 sq km under that of China. The state is bounded by Pakistan, Afghanistan and China from the West to the East. As per Census 2011, total population of the state stands at 1,25,48,926, constituting 1.04 per cent of total population of India. The population density in the state stands at 124 persons per sq km, lower as compared to all-India level of 382 persons per sq km. The sex ratio of the state is 883 females per 1,000 males, lower as compared to all-India level of 940 females per 1,000 males. The literacy rate in the state also stands lower as compared to all-India level. The literacy rate in Jammu and Kashmir stands at 68.7 per cent (78.3 per cent for males and 58.0 per cent for females), while it is 74.0 per cent (82.1 for males and 65.5 per cent for females) for all-India. As per the estimates by Planning Commission of India for the year 2004-05, 5.4 per cent of total population in the state are below poverty line. The poverty ratio is higher in urban areas than rural areas. The poverty ratio in urban areas stands at 7.9 per cent, whereas it is 4.6 per cent in rural areas. As per Census 2001, the total workforce as percentage of total population in Jammu and Kashmir is 37.0 per cent. Jammu and Kashmir is basically an agrarian economy. As per Census 2001, 18.4 lakh persons, i.e., 49 per cent of total workforce comprising 15.9 lakh cultivators and 2.5 lakh agricultural labourers depend directly on agriculture.

Jammu and Kashmir has three regions *viz.*, Jammu, Kashmir and Ladakh, and two divisions, *viz.*, Jammu and Kashmir. There are at present 22 districts in the state—10 in Jammu region, 10 in Kashmir region and two in Ladakh region. The districts under Jammu region are Kathua,

Jammu, Samba, Udhampur, Reasi, Rajouri, Poonch, Doda, Ramban and Kishtwar, whereas districts under Kashmir region are Anantnag, Kulgam, Pulwama, Shopian, Budgam, Srinagar, Ganderbal, Bandipora, Baramulla and Kupwara. The two districts of Ladakh region are Kargil and Leh. The state has 82 *tehsils*, 142 blocks, 6,886 villages and 68 urban areas. Srinagar is the summer capital, whereas Jammu is the winter capital of the state.

State Domestic Product (SDP) and Per Capita Income

The SDP and the per capita income of Jammu and Kashmir have witnessed a continuous increase over the years. The real gross state domestic product (GSDP) has been growing by more than 6 per cent since 2005-06 (Table 10.1).

Table 10.1

State Domestic Product and Per Capita Income: Jammu and Kashmir

Item	*Year*				
	2004-05	*2005-06*	*2006-07 (QE)*	*2007-08 (PE)*	*2008-09 (PE)*
1	*2*	*3*	*4*	*5*	*6*
GSDP at current prices (Rs crore)	24265 (9.3)	26537 (9.4)	29030 (9.4)	31793 (9.5)	34805 (9.5)
GSDP at constant 1999-2000 prices (Rs crore)	19234 (5.2)	20421 (6.2)	21698 (6.3)	23060 (6.3)	24471 (6.1)
NSDP at constant 1999-2000 prices (Rs crore)	16519 (5.4)	17497 (5.9)	18557 (6.1)	19687 (6.1)	20889 (6.1)
Per capita NSDP at constant 1999-2000 prices (Rs)	15414 (3.8)	16086 (4.4)	16817 (4.5)	17590 (4.6)	18405 (4.6)

Note: QE: Quick Estimates. PE: Preliminary Estimates.
Figures in parentheses are growth rates in per cent.

Source: Directorate of Economics and Statistics, Jammu and Kashmir.

Sectoral composition and growth in SDP: The contribution of services sector to NSDP has been highest in Jammu and Kashmir. The share of agriculture and allied activities sector has continuously declined, whereas that of industry has continuously increased (Table 10.2).

Table 10.2

Sectoral Composition of NSDP: Jammu and Kashmir (At Constant 1999-2000 Prices)

(Per cent)

Sector	Year				
	2004-05	2005-06	2006-07 (QE)	2007-08 (PE)	2008-09 (PE)
1	2	3	4	5	6
Agriculture and allied activities	32.1	30.7	29.8	28.6	27.4
Industry	22.0	22.7	23.7	24.9	25.9
Services	45.9	46.6	46.5	46.6	46.7

Note: QE: Quick Estimates. PE: Preliminary Estimates.

Source: Directorate of Economics and Statistics, Jammu and Kashmir.

In Jammu and Kashmir, industry has been the fastest growing sector followed by services sector as evidenced by sectoral growth in NSDP at constant (1999-2000) prices (Table 10.3). The leading contributing sector in growth of industry has been mining & quarrying followed by manufacturing and construction, whereas in growth of services sector, the leading sectors are transport, storage & communication, trade, hotels & restaurants and banking & insurance (Annexure Table A-10.1).

Table 10.3

Sectoral Growth in NSDP: Jammu and Kashmir (At Constant 1999-2000 Prices)

(Per cent)

Sector	Year					
	2003-04	2004-05	2005-06	2006-07 (QE)	2007-08 (PE)	2008-09 (PE)
1	2	3	4	5	6	7
Agriculture and allied activities	7.3	1.1	1.3	2.9	1.8	1.8
Industry	5.0	18.8	9.5	10.4	11.4	10.7
Services	3.7	2.9	7.4	6.0	6.1	6.3

Note: QE: Quick Estimates. PE: Preliminary Estimates.

Source: Directorate of Economics and Statistics, Jammu and Kashmir.

Gross District Domestic Product (GDDP) and Per Capita GDDP

As per estimates for the year 2007-08 at constant (1999-2000) prices for 14 districts in the state, Jammu has the highest GDDP and per capita GDDP followed by Srinagar, whereas Kargil and Kupwara have the lowest GDDP and per capita GDDP respectively (Table 10.4).

Table 10.4

Gross District Domestic Product (GDDP) and Per Capita GDDP (2007-08): Jammu and Kashmir (At Constant 1999-2000 Prices)

District	GDDP (Rs crore)	Per Capita GDDP (Rs)
1	2	3
Anantnag	2190	16782
Baramulla	2347	18092
Budgam	1181	16965
Doda	1403	18484
Jammu	5075	28997
Kargil	323	14486*
Kathua	1498	25355
Kupwara	1048	14225
Leh	376	18668*
Poonch	679	16549
Pulwama	1246	17455
Rajouri	881	16710
Srinagar	3027	22809
Udhampur	1787	21904
Jammu and Kashmir	23060	20604

Note: *: Adjusted figure.

Source: *Economic Survey 2010-11*, Government of Jammu and Kashmir.

III

Status of Financial Inclusion in Jammu and Kashmir

Growth of Banking Sector

The banking sector in Jammu and Kashmir state has witnessed a significant expansion over the years. The number of bank offices, which was 821 at end-December 2001, increased to 978 at end-December 2009. The deposits per bank office as well as credit per bank office witnessed an improvement in the period 2001 to 2009. The deposits per bank office and credit per bank office, which was Rs 12.9 crore and Rs 4.9 crore respectively at end-December 2001, increased to Rs 31.6 crore and Rs 15.1 crore respectively at end-December 2009. The credit-deposit (C-D) ratio, which was 38.2 per cent at end-December 2001, rose to 47.8 per cent at end-December 2009 (Table 10.5).

Table 10.5

Growth of Banking Sector: Jammu and Kashmir

Year (As at End-December)	Bank Offices (No.)	Deposits per Bank Office (Rs crore)	Credit per Bank Office (Rs crore)	C-D Ratio (per cent)
1	2	3	4	5
2001	821	12.9	4.9	38.2
2002	832	14.7	5.3	36.4
2003	840	16.1	6.3	38.8
2004	854	18.2	7.1	39.1
2005	852	20.2	8.9	44.3
2006	866	22.8	11.0	48.3
2007	906	25.2	12.6	49.8
2008	944	27.4	13.6	49.6
2009	978	31.6	15.1	47.8

Source: *Quarterly Statistics on Deposits and Credit of Scheduled Commercial Banks*, Reserve Bank of India. Author's calculations.

During the period 1999 to 2009, the number of deposits and credit accounts witnessed a positive annual growth of 5.0 per cent and 6.8 per cent respectively in Jammu and Kashmir. During the same period, the rural areas showed the lowest annual growth in number of deposits and credit accounts with 3.3 per cent and 4.2 per cent respectively as compared to semi-urban and urban areas of Jammu and Kashmir, indicating higher growth of banking sector towards urban and semi-urban areas. During the same period, the annual growth in deposits accounts in rural areas of Jammu and Kashmir was lower as compared to that in northern region (4.0%) and all-India level (5.0%); however, the growth in credit accounts was higher in rural areas of Jammu and Kashmir as compared to that in northern region (3.9%) and all-India level (3.3%) (Table 10.6).

Table 10.6

Population Group-wise Deposits and Credit Accounts in Jammu and Kashmir vis-à-vis Northern Region and All-India

Population Group	*Deposits Accounts (No.)*		*Credit Accounts (No.)*		*CAGR (per cent)*	
	1999	*2009*	*1999*	*2009*	*Deposits Accounts 1999-2009*	*Credit Accounts 1999-2009*
1	*2*	*3*	*4*	*5*	*6*	*7*
Rural						
Jammu and Kashmir	2241947	3116763	167721	254192	3.3	4.2
Northern region	18869570	27871250	2470956	3623888	4.0	3.9
All-India	122660091	199695080	24473040	33822539	5.0	3.3
Semi-urban						
Jammu and Kashmir	544228	1659996	39514	127967	11.8	12.5
Northern region	16327384	23722562	1357952	2388250	3.8	5.8
All-India	112375849	169724911	14457568	24792743	4.2	5.5
Urban/Metropolitan						
Jammu and Kashmir	1582266	2330740	97514	205928	3.9	7.8
Northern region	35621057	58835279	2180321	5653429	5.1	10.0
All-India	170871985	292882413	13374848	51440895	5.5	14.4
Total						
Jammu and Kashmir	4368441	7107499	304749	588087	5.0	6.8
Northern region	70818011	110429091	6009229	11665567	4.5	6.9
All-India	405907925	662302404	52305456	110056177	5.0	7.7

Note: There is no metropolitan centre in Jammu and Kashmir.

Source: *Basic Statistical Returns of Scheduled Commercial Banks in India*, Reserve Bank of India. Author's calculations.

Geographic Outreach

In Jammu and Kashmir, the outreach of banking sector is more towards its major cities and districts *viz.*, Srinagar and Jammu. The average area per bank branch for Jammu and Kashmir stands at 104.2 sq km (as at end-March 2009), whereas average area per ATM is 342.2 sq km (as at end-June 2010). Among 22 districts of the state, in terms of average area per bank branch, Srinagar ranks at the top position with 7.9 sq km, while Leh stands at the bottom position with 2,819.4 sq km. In terms of average area per

ATM, Jammu stands at the highest position with 15.1 sq km, while Leh ranks at the lowest position with 5,012.2 sq km (Table 10.7).

Table 10.7

Outreach of Banking Sector: Jammu and Kashmir

District	*Geographic Outreach*		*Demographic Outreach*			
	*Average Area per Bank Branch** *(sq km)*	*Average Area per ATM (sq km)*	*Average Population per Bank Branch*('000)*	*Average Population per ATM @('000)*	*Percentage of Population having Deposits Account**	*Percentage of Population having Credit Account**
1	2	3	4	5	6	7
1. Anantnag	45.6	132.6	14.3	45.1	43.6	4.6
2. Bandipora	24.9	199.0	27.2	200.3	24.8	2.1
3. Baramulla	45.5	149.6	10.9	38.6	44.6	4.8
4. Budgam	38.1	80.6	20.8	46.9	34.6	3.3
5. Doda	157.1	373.1	20.8	45.3	36.1	2.7
6. Ganderbal	45.4	174.2	11.4	44.9	45.0	4.1
7. Jammu	11.7	15.1	8.4	11.1	109.8	7.8
8. Kargil	1276.0	2339.3	13.4	25.2	45.1	3.1
9. Kathua	49.1	250.2	12.4	64.8	60.0	3.4
10. Kishtwar	967.1	1934.3	29.4	60.4	36.6	2.5
11. Kulgam	39.5	355.7	19.7	164.2	25.7	2.3
12. Kupwara	54.1	396.5	18.2	137.3	32.4	2.9
13. Leh	2819.4^	5012.2^	9.0	16.5	86.6	5.0
14. Poonch	83.7	836.5	23.0	235.9	37.1	3.3
15. Pulwama	31.0	90.5	15.6	46.6	40.2	4.4
16. Rajouri	65.8	239.1	14.9	55.6	43.0	3.2
17. Ramban	84.1	336.5	16.6	68.0	40.1	2.0
18. Reasi	73.9	130.8	13.3	24.1	39.7	2.7
19. Samba	32.5	75.8	12.0	28.5	69.3	3.6
20. Shopian	19.5	156.0	16.3	133.8	31.3	3.7
21. Srinagar	7.9	15.4	8.4	16.3	101.1	9.7
22. Udhampur	63.4	107.5	14.5	27.3	50.2	3.6
Jammu and Kashmir	104.2^^	342.2^^	12.9	31.6	56.8	4.7

Note: *: As at end-March 2009. @: As at end-June 2010.
^: Excludes area under illegal occupation of China.
^^: Excludes areas under illegal occupation of Pakistan and China.

Source: 1. *Digest of Statistics 2008-09*, Government of Jammu and Kashmir.
2. *Branch Banking Statistics*, 2010, Reserve Bank of India.
3. *Basic Statistical Returns of Scheduled Commercial Banks in India*, 2010, Reserve Bank of India.
4. Number of ATM figures provided by various banks operating in Jammu and Kashmir state.
5. Author's calculations.

Demographic Outreach

The average population per bank branch for Jammu and Kashmir state stands at 12.9 thousand persons (as at end-March 2009), whereas average population per ATM is 31.6 thousand persons (as at end-June 2010). In terms of average population per bank branch, Srinagar and Jammu with 8.4 thousand persons hold the top position, while Kishtwar with 29.4 thousand persons holds the lowest position. In terms of average population per ATM, Jammu ranks the highest position with 11.1 thousand persons, while Poonch stands at the lowest rank with 235.9 thousand persons. In Jammu and Kashmir, 56.8 per cent of total population are having deposits accounts, whereas only 4.7 per cent population have their credit accounts. In Jammu, highest 109.8 per cent population are having deposits accounts, while only 24.8 per cent population have their deposits accounts in Bandipora. Srinagar with 9.7 per cent of population having credit accounts ranks at the highest position, while Ramban with only 2.0 per cent of total population having their credit accounts ranks the lowest position (Table 10.7).

Position of Unbanked Villages

The Jammu and Kashmir State Level Bankers' Committee (J&KSLBC) has identified 795 unbanked villages with population of 2,000 and above as per Census 2001 (i.e., 11.5 per cent of total villages in the state). The percentage of unbanked villages to total number of villages is highest in Ramban with 36.5 per cent followed by Poonch with 31.8 per cent (Table 10.8).

Deposits-GDDP Ratio and Credit-GDDP Ratio

As per estimates for the year 2005-06, deposits-GDDP ratio was highest for Srinagar (129.5%) followed by Jammu (107.7%), whereas it was lowest in Kupwara (26.3%) preceded by Anantnag (34.1%). The credit-GDDP ratio was highest for Srinagar (113.2%) followed by Jammu (32.7%), whereas it was lowest for Kargil (5.1%) after Doda (6.0%). The contribution of banking (including insurance) sector to GDDP is highest in Jammu with 7.8 per cent followed by Srinagar (6.3%) (Table 10.8). This is also an indication of banking growth towards major cities and districts in Jammu and Kashmir.

Table 10.8

Outreach of Banking Sector: Jammu and Kashmir

District	*Deposits-GDDP Ratio* (per cent)*	*Credit-GDDP Ratio* (per cent)*	*C-D Ratio# (per cent)*	*Unbanked Villages@ (No.)*	*Contribution of Banking (including Insurance) Sector to GDDP* (per cent)*
1	2	3	4	5	6
1. Anantnag	34.1	12.4	41.9	76 (19.2)	2.3
2. Bandipora	-	-	59.6	29 (23.4)	-
3. Baramulla	36.2	12.5	51.4	54 (10.1)	2.0
4. Budgam	46.6	17.1	48.0	62 (13.0)	2.4
5. Doda	34.3	6.0	17.8	23 (5.8)	0.7
6. Ganderbal	-	-	58.2	38 (27.9)	-
7. Jammu	107.7	32.7	34.4	87 (9.8)	7.8
8. Kargil	42.6	5.1	14.6	0 (0.0)	1.0
9. Kathua	43.7	16.3	34.2	42 (7.1)	2.8
10. Kishtwar	-	-	15.1	34 (21.8)	-
11. Kulgam	-	-	43.7	38 (14.7)	-
12. Kupwara	26.3	6.2	45.6	55 (14.6)	1.2
13. Leh	78.5	12.2	18.8	0 (0.0)	2.9
14. Poonch	38.0	6.9	22.2	56 (31.8)	1.6
15. Pulwama	36.4	16.3	44.1	40 (11.9)	1.3
16. Rajouri	44.9	7.2	24.3	55 (14.1)	1.5
17. Ramban	-	-	18.5	35 (36.5)	-
18. Reasi	-	-	29.3	4 (1.6)	-
19. Samba	-	-	46.8	3 (0.9)	-
20. Shopian	-	-	56.1	20 (8.7)	-
21. Srinagar	129.5	113.2	82.0	13 (9.6)	6.3
22. Udhampur	44.3	8.8	23.7	31 (8.8)	2.6
Jammu and Kashmir	64.7	28.6	47.8	795 (11.5)	3.7

Note: *: At constant (1999-2000) prices for the year 2005-06.

@: Number of unbanked villages with population over 2000 as per Census 2001.

#: As at end-December 2009.

-: Indicates that corresponding district was not in existence for the corresponding year.

Figures in parentheses are percentage share of unbanked villages to corresponding districts/state.

Source: 1. *Quarterly Statistics on Deposits and Credit of Scheduled Commercial Banks*, Reserve Bank of India.

2. *Economic Survey 2009-10*, Government of Jammu and Kashmir.

3. Jammu and Kashmir State Level Bankers' Committee.

4. Author's calculations.

Position of No-Frills Accounts

As at end-March 2011, banks in Jammu and Kashmir had opened 10,53,121 no-frills accounts with a deposit amount of Rs 167.42 crore. Out of these accounts, 69.8 per cent accounts were opened by private sector banks followed by RRBs (19.2%), public sector banks (7.2%) and cooperative banks (3.8%).

Performance under Kissan Credit Cards (KCCs) Scheme

As at end-March 2011, banks in Jammu and Kashmir had issued 1,43,048 Kissan Credit Cards (KCCs). As per the figures of J&KSLBC, the performance by banks and financial institutions operating in Jammu and Kashmir state under KCCs scheme *vis-à-vis* Annual Credit Plans during the last eight years from 2002-03 to 2009-10 was not satisfactory. The financial achievement was highest in 2002-03 with 47 per cent, thereafter, it had been lower.

Position of General Credit Cards (GCCs)

RRBs in the state are playing the leading role in issuing General Credit Cards (GCCs). As at end-March 2011, out of 13,231 GCCs issued in the state, 91.1 per cent cards were issued by RRBs.

IV

Financial Inclusion: Cross States/UTs Comparison

The present section analyses the status of financial inclusion in Jammu and Kashmir state with cross states/UTs comparison in terms of outreach of banking sector.

The cross states/UTs comparison shows that the demographic outreach of banking sector in Jammu and Kashmir is in better position as compared to all-India level. As at end-March 2009, the average population per bank branch stood at 13 thousand persons for Jammu and Kashmir, whereas it was 15 thousand persons for all-India. However, in terms of geographic outreach of banking sector, Jammu and Kashmir is in a worse position as compared to all-India. As at end-March 2009, average area per bank branch in Jammu and Kashmir stood at 104.2 sq km, whereas it was 39.7 sq km for all-India. In

Table 10.9

Outreach of Banking Sector: Cross States/UTs Comparison
(As at End-March 2009)

State/UT	Share in All-India Population (per cent)	Average Population per Bank Branch ('000)	Average Area per Bank Branch (sq km)	Percentage of Population having Deposits Account	Percentage of Population having Credit Account	Deposits per Account (Rs)	Credit per Account (Rs)	Per Capita Deposits (Rs)	Per Capita Credit (Rs)
1	2	3	4	5	6	7	8	9	10
Andaman and Nicobar Islands	0.04	11	222.9	56.8	5.3	53608	182707	30438	9652
Andhra Pradesh	7.17	13	42.2	72.4	14.4	36264	175117	26251	25293
Arunachal Pradesh	0.10	16	1101.9	43.0	4.7	68603	160494	29496	7525
Assam	2.57	22	57.0	38.5	4.4	34179	116247	13170	5072
Bihar	8.19	25	24.6	28.5	4.0	32178	61404	9156	2453
Chandigarh	0.11	4	0.4	173.3	14.7	123693	1679303	214418	246526
Chhattisgarh	2.03	20	111.1	34.4	4.0	48269	191297	16591	7687
Dadra and Nagar Haveli	0.03	11	20.5	70.9	1.6	34412	277405	24415	4425
Daman and Diu	0.02	11	6.2	91.7	1.8	55230	548709	50629	9766
Delhi	1.50	8	0.7	142.1	15.3	207890	1333188	295368	203649
Goa	0.14	4	9.1	200.6	11.2	71318	340365	143034	38140
Gujarat	4.95	13	45.2	64.9	5.6	50160	369018	32539	20721
Haryana	2.12	11	20.6	70.3	6.6	50263	326583	35356	21697
Himachal Pradesh	0.57	7	58.6	81.9	8.4	43511	164618	35656	13753
Jammu and Kashmir	0.98	13	104.2*	62.3	5.1	41183	235331	25645	12093
Jharkhand	2.64	18	46.8	41.3	4.3	43569	133107	18002	5769
Karnataka	5.01	10	33.3	75.4	14.6	58439	234025	44078	34067

contd...

...contd...

1	2	3	4	5	6	7	8	9	10
Kerala	2.93	9	9.6	85.0	16.7	46663	141529	39667	23695
Lakshadweep	0.01	6	2.9	57.9	6.2	110417	55656	63939	3444
Madhya Pradesh	6.02	18	77.9	37.2	5.0	38567	164002	14347	8230
Maharashtra	9.44	14	40.8	63.3	25.4	143878	326696	91100	83100
Manipur	0.21	33	279.1	20.6	3.1	51163	122863	10545	3799
Meghalaya	0.22	13	111.6	35.8	4.5	67764	152159	24237	6849
Mizoram	0.08	11	226.7	33.0	6.1	54730	170093	18049	10446
Nagaland	0.19	26	192.8	21.9	4.2	71620	116122	15671	4827
Orissa	3.45	15	57.9	43.0	7.7	40726	115858	17517	8906
Puducherry	0.11	9	3.9	93.6	16.2	46021	136563	43097	22152
Punjab	2.33	8	15.5	96.2	7.7	46220	377672	44487	29220
Rajasthan	5.66	17	87.8	41.9	5.3	33368	212996	13980	11271
Sikkim	0.05	8	99.9	48.2	6.1	87598	288539	42180	17542
Tamil Nadu	5.73	11	22.1	78.4	19.2	47023	207222	36874	39859
Tripura	0.30	17	49.2	48.1	8.6	37080	63798	17820	5472
Uttar Pradesh	16.69	20	24.9	48.5	4.6	28010	123431	13577	5735
Uttarakhand	0.83	9	49.4	72.1	7.5	64455	157660	46474	11753
West Bengal	7.57	18	17.7	53.1	4.5	49006	352922	26012	15798
All-India	100.00	15	39.7*	57.1	9.5	59217	258751	33786	24532

Note: *: Excludes area under illegal occupation of Pakistan and China.

Source: 1. Projected population figures for 2009 provided in Census 2001.

2. *Basic Statistical Returns of Scheduled Commercial Banks in India*, Reserve Bank of India.
3. *Branch Banking Statistics*, Reserve Bank of India.
4. Author's calculations.

terms of percentage of population with deposits accounts, Jammu and Kashmir is in better position as compared to all-India level, whereas it is lagging behind all-India level in percentage of population having credit accounts, deposits per account, credit per account, per capita deposits and per capita credit (Table 10.9).

V

Financial Inclusion Index (FII): Across States/UTs and Districts of Jammu and Kashmir

With a view to assess the status and progress of financial inclusion across all states/UTs and all districts of Jammu and Kashmir, an attempt has been made in this section to construct a Financial Inclusion Index (FII) that can capture all dimensions of financial inclusion including 'coverage', 'access and availability' and 'use' of financial services.

Financial Inclusion Index: Methodology and Data

The methodology adopted to construct FII is similar to the one adopted by United Nations Development Programme (UNDP) for constructing the Human Development Index (HDI) up until its Report 2009. First, a dimension index of the indicators used to capture financial inclusion has been constructed, and then the FII is computed as a weighted average of the dimension indices.

The dimension index for the ith dimension, D_i has been computed by the following formula:

$$D_i = (X_i - X_{min})/(X_{max} - X_{min})$$

Where,

D_i = Dimension Index,

X_i = Actual value of ith dimension,

X_{min} = Minimum value of ith dimension and

X_{max} = Maximum value of ith dimension.

The FII is the weighted average of the dimension indices, where the weights are equal. The formula for calculating FII is given as under:

Financial Inclusion Index (FII) $= 1/n. \sum D_i$

Where,

D_i = Dimension Index and

n = Number of dimensions.

Dimensions of financial inclusion: The FII is a summary measure of financial inclusion. It measures the average achievements in a state/UT or district in the following three dimensions of financial inclusion:

1. *Coverage:* An inclusive financial system should have a broader coverage. To capture coverage, percentage of population having deposits account and percentage of population having credit account have been used as proxy measures.
2. *Access and availability:* An inclusive financial system should be easily accessible to its users. The average population per bank branch has been used as a proxy measure to capture this dimension.
3. *Usage:* An inclusive financial system should be utilised as much as by its users. To capture this dimension, deposits per account, credit per account, and credit per office have been used as proxy measures.

Data Sources: The FII for all states/UTs and all districts of Jammu and Kashmir have been computed for the years 2002 and 2009. To calculate coverage and usage dimension indices, the data on number of offices, deposits, credit, deposits and credit accounts for all states/UTs and all districts of Jammu and Kashmir have been obtained from *Basic Statistical Returns of Scheduled Commercial Banks in India*, Reserve Bank of India, while the population figures for all states/UTs and all districts of Jammu and Kashmir have been taken from projected population figures provided in Census 2001, Government of India and projected population figures provided by Directorate of Economics and Statistics, Government of Jammu and Kashmir in its *Digest of Statistics 2008-09* respectively. To calculate access and availability dimension index, the data on average population per bank branch for all states/UTs and the number of bank branches for all districts of Jammu and Kashmir have been taken from *Branch Banking Statistics*, Reserve Bank of India. The *Digest of Statistics 2008-09* is also the source of data for population figures for the years 2002 and 2009 for calculation of access and availability dimension index for all districts of Jammu and Kashmir.

Financial inclusion classifications: The FII theoretically takes values between zero (0) and one (1), i.e., $0 \leq \text{FII} \leq 1$. The value '0' can be interpreted as indicating 'no financial inclusion', while the value '1' indicating 'complete financial inclusion'. The financial inclusion classifications adopted are similar to the human development classifications by UNDP in its Report 2009—very high, high, medium and low. However, for analytical purposes low FII value classification has been classified into two sub-categories—low and very low financial inclusion (Table 10.10).

Table 10.10

Financial Inclusion Classification

FII Value		*Classification*
(A)	$0.900 \leq \text{FII} \leq 1$	Very high financial inclusion
(B)	$0.800 \leq \text{FII} < 0.900$	High financial inclusion
(C)	$0.500 \leq \text{FII} < 0.800$	Medium financial inclusion
(D)	$0 \leq \text{FII} < 0.500$	Low/very low financial inclusion
(D.i)	$0.200 \leq \text{FII} < 0.500$	Low financial inclusion
(D.ii)	$0 \leq \text{FII} < 0.200$	Very low financial inclusion

Source: UNDP. Author's calculations.

Financial Inclusion Index (FII)—Status and Progress: Cross States/UTs Comparison

Cross states/UTs comparison of status and progress of financial inclusion shows that most of the states fall under low/very low FII category. In 2002, out of 35 states/UTs, 32 states/UTs were under low/very low FII category—13 under low FII category, and 19 under very low financial inclusion category. Chandigarh was at the top position followed by Goa and Delhi. Jammu and Kashmir was at 19th position with 0.185 FII value under very low financial inclusion category (Table 10.11).

Similarly, in 2009, 32 states/UTs were under low/very low financial inclusion category—13 under low financial inclusion category, and 19 under very low financial inclusion category. Chandigarh was at the top position followed by Delhi and Goa. Jammu and Kashmir slipped to 20th position with 0.163 FII value under very low financial inclusion category (Table 10.12).

Table 10.11

Financial Inclusion Index: 2002—State/UT-wise

FII Rank	State/UT	Financial Inclusion Index Value	Dimension Index		
			Coverage Index	Access and Availability Index	Usage Index
High financial inclusion					
1.	Chandigarh	0.857	0.983	0.745	0.842
Medium financial inclusion					
2.	Goa	0.694	0.878	1.000	0.203
3.	Delhi	0.649	0.713	0.330	0.904
Low financial inclusion					
4.	Kerala	0.368	0.656	0.335	0.113
5.	Maharashtra	0.323	0.294	0.142	0.532
6.	Punjab	0.318	0.457	0.334	0.162
7.	Karnataka	0.311	0.552	0.263	0.119
8.	Puducherry	0.302	0.534	0.239	0.132
9.	Himachal Pradesh	0.292	0.359	0.446	0.070
10.	Tamil Nadu	0.282	0.487	0.195	0.163
11.	Lakshadweep	0.254	0.177	0.512	0.073
12.	Daman and Diu	0.243	0.228	0.285	0.217
13.	Andhra Pradesh	0.238	0.466	0.158	0.090
14.	Uttarakhand	0.236	0.324	0.305	0.079
15.	Sikkim	0.224	0.132	0.256	0.285
16.	Tripura	0.205	0.484	0.098	0.034
Very low financial inclusion					
17.	Gujarat	0.192	0.226	0.174	0.177
18.	Haryana	0.190	0.282	0.179	0.109
19.	Jammu and Kashmir	0.185	0.214	0.221	0.121
20.	Andaman and Nicobar Islands	0.182	0.185	0.242	0.120
21.	Mizoram	0.168	0.082	0.251	0.171
22.	West Bengal	0.152	0.246	0.095	0.116
23.	Orissa	0.150	0.281	0.121	0.047
24.	Meghalaya	0.147	0.126	0.201	0.115
25.	Dadra and Nagar Haveli	0.128	0.096	0.072	0.217
26.	Rajasthan	0.116	0.170	0.110	0.069
27.	Jharkhand	0.111	0.175	0.089	0.071
28.	Madhya Pradesh	0.108	0.146	0.103	0.077
29.	Arunachal Pradesh	0.101	0.117	0.128	0.057
30.	Uttar Pradesh	0.093	0.179	0.064	0.035
31.	Chhattisgarh	0.077	0.083	0.068	0.079
32.	Assam	0.059	0.095	0.049	0.031
33.	Nagaland	0.058	0.004	0.000	0.170
34.	Bihar	0.047	0.088	0.035	0.018
35.	Manipur	0.029	0.009	0.002	0.077

Source: Author's calculations.

Table 10.12

Financial Inclusion Index: 2009—State/UT-wise

FII Rank	*State/UT*	*Financial Inclusion Index Value*	*Dimension Index*		
			Coverage Index	*Access and Availability Index*	*Usage Index*
High financial inclusion					
1.	Chandigarh	0.810	0.699	1.000	0.731
Medium financial inclusion					
2.	Delhi	0.661	0.624	0.431	0.929
3.	Goa	0.623	0.702	1.000	0.166
Low financial inclusion					
4.	Maharashtra	0.442	0.619	0.187	0.519
5.	Lakshadweep	0.324	0.200	0.621	0.153
6.	Puducherry	0.323	0.510	0.368	0.092
7.	Tamil Nadu	0.321	0.531	0.276	0.156
8.	Kerala	0.318	0.497	0.368	0.089
9.	Punjab	0.305	0.339	0.431	0.146
10.	Karnataka	0.300	0.424	0.317	0.160
11.	Himachal Pradesh	0.297	0.312	0.512	0.067
12.	Sikkim	0.262	0.171	0.431	0.185
13.	Uttarakhand	0.246	0.266	0.368	0.106
14.	Andhra Pradesh	0.243	0.413	0.212	0.103
15.	Haryana	0.221	0.244	0.276	0.144
16.	Daman and Diu	0.218	0.201	0.276	0.176
Very low financial inclusion					
17.	Gujarat	0.193	0.207	0.212	0.158
18.	Andaman and Nicobar Islands	0.183	0.178	0.276	0.095
19.	Mizoram	0.166	0.130	0.276	0.092
20.	Jammu and Kashmir	0.163	0.190	0.212	0.087
21.	Dadra and Nagar Haveli	0.160	0.140	0.276	0.065
22.	Meghalaya	0.141	0.103	0.212	0.107
23.	West Bengal	0.139	0.151	0.115	0.153
24.	Orissa	0.138	0.190	0.166	0.059
25.	Arunachal Pradesh	0.130	0.127	0.147	0.117
26.	Tripura	0.128	0.223	0.130	0.033
27.	Rajasthan	0.114	0.137	0.130	0.077
28.	Madhya Pradesh	0.100	0.118	0.115	0.067
29.	Jharkhand	0.097	0.115	0.115	0.062
30.	Chhattisgarh	0.090	0.089	0.090	0.092
31.	Uttar Pradesh	0.088	0.141	0.090	0.033
32.	Assam	0.073	0.108	0.069	0.042
33.	Nagaland	0.070	0.057	0.037	0.115
34.	Bihar	0.044	0.072	0.044	0.017
35.	Manipur	0.036	0.031	0.000	0.076

Source: Author's calculations.

District-wise FII: Jammu and Kashmir

District-wise FII indicates that most of the districts of Jammu and Kashmir fall under low/very low FII category. In 2002, out of existing 14 districts in the state, five were under low FII category, and six under very low financial inclusion category. Srinagar with 0.847 FII value was at the top position followed by Jammu and Leh, while Kupwara was at the bottom (Table 10.13). In 2009, out of 22 existing districts in the state, 19 were under low/very low financial inclusion category. The FII value for Srinagar showed a significant improvement and it was 0.979. Jammu and Leh held second and third position respectively. Bandipora was at the lowest position in the same year (Table 10.14).

Table 10.13

Financial Inclusion Index: 2002—District-wise (Jammu and Kashmir)

FII Rank	*District*	*Financial Inclusion Index Value*	*Dimension Index*		
			Coverage Index	*Access and Availability Index*	*Usage Index*
High financial inclusion					
1.	Srinagar	0.847	0.842	0.697	1.000
Medium financial inclusion					
2.	Jammu	0.631	0.854	0.665	0.375
3.	Leh	0.596	0.432	1.000	0.357
Low financial inclusion					
4.	Kathua	0.420	0.522	0.620	0.118
5.	Udhampur	0.318	0.437	0.382	0.135
6.	Baramulla	0.258	0.183	0.504	0.088
7.	Budgam	0.223	0.312	0.211	0.146
8.	Kargil	0.205	0.095	0.293	0.228
Very low financial inclusion					
9.	Rajouri	0.198	0.247	0.336	0.010
10.	Pulwama	0.173	0.187	0.185	0.146
11.	Anantnag	0.100	0.151	0.058	0.090
12.	Poonch	0.090	0.174	0.000	0.097
13.	Doda	0.076	0.096	0.019	0.112
14.	Kupwara	0.040	0.000	0.085	0.035

Source: Author's calculations.

Table 10.14

Financial Inclusion Index: 2009—District-wise (Jammu and Kashmir)

FII Rank	*District*	*Financial Inclusion Index Value*	*Dimension Index*		
			Coverage Index	*Access and Availability Index*	*Usage Index*
Very high financial inclusion					
1.	Srinagar	0.979	0.948	0.988	1.000
Medium financial inclusion					
2.	Jammu	0.779	0.878	1.000	0.460
3.	Leh	0.619	0.559	0.897	0.402
Low financial inclusion					
4.	Samba	0.419	0.370	0.577	0.310
5.	Baramulla	0.371	0.298	0.678	0.137
6.	Kathua	0.346	0.298	0.548	0.191
7.	Ganderbal	0.333	0.255	0.628	0.117
8.	Anantnag	0.299	0.279	0.422	0.196
9.	Reasi	0.299	0.137	0.483	0.275
10.	Kargil	0.295	0.192	0.477	0.218
11.	Udhampur	0.275	0.258	0.407	0.159
12.	Pulwama	0.270	0.246	0.355	0.209
13.	Shopian	0.245	0.148	0.320	0.268
14.	Rajouri	0.238	0.190	0.387	0.138
Very low financial inclusion					
15.	Ramban	0.186	0.090	0.308	0.161
16.	Doda	0.143	0.113	0.165	0.150
17.	Budgam	0.140	0.147	0.166	0.106
18.	Poonch	0.138	0.159	0.111	0.145
19.	Kupwara	0.134	0.107	0.244	0.052
20.	Kulgam	0.104	0.025	0.195	0.092
21.	Kishtwar	0.068	0.105	0.000	0.098
22.	Bandipora	0.041	0.010	0.033	0.078

Source: Author's calculations.

VI

Initiatives towards Financial Inclusion in Jammu and Kashmir

In this section, the various initiatives being taken especially by the Reserve Bank and the J&KSLBC towards achieving 100 per cent financial inclusion in the state have been presented.

Reserve Bank

As part of initiatives towards financial inclusion, as on March 2011, the Reserve Bank had adopted 11 villages for 100 per cent financial inclusion in Jammu and Kashmir state. Out of these villages, nine are in Jammu division and two in Kashmir division. The Reserve Bank had organised outreach progammes at these villages to ensure 100 per cent financial inclusion through information and communication technology (ICT) initiative by issuance of smart cards through the banking correspondent (BC) model for achieving the objectives of financial inclusion and providing doorstep banking services to the financially excluded comprising rural poor, small and marginal farmers and underpriviledged classes of the society.

The Reserve Bank has also been organising financial literacy and awareness programmes at different locations of the state. In these programmes, people are told about the economy in general and the various functions and role of the Reserve Bank in the Indian economy, the benefits and important aspects of financial inclusion, etc.

Financial Literacy and Credit Counselling Centres (FLCCCs)

As on April 2011, two FLCCCs were opened in Jammu and Kashmir. Both FLCCCs sponsored by the State Bank of India are locate in Jammu division.

Jammu and Kashmir State Level Bankers' Committee (J&KSLBC)

J&KSLBC has also been playing an important role towards achieving the goal of 100 per cent financial inclusion in the state. In this direction,

J&KSLBC has identified 795 unbanked villages in 20 districts (115 blocks) out of 22 districts with a population over 2,000 as per Census 2001 in the state to ensure financial inclusion in these villages. To ensure financial inclusion, these villages have been allocated to various commercial banks including RRBs and cooperative banks *viz.*, J&K Bank, State Bank of India, Punjab National Bank, Punjab & Sind Bank, State Bank of Patiala, UCO Bank, Allahabad Bank, Central Bank of India, Ellaquai Dehati Bank, J&K Grameen Bank, J&K State Cooperative Bank, Jammu Central Cooperative Bank, Anantnag Central Cooperative Bank and Baramulla Central Cooperative Bank. Most of the unbanked villages have been allocated to J&K Bank as its banking coverage is highest in the state.

VII

Concluding Observations and Policy Recommendations

Towards achieving 100 per cent financial inclusion in the state, combined efforts by banking sector led by the Reserve Bank and the Government (State and Central) should be more intensified. The RRBs and cooperative banks with commercial banks should be more encouraged to bring unbanked population under the umbrella to finance. For this they should be provided adequate infrastructural facilities and incentives.

One of the major reasons for low financial inclusion in the state has been lack of awareness about importance and various benefits of financial services among people especially residing in rural areas involved in agriculture and small businesses, marginal section and poor people. Keeping this in view, more financial literacy and awareness campaigns should be organised amongst these people by the Reserve Bank and banking sector.

References

Beck, Demirgüç-Kunt and Martinez Peria (2007). "Reaching Out: Access to and Use of Banking Services Across Countries", *Journal of Financial Economics* 8.

Chakravarty, Satya R. and Rupayan Pal (2010). *Measuring Financial Inclusion: An Axiomatic Approach*. Indira Gandhi Institute of Development Research (IGIDR). March.

European Commission (2008). *Financial Services Provision and Prevention of Financial Exclusion*. March.

Government of Jammu and Kashmir (n.d.). *Economic Survey of Jammu and Kashmir 2009-10*.

————. (n.d.) *Digest of Statistics of Jammu and Kashmir 2008-09*.

Jammu and Kashmir State Level Banker's Committee (J&KSLBC) (2010). *Thematic SLBC Meeting on Kisan Credit Scheme in the state*. May. Available on *www.jkslbc.com*.

————. (n.d.). *Financial Inclusion*. Available on *www.jkslbc.com*.

Leeladhar, V. (2005). *Taking Banking Services to the Common Man: Financial Inclusion*. December. Available on *www.rbi.org.in*.

Leyshon, Andrew and Nigel Thrift (1995). *Geographies of Financial Exclusion: Financial Abandonment in Britain and the United States*. Royal Geographical Society (with the Institute of British Geographies).

Measuring Banking Sector Outreach. Available on *http://siteresources.worldbank.org*

Mehrotra, Nirupam, V. Puhazhendhi, Gopakumaran Nair G. and B.B. Sahoo (2009). *Financial Inclusion: An Overview*. National Bank for Agriculture and Rural Development (NABARD).

Mohan, Rakesh (2006). *Economic Growth, Financial Deepening and Financial Inclusion*. November. Available on *www.rbi.org.in*.

National Bank for Agriculture and Rural Development (NABARD) (2008). *Report of the Committee on Financial Inclusion*. January.

Pal, Rupayan (2009). *Outreach of Banking Services, Infrastructure Penetration, Labour Regulation and Industrial Growth: Evidence from Indian States*. Indira Gandhi Institute of Development Research (IGIDR). January.

Reserve Bank of India (n.d.). *Basic Statistical Returns of Scheduled Commercial Banks in India*.

Sarma, Mandira (2008). *Index of Financial Inclusion*. Indian Council for Research on International Economic Relations (ICRIER). June.

Sarma, Mandira and Jesim Pais (2008). *Financial Inclusion and Development: A Cross Country Analysis*. Indian Council for Research on International Economic Relations (ICRIER). September.

Subbarao, D. (2009). *Financial Inclusion: Challenges and Opportunities*. Remarks at the Bankers' Club in Kolkata. December 9. Available on *www.rbi.org.in*.

Annexure Table A-10.1

Sectoral Growth in NSDP: Jammu and Kashmir (At Constant 1999-2000 Prices)

(Per cent)

Sector	Year					
	2003-04	2004-05	2005-06	2006-07 (QE)	2007-08 (PE)	2008-09 (PE)
1	2	3	4	5	6	7
A. Agriculture and allied activities	**7.3**	**1.1**	**1.3**	**2.9**	**1.8**	**1.8**
1.1 Agriculture including livestock	9.2	1.1	1.1	3.0	1.7	1.7
1.2 Forestry & logging	-10.7	0.4	4.9	1.9	2.4	2.4
1.3 Fishing	0.2	0.0	0.7	0.3	0.3	0.3
B. Industry	**5.0**	**18.8**	**9.5**	**10.4**	**11.4**	**10.7**
2. Mining & quarrying	4.3	21.3	22.5	26.4	23.4	19.6
3. Manufacturing	3.8	54.5	9.6	18.3	11.7	11.0
3.1 Manu-registered	9.4	139.1	11.5	17.4	12.8	12.8
3.2 Manu-unregistered	0.8	4.3	6.9	19.5	10.3	8.4
4. Construction	5.5	22.4	10.0	11.5	14.6	12.8
5. Electricity, gas & water supply	4.6	-17.5	6.7	-5.9	-5.6	-3.5
C. Services	**3.7**	**2.9**	**7.4**	**6.0**	**6.1**	**6.3**
6. Trade, hotels & restaurants	6.7	9.4	12.7	7.4	9.8	9.2
7. Transport, storage & communication	13.0	9.1	48.1	12.4	19.2	18.5
7.1 Railways	971.8	-87.5	44.1	45.5	19.2	-
7.2 Transport by other means	2.7	2.6	18.1	5.7	19.3	-
7.3 Storage	873.9	-90.6	31.7	-5.8	19.2	-
7.4 Communication	24.2	14.9	71.6	16.0	19.3	-
8. Banking & insurance	-0.6	8.6	3.5	21.6	11.2	8.9
9. Real estate, ownership of dwellings & business services	0.7	3.4	-6.5	-2.2	-1.8	-1.3
10. Public administration	-2.6	-5.5	1.1	0.8	-1.2	-1.5
11. Other services	9.8	3.2	3.2	3.5	3.3	4.6

Note: QE: Quick Estimates.
PE: Preliminary Estimates.

Source: Directorate of Economics and Statistics, Jammu and Kashmir.

11 Financial Inclusion in Kerala

V. DHANYA[1]

Introduction

The importance of financial inclusion in ensuring inclusive growth is well accepted in academic and policy circles. Both Reserve Bank of India and Government have been pursuing this goal over the last several decades through building the rural cooperative structure in the 1950s, the social contract with banks in the 1960s and the expansion of bank branch networks in the 1970s and 1980s (Subbarao, 2009). Irrespective of the efforts, a large section of population continued to be outside the banking framework. To bring the excluded population to the banking fraternity a more direct approach was taken by Reserve Bank of India in recent years.

The Reserve Bank launched a financial inclusion drive targetting one district in each state for 100 per cent financial inclusion. Accordingly, Palakkad district of Kerala became the first district in the country to be declared 100 per cent financially inclusive in September 2006. Subsequently, all the districts in Kerala were declared 100 per cent inclusive in June 2007, the third state to achieve 100 per cent financial inclusion after Goa and Himachal Pradesh. Accordingly, every single household in Kerala has been brought under banking network with at least one member

1. The views expressed in this paper are of the author herself and not of the organisation she is working with. The author is grateful to Dr D. Subbarao, Governor Reserve Bank of India for instructing her to take up the study. Sincere thanks to Suma Varma, Regional Director, RBI, Kerala, K.U.B Rao, Adviser, DEPR, C.V. George, GM (O-i-C) RBI, Kochi and G.J. Raju, DGM, RPCD, Thiruvananthapuram for the constant support and valuable suggestions for consolidating the study. Special thanks to Harold James, Manager, RBI Kochi for helping in the field visits. The support provided by DEPR staff and Antony Joseph is also acknowledged. Whole hearted cooperation has been received from the four surveyed district's lead district managers, lead bank officers, officials of district cooperative banks, NABARD, Attapady Hills Area Development Society officials and Kudumbashree officers and members.

of each family having a bank account. At present, Kerala has moved a long way from just opening an account to more active use of banking services. A lot of factors have contributed to this and in the study we look at the determining factors that shaped the financial inclusion in Kerala. In particular, we examine the nature and characteristics of Kerala that helped it to make considerable headway in financial inclusion when compared to the rest of the country.

Scheme and Methodology of the Study

Section I of the study looks into the concept of financial inclusion. In Section II, analysis of financial inclusion in Kerala *vis-à-vis* other states is made using various indicators of financial inclusion. Section III examines the unique characteristics of the state that made it more inclusive. It also examines the prospects of replicating Kerala's success in other states. The results of the Primary Survey are incorporated in Section IV. Section V gives the concluding remarks.

Both secondary and primary data sources are used for the study. Section I and II are based on secondary sources. Section III and IV largely depends on primary data/information collected through field visits, surveys, interviews and discussions with stakeholders. Four districts of the state are selected for field survey, *viz.*, Palakkad, Ernakulam, Kollam and Malappuram.

I

Financial Inclusion: Conceptual Issues

Access to finance is generally looked upon as a prerequisite for better economic well-being in terms of its role in promoting employment, economic growth and poverty reduction and social cohesion (GoI, 2008). While banking services in general have increased both in coverage and in variety over the years, a large section of population is still excluded from the formal financing channel. Prolonged and persistent deprivation of banking services to a large segment of the population leads to a decline in investment and has the potential to fuel social tensions causing social exclusion (Mehrotra *et al.*, 2009). Lack of finance is often seen as the critical element underlying persistent income inequality, as well as slower growth (World Bank, 2008). Giné and Townsend (2004) through their analysis on Thai economy showed that the greatest quantitative impact of financial deepening and financial access on income inequality came through indirect labour market effects.

While financial exclusion can be an individual choice, all those who desire to have access to finance should be given ample opportunity to avail the services. In the report *Building Inclusive Financial Sectors for Development* (2006), more popularly known as the Blue Book, the United Nations (UN) points out that an inclusive financial sector would provide access to credit for all 'bankable' people and firms, insurance for all insurable people and firms and savings and payments services for everyone.

Rangarajan Committee Report (GoI, 2008) has defined financial inclusion as the process of ensuring access to financial services and timely and adequate credit where needed by vulnerable groups such as weaker sections and low income groups at an affordable cost. The various financial services include savings, loans, insurance, payments, remittance facilities and financial counselling/advisory services by the formal financial system. Within these various services, it is the availability of adequate credit that is considered to be the most important indicator of financial inclusion, probably because lack of finance is often associated with underdevelopment.

While the concept of financial inclusion is a whole encompassing one, the actual financial inclusion declared so far has been questioned by many. It is often pointed out that many accounts that were opened to satisfy the financial inclusion drive are lying dormant. Most of the accounts were opened for achieving the target of 100 per cent coverage in terms of accounts opened by every household. Realising the need to go beyond the simple definition of financial inclusion, Reserve Bank of India in its *Annual Policy Statement 2007-08* announced that an evaluation of the progress made in the districts that have reported 100 per cent financial inclusion should be taken up by independent external agencies. Accordingly, studies were conducted in 26 districts in the states of Andhra Pradesh, Gujarat, Himachal Pradesh, Karnataka, Orissa, Punjab, Rajasthan and West Bengal. The findings reveal that although the State Level Bankers' Committees

(SLBCs) have declared several districts as 100 per cent financially included, actual financial inclusion has not been to that extent in all the districts. Further, most of the accounts that have been opened as part of the financial inclusion drive have remained inoperative without any transactions in the accounts. Recognising the limitations of defining achievement of financial inclusion in terms of number of bank accounts opened, the definition of financial inclusion was widened to include/imply provision of all financial services like credit, remittance and overdraft facilities for the rural poor.

II

Status of Financial Inclusion in Kerala

Kerala has a long history of development of banking and finance which has evolved in line with the development needs of the state. Kerala's external relations initially through the trade channel and later through migration played a major role in development of banking services in the state. Traditionally, both formal and informal financial structures co-exist in Kerala with commercial banks, cooperatives, non-banking finance companies (NBFCs), all-India financial institutions (AIFIs) on the one hand and the informal moneylenders and chit funds on the other side, playing a major role in the development process of the state.

Lack of physical access or the geography of the banking structure is the most often cited reason for financial exclusion. Hence, geographic distance to the nearest branch, or the density of branches relative to the population, can provide a first crude indication of geographic access or lack of physical barriers to access (Beck and Peria, 2007). In Kerala, the accessibility of banking is high in terms of the intensity of branches, which contributed significantly to bring the population within the purview of formal finance. The average population per bank branch[2] in Kerala was 8,139 as on March 2010 as against the national average of 14,073.

As on March 2010, the total number of branches of scheduled commercial banks (SCBs) in Kerala stood at 4,227, accounting for 5.0 per

2. Population per bank branch is calculated using the estimated mid-year population figures from Central Statistical Organisation (CSO).

cent of total bank branches in the country. The distribution of branches in Kerala is skewed towards semi-urban category which accounts for 66.9 per cent of total bank branches in Kerala followed by urban branches at 25.0 per cent and rural branches at 8.1 per cent. However, considering the fact that the difference in economic conditions in rural and semi-urban is very narrow in Kerala, this skewed nature of branch distribution cannot be taken as a sign of financial exclusion in Kerala. In fact, there is more equitable distribution of deposit and credit in Kerala among the semi-urban and urban branches compared to all-India figure where a major part of deposit mobilised and credit deployed comes from the urban/metro region (Table 11.1).

Table 11.1

Distribution of Branches and Banking Services across Regions as on March 2010

Regions/Items	*Rural*			*Semi-Urban*			*Urban/Metropolitan*		
	Offices	*Deposits*	*Credit*	*Offices*	*Deposits*	*Credit*	*Offices*	*Deposits*	*Credit*
All-India	38.4	9.2	7.5	24.2	13.4	9.6	37.3	77.4	83.0
Northern region	35.0	8.6	6.7	20.9	9.4	6.8	44.1	82.0	86.5
Northeastern region	54.7	17.7	22.4	25.3	33.2	32.9	20.0	49.1	44.8
Eastern region	53.5	17.6	13.6	18.4	18.0	10.6	28.1	64.3	75.8
Central region	47.2	18.4	19.6	21.2	17.7	17.6	31.6	63.9	62.8
Western region	29.8	3.6	2.5	22.2	6.9	3.9	48.0	89.5	93.6
Southern region	28.6	8.0	8.8	32.9	21.0	15.9	38.5	71.0	75.3
Andhra Pradesh	35.4	9.8	11.7	23.8	17.0	13.2	40.8	73.2	75.1
Karnataka	5.7	2.1	8.8	20.8	10.0	8.9	43.7	82.5	82.3
Kerala	8.1	4.1	4.7	66.9	53.0	46.2	25.0	42.9	49.1
Tamil Nadu	28.3	9.0	7.5	32.0	18.9	14.1	39.7	72.1	78.4

Source: Quarterly Statistics on Deposits and Credits of Scheduled Commercial Banks, RBI.

Various indicators of banking penetration also reveal better financial inclusion than in the rest of the country (Table 11.2). Both per capita credit and per capita deposits are higher in Kerala than the all-India level all through the time period taken for analysis. On the other hand, deposit per account and credit per account is higher at the all-India level showing lower utilisation in Kerala. However, the above two parameters, together show a more equitable distribution of resources among the account holders in Kerala than the rest of the country.

Table 11.2

Banking Penetration in Kerala and India

	2001		*2005*		*2009*		*2010*	
	India	*Kerala*	*India*	*Kerala*	*India*	*Kerala*	*India*	*Kerala*
Deposit per office (Rs lakh)	1,406	1,314	2,497	1,914	4,794	3,240	5,479	3,563
Credit per office (Rs lakh)	797	568	1,647	1,046	3,481	1,936	3,983	2,266
Per capita deposits (Rs)	9,174	13,842	15,861	20,874	33,786	39,565	38,930	43,781
Per capita credits (Rs)	5,203	5,987	10,464	11,407	24,532	23,634	28,302	27,842
Deposit per account (Rs)	22,182	21,495	37,422	26,682	59,217	46,663	NA	NA
Credit per account (Rs)	102,824	51,638	149,379	81,564	258,751	141,529	NA	NA
Population per branch	15,327	9,493	15,740	9,167	14,191	8,190	14,073	8,139

Source: Calculations based on *Basic Statistical Returns*, various issues.

Various studies using NSSO data have shown that Kerala's indebtedness to formal credit channel is above the national average (Suran and Narayana, 2009; Chavan, 2005). As per the NSSO (2003) data, 45.9 million farmer households in the country (51.4%) do not access credit either from institutional or non-institutional sources. Only 27 per cent of total farm households are indebted to formal sources. Among these, one-third borrows from informal channels also. On the other hand, Kerala's indebtedness to formal channels is high compared to not only the All-India average but also to other South Indian states. In Kerala, 82.3 per cent of the debt is from the formal credit channels and SCBs contribution is nearly 50 per cent.

Similarly, Kerala ranked first in the Financial Inclusion Index constructed by Mehrotra *et al.* (2009) for the year 2006 capturing various dimensions of financial inclusion. The parameters selected were: (i) coverage measured in terms of number of rural offices, (ii) access and availability measured by number of rural deposit accounts, (iii) input of the banking system measured by volume of rural deposits and (iv) use/output of banking system measured by volume of rural credit.

Thus, our analysis using various parameters of inclusiveness showed better financial inclusion in Kerala compared to rest of India. A more detailed analysis of the extent of financial inclusion is carried out in Section IV using the primary survey results. In the following section we examine the factors that have shaped the extent of financial inclusion in the state.

III

Factors affecting Financial Inclusion in Kerala

A whole gamut of factors, positively contributed to bring about financial inclusion in the state. Historically, Kerala was linked with the external world through trade channels. The location of the region on the Arabian Sea coast permitted trading and cultural relations with outside world. The Kerala ports developed into centres of trade between the Arab countries, North Africa and the Roman Empire (Kerala Council for Historical Research, 2010 as cited in George, 2011; Tharakan, 2005). As a result of such trade, use of money and different types of coins increased in this region, leading to minting of coins in Kerala (Tharakan, 2005). Later on during the colonial period, Kerala was known for its spices and other cash crops. All these promoted banking business in Kerala and during 1926-1930, Travancore[3] alone accounted for about one-fifth of the total number of banks in British India. The average area served by an office of a commercial bank in Travancore-Cochin in December 1949 was 18 square miles as against 222 for the country as a whole (George, 2011). Again, the average population served by a commercial bank was 16,000 as against 65,000 for the country as a whole (Government of India, 1953 as quoted in George, 2011). Thus, historically, Kerala had the locational advantage in banking business compared to other states. This was facilitated by the economic conditions as a trading centre which again was due to its natural geographic advantage.

---

3. Kerala state was formed on November 1st 1956 on linguistic basis amalgamating Travancore, Cochin and Malabar regions.

Embedded from its historical advantage, Kerala's success in financial inclusion is contributed by many factors. In the following sub-section we list out in detail the most prominent factors that promoted financial inclusion in the State.

Socioeconomic Conditions in Kerala

Kerala has a favourable socioeconomic base conducive for financial inclusion. Kerala made significant strides in improving the standard of living, reflected in the various indicators of social development (Annexure Table A-11.1), which are comparable even to that of developed countries. In fact, Kerala's success in financial inclusion should also be viewed as a natural extension of the already achieved social and cultural inclusion. Kerala traditionally had a system of health and educational institutions which were made accessible even to the lower strata of the society. Achievements such as low infant mortality, low levels of population growth and high levels of literacy and education have played a significant role in promoting social and economic development in the state. Kerala has achieved 100 per cent literacy in the year 1991 at the time when the national average was below 50 per cent. Further, political awareness among the common people in Kerala is high, making them aware of their rights.

Another social condition that has helped is the relatively high social status enjoyed by the women which is reflected in the sex ratio favourable to women. Kerala has 1,084 females against 1,000 males as compared to 914 at the all-India level. Most women also have post office deposit schemes which made them aware of the advantages of savings, a service associated with banks.

The high literacy and educational qualifications increased the reading habits of the people. In fact, Kerala has one of the highest rates of circulation of newspaper dailies in the country. Malayalam newspapers were the seventh most circulated newspapers in regional languages in India during 2007-08 and second in terms of per capita circulation. The habit of reading newspapers and the discussions in small shops used to be a common scene in earlier days. This facilitated an informal platform for knowledge and information sharing. Further, the high literacy and education facilitated better awareness, making financial literacy and awareness campaigns more worthwhile in the state.

The high wage structure has also played a role in increasing banking habits among the people. According to the Labour Bureau Report on the Working of the Minimum Wages Act, 1948—for the year 2008, almost in all the scheduled employments, the highest wages are being paid in the state of Kerala than the rest of the country. The high wages received give an impetus to save which brings them to the banking network. On the other hand, the consumerist nature of Keralites also propelled the use of banking services in the credit side. As per the NSSO data, Kerala ranks first in terms of the per capita consumption expenditure. The consumerist nature is further substantiated by the high share of personal loans in total bank credit structure. During 2008-09, personal loans accounted for 41.4 per cent of total bank credit deployed in the state.

Migration to many parts of the world and more particularly to Middle East has resulted in the common people having closer access to financial institutions. The non-resident population constitutes 26.4 per cent of the total workforce of the state and contributes significantly to the economic activities of the state. While in the initial years, informal channels were largely used for transfer of money, formal channels gained prominence soon. Studies at the all-India level have pointed out that with the liberalisation of exchange rate regime and the development of e-banking services facilitating instantaneous transfer facilities, the use of formal means for remittances have increased (Jadhav and Singh, 2006). Further, reduction in the cost of transfer of remittance through the formal channels and the deepening of the payment infrastructure has considerably reduced the incentives for informal transfers (Singh, 2010).

Role of Cooperatives

The cooperative sector has been playing a distinct and significant role in the process of socio-economic development of the state with special focus on rural population and their livelihood by making available agricultural credit at affordable cost. Kerala State Cooperative Bank Ltd. (KSCB) forms the apex body in the state rural cooperative structure. At present there are 20 branches in the state. At the second tier of the rural cooperative system is the District Cooperative Banks (DCBs). As of March 2009, there were 14 DCBs having around 600 branches across Kerala. Out of these, 10 were profit-making and four loss-making. Many of the DCBs are functioning efficiently and some have migrated to core banking. Primary agricultural credit societies (PACSs) which form the base of rural cooperative structure is quite strong in Kerala and during 2009 there were 1,608 PACSs in Kerala. Similarly, there were 14 branches of Kerala State Co-operative Agricultural and Rural Development Bank Ltd. (KSCARDB) and 48 Primary Co-operative Agricultural and Rural Development Bank Ltd. (PCARDB) during 2009.

The state-wise distribution of cooperative credit is given in Table 11.3. The total credit of the cooperative sector includes loan outstanding of KSCBs, DCBs, PACS, KSCARDB and PCARDB. Southern region accounted for the major share in total cooperative credit with a share of 35.2 per cent as on March 2009. However, in terms of individual states, Maharashtra came first in terms of cooperative credit with a share of 17.9 per cent in 2009 followed by Kerala (12.0%) and Tamil Nadu (9.4%).

Table 11.3

Region/State-wise Distribution of Cooperative Credit
(Percentage Share)

Region/State		*2008*	*2009*
Central region		11.7	10.9
	Madhya Pradesh	5.4	5.3
Northern region		22.7	21.8
	Haryana	7.6	7.2
	Punjab	6.9	7.4
	Rajasthan	5.6	5.1
Eastern region		9.3	8.2
	Orissa	6.1	4.0
	West Bengal	3.3	3.3
Western region		24.5	23.3
	Gujarat	5.8	5.3
	Maharashtra	18.6	17.9
Southern region		33.1	35.2
	Andhra Pradesh	8.0	6.6
	Karnataka	5.9	7.1
	Kerala	10.5	12.0
	Tamil Nadu	8.5	9.4
Northeastern region		0.5	0.5

Note: Only states having major share are included.

Source: Calculations based on NABARD *Annual Report, 2009-10*, RBI *Report on Trend and Progress of Banking in India*.

Kerala's role in cooperative credit becomes predominant when the outstanding loans and advances of PACS are taken into account. As on March 2009, Kerala accounted for 23.5 per cent of total PACS credit in the country. Southern region as a whole accounted for nearly half (47.7%) of the PACS credit in the country. While individual states' share in overall cooperative credit shows their relative importance, it is necessary to look into the share of cooperative credit in total credit disbursement of the states to understand the importance of cooperatives in the state's economy. Table 11.4 is an attempt on this aspect.

Table 11.4

Share of Cooperative Credit in Total Credit Disbursed: State-wise as on March 2009

Share Percentage	*States*
20% and above	Himachal Pradesh, Haryana, Orissa, Kerala
10% to 20%	Chhattisgarh, Madhya Pradesh, Uttarakhand, Punjab, Rajasthan
5% to 10%	Uttar Pradesh, Bihar, West Bengal, Gujarat, Andhra Pradesh, Karnataka, Tamil Nadu

Source: Calculated from RBI data.

As seen from Table 11.4 cooperative credit plays a major role in northern states like Himachal Pradesh and Haryana. With the exception of Kerala, share of cooperative credit in the total credit disbursement of the states is lower in the South Indian states. As on March 2009, Himachal Pradesh ranked highest (26.7%) in terms of the importance of cooperative credit in the state credit structure followed by Kerala (24.8%) and Haryana (23.1%).

The above analysis shows that cooperative credit structure is stronger in Kerala compared to other states with far greater outreach than the SCBs in terms of coverage in rural areas. According to SLBC, Kerala, there are 120 unbanked villages in Kerala with a population of more than 2,000. This classification does not take into account the presence of PACSs. If PACSs are also taken into account, then the number of unbanked villages in Kerala will come down drastically.

Very often the consumption needs of the society which otherwise are not met by the scheduled banks are met through the cooperative structure.

The satisfaction to the beneficiaries arising from simplified loaning procedures and active participation of members in the affairs of the society acts as further incentive to be part of the cooperative credit structure.

Various initiatives have been taken by District Cooperative Banks and State Cooperative Banks to improve the financial inclusion in the state. Notable are the efforts by Ernakulam District Co-operative Bank Ltd. (EDCBL) and Palakkad District Co-operative Bank Ltd. (PDCBL). EDCBL operates 'Bank on Wheels' (mobile bank) in the Agricultural Urban Wholesale Market at Maradu, a suburb of Ernakulum to extend financial services to the producers and traders whose banking requirements are often after the regular banking hours. Similarly, PDCBL opened mobile banking facilities in the predominantly ST region of Attapadi. The Pudur village in Palakkad district was otherwise completely excluded from the banking services, even PACSs were absent in the village. The villagers had to come to Agali branch, which is around 20 kilometres away, to avail banking services. The transportation facilities to ST holdings were poor and the entire process of communicating used to take on an average three days. The mobile branch functions six days in a week covering six places in the Attapadi area each day, extending banking services to the otherwise unbanked areas.

Role of Kudumbashree and other SHGs

An important step to bring financially excluded people within the fold of formal financial sector was the promotion of microfinance in India. The SHG-bank linkage programme (SBLP) was launched by NABARD in 1992, with policy support from the Reserve Bank, to facilitate collective decision-making by the poor and provide 'door step' banking. Banks, as wholesalers of credit, were to provide the resources, while the NGOs were to act as agencies to organise the poor, build their capacities and facilitate the process of empowering them (RBI, 2008).

However, in Kerala, SBLP followed a different mode of functioning with active support from the government. In fact, the alternative channel played a major role in promoting financial inclusion in Kerala. Unlike other states where microfinance activities are carried out through NGOs/ microfinance institutions (MFIs), a major portion of microfinance is routed directly to SHGs through the Kudumbashree Mission, a women based participatory poverty eradication programme jointly initiated by Government of Kerala and NABARD, avoiding the middleman and thus, the exorbitant interest rates associated with it. It was launched by the Government of Kerala in 1998 for wiping out absolute poverty from the state through concerted community action under the leadership of local self-governments (LSGs). Built around three critical components, microcredit, entrepreneurship and empowerment, the Kudumbashree initiative has brought to the forefront the less privileged women. The role it played in Kerala's society is visible from the number of Kudumbasree members coming forward to contest in the last LSG elections. By addressing the basic needs of the less privileged women, Kudumbashree offered them avenues to lead a more dignified life.

Under this, weekly collections were made from the members of neighbourhood groups[4] (NHGs) and the savings are pooled together and given out as loans to the most deserving. These loans have been used for purposes ranging from covering hospital expenses to meeting working capital needs for microenterprises. In fact, various studies have pointed out that the credits from the NHGs were mostly used for consumption purposes. However, considering the fact that a great amount of dealings with moneylenders is to meet the consumption requirements, the availability of credit at a lower interest rate have helped to reduce the dependency on moneylenders to a great extent. The survey results also showed that a large number of people now depend on the SHGs in case of any emergency (discussed in Section IV). Further, the SBLP has helped NHGs to augment their existing resources collected through thrift.

Further, interest subsidy scheme was also introduced by the Government as an added incentive to the NHGs. As per the scheme, all commercial and cooperative banks that are prepared to lend to Kudumbashree NHGs under the SBLP at 9 per cent or below, will be participants in the scheme. As on March 2011, five banks and two RRBs[5] have entered in MoU with the Executive Director of Kudumbashree. The interest subsidy would be provided as annual installments to the banks.

---

4. SHGs under Kudumbashree Mission are called neighbourhood groups (NHGs).
5. State Bank of Travancore, Syndicate Bank, Canara Bank, North Malabar Grameen Bank, South Malabar Grameen Bank, Central Bank of India and Punjab National Bank.

The more recent joint liability groups (JLGs)[6] for farming is also brought under the ambit of the scheme.

Microcredit in Kerala is largely financed directly through the SHGs, which reveals its importance among Kerala's microfinance structure (Table 11.5). Out of the total microcredit disbursed as on March 2009, 63.6 per cent was disbursed directly through the SHGs.

To increase the NHG-bank linkage and also to improve general financial awareness, a 'Financial Literacy Campaign' was carried out by the Kudumbashree Mission. Learning from the success of Kudumbashree, other state governments have followed the path like 'Velugu' in Andhra Pradesh, 'Sakhi Mandal' in Gujarat, 'Mahalir Thittam' in Tamil Nadu etc. With the success of Kudumbashree NHG model, there are a number of NGOs and MFIs that operate in Kerala. However, compared to Kudumbashree, their operations are limited. But, this has resulted in an increase in multiple memberships with repayment often done by rotating funds from different channels or none at all.

Implementation of NREGA

Another factor that has played a major role in improving the financial inclusion in Kerala is the successful implementation of National Rural Employment Guarantee Act (NREGA). The NREGA was passed by the Government of India in 2005 as a national initiative to promote employment opportunities in the rural areas and thereby enhancing livelihood security. As per this, payment to the workers can be made through bank accounts or post office. In Kerala, NREGA was first implemented in two districts, *viz.*, Palakkad and Wayanad in 2006. Later on, it was extended to two more districts and since January 2009, it has been implemented in all the districts in Kerala. NREGA made it mandatory for the state governments to come out with a Rural Employment Guarantee Scheme and in Kerala, the Kerala Rural Employment Guarantee Scheme (KREGS) became effective from January 31, 2006. A major feature of KREGS was to promote direct payment to the workers through individual

6. JLGs is a recent entrant where 4 to 5 members form the group. Unlike the SHGs which can function as a micro credit group, JLGs are formed with the intention of entering into productive purpose. It can be created for either aricultural group or an enterprise group.

Table 11.5

Mode of Payment of Microcredit in Kerala (As on March 2009)

		Total SHGs	*Under Government Sponsered Schemes*	*Exclusive Women SHGS*
SHGs financed under bank linkage programme	No	216,648 (61.0)	65,839 (84.0)	191,805 (61.0)
	Amount	153,051 (63.6)	65,218 (88.8)	134,888 (63.5)
SHGs financed directly through NGO facilitation	No	61,115 (17.3)	12,829 (16.3)	54,102 (17.2)
	Amount	40,946 (17.0)	6,901 (9.4)	37,480 (17.6)
SHGs financed through NGOs	No	75,812 (21.4)	NA	68,982 (21.9)
	Amount	46,698 (19.4)	1,360 (1.9)	40,144 (18.9)
Total bank finance	No	353,575 (100.0)	78,668 (100.0)	314,889 (100.0)
	Amount	240,696 (100.0)	73,479 (100.0)	212,512 (100.0)

Note: Figures in parenthesis refer to percentage share to total bank finance.
Source: SLBC Kerala.

bank accounts. This feature gave a major boost to the drive for financial inclusion in Kerala. A number of no-frills accounts which were opened were utilised for payment of wages. In fact, implementation of NREGA in Palakkad district helped it to become the first district in India to achieve 100 per cent financial inclusion.

Institutional Interventions

Proactive role of institutions like that of the state government, SLBC, SCBs, RRBs and RBI played a major role in improving the access to financial services in the state. In many cases, it was the harmonious working of bankers and developmental agencies in tandem with the state government initiatives that resulted in a deep-rooted inclusion in the state. The SLBC provided the required platform for the deliberations regarding various issues.

The SBLP in Kerala met with such huge success in terms of its coverage mainly because of the strong organisational set up which is closely monitored by the Kudumbashree Mission, a part of Government machinery. Again, at the *panchayat* level, the LSG is actively engaged in implementing various government schemes through the banking channel. Many of centrally sponsored schemes like Indira Awas Yojana (IAY), Swarna Jayanti Sahari Rozgar Yojana (SGSRY) and NREGP were all implemented with the active support and participation of LSGs. Further, the implementation of EMS housing loan scheme by the state government played a major role in financial inclusion in the state. The loan was given through the cooperative banks and PACSs and for availing the loan, it became mandatory to open bank accounts. Here again, LSG played an important role as the actual implementation of the programme was rested with them.

Similarly, the various initiatives taken by the SCBs and cooperative banks in the state also helped to promote financial awareness, education and inclusion. Some commercial banks have adopted villages to make them 'moneylender free villages'. To improve financial awareness among the public, Financial Literacy and Credit Counselling Centres (FLCCs) were opened in each district of Kerala under the aegis of respective lead bank. Business correspondents were used to improve the services provided in villages.

The NABARD also has played a significant role in promoting financial inclusion by bringing poor rural households to the formal financing channels through SBLPs, JLGs, Farmers' club etc. With an aim to achieve total financial inclusion by 2012, NABARD has introduced a scheme to support the capacity building needs of business correspondents (BCs) and business facilitators (BFs) of banks.

Above all, RBI through its various policies and initiatives played a lead role in the state for promoting financial inclusion. As per the RBI norms, many no-frills accounts and Kisan Credit Cards (KCCs), were opened in the state. As on March 2011, 27 lakh no-frills accounts were opened in the state and 205 villages were covered under ICT based financial inclusion with 200 BC/BFs operating at the state. Similarly, about one lakh General Credit Cards (GCCs) and four lakh KCCs were issued in the state.

Top priority was given to the financial outreach programmes where the public was made aware of the banking services. Further, interactions with Banking Ombudsman also brought people closer to the banking fraternity. Priority was given to deepening financial literacy among school children and college students to help them in acquiring basic proficiency in financial concepts.

IV

Survey Results

While the secondary sources throw light on the features of financial inclusion in Kerala, a survey was carried to get an in-depth view. The following four districts in Kerala were selected for the survey based on various parameters.

(i) Palakkad—being the first 100 per cent financially inclusive district.

(ii) Ernakulam—being the commercial capital of Kerala.

(iii) Kollam—having more SC and fishermen population who are generally perceived to be outliers of Kerala's economic growth.

(iv) Malappuram—being educationally backward but traditionally receiving high remittances.

Irrespective of the difference in economic development of the districts, financial inclusion is more or less uniform across Kerala. Hence, we assume the results from the survey are representative of the entire state. Sample size of the survey is 1,000, 250 each from each district. Two *panchayats* were taken from each district and survey was carried out among the relatively poor sections of the population. We did not strictly follow the APL/BPL classification as we thought it is also necessary to include people who remain on the fringes of the poverty line.

Profile of Respondents

The average age of respondents was 49, and 56 per cent of the respondents were male and 44 per cent were female. About 90 per cent of respondents were having some form of landholding. Ten per cent of respondents were staying in rented houses or rooms. This is especially true in the case of Palluruthy area which comes under the Corporation of Cochin and Sakthikulangara, a fisherman hamlet in Kollam district. Majority of respondents fall under the landholding category of 5 to 25 cents showing that they have some assets as security. However, only 31.4 per cent were having agricultural land. About 24.5 per cent of the respondents were getting some form of government funds and 77.8 per cent received funds through post office and 17 per cent through banking channel.

As pointed out earlier, physical access is a major factor determining inclusion. The survey results show that 93.0 per cent of respondents had bank offices within 5 kilometres while 5 per cent had it within 6 to 10 kilometres.

The survey results substantiated the findings of the study on the importance of SHGs, NREGA, cooperative structure and general awareness as determining factors of financial inclusion in the state. About 52.2 per cent of the respondents were members of SHG. About 97 per cent of SHG members pointed out that their membership in SHGs have increased their awareness on banking and 44.5 per cent of SHG members have opened individual bank accounts after becoming members of SHGs. In fact, our interactions with SHG groups also revealed that they are given classes on financial matters including book keeping, maintaining accounts with banks and various Government and NABARD schemes and the services offered by banks.

The importance of cooperative sector in Kerala's financial inclusion was also substantiated by the survey results. Figure 11.1 gives the percentage distribution of accounts among different categories. Cooperative sector accounted for the major share followed by nationalised banks. Others which include accounts with SHGs, Kerala State Financial Enterprises, other chit funds, post office accounts, etc., also contributed to 2.1 per cent of total accounts. RRBs accounted for 16.4 per cent. The presence of RRBs is significant in northern Kerala as most of the RRB branches are functioning in that region. However, in recent years, they have started branches in south Kerala also.

Figure 11.1

Percentage Distribution of Bank Accounts among Respondents

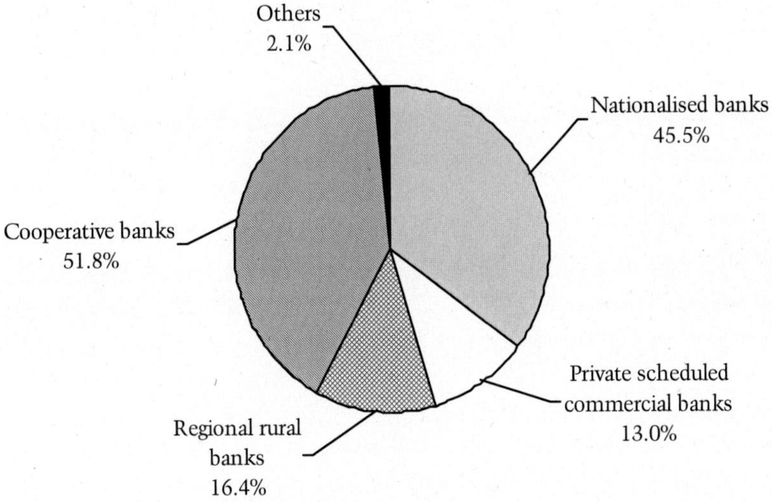

Note: The percentages will not add to 100 due to the existence of multiple accounts.

NREGA also contributed significantly to financial inclusion drive in Kerala. About 27.4 per cent of respondents were members of NREGA and received funds through the banks and cooperative sector. Further, 24.5 per cent of population are receiving funds from Government under welfare programmes and one-fifth of them are receiving it through bank. A major share is received through post offices.

Irrespective of the high financial inclusion indicators, majority of the respondents still depend on informal channels in case of any emergency (Figure 11.2). Nevertheless, among the informal channels, moneylender came only third after relatives and friends and SHGs. The procedural delay associated with formal channels act as hindrance in approaching them in case of emergency. Here again, it may be noted that respondents have more access to cooperative sector than scheduled commercial banks in an emergency.

Figure 11.2

Sources of Funds in Case of Emergency

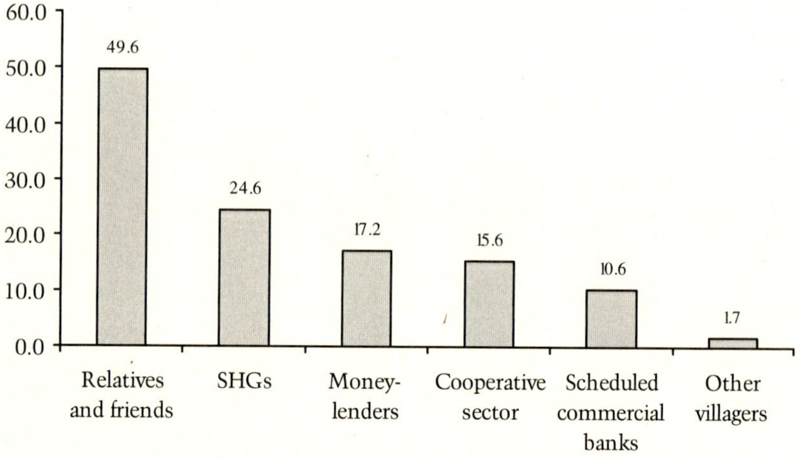

Note: Figures need not add up to 100 due to more than one choice indicated by the respondent.

Irrespective of the fact that, there is utilisation of financial channel by the respondents, most of them follow traditional ways of going to the bank branch for withdrawal of money. 73.6 per cent of respondents personally go and withdraw money from their accounts while 18.75 per cent use ATMS. While this shows the persistence of traditional ways for withdrawing money, it also reveals the capability of the person to do banking business on his own. More than half of the respondents were confident in filling the forms themselves without any external help.

The high literacy rate in Kerala has played a major role in bringing people close to the banking channels. Survey results showed that the financial awareness among the respondents was generally high. About 80.3 per cent of the respondents were aware of the consequences of non-repayment of loan. About 43 per cent knew the method of filing complaints against banks. The usual response on this was that the facility to register complaints is displayed in the branch and a complaint register is also maintained. A few were aware of the banking ombudsman scheme.

Thus, our survey results show that Kerala is witnessing rapid strides in financial inclusion with people actually utilising banking services in a big way. Majority of the people have availed banking services in one form or the other. The implementation of NREGA, SHG movement and the various policies taken by the banking fraternity and the Government has indeed resulted in better inclusion among the poor.

V

Conclusion

The study was an attempt to look into the extent of financial inclusion and the factors that promoted financial inclusion in the state. The analysis showed that there are certain unique features of Kerala that helped it to achieve financial inclusion. Kerala's history of having trade ties with external world and later on migration necessitated the need for formal financing channels. Banking penetration in Kerala, thus, is historically high compared to other states and the wide network of branches along with the strong cooperative structure played a major role in achieving better financial inclusion. Further, the high social development indicators like level of literacy, education, etc., gave Kerala an unparalleled advantage in creating financial awareness. In fact, financial awareness preceded financial inclusion in the state which acted as a base for the later concerted efforts on the part of RBI, Government and banking fraternity for promoting financial inclusion. Kerala's path to financial inclusion shows that utmost importance should be given to financial literacy and awareness initiatives for successful implementation of various programmes for financial inclusion.

Thus, Kerala's achievement in financial inclusion has to be seen as a natural extension of already achieved inclusion in various social and economic indicators. The local conditions and institutional structure played a major role in shaping Kerala's financial inclusion. Hence, the study points to the need for differentiated policy prescriptions depending on the conditions of each state. At the same time, it also throws light on the need for special efforts on the part of those states that lag behind in social development, particularly, in literacy and education, to provide awareness campaigns among the poor. Concerted action on the part of LSG and banking fraternity should be made in this regard.

The SBLP followed by the state facilitated to a great extent the inclusion of women into the banking channel. In fact, the role played by the organisation in training and directing the groups, virtually providing handholding can be emulated in other states. The implementation procedure of NREGA followed in the state also helped in improving financial inclusion in a major way. All payments relating to NREGA were routed through banking channels which made it imperative for the account holders to use their accounts for receiving wages. Further, constant interaction with the banks also helps in improving awareness on banking services. For states which are having low penetration of bank offices, BC/BF model can be used in providing NREGA wages and other Government funds. Here again, the issues of connectivity and the use of technology comes to picture which has to be addressed by the concerned authorities.

The technology induced financial inclusion can play a major role in further progress towards achieving that goal. It can reduce the operating cost associated with opening of new bank branches and also the man power shortage experienced by banks. However, the usage of technology and communication in any place depends on the infrastructure, in particular, the connectivity available at the place. In many remote villages, connectivity is a problem and thus limits the financial inclusion drive through information and communication technology. Further, the lack of awareness of the programme among the public regarding the model and the difficulty in accepting a person acting as 'bank' acts as hindrance to get the desired result. Again, the general skepticism on technology can also pull back a person from opening account with a BC. Further, the usability of this will depend on the extent of financial services that can be accessed through a Smart Card. For example, if the pensions and other benefits from the Government can be channelised through this system, there will be greater demand for the model. Thus, a move to meaningful financial inclusion calls for innovative approaches for ensuring better coverage of financial services.

References

Beck, Demirgüç-Kunt and Martinez Peria (2007). "Banking Services for Everyone? Barriers to Bank Access and Use around the World", *Policy Research Working Paper* 4079. Washington, DC: World Bank.

Chavan, Pallavi (2005). "How 'Inclusive' Are Banks under Financial Liberalisation?", *Economic and Political Weekly*, October 22.

George, K.K. (2011). "Kerala Economy: Growth, Structure, Strength And Weakness", *CSES Working Paper* No. 25. Cochin: Centre for Socio-economic & Environmental Studies.

Gine, Xavier and Robert Townsend (2004). "Evaluation of Financial Liberalisation: A General Equilibrium Model with Constrained Occupation Choice", *Journal of Development Economics* 74 (2).

Government of India (2008). *Report of the Committee on Financial Inclusion. http://www.nabard.org/pdf/report_financial/Full%20Report.pdf*

Jadhav, Narendra and Bhupal Singh (2006). ''Worker's Remittances as Stable Financial Flows: Some Evidence from India'', *Labour and Development* 11-12(1 & 2).

Mehrotra, *N., V. Puhazhendhi, G.G. Nair and B.B. Sahoo* (2009). "Financial Inclusion: An Overview", *NABARD Occasional Paper 48*. Mumbai: National Bank for Agriculture and Rural Development.

Reserve Bank of India (2008). "The Banking Sector in India: Emerging Issues and Challenges", *Report on Currency and Finance* 2006-08. Mumbai.

Singh, Bhupal (2010). "Workers' Remittances to India: An Examination of Transfer Cost and Efficiency", *International Migration* 48(5).

Subbarao, D. (2009). "Financial Inclusion: Challenges and Opportunities", Speech delivered at Bankers' Club in Kolkata, December 9.

Suran, B.S and D. Narayana, (2009). "The Deluge Of Debt: Understanding The Financial Needs of Poor Households", *CDS Working Paper* 412. Thiruvananthapuram: Centre for Development Studies.

Tharakan, Michael (2005). "Evolution of Economy and Society in Kerala: A Long Term Perspective", *Kerala Economy: Trajectories, Challenges and Implications*. Cochin: Directorate of Publication and Public Relations, Cochin University of Science and Technology. pp.11-24.

United Nations (2006). *Building Inclusive Financial Sectors for Development*. New York.

World Bank (2008). "Finance for All? Policies and Pitfalls in Expanding Access", *World Bank Policy Research Report*. Washington DC.

Annexure Table A-11.1

Demographic, Social and Human Development Indicators of Kerala

Sl. No.	*Particulars*	*Year*	*All-India*	*Kerala*
1.	Population and demographic features			
	Population: Kerala' share in all-India (%)	2011		2.76
	Rate of growth of population	2001-2011	17.6	4.9
	Total population (no. crore)	2011	121.01	3.33
	Male (no. crore)	2011	62.3	1.6
	Female (no. crore)	2011	58.7	1.7
	Death rate (per 1,000)	2008	7.4	6.6
	Birth rate (per 1,000)	2008	22.8	14.6
	Infant mortality rate (per 1,000 live births) (all)	2008	53.0	12.0
	Life expectancy at birth: Male	2002-2006	62.6	71.4
	Female	2002-2006	64.2	76.3
2	Literacy rate (persons)	2011	74.0	93.9
	Male	2011	82.1	96.02
	Female	2011	65.5	91.98
3	People below poverty line (total) (%)	2004-05	27.5	15.0
	Rural (%)	2004-2006	28.3	13.2
	Urban (%)	2004-2007	25.7	20.2
4	Human development index	2005	0.619	0.773
5	Employment Work participation rate (%)	2004-05		
	Rural male		54.6	55.9
	Rural female		32.7	25.6
	Urban male		54.9	54.7
	Urban female		16.6	20.0
	Unemployment rate (%)	1999-2000	3.1	12.0

Source : i) *Economic Survey*, Government of India.

ii) *Economic Review*, State Planning Board, Government of Kerala.

12

Financial Inclusion in West Bengal

SADHAN KUMAR CHATTOPADHYAY[1]

I

Introduction

The concept of financial inclusion can be traced back to the year 1904 when cooperative movement took place in India. It gained momentum in 1969 when 14 major commercial banks of the country were nationalised and lead bank scheme was introduced shortly thereafter. Branches were opened in large numbers across the country and even in the areas which were hitherto being neglected. Even after all these measures a sizable portion of the population of the country could not be brought under the fold of banking system. In fact, there is a severe gap in financial access which needs special attention. Studies have proved that lack of inclusion or rather exclusion from the banking system results in a loss of one per cent to the GDP. Thus, financial inclusion is not just a sociopolitical imperative but also an economic one. Realising the gravity of the problem, Reserve Bank in its *Mid Term Review of Monetary Policy* (2005-06), urged the banks to make financial inclusion as one of their prime objectives.

The concept of financial inclusion is not unique in India. The message of its positive impact is wide-spread across the globe. Most of the literature on banking sector outreach focus on its effect through cross-country evidence (Pechey and Roe, 2006; Beck *et al.*, 2006; Claessens,

---

1. The views expressed in this paper are of the author and not of the organisation he is working with. The author wishes to express his sincere thanks to S. Karuppasami, ED of RBI for his encouragement and also giving him the opportunity to do the survey. He would also like to express his deep gratitude towards C.D. Srinivasan, CGM, RPCD, RBI and Ashok Chatterjee, Assistant Adviser, DSIM, Kolkata for their useful guidance and cooperation in various stages of the study.

2006; Anderloni and Carluccio, 2007). Some of the studies which are important in this respect are Beck *et al.* (2007), Honohan (2004a), Galor and Zeira (1993), Klapper, Laeven and Rajan (2006) and Rajan and Zingales (2003). World Bank has also done a study on this subject for rural India and found that about 40 per cent of households have deposit accounts, 20 per cent have outstanding loans and only 15 per cent have any insurance (Basu, 2006).

Financial exclusion is broadly defined as the lack of access by certain segments of the society to suitable, low-cost, fair and safe financial products and services from mainstream providers. Thus, the essence of financial inclusion is to ensure that a range of appropriate financial services is available to every individual and enable them to understand and access those services. Apart from the regular form of financial intermediation, it may include a basic no-frills banking account for making and receiving payments, a savings product suited to the pattern of cash flows of a poor household, money transfer facilities, small loans and overdrafts for productive, personal and other purposes, insurance (life and non-life), etc. In fact, the main reasons for financial exclusion, from the demand side are lack of awareness, low income, poverty and illiteracy; and from the supply side is distance from branch, branch timings, cumbersome documentation and procedures, unsuitable products, language, staff attitudes, etc. Due to all these procedural hassles people feel it easier to take money from informal credit sources, but it results in compromised standard of living, higher costs, and increased exposure to unethical and unregulated providers and vulnerability to uninsured risks. Thus, financial inclusion does not mean merely opening of saving bank account but signifies creation of awareness about the financial products, education and advice on money management, offering debt counselling, etc., by banks. Every society should ensure easy access to public goods. Therefore, banking service being a public good should also be aimed at providing service to the entire population.

With this background, the major objective of the paper is to examine the extent of financial inclusion in West Bengal. Financial inclusion is meant to include all the sections of the society, who are mainly out of the net of the financial institutions. Since it is difficult to cover all the sections of the society in our study, we concentrate only on the rural sector because of its enormity on the one hand and significance on the other. Agriculture, being the vast sector of the economy, has a larger implication of financial inclusion. For example, improvement in rural infrastructure in terms of electricity, road, telecommunications, etc., is expected to establish a better overall supply chain management and enhance productivity of physical resources in the rural areas and value addition in agriculture. These developments would lead to much greater demand for banking services in the rural areas. Section II deals with background of the State of West Bengal followed by the index of financial inclusion which is discussed in Section III. Section IV deals with the findings of the survey which has been undertaken in three districts of the State. Section V concludes the study.

II

Background of the State

As per 2001 Census, the state of West Bengal has a total population of 8 crore out of which around 72 per cent are rural. Around 45.54 lakh people in the state are cultivators and 45.23 lakh are agricultural labourers. In line with the trend as set at the national and international level, West Bengal is also not laggard in outreach activity. The number of accounts per branch in the state has increased from 5,046 in 1980-81 to 8,966 in 2009-2010 (Annexure Table A-12.1). However, out of 18 districts in the state only five districts are above the average. The number of accounts per 100 adult persons has also, increased from 40 to 77 in the state during the period. Here also only five districts are above the average. Further, number of adult population per branch has decreased from 12,697 to 11,665 during the same period. On the other hand, although per capita deposit and credit have increased during the three decades period, C-D ratio remained very low in almost all the districts except North 24-Parganas and Kolkata (Annexure Table A-12.2). As per the directives of the Government and Reserve Bank of India (RBI), several steps have been taken in the state in order to increase financial inclusion. The state has already identified all the districts for 100 per cent financial inclusion, which means every household should have got at least one bank account.[2] Some of the important

2. However, the definition of financial inclusion has changed to a larger extent. Now the 100 per cent financial inclusion means ensuring banking access facilities to all the households of the village with a population of 2,000 or more.

initiatives taken so far in the State are introduction of 'no-frills account', introduction of Kisan Credit Card (KCC) Scheme, introduction of General Credit Card (GCC) Scheme, introduction of SHG-bank linkage programme (SBLP), introduction of business facilitator (BF) and business correspondent (BC) model, etc.

III

Index of Financial Inclusion

The term banking sector outreach or financial inclusion refers to the access to banking services and their use by households and firms (Beck *et al.*, 2006). There are various dimensions to access: availability of financial services, cost of access, range, type and quality of financial services offered (Claessesns, 2006). Access is not synonymous to use. Economic agents might decide not to use accessible financial service, either for socio-economic reasons, or because opportunity costs are too high (Beck *et al.*, 2006). The counter part of access is exclusion. Financial exclusion may be caused by: (1) 'geographic limitations' due to under-provision of banking services in remote and scarcely populated areas, (2) 'socioeconomic limitations' when financial services appear inaccessible to specific income, socio or ethnic groups, or (3) 'limitations of opportunity', when new or small firms with profitable projects are credit rationed because of lack of information and collaterals (Beck and de la Torre, 2006; Anderloni and Carluccio, 2007: 9).

So far, the literature on financial sector development has focused primarily on the dimension of depth, its measurement, determinants and its economic impact. Little is known about the breadth or the outreach of financial systems across countries, its determinants and impact on development. This is partly due to inadequacy of data (see Honohan, 2004b).

To measure financial inclusion, several proxy indicators have been used in the literature (Table 12.1). Proxi (i) measures access to and use of bank accounts. Full access may be reached, if the number of accounts per adult is above 0.5 (Peachy and Roe, 2006). The penetration of banks' physical outlets (branches, ATMs) is measured by (ii)–(v). While higher geographic branch and ATM penetration indicate smaller distance and thus easier geographic access, higher demographic branch and ATM penetration indicates easier access because of fewer potential clients per outlet. The use of loans and deposit is measured by (vi)–(ix). A higher demographic loan or deposit penetration indicates larger use, and higher loan or deposit-income ratios signal that these services may only be affordable to larger enterprises or wealthier individuals. The loan-income ratio is above 2 in rich countries, but above 8 in poor countries (Beck *et al.,* 2006). Alternative measures of deposit penetration are the deposit-GDP ratio or the cash-deposit ratio. According to Peachy and Roe (2006), an economy has reached full access, if the deposit-GDP ratio is 100 per cent or the Cash-Deposit ratio is below 20 per cent. This measures the development of the financial system rather than deposit penetration. For the indicators (ii)-(ix), a country may be considered approaching full access, if its outreach indicator lies above the mean value in developed countries (Beck and de la Torre, 2006).

Table 12.1

Indicators of Banking Sector Outreach

	Indicator	*Measurement*
(i)	Bank accounts per adult	Number of bank accounts per adult
(ii)	Geographic branch penetration	Number of branches per 1000 km^2
(iii)	Demographic branch penetration	Number of branches per 1,00,000 people
(iv)	Geographic ATM penetration	Number of bank ATMs per 1000 km^2
(v)	Demographic ATM penetration	Number of bank ATMs per 1,00,000 people
(vi)	Demographic loan penetration	Number of loans per 1,00,000 people
(vii)	Loan-income ratio	Average size of loan to GDP per capita
(viii)	Demographic deposit penetration	Number of deposits per 1,00,000 people
(ix)	Deposit-income ratio (or deposit-GDP Ratio)	Average size of Deposits to GDP per capita (or total bank deposits to GDP)
(x)	Cash-Deposit ratio	Cash in circulation to total bank deposits

Source: Conrad *et al.* (2008).

Thus, several indicators have been used to assess the extent of financial inclusion. However, the indicators discussed above, while used individually, provide only partial information on the inclusiveness of the financial system of an economy. Using individual indicators can lead to misleading picture of the extent of financial inclusion in an economy. Therefore, any single indicator fails to adequately capture the extent of financial inclusion.[3] In order to address this problem, we have developed an index of financial inclusion, which is able to capture information on several aspects in one single number. Such a measure is useful to compare the levels of financial inclusion across economies and across states within countries at a particular time period. It can be used to monitor the progress of policy initiatives for financial inclusion in a country over a period of time. In this paper, first we calculate state-wise index of financial inclusion (IFI) and then we calculate IFI for the state of West Bengal at the district level which is the main focus of our study. It may be stated in this regard that unless we know the level of financial inclusion at the state level, it will be difficult to get a comparable position of financial inclusion in West Bengal. That's why by calculating the IFI at the state level, we can understand the comparable position of West Bengal *vis-à-vis* the rest of the states in the country. The IFI satisfies the following criteria:

(i) It should incorporate information on as many aspects (dimensions) of inclusion as possible.

(ii) It should be easy and simple to compute.

(iii) It should be comparable across countries/states.

The proposed IFI takes values between 0 and 1, zero indicating lowest financial inclusion (i.e., complete financial exclusion) and 1 indicating complete financial inclusion.

Methodology

Since inclusive financial system is judged from several dimensions, we follow a multidimensional approach while constructing the index of financial inclusion (IFI). Our approach is similar to the one used by Sarma (2008). UNDP (United Nations Development Programme) has also used similar kind of approach for computation of some well known development indexes such as HDI, the HPL, the GDI and so on.[4] As in the case of these indexes, IFI is computed by first calculating a dimension index for each

---

3. Details may be found in Sarma (2008).
4. For details see Technical Note in UNDP's Human Development Reports available at *<www.undp.org>*.

dimension of financial inclusion. The dimension of index for the ith dimension, $d_{i,}$ is computed by the following formula.

$$d_i = \frac{A_i - m_i}{M_i - m_i} \quad (1)$$

where,

A_i = Actual value of dimension i.

m_i = minimum value of dimension i.

M_i = maximum value dimension i.

Formula (1) ensures that $0 \leq d_i \leq 1$. Higher the value of d_i, higher the state's achievement in dimension i. If n dimension of financial inclusion are considered, then a state i will be represented by a point $D_i = (D_1, D_2, \ldots\ldots D_n)$ on the n-dimensional Cartesian space.

In the n-dimensional space, the point O = (0, 0,......0) represents the point indicating the worst situation while the point I = (1, 1, ...,1) represents the highest achievement in all dimensions. The index of financial inclusion, IFI_i, for the i-th state, then is measured by the normalised inverse Euclidean distance of the point D_i from the ideal point I = (1, 1, ...,1). The exact formula becomes,

$$IFI_i = 1 - \frac{\sqrt{(1-d_1)^2 + (1-d_2)^2 + \ldots + (1-d_n)^2}}{\sqrt{n}} \quad (2)$$

In formula (2), the numerator of the second component is the Euclidian distance of D_i from the ideal point I, normalising it by $\sqrt{n}$ and subtracting from 1 gives the inverse normalised distance. The normalisation is done in order to make the value lie between 0 and 1 and the inverse distance is considered so that higher value corresponds to higher financial inclusion.

In this paper, we consider three basic dimensions of an inclusive financial system—banking penetration (BP), availability of the banking services (BS) and usage of the banking system (BU). The main reasons for selecting these dimensions are data availability and recent development in the literature.[5]

Banking Penetration (Dimension 1)

This is one of the most important indicators of financial inclusion. Ideally, inclusive financial system should penetrate widely amongst its users. The size of the banked population, i.e., number of adult population having a bank account is a measure of the banking penetration of the system. Thus if every adult person in an economy has a bank account, then the value of this measure would be equal to 1. In the absence of the data on banked population, we use number of bank accounts as a proportion of the total population as an indicator of this dimension. However, we use both deposit account and credit account or loan account as the indicators of banking penetration.

Availability of Banking Services (Dimension 2)

Under an inclusive financial system, banking services should be easily available to its users. Availability of services can be indicated by the number of bank outlets (per 1000 population) and/or by the number of ATM per 1000 people, or the number of bank employees per customer. In India, there is another concept introduced in the banking system which is known as banking correspondence (BC) model in order to provide the banking services to the people of the nation. In the absence of data on the number of ATMs and number of BCs appointed, we use the number of bank branches per 1000 adult population and also number of branches per square km to measure the availability dimension.[6]

Usage (Dimension 3)

This dimension emerges from the concept of 'underbanked' or 'marginally banked' people, as observed by Kempson *et al.* (2004). It

5. One could think of taking some other dimensions, like timeliness, affordability etc. However, due to non-availability of such information we could not incorporate these dimensions in the present study.

6. Although Sarma (2008) mentioned that the number of staff per customer can be an important indicator of availability of banking service, we do not support this view. This is because in the age of technology number of staff perhaps does not matter.

observes that 'in some apparently very highly-banked countries, a number of people with bank account are nonetheless making very little use of the services on offer'. Thus merely having a bank account does not ensure that the system is inclusive; it is also imperative that the banking services are adequately utilised. In order to incorporate the usage dimension in our index, we consider two basic services of the banking system—outstanding credit and deposit. Accordingly, the volume of outstanding deposit and credit as proportion of the net district domestic product (NDDP) has been used to measure this dimension.

Thus, considering the above three dimensions—penetration, availability and usage—we can represent a state i by a point (p_i, a_i, u_i) in the three dimensional Cartesian space, such that, $0 \leq p_i, a_i, u_I \leq 1$, where p_i, a_i and u_i denote the dimension indexes for the state i computed using formula (1). In the three-dimensional Cartesian space, the point (0, 0, 0) will indicate the worst situation (complete financial exclusion) and the point (1, 1, 1) will indicate the best or ideal situation (complete financial inclusion).

The IFI for the state i is measured by the normalised inverse Euclidean distance of the point (p_i, a_i, u_i) from the ideal point (1, 1, 1). Algebraically,

$$IFI_i = 1 - \frac{\sqrt{(1-p_i)^2 + (1-a_i)^2 + (1-u_i)^2}}{\sqrt{n}} \qquad (3)$$

Data

Since the initiatives on financial inclusion in India were taken during 2005-06, we have computed the index from 2006-07 till 2009-10. First, we have computed the index for 23 states of India along with all-India average. Then we have computed the indcx for 18 districts of West Bengal for which data are available. All banking data have been taken from Banking Statistics of Reserve Bank. Data on adult population and geographical area of the states have been taken from Census of India and figures on net districts domestic products have been taken from the Bureau of Applied Economics and Statistics, Government of West Bengal.

Results

Using data on all three dimensions (penetration, availability and usage) for 23 states and 18 districts for the years 2006-2009, IFI values have been computed and averaged for four years.

Depending on the values of IFI, states and districts are categorised into three categories, *viz.*:

(i) $0.5 < \text{IFI} \leq 1$ – high financial inclusion

(ii) $0.3 \leq \text{IFI} < 0.5$ – medium financial inclusion

(iii) $0 \leq \text{IFI} < 0.3$ – low financial inclusion

State-wise Financial Inclusion

In the group of 23 states for which a three-dimensional IFI has been estimated by using data on three dimensions of financial inclusion, Kerala leads with the highest value of IFI followed by Maharashtra and Karnataka (Table 12.2). However, only three states, *viz.*, Kerala, Maharashtra and Karnataka belong to the high IFI group with IFI values of 0.5 or more. Another six states, *viz.*, Tamil Nadu, Punjab, Andhra Pradesh, Himachal Pradesh, Sikkim and Haryana form the group of medium IFI states with IFI values between 0.3 and 0.5. In fact, all-India average IFI also falls under this category. All other states have a low IFI values, ranging between 0.0 and 0.3. It is interesting to note that all the southern states are at the high or medium level of financial inclusion and except Sikkim all the eastern, northeastern and central states are in the low level of financial inclusion. On the other hand, West Bengal and Gujarat rank 11th and 12th, respectively in financial inclusion. Further, out of seven northeastern states, three states belong to the lowest rank of financial inclusion.

District-wise Financial Inclusion in West Bengal

Now coming to the West Bengal scenario, it is observed that in the group of 18 districts for which a three-dimensional IFI has been computed by using data on three dimensions of financial inclusion, Kolkata leads with the highest value of IFI followed by Darjeeling (Table 12.3). However, only one district, *viz.*, Kolkata belongs to the high IFI group with IFI values

Table 12.2

State-wise Index of Financial Inclusion

State	*D1 (Penetration)*	*D2 (Availability)*	*D3 (Usage)*	*IFI*	*IFI Rank*
High financial inclusion (0.5-1)					
Kerala	0.70	0.81	0.28	0.54	1
Maharashtra	0.62	0.29	1	0.53	2
Karnataka	0.72	0.47	0.46	0.53	3
Medium financial inclusion (0.3-0.5)					
Tamil Nadu	0.70	0.43	0.38	0.48	4
Punjab	0.45	0.69	0.29	0.45	5
Andhra Pradesh	0.56	0.30	0.41	0.41	6
Himachal Pradesh	0.42	0.40	0.18	0.33	8
Sikkim	0.28	0.33	0.34	0.32	9
Haryana	0.39	0.50	0.12	0.32	10
All-India	0.27	0.22	0.55	0.33	7
Low financial inclusion (<0.3)					
West Bengal	0.24	0.38	0.23	0.28	11
Gujarat	0.32	0.30	0.16	0.26	12
Uttar Pradesh	0.28	0.31	0.15	0.24	13
Meghalaya	0.21	0.28	0.14	0.21	14
Tripura	0.31	0.22	0.08	0.20	15
Orissa	0.26	0.23	0.11	0.20	16
Rajasthan	0.25	0.22	0.12	0.19	17
Arunachal Pradesh	0.20	0.16	0.14	0.17	18
Mizoram	0.13	0.26	0.09	0.16	19
Madhya Pradesh	0.18	0.21	0.08	0.16	20
Bihar	0.15	0.24	0.08	0.15	21
Assam	0.17	0.17	0.07	0.13	22
Nagaland	0.03	0.04	0.07	0.05	23
Manipur	0.00	0.01	0.01	0.01	24

Note: Author's own calculations.

of 1.0. All other districts have a low IFI values, hovering between 0.0 and 0.3. It is interesting to note that no district is falling under the medium level of financial inclusion. Thus, the IFI values clearly indicate that level of financial inclusion is significantly low in West Bengal.

Table 12.3

Index of Financial Inclusion: Using Three Dimensions of Financial Inclusion (Four-year Average)

State	*D1 (Penetration)*	*D2 (Availability)*	*D3 (Usage)*	*IFI*	*IFI Rank*
High financial inclusion (0.5-1)					
Kolkata	1.00	1.00	1.00	1.00	1
Low financial inclusion (< 0.3)					
Darjeeling	0.23	0.10	0.10	0.14	2
Birbhum	0.16	0.06	0.03	0.08	3
Bardhaman	0.13	0.06	0.06	0.08	4
Haora	0.10	0.05	0.07	0.07	5
Hugli	0.10	0.04	0.04	0.06	6
Bankura	0.12	0.04	0.02	0.06	7
North 24-Parganas	0.09	0.03	0.06	0.06	8
Koch Bihar	0.13	0.03	0.01	0.05	9
Midnapore	0.09	0.04	0.02	0.05	10
Maldah	0.09	0.04	0.01	0.05	11
Nadia	0.08	0.01	0.02	0.04	12
Puruliya	0.06	0.03	0.02	0.04	13
Dakshin Dinajpur	0.07	0.02	0.01	0.03	14
Jalpaiguri	0.07	0.01	0.02	0.03	15
Uttar Dinajpur	0.05	0.00	0.01	0.02	16
Murshidabad	0.05	0.01	0.01	0.02	17
South 24-Parganas	0.02	0.00	0.01	0.01	18

Note: Author's own calculations.

IV

Survey of Financial Inclusion in West Bengal

As mentioned above, a survey on financial inclusion was conducted in three districts of West Bengal in order to understand the nature and extent of financial inclusion in the state. The objective of the study was primarily to identify the extent of financial exclusion of the rural Bengal. Besides, the study has focused, *inter alia*, on some socioeconomic indicators like occupation, literacy, landholding pattern in rural areas, rural indebtedness and people's opinion about banking services in India in general and West Bengal, in particular.

Methodology

Data have been collected from the various households in two/three blocks in each of the three districts of East Midnapore, Birbhum and Murshidabad in West Bengal. Selection of these three districts was based on the level of developments of these districts. Out of these three districts, East Mindnapore is relatively better developed and Murshidabad is moderately developed, whereas Birbhum is lesser developed.[7] So, in a way, these three districts indicate the overall picture of the state. Selection of households has been done on a random basis. However, the occupations of the households are mixed, i.e., they are a mix of farmers, landless labourers, small traders etc. In fact, the districts that have been chosen have some unique features of their own by the geographical position, the level of trade activities in East Midnapore, large composition of tribal population and unbanked areas in the district of Birbhum and the border of Murshidabad adjacent to Bangladesh having a strong base of minority people of Muslims, and having a predominant occupation of *bidi*-making. A total of 329 households (HHs), in three districts of East Midnapore (103 HHs), Birbhum (108 HHs) and Murshidabad (118 HHs) have been taken up for the survey. The relevant questionnaire with around 60 questions was prepared encompassing various issues like occupation, level of literacy, rural indebtedness and present situation of financial inclusion, landholding pattern etc.

Occupational Structure and Landholding Pattern

The survey results revealed that over 44 per cent of the population in the three districts surveyed is dependent on cultivation. The result has revealed that 34.3 per cent households occupy land holdings in the size below 1.0 acre on an average. Little over 61 per cent of the households in East Midnapore are marginal farmers occupying land size below 1.0 acre, whereas in Birbhum and Murshidabad around 21.0 per cent and 23.0 per cent, respectively are having land size less than 1.0 acre. Further, around 43.0 per cent people are landless in three districts (Table 12.4). District-wise, Murshidabad district has the highest landless labourers (33.1%),

7. As per the data published by Bureau of Applied Economics and Statistics, Government of West Bengal, the per capita income of East Midnapore was Rs 27,927 in 2007-08, Murshidabad's was Rs 18,720 and Birbhum's was Rs 17,847.

followed by Birbhum (25.0%) and East Midnapore (8.7%). Households have an average family size of around 5.5 members with 1.41 earning members. District-wise, East Midnapore has the highest family size and Birbhum has the lowest family size. Further, each household with 5.5 family size has 1.4 earning member, implying very high dependency ratio in these districts.

Table 12.4

Occupational Structure and Landholding Pattern

(Per cent)

District	*No. of Households (HHs)*	*Occupation*				*Area of Land (Acres)*		*No. of Family Members*	*No. of Earning Members*
		Cultivation	*Business*	*Service*	*Landless Labour*	*0-1*	*1-2.5*		
1	*2*	*3*	*4*	*5*	*6*	*7*	*8*	*9*	*10*
East Midnapore	103	54.4	18.4	7.8	8.7	61.2	6.8	6.5	1.5
Birbhum	108	44.4	24.1	2.78	25.0	21.3	18.5	4.6	1.36
Murshidabad	118	34.7	33.9	16.1	33.1	23.0	13.6	5.4	1.36
Total	329	44.1	49.1	17.2	43.1	34.3	13.1	5.5	1.41

Note: Author's own calculations.

Survey Results

The survey has revealed that about 61.7 per cent of the households had opened an account with a commercial bank or RRB or a cooperative society. Of this, district of East Midnapore has shown an encouraging figure with 72.8 per cent of the households having a bank account, while for the district of Birbhum, the figure has been dismally placed at 51.9 per cent and the district of Murshidabad has shown the overall average of 61.0 per cent. Among these three districts, East Midnapore has the highest percentage (86.4%) of adequate banking facilities in the locality. Average monthly income of the family was found to be highest in Murshidabad followed by East Midnapore and Birbhum. It has been observed that the poor result in respect of bank account in the district of Birbhum can be attributed to the prevalence of savings accounts in the post offices where the proceeds of NREGA accounts are routed through these post office savings accounts. The result may seem to be less encouraging if the households in a village adopted by NABARD where all the households have bank accounts under a self-help group (SHG) are excluded from the survey. The main reason cited by the respondents for less number of bank account was low income level which is insufficient to maintain even their minimum level of consumption.

About 77.5 per cent households have admitted adequate banking facilities in the locality and 90.6 per cent households operate their bank accounts by personal visits while only 5.9 per cent households use the ATM cards. So far as income levels of the households are concerned, the distribution is much skewed at an average of Rs 3530.10 per family and for Birbhum, it is Rs 2485.90 only and about 9.12 per cent of the surveyed households receive pension through Government Pension Scheme (Table 12.5).

Table 12.5

Banking Habits

(Per cent)

District	*Average Monthly Income (Rs)*	*Any Assistance through Pension of Government Scheme*	*Banking Facilities Adequate in the Locality*	*Any Bank Account by Any of the Family Members*	*Mode of Operation of Bank Account*		*Whether Satisfied with the Arrangement*
					ATM	*Personal Visit to Bank*	
1	*2*	*3*	*4*	*5*	*6*	*7*	*8*
East Midnapore	3,448.0	10.7	86.4	72.8	5.3	77.4	88.0
Birbhum	2,485.9	12.1	75.0	51.9	3.6	91.1	92.2
Murshidabad	4,812.0	5.1	72.0	61.0	8.4	93.1	98.6
Total	3,530.1	9.1	77.5	61.7	5.9	90.6	98.1

Note: Author's own calculations.

Rural Indebtedness

The survey has revealed that moneylenders are still a dominant source of rural finance despite wide presence of banks in rural areas and in about 66.5 per cent cases finance is received from village moneylenders at exorbitantly high rate of interest (around 10-20 per cent per month) as detailed in Table 12.7. In 28.1 per cent cases, collateral security is required to be furnished by the borrowers. Among these three districts, dependence on moneylenders is lowest in East Midnapore district and highest in Birbhum. However, in the district of East Midnapore, moneylenders are more formal than two other districts. This is because, in the case of former, around 88.6 per cent of households pay interest to the moneylenders, followed by Birbhum and Murshidabad. In the latter two districts, moneylenders are giving loans with some terms and conditions. Sometimes they do not insist on collateral; but if the loan is not repaid within the time limit then interest rate may go up even to double. In some other cases, loan is provided by the local moneylenders to the borrowers with the condition that the latter would provide their labour at the time of their need, mostly during the sowing or harvesting season. In local term it is called *'bandha munish'*. It is normally observed that mostly the villagers take loan from the local moneylenders for consumption purposes. It can be observed that around 63.4 per cent of the people pay interest to the moneylenders (Table 12.6).

In the case of East Midnapore district, in 49.5 per cent cases, people take loans from the village moneylenders due to the fact that the area is extremely busy in agriculture, trade and allied activities and due to the existence of SHGs. The area has a distinct advantage of having a nearby fishing harbour, cashew nut cultivation and processing factories and plenty of youth engaged in restaurants within the country and overseas. In the district of Murshidabad, it was observed that a big section of the population (mostly women) is engaged in *bidi* industry which is very popular in the district. It is also observed that although dependence on moneylenders in Birbhum is highest among the three, the number of cases where interest is paid is relatively low. This is simply because moneylenders are providing loans to the villagers with different term and conditions.

Data suggest that 76.0 per cent of households are willing to take loan from the banks due to comparatively lower interest rates. About 51.4 per cent households have availed loan from the commercial banks, while 37.1 per cent households have availed the same from the RRBs. In case of the district of Birbhum, having a sizeable tribal population, loans floated by commercial banks and cooperative banks are very less due to the fact that the families do not have any meaningful income and they lack direction in business plans.

Table 12.6

Extent of Rural Indebtedness

(*Per cent*)

District	*Source of Debt in Need*			*No. of Households where Interest is Paid*	*No. of Households where Collateral Security has been Furnished*	*No. of Households Willing to take Bank Loan*	*Any Loan from Money-lenders*	*If Taken, from which Bank*		
	Relative	*Friends*	*Money-lender*					*Com. Bank*	*RRB*	*Coop. Bank*
1	*2*	*3*	*4*	*5*	*6*	*7*	*8*	*9*	*10*	*11*
East Midnapore	8.7	18.5	49.5	88.6	49.4	65.1	51.1	66.6	7.13	26.1
Birbhum	9.3	3.8	64.8	53.6	20.2	79.6	42.6	34.7	63.2	2.1
Murshidabad	13.8	33.0	53.2	51.1	17.1	82.2	33.1	64.3	35.7	-
Total	12.5	21.1	66.5	63.4	28.1	76.0	41.7	51.4	37.1	11.5

Note: Author's own calculations.

Table 12.7

Incidence of Interest Rates of Moneylenders in Rural Areas

Range (Rs) (Per cent per Month)	*East Midnapore (No. of Cases)*	*Birbhum (No. of Cases)*	*Murshidabad (No. of Cases)*
2 – 3	30	8	5
>3 – 5	19	8	10
>5 – 7	5	1	1
>7 – 10	5	25	23
>10 – 20	3	3	3
Total	62	45	42

Note: Author's own calculations.

Results reveal that 73.2 per cent households have their nearest branch of the bank within a distance of 5 kms and 70.2 per cent households find the behaviour of the banks is friendly and 22.5 per cent of households find that the banks are either indifferent or non-cooperative in its approach. Around 95.8 per cent households place their faith in Indian banking system and in 72.9 per cent of the cases, friends and relatives is still a dominant source of information in banking. About 79.9 per cent households seek simplification of procedures and documentation for getting loans and this has become a great reason for dominance of village money-lenders (Table 12.8).

The survey has further revealed that 32.2 per cent households are not aware of the opportunities of the bank loans at a lower rate of interest and this again points to the need of spread of financial literacy in the rural areas. During the survey, it has been observed that, on some occasions, people do not know whether they can deposit their own money for saving in the bank accounts opened for the receipt of their NREGA proceeds.

V

Conclusion

The issue of financial inclusion has received large importance in India during the recent years. India had invested considerable amount of resources in expanding its banking network with the objective of reaching to the people. During the last 40 years huge infrastructure has been created

Table 12.8

People and Indian Banking

District	Whether Aware of Lower Interest Rates in Banks	Whether getting Bank Loans Difficult	If yes, Reasons for			Percentage of Surveyed Households who have Faith in Indian Banks	Distance to Nearest Bank (in kms)		Behaviour of Bank Employees		
			Form Fill-up Difficult	Insistence on Collateral Security	Lack of Business Plan		<5	6-10	Friendly	Indifferent	Non-Cooperative
1	2	3	4	5	6	7	8	9	10	11	12
East Midnapore	77.7	46.6	43.7	30.1	25.3	89.3	79.6	20.4	85.4	1.9	4.8
Birbhum	77.8	69.5	41.7	55.6	16.7	99.0	74.1	25.9	73.1	11.1	7.4
Murshidabad	50.8	67.8	52.5	76.3	17.8	98.3	66.9	23.7	54.2	24.6	15.3
Total	68.1	61.7	49.2	55.1	19.7	95.8	73.2	17.1	70.2	13.1	9.4

Source: Author's own calculation.

in the banking sector. However, this large infrastructure that has penetrated even remote rural areas has been able to serve only a small part of the potential customers. While India is on a very high growth path, almost at the two-digit level, majority of the people are out of the growth process. This is neither desirable nor sustainable for the nation. We also know that one of most important driving forces of growth is institutional finance. Therefore, it is now realised that unless all the people of the society are brought under the ambit of institutional finance, the benefit of high growth will not percolate down and by that process majority of the population will be deprived of the benefits of high growth. Thus, financial inclusion is not only sociopolitical imperative but also an economic one. It is observed from the study that the achievement of financial inclusion in West Bengal is not significant. Although some improvement in respect of some parameters might have been taken place, this is not sufficient to conclude that financial inclusion has taken place in the state.

We have developed an index of financial inclusion using data on three dimensions of financial inclusion. This is useful to monitor the progress of policy initiatives for financial inclusion in a country/state over a period of time. The result shows that in the group of 18 districts for which a three-dimensional IFI has been estimated by using data on three dimensions of financial inclusion, Kolkata leads with the highest value of IFI followed by Darjeeling district. Only one district, *viz.*, Kolkata belongs to the high IFI group with IFI values of 1.0. All other districts have a low IFI values, hovering between 0.0 and 0.3. It is also observed that the level of financial inclusion in West Bengal is very low as against the rest of the major states of the country. In fact, no significant achievement has taken place in financial inclusion in the state since 2005-06 (period of commencement of the initiatives in the country). This is confirmed by the survey we have conducted in the three districts of West Bengal, *viz.*, East Midnapore, Birbhum and Murshidabad. The survey results revealed that over 44 per cent of the population in the three districts surveyed is dependent on cultivation. About 61.7 per cent of the households had opened an account with a commercial bank or RRB or a cooperative society. Remaining 38 per cent feel that they do not have sufficient income to open an account in the bank. About 77.5 per cent of the respondents feel that that there are adequate banking facilities in the locality. The survey has revealed that moneylenders are still a dominant source of rural finance despite wide presence of banks in rural areas and in about 66.5 per cent cases finance is received from village moneylenders at exorbitantly high rate of interest. In 28.1 per cent cases, collateral security is required to be provided by the borrowers. It is found that 76.0 per cent households are willing to take loan from the banks due to comparatively lower interest rates in the banks and 51.4 per cent households have availed loan from the commercial banks, while 37.1 per cent households have availed the same from the RRBs. In case of the district of Birbhum, having a sizeable tribal population, loans floated by commercial banks and cooperative banks are very less due to the fact that the families do not have any meaningful income and lack of direction in business plans.

Results reveal that 73.2 per cent households have their nearest branch of the bank within a distance of 5 kms. The survey has further revealed that 32.2 per cent households are not aware of the opportunities of the bank loans at a lower rate of interest and this again points to the need of spread of financial literacy in the rural areas.

In a nutshell, it is observed that although various measures have been undertaken for financial inclusion, the success is not found to be noteworthy. However, only supply-side factor is not responsible for the financial exclusion. Demand-side factors are also equally responsible. Thus, there is a need to solve both these problems with the help of appropriate policies. Banks should look at financial inclusion both as a business opportunity and as a social responsibility. Apart from formal banking institutions the role of the SHG movement and microfinance institutions (MFIs) is important to improve financial inclusion. However, some regulatory procedures for MFIs may have to be evolved in consultations with MFIs, consumers and the government. Political interference in the financial system should be avoided in order to maintain the viability of the formal financial institutions. The risk elements of small and marginal farmers and other vulnerable groups have to be taken into account in framing policies for financial inclusion. Banking correspondent (BC) model has to be made more effective, by involving more local people. Proper BC model can take care of problems of supply and demand factors to a greater extent. In fact, providing the banking service is not sufficient. Many rural people still are not aware of banking products and they are reluctant to take the advantage of banking facilities. Therefore, financial literacy among the rural people is important. This apart, because of various formalities involved in availing loans etc., they are scared of going to bank and hence fall back upon the moneylenders. But since BC is recruited from the local people they can solve these problems. On the one hand, they can do the formalities on behalf of the illiterate or semi-literate people and on the other, they would educate them how to benefit from the banking service in an effective manner. Above all, a wholehearted effort is called for from all the corners of the society, *viz.*, banks, beneficiaries and regulators in order to make financial inclusion more meaningful and effective.

References

Anderloni, L. and E.M. Carluccio (2007). "Access to Bank Accounts and Payment Services", in L. Anderloni, M.D. Braga and E.M. Carluccio (eds.), *New Frontiers in Banking Services*, Berlin *et al.*: Springer. pp.5-105.

Baltagi, B.H. (1999). *Econometrics*. Second (revised) edition. Berlin *et al*.: Springer,. pp.189-201.

Basu, P. (2006). *Improving Access to Finance for India's Rural Poor.* Washington, DC: The World Bank.

Beck, T., A. Demirguc-Kunt and M.S. Martinez Peria (2006). *Reaching Out: Access and Use of Banking Services Across Countries.* Washington D.C.: World Bank. July.

Beck, T., A. Demirguc-Kunt and R. Levine (2007). "Finance, Inequality and the Poor", *Journal of Economic Growth* 12: 27-49.

Beck, T. and A. de la Torre (2007). "The Basic Analytics of Access to Financial Services", *Financial Markets, Institutions and Instruments* 16.

Beck, T., A. Demirguc-Kunt, M. Peria and M. Soledad (2006). "Banking Services for Everyone? Barriers to Bank Access and Use Around the World", *Working Paper Series* No. 4079. World Bank Policy Research.

Claessens, S. (2006). "Access to Financial Services: A Review of the Issues and Public Policy Objectives", *The World Bank Research Observer* 21(2): 207-40.

Conrad, A., D. Neuberger and M. Schneider-Reißig (2008). "Geographic and Demographic Bank Outreach: Evidence from Germany's Three-Pillar Banking System", *Working Paper* No. 98. University of Rostock.

Galor, O. and J. Zeira (1993). "Income Distribution and Macroeconomics", *Review of Economic Studies* 60: 35–52.

Honohan, P. (2004a). "Financial Developoment, Growth and Poverty: How Close are the Links?", in Charles Goodhart (ed.), *Financial Development and Economic Growth: Explaining the Links*. London: Palgrave.

———. (2004b). "Data on Microfinance and Access: Thinking about what is Available and What is Needed". World Bank. *mimeo.*

Kempson E, A. Atkinson and O. Pilley (2004). "Policy Level Response to Financial Exclusion in Developed Economies: Lessons for Developing Countries", *Report of Personal Finance Research Centre.* University of Bristol.

Klapper, L., L. Laeven and R. Rajan (2006). "Entry Regulation as Barrier to Entrepreneurship", *Journal of Financial Economics* 82: 591–629.

Peachy, S. and A. Roe (2006). "Access to Finance—What does it Mean and how do Savings Banks Foster Access: A Study for the World Savings Banks Institute", *Perspectives* No. 49. Oxford Policy Management.

Rajan, R. and L. Zingales (2003). *Saving Capitalism from the Capitalists.* Crown Business Division of Random House.

Sarma, M. (2008). "Index of Financial Inclusion", *Working Paper* No. 215. New Delhi: ICRIER.

Annexure Table A-12.1

District-wise Outreach of Scheduled Commercial Banks in West Bengal

Name of Districts	*No. Accounts per Branch*				*No. of Accounts per 100 Adult Persons**				*No. of Adult Population per Branch**			
	1980-81	*1990-91*	*2000-01*	*2009-10*	*1980-81*	*1990-91*	*2000-01*	*2009-10*	*1980-81*	*1990-91*	*2000-01*	*2009-10*
Bankura	2,856	3,705	5,520	7,112	13	36	49	55	22,025	10,276	11,286	12,863
Bardhaman	5,103	6,464	7,528	8,724	35	66	68	76	14,763	9,802	11,011	11,501
Birbhum	2,146	3,331	5,304	7,715	14	40	55	69	14,918	8,285	9,646	11,119
Dakshin Dinajpur	2,968	14,805	3,714	5,846	18	108	27	37	16,308	8,941	14,065	16,688
Darjiling	3,817	6,625	7,011	8,166	38	81	81	96	10,087	8,224	8,610	8,470
Haora	5,405	7,918	10,331	10,430	41	63	87	82	13,228	12,488	11,904	12,652
Hugli	5,658	6,774	9,251	10,375	37	71	73	78	15,458	9,600	12,620	13,313
Jalpaiguri	3,309	4,205	5,755	8,069	14	35	41	50	23,717	12,024	14,033	16,012
Koch Bihar	2,963	3,200	4,387	6,782	13	25	35	45	23,065	12,662	12,585	14,978
Kolkata	7,163	10,252	10,348	10,064	226	312	334	301	3,168	3,289	3,098	3,345
Maldah	2,640	3,092	4,540	7,042	10	28	39	51	25,595	10,981	11,559	13,751
Murshidabad	3,154	3,847	5,641	8,247	41	33	41	28	7,684	11,823	13,715	28,965
Nadia	4,462	5,225	7,509	9,174	22	43	50	53	19,973	12,253	15,150	17,418
North 24 Parganas	6,146	8,465	11,373	11,662	68	84	90	48	10,344	13,492	15,546	14,825
Midnapore	3,200	3,858	5,345	4,051	12	35	46	31	26,235	11,000	11,520	13,173
Puruliya	2,401	4,355	5,702	6,808	13	35	45	48	18,709	12,575	12,728	14,115
South 24 Parganas	6,146	5,200	7,912	8,775								
Uttar Dinajpur	2,968	7,164	3,952	6,306								
West Bengal	5,046	6,265	8,095	8,966	40	68	75	77	12,697	9,173	10,800	11,665

Annexure Table A-12.2

District-wise Pattern of Deposits, Loans and C-D Ratio

	Per Capita Deposits				*Per Capita Credits*				*C-D Ratio*			
	1980	*1990*	*2000*	*2009*	*1980*	*1990*	*2000*	*2009*	*1980*	*1990*	*2000*	*2009*
24 Parganas N	543	30	6,101	5,018	85	15	783	4,213	15.6	49.0	12.8	84.0
24 Parganas S									15.6	56.3	15.7	32.4
Bankura	211	1,045	4,201	12,408	58	375	969	3,696	27.3	35.9	23.1	29.8
Bardhaman	842	3,030	9,981	28,502	291	923	2,202	9,073	34.5	30.5	22.1	31.8
Birbhum	277	1,250	5,003	14,694	86	512	1,283	4,323	30.9	40.9	25.7	29.4
Dinajpur	144	124	2,421	7,620	64	150	737	3,932	44.1	121.2	30.4	51.6
Darjiling	998	3,409	12,849	33,367	278	1,429	3,268	19,545	27.9	41.9	25.4	58.6
Haora	973	2,744	10,227	27,532	207	759	1,758	7,961	21.3	27.7	17.2	28.9
Hugli	727	2,777	7,747	21,517	163	912	1,297	5,209	22.4	32.8	16.7	24.2
Jalpaiguri	316	1,468	5,107	11,742	143	577	934	4,113	45.2	39.3	18.3	35.0
Koch Bihar	206	74	2,756	7,711	67	90	900	4,215	32.6	121.3	32.6	54.7
Kolkata	11,970	36,288	97,946	317,005	9,288	24,340	67,276	276,363	77.6	67.1	68.7	87.2
Maldah	155	106	3,452	10,173	76	124	888	4,652	49.1	116.7	25.7	45.7
Murshidabad	717	82	3,295	5,476	230	61	890	1,996	32.1	74.2	27.0	36.4
Nadia	366	73	4,812	12,988	123	41	1,012	3,778	33.7	56.7	21.0	29.1
Midnapore	448	124	9,903	15,859	108	93	2,120	5,177	24.0	74.9	21.4	32.6
Puruliya	247	109	4,475	12,115	58	50	841	2,618	23.4	45.5	18.8	21.6
West Bengal	1,522	3,698	13,190	34,336	866	2,200	5,858	22,876	56.9	59.5	44.4	66.6

Annexure 12.1

Some Socioeconomic Observations as Evident in Course of the Survey on Financial Inclusion in Select Districts in West Bengal

District: East Midnapore

Tamluk Area is well connected with railway and road transport—basically agricultural area—rice, coconut and processing of betel nut, betel leaf, village handloom, nearby fishing harbour fish market and cashew nut.

BPL: Complaint - 5/7 days a year – NREGA job
Rs 2/- per kg. rice
1100 gm per head

Banking Aspects:

East Midnapore - Lead Bank - UBI, Tamluk

1. A branch in Nim Touri has arranged for opening of 'no-frills' accounts.
2. Zero balance accounts are being opened in UBI for children of *bidi* workers in the area.
3. Complaint has been raised on the issue of existence of middlemen between the banks and the borrowers. Borrowers complain that without any help of the middlemen, no loan can be obtained (Commission – Rs 1,000/- for Rs 10,000/- loan).
4. Much of the accounts are opened for reason of NREGA payments.
5. Agents very often ask the borrowers to purchase a LIC policy if they intend to have a loan from a bank.
6. Loans in the area from the land development banks.
7. Some NREGP accounts in post offices.
8. Most of the daily wage earners are *bhag-chasi* (sharecroppers) attached to landowners from whom they get temporary short term loans.

9. Loan Savings due to low income levels of the households (HHs) in the area.
10. In many of the cases, people are not able to repay the bank loans.
11. In Deulihat village in Ramnagar–I in East Midnapore, there are some SHGs operating the area and PNB is extending loans in a regular way and local *panchayat* has played a good role.
12. In this area, much of the SB accounts are SHG-induced.
13. Women are taking interest in banking activities in a greater way as the youth in the area are engaged overseas and other metropolitan cities of India in restaurant, diamond cutting and gold polishing. Even women are using ATM to withdraw money arising out of foreign remittances into the locality.
14. To get loans from the village moneylenders, they are to keep gold ornaments, watches, bicycles etc. In case of gold, rate of interest is comparatively lower.
15. Not getting money from ATM as it becomes non-functional due to being out of order. Bank's attitude is non-cooperative and sample no. 88 is not happy with loan facility. Most of the banks are reluctant to float loans.
16. PNB is the only service commercial bank in the area in the business locality. Villagers agree that there is a need for another branch within a span of 15 kms.

District: Birbhum

Area Surveyed - Predominantly agricultural track mixed with small trade and handloom in silk sarees and famous Shantiniketan handicrafts and design.

Some Socioeconomic Features:

1. Nirvoypur—a tribal village adopted by NABARD had strived to develop itself by forming SHGs in Md. Bazar Block in Birbhum under the guidance of umbrella of Angargaria Srijoni Siksha Niketan. It has offered manifold directions in occupation—

poultry farming—vermi-post culture essence—*agarbatti* stick making, making of seed ornaments—the villagers once migrated from other villages.

2. Predominantly *bargadars* (Sharecroppers).
3. People are not happy with the stipulation on minimum balance requirement imposed by the banks.
4. At present seven SHGs are operating in the village.
5. A loan to be sanctioned to a villager only when all the outstanding loans are fully repaid—seemingly a self-framed rule made by the Branch Manager, UCO, Rajnagar Branch, Birbhum.
6. Male counterpart addicted to liquor. So women joining the SHG keep the passbook with SHG office and keep savings secret.
7. Some instances where people have applied for Kisan Credit Card (KCC) but they have been denied on the plea of pressure of workload at the branches.
8. Mayurakshi Gramin Bank has the major share in floatation of small loans in the area.
9. SHG in rice processing.
10. Moneylenders still play a greater role in rural finance. Rate of interest ranges from 24 per cent per annum to as high as 240 per cent per annum. People do not hesitate to take loans at such exorbitant rate of interest. The reason forwarded by them for such costly loan is that they take a very short-term loan, say for 5 to 6 months before the harvesting season and repay it when crop is reaped. Thus, the loan from the moneylenders is hassle-free and do not require any document except some collateral security like gold ornaments, bicycles, and some valuable utensils.

    In view of the above, the banks may deliver such short-term loans to the farmers artisans under close supervision where the tenure of credit delivery and repayment may be limited to six months as it is done in case of moneylenders. Because they can repay when they have money at hand and do not find time to think to be a loan defaulter.

District: Murshidabad

1. Sample No.17.

   SBI sanctioned Rs 18,000/- out of Rs 50,000/-

   Yield is more in jute in comparison to paddy and price (assured) is high for jute also.

2. Sample No.72.

   He does not know that he can deposit his own money into the NREGA account.

   Lack of financial education.

3. Sample No.80.

   i) Harrassment for getting money under SHG.

   ii) Subsidy not received.

   iii) Complaint against Branch Manager, Paschim Bangla Gramin Bikash Bank, Sanko Bazar Branch.

   iv) Delay in getting money under NREGA.

4. Sample No.34.

   Rural Bengal has seen acute shortage of labour supply as some people in BPL list prefer to stay idle when they can manage their out-of-pocket expenses by selling a part of rice so obtained from the ration shops at Rs 2 per kg. This resembles the findings of the 2010 Nobel Laureates' view on 'Search Theory' which states that where unemployment benefits are too generous, people will delay accepting job offers. This has a serious implication for the rural labour market when prices tend to increase to have a bearing on general price level.

Section IV

Structural Issues

13 Structural Transformation in Punjab Economy

NAVEEN KUMAR[1]

Introduction

The remarkable changes that the country has witnessed in surprisingly few years makes it relevant to study the transformations being in motion at the sub-national level to appreciate regional growth dynamics and their interlinkages to change in overall economic policy during 1991. While the general underpinning of changes everywhere have been the unleashing of market forces as natural corollary to the process of globalisation, liberalisation and privatisation, post-1991, their impact and visibility, differs both at national and state level and also at rural and urban level. While there is no doubt that the changes have been able to resolve a few long standing structural issues, however, the journey itself has created new problems and challenges.

Punjab, credited with ushering green revolution in agriculture, thus, contributing to self-sufficiency in food security has traversed a long path with current economy struggling with some deep entrenched problems undermining its potential. Punjab is one of the least poverty stricken states with its record of fivefold decline in poverty ratio within about 30-year period. The primary credit to this achievement goes to Green Revolution which began in the mid-sixties and ushered into the era of economic prosperity in the rural economy of Punjab. There was a dramatic improvement in agriculture productivity which resulted into a rise in per capita income. However, the economy of Punjab has experienced a down-turn in the post-reform period. The overall significance of agriculture in the

1. The views expressed in this paper are of the author himself and not of the organisation he is working with.

state has declined over time. This signalled the gradual withering of gains from Green Revolution and the agriculture sector witnessed a halt in productivity.

In Punjab, there are some structural issues that have emerged in recent years like changing structure of state economy with declining importance of agriculture, comparative lower economic growth, unsustainable state finances, structural rigidities, low human capital development, demand and supply factors etc., which are undermining the true potential of Punjab economy. After more than 40 years of adoption of the Green Revolution strategy, the agricultural sector is in an acute state of crisis, raising serious questions about future sustainability in output and livelihoods. This crisis manifests itself in a number of ways: stagnating crop yield and farm incomes, buildup in the levels of indebtedness amongst the farmers, general economic distress and environmental damage. In this background, the present study attempts to decipher structural transformation of state and also address some long standing issues to provide some fresh insights and solutions.

Organisation of Paper/Sections

Section I undertakes a comprehensive review of the literature on regional studies especially on Punjab economy. Section II presents account of growth performance observed in last three decades and also deals with issues of structural changes in state economy. The issues pertaining to the pattern of agriculture development and productivity are set out in Section III. Section IV discusses the trend in finances of the state. Policy suggestion for improving the state of the economy of Punjab is discussed in Section V. Concluding observations are presented in Section VI.

I

Literature Survey

One of the primary causative factors generating structural changes across states was policy of economic reforms pursued post-1991. In the Indian context with wide regional variations in terms of socioeconomic development, economic reforms have been initiated at different levels across states. Most of the economic reforms have been pursued in the industrial sector, the spread and growth of which show considerable regional variations (Bhanumurthy and Mitra, 2004). The rationale of the various economic reforms initiatives at the national level such as abolition of industrial licensing and other types of controls over private investment, liberalisation of trade policy, financial sector reform, etc., was that they would increase efficiency and lead to higher factor productivity (Ahluwalia, 2000). Ahluwalia in the same paper titled 'State Level Performance under Economic Reforms in India' provides an excellent exposition of dynamics of economic reforms on differential response of states' economies. He argues that since these policies are generally applicable to all states, there is a natural presumption that they would provide efficiency gains for all these states, which should increase the growth potential of each state. The reforms generate potential gains for each state and while some states may benefit more than others, the reforms do not hurt any states. However, it is important to recognise that even though the reforms themselves are non-discriminatory, they will affect states differently because of differences in state-specific characteristics and this could lead to a deceleration in growth in some states.

Various studies have been undertaken in past analysing the economic performance of Punjab economy. Some of them have been quoted in the following paragraphs to revisit the analysis and issues raised in them. Lakhwinder Singh (2010) maintains that the economic development experience of the economy of Punjab state since the advent of Green Revolution remained quite dynamic. However, the state economy has experienced a downturn in its economic development in the post-reform period compared with acceleration of economic growth of the Indian economy as well as other dynamic states. Therefore, a legitimate question arises that why Punjab economy could not develop at a rate that has been experienced by the Indian economy. Singh in the same paper titled 'Post-Reform Economic Development in Punjab: Constraints and Remedies' explores economic development experience of the economy of Punjab in a comparative perspective to arrive at the factors that have contributed to the downturn in economic growth during the post-reform period. The post-reform economic growth pattern of Punjab economy clearly brings out that the dominant sectors of the state like agriculture, registered manufacturing, electricity, real estate, public administration and others services, which contributed 68.52 per cent of the net state domestic product (NSDP) at the beginning of the reform period, have experienced deceleration in economic growth. Upinder Sawhney (2008) in her study titled 'Growth of Services Sector in a Predominantly Agricultural Economy of Punjab' concludes that in view of the fact that the growth of the primary sector in Punjab is slow, the state certainly needs to generate gainful off-farm opportunities. The industrial development of the state has not been very encouraging in the last decade and a half, so the tertiary sector needs to be tapped to promote the growth of income and employment in the state.

The decelerating economic growth is essentially rooted in the irrational pattern of investment and declining developmental expenditure and compounded by the crisis in agriculture, due to marginalisation of the small farmer and population pressure on land (Singh and Singh, 2002). Lakhwinder Singh and Sukhpal Singh in their same paper titled 'Deceleration of Economic Growth in Punjab: Evidence, Explanation and a Way Out' concludes that factors especially capital accumulation, technological breakthroughs and human capital are constraining further growth and the sustenance of the earlier growth momentum of the state economy. This is evident even in the crisis of the farm sector especially at the technological plane and in the rising costs to maintain the existing level of productivity. The recent spate of suicides among farmers in India today is a manifestation of an underlying crisis in agriculture which is a result of the marginalisation of agrarian economy in national policy since the economic reforms of the 90s (Posani, 2009).

A few studies have examined the sustainability aspect of agriculture in the state. Kohli and Singh (1997) contend that growth in Punjab has been closely associated with the well-known 'Green Revolution', which saw the development and adoption of new, high-yielding varieties (HYVs) of wheat, rice and other food crops. During the period of 1990s, the Green Revolution technology has shown signs of fatigue. Productivity growth stagnated along with near freeze of prices, which resulted into the decline of agriculture sector's contribution to the state income. The rural economy of Punjab has been undergoing structural transformation. However, the dependence of the rural population in general and of rural labour in particular, on earning their livelihood from the rural economy continues.

This process of rural transformation has perpetuated distress among the rural workforce (Singh *et al.*, 2007). The low growth of agriculture sector and high dependence of workforce are expected to further worsen the working and living conditions of the rural workforce. This will act as a disincentive for the migratory workforce which usually comes to the rural areas of Punjab for finding much-needed livelihood. This will either divert these flows to other fast growing states of India or will suffer because of non-availability of necessary skills required to be absorbed in the urban areas.

II

Growth Performance and Structural Changes in State Income

Since its phenomenal growth in the 1960s, Punjab is now facing an uncertain economic prospect. It was a widely held belief that in the post-economic reform era in India, not only its past performance and the lead of Punjab would continue but also, it would get a big push towards the road to economic prosperity. However, in the post-reform period the performance of the Indian economy in general and of some of the states, which have overtaken Punjab so far as per capita income is concerned, has improved while that of Punjab has lagged behind. The post-reform period economic growth has further exposed the weaknesses in the pattern of growth in Punjab and raised a pertinent question as to why Punjab's economic performance has lagged far behind.

Analysing Growth Pattern

Table 13.1 provides the rate of growth of GSDP of 15 states for the pre-reform period i.e., period from 1981-82 to 1990-91 and post-reform period from 1991-92 to 2008-09. The table reveals that the GSDP of Punjab grew by 5.28 per cent in pre-reform period higher than both 1990s and 2000s. The growth rate in post-reform period during both periods was lower than national GDP growth and also lower than average growth of all the 15 states taken together in the table. Though there is marginal difference between pre- and post-reform growth rate of Punjab, a comparative picture of performance of other states underlines the missed opportunity in terms of seizing advantage from economic reforms as others have done.

Table 13.1

Relative Economic Performance of States during Pre- and Post-Reform Period

States	Annual Rate of Growth of GSDP (Per cent)			
	Pre-Reform	Post-Reform		
	1981-82 to 1990-91	1991-92 to 2008-09	1991-92 to 1999-2000	2000-2001 to 2008-09
1. Andhra Pradesh	6.43	6.56	5.37	7.75
2. Bihar	4.93	5.73	2.57	8.88
3. Gujarat	5.94	8.16	7.57	8.83
4. Haryana	6.63	6.90	4.81	9.00
5. Himachal Pradesh	5.10	6.62	5.91	7.33
6. Karnataka	5.21	7.17	7.56	6.77
7. Kerala	3.67	6.80	5.84	7.76
8. Madhya Pradesh	5.22	4.50	5.48	3.41
9. Maharashtra	6.12	6.91	7.03	6.77
10. Orissa	3.32	6.34	4.89	7.78
11. Punjab	5.28	4.90	4.82	4.97
12. Rajasthan	8.08	6.30	5.70	6.89
13. Tamil Nadu	5.72	6.26	6.33	6.18
14. Uttar Pradesh	5.06	4.39	3.80	4.98
15. West Bengal	4.40	6.59	6.76	6.42
GSDP of 15 states	5.36	6.17	5.70	6.70
GDP (national accounts)	5.40	6.87	5.73	7.22

Note: Growth rate for states have been calculated from the spliced data.

Source: Central Statistics Organisation, GoI.

An interesting fact which can be noticed from Table 13.1 is that the predominantly agricultural states like Punjab and Haryana witnessed a deceleration of economic growth in the following years of economic reforms. However, Haryana improved upon its growth during 2000-01 to 2008-09 period registering a growth of 9.0 per cent which is highest growth registered by any state among selected 15 major states in the table, while Punjab continued to languish with poor growth performance in second decade of economic reform. This depicts the contrasting tale of two states that have both shared the gains of Green Revolution earlier, but which have adjusted to requirements of new economy differently and have now different growth trajectory. Even a state like Bihar which has very low per capita income and was badly performing during the first decade of reforms period has surpassed Punjab by wide margin with growth rate of 8.9 per cent during 2000-2001 to 2008-09. Among 15 selected major states in Table 13.1, barring Uttar Pradesh and Madhya Pradesh, other 12 states have recorded higher growth than Punjab in post-reform period, i.e., during 1991-92 to 2008-09 which further empirically proves the marginalisation of the state in post-reform period. The relative degradation of state is further exemplified by the fact that growth performance of the state was better than eight states in pre-reform period among 15 selected states in Table 13.1. Thus, the relatively better position of Punjab during Pre-reform period has given way to deceleration in its growth and of overall improvement in majority of states during post-reform period.

The economic growth in Punjab during pre-reform period during 1981-82 to 1990-91 was more or less in conformity with the trend observed at the national level (Figure 13.1). In fact the average annual growth rate at 4.8 per cent was only marginally lower than 5.4 per cent growth for all-India, with growth in Punjab being higher in six years of the 10 years during pre-reform period as evident from multiple intersecting points of the growth curve of Punjab and all-India. This is in sharp contrast to post-reform trend when the growth at all-India level remained higher than Punjab's growth rate consistently for 18 consecutive years from 1992-1993 to 2009-10. In fact, during post-reform period the gap between Punjab and all-India widened with Punjab's growth rate at 4.9 per cent which was almost same as that of pre-reform period and 6.5 per cent growth for all-India indicating substantial improvement in growth scenario in the post-reform era. Thus, the economy of Punjab failed to improve its growth performance of the 1980s in post-reform era in comparison of substantial pickup in growth in the period immediately after the initiation of economic reforms. The spurt in overall growth momentum picked up further in the last seven years of 2000s which though was similar as in Punjab, was however still way behind the all-India trend.

Figure 13.1

Trend of Growth Rate in Punjab vis-à-vis All-India

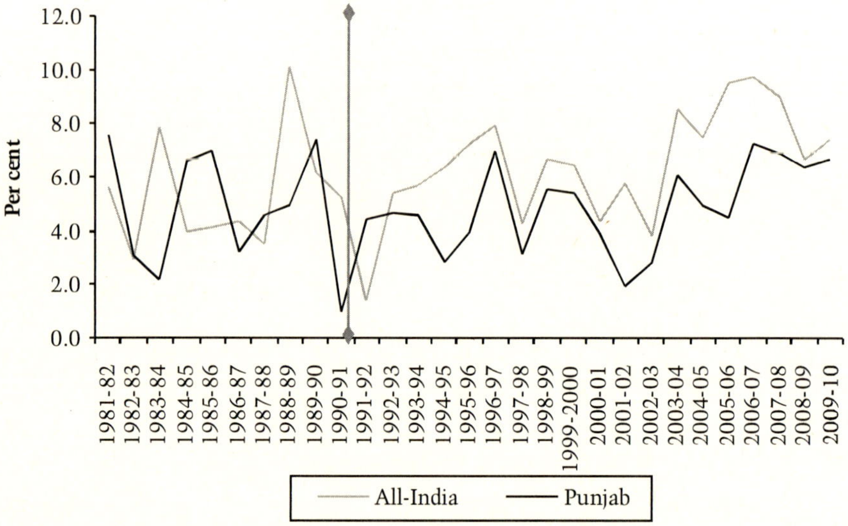

Source: CSO.

The agriculture sector during 1981-82 to 1990-91 has recorded a growth of 5.0 per cent which was substantially higher than the growth rate of 3.0 per cent recorded during the first decade of the economic reform. In fact, the agriculture sector growth rate at 2.6 per cent during second decade of reforms was almost half than that of the pre-reform period (Table 13.2). The reason for this deterioration of agricultural growth scenario in Punjab has been stagnation in productivity level, growing ecological constraints and unfavourable market signals in post-reform era. In terms of volatility as measured by coefficient of variation (CV), there was marginal difference between pre- and post-reform growth trend (Table 13.3). But in both the periods, the value of CV was lower than all-India value which basically is on account of the fact that Punjab has more than 90 per cent irrigated cultivable land in contrast with two-third of the area in the country being dependent on monsoon rains. The industrial sector has also shown similar decadal trend with the growth momentum of 1980s being lost in the subsequent years as observed in the manufacturing sector whose growth declined from 9.1 per cent in 1980s to 6.4 per cent in 1990s and finally to 5.7 per cent in 2000s. It is to be noted that CV for industrial sector in Punjab almost remained same during both pre- and post-reform period,

Table 13.2

Sectoral Growth Trend in Punjab during 1981-82 to 2009-10

	Pre-Reform	*Post-Reform*	
	1981-82 to 1990-91	*1991-92 to 2000-01*	*2001-02 to 2009-10*
I. Agriculture and allied activities	**4.9**	**3.1**	**2.6**
of which:			
Agriculture	5.0	3.0	2.6
Forestry and logging	0.2	4.1	1.1
Fishing	15.5	17.0	5.4
II. Industry	**9.1**	**6.2**	**6.1**
Mining and quarrying	18.7	-3.7	47.5
Manufacturing	9.1	6.4	5.7
Electricity, gas and water supply	9.3	5.5	7.6
III. Services	**3.5**	**5.3**	**6.8**
Construction	1.0	7.9	10.3
Transport, storage and communication	7.4	11.4	12.3
Trade, hotels and restaurants	2.9	5.0	4.8
Banking and insurance	12.2	9.8	11.7
Real estate, ownership of dwellings and business services	2.2	2.3	2.7
Public administration	7.3	5.8	5.3
Other services	2.5	3.0	3.0
Total GSDP	4.8	4.5	5.3

Source: CSO.

however, for all-India the same increased from 0.32 during 1980-81 to 1990-91 at 0.56 during 1991-92 to 2009-10 signifying increased volatility though with marginally reduced growth rate. It was services sector which recorded opposite trend to that recorded by agriculture and industrial sector, registering significant upswing in growth in both decades of the post-reform period. Within the services sector, the construction sector accelerated considerably with almost eightfold increase in growth rate from 1.0 per cent during 1981-82 to 1990-91 to 7.9 per cent in first decade of economic reforms and further peaked up to 10.3 per cent during the second decade of economic reform, clearly showing the positive impact of economic reforms which has spurred economic activities considerably including infrastructural activities prompting higher construction. The other sub-sectors that recorded double digit growth were transport, storage and communication and banking and insurance sector. The services sector growth in Punjab were more volatile than all-India as measured by CV during both pre- and post-reform period. In fact, during this period CV increased from 0.28 to 0.39. At all-India level also CV increased from 0.17 to 0.25, signifying that increased growth rate of services achieved during post-reform period was accompanied by higher volatility.

Table 13.3

Trend in Coefficient of Variation of Sectors of Punjab vis-à-vis All-India

	Pre-Reform: 1981-82 to 1990-91		Post-Reform: 1991-92 to 2009-10	
	All-India	Punjab	All-India	Punjab
Agriculture & allied activities	1.55	1.02	1.56	1.06
Industry	0.32	0.51	0.56	0.52
Services	0.17	0.28	0.25	0.39
GDP/GSDP	0.41	0.49	0.32	0.32

Source: CSO and Author's own calculations.

Structural Transformation

During 1980-81, Punjab was predominantly an agriculture based economy with the agriculture sector constituting 42.2 per cent share in GSDP. In fact the share of agriculture sector works out to be four times that of industrial sector. The Green Revolution had driven the agriculture sector to register impressive growth in 1970s and 1980s to such level that agriculture sector overtook services sector in terms of share in GSDP and maintained this lead till 1994-95 (Figure 13.2). In fact, the share of agriculture sector has started falling in the last two decades only after remaining stagnant in preceding decade. During 1980-81 to 1990-91, the industrial sector added to its share by around five percentage point mostly at the cost of services sector. Thus, this period has unique dynamics when the industrialisation made strong headway together with continued dominance of agriculture. However, the services sector did not have any rising sector during the period to provide the stimulus and instead the sub-sectors of services sector like construction, trade, hotel, restaurants and real estate sector witnessed fall in their share. In the subsequent decade, the situation reversed as the share of services started rising while the share of agriculture started falling. In the same period the share of industrial sector reached the decadal peak witnessing continued growth in the share of the sector. In fact, the gap between share of services and agriculture sector widened to 6.6 percentage point during 1999-2000 as compared to zero difference in 1984-85. A graphic glimpse of Figure 13.2 provides this interesting trend of changing structure of the Punjab economy with changing slope of services sector in two time interval. For initial years, the slope is horizontal implying stagnancy which changes to relatively steeper curve for the next two decades implying faster decline in the share of agriculture sector. For the period between 1995-96 and 2009-10, the slope of agriculture and services sector were inclined opposite to each other with services sector having positive slope and agriculture sector having negative slope leading to increasing gap between these two. While the share of agriculture sector was declining, the share of services sector was rising culminating into a gap of 22.6 percentage point between these two in 2009-2010. It is to be noted that fall in the share of agriculture sector has been mostly offset by the rise in share of services sector and the share of industrial sector remained almost unchanged during the last decade.

Figure 13.2

Structural Changes in Punjab Economy in 30 Years

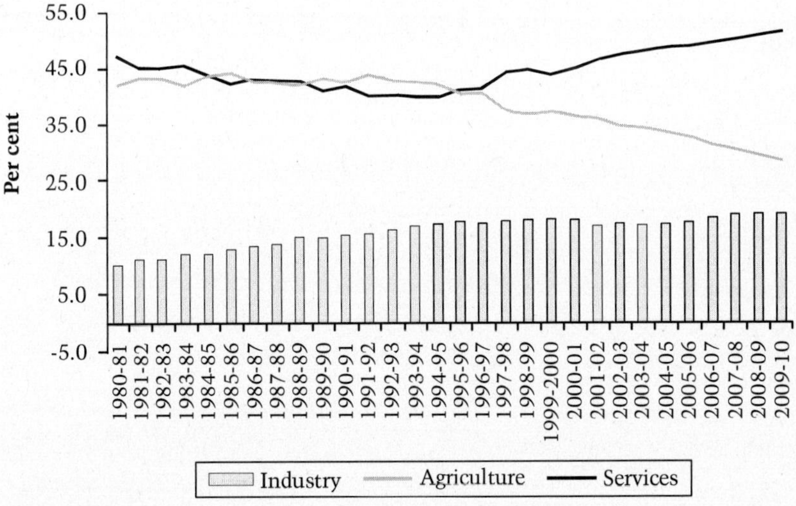

Source: CSO.

A comparison of Punjab with all-India trend in term of changes in share of broad sector of economy depicts an interesting tale. It may be noted from Table 13.4, that share of agriculture was very high in both Punjab and at all-India level in 1980-81, which though reduced significantly in both the cases in the following decades, still, the share of agriculture in Punjab at 29.0 per cent is almost twice that of 14.6 per cent at all-India level in 2009-10. Thus, agriculture is still playing an important role in Punjab economy while in other advanced states' agriculture primacy has rapidly faded. Another interesting trend is relative stagnation of industrial sector during the 30-year period in India compared to rise of its share from 10.4 per cent in 1980-81 to 19.4 per cent in 2009-10 in Punjab, signalling better industrial activities. This is a very important trend as India's structural transformation is believed to have missed critical stage of industrialisation as a step from primary activities to tertiary activities. In Punjab on the contrary, significant portion of fall in agriculture sector has been grabbed by industrial sector during the last three decades. This trend should be comforting as equitable economic structure provides wider basis for overall development of different sectors of the state economy ensuring sustainability of growth in the long run. The experience at national level of missing expansion of manufacturing sector capacities have been avoided to a great extent in Punjab, thus, theoretically putting it at better prospects for balanced growth in future. The services sector have expanded at a rapid pace to jump from 44.6 per cent share in GDP in 1980-81 to 64.9 per cent in 2009-10 at all-India level. The services sector share in Punjab in 1980-1981 was greater than that of all-India. But the progress since then has

Table 13.4

Comparative Structural Transformation of Punjab vis-à-vis All-India

(Per cent)

		Punjab	*All-India*
1980-81	Primary	42.2	37.9
	Secondary	10.4	17.4
	Tertiary	47.4	44.6
2009-10	Primary	29.0	14.6
	Secondary	19.4	20.5
	Tertiary	51.6	64.9

Source: CSO.

been discouraging with initial spell of fall during 1980s and rising only in the last 15 years. Still during the three-decade period, increase of 4.2 per cent is insignificant in comparison with the national trend. Thus, while the national economy has become service dominated, the sectoral distribution in Punjab appears more balanced at present.

For detailed examination of changes in the share of different sectors, an interval of five-year period has been taken in Table 13.5. It may be observed from the table that share of agriculture sector increased during 1980-81 to 1985-86, but for the next five years it declined. Thus, for overall pre-reform period the share of agriculture remained stagnant while the share of forestry and logging declined. In the subsequent years i.e., post-reform period, the declining trend continued and the share of agriculture fell from 42.1 per cent in 1990-91 to 28.5 in 2009-10, an overall decline of 13.6 per cent which is quite substantial for an economy like Punjab. From the above facts it is quite apparent that economic reforms have created a scenario where agriculture has lost its importance while other sectors of the economy grew relatively faster. In the pre-reform period, manufacturing sector share had risen from 8.4 per cent in 1980-81 to 12.5 per cent in 1990-91, a sharp rise by 4.1 per cent in 10 years. This is both an interesting and puzzling trend as this rise in share was at the cost of decline in share of services sector by 5.5 percentage point during the same period. Thus, during the pre-reform period, the overall trend for the economy was stagnant share of agriculture sector and falling share of services sector while rising share of industrial sector. The fall in share of services sector was mainly driven by the poor performance of sub-sectors like construction, real estate, trade and hotels. However in the post-reform period, the share of services sector rose sharply from 41.9 per cent in 1990-1991 to 51.6 per cent in 2009-10, marking a break from earlier historical trend. The sub-sectors which led to this trend were construction sector, transport, communication, banking and insurance, much in alignment with the national trend. Thus, the post-reform period which had liberal policy regime in most of the sub-sectors of services especially telecommunication, banking and insurance led their faster growth both at national and state level. The growing trend of services orientation of economy is a globally driven phenomenon which has reached even at the sub-national level due to opening up of the economy.

Table 13.5

Share of Different Sub-Sectors of the Economy in Punjab during Pre- and Post-Reform Period

(Per cent)

	Pre-Reform			Post-Reform			
	1980-81	1985-86	1990-91	1995-96	2000-01	2005-06	2009-10
I. Agriculture and allied activities	**42.2**	**44.5**	**42.5**	**40.8**	**36.6**	**33.0**	**29.0**
of which:							
Agriculture	41.6	44.0	42.1	40.3	36.0	32.3	28.5
Forestry and logging	0.5	0.4	0.3	0.3	0.3	0.3	0.2
Fishing	0.0	0.0	0.1	0.2	0.3	0.4	0.3
II. Industry	**10.4**	**13.1**	**15.6**	**17.9**	**18.2**	**18.0**	**19.4**
Mining and quarrying	0.0	0.0	0.0	0.0	0.0	0.0	0.0
Manufacturing	8.4	10.7	12.5	14.7	14.9	14.6	15.4
Electricity, gas and water supply	2.0	2.5	3.0	3.3	3.3	3.3	4.0
III. Services	**47.4**	**42.4**	**41.9**	**41.3**	**45.1**	**49.1**	**51.6**
Construction	5.8	4.5	4.0	4.4	4.9	6.3	7.3
Transport, storage and communication	2.2	2.3	2.8	3.3	5.2	7.7	9.2
Trade, hotels and restaurants	14.5	12.8	12.1	11.8	12.5	12.8	12.0
Banking and insurance	1.5	1.9	2.9	3.3	4.5	5.0	7.5
Real estate, ownership of dwellings and business services	7.4	6.6	5.7	5.2	4.6	4.3	3.7
Public administration	3.4	3.2	4.3	3.9	4.7	4.7	4.7
Other services	12.6	11.1	10.1	9.4	8.7	8.2	7.2
Total GSDP	100	100	100	100	100	100	100

Source: CSO.

III

Agricultural Transformation

Agriculture continues to be the backbone of the state economy of Punjab providing employment to majority of people and also generating trading in surplus produce. Maintaining healthy agricultural growth is a prerequisite for the overall development of the state as others sectors are dependent for input, market and income. The food security at the national level also hinges on the state agriculture performance. Punjab has enjoyed a distinct comparative advantage in comparison to other states in agricultural development and this is reflected in its contribution to the national output. During 2009-10, Punjab accounted for 18.8 per cent of the country's wheat production, 12.6 per cent of rice production and 12.4 per cent of food grain output (Figure 13.3) and also contributed substantially in the central pool. During the last 20 years, the Punjab's share in India's wheat production has come down and the decline has mainly been in the last decade, i.e., 2000s, while the share of rice has marginally improved during the last two decades indicating preference for rice cultivation and also pickup in wheat cultivation in other states of the country. The food grain's share has not seen much change in the last 20 years marking the end of the trend of Punjab's rising share as a consequence of the spurt in food production contributed by the Green Revolution in the state. The other interpretation is that Green Revolution has now spread to other parts of country bringing some sense of equality. The above trend also raises concerns regarding productivity. Punjab which took lead in agricultural production due to

Figure 13.3

Trend of Main Crops of Punjab in Percentage Share of All-India in Last Two Decades

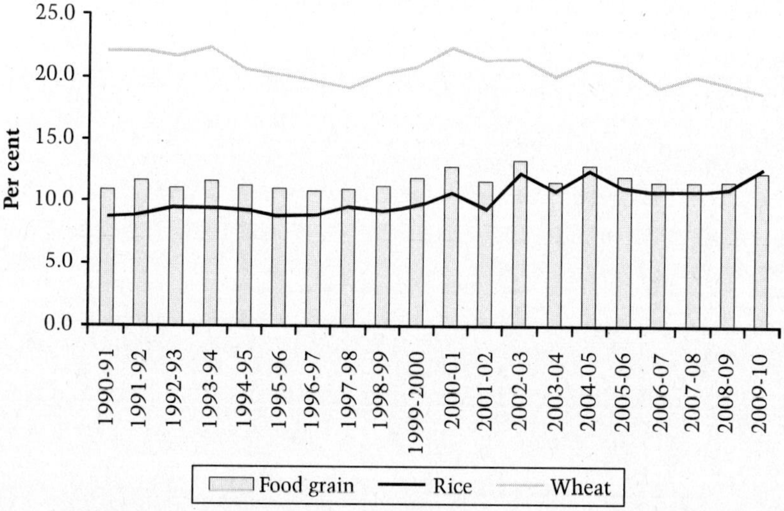

Source: *Handbook of Statistics on Indian Economy*, RBI.

earlier adoption of technological breakthrough reaped rich dividends for some years but eventually exhausted the gains, while other states also caught up. Unable to come up with new technological breakthrough or major innovation in production processes, agriculture in Punjab remained stagnant leading to unchanged share in the last 20 years.

The importance of agriculture sector in Punjab economy was very much evident in 1980s when it defied national trend of declining share of agriculture in GDP, and instead share of agriculture in GSDP in Punjab rose from 42.2 per cent in 1980-81 to 44.0 per cent in 1991-92. During the same corresponding period, at all-India level there was a decline of 7.6 per cent in share of agriculture in GDP, signifying the rapid economic restructuring under process in the economy. This pre-reform period dynamics in Punjab showed the continued momentum in agriculture sector on account of Green Revolution. This was the stage when the technological diffusion of Green Revolution era was picking up and other sectors of the economy were not growing at a comparable pace. However, thereafter Punjab's agriculture sector rapidly lost its share in the next two decades and grew at the pace comparable to that at the all-India level. The gains of Green Revolution dissipated during this period. At present, the share of agriculture in GSDP of Punjab at 29.0 per cent is almost double than the all-India's share of 15.6 per cent indicating the relative importance of agriculture in Punjab economy as compared to national economy.

The agriculture growth in Punjab was higher in pre-reform period, i.e., in 1980s than post-reform period on account of continued momentum of Green Revolution of 1970s and wider diffusion of new technology. However, the growth witnessed during this period was highly volatile. In fact, the CV for period 1981-82 to 1990-91 was 1.02, while annual average growth rate was 5.0 per cent for the same period. In the subsequent decade, i.e., post-reform period A, though the volatility of growth further increased as measured by CV at 1.28, the average annual growth rate dropped to 3.0 per cent during 1991-92 to 2000-01 (Figure 13.4). In the period 2001-02 to 2009-10, i.e., post-reform period B, although growth became least volatile in the last three decades with CV at 0.80, the growth also slumped to lowest level of average annual growth of 2.5 per cent.

Figure 13.4

Trend in Agriculture Growth in Punjab in Last Three Decades

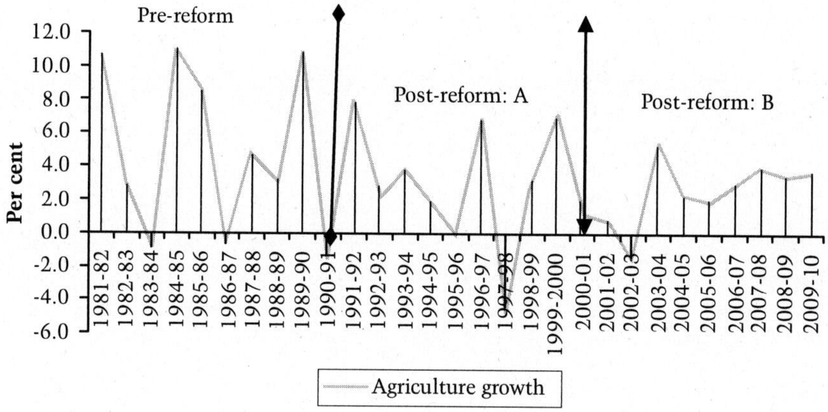

Source: CSO.

Trend in Area, Production and Productivity

Currently, wheat and rice have a combined share of about 98 per cent in food grain production, cover over three quarters of the cropped area and have more than 85 per cent contribution in total agricultural output in the state. In fact, the rise in crop intensity over these years has mainly benefitted wheat and rice crop (Table 13.6). The present agriculture cropping pattern in the state is dominated by the wheat-paddy rotation causing degradation in soil fertility and fall in the underground water table. Wheat and paddy cover major portion of the gross cropped area as area

Table 13.6

Net Sown Area and Cropping Intensity

Year	*Net Sown Area ('000 hectare)*	*Cropping Intensity*
1960-61	3757	126
1970-71	4053	140
1980-81	4191	161
1990-91	4218	178
1996-97	4234	185
2000-01	4264	186
2008-09	4171	190

Source: *Statistical Abstract of Punjab* (various years), Government of Punjab.

under these two crops has increased to 79 per cent in 2008-09 from 47 per cent in 1970-71. Therefore, it will be worthwhile to study the trends of these two crops to understand the overall agriculture dynamics.

It may be observed in the Table 13.7 that there has been an increase of 974 thousand hectare and 1,625 thousand hectare acreage in wheat and rice crops, respectively, during the period 1970-71 to 1990-91 signifying the dominance of new crops of Green Revolution. However, increases in the production of rice and wheat have come at the expense of other crops such as cotton, oilseeds, maize and millets. Essentially, all high potential available land has been sown with wheat and paddy, and the limit of further land expansion is exhausted. Thus, in the ensuing two decades only rice has shown some addition in acreage, though the rate of increase has halved. On the other hand, the net addition of land for cropping of wheat has almost stagnated, a sign of fatigue of gains from new technology and also some adverse market development and rise of better return yielding rice crop with attendant facility of irrigation. Overall, sustained economic growth, increasing urbanisation, expanding trade liberalisation and globalisation, and changing lifestyle patterns are shifting consumption patterns in the economy away from basic staples such as wheat and rice, towards high-value agricultural commodities. This pattern though is not reflected at macro level in terms of large scale shifts in cropping pattern, however, diversified cropping including diversification toward high-value commodities—*basmati* and fine long-grained rice, durum wheat and

Table 13.7

Area and Production of Wheat and Rice in Punjab in Selected Years, 1970-71 to 2009-10

Years	*Wheat*			*Rice*		
	Area ('000 ha)	*Production (million tonne)*	*Yield (kg/hectare)*	*Area ('000 ha)*	*Production (million tonne)*	*Yield (kg/hectare)*
1970-71	2299	4.9	2131.4	390	0.7	1794.9
1980-81	2812	7.7	2738.3	1183	3.2	2705.0
1990-91	3273	12.2	3727.5	2015	6.5	3225.8
2000-01	3408	15.6	4577.5	2612	9.2	3522.2
2009-10	3522	15.2	4315.7	2802	11.2	3997.1

Source: *Statistical Abstract of Punjab*, (various years), Government of Punjab.

cultivation for agro-processing should be more evident in the coming years. However, the relative attractiveness of wheat and rice to provide stable income is deterrent for faster adoption of newer cropping pattern in favour of floriculture, horticulture, dairying, fishing, etc. Still, the stagnant level of acreage over two decades for wheat definitely indicates intrinsic structural changes underway in Punjab agriculture.

The tangible benefits from Green Revolution are reflected in the quantum jump in the production of wheat from 4.9 million tonne in 1970-1971 to 12.2 million tonne in 1990-91, i.e., an increase of 145 per cent. The rise in production of rice was more remarkable at more than eightfold increase in production from 0.7 million tonne in 1970-71 to 6.5 million tonne in 1990-91. This difference in production trend of wheat and rice was mainly on account of early start by wheat in comparison to rice as startup in new technology package. However, rice picked up fast in the subsequent years benefitting from expanding irrigation facilities, rising acreage and increasing productivity during this period. The production of wheat witnessed marginal increase in 1990-91 to 2000-01, i.e., an increase of only 3.4 million tonne in these 10 years. Thereafter, the trend reversed to a marginal fall in production from 15.6 million tonne in 2000-01 to 15.2 million tonne in 2009-10. This in a way marked the end of dominance of wheat crop in Punjab agriculture. It is, however, to be noted that this deterioration in wheat production was more of compulsion rather than their choice. Overall, the acreage for wheat has reached the peak level where there was no land left for other inferior crops to be diverted to wheat crop to drive commercial benefits. The primary reason underlying this unfavourable scenario is the stagnant productivity of wheat. This itself is primarily on account of lack of technological breakthrough in the subsequent years of Green Revolution, ecologically unsustainable practices and adverse market signals in changing demand composition.

Analysing Productivity Pattern

The primary reason for the ushering of prosperity in Punjab has been on account of sharp upturn in productivity of main cultivation crop, i.e., wheat and rice benefitting from Green Revolution in the late 1960s. The package which led to this transformation had components relating to all stages of cultivation like inputs, harvesting, credit, marketing and role of institutional support. The main technological breakthrough was new varieties of seed having enhanced capacity to give far better yield with a set of input and conditions including intense irrigation, chemical fertilisers, pesticides and semi-arid conditions. The initial results enthused all the major stakeholders including agricultural scientist, farmers and policy-makers to introduce this package technology in area which were suitable according to overall requirement of new cultivation technology. Punjab being in semi-arid region with vast network of irrigation suited climatically and geographically for requirements of new varieties of crop. However, with time, first the stage of saturation came in the productivity of major crops signifying structural constraints being manifested in technological limits and finally stagnation and retrogression also set in. In fact, Punjab being the leading state in terms of productivity in all these years has compromised on ecological sustainability and only concentrated on maximum utilisation of natural resources is now facing constraints like groundwater depletion and micronutrient deficiency (Table 13.8).

It will be really difficult to break the current stagnation in production and productivity of wheat and rice, as most of the growth factors stand exhausted. Further expansion of area under cereals has very little scope; expansion of the irrigated area has reached a virtual dead end and may even fall due to the fast depleting groundwater level. Fertiliser intensity may also decrease if fertiliser subsidy is reduced. Public and private investment in agriculture is declining. HYV wheat and rice seeds have almost exhausted their potential, and are under threat of ruin by crop diseases. Given so many negative factors and constraints, even sustaining the current level of wheat and rice production will require considerable effort and will test the ingenuity of farmers and the government apparatus. Even in the case of wheat and rice crops, for which tried and tested high yield potential HYV seeds are available, the scope of area expansion is limited. A saturation point in area under these two crops seems to have been reached by the closing years of the 20th century.

Table 13.8

Region-Specific Factors Causing Low Productivity

Agro-Climatic Region	*States/Parts of States*	*Region-Specific Constraints*
Western Himalayan region-I	J&K, HP, Uttarakhand	Severe soil erosion, degradation due to heavy rainfall/floods and deforestation, low SRRs, poor road, poor input delivery, inadequate communication infrastructure and marketing
Eastern Himalayan region-II	Assam, NE states, Sikkim	Aluminium toxicity and soil acidity, soil erosion and floods, shifting cultivation, low SRRs, non-availability of electricity, poor road, poor input delivery system and communication infrastructure
Lower and middle gangetic plains region-III and IV	West Bengal, Bihar, Eastern UP	Flood/waterlogging, improper drainage, salinity/alkalinity, arsenic contamination, low SRRs, non-availability of electricity, high population growth, poor road and communication infrastructure
Upper and trans-gangetic plains region-V and VI	Western UP, Punjab, Haryana	Groundwater depletion, decreasing total factor productivity, micro-nutrient deficiency, non-availability of electricity and high population density
Eastern plateau and hills region-VII	Orissa, Jharkhand, Chhattisgarh	Moisture stress, drought and soil acidity, iron toxicity, low SRRs, non-availability of electricity, high population growth, poor road, poor input delivery and communication infrastructure

Note: SRR: Seed Replacement Rate.

Source: Eleventh Five Year Plan Document, Planning Commission, Government of India.

Agricultural Prospects

Punjab agriculture is clearly at a crossroad. Agriculture is dominated by wheat and rice, which now cover over three quarters of cropped area and account for 85 per cent of the gross value of crop output. However, the yield level has hit saturation point for both these crops in the last decade though rice is performing relatively better. The changes witnessed in the economy has resulted in a shift in basic consumption pattern with high value agriculture commodities becoming prominent driving consumer demand away from traditional crops. The state has been experiencing increasing stress on natural resources. Fertiliser, especially nitrogen, is being used at levels exceeding the recommended amounts, contributing to imbalances among nutrients (too much N relative to P and K), and micronutrient deficiencies, resulting in low marginal returns to fertiliser. Largely due to paddy cultivation, groundwater levels have been falling, especially in the central zone at a rate of almost one quarter metre per year. Large areas are being lost to salinity and waterlogging, especially in the southwestern cotton zone. Thus, the sustainability of agriculture is under threat.

Given the fact that the constraints inhibiting the productivity growth are structural, ecological, economical and institutional, it will be better to focus on alternatives which are contemporary and farmer-friendly. In fact, in Punjab there is a need to shift to a new production profile away from common rice and wheat varieties and focus on high value crops such as *basmati* rice and durum wheat. Diversifying their crop base into crops like soyabean and maize and increasing the production of livestock and poultry will help in reducing the pressure on land. It is also important to integrate high yielding short-duration legumes into the existing rice-wheat cropping system in order to have positive environmental benefits. Fruits and vegetables such as okra, eggplant and potatoes can be produced for domestic markets. Developing dairy industries to produce milk and milk products for the urban centres of north India is another way of diversifying the crop base in Punjab. In addition, where water availability is not a problem, development of inland fisheries is also a possibility. More and more quality seeds for production in agriculture is becoming a serious need. Punjab farmers with their ability to maintain high quality production systems can become involved in producing seeds for the rest of the country. In summary, Punjab's non-traditional export needs to go up in line with the trend that is happening in the rest of India. Value addition is an essential part of transforming Punjab agriculture. Hubs of processed wheat products around modernised private industries can be developed to produce *dalia*, *atta*, *maida*, *suji*, biscuits, pasta in place of whole wheat. Transporting processed wheat products is much more cost-effective than transporting whole grains. The use of soyabean and maize for the livestock industry to produce high value livestock products should be a priority. Processing plants for processing vegetables and fruits and for processing dairy and poultry are also economically efficient ways of diversifying the agricultural base. Expanding crop diversification and increasing agro-industrialisation requires the building of a golden triangle with farmer, agro-industry and the banker as the corners of the triangle. Market reforms related to rationalisation of input subsidies and removal of restrictions in terms of stocking limits, movements and levies in transporting food grains should be implemented.

IV

Examining State Finances

Analysts opine that some deep-rooted fiscal issues are becoming stumbling block in sustainable economic development of Punjab. Debt liability of the state has been burgeoning continuously over the years (Figure 13.5). The debt burden of the state has acquired unmanageable proportion. Vast losses incurred by the State Electricity Board due to provision of free power, low irrigation charges, uneconomic transport fares have all combined to produce unduly low returns on decades of past investments. The total debt stock of the state has risen from Rs 32,496

Figure 13.5

Trend in Public Debt of the State Government

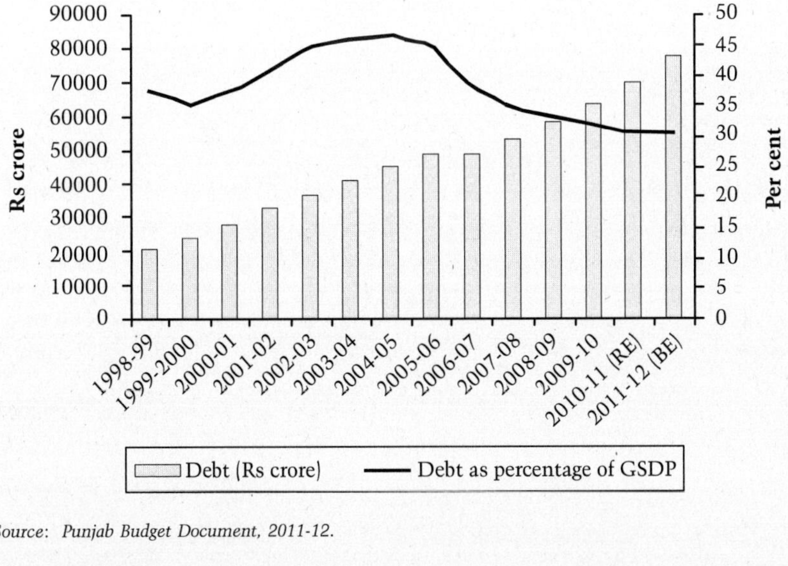

Source: Punjab Budget Document, 2011-12.

crore in 2001-02 to Rs 77,585 (as on 31st March) in the budget estimates of 2011-12. The liability for servicing this debt is also increasing in tandem. However, it is comforting that the state has been able to improve the debt-GSDP ratio from 38.13 per cent in 2006-07 to 33.01 per cent in 2008-09. This is likely to improve further to 30.43 per cent by the end of 2011-12. Thus, improvement in debt-GSDP ratio in second half points to improved growth scenario in the state implying enhanced resource capability to service the debt.

The fiscal situation of the state for the last many years has been characterised by burgeoning debt, consequent higher interest outgo, increase in non-plan revenue expenditure and low share of state in Central taxes. The situation also aggravated due to the fact that Twelfth Finance Commission did not recommend any revenue deficit grant to the state beyond 2007-08. The implementation of recommendation of the Pay Commission has put added strain on the state's resources. The Government has been constrained in achieving its desired levels of public investment and spending on account of the huge debt burden of the state. The state's borrowings have increased over the last few years to finance the revenue deficit and fund its plan expenditure. The factors which have adversely impacted the state's fiscal situation are ever increasing salaries and wage bills of the employees, mounting debt burden, heavily subsidised social and economic services, slow growth of revenue and loss-making public sector undertakings (PSUs). The galloping rise in non-development expenditure in last two decades has also distorted expenditure priorities and is also an outcome of accumulation of debt burden (Figure 13.6).

Punjab has been under fiscal stress since 1987-88, when it became a revenue deficit state (Figure 13.7). During 1990s, there was steep rise in revenue deficit with a fourfold increase in level of revenue deficit witnessed during 1990-91 to 1999-2000. The revenue deficit further increased in first part of 2000s but steeply fell to low level for two consecutive years i.e., 2005-06 and 2006-07. Thereafter, it has again resumed to higher level at Rs 5,251 crore in 2009-10, the highest value in the series till then. However, there has been a sharp turnaround in the scenario with revenue deficit budgeted at Rs 3,379 crore in 2011-12 i.e., decline by 35.6 per cent from 2009-10 value. The state's revenue deficit is evidently high, primarily

Figure 13.6

Trend in Non-Development Revenue Expenditure

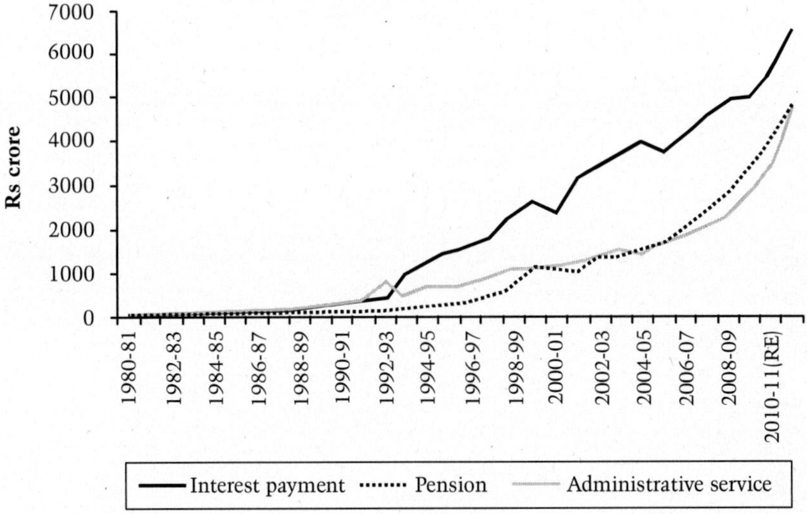

Source: *Handbook of Statistics on State Government Finances, 2010* and Budget Documents of Punjab Government (various issues).

Figure 13.7

Trend in Revenue Deficit in Last Three Decades

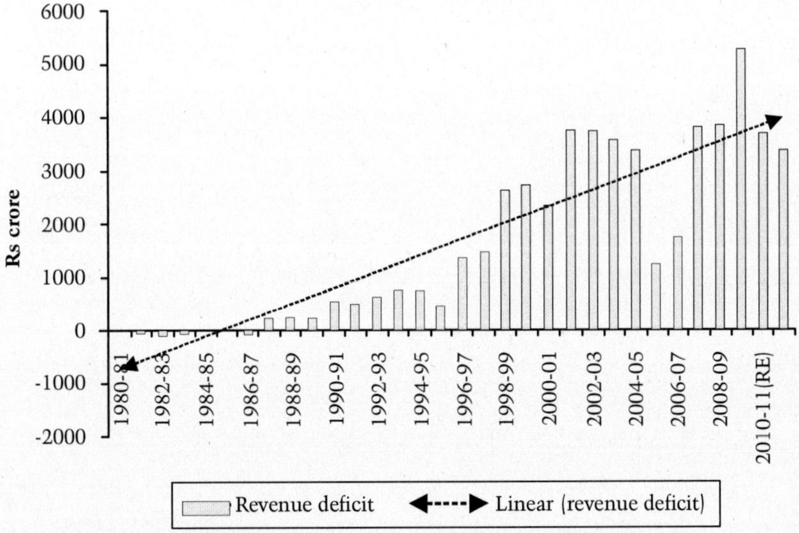

Source: *Handbook of Statistics on State Government Finances, 2010* and Budget Documents of Punjab Government (various issues).

on account of the high expenditure on salaries, pensions and servicing of debt. The total interest payment from revenue account is budgeted to increase from Rs 4,902 crore in 2008-09 to Rs 6,530 crore in 2011-12.

However, revenue deficit as per cent of GSDP has shown improvement in the last decade with its level of 4.7 of GSDP in 2001-02 falling to 2.63 per cent of GSDP in 2009-10, a significant improvement within eight years signifying some steps taken by state government especially in light of state fiscal responsibility bill (Figure 13.8). This is further budgeted to improve at 1.33 per cent in 2011-12. The gross fiscal deficit has also followed the same trend being mainly driven by the similar forces. From the above analysis, it is evident that the state has made some progress in fiscal consolidation in the past 7-8 years in terms of reducing revenue/fiscal deficit and also total outstanding debt as percentage of GSDP. However, in terms of absolute values these have shown an increasing trend.

The state government should further consolidate its fiscal position. Fiscal prudent measures would require cutting down subsidies on power and water, levy of property tax, disinvestment of PSUs that are in the red, plugging of losses suffered by the transport department. These would be politically difficult to implement but expenditure restructuring is a must for bringing in shape the fiscal condition and reducing the debt further. On

Figure 13.8

Trend in Revenue and Fiscal Deficit as Per cent of GSDP

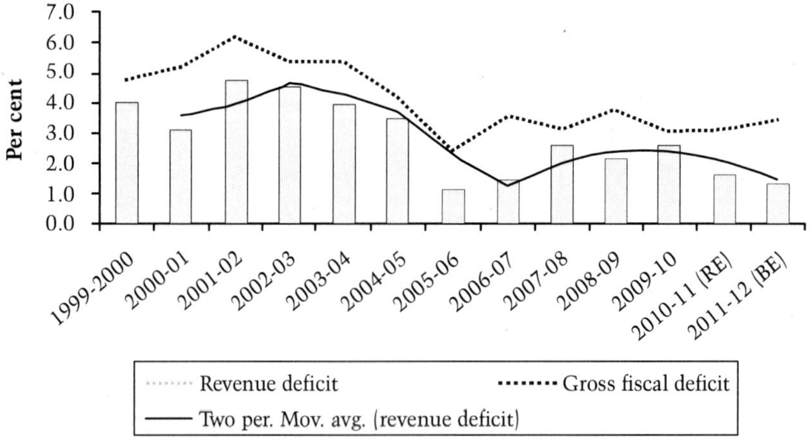

Source: *Punjab Budget Document, 2011-12.*

revenue side also, new innovative measures in raising taxes from the state income need to be introduced.

V

Recommendations

The analysis in the paper had made starkly clear the necessity to bring changes in economy so as to break current status quo to facilitate Punjab traverse new path of development and prosperity. The most significant indicator of current development of state economy is structural composition of different sectors. In the previous section it has been observed that the Punjab's sectoral composition is relatively skewed in favour of agricultural sector in comparison to all-India. Therefore, the agriculture sector has to have prominence in policy space in terms of providing newer impetus and replicate another Green Revolution so as to break the stagnancy in agricultural production and productivity. In terms of finding new solution to pertinent problems of Punjab economy, an exercise of SWOT analysis would be helpful in focusing on key strategic areas while improving upon deficiencies (Table 13.9). In the table, it appears that policies should focus on opportunities in different sectors so as to harness the advantages that are unique to the state. Contract farming is one of the areas which can help reap huge benefits of economies of scale and specialisation besides bringing newer technology in farming. Its success requires newer production structure with appropriate contract and tenancy laws. Similarly, food processing industries have promising prospects in state and enabling measures can lead to its wider outreach.

The conclusion emerging from different sections of the paper has a common thread in terms of trend observed in the last three decades, significance of economic reforms in impacting performance of different sectors and the need for the state economy to adjust to the priorities of new policy regime putting premium on competition and productivity. Investment promotion and creation of enabling framework are the two effective solutions for rejuvenating the economic activity in Punjab. Thus, any recommendation has to take care of the reality of new policies being pursued at Centre so that the state policies compliment them. It may be noted that the table on SWOT also forms base for deriving the recommendations:

A multipronged strategy is suggested to obviate the current difficulties in agriculture sector and usher transformation to bring farm prosperity with the following components.

Table 13.9

SWOT Analysis for Punjab

Sector	*Strengths*	*Weaknesses*	*Opportunities*	*Threats*
Agriculture	• Fertile land and good irrigation facilities • Concerned government	• Adverse climatic effects and uncertainties • Low investments	• Development of food processing and storage industries • Contract farming	• Exploitation of natural resources beyond sustainable levels • Movement to industry and services sector
Industry	• Good base of traditional industries • Hardworking and entrepreneurial people	• Agriculture based industry • Severe power shortages • Low investments • Weak enforcement of policies • High land costs • Landlocked and away from major markets	• Huge potential for value added industry • Room for improving the productivity by investing in advanced technologies	• Competition from other progressive states • Labour crunch
Services	• Strong human resource pool and technical base • Well developed tourism sector • Good base of traditional and financial services	• Dominated by traditional services • Lower female literacy rate	• Low service base compared with national average • Development of strategic business services • IT and ITES	• Competition from other progressive states

Source: Adapted from Assocham's Research Bureau Report.

First, the state should focus on replicating its success achieved in realising Green Revolution. This requires a genuine policy boost essentially for identifying, adapting and assimilating the relevant outcomes of the scientific research available. Further, agriculture special economic zones (SEZs) should be the ideal channel for taking up capital intensive high value organic agriculture in the state.

Second, the subsidies need to be rationalised according to current realities. Currently, the implicit subsidy with respect to free of charge electricity and subsidised irrigation charges has resulted into usage of tube well set with higher than required capacity sucking unaccounted groundwater. This has resulted into overexploitation of groundwater resources and undesirable cropping pattern unsuitable to the state agro-climatic location. The fertiliser subsidy has resulted into unbalanced NPK ratio undesirable for both crop and soil fertility. Subsidies need to be rationalised so that overall production structure readjust to the present requirement ensuring both ecological and economic sustainability.

Third, Punjab has enormous potential for the development of value added food products for both domestic and foreign markets. The state should focus not only on the production of food grains but also their processing for value addition and marketing. Facilitating the operation of new institutions and strengthening the linking of farmers to processors and retailers, which would unleash a wave of high value crop value-added activity to satisfy the rapidly growing demand.

Fourth, infrastructure needs a major overhaul in the state. Irrigation and watershed management is an immediate requirement in order to stop overexploitation of water resources in the state. Alongside, a definite roadmap for improving transport infrastructure, storage facilities, logistics, power, communications and marketing is required. Punjab needs to prepare and implement an appropriate time-bound comprehensive programme with the above objectives on an urgent basis.

Fifth, reforming irrigation by focusing on better utilisation of the irrigation potential already created, establishing and promoting water-user associations to improve maintenance and equitable allocation of water, make them truly participatory, and devolve powers by the irrigation department, gradually increasing pricing to at least cover operations and maintenance (O&M) costs and devolving solution to local/sub-zonal problems to correct regional inequalities.

Sixth, institutional innovations such as warehouse receipt system, futures trading and commodity exchanges should be established to tap international markets. Crop insurance programmes that will help farmers to protect themselves from the volatility of international markets as well as from vagaries of monsoon should be implemented and the success of the programmes such as on Kisan Credit Cards (KCCs) should be expanded. Developing institutions for certifying quality characteristics of agricultural produces will go a long way in enabling farmers to reach out to international markets. Institutional reforms, particularly in input supplying agencies and in irrigation systems should be undertaken.

Finally, encouraging farmers' associations and cooperatives to build collective bargaining power and to enter into contracts with agro-processors and supermarkets is essential for adding value to the products produced by farmers. Getting the bankers, entrepreneurs and farmer leaders on the same table and meeting their needs in order to make progress will be essential in the near future. Last but not the least, getting the legislation cleaned up for all the controls that are pulling down the agricultural economy will be important.

The state needs to focus on the development of new age industries like engineering, biotechnology, food processing and gems and jewellery sectors. Punjab needs to prepare a policy for attracting big industrialists in investing in these sectors. These sectors on being properly developed will make the state as the R&D hub of India.

Punjab should focus on developing IT and ITES industry in the state. Punjab has a number of important tourist places to attract both national and international tourists into the state. Some of these places are losing their relevance owing to their management and environmental degradation as well due to increased competition from the neighbouring states. The state government needs to prepare a strategy and infrastructure in order to attract maximum number of tourists in future.

The externalities attached with some of the services sector are immense. Education and health services add value to human capital and if harnessed effectively to the benefit of the society, can give extraordinary returns. Credit facilities go a long way in providing an impetus to the growth of economic activities. Thus, strategic focus on few select services sub-sectors suited to state endowment and conveniently placed in domestic and world market can bring faster prosperity as long as complementary infrastructural support is also provided.

VI

Concluding Observations

In Punjab, the wave of economic transformation has been operating as elsewhere though the direction and pace has not always been aligned to national trend. Thus, in Punjab also the prominence of agriculture faded with fall in its share in economy to some extent. In fact, the stagnating agricultural productivity and saturation in extension of crop acreage led to this decline in post-reform period. However, the fall in share of agriculture at all-India was sharper. In the final analysis, it appears that agriculture was still maintaining its importance in the Punjab economy in comparison to relatively lower share of agriculture in the economy at all-India level. Thus, given the fact that majority of workforce is dependent on agriculture sector, we have more reasons to take it seriously in any policy prescriptions for Punjab. Another interesting trend is relative stagnation of secondary sector during 30-year period in all-India compared to rise in share of industrial sector in GSDP from 10.4 per cent in 1980-81 to 19.4 per cent in 2009-10 in Punjab, signalling better industrial activities. This is a very important trend as India's structural transformation is believed to have missed critical stage of industrialisation as a step from primary activities to tertiary activities. In Punjab on the contrary, significant portion of fall in primary sector has also been grabbed by secondary sector during the last three decades. This trend should be comforting as balanced sectoral structure provide wider basis for development of different sectors of state economy ensuring sustainability of growth in the long run.

The economic reforms of 1991 had an overwhelming influence on the institutions and policy apparatus even at the subnational level. Overall, different sectors of state economy have responded differently as seen in previous sections. The experience of the Punjab economy shows that reforms can be hindered by the fact that important stakeholders can have rather different, and often opposing, views about essential facts, causal mechanisms and appropriate policy solutions. The structural reforms and stabilisation policies initially focused on industry, tax reforms, foreign trade and investment, banking and capital markets. The economic reforms did not include any specific package specifically designed for agriculture. It was viewed that freeing agricultural markets and liberalising external trade in agricultural commodities would provide price incentives leading to enhanced investment and output in the sector, while broader trade liberalisation would shift intersectoral terms of trade in favour of agriculture.

The changing policy dynamics at Centre and state has not impacted agriculture sector favourably as some deep-rooted structural problems have cropped up which are insensitive to policy solutions and packages. In Punjab agriculture production has reached a plateau. The soil health in the state has been deteriorating with the adoption of rice-wheat rotation. In a nutshell, the agriculture faces problems as the net area sown and irrigated areas have been fully exploited and the cropping intensity has reached a saturation point from where further scope is minimal. Domination of wheat-paddy in food grains, stagnating productivity, in the absence of breakthrough in new high yielding varieties, strains on marketing infrastructure, dwindling groundwater resources, decline in profitability etc., are the major concerns which demand immediate attention. Diversification could be the answer, but would require fundamental changes in incentives, institutions and investments. If Punjab does not rationalise incentives, create new institutions and reinvigorate the existing institutions and increase investments significantly, it will suffer declining income and employment and irreversible environmental degradation.

The current scenario also pose difficult phase for Punjab economy where it is confronted with multiple problems at different fronts of the economy. The structural problems in the economy having acquired crisis proportion requiring immediate actions and solutions. The spillover effect of economic crisis to social crisis though delayed is more harmful and dangerous. The current rural distress on account of mounting debt burden is a manifestation of such a spillover effect of multidimensional crisis having combination of economic factors such as economic hardship of the peasant households, crop failure, unemployment, etc. The extreme distress shown by farmers in some instances is in fact an indicator of weakening of production process, institutional structure, market and state support showing deep-rooted problems in state economy requiring urgent revamp. Finally, the past history of Punjab shows its resilient character as it quickly recovered from Partition wounds to produce miracle in agriculture sector transforming the food security scenario of whole country by quantum leap in productivity of select food grains during Green Revolution. Given the fact that gains in agriculture sector are now withering away, the state needs to reposition itself according to the requirements of new knowledge based economy by harnessing human potential. In the end, it can be concluded that Punjab is at crossroads where its choice of alternative solutions to the structural problems will determine its position and growth trajectory in the coming years.

References

Ahluwalia, Montek S. (2000). "State Level Performance under Economic Reforms in India", Paper presented at the Centre for Research on Economic Development, Stanford University.

Bhanumurthy, N.R. and Arup Mitra (2004). *Economic Growth, Poverty and Reforms in Indian States*. New Delhi: Institute of Economic Growth.

Ghosh, Anjan, Jayanta Roy and Aditi Nayar (2010). *Fiscal Consolidation: Challenges for Indian States*. ICRA, December.

Ghuman, Ranjit Singh (2008). "Socio-economic Crisis in Rural Punjab", *Economic & Political Weekly*, February.

Gill, Sucha S. (2005). *Economic Distress and Farmers Suicides in Rural Punjab*. Patiala: Punjabi University.

International Food Policy Research Institute (IFPRI) (2007). *Report: Withering Punjab Agriculture - Can it regain its leadership?*. March, New Delhi.

Kohli, Deepali Singhal and Nirvikar Singh (1997). *The Green Revolution in Punjab, India: The Economics of Technological Change*. NCAER, September.

Posani, Balamuralidhar (2009). *Crisis in the Countryside: Farmer Suicides and the Political Economy of Agrarian Distress in India*. London: Development Studies Institute.

Sawhney, Upinder (2008). "Growth of Services Sector in a Predominantly Agricultural Economy of Punjab", *Political Economy Journal of India*, January-June.

———. (2005). *Fiscal Reforms at the Sub-National Level: The Case of Punjab*. New Delhi: National Institute of Public Finance and Policy.

Shergill, H.S. (2008). *Economics of Food Self-Sufficiency*. Chandigarh: Institute for Development and Communication (IDC).

Singh, Lakhwinder (2010). "Post-reform Economic Development in Punjab: Constraints and Remedies", *MPRA Paper* 26741, Germany: University Library of Munich.

———. (2006). *Deceleration of Industrial growth and Rural Industrialisation Strategy for Indian Punjab*. Patiala: Punjabi University, November.

Singh, Lakhwinder, Ranjit Singh and Ranjit Singh Ghuman (2007). *Changing Character of Rural Economy and Migrant Labour in Punjab.* Patiala: Punjabi University, Department of Economics.

Singh, Lakhwinder and Sukhpal Singh (2002). "Deceleration of Economic Growth in Punjab: Evidence, Explanation and a way out", *Economic and Political Weekly*, February.

14 Social Sector Expenditure across States

AVDHESH KUMAR SHUKLA[1]

I

Introduction

The ultimate objective of development planning is human development or increasing social welfare and well-being of the people of a nation. This goal is important because the sustainability of the development process hinges on the quality of life enjoyed by the people. A healthy and educated population leads to increased productivity, which, in turn, can contribute effectively to output growth. Development strategies, therefore, needs continuous strive for broad-based improvement in standards of living. High growth is essential to generate resource for social spending (*Economic Survey, 2009-10*). Moreover, spending on social sectors is important because it tends to benefit the poor relatively more than the rich and because, arguably, it increases the human capital of economy, which can produce direct growth effects and indirect spillover benefits for rest of the economy (Reza Baqir, 2002).

In recent years, particularly after economic reforms, India witnessed rapid economic growth in terms of per capita as well as gross domestic product. Like many other emerging economies, India also vouch to eradicate poverty, illiteracy, malnutrition, mass hunger and other social problems. In India, the state governments, due to their operational advantage to local issues, are entrusted with the major responsibilities related to social expenditure. This article has analysed social sector

1. The views expressed in this paper are of the author himself and no way represent the views of the organisation he is working with.

expenditure of 16 major non-special category states[2] of India, i.e., Bihar, Uttar Pradesh, Madhya Pradesh, Jharkhand, Rajasthan, Orissa, Chhattisgarh, West Bengal, Andhra Pradesh, Karnataka, Tamil Nadu, Kerala, Gujarat, Punjab, Maharashtra, and Haryana. Study has excluded the special category states from analysis, as share of social sector expenditure in their total expenditure is significantly high. One non-special category state, Goa has also been excluded from the study as it is very small and its per capita income is comparatively very high *vis-à-vis* other states. Combined share of these states in total population of India is about 92 per cent whereas they contributed about 82 per cent in net national domestic product. In terms of population below poverty line, share of these states was about 95 per cent. Improvement in social sector indicators of these states will have a very significant impact on overall human development of India.

In terms of per capita income and growth, these states are at different stages of development (Table 14.1). Per capita income of richest state, Haryana is more than five times of the per capita income of Bihar, the poorest state. During 2008-09, per capita income of eight states among studied states is below national per capita income, whereas per capita income of other eight states is above the national average. In terms of percentage of population living below poverty line (BPL), during 2004-05 share of BPL population in Orissa was 46.40 per cent as against to 8.40 per cent in Punjab during the same period. In terms of infant mortality rate (IMR) also there exists a wide variation across the studied states. In 2008, as against to IMR of 12 per thousand live births in Kerala, it was 70 in Madhya Pradesh and 67 in Uttar Pradesh. It is a proven fact that the government expenditure on social sector has a positive impact on various social sector indicators. High social sector indicators indicate the availability of better quality of human resource in the economy, which is a precondition for higher economic growth.

2. Twelfth Finance Commission has divided the states into two categories of special states and non-special states. Special states receive 90 per cent of their resources from Union government.

Table 14.1

Select Socioeconomic Indicators of Major States

State	*Per Capita Income (at Current Prices) (in Rupees) 2008-09*	*Per Capita Income (at Constant Prices) (in Rupees) 2008-09*	*Number Persons below Poverty Line (in Lakh)#*	*Percentage of Population below Poverty Line#*	*Infant Mortality Rate (per Thousand Live Births (2008)*	*Gross Enrollment Ratio in Classes VI to VIII (2006-07)*
Andhra Pradesh	40,902	27,362	126.10	15.8	52	75.5
Bihar	13,663	10,206	369.15	41.40	56	39.0
Chhattisgarh	34,483	19,521	90.96	40.90	57	87.6
Gujarat	57,619	35,747	90.69	16.80	50	75.4
Haryana	68,914	41,896	32.10	14.00	54	80.3
Jharkhand	21,465	16,294	116.39	40.30	46	52.3
Karnataka	40,998	27385	138.89	25.00	45	88.8
Kerala	49,316	35,457	49.60	15.00	12	98.9
Madhya Pradesh	20,287	14,446	249.68	38.30	70	96.0
Maharashtra	57,908	39,732	317.38	30.70	33	101.5
Orissa	29,464	18,212	178.49	46.40	69	74.8
Punjab	52,879	33,198	21.63	8.40	41	69.0
Rajasthan	27,001	19,708	134.89	22.10	63	79.6
Tamil Nadu	45,058	30,652	145.62	22.50	31	109.2
Uttar Pradesh	18,214	12,481	590.03	32.80	67	53.6
West Bengal	36,322	24,720	208.36	24.70	35	89.7
All-India	37,490	25,494	3,017.20	27.50	53	73.8

Note: # Based on Uniform Recall Period Consumption.

Source: *Handbook of Statistics on Indian Economy, 2009-10*, Reserve Bank of India; *Economic Survey 2009-10*.

Present study has attempted to compare and analyse the trend of social sector expenditure by the state governments. Study has also attempted to analyse the determinants of social sector expenditure with help of a panel data econometric exercise. For analysis purpose, study has divided these states into two broad categories on basis of their per capita income of 2008-09. Accordingly, study has assumed Andhra Pradesh, Gujarat, Haryana, Karnataka, Kerala, Maharashtra, Punjab and Tamil Nadu as developed states whereas Bihar, Chhattisgarh, Jharkhand, Madhya Pradesh, Orissa, Rajasthan, Uttar Pradesh and West Bengal as underdeveloped states. It would be worth to mention that 64 per cent poor of India reside in these underdeveloped states.

The study has seven sections. Section II has briefly outlined the achievements of various developmental goals of these states in light of millennium development targets. Section III has surveyed the existing literature related to the topic and has covered a brief theoretical perspective on the subject. Section IV has given stylised facts related to social sector expenditure by the state governments. Section V has analysed fiscal parameters of state governments and their movement *vis-à-vis* social sector expenditure. In this section, an attempt has been made to ascertain the variables, which determine the social sector expenditure by the state governments with the help of panel data analysis. Section VI has covered the role of Finance Commissions. Section VII has given concluding observations of study.

Data and Methodology

For analysis, study has used data related to state governments' budgets published in *Handbook of Statistics on State Government Finances 2010* of the Reserve Bank of India. It has also used Central Statistical Organisation (CSO) data for net state domestic product (NSDP) at current prices and per capita income at current prices in studied states. Series of domestic product and per capita income for studied period have been prepared by splicing of data of previous base years. Data, used in study, have taken from the *Handbook of Statistics on Indian Economy 2009-10* published by the Reserve Bank of India. The budget data provides information on expenditure by the state governments on various social services including education and health. In this study, mainly we have used aggregate social sector expenditure[3] data for analysis but at some places, revenue account expenditure has also been used, which have appropriately indicated there. All econometric exercises mentioned in the paper have been conducted with help of E-views 6 package.

---

3. Conventionally, social sector expenditure of the state governments comprises expenditure on a number of heads *viz.*, education, sports, art and culture, medical and public health, family welfare, water supply and sanitation, housing, urban development, welfare of backward classes of society, labour and labour welfare, social security and welfare, nutrition, relief on account of natural calamities, etc. In most parts of this study, aggregate social sector expenditure have been used. However, where data of expenditure on education and health services have been used it pertains to expenditure of revenue account only.

II

Millennium Development Goals: Some Stylised Facts related to Indian States

The Millennium Declaration of the United Nations set 2015 as the time line for achieving most of the Millennium Development Goals (MDGs), which provide quantitative benchmarks for eradication of extreme poverty, hunger, illiteracy and diseases apart from achieving gender equality and empowerment of women, environmental sustainability and global partnership for development. The CSO has carried out a mid-term appraisal of India's progress towards attainment of MDGs in its report *Millennium Development Goals—India Country Report 2009*. The report has analysed in detail the status of achievement of all 12 MDG indicators relevant to India.[4] Analysis in following paragraphs is based on data/information available in that report.

Eradication of Extreme Poverty and Hunger

India is witnessing decline in incidence of poverty. It has declined from 55 per cent in 1973-74 to 36 per cent in 1993-94 and further to 27.5 per cent in 2004-05. This trend indicates that India is on track to achieve the target of halving the proportion of people below the poverty line by 2015. However, this improvement is not homogeneous across the states. Among the states, there are 21 states/UTs, which are going to be early achiever of poverty headcount ratio (PHR) targets of halving their 1990 poverty levels. Four states/UTs are either on track or slightly slow at achieving the target. Seven states/UTs are relatively slow in progress. Although, the number of early achieving states is more than the states, which are slow or on track, but together overall progress of the country outweighed by slow progress of the more populated and bigger states. Among the major states that are on fast track are Gujarat, Kerala, Tamil Nadu and West Bengal while Andhra Pradesh, Karnataka, Punjab and Rajasthan are the major states that are just on track. As against to this

4. MDG have set 18 targets but six are not relevant to India as they are mainly related to the landlocked/island/least developed countries and also for the developed countries.

Bihar, Haryana, Madhya Pradesh, Maharashtra, Orissa, Uttar Pradesh, Chhattisgarh and Jharkhand will fail to achieve the target. It may be mentioned that majority of states which will achieve the target are comparatively small and less significant whereas lagging states are considerably bigger. As illustrated earlier in the article majority of below poverty population reside in these states (refer Table 14.1).

Halving Proportion of People who Suffer from Hunger between 1990 and 2015

According to CSO report, among major states, only Punjab and Tamil Nadu are early achievers whereas Andhra Pradesh, Karnataka and Maharashtra are just on track. Except for these states, all other major states will fail to meet the target of MDG.

Universal Primary Education

According to mid-term appraisal report, country as whole is on track to meet the target of universal enrollment well before 2015. However, Uttar Pradesh, Bihar and Jharkhand are lagging.

Child Mortality Rate

MDG targets to reduce the under five years child mortality (U5MR) by two-third, between 1990 and 2015. India is likely to miss the target. Among studied states, it is higher in Bihar, Madhya Pradesh, Rajasthan and Uttar Pradesh. Haryana, Kerala, Tamil Nadu and Gujarat are on track to achieve it.

III

Theoretical Perspective and Literature Survey

Spending capacity of state governments and their expenditure on social sector has received wide attention among academicians and policy-makers. Hong and Ahmed (2009) used panel data for 14 Indian states (from 1990 to 2002 period) and concluded by econometric evidence that state government's fiscal policies have important implications for per capita NSDP growth. The share of public goods expenditures in total state government expenditures has a large positive and significant impact on per capita NSDP growth. Reallocation of funds to increase the share of public goods expenditures could on average lead per capita income growth rate to increase by up to 2.7 percentage points. They further pointed out that the share of other developmental expenditures has a significant positive effect on growth, but the effect is only about one-half of the shares of public goods spending. Another finding is that state fiscal policies also have significant impacts on poverty reduction.

However, Chakraborty *et al.* (2009) concluded that in the post-economic liberalisation era in India, fiscal reforms at Centre and the financial sector reforms in country have adversely affected sub-national finances. The Centre's fiscal consolidation measures contributed to sharp decline in the vertical transfers and liberalisation has increased interest rate differentials, which has widened the states' resource gap through an increase in interest outgo on the debt stock. Further, they concluded that though there are sharp interstate differences, the fiscal and macro-policy shocks have reduced the fiscal space across states with varying degrees. According to them, the sub-national fiscal space is shrinking in face of an increase in cost of borrowing.

In an article published in *Economic and Political Weekly*, Isaac and Ramakumar (2006) concluded that due to passing of fiscal responsibility legislation in accordance with recommendations of successive Finance Commissions, states have accumulated huge cash surpluses. This, according to them, has led to decline in social sector expenditure by the state governments. Sethi (2009) also concluded that strict framework, which has been recommended by the Thirteenth Finance Commission for state governments might prove detrimental for underdeveloped states in enhancing their social sector expenditure. According to her, in pressure to meet the time-bound targets, these states have been compelled to neglect the very sectors that can pull them out of their present status of being the 'least developed states'. Sen and Karmakar (2007) though accepted the view, that in short and medium terms most of the committed non-developmental expenditures cannot be reduced drastically and macroeconomic performance also cannot be improved suddenly through actions at the state level alone, but an important method of managing resources to finance consistent and balanced human development lies in the reprioritisation of current expenditure in accordance with the urgent needs and shortfalls in particular areas. Such reprioritisation should also lead the states to a better macroeconomic future, through improvements in key areas. They suggested that state governments should use standard consumer theory while prioritising their policy preferences according to utility maximisation subject to the budget constraint. According to them biggest problem for governments is that this utility function is missing.

Bhatt and Jain (2004) in a study on relationship between income and health care expenditure at state level computed the income elasticity of health care expenditure by the state governments. According to them, it was only 0.68, which suggests that every one per cent increase in state per capita income will lead only .68 per cent increase in health care expenditure. They found that, as against to this, income elasticity of private expenditure on health care is about 1.95. However, this study had covered only the relationship between public health care expenditure by the state governments and per capita income. Study has not analysed the impact of fiscal indicators on health expenditure.

Tsujita (2005) found that economic reforms largely did not have a major negative impact on expenditures. In fact he concluded that there was a positive impact on some states, which often were those that received more foreign aid than other states. By the late 1990s, states expending more on the social sector changed from states with a traditionally strong commitment to the social sector, such as Kerala, to states having higher revenues including aid from outside the country. He focused mainly on two issues: 1) whether or not economic reforms were a turning point for the changes in expenditures and 2) what were the reasons for the changes. He concluded that downward trends in social sector expenditure by state governments were not simply the result of economic reforms, but were continuing trends from the pre-economic reform period. According to him, there were three major reasons for decline in social sector expenditure by the state governments during 1980s. First, the Reserve Bank of India (RBI) strengthened its overdraft regulation in 1985. Second, state governments increased civil servant salaries and pensions in the mid-1980s following the recommendations of the Fourth Central Pay Commission. This increase coupled with rising interest payments on the states' growing debt issues meant that development expenditures had to be reduced in order to pay for salaries and pensions in non-development expenditures. As already pointed out, most of the states started to reduce development expenditures in the mid-1980s, which means that social service expenditures have been sacrificed since the mid-1980s. Third, the reduction of transfers from the Central government since the mid-1980s has also played a role in the decline of social sector expenditures. Prabhu and Sarkar (2001) pointed out that sharp jump in budgeted revenue gap of state governments, which quantifies the extent that states are dependent on resources over which they have no control, seems to coincident with an expenditure shift in a given fiscal year. In all states having a year of significant downward shift in social services expenditures, that year has coincided with increasing resource gap or is one year earlier. This implies that state governments adjusted social service expenditures in the year or one year after having obtained fewer resources they did not control. They concluded that revenue has played an important role in the level and trend of state expenditures for social services since the mid-1980s.

Dev and Mooij (2002) concluded that social sector expenditure by the state governments during 1990s declined, mainly due to decline in financial resources transferred from the Centre to the states. They pointed out that due to this, social sector expenditure by the Central government has increased. They also pointed out that in most states, social sector expenditure has not increased very much in the first half of the 1990s, but in the second half there has been an increase, in terms of per capita real expenditure. They had divided states in three groups, *viz.*, rich income, middle income and poor income states. The rich and middle income states have done better than the poor states, but there are also huge variations within income groups. Within the group of middle income states, West Bengal is an outlier, in the sense that its social spending has increased much less than that of the other middle-income states, while the absolute level is also not very high. Within the group of poor states, the performance (in terms of spending) of Madhya Pradesh, Orissa and Rajasthan has increased considerably, especially after the mid-1990s, while Bihar and Uttar Pradesh did less well. In general, the situation of three states (Bihar, Uttar Pradesh and West Bengal) is worrying because both levels and growth of expenditure on social services are lower in these states. In the case of Madhya Pradesh, Orissa and Rajasthan, levels are lower in spite of reasonable growth in social service expenditures.

There are a few studies, which have examined the convergence of state governments' expenditure on social sector also. *State Finance: A Study of Budgets 2009-10* examined beta and alpha convergence of various indicators of social sector expenditure. It concluded that levels of per capita capital outlay, development expenditure and social sector expenditure have shown some convergence across the states, as their respective coefficients are negative as well as statistically significant. However, within social sector expenditure, the coefficient equations tested for per capita expenditure on rural development is negative but not statistically significant indicating convergence not supported by statistical confidence. Among the broad expenditure categories, the rate of convergence as denoted by beta shows that per capita social sector expenditure had the highest rate of convergence across states during 1980-81 and 2008-09 followed by per capita development expenditure.

Economic literature as illustrated above indicates that although authors have accepted the fact that social sector expenditure is falling but there is no unanimity about its causes. Some authors have pointed out that due to economic reforms, committed expenditure in form of interest outgo has increased which has led to shrinking of social sector expenditure. Whereas some have pointed out that decline of social sector expenditure of states started much before commencement of economic reforms. These studies pointed out that social sector expenditure of states declined due to: i) implementation of hike in salaries of civil servants in view of various Pay Commissions recommendations and ii) overdependence of states on budget revenue gap. Decline in Central transfers has also been cited as reason in some studies.

IV

Expenditure Pattern on Social Sector by the State Governments: Some Stylised Facts

Government expenditure can be analysed in three distinct ways, *viz.*, as percentage of aggregate expenditure, as percentage of domestic product (income) and third as per capita expenditure. Data relating to the state government's expenditure on social sector reveal following facts.

Social Sector Expenditure as Percentage of Aggregate Expenditure

During the period 1980-2010, social sector expenditure as percentage of aggregate expenditure (SSE-AE) across the states has varied considerably. During the second half of 1980s, SSE-AE witnessed significant increase in all the states *vis-à-vis* first half of the decade (Figure 14.1a). However, SSE-AE of developed states, barring Karnataka and Maharashtra where it has increased marginally, witnessed decline during first half of 1990s and this trend of decline was continued up to end of first half of 2000s. This trend of decline in SSE-AE reversed only in second half of 2000s once fiscal situation of these states improved considerably.

In underdeveloped states, SSE-AE increased until end of second half of 1990s in Bihar, Madhya Pradesh and Orissa; however, in Uttar Pradesh and West Bengal it witnessed consistent decline during 1990s. At the same time, it remained stagnant in Rajasthan. During the second half of 2000s, SSE-AE of these states increased again (Figure 14.1b).

During studied period, SSE-AE of underdeveloped states as a group was higher than that of developed states as a group. However, at state level, as mentioned earlier wide variations exist. Among developed states during 1980-1985, SSE-AE was highest for the state of Kerala (42.10%) followed by Andhra Pradesh (36.46%) and Tamil Nadu (35.35%). Among the developed states Haryana (24.67%) followed by Punjab (26.43%) and Maharashtra (28.71%) were at bottom. During the same period (i.e., 1980-1985) under the underdeveloped category states, SSE-AE was highest for West Bengal (39.28%). For other underdeveloped states, SSE-AE was in a range of 28.03

per cent to 33.98 per cent. In fact, if we exclude West Bengal from underdeveloped states category during 1980-1985, SSE-AE in these states was significantly lower than the developed states.

Figure 14.1

Social Sector Expenditure as Percentage to Aggregate Expenditure

(a)

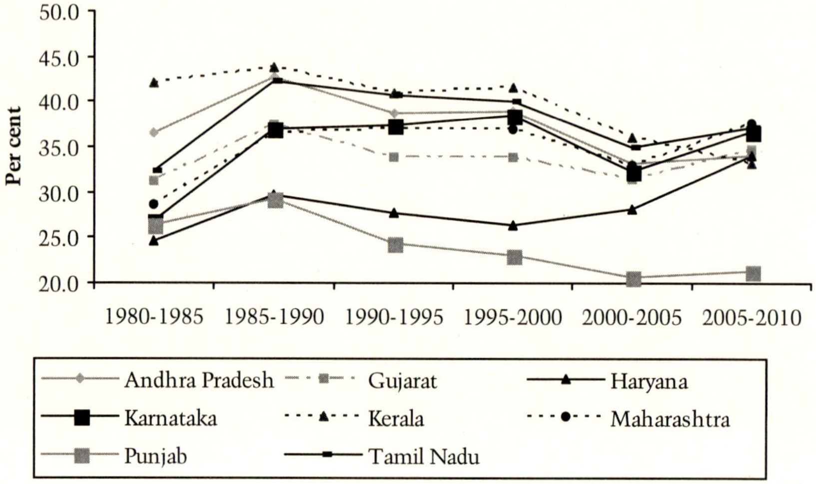

(b)

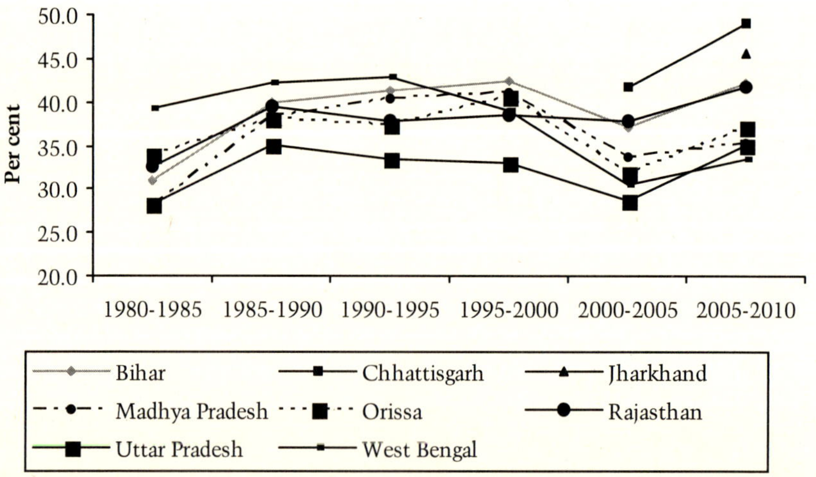

During the period 2005-2010, SSE-AE of developed states (barring Punjab that witnessed steep decline in it and was at 21.70 per cent, lowest in country) witnessed a convergence in a range of 33.54 per cent (Kerala) to 39.43 per cent (Maharashtra). During the studied period Kerala, West Bengal, Punjab and Andhra Pradesh were the states, which witnessed decline in SSE-AE. Barring these four states, SSE-AE of all other states was higher during 2005-2010 in comparison with 1980-1985. During the period, though, SSE-AE of underdeveloped states has increased during 2005-2010 period but its dispersion has also increased.

A plot of coefficient of variation (CV) of SSE-AE indicates that disperson of share of expenditure on social sector has a gradually increasing trend over the years (Figure 14.2). Although after 2003-04 it witnessed steep decline from its peak and since 2006-07 it has remained below the trend.

Figure 14.2

Coefficient of Variation of SSE as Per cent of AE

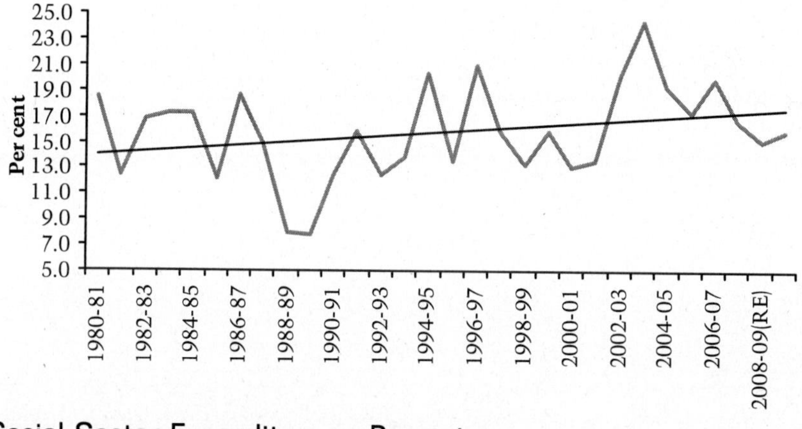

Social Sector Expenditure as Percentage of Net Domestic Product

Social sector expenditure by the state governments as percentage of net state domestic product (SSE-NSDP) during the studied year has witnessed an increasing trend over the years. Although this increasing trend was not smooth, first it increased during second half of 1980s and then it witnessed decline during 1990s. The trend in decline was reversed only in early years of 2000s. Increase in SSE-NSDP was higher in case of underdeveloped states *vis-à-vis* developed states (Figure 14.3).

Figure 14.3

Social Sector Expenditure by the State Governments as Percentage of State Income

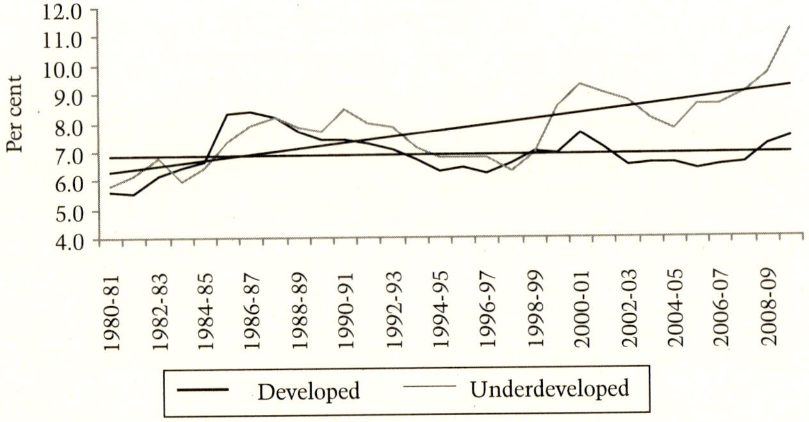

At the states level, during 2005-2010, in developed category states, SSE-NSDP was higher than the average of group in Andhra Pradesh, Karnataka, Tamil Nadu and Maharashtra. Whereas it was lower in Punjab, Haryana, Gujarat and Kerala. Here, it may be mentioned that till the end-2005, SSE-NSDP of Kerala was highest amongst developed category states; however, during 2005-2010 period it witnessed moderation and SSE-NSDP was lower than average of developed category states (Figure 14.4a). Among developed states Punjab and Haryana have lowest SSE-NSDP. Historically also SSE-NSDP of these two states was lowest. In underdeveloped category states, Bihar witnessed fastest growth in SSE-NSDP during 2000s (Figure 14.4b). During 2000-2010 period, SSE-NSDP of all underdeveloped states barring Orissa and West Bengal increased.

Figure 14.4

Social Sector Expenditure as Percentage of Net State Domestic Product

(a)

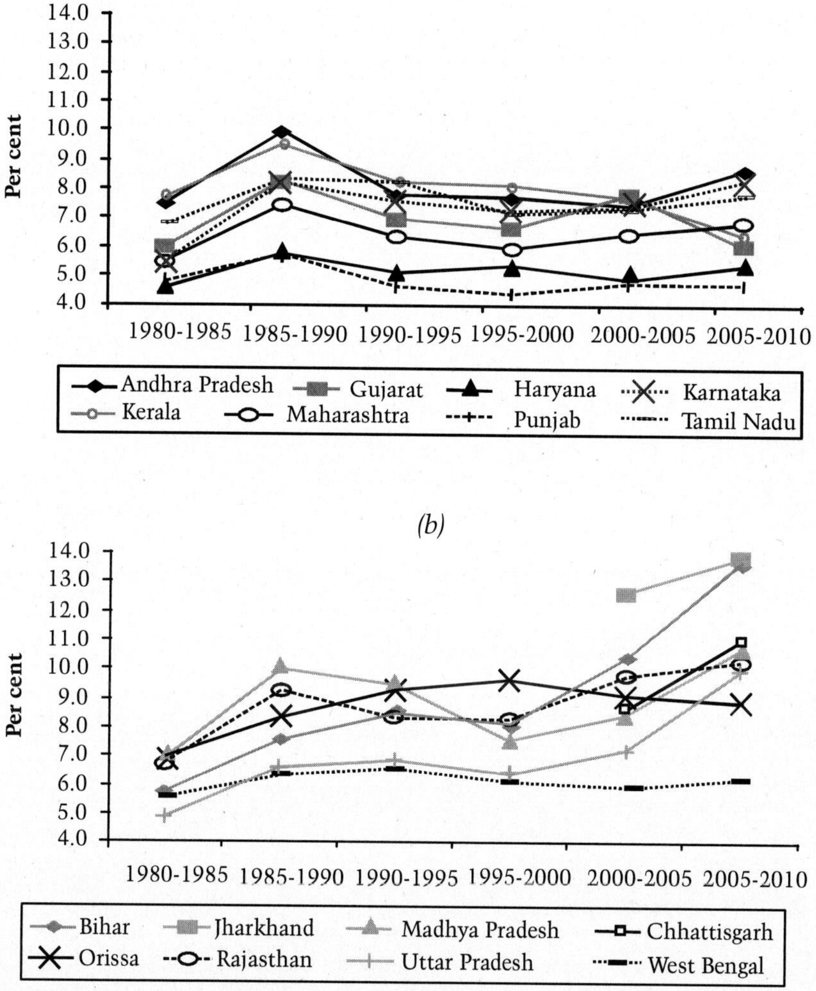

Per Capita Social Sector Expenditure

Per capita social sector expenditure (PC-SSE) is a better indicator of social sector expenditure *vis-à-vis* other two variables i.e., SSE-AE and SSE-NSDP. Analysis of per capita social sector expenditure by the state governments indicates that although underdeveloped states spend more in terms of SSE-AE and SSE-NSDP, but in per capita terms almost all underdeveloped states spend less than the developed states (Figure 14.5). In terms of PC-SSE during 2005-2010, Bihar was at the bottom among all states followed by Uttar Pradesh at number two from bottom.

Figure 14.5

Per Capita Expenditure on Social Sector by States

(a)

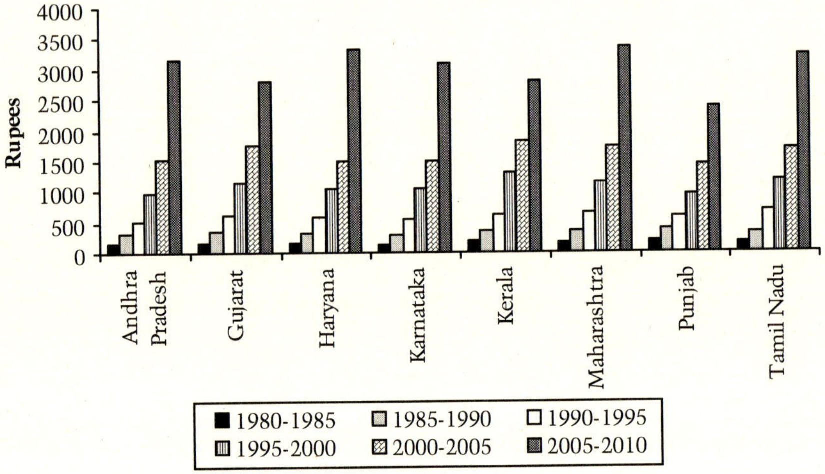

(b)

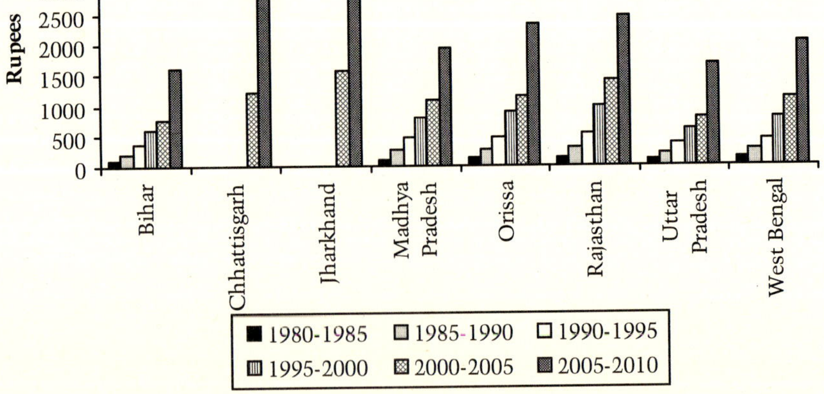

Scatter graph given in Figure 14.6 indicates that there is a strong positive relationship between social sector expenditure of state governments and per capita income of those states. During the studied period, i.e., 1980-81 to 2009-10, nominal NSDP at factor cost of developed states increased by an annual growth rate of 13.86 per cent per annum as against to 12.56 per cent annual growth rate achieved by underdeveloped states. During this period, population growth of underdeveloped states *vis-à-vis* developed states was also marginally high. Due to this even though developed states, in terms of SSE-NSDP and SSE-AE were spending less on social sector, but their per capita social sector expenditure was higher *vis-à-vis* underdeveloped states. This indicates that low level of per capita income of underdeveloped states also limit their ability to raise social sector expenditure.

Figure 14.6

Social Sector Expenditure (Revenue) and Per Capita Income (At Current Prices)

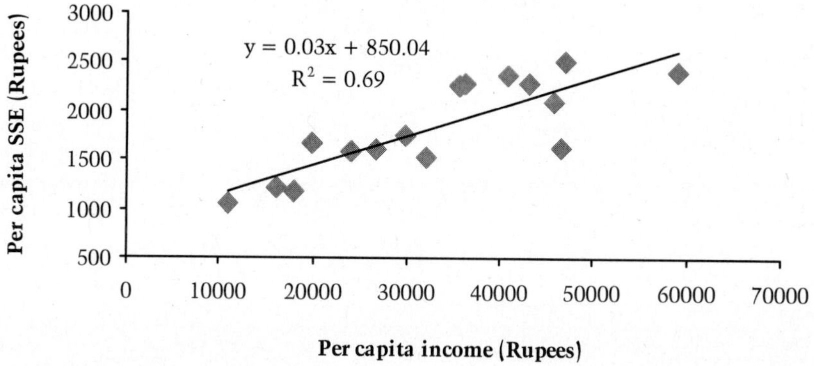

During the studied period, it has been observed that underdeveloped states did not witness any major change in their rankings in terms of PC-SSE (Figure 14.7). Bihar, Uttar Pradesh and Madhya Pradesh remained at the bottom during 2005-2010 as they were during 1980-1985 period. In this category, only major upheaval was slipping of West Bengal from being top spender on social sector during 1980-1985 to fifth place during 2005-2010. States of Chhattisgarh and Jharkhand were formed in the year 2000, due to this comparable data of early years for them are not available. However, it can be assumed that their PC-SSE was equal to their parent state's PC-SSE and with this assumption it may be easily concluded that Chhattisgarh and Jharkhand have witnessed higher increase in PC-SSE. In fact during 2005-

2010, PC-SSE of Chhattisgarh was second highest in country after Maharashtra.

As against to underdeveloped states, developed states witnessed major changes in PC-SSE ranking, during the studied period. During 1980-1985, Kerala and Punjab were at the top in ranking followed by Gujarat (Figure 14.7b); however, during 2005-2010 period these states were replaced from top ranking by Maharashtra, Haryana and Tamil Nadu. In fact Punjab, Kerala and Gujarat are at bottom during 2005-2010 (Figure 14.7a).

Figure 14.7

Change in Per Capita Expenditure on Social Sector by States

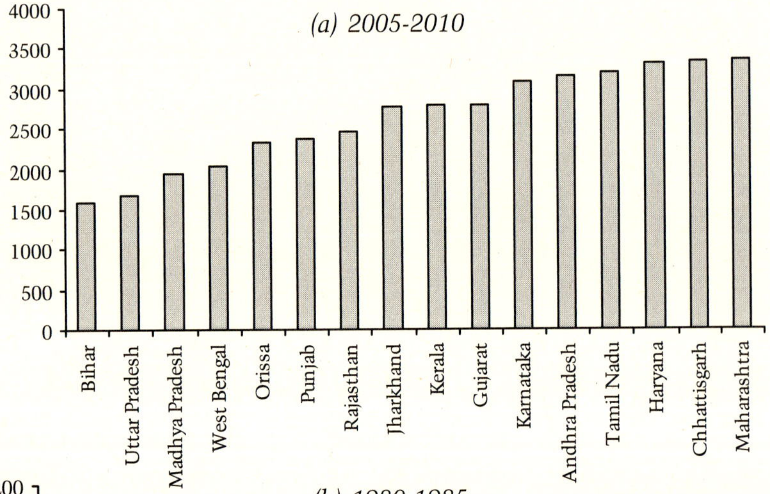

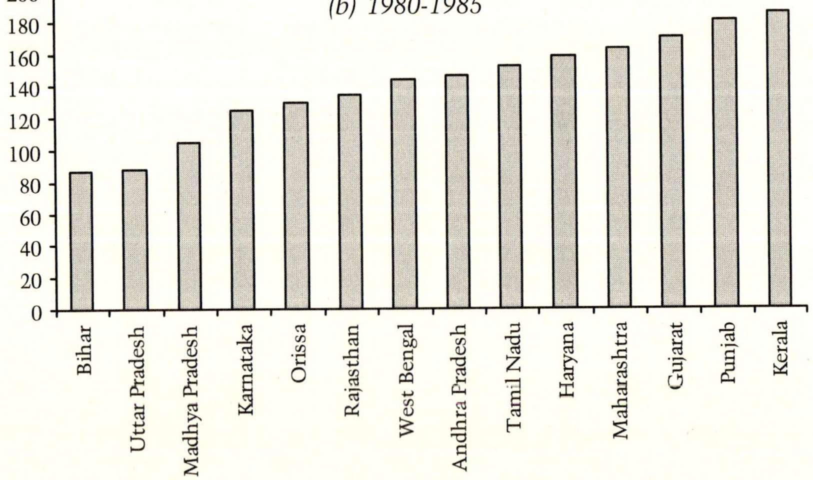

Analysis of CV of PC-SSE of studied states during 1980-81 to 2009-10 period indicates that over the years, across the states inequality of expenditure on social sector has been moving in a range (Figure 14.8). Although it is not increasing but it has also not shown any moderation.

Figure 14.8

Coefficient of Variation of Per Capita Social Sector Expenditure by the State Governments

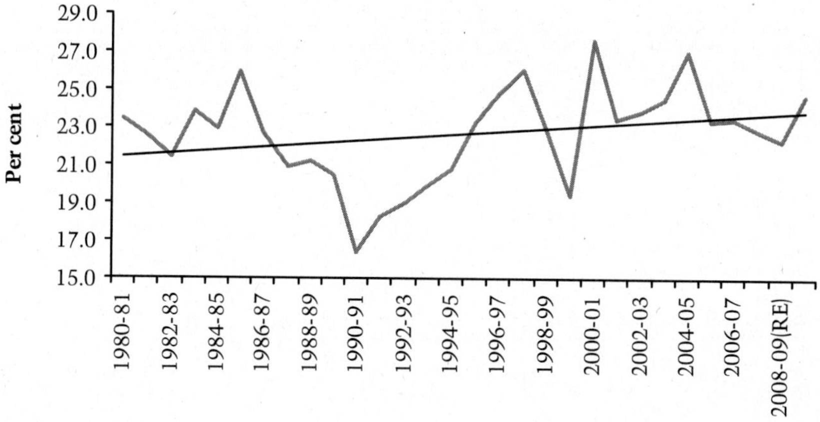

V

Fiscal Scenario of States and Social Sector Expenditure

This section has briefly analysed movement of various fiscal indicators, *viz.*, revenue receipts (Central transfers and own revenue), deficit situation, etc., of states and their impact on social sector expenditures. Own revenue of any state is a function of a number of variables, *viz.*, tax base of the state, ability of tax administration to exploit the tax base, collection of user charges on the services rendered by the public utilities, etc. Data related to own revenue of states indicate that during the studied period own revenue as percentage of NSDP of developed states was higher than that of under-developed states barring a few years during middle of 1990s. Figure 14.9 indicates that share of Central taxes and grant-in-aid as percentage of NSDP of developed states has hovered around four per cent during the studied period; however, it was less than four per cent during 1989-90 to 2005-06 periods when it varied between

2.85 per cent (1998-99) to 3.97 per cent (1992-93). During the same period, share of Central taxes and grant-in-aid of revenue in NSDP of underdeveloped states was irregular. In 1992-93 it increased to 8.31 per cent of NSDP as against to 6.20 per cent in 1980-81 and from there it declined to 4.75 per cent in 1998-99. From 1998-99 onwards it increased further and in 2009-10 it was 10.23 per cent of NSDP.

Figure 14.9

Central Taxes and Grant-in-Aid as Percentage of NSDP

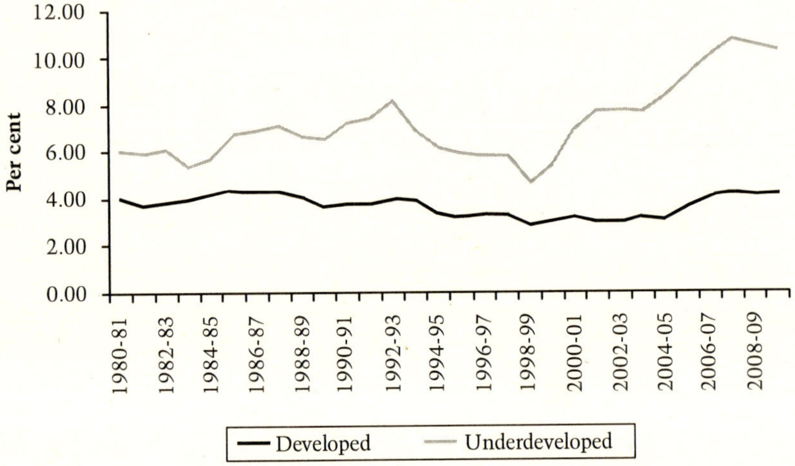

Due to favourable central transfers, total revenue receipts as percentage of NSDP of underdeveloped states is higher than that of developed states (Figure 14.10).

Revenue deficit indicates the shortfall of revenue receipts over revenue expenditure. Revenue deficit as percentage of NSDP (RD-NSDP) for all states witnessed deterioration from second half of 1980s, and this deterioration continued until end of 2000-2005 in majority of states (Figure 14.11). However, due to enactment of Fiscal Responsibility Legislation by states, in view of recommendations of Twelfth Finance Commission, revenue deficit witnessed a turnaround. During 2006-07 and 2007-08, both category of states witnessed surplus on revenue account. Even during 2008-2009 and 2009-10, which were crisis years, a number of states, *viz.*, Andhra Pradesh, Bihar, Jharkhand, Karnataka, Madhya Pradesh and Uttar Pradesh, reported surplus in revenue accounts.

Figure 14.10

Total Revenue as Percentage of NSDP

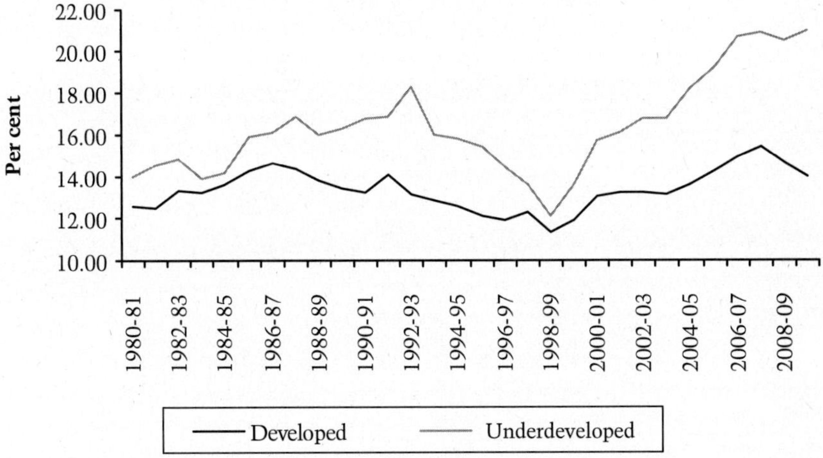

Figure 14.11

Revenue Deficit (+)/Surplus (-) as Percentage of NSDP

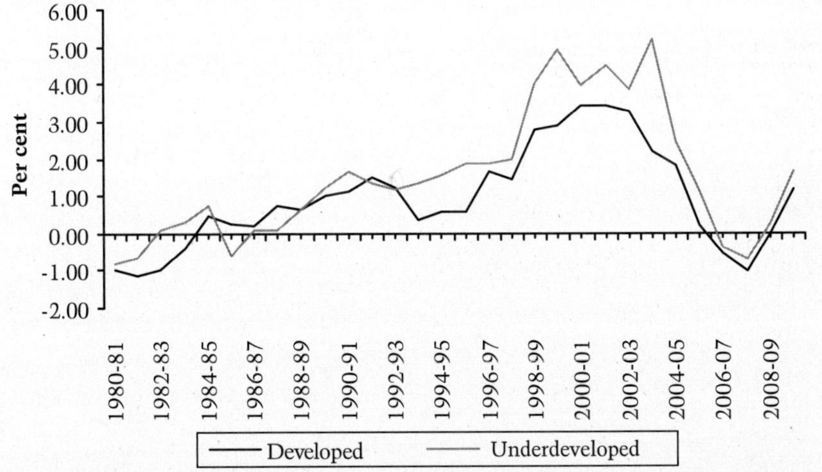

For purpose of analysis, entire studied period may be divided into four parts, i.e., a) 1980-1986, when states were reporting revenue surplus, b) 1986-1998, low revenue deficit scenario, c) 1998-2005 period, when states witnesed very high revenue deficit scenario and d) 2005-2008, when revenue deficits of states declined sharply and witnessed moderate surpluses. Rajmal (2006) has divided 1980-2004 period in three parts, i.e., 1980-1986, 1986-1998 and 1998-2004, on basis of deficit scenario witnessed by the states. According to him, revenue deficit as percentage to NSDP of states increased due to stagnation or decline in their own revenue and Central transfers and increase in committed non-developmental revenue expenditure. Interest payments, expenses towards administrative services, wages and salaries, pensions and subsidies given by the states led the revenue expenditure to grow significantly (Rajmal, 2006). At individual state level, both category states, i.e., developed as well as underdeveloped, can further be divided into two additional categories according to level of revenue deficit prevailing in those states as high revenue deficit states and low revenue deficit states. In developed category states Punjab, Kerala and Gujarat may be defined as high revenue deficit states, whereas in underdeveloped category states West Bengal, Uttar Pradesh and Orissa may be defined as high deficit states. Here, it may be pointed that Gujarat witnessed improvement in revenue deficit scenario and it reported modest surplus during 2005-2008 before slipping in deficit during 2008-2010.

Analysis of correlation of states' own revenue and Central transfers to states indicates that revenue of underdeveloped states are highly positively correlated (Correlation is .77) with Central transfers during the studied period (Figure 14.12). Due to this any decline of Central transfers has a severe impact on overall revenue of these states. In comparison to underdeveloped states, correlation between own revenue of developed states and Central transfers to them is lower although positive (correlation is .31 in case of developed states). This indicates that in case if Central government's revenue receipts decline, it will impact revenue receipts of underdeveloped states more adversely *vis-à-vis* developed states. This may lead to higher revenue deficit in underdeveloped states during such years when Central transfers are low.

Figure 14.12

Relationship of States' Own Revenue and Central Transfers

(a) Underdeveloped States' Own Revenue and Transfers as Percentage of NSDP

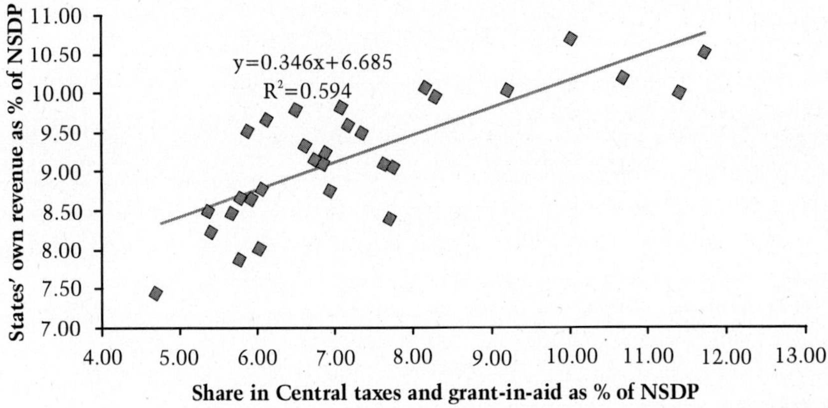

(b) Developed States' Own Revenue and Central Transfers as Percentage of NSDP

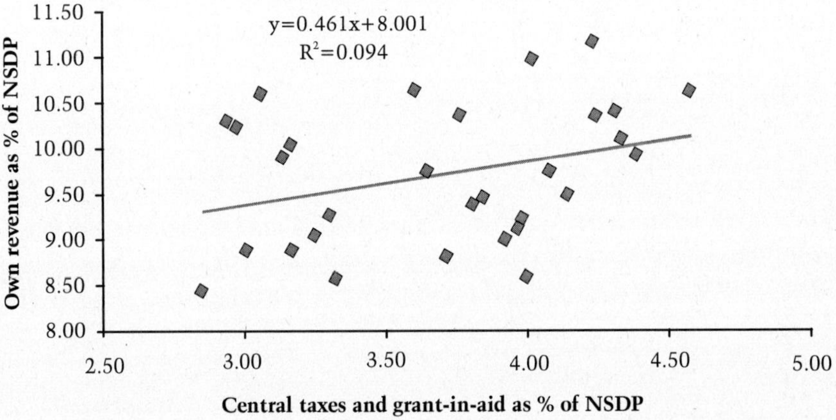

Determinants of Social Sector Expenditure of State Governments: A Panel Data Analysis

As mentioned in introductory paragraphs, the study has undertaken a panel data analysis to analyse the determinants of social sector expenditure by the state governments. Given below are the variables, methodology and results of analysis.

Variables: The variables that have been used in panel data analysis are explained below:

SSEit: Social sector expenditure of state governments as percentage of net state domestic product at current prices.

CTGit: Central transfers to state governments (taxes as well as grant-in-aid of revenue) as percentage of net state domestic product at current prices.

OTRit: Own revenue of states as percentage of net state domestic product at current prices.

RDit: Revenue deficit of states as percentage of net state domestic product at current prices.

Model: For econometric exercise, present study has used following fixed effect model (Equation 1). Before discussing about the model, it would be appropriate to mention that cross-section specific redundant fixed effect is significant at 1 per cent level of significance (Table 14.2).

$$SSE_{i,t} = C_1 + C_2^{*}CTG_{i,t} + C_3^{*}OTR_{i,t} + C_4^{*}RD_{i,t} + C_5^{*}SSE_{i,t(-1)} + C_6^{*}RD_{i,t(-1)} + (a_i + u_{it}) \quad \ldots (1)$$

Table 14.2

Redundant Fixed Effects Tests

Effects Test	*Statistic*	*d.f.*	*Prob.*
Cross-section F	12.802058	(13,387)	0.0000

Output of regression analysis is given in Table 14.3. Analysis of panel data of 14 states[5] shows that all variables used in analysis are significant at 1 per cent level of significance and signs of their coefficients are on expected lines. From Table 14.3, it is evident that Central government transfers to the state governments and own revenues are an important source of variation in expenditure of social sectors by the state governments. Lagged values of social sector expenditure are also a very important explanatory variable of social sector expenditure of state governments. It indicates that high social sector expenditure in state leads to further increase in social sector expenditure by governments. Revenue deficit (RD) has a very important impact on social sector expenditure. RD has a positive impact during the first year of expenditure; however, it affects adversly to social sector expenditure from next year onwards. One possible explanation of this could be very low return on social sector expenditures.

Table 14.3

Determinants of Social Sector Expenditure of State Governments

Variable	*Coefficient*	*Std. Error*	*t-Statistic*	*Prob.*
C	0.704568	0.223987	3.145569	0.0018
CTGit	0.456401	0.021158	21.57115	0.0000
RDit	0.305567	0.021255	14.37636	0.0000
OTRit	0.178914	0.018353	9.748209	0.0000
SSEit(-1)	0.303185	0.033041	9.176003	0.0000
RDit(-1)	-0.123338	0.022048	-5.594045	0.0000

Cross-section fixed effects of states on social sector expenditures are depicted in Figure 14.13. According to it, poor states have negative coefficient. This indicates low own revenue capacity of poor states is a big constraint in the way of increasing their social sector expenditure. In developed states category also Punjab and Haryana have negative coefficients but that could be due to their historically low level of social sector expenditure. In the next section, one brief attempt has been made to see how successive Union Finance Commissions have tried to fill this gap in social sector expenditure between developed and underdeveloped states.

5. Two states Jharkhand and Chhattisgarh are included in panel analysis as they became state in year 2000 and their data related to expenditure are available from then onwards.

Figure 14.13

Coefficient of Cross-Section Dummies

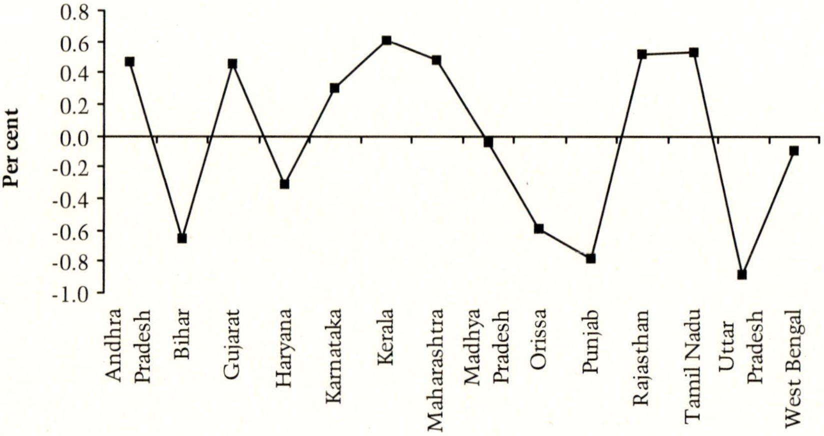

VI

Finance Commission Reports and Social Sector Expenditure by State Governments

Finance Commissions (FCs) are hallmark of India's fiscal federalism. Various Finance Commissions have provided guidance to evolution of the Central-state and interstate fiscal relationship along with recommending formula of distribution of resources between the Centre and states and among the states. As the system of grants has evolved in India, grants flow from the Centre to the states in three ways. The first consists of grants-in-aid given under the recommendations of the Finance Commission. The second category consists of plan grants covering Central assistance for state plans as decided by the Planning Commission, as well as the plan grants given by the Central ministries for implementation of plan schemes. The third type of grants, which is much smaller in magnitude, essentially consists of discretionary grants given by the Central ministries to states on the non-plan side (FC-XII).

Sufficiency of resources is a precondition for sustainability of any kind of expenditure by any government in long run. In total resource transfers recommended by the FCs, from the First to the Twelfth, tax devolution accounted for an average of over 84 per cent. The share of tax devolution in the total transfers recommended varied from 73.9 per cent by FC-VI to 92.3 per cent by FC-VII. In the total transfers recommended by FC-XII, tax devolution accounted for 81.1 per cent as compared to the 86.5 per cent share recommended by FC-XI (Table 14.4). As regards the determination of the *inter se* shares of the states, the basic objective of the FC transfers has been to: (i) correct the differentials in revenue capacity and cost disability factors inherent in the economies of the states and (ii) foster fiscal efficiency among the states. The criteria used for these purposes can be grouped under: (a) factors reflecting needs, such as population and income measured either as distance from the highest income or as an inverse; (b) cost disability indicators such as area and infrastructure distance and (c) fiscal efficiency indicators such as tax effort and fiscal discipline (RBI, 2011). As mentioned in previous paragraph that, in general, finance commissions have used equity and efficiency as the two guiding principles while recommending *inter se* shares of states in tax devolution. In order to achieve equity and efficiency of distribution among states in general, finance commissions have used population, area, fiscal capacity distance and fiscal discipline or their proxies as criteria. It indicates that over the years, resource transfers from Centre to states have become more favourable to underdeveloped states (refer Figure 14.9).

Table 14.4

Transfers Recommended by Finance Commissions

(In Rs crore)

Commission	*Period*	*Grant-in-Aid*		*Share in Taxes*		*Total Amount*
		Amount	*% Share*	*Amount*	*% Share*	
Seventh	1979-1984	1609.92	7.72	19233.05	92.28	20842.97
Eighth	1984-1989	3769.43	9.55	35682.58	90.45	39452.01
Ninth	1989-1995	11030.38	9.96	99667.64	90.04	110698.02
Tenth	1995-1900	20300.30	8.96	206343.00	91.04	226643.30
Eleventh	2000-2005	58587.39	13.47	376318.01	86.53	434905.40
Twelfth	2005-2010	142639.60	18.87	613112.02	81.13	755751.62
Thirteenth	2010-2015	318581.00	18.03	1448369.00	81.97	1766950.00

Note: 1. Only studied period has been covered. 2. Ninth Finance Commission covered six years, and in addition also provided Plan grants of Rs 9000.83 crore (not included above).

Source: *Report of Twelfth Finance Commission* and *Report of Thirteenth Finance Commission*.

In their recommendations, FCs have given high importance to improvement of social services in states, particularly in underdeveloped states. While recommending tax devolution to states, FCs use a number of variables and their proxies (including level of supply of social services in states) but some states suffer with a number of disabilities, which are not possible to address fully by the devolution formula only. In view of this, grant-in-aid of revenue has emerged as an important source of fund flow, particularly to meet special expenditures in poorer states. FC-I had devised a broad framework for devolution of grant-in-aid of revenue to states.[6] Along with other criterion deficiency of availability of social services among the states was a major indicator. FC-I gave very high importance to primary education and recommended grant-in-aid of revenue for eight states[7] which were at bottom in terms of percentage of children in age group of 6 to 11 years attending school. Successive FCs accepted the broad guidelines used by FC-I, while recommending grant-in-aid of revenue, with some modifications. Although, FCs were recommending higher allocation for social services but from FC-VI onwards disparities in the provision of administrative and social services were sought to be corrected through the mechanism of upgradation grants which become part of their term of references (Ninth Finance Commission, FC-XI).

The Eighth Finance Commission (FC-VIII) provided grants for two developmental sectors, *viz.*, education and health, besides for certain non-

6. According to First Finance Commission, the budgetary needs of the state should be an important criteria for determining the assistance required by the states, but that in arriving at the needs, appropriate allowances have to be made based on a number of considerations. The first consideration was that the budget should be reduced to a standard form by eliminating non-repetitive items. Second, due consideration should be given to tax effort by the state and the extent to which the state itself had made efforts to raise resources in relation to its tax potential. Third, allowance should be made for the scope for economy in expenditure. Fourth, the system of grant-in-aid should be designed to avoid large disparities in the standard of basic social services. Fifth, grant-in-aid may be given to help individual states to meet their special burdens, if such burdens are national concerns and if they are likely to cause undue strain on the states' finances. Sixth, grant-in-aid may be given for broad national purposes with a view to further any beneficent service of primary importance in regard to which it is in national interest to assist the less advance states to go forward (FC-III, Chapter 9).

7. These states were Bihar, Hyderabad, Punjab, Orissa, Madhya Bharat, Madhya Pradesh, Patiala and East Punjab State Union and Rajasthan.

developmental sectors. In addition, it provided grants to some states towards special problems too. The terms of reference of the FC-IX did not make any specific mention of the upgradation or special problem grants. In its first report (1989-90), however, it made a provision for upgradation as well as special problem grants. However, in its second report (1990-1995), it did not make any such exclusive provision. FC-X was specifically asked to consider the requirements of the states for upgradation in non-developmental sectors. It recommended upgradation grants for those states that were assessed by it to be in pre-devolution deficit on revenue account. The sectors covered by it for these grants were non-developmental as well as developmental (education). It also provided special problem grants to all the states. FC-XI also recommended grants for upgradation of health services and elementary education in states along with other administrative services.

Twelfth Finance Commission (FC-XII) adopted equalisation approach to fill the gap in per capita expenditure on education and health by many states *vis-à-vis* their group states. According to FC-XII, while the amount of transfer required for a full application of the equalisation approach would have too large, it had decided to focus on two critical areas of deficiencies, namely, education and health. But only a partial correction could be made, because of large disparity between the relevant group average and the actual per capita expenditure of some of the constituent states, particularly those having low fiscal capacity and large population. In the estimation of grants, care was taken about those states, which were unable to allocate on education and health an amount equal to the group average, as measured in relation to the aggregate revenue expenditure, including both plan and non-plan. FC-XII recommended grant-in-aid of revenue for education of Rs 10171.65 crore to eight states, *viz.*, Assam, Bihar, Jharkhand, Madhya Pradesh, Orissa, Rajasthan, Uttar Pradesh and West Bengal. It also recommended grant-in-aid of revenue of Rs 5887.08 crore for health sector to Assam, Bihar, Jharkhand, Madhya Pradesh, Orissa, Uttar Pradesh and Uttarakhand. However, FC-XII acknowledged the fact that this amount is not sufficient to fill the gap required to equalise the expenditure of these states with other non-special category states. Thirteenth Finance Commission (FC-XIII) has also recommended grants of Rs 24,068 crore for elementary education in pursuance of the goal of universalisation of elementary education, underpinned by the constitutional right of all children, in the age group 6 to 14, to free and compulsory schooling. This targetted grant is designed to help states to overcome their resource constraint in funding this sector, while the national character of the programme is underscored by ensuring that all states receive a share of this grant. FC-XIII has not recommended any grant-in-aid for health service.

Discussion in above paragraphs indicates that FCs have attached very high priority to improvement of social services in states in general and backward states in particular. However, as also specified successively in terms of references to FCs, they have accorded very high priority to fiscal consolidation of states. Our analysis indicates that huge imbalances in fisc have affected social sector expenditure very adversely. Accordingly, priority attached to fiscal consolidation of states by successive Finance Commissions is a right step. Like FC-XI and FC-XII, FC-XIII has also given very high priority to fiscal consolidation and recommended fiscal consolidation plan for Central and state governments, which have deteriorated due to global crisis.

VII

Conclusion

Expenditure on social sector by the state governments has a very important role to play in nurturing overall human resource of the country. Analysis in above paragraphs indicates that in the long run, sustained high revenue deficit affects states' spending capacity on social sector and human development projects adversely. It affects more adversely in case of underdeveloped states, those trapped in vicious cycle of low per capita income and low social sector expenditure. Our analysis indicates that even though underdeveloped states spend more in terms of percentage of NSDP but due to higher population of these states in general and higher concentration of poverty in particular, leads to lower per capita disbursement on social sector. This reflects in their underperformance in achievement of various MDG goals also. Successive FCs have given very high priority to fill the gap of the availability of social services among the states; however, it seems resources devolved by them are not sufficient.

India has one of the world's youngest populations. As mentioned by FC-XIII, this is a one-time demographic dividend, which needs to harness through appropriate investments in human development, particularly in education and public health, so that the country, after undertaking its long-term development transformation, is then able to cater to the challenges that this dividend poses—that of an ageing population. In order to reap the benefits of demographic dividend, states have to articulate their preferences and goals very clearly. Although in short-term, underdeveloped states may not be able to spend as much as developed states are doing but they can still make a sizeable difference by improved targetting to these sectors.

The imperatives of urbanisation, empowerment of India's villages and improved information flows have collectively increased the expectation and demand for public and merit goods (FC-XIII). Poor states can fulfill these expectations of masses by improving their expenditure on social services, improving the local governance and fine-tuning the delivery mechanism. States have to consolidate their fiscal position as human resource development process has a very long gestation period, due to which large amount of financial resources will be required in future also. States in general and underdeveloped states in particular have to improve their tax administration system. However, our panel data analysis proves that Central transfers are the most important source of social sector expenditure by the states and as poor states cannot increase their own revenue in short time, enhancement of Central transfers to poor states is a precondition for increasing social sector expenditure in those states.

References

Baqir, Reza (2002). "Social Sector Spending in a Panel of Countries", *IMF Working Paper* WP/02/35.

Bhatt, Ramesh and Nishant Jain (2004). "Analysis of Public Expenditure on Health Using State Level Data", *Working Paper* WP 2004-06-08, Ahmedabad: Indian Institute of Management.

Brooks, Chris (2008). "Panel Data", in *Introductory Econometrics for Finance*. Cambridge Publication. pp.488-89.

Chakraborty, Pinaki, Anit N. Mukherjee and H.K. Amarnath (2009). "Macro Policy Reform and Sub-National Finance: Why Is the Fiscal Space of the States Shrinking?", *Economic and Political Weekly* xliv (14): 38-44.

Dev, S. Mahendra and Jos Mooij (2002). "Social Sector Expenditures in the 1990s: Analysis of Central and State Budgets", *Economic and Political Weekly*, March 2.

Government of India (2010a). "Human Development, Poverty and Public Programmes", *Economic Survey*, 2009-10. p.270.

———. (2010b). *Millennium Development Goals—India Country Report 2009.* Central Statistical Organisation, Ministry of Statistics and Programme Implementation.

———. *Report of Finance Commission* (various reports). Ministry of Finance.

Hajra, Kumudini, Rajeev Jain and Dhirendra Gajbhiye (2009). "Determinants of Surplus Cash Balances of States in India: A Panel Data Analysis", *Reserve Bank of India. Staff Studies* No. 9.

Hong, Houqi and Sadiq Ahmed (2009). "Government Spending on Public Goods: Evidence on Growth and Poverty", *Economic and Political Weekly* xliv(31): 102-108.

Isaac, T.M. Thomas and R. Ramakumar (2006). "Why Do the States Not Spend?: An Exploration of the Phenomenon of Cash Surpluses and the FRBM Legislation", *Economic and Political Weekly* 41(48): 4965-4976. December 2.

Mohan, Rakesh (2005). "Human Development and State Finances", *Reserve Bank of India Bulletin* LIX, December.

Pattnaik, R.K., R.D. Bangar, S.M. Pillai and Rekha Sharma (1994). "Resource Gap of the State Governments: Measurement and Analysis", *Reserve Bank of India Occasional Papers* 15(4).

Prabhu, K. Seeta and P.C. Sarkar (2001). "Financing Human Development in Indian States Trends and Implications (1974/75- 1995/96)", *The Asian Economic Review* 43(1).

Rajmal (2006). "State Finances and Effectiveness of Policy Measures: An Analysis of Indian States", *Reserve Bank of India Occasional Papers* 27(1 and 2): 141-175. Summer and Monsoon.

Reserve Bank of India (2011). *State Finances: A Study of State Budgets: 2010-11.*

———. (2010). *Handbook of Statistics on State Government Finances.*

———. *Handbook of Statistics on Indian Economy* 2009-10.

———. *State Finances: A Study of Budgets*: 2008-09.

———. *State Finances: A Study of Budgets*: 2009-10.

Sen, Tapas K. and Krishanu Karmakar (2007). "Reprioritisation of Public Expenditure for Human Development", *www.nipfp.org.in/working_paper/wp_2007_hd_50.pdf.*

Sethi, Tanya (2009). "Can Poor States Afford the Fiscal Responsibility Legislation?", *Economic and Political Weekly* xliv(41): 18-22.

Tsujita, Yuko (2005). "Economic Reforms and Social Sector Expenditures: A Study of Fifteen Indian States 1980/81—1999/2000", *Discussion Paper* No. 31, Japan: Institute of Developing Economies.

15 Issues in Services Sector
A Case Study of Delhi

JAYANTA KUMAR MALLIK and
MONIKA KATHURIA[1]

Introduction

The rapid pace of expansion of activity in the services sector in recent years has been one of the key drivers of the overall GDP growth in India. According to World Bank *(World Development Indicators, 2011)*, the annual average growth rate of 9.5 per cent in the output in the services sector in India during 2000-2009 was more than thrice the rate of growth in world output of services and it was higher than the growth in other sectors of the Indian economy. Notwithstanding the impressive record, the literature is beset with scepticisms about the future growth of this sector. A number of eminent scholars have expressed concerns about the unusually high growth in the services sector, which is neither attributable to the impulse transmitted by the material producing sectors and nor is it accompanied by proportionate increase in labour absorption. There are also a number of studies which have documented the success story of India's services sector and have tried to allay the concerns surrounding the growth and the employment potential of this sector. However, the continued growth of output and employment in the services sector, according to them, would depend upon a variety of conditions, the fulfillment of which may not be all that easy. The moot question is why so much of scepticism about the future of a sector that has been performing so well? A related question is what gives rise to the differences in the perception regarding the growth performance or employment potential of the services sector?

---

1. The views expressed in this paper are of the authors and not of the organisation they are working with.

This paper addresses these issues drawing on a case study of Delhi. In 2009-10, Delhi occupied ninth place among 32 states/UTs in terms of the size of net state domestic product (NSDP). The growth rate of NSDP in Delhi over the period 1993-94 to 2009-10 was higher than that in all other states/UTs of India with the exception of five small state/UTs, *viz.*, Chandigarh, Goa, Puducherry, Sikkim and Uttarakhand. The absolute value of the NSDP from the services sector in only seven states was larger than that of Delhi in 2009-10. The process of structural transformation in Delhi—agriculture nearing extinction, mining conspicuous by its absence and the relative size of manufacturing now one-fourth of what it used to be in the early 1990s—has been dramatic. In fact, Delhi is tending to be a services economy with the services sector (including construction) accounting for 93 per cent of the NSDP. Given the national capital territory (NCT) status, Delhi may not be a model to be emulated by other states/ UTs. However, an enquiry into the process of growth of services sector in Delhi would be useful from the analytical point of view. In fact, the virtual absence of agriculture gives Delhi the unique position for addressing the empirical issues concerning employment generation.

The rest of the paper has been organised as follows. Section I presents a brief review of literature setting out the issues concerning the growth of services sector in India. Section II analyses the pattern of growth in economic activity in Delhi over the last three decades. Section III revisits the issues and Section IV presents the main conclusions.

I

Issues

The theories of structural transformation provide insight into the changing significance of different sectors of an economy as it grows. Initially, agriculture remains the most important sector in an economy. As the income per capita rises, agriculture loses its primacy, giving way first to a rise in industrial sector and then to the service sector. The consecutive shifts are called as industrialisation and post-industrialisation. All the growing economies are likely to go through these stages, which are attributable to the structural changes in consumer demand and in relative labour productivity in the three sectors. The shares in output and employment of the three sectors change in this pattern. The historical experience of not only developed countries but also developing countries appears to support the case for there being a universal pattern (Soubbotina and Sheram, 2000 and Mazumdar, 2010).

Sustainability of Services-led Growth

The economic growth in India has been described as services-led that has bypassed the phase of industrial growth. The analysis of sectoral composition of GDP and employment for the period 1950-2000, shows that there has been 'tertiarisation' of the production and employment in India; while agriculture and manufacturing sectors have experienced phases of deceleration, stagnation and growth, the tertiary sector exhibited a uniform growth trend over this period (Joshi, 2008). India has been an 'outlier' in terms of its services sector growth since the turn of the 21st century (Shingal, 2010).

While a lot of research has been devoted to explaining the 'services revolution' in India, a number of observers have expressed scepticism regarding the long-term sustainability of the growth of services sector in India. The scepticism is rooted in the perception regarding the disproportionately high growth in the services sector that 'cannot be readily attributed to any impulse transmitted by the sectors engaged in material production' and that the growth of income in the services sector is not accompanied by proportionate increase in the absorption of the working force (Mitra, 1988). It has also been argued that the generation of excess demand due to the growth in services income unaccompanied by commensurate growth in commodity sectors is expected to lead to high inflation and rising imports. The disproportional growth of services sector is also expected to have implications for income distribution unless appropriate changes in production techniques and investment allocation for commodity sectors are made (Bhattacharya and Mitra, 1990). Questions have been raised about the plausibility and sustainability of services sector growth, based on the past trends and the growth records in other countries (Acharya, 2002 and 2003). The high dependence on services for GDP growth and on agriculture for employment is perceived as a source of vulnerability (Gokarn, 2011).

One also comes across a number of studies highlighting the positive developmental implications of the services sector and trying to allay the concerns surrounding the growth of this sector. Hansda (2002) analyses the backward and forward linkages of services sector using input output tables for the Indian economy. The study points out that the services sector is more growth inducing than industry or agriculture. The study, however, notes that since the multiplier value remains less than one for all activities including services, the expansionary potential of services-led growth may not be overemphasised unless accompanied by growth impulses from other sources. Karmakar (2008) observes that services contribute to economic growth as inputs into production process as also by offering cheaper final services to individuals and business consumers. The study observes that India exhibits revealed comparative advantage (RCA) in services relative to goods and that the RCA in services has been rising sharply since the mid-1990s. The study also notes that India has contributed to increasing FDI flows from Asia to developed countries, adding a new dimension to its rising competitiveness in this sector. Using state-level data, Shingal (2010) argues that the growth in services sector has positive implications for income distribution. The study finds that even though per capita income is not converging across Indian states, per capita services are converging. The study concludes that the benefits from services growth are being distributed more widely than may be perceived. Eichengreen and Gupta (2011) present a case for continued high future growth of services conditional upon other circumstances. The study notes that while growth of service sector in India has been unusually rapid, whether the output in this sector would continue to grow in excess of international norms will depend on the continued expansion of modern services (business services, communication and banking) as also on the application of modern information technology to more traditional services (retail and wholesale trade, transport and storage, public administration and defence). The study reports the empirical finding that the services segments which were both liberalised and tradable grew 7-8 percentage points higher than the non-tradable/non-liberalised services during 1980-2007, arguing for a liberalised policy regime.

Low Labour Absorption in Services Sector

At the conceptual level, it is argued that the growth of the service sector can help in making development more sustainable by creating more employment opportunities as services activities involve lower mechanisation. While this leads to growth of employment in the services sector, employment in agriculture and industry declines because of technological progress. Eventually, the services sector replaces the industrial sector as the leading sector of the economy. Further, at the sub-sector level, services activities such as telecommunications and business services are characterised by a high level of business dynamics as demonstrated by high rates of new firm creation, rapid growth of successful new firms, and reallocation of resources from declining to growing firms. This is expected to result into rapid employment generation (Soubbotina and Sheram, 2000 and Pilat, 2005).

In the Indian context, however, the low labour absorption in the services activities has been one of the major concerns surrounding the growth of this sector. It has been observed that sectors having large potential for employment generation, such as, construction, transport and professional services have grown slowly; on the other hand, the sectors such as software services and communications and financial business services, which have grown rapidly, have a low potential for job creation. The employment in services sector is concentrated in the informal sector, personal services and public administration which have limited spillovers and limited scope for productivity improvement. Furthermore, the IT and communication sectors employ very little unskilled and semi-skilled labour, which is in surplus in a labour-abundant country like India (Banga, 2006). Eichengreen and Gupta (2011), however, report that the mix of skilled and unskilled labour in manufacturing and services activities is becoming similar.

The concerns regarding the future growth and employment potential in the services sector have apparently found recognition in planning and policy formulation. The Draft Approach Paper to the Twelfth Plan has set growth targets of 9.8 per cent in manufacturing and 10.0 per cent in services for the GDP growth target of 9.0 per cent during the Twelfth Plan (which is a restatement of the Eleventh Plan target); for a higher GDP growth (9.5%), the growth target for the manufacturing sector is much higher (11.5%) while the target for the services sector is the same (10.0%). In either case, the growth targets for the manufacturing sector for the Twelfth Plan period imply sharp acceleration *vis-à-vis* the achievements during the Eleventh Plan period (7.7%). For the services sector, the growth targets for the Twelfth Plan entail no change from the achievement in the Eleventh Plan. The National Manufacturing Policy that was approved by the Union Cabinet on October 25, 2011 envisages a growth rate of 12-14 per cent for the manufacturing sector, aimed at raising its share in GDP to at least 25 per cent by 2022 (from 16 per cent at present) and creating 100 million additional jobs by that year.

II

The Case of Delhi

With a population share of 1.4 per cent (as per 2011 Census), Delhi accounted for 3.8 per cent of India's NDP at current prices in 2009-10. The per capita income in Delhi at Rs 1.17 lakh in 2009-10 was next only to Goa and Chandigarh. Comparable data on NSDP in respect of 32 states/ UTs of India are available for the period 1993-94 to 2009-10. In 1993-94, the NSDP of 13 states was larger than that of Delhi. In 2009-10, only eight states had NSDP higher than Delhi. The improvement in the ranking of Delhi in this regard by five places is unmatched. Between 1993-94 and 2009-10, the NSDP of Delhi at current prices grew nearly tenfold—a compound rate of 16.1 per cent per annum. This was faster than the growth in all other major states/UTs of the country with the exception of only five small states/UTs, *viz.*, Chandigarh, Goa, Puducherry, Sikkim and Uttarakhand (Table 15.1).

The Size of Services Sector

In the analysis of the structural change in output, the classification of activity is generally done by grouping them under: (a) primary-secondary-tertiary or (b) agriculture-industry-services sectors. The normal practice in recent times is the adoption of the second approach. However, the sector classification of construction—whether to include it in industry or in services—remains an unsettled issue. While the practice in this regard

Table 15.1

NSDP at Current Prices

(Rs crore)

Sl No.	State/UT	Value			Rank		
		1993-94	2009-10	CAGR (in %)	1993-94	2009-10	Shift
1	2	3	4	5	6	7	8
1.	Andaman & Nicobar Islands	468	3524	13.4	31	32	-1
2.	Andhra Pradesh	51665	426816	14.1	3	3	0
3.	Arunachal Pradesh	812	6276	13.6	29	29	0
4.	Assam	13477	81691	11.9	16	18	-2
5.	Bihar	20780	160213	13.6	12	14	-2
6.	Chandigarh	1371	15842	16.5	24	23	1
7.	Chhattisgarh	12163	93245	13.6	18	16	2
8.	Delhi	18967	207180	16.1	14	9	5
9.	Goa	2002	22283	16.3	22	22	0
10.	Gujarat	42560	370400	14.5	6	5	1
11.	Haryana	19422	195762	15.5	13	11	2
12.	Himachal Pradesh	4250	35593	14.2	21	20	1
13.	Jammu & Kashmir	5500	35187	12.3	19	21	-2
14.	Jharkhand	13403	83744	12.1	17	17	0
15.	Karnataka	36982	305039	14.1	7	7	0
16.	Kerala	23851	202487	14.3	11	10	1
17.	Madhya Pradesh	33937	192333	11.5	8	12	-4
18.	Maharashtra	101767	817891	13.9	1	1	0
19.	Manipur	1141	7436	12.4	27	28	-1
20.	Meghalaya	1309	11229	14.4	25	25	0
21.	Mizoram	618	5078	14.1	30	30	0
22.	Nagaland#	1251	9670	13.6	26	27	-1
23.	Orissa	16185	134242	14.1	15	15	0
24.	Puducherry	829	10089	16.9	28	26	2
25.	Punjab	27068	173169	12.3	10	13	-3
26.	Rajasthan	28977	225730	13.7	9	8	1
27.	Sikkim	364	4144	16.4	32	31	1
28.	Tamil Nadu	51643	424724	14.1	4	4	0
29.	Tripura	1619	12734	13.8	23	24	-1
30.	Uttar Pradesh	70935	458162	12.4	2	2	0
31.	Uttarakhand	5109	58047	16.4	20	19	1
32.	West Bengal	48398	364111	13.4	5	6	-1
	All-India (NDP)	697992	5477557	13.7			

Note: # NSDP of Nagaland for 2009-10 has been extrapolated using average growth during 2006-07 to 2008-09.

Source: Website of CSO, MoSPI: *State Domestic Product and Other Aggregates*, 1993-94 series and 2004-05 series.

differs, two-way classification of construction (one that includes it under industry and the other includes it under services) has been used in some cases (RBI, 2003; Mazumdar, 2010 and Government of India, 2011). Mazumdar (2010) mentions that there are some practical problems associated with including construction in industry sector and to circumvent the problem, he uses the parallel classification scheme. However, he observes that the pattern of movement of the share of industry sector excluding construction in GDP is more representative of the pattern exhibited by the entire industrial sector except construction, as the construction segment exhibited different patterns. The distinguishing movement of the share of construction or its growth rate *vis-à-vis* the rest of industry is more pronounced in the case of Delhi as it would be evident from the discussion in the subsequent sections. This paper also uses a two-way classification of construction to facilitate comparison of the growth rate or the relative share of the services sector in Delhi with the similar estimates at the national level as also in other research studies. For succinctness, however, in the discussion that follows, the services sector would imply that it includes construction unless specified otherwise.

The overall share of the services sector in the NSDP of Delhi at 93 per cent in 2009-10 was substantially higher than its share of 66 per cent in the net domestic product (NDP) of India (Table 15.2). The value of NSDP originating from the services sector in Delhi accounted for 5.3 per cent of the NDP of India from this sector in 2009-10. The size of the services sector in only seven states (*viz.*, Andhra Pradesh, Gujarat, Karnataka, Maharashtra, Tamil Nadu, Uttar Pradesh and West Bengal) was larger than that of Delhi. Delhi (along with Chandigarh) occupied the top place in terms of the relative share of the services sector in NSDP. However, when construction is excluded, the share of services sector in Chandigarh was larger than that in Delhi.

In terms of the structure of output, Delhi is comparable to the high income economies of the world (Table 15.3). It would indeed appear from the subsequent discussion that Delhi is already into post-industrialisation (or becoming less reliant on industry), a phase that characterises the high income countries.

Table 15.2

NDP/NSDP from Services at Current Prices: 2009-10

(Value: Rs crore)

Sl. No.	State/UT	Services (Excl. Construction)	Services (Incl. Construction)	% Share of 3 in NSDP	% Share of 4 in NSDP
1	2	3	4	5	6
1.	Maharashtra	495878	557540	61	68
2.	Tamil Nadu	264418	306025	62	72
3.	Uttar Pradesh	223036	270915	49	59
4.	Andhra Pradesh	224856	269298	53	63
5.	West Bengal	216087	239185	59	66
6.	Gujarat	175021	206865	47	56
7.	Karnataka	168585	198090	55	65
8.	Delhi	172783	193363	83	93
9.	Kerala	127483	154403	63	76
10.	Rajasthan	109129	137966	48	61
11.	Haryana	103137	124170	53	63
12.	Bihar	98206	114872	61	72
13.	Madhya Pradesh	90820	109086	47	57
14.	Punjab	71144	85180	41	49
15.	Orissa	69262	80237	52	60
16.	Assam	40951	45497	50	56
17.	Jharkhand	36840	45205	44	54
18.	Chhattisgarh	35780	44660	38	48
19.	Uttarakhand	32016	37252	55	64
20.	Himachal Pradesh	14946	23183	42	65
21.	Jammu & Kashmir	16136	22938	46	65
22.	Chandigarh	13512	14736	85	93
23.	Goa	10039	12492	45	56
24.	Tripura	6997	9257	55	73
25.	Meghalaya	5686	7388	51	66
26.	Nagaland#	5640	6854	58	71
27.	Puducherry	5013	5904	50	59
28.	Manipur	3194	5054	43	68
29.	Arunachal Pradesh	2699	3973	43	63
30.	Mizoram	2991	3763	59	74
31.	Andaman & Nicobar Islands	1896	2975	54	84
32.	Sikkim	2069	2649	50	64
	All-India (NDP)	3139789	3614842	57	66

Note: # NSDP of Nagaland for 2009-10 has been extrapolated using average growth during 2006-07 to 2008-09.

Source: Website of CSO, MoSPI: *State Domestic Product, 2004-05* State Series.

Table 15.3

Structure of Output: 2009

(Share in Per cent)

Region/Country/State	*Agriculture*	*Industry*	*Manufacturing*	*Services*
1	*2*	*3*	*4*	*5*
World	3	27	17	70
High income	1	25	16	74
Belgium	1	22	14	78
Denmark	1	22	13	77
France	2	19	11	79
Hong Kong SAR	...	8	2	92
Singapore	...	26	19	74
Sweden	2	25	16	73
Switzerland	1	27	19	72
UK	1	21	11	78
US	1	21	13	77
Low & middle income	10	35	21	55
India	18	27	15	55
Delhi*	1	17	6	82

Notes: Manufacturing is a sub-sector of industry.

* Data for Delhi pertains to fiscal year 2009-10.

Source: World Bank, *World Development Indicators, 2011* and CSO.

The absolute size of the NSDP originating from banking and insurance sector in Delhi was the second largest (after Maharashtra) amongst the 32 state/UTs in India in 2009-10. The relative share of this component in the NSDP of Delhi at 16.2 per cent was the highest for any state/UT in the country (Table 15.4). According to the Reserve Bank of India (*Quarterly Statistics on Deposits and Credit of Scheduled Commercial Banks,* March 2011), Delhi accounted for 11.8 per cent of the total deposit and 13.9 per cent of the total credit of all scheduled commercial banks (SCBs) at end-March 2011. Delhi also occupies a prominent position in the insurance segment. According to the Insurance Regulatory and Development Authority (*Annual Report, 2009-10*), Delhi accounted for about 20 per cent of the total number of registered brokers as on August 18, 2010 and about 9 per cent of the gross direct premium income of the insurance companies in the country during the year 2009-10.

Table 15.4

NSDP from Banking and Insurance at Current Prices: 2009-10

Sl. No.	*State/UT*	*Value in Rs Crore*	*Share in NSDP (In %)*
1	*2*	*3*	*4*
1.	Maharashtra	91442	11.2
2.	Delhi	33575	16.2
3.	Tamil Nadu	29268	6.9
4.	West Bengal	22218	6.1
5.	Andhra Pradesh	20634	4.8
6.	Gujarat	20518	5.5
7.	Karnataka	19982	6.6
8.	Uttar Pradesh	17928	3.9
9.	Kerala	11782	5.8
10.	Rajasthan	9123	4.0
11.	Punjab	8733	5.0
12.	Madhya Pradesh	7405	3.9
13.	Haryana	6848	3.5
14.	Orissa	4910	3.7
15.	Bihar	4336	2.7
16.	Assam	3197	3.9
17.	Chhattisgarh	2544	2.7
18.	Jharkhand	2541	3.0
19.	Chandigarh	2241	14.1
20.	Uttarakhand	1963	3.4
21.	Jammu & Kashmir	1641	4.7
22.	Himachal Pradesh	1404	3.9
23.	Goa	1359	6.1
24.	Puducherry	401	4.0
25.	Tripura	339	2.7
26.	Meghalaya	289	2.6
27.	Nagaland#	176	1.8
28.	Arunachal Pradesh	149	2.4
29.	Manipur	136	1.8
30.	Mizoram	136	2.7
31.	Sikkim	96	2.3
32.	Andaman & Nicobar Islands	60	1.7
	All-India (NDP)	**325768**	**5.9**

Note: # NSDP of Nagaland for 2009-10 has been extrapolated using average growth during 2006-07 to 2008-09.

Source: Website of CSO, MoSPI, *State Domestic Product, 2004-05* State Series.

Structural Change

The structure of economic activity in Delhi has changed dramatically during the last two decades. It would be observed from Figure 15.1 that the relative shares of agriculture and manufacturing have declined sharply, especially since the mid-1990s. Contemporaneously, the services activities (most notably, real estate, ownership of dwellings and business services) have gained prominence. Figure 15.2 portrays the time plots of two series on ratios of services NSDP to industry NSDP—one includes construction in services while the other includes it in industry—for the period from 1980-81 to 2009-10. Both the series exhibit an upward drift in the mid-1990s and the drift is more pronounced in the series that treats construction as part of the services sector.

With the rapid pace of urbanisation taking its toll on arable land, the share of agriculture sector in NSDP of Delhi declined from 4.4 per cent in 1990-91 to 0.7 per cent in 2009-10 (Table 15.5). Mining is a minor economic activity in Delhi due to its topography. It was further curtailed by Court orders imposing a ban on quarrying of stone and extraction of *badarpur* within the territories of Delhi. Only sand was being extracted from river bed of Yamuna till 2004-05, which has been halted by the sole licensee i.e., Delhi State Industrial Development Corporation (DSIDC) since 2005-06 (Government of NCT of Delhi, 2011). The share of manufacturing in NSDP of Delhi fell to 5.2 per cent in 2009-10 from 19.5 per cent in 1990-91. Contextually, Delhi has been grappling with the problems of manufacturing units functioning in non-conforming residential areas and pollution caused by industrial units. In 1996, the Supreme Court gave directions to Delhi for: (a) shutting down of hazardous, noxious, heavy and large industries; (b) closing down of hot-mix plants and brick kilns in Delhi and (c) relocating the manufacturing units in residential areas not conforming to the *Master Plan of Delhi 2021* (MPD-2021). Consequently, Delhi government framed an industrial relocation scheme in October 2006, whereby 27,905 units were declared eligible for allotment of industrial plots or flats in various locations. By July 2009, 17,801 units had completed all legal formalities while 16,667 had taken physical possession although only about 5,000 units had started actual construction work on the site (Government of NCT of Delhi, 2010).

Figure 15.1

Activity-wise Distribution of NSDP: Delhi

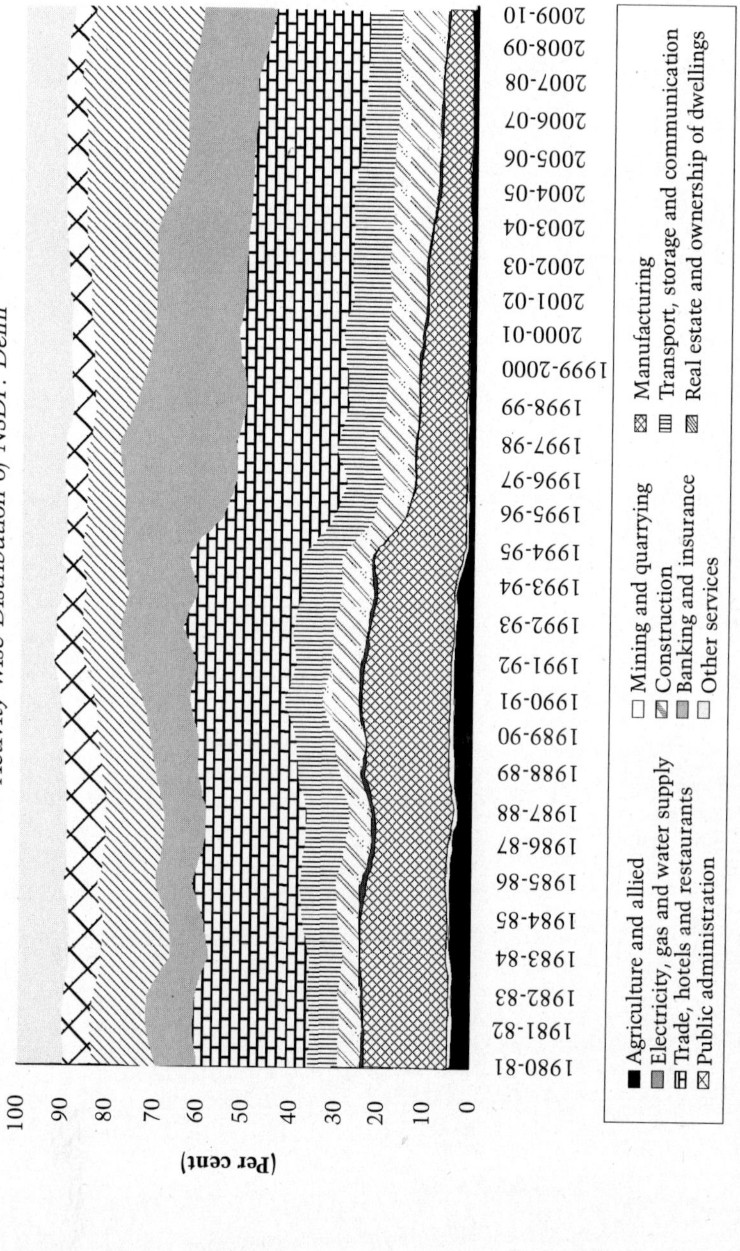

Source: Website of CSO, MoSPI: *State Domestic Product*, 1980-81, 1993-94, 1999-2000 and 2004-05 State Series.

Figure 15.2

Ratio of Services NSDP to Industrial NSDP: Delhi

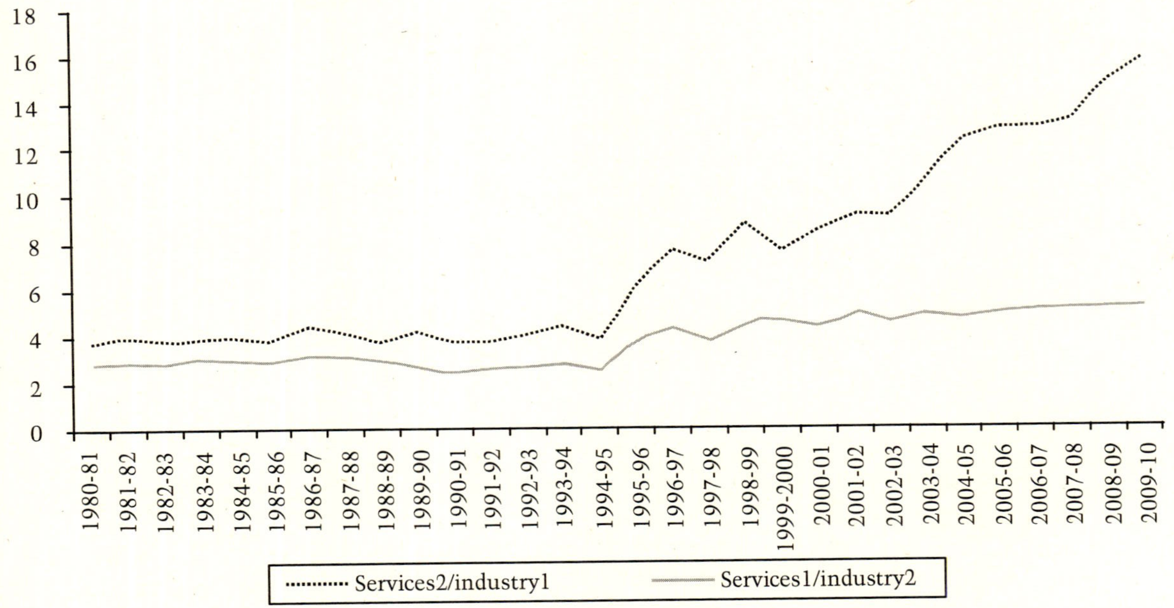

Notes: Industry1- Industry without construction and Industry2- Industry with construction.

Services1- Services without construction and Services2- Services with construction.

Source: Website of CSO, MoSPI: *State Domestic Product*, 1980-81, 1993-94, 1999-2000 and 2004-05 State Series.

Table 15.5

Activity-wise Distribution of NSDP/NDP at Current Prices

(Per cent)

Activity	Delhi (NSDP)				All-India (NDP)			
	1980-81	1990-91	2000-01	2009-10	1980-81	1990-91	2000-01	2009-10
1	2	3	4	5	6	7	8	9
Agriculture and allied	4.1	4.4	1.5	0.7	37.8	31.1	24.8	18.5
Mining and quarrying	0.3	0.4	0.0	0.0	1.7	2.4	2.1	2.1
Manufacturing	18.4	19.5	9.4	5.2	15.7	15.4	13.7	12.7
Electricity, gas and water supply	1.8	0.5	0.9	0.7	1.0	1.1	1.4	0.7
Construction	4.7	8.2	7.9	9.9	4.8	5.8	6.3	8.7
Transport, storage and communication	6.9	8.6	9.4	7.3	3.4	5.2	6.9	7.7
Trade, hotels and restaurants	23.2	20.2	22.7	20.2	12.3	13.7	15.9	17.7
Banking and insurance	9.8	11.2	19.0	16.2	3.3	4.3	5.9	5.9
Real estate, ownership of dwellings & business services	13.5	9.8	13.1	23.2	6.9	7.7	7.5	11.3
Public administration	7.2	8.0	5.1	5.3	5.0	5.6	6.6	6.3
Other services	10.1	9.2	10.9	11.2	8.2	7.8	8.9	8.5
Total NSDP	100.0	100.0	100.0	100.0	100.0	100.0	100.0	100.0
Services (including construction)	75.5	75.3	88.2	93.3	43.9	50.0	58.1	66.0
Services (excluding construction)	70.8	67.1	80.2	83.4	39.1	44.2	51.7	57.3

Source: Website of CSO, MoSPI: *State Domestic Product*, 1980-81, 1993-94, 1999-2000 and 2004-05 State Series.
National Accounts Statistics, Back Series 2007 (1950-51 to 1999-2000), *National Accounts Statistics* 2008 and 2011.

Between 1990-91 and 2009-10, the services sector in Delhi posted a gain of about 18 per cent in the relative share in NSDP; this was in line with the increase of 16 per cent in its share in all-India NDP. Among the sub-sectors, the activities in banking and insurance and construction in Delhi gained prominence over the same period, which are broadly comparable to the patterns witnessed at the all-India level. The share of trade, hotels and restaurants remained unchanged at 20.2 per cent; at the all-India level, the share of this sector improved from 13.7 per cent in 1990-91 to 17.7 per cent. Among others, the share of 'real, estate, ownership of dwellings and business services' in the NSDP of Delhi increased from 9.8 per cent in 1990-91 to 23.2 per cent in 2009-10; this was significantly more pronounced than the increase witnessed at the all-India level. With the abundance of skilled workforce, Delhi is considered to be ideal for the knowledge-based activities, such as IT, ITes, financial and business services and designing, etc. In the *National Science Report 2005*, Delhi emerged as the country's best in terms of the intensity of core human resources in science and technology (HRST) personnel (NCAER, 2005).

III

Revisiting the Issues

Sustainability of the Growth of Services Sector

Notwithstanding the findings of a number of recent studies documenting the success stories of India's services sector, the phenomenon of disproportional growth of services activities is an issue that merits attention. In fact, the disproportionality in the pattern of growth has increased in recent times. At the all-India level, the rate of growth of NDP in the services sector improved to 8.9 per cent during 1995-2010 from 6.2 per cent recorded during 1981-1995. Contemporaneously, the growth in commodity producing sectors (agriculture plus industry) fell from 4.2 per cent to 4.1 per cent. If one takes a more recent period, the growth rate in the services sector at 10.2 per cent during 2005-2010 was almost twice the rate of growth in commodity production. The divergence between the growth in the services sector and the commodity producing sectors during the period 1995-2010 (or during the 2005-2010 period within that) is even more pronounced in the case of Delhi (Table 15.6).

Table 15.6

Growth Rate in Activity at Constant Prices

(Average annual per cent change)

Sectors	Delhi (NSDP)				All-India (NDP)			
	1981-1995	1995-2010	1995-2005	2005-2010	1981-1995	1995-2010	1995-2005	2005-2010
1	2	3	4	5	6	7	8	9
Agriculture and allied	-0.4	0.4	1.3	-1.4	3.4	2.4	2.3	2.7
Mining and quarrying	2.3	30.8	43.9	-	6.3	3.5	4.9	0.8
Manufacturing	10.7	2.1	0.1	6.1	5.6	6.9	5.7	9.2
Electricity, gas and water supply	8.6	12.9	1.4	36.0	8.9	5.9	5.4	6.9
Construction	7.9	10.6	12.8	6.3	4.2	8.2	7.8	8.9
Trade, hotels and restaurants	8.8	6.7	5.5	9.0	6.0	8.7	8.5	9.0
Railways	4.4	13.6	11.7	17.5	4.3	7.9	6.6	10.5
Transport by other means	10.7	3.9	3.7	4.4	6.8	7.9	8.0	7.7
Storage	-1.9	3.3	-0.1	10.1	2.9	4.2	2.6	7.6
Communications	9.4	17.4	18.2	15.6	7.2	26.3	24.9	29.1
Banking and insurance	13.4	13.5	12.0	16.5	10.3	11.1	8.8	15.8
Real estate, ownership of dwellings & business services	5.9	10.3	9.5	12.0	9.8	7.3	6.2	9.4
Public administration	5.2	9.3	8.5	10.9	5.3	8.0	7.0	10.0
Other services	5.6	8.3	6.2	12.5	5.3	7.2	7.3	6.9
NSDP/NDP	**8.1**	**8.5**	**7.3**	**10.8**	**5.1**	**6.9**	**6.1**	**8.4**
Memo								
Industry (with construction)	9.6	5.0	4.2	6.4	5.4	6.8	6.1	8.2
Industry (without construction)	10.6	2.1	-0.1	6.6	5.9	6.3	5.5	7.9
Services (with construction)	7.9	9.6	8.8	11.2	6.2	8.9	8.2	10.2
Services (without construction)	8.1	9.6	8.6	11.7	6.6	9.0	8.3	10.4
Commodity producing (agri+ind-with const.)	8.2	4.7	4.0	6.0	4.2	4.7	4.1	5.9
Commodity producing (agri+ind-without const.)	8.7	1.8	-0.1	5.6	4.2	4.1	3.5	5.2

Source: Website of CSO, MoSPI: *State Domestic Product*, 1980-81, 1993-94, 1999-2000 and 2004-05 State Series.
National Accounts Statistics, Back Series 2007 (1950-51 to 1999-2000), *National Accounts Statistics*, 2008 and 2011.

Recent studies have attributed the high growth of services sector in India since the mid-1990s to a number of factors, such as, economic reforms, globalising world, internationalisation of business, technological advancements, growing income, changes in lifestyle and so on (Pilat, 2005; Karmakar, 2008). While these are true, the revisions in the data have, to some extent, contributed to the changes in the perception regarding the growth of the services sector.

To substantiate the point, it may be mentioned that the high growth in services and in the sub-sectors within that in recent years was associated with the sharp upward revision in the data. At the all-India level, GDP at factor cost at current prices for the year 1993-94 was revised upwards by 9.0 per cent, reflecting the long gap of 13 years in the revision and significant methodological changes, notably the use of workforce estimates from NSS Survey (50th Round: 1993-94) in place of the Population Census (which was the practice earlier). The upward revision in the GDP originating from the services sector in that year was of the order of 13.1 per cent. The magnitude of the revision in the GDP was relatively less for the subsequent two series (1.7 per cent for the year 1999-2000 and 3.1 per cent for the year 2004-05). However, the revisions in the services sector were sharper (4.0 per cent for the year 1999-2000 and 4.6 per cent for the year 2004-05). The revision in the sub-sectors within the services sector in 2004-2005 was sharper in real estate, ownership of dwellings & business services, construction and transport by other means (Table 15.7).

In the case of Delhi, the upward revision in the GSDP in 2004-05 by 9.0 per cent was relatively sharper with the GSDP in the services sector having been revised upwards by 11.6 per cent. The sub-sectors within services that underwent larger upward revision are: storage, real estate, ownership of dwellings & business services, construction and trade, hotels and restaurants (Table 15.8).

To what extent the revision in data series affects the growth rates can be appreciated by making a comparison of the data from the original series and the linked series for the period from 1950-51 to 1998-99 that the CSO released in 2007, making them comparable with the series having 1999-2000 as the base year. The real estate, ownership of dwellings & business services segment witnessed sharp upward revision in all the benchmark years observed at the all-India level as well as in Delhi. The divergence

Table 15.7

Revisions in GDP at Factor Cost at Current Prices: All-India

(Rs crore)

Sector	1993-94			1999-2000			2004-05		
	1980-81 Series	1993-94 Series	% Change	1993-94 Series	1999-2000 Series	% Change	1999-2000 Series	2004-05 Series	% Change
1	2	3	4	5	6	7	8	9	10
Agriculture and allied	223705	242438	8.4	461964	454061	-1.7	552422	560308	1.4
Mining and quarrying	16818	19702	17.1	41298	41594	0.7	84776	84954	0.2
Manufacturing	127646	126697	-0.7	266704	264113	-1.0	453603	453225	-0.1
Electricity, gas and water supply	18879	18968	0.5	42299	44732	5.8	59892	61905	3.4
Construction	40699	40433	-0.7	105297	105149	-0.1	212807	229932	8.0
Trade, hotels and restaurants	98024	110995	13.2	246037	254143	3.3	461287	477299	3.5
Railways	9648	9648	0.0	15623	19504	24.8	29645	29118	-1.8
Transport by other means	37066	38314	3.4	81855	82377	0.6	159385	170347	6.9
Storage	569	608	6.9	1262	1427	13.1	2161	1959	-9.3
Communications	8813	9420	6.9	25567	28446	11.3	53595	49174	-8.2
Banking and insurance	43570	41665	-4.4	119075	105662	-11.3	167831	171098	1.9
Real estate, ownership of dwellings & business services	23575	47918	103.3	101484	127090	25.2	237250	264686	11.6
Public administration	39950	43094	7.9	116686	119671	2.6	173491	177119	2.1
Other services	43912	49177	12.0	136687	144323	5.6	229556	236475	3.0
GDP	**732874**	**799077**	**9.0**	**1761838**	**1792292**	**1.7**	**2877701**	**2967599**	**3.1**
Services (incl. construction)	345826	391272	13.1	949573	987792	4.0	1727008	1807207	4.6
Services (excl. construction)	305127	350839	15.0	844276	882643	4.5	1514201	1577275	4.2

Source: Website of CSO, MoSPI.
Brochures on series of *National Accounts Statistics* (Base Year: 1993-94, 1999-2000 and 2004-05).

Table 15.8

Revisions in GSDP at Factor Cost at Current Prices: Delhi

(Rs lakh)

Sector	1993-94			1999-2000			2004-05		
	1980-81 Series	*1993-94 Series*	*% Change*	*1993-94 Series*	*1999-2000 Series*	*% Change*	*1999-2000 Series*	*2004-05 Series*	*% Change*
1	*2*	*3*	*4*	*5*	*6*	*7*	*8*	*9*	*10*
Agriculture and allied	86031	79480	-7.6	72130	76152	5.6	87826	109448	24.6
Mining and quarrying	1561	1421	-9.0	172	179	4.1	451	453	0.4
Manufacturing	356666	355108	-0.4	559853	630048	12.5	871033	732602	-15.9
Electricity, gas and water supply	36690	29763	-18.9	8647	67334	678.7	141436	141606	0.1
Construction	138663	143988	3.8	310211	310788	0.2	862052	975668	13.2
Trade, hotels and restaurants	366609	432711	18.0	1020190	1174806	15.2	1929663	2106249	9.2
Railways	11733	11733	0.0	22147	25569	15.5	56732	48337	-14.8
Transport by other means	153005	144169	-5.8	325431	318965	-2.0	498567	535177	7.3
Storage	4119	1252	-69.6	1175	2482	111.2	3529	5531	56.7
Communications	70572	71114	0.8	163703	237767	45.2	331281	297405	-10.2
Banking and insurance	334980	328218	-2.0	1403680	1166049	-16.9	1583259	1636236	3.3
Real estate, ownership of dwellings & business services	165050	189611	14.9	530508	614725	15.9	1468670	1952309	32.9
Public administration	126101	114416	-9.3	315685	328004	3.9	514827	599954	16.5
Other services	139510	196195	40.6	567433	569148	0.3	855990	891477	4.1
GSDP	**1991290**	**2099179**	**5.4**	**5300965**	**5522016**	**4.2**	**9205316**	**10032452**	**9.0**
Services (incl. construction)	1510342	1633407	8.1	4660163	4748303	1.9	8104570	9048343	11.6
Services (excl. construction)	1371679	1489419	8.6	4349952	4437515	2.0	7242518	8072675	11.5

Source: Website of CSO, MoSPI.
State Domestic Product, 1980-81, 1993-94, 1999-2000 and 2004-05 State Series.

between the original series and the linked series and the jump that occurred in 1993-94 in the GDP from this sector can be observed from Figure 15.3 and Figure 15.4. The growth rate in GDP at current prices in

Figure 15.3

GDP of Real Estate, Ownership of Dwellings & Business Services at Current Prices

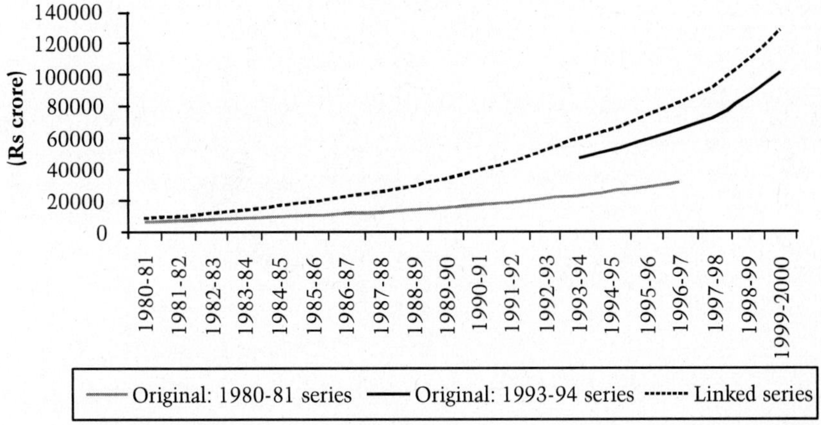

Source: CSO, MoSPI.

Figure 15.4

GDP of Real Estate, Ownership of Dwellings & Business Services at Constant Prices

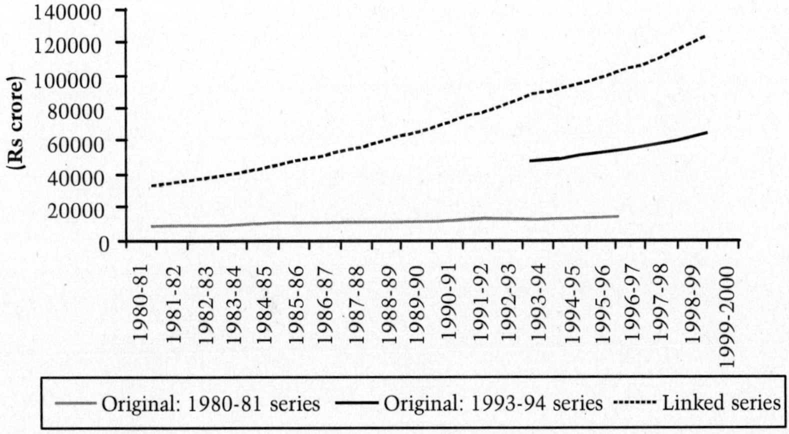

Source: CSO, MoSPI.

real estate, ownership of dwellings & business services during the period 1981-1993 was 9.3 per cent in the original series and this turned out to be 14.8 per cent in the linked series. The growth in GDP at constant (1999-2000) prices for the same sector, which was 3.6 per cent as per the original series, turned out to be 8.1 per cent as per the linked series (Table 15.9).

Table 15.9

Growth Rate of GDP from Real Estate, Ownership of Dwellings and Business Services

(Annual average, percentage change)

Period	*Current Price*		*Constant Price*	
	Original Series	*Linked Series (Base Year 1999-2000)*	*Original Series*	*Linked Series (Base Year 1999-2000)*
1	*2*	*3*	*4*	*5*
1981-1993	9.3	14.8	3.6	8.1
1993-2000	12.7	13.6	5.0	6.3
1981-2000	10.6	14.4	4.1	7.5

Source: CSO, MoSPI, *National Accounts Statistics Back Series 2007* (1950-51 to 1999-2000), 1980-81 and 1993-94 series.

The crucial point that comes out of the above analysis is that the relatively low growth of the services sector during the earlier periods (based on the original series) was on account of underestimation. It would be of interest to note that the earlier studies that expressed scepticism about the sustainability of the growth in the services sector were based on the old or original data series while some of the recent studies which have mentioned about consistent growth in services sector are the ones that have used the data from the linked series of NAS released by the CSO in 2007.

No such linked series is available for the states and UTs. However, the available information regarding the revisions in the GSDP emanating from the services sector in Delhi (8.1 per cent in 1993-94 and 11.6 per cent in 2004-05) would suggest that the divergence in the growth estimates would be substantial in the event of availability of such linked series. This calls for refinements in the data series on state domestic product along with such refinements done in the case of all-India GDP/NDP. This is important in the context of the increasing emphasis being placed on understanding the micro foundations of macroeconomic growth through sector- and region-specific studies.

Jobless Growth

The quinquennial surveys on employment and unemployment conducted by the National Sample Survey Office (NSSO) constitute the primary source of data on various parameters of labour force, workforce and employment at the national and state levels. The perceptions regarding the low labour absorption in the services sector and the changes therein as one gets from the past studies were mainly on account of the data from various Rounds of the NSS surveys, which often tended to be surprising.

The results from NSS 55th Round (1999-2000) showed deceleration in the growth rate of aggregate employment to less than 1 per cent per annum during the period 1993-94 to 1999-2000 from that of 2 per cent per annum during the period 1983 to 1993-94 and this led to concerns about the phenomenon of 'jobless growth'. The perception changed in the latter years, as the results from NSS 61st Round (2004-05) showed acceleration in the growth rate of employment to 2.9 per cent during the period 1999-2000 to 2004-05 with 60 million jobs having been added during that period. The employment elasticity at the aggregate level tripled to 0.48 during the period 1999-2000 to 2004-05 from 0.15 during the period 1993-94 to 1999-2000. Change in the employment elasticity in agriculture (from 0 to 1.52) and in mining (from 0 to 0.82) between these two periods were rather surprising (Rangarajan *et al.*, 2007). Although the overall employment elasticity was just 0.48, it was reasonably high (and increasing) in certain categories of services: 0.94 in financing, insurance, real estate and business services followed by 0.88 in construction (Karmakar, 2008).

The results of the 66th Round of the NSS carried out during 2009-10 indicate that the trends are again different. The aggregate employment at 459 million in 2009-10 recorded an increase of a little over 1 million from the level of 2004-05 (or a compound rate of 0.05 per cent per annum over the five-year period). The labour force participation rate (LFPR) fell from 430 per thousand in 2004-05 to 400 per thousand in 2009-10; the size of labour force declined, *albeit* marginally; and the unemployment rate dropped from 23 per thousand in 2004-05 to 20 per thousand in 2009-10 (Table 15.10). The publication of these data has given rise to serious concerns. The decline in the labour force at the all-India level is due mainly to the withdrawal of rural female from agriculture. Even then, an overall decline in the labour force at a time when both population and GDP are growing is difficult to explain (Rangarajan *et al.*, 2011).

Table 15.10

Employment and Unemployment

(In million)

	*Delhi**		*All-India*		*CAGR*	
	2004-05	*2009-10*	*2004-05*	*2009-10*	*Delhi**	*All-India*
Projected population	14.6	17.0	1092.9	1174.1	3.10	1.44
Labour force	5.1	5.8	469.0	468.8	2.57	-0.01
Workforce	4.9	5.7	457.9	459.0	3.04	0.05
LFPR	351	342	430	400		
WPR	334	333	420	392		
UR	48	26	23	20		

Notes: *: Figures pertain to urban Delhi.
1. Figures on employment and unemployment pertains to usual (principal and subsidiary) status.
2. Labour Force Participation Rate (LFPR) is defined as the number of persons/person-days in the labour force per 1,000 persons/person-days.
3. Worker Population Ratio (WPR) is defined as the number of persons/person-days employed per 1,000 persons/person-days.
4. Unemployment Rate (UR) is defined as the number of persons/person-days unemployed per 1,000 persons/person-days in the labour force (which includes both the employed and unemployed).

Sources: 1. NSSO, NSS 66th Round (2009-10), NSS 61st Round (2004-05).
2. Office of Registrar General and Census Commissioner, *Population Projections for India and States: 2001-2026*.

In Delhi, however, employment recorded a stronger growth and the unemployment rate exhibited a sharper decline between 2004-05 and 2009-10. The size of labour force in Delhi increased unlike the decline witnessed at the all-India level, as Delhi experienced a higher rate of growth in population (Table 15.10).

The industry-wise distribution of output and employment for 2004-05 and 2009-10 throw up certain interesting patterns, some are on the expected lines while some appear to be counter-intuitive (Table 15.11). Before discussing the trends, it may be mentioned that the industry classification in the 66th Round of NSS (2009-10) relates to NIC-2004 and it differs from that of NIC-1998 used in the 61st Round (2004-05). For comparison purposes, the data on certain industries have been regrouped.

That apart, thc industry-wise distribution of employment for Delhi relates to urban population as comparable data on aggregate (urban plus rural) for the states/UTs are not available for the 61st Round of NSS. This in any case may not pose a serious problem in the analysis, as 98 per cent of the total population of Delhi belonged to the urban area as per 2011 Census.

At the all-India level, the shifts in sectoral share of employment—decline in agriculture and manufacturing and increase in services—broadly correspond to the changes in the relative shares of the respective sectors in output. Over the five-year period from 2004-05 to 2009-10, the share of services sector in employment increased by about 6 percentage points. However, a large portion of this increase was on account of construction. While the share of construction in employment increased by 4 percentage points, its share in NDP increased only marginally. If construction is taken out, the share of services sector in total employment increased by about 2 percentage points. The overall share of services sector in employment in 2009-10 (35 per cent including construction and 25.4 per cent excluding construction) was roughly half of its share in NDP (66 per cent including construction and 57.3 per cent excluding construction). Notwithstanding the decline, the share of agriculture in employment remained at a high of 53.2 per cent in 2009-10, roughly thrice its share in NDP (Table 15.11).

In Delhi, however, the overall share of the services sector in employment in 2009-10 (71.2 per cent including construction or 68.2 per cent excluding construction) maintained a better proximity to its share in NSDP (Table 15.11). Over the five-year period (2004-05 to 2009-10), the share of services sector (including construction) in employment recorded a decline; excluding construction, the share increased marginally. Among the sub-sectors, the share of transport, storage & communication, trade, hotels & restaurants and financial intermediation and real estate and ownership of dwellings in employment increased while construction and community, social and personal services recorded declines. The sharp decline in the relative share in employment of construction in Delhi from 6.3 per cent in 2004-05 to 3.0 per cent in 2009-10 was not associated with any decline in its share in output and it was opposite to the increase observed at the all-India level. Furthermore, the share of construction in employment in 2009-10 was less than one-third of its share in output whereas at the all-India level, the share of this sector in employment was higher than its share in

Table 15.11

Distribution of Employment and Output

(Per cent)

Activity	Delhi*				All-India			
	Employment		Output		Employment		Output	
	2004-05	2009-10	2004-05	2009-10	2004-05	2009-10	2004-05	2009-10
1	2	3	4	5	6	7	8	9
Agriculture and allied	0.1	0.1	1.1	0.7	58.5	53.2	19.9	18.5
Mining and quarrying	0.0	0.1	0.0	0.0	0.6	0.6	2.7	2.1
Manufacturing	25.5	28.4	6.7	5.2	11.8	11.0	13.1	12.7
Electricity, gas and water supply	0.1	0.0	0.7	0.7	0.3	0.3	1.3	0.7
Construction	6.3	3.0	9.9	9.9	5.6	9.6	8.2	8.7
Transport, storage and communication	8.2	9.4	8.6	7.3	3.9	4.3	8.3	7.7
Trade, hotels and restaurants	26.8	30.9	22.0	20.2	10.2	10.8	17.5	17.7
Financial intermediation and real estate and ownership of dwellings	8.5	12.4	36.6	39.4	1.6	2.1	15.0	17.2
Community, social and personal services	24.3	15.5	14.3	16.5	7.6	8.2	14.2	14.8
Memo								
Services (including construction)	74.1	71.2	91.5	93.3	28.8	35.0	63.1	66.0
Services (excluding construction)	67.8	68.2	81.6	83.4	23.3	25.4	54.9	57.3

Note: Output relates to current price estimates of NSDP in case of Delhi and NDP for all-India.

* Relates to urban region.

Source: NSS 66th Round (2009-10), NSS 61st Round (2004-05); and CSO (MoSPI).

output. Among the commodity producing sectors, the share of agriculture in employment at 0.1 per cent in Delhi was lower than its share in NSDP while the share of manufacturing in employment at 28.4 per cent was more than five times its share in NSDP. Moreover, the share of manufacturing in employment increased over time in contrast to the decline in its share in NSDP.

The low share of construction in employment (and its decline) would perhaps be indicative of the high (and growing) level of mechanisation in this activity in Delhi. The relatively high share of manufacturing in employment would signify that this activity in Delhi—dominated by low-skill intensive, small-scale units in the unorganised sector—is (and becoming) more labour-intensive. In other words, the productivity of workers in the manufacturing sector in Delhi is low (and falling). As against that, the productivity of workers increased in community, social and personal services, as this segment witnessed sharp decline in the share in employment along with increase in the share in output. However, drawing ready inferences from official data can be misleading, as past studies have opined. In the case of all-India data, it is believed that a significant portion of the workforce accounted for the agricultural/rural employment is working in the unorganised services sectors both in rural and urban areas (Karmakar, 2008). The near absence of agriculture precludes such a possibility in Delhi. However, whether the NSS figures on employment or for that matter the estimates on state domestic product in construction and manufacturing sectors in Delhi are realistic or not would need further detailed analysis.

IV

Concluding Observations

The structural change in the output in Delhi over the last two decades has been dramatic and this is attributable to various pull and push factors. On the one hand, the process of disappearance of agriculture and mining and the reduction in the dependence on industry represent the growing needs of a city state, aimed at relieving the pressure on the environment. This is the push factor for the growth in services activities. On the other hand, availability of skilled labour force and better infrastructure—the pull factors—propelled the growth of services activities, notably in IT, ITes, finance and business services segments. The economy of Delhi has grown rapidly—racing ahead of several major states—on the back of the services sector, taking advantage of the national level reform measures undertaken since 1991.

As regards the issues surrounding the growth of the services sector in India, this paper underscores the need for strengthening the database that would support decision-making. The refinements made in National Accounts Statistics with the release of the revised (linked) series in 2007 had led to a change in the perception regarding the growth of the services sector—from what was viewed as an implausible and unsustainable rate of growth to that of a consistent pattern of growth. However, no such refinement has been made to the data on state domestic products and this causes difficulties in the analyses of growth and structural change across states/UTs. Revision in the data on state income commensurate with the National Accounts Statistics would facilitate preparation of policy-supportive research studies.

On the concerns regarding the 'jobless growth', the paper observes that employment in Delhi recorded a sharp growth over the period 2004-05 to 2009-10, whereas the growth in employment in the country as a whole was abysmally low. Yet another interesting finding is that, there is a better correspondence between employment and output in the services sector in Delhi unlike the wide divergence observed at the national level. However, the patterns in output and employment in construction and manufacturing are puzzling. Whether the NSS figures on employment or the estimates on state domestic product in these cases are realistic or not, would need further analysis. This would form part of the agenda for research in future.

References

Acharya, Shankar (2002). "Macroeconomic Management in the Nineties", *Economic & Political Weekly* 37(16): 1515-1538, April 20-26.

———. (ed.) (2003). *India's Economy: Some Issues and Answers*. New Delhi: Academic Foundation.

Banga, Rashmi (2006). "Critical Issues in India's Services-led Growth", *Asian Development Bank, INRM Policy Brief* No.2.

Banga, Rashmi and Bishwanath Goldar (2004). "Contribution of Services to Output Growth and Productivity in Indian Manufacturing: Pre and Post Reforms", *Working Paper No.*139, Indian Council for Research on International Economic Relations, July.

Bhattacharya, B.B. and Arup Mitra (1990). "Excess Growth of Teritiary Sector in Indian Economy: Issues and Implications", *Economic & Political Weekly* 25(44): 2445-2450, November 3.

Eichengreen, Barry and Poonam Gupta (2011). "The Services Sector as India's Road to Economic Growth", *Working Paper No.*16757, Cambridge: National Bureau of Economic Research.

Government of India (2011). *Economic Survey, 2010-11.*

Government of NCT of Delhi (2010). *Industrial Policy for Delhi, 2010-2021.*

———. (2011). *Estimates of State Domestic Product 2010-11* (Base Year: 2004-05).

Gokarn, Subir (2011). "Growth, Resilience and Reforms: Reflections on Post-crisis Policy Challenges", The 45th A.D. Shroff Memorial Lecture delivered at Indian Merchant Chamber, Mumbai, 2nd November.

Hansda, Sanjay Kumar (2002): "Sustainability of Services-Led Growth: An Input Output Analysis of the Indian Economy", *RBI Occasional Papers.*

Joshi, Seema (2008). "Services Sector in India's Economy: Performance, Problems and Prospects", *Country Paper*, Project No.08-RP-38-GE-STM-B, *Asian Productivity Organisation*, June.

Karmakar, Suparna (2008). "An Open Services Regime: Recipe for Jobless Growth?", *Working Paper No.*210, Indian Council for Research on International Economic Relations, March.

Mazumdar, Surajit (2010). "Industry and Services in Growth and Structural Change in India: Some Unexplored Features", *Working Paper No.*2010/02, Institute for Studies in Industrial Development.

Mitra, Ashok (1988). "Disproportionality and the Services Sector: A Note", *Social Scientist* 179, April.

NCAER (2005). *India Science Report.*

Pilat, Dirk (2005). "Introduction and Synthesis", in *Enhancing the Performance of the Services Sector. OECD.*

Rangarajan, C., Padma Iyer Kaul and Seema (2011). "Where Is the Missing Labour Force?", *Economic and Political weekly* XLVI (39): 68-72. September 24-30.

———. (2007). "Revisiting Employment and Growth", *ICRA Bulletin, Money & Finance.* September.

Reserve Bank of India (2003). "Construction: Industry or Services?", Box II-6 in *Annual Report, 2002-03.*

Shingal, Anirudh (2010). *Services Growth and Convergence: Getting India's States Together*. Electronic copy available at *http://ssrn.com/abstract=1690162*

Soubbotina, T.P. and K.A. Sheram (2000). "Beyond Economic Growth: Meeting the Challenges of Global Development", *WBI Learning Resources Series*, The World Bank, October.

16 Regional Dimensions of Realty Sector in India

R. KAUSALIYA and SURAJ S.

I

Introduction

The realty sector in India is of great importance given its linkages with various sectors of the economy. It has caught the attention of policy-makers world over. India is no exception. In the wake of recent global financial crisis that emerged from asset prices bubble, the realty sector has assumed renewed importance, especially in the context of monetary policy formulation. The sharp and rapid rise and fall of asset prices, especially, the realty prices may have systemic effect from the point of view of price stability and financial stability and thereby macroeconomic stability of an economy. The asset price bubble is a serious monetary concern of the central banks across the world, particularly in the post-global financial crisis scenario. In this context, the present study is an attempt to draw the trends in the realty sector including housing and commercial real estate across the major states of India to identify various regional dimensions of the sector.

The period of the current study from 1999-2000 to 2008-09 is considered significant to draw lessons on regional dimensions of growth as this post-reform phase marked the highest growth experienced by the Indian economy supported by more or less stable macroeconomic environment except 2008-09 on account of global financial crisis. As the availability of reliable data on the prices and quantity of real estate across the states is limited, the focus of the study is to comprehend the trends and developments of the realty sector by analysing the co-movements of the other related macroeconomic variables.

The study is structured into six sections. Following introduction, Section II sets out the literature review of the study. Theoretical framework and methodology of the study is detailed in Section III. In order to understand the growth in realty sector across states, Section IV provides analysis on the structural changes in regional growth witnessed across the Indian states and the relative contribution of realty sector to each regional economy. Section V examines the regional trends in the bank credit for housing across the states with an empirical analysis besides analysing the trends in housing prices of major centres across states. The inferences drawn from the analysis is summarised as conclusion in Section VI.

II

Literature Review

Demand for any type of real estate has at least three components such as type of occupancy, i.e., owner-occupied or rental, property characteristics and quality and locational characteristics. The drivers of real estate demand may differ by property type. The drivers of demand for office space are different from the drivers of demand for retail space or the drivers of demand for industrial space. Therefore, rent also plays a vital role in property valuation. However, effective demand for property is basically driven by purchasing power and therefore income and credit growth is critical for generating demand for real estate. The potential growth of credit could also influence the demand in the realty sector which may be for the purpose of investment in the physical assets or for real housing. The role of money and credit plays a major role in the determination of assets prices accelerated by speculations (Kindleberger, 1978). Many studies reinstated the role of credit on assets price bubbles in the backdrop of the burst of such bubbles unstabilising many economies at different periods of their economic history. The negative and positive asset price bubbles and the role of monetary policy and credit growth relationships suggests that greater the uncertainty regarding the monetary policy and the amount of aggregate credit growth greater is the bubble (Allen and Gale, 2000). The prominent role of money and credit to assess developments in asset prices which in turn pose threat to price and economic stability and therefore, the assessment of money and credit plays an important role in shaping the medium to long-term outlook for price developments (ECB, 2005). The use of asset price misalignments in guiding central bank policy is discussed much in the literature by Cecchetti *et al.* (2000). Cecchetti *et al.* (2002) suggests that macroeconomic performance can be improved if monetary policy reacts to asset price misalignments in addition to reducing the probability of bubbles arising at all. However, in the aftermath of the global financial crisis, the revisiting of the debate on asset price bubbles and monetary policy highlights that as the monetary policy works with a lag the direct linkage between them is weak and therefore regulatory and supervisory policies, rather than monetary policies, would have been more effective means of addressing the run-up in house prices (Bernanke, 2010).

Research on housing market in India is scarce due to the dearth of adequate information. According to the latest report by Cushman and Wakefield (2010), the global real estate consultant, the pan-India residential demand for the period 2010-2014 is estimated to be about 4.25 million units of which mid-range and affordable sectors continue to capture a significant share of 70 per cent. However, there are few studies which found the housing demand in India inelastic with respect to income and price; the income elasticity was estimated as 0.75 while price elasticity is slightly less than unity (Tiwari and Parikh, 1998). Further, on the potential threat of asset price, bubbles to the India economy, the empirical study based on the monthly data suggests that housing prices are significantly more sensitive to permanent interest rate shocks than shocks to credit growth (Joshi, 2006). The study further suggests that the housing market in India at present remains fairly well equilibrated if seen in terms of the proximity of the actual housing prices and the estimated long run equilibrium housing prices. This implies that the risk of speculation in the market is not yet materially significant. However, as a mark of caution, since the empirical results indicate that housing prices are significantly much more sensitive to permanent interest rate shocks than shocks to credit growth, the stance of monetary policy particularly that reflected by the setting of the policy rate appears to be the single most important arbiter of the future growth of the housing market. Besides, as income growth explains quite little about variations in housing prices, observing the possibility of some adverse selection in overall bank financing of the housing sector cannot be completely ruled out.

The linkage between housing sector GDP in India and household sector leverage and public sector banks (PSB) housing has been studied and the income and price elasticity of demand is also estimated as less than unity (Bhandopadhay, *et al.*, 2008). The study finds that net 68 million Indians will require independent housing and thereby they will add to the housing demand of the nation due to age-demographic effect by 2015. In case of urban population, the additional need for housing would be 31 million (1/3rd of 94 million). The study also has done projections of realised demand for housing through credit supply channel till 2012. Following this method, forecast for additional demand for housing for 2012-13 is around 6.79 million. The study found linkage between housing sector GDP and household sector leverage and PSBs housing loan disbursement, as also found evidence of linkage between house hold leverage and GDP. Further, the house price index (computed by the study) moves in with the economic cycle and it becomes more evident when the growth profile is matched with the expansion in bank credit growth to housing (especially during 2004 onwards when banks stepped up the lending to housing segment). The study by Sahu (2010) shows that demand for housing finance is high and growing faster among all income size sub-groups within low-income groups. The study by Mahalik and Mallick (2009) using cointegration test and vector error-correction model (VECM), finds that in the long run, real income significantly and positively influences the housing prices while real non-food bank credit adversely influences it. The net impact is a rise in housing prices on account of rising demand reflected in the increased income. However, the variance decomposition results suggest that it is the shocks to the non-food bank credit which mainly explains the variability in housing prices besides its own shocks being the most influential among the factors suggesting that the role of credit availability cannot be underestimated in the dynamic behaviour of housing prices in emerging economies. Needless to mention, it is therefore necessary to take this factor into due account while developing policy approaches in relation to the housing sector. In view of the above the present study is a pioneer attempt to draw a geographical distribution of the trends and developments in the realty sector among select states in India through analysing bank credit and other related macroeconomic variables.

III

Theoretical Framework and Methodology

The major factors determining trends in demand for real estate are demographic factors such as increase in population either due to higher birth rates prevailing or increased migration as well as other factors like income, price, cost and availability of credit, etc. In Indian context, demand for real estate arising out of the increase in population due to higher birth rates could be separated from other factors as most of the Indian states historically followed a high birth rate and subsequently experienced a declining trend in birth rates due to stringent follow up of demographic policies pursued by the government after the country's Independence. However, migration inward and outward added to the demand of real estate in various developing cities apart from the metro cities. In this context, this study is an attempt to analyse realty sector developments in order to identify any converging trends in the realty demand experienced across the states. The observations in this regard may also help in analysing the co-movements of related macroeconomic variables with the realty sector variables. The study attempts to analyse the available indicators in a theoretical framework based on simple form of theory of demand in order to comprehend the trends and developments of the realty sector across the select states of India.

Recent academic and research studies are focused more on the role of interest rates and credit rather than income in analysing the housing credit and asset price movements which in turn molds the market conditions to a boom-bust cycle. The importance of availability of credit and the terms of credit in measuring the demand for housing could not be denied *vis-à-vis* income and other characters (Gelfand, 1970). The factors which appear to be important for the growth of housing market consisting of income growth mix of monetary policy, tax and regulatory incentives and procedural ease of loan disbursals, etc., and its significance in sustaining financial stability has been recognised following significant credit growth during a period of low interest rate (Joshi, 2006). Many industrialised countries have experienced extraordinarily strong rates of money and credit growth accompanied by strong increases in house prices (ECB, 2008). The demand for real estate properties, particularly for the private homes, depend primarily on earning capacity of the prospective owner, his borrowing capacity, interest rate structure and taxation policy, etc. The impact of property prices on bank credit is found to be significantly positive and therefore the challenge central bankers face is in ensuring rapid credit growth not leading to bubbles, however, almost three-fifths of the overall variation in housing prices can be explained by innovations in the housing market itself and the combined effect of other explanatory factors, such as GDP, interest rates, bank credit and equity prices, accounts for the rest (RBI, 2010). In this context, since there is a paucity of data on housing prices across the states, bank lending being one of the major sources of real estate funding in India, the Study is attempting to identify the trends in realty sector using bank credit *vis-à-vis* changes to the related macro-economic variables across the select states.

In general, the demand for housing could be influenced by many factors such as income, price level, availability of credit and level of interest rate, etc., apart from the factors related to taste and preferences. The study adopted a pooled regressive methodology to indentify the relative significance of explanatory variables such as income, availability of credit, and interest rate in determining the demand for housing credit across the states using data for the period 1990 to 2008 which witnessed high growth in the Indian economy, and the pooled regression model could be given as follows:

$$Y_{it} = \alpha + \beta_{it} X_{it} + e_{it} \qquad ...(1)$$

As simple pooled regression may be subjected to omitted variable bias, therefore the explanatory power is limited. In the panel data analysis in which the cross-sectional data is heterogeneous, a pooled OLS regression would not be sufficient to explain whether all the states have a common intercept for the relationship among the regressors factoring the period and crosss-section effects. The general functional form including the cross-section and period-specific effects for identyfying fixed or random effect is as follows.

$$Y_{it} = \alpha + X_{it} \beta_{it} + \mu_i + \lambda_t + e_{it} \qquad ...(2)$$

where in Y_{it} represents the dependent variable, X_{it} independent variables μ_t and λ_t represents cross-section and period effects of associated unobserved variables with the respective dummies, e_{it} the remainder disturbance (capturing everything that is left unexplained about Y_{it}), i cross-sectional units observed for dated periods—(the number of states) and t the period of time. The model with dummy variables takes the functional form as follows depending on the model specifications.

$$Y_{it} = \alpha + X_{it}\,\beta_{it} + \mu_i D1_i + \mu_i D2_i + \ldots\ldots + \mu_I DN_I + e_{it} \qquad \ldots(3)$$

The selection of fixed or random model, the analysis for consistency and efficiency depends basically on the nature of data used for analysis and the related tests. The details regarding model specification is described in the empirical section.

Data and Methodology

The data for the study is mostly drawn from Central Statistical Office (CSO). The data is at a single base price of the year 1999-2000, thus making the comparative analysis across the states more realistic. Due to the non-availability of separate data on the value of real estate construction and real estate business activity, the realty sector GSDP described in the study is defined as combined GSDP of construction industry and real estate, ownership of dwellings and business services. Construction industry, in India, for the purpose of estimating domestic product, has been taken to include the whole of construction activity (contractual as well as own account) and covers 45 construction activities which include development of infrastructure excluding demolition activity. Real estate, ownership of dwellings and business services cover major economic activities including: (i) ownership of dwellings (occupied residential houses), (ii) real estate services (activities of all types of dealers such as operators, developers and agents connected with real estate) and includes the imputed value of owner-occupied dwellings apart from other business services. The empirical analysis of the study followed a pooled regressive methodology to indentify relative changes in housing bank credit with respect to changes in the related macroeconomic variables such as income, availability of credit, and interest rate across these states. Despite the limitations of using banks' credit for the analysis of housing demand as it is highly urbanised in nature and may not be uniform across the states and is only one among sources of finance for housing, the study considered it due to the lack of reliable data on housing or similar parameters across the states.

The model has taken the data on state revenue from stamp duties and registration across the states as a proxy for movements in realty prices due to its likely positive relationship with the realty prices, assuming there is no understatement of prices despite differences in rates of duties and registration across the states. Since the period of analysis is restricted to the period from 1990 to 2008, the regression analysis may be subjected to the limitations arising from using less number of observations. The study also pursues various statistical tools to analyse the relative changes in variables related to the realty sector *vis-à-vis* the overall growth of these regional economies. The data for bank credit as well as housing credit and data on state revenue from registration and stamp duties and the data for interest rate which is the advance rate of SBI (as the biggest scheduled commercial bank) are taken from various RBI publications. It may be mentioned that although the interest rate (base rate) prevailing in the economy may be less than the advance rate of SBI (base rate + markup), the same was chosen under the consideration that it is the most likely representative of effective level of interest rate on housing credit for common public. The choice of the states for the study is in terms of their contributions to the national growth with a view to obtain the cross-section of the developments across the states (Table 16.1).

Table 16.1

Regional Trends in Economic Growth: Ranking of States

States	*Share to National GDP 1999-2000*	*Rank in Share to National GDP*	*Share to National GDP 2008-09*	*States*
Maharashtra	13.9	1	9.0	Maharashtra
Uttar Pradesh	9.8	2	5.5	Uttar Pradesh
West Bengal	7.6	3	5.1	Andhra Pradesh
Tamil Nadu	7.5	4	4.8	West Bengal
Andhra Pradesh	7.2	5	4.6	Tamil Nadu
Gujarat	6.1	6	4.3	Gujarat
Karnataka	5.7	7	3.7	Karnataka
Rajasthan	4.6	8	2.9	Rajasthan
Madhya Pradesh	4.5	9	2.7	Kerala
Kerala	3.9	10	2.4	Delhi
Punjab	3.8	11	2.4	Madhya Pradesh
Delhi	3.1	12	2.3	Haryana
Haryana	2.9	13	2.1	Bihar
Bihar	2.8	14	2.1	Punjab
Orissa	2.4	15	1.7	Orissa
Assam	1.9	16	1.1	Assam
Total share in national GDP	87.7		56.7	

Source: Central Statistical Office.

IV

Regional Dimensions of Economic Growth

The changes in the growth process during the period witnessed across the states enabled substantial growth of the regional economies reflected in higher per capita income growth. With the changes in the composition of growth as visible at the national level, the states also observed increased share of services in GSDP growth while the share of primary sector witnessed a decline across the states during the period. It has been observed that the states where steepest decline in the primary sector was registered also recorded highest increase in the share of services in their economic growth. Reflecting the increasing regional spread of industrialisation, the share of the secondary sector also witnessed reasonable increase in most of the states other than the traditionally industrialised states during the period. Among the select major states barring the Delhi with 83.5 per cent share of tertiary sector, Kerala recorded highest share with 62.6 per cent followed by Maharashtra and Tamil Nadu with 60.6 per cent each. However, the pace of growth of tertiary sector varied across the states (Figure 16.1).

Figure 16.1

Changes in Sectoral Shares: 2000-2008

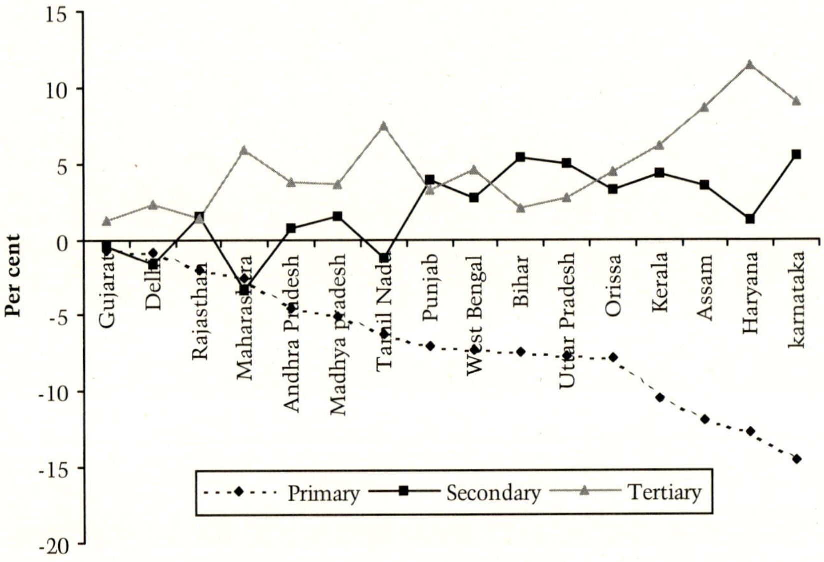

Source: Central Statistical Office (CSO).

The growth in per capita income as well as the growth in population either due to increase in total birth or increase in migrant population may push up the demand for real estate. The acceleration in growth driven by the structural changes is also reflected in the per capita income levels of the states. The per capita income is highest in case of Delhi though it may not be comparable with other major states. Among the major states barring Delhi, the highest level of per capita income was recorded by Haryana followed by Kerala as on 2008-09 (Table 16.2).

Table 16.2

Per Capita Income Levels: Ranking of States

(Amount in Rupees)

States	*1999-2000*	*Rank*	*States*	*2008-09*
Delhi	38913	1	Delhi	64819
Punjab	25631	2	Haryana	41896
Haryana	23222	3	Kerala	35457
Maharashtra	23011	4	Maharashtra	35033
Kerala	19461	5	Gujarat	33608
Tamil Nadu	19432	6	Punjab	33198
Gujarat	18864	7	Tamil Nadu	30652
Karnataka	17502	8	Karnataka	27526
West Bengal	15888	9	Andhra Pradesh	27362
Andhra Pradesh	15427	10	West Bengal	24720
Rajasthan	13619	11	Rajasthan	19708
Madhya Pradesh	12384	12	Orissa	18212
Assam	12282	13	Assam	16272
Orissa	10622	14	Madhya Pradesh	14918
Uttar Pradesh	9749	15	Uttar Pradesh	12637
Bihar	5786	16	Bihar	10206

Note: Per capita income in 1999-2000 prices.
Source: CSO.

Though per capita income level does not really provide the overall increase in income across the population, however, the changes in per capita level across the state definitely provides an indication of overall level of income growth during the period. Therefore, the changes in the per capita income across the states play a critical role in characterising the demand conditions prevailing in the regional economies. During the period under study, the increase in per capita income level was observed across the states reflecting the convergence of the regional growth in India (Figure 16.2).

Figure 16.2

Average Annual Growth in Per Capita Income

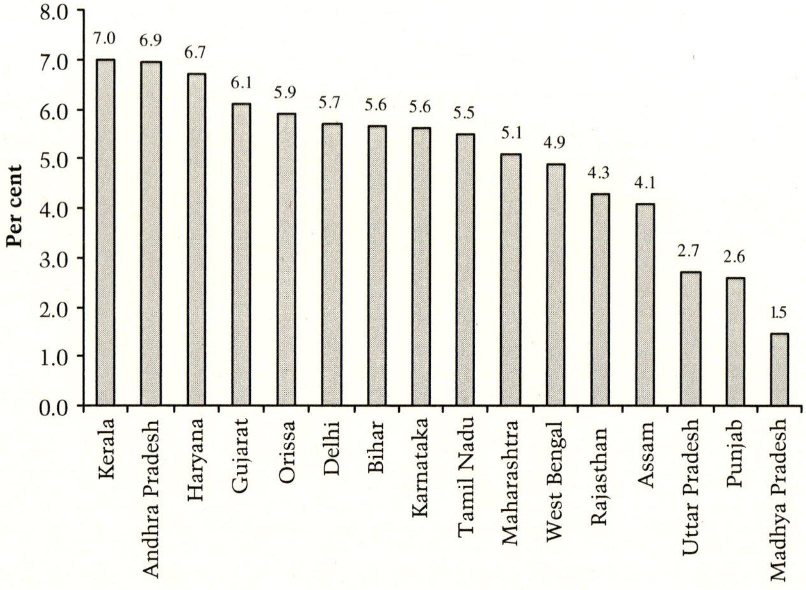

Source: CSO.

In the context of acceleration of growth of regional economies spearheaded by the structural changes in the composition of growth, the current study is an attempt to analyse the developments in realty sector in the above select regional economies in relation to the changes in the per capita income levels and the bank credit. As the per capita income and the credit availability are the major driving factors in determining the demand in realty sector, an analysis based on per capita income and bank credit *vis-à-vis* the developments in the realty sector may help in identifying the underlying demand conditions in the realty sector across the states.

Realty Sector GSDP and State Revenues

The size and the magnitude of realty sector across the states significantly contribute in analysing relative changes and their relationships of macroeconomic variables and the realty sector in particular with a regional dimension. Realty GSDP across the states witnessed substantial increase during the period leading to increased share of realty sector in the economic growth. With regard to the size of the realty sector across the select states in terms of its share in the economic growth, Kerala has the biggest realty sector followed by Delhi, Karnataka and Haryana (Figure 16.3).

Figure 16.3

Regional Dimension of Realty Sector Growth

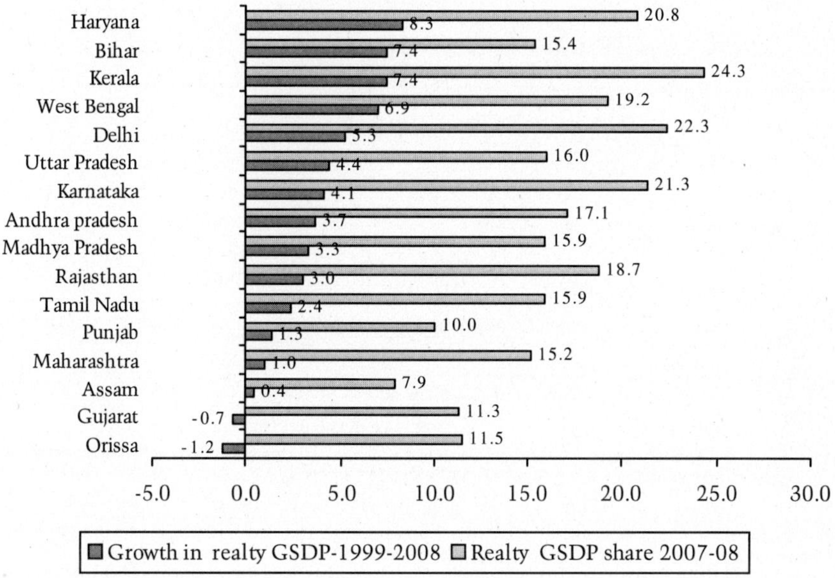

Source: CSO.

The determinants factored in changing the demand with regard to real estate, would be prices and income, same as in the case of any other goods envisaged by the demand theories. However, trends in real estate price across the states and within the state is highly varied due to the diversified nature of supply and demand forces driven by highly localised prospects. Therefore, the magnitude of the realty sector across the states is observable in terms of their share of revenue generated from the real estate business in the form of stamp duties and registration fees to the total all-India revenue generated in this regard. Accordingly, the magnitude of realty sector in terms of state's share in all-India total revenue generated, reveals that Maharashtra generates largest revenue from the realty sector in India (Figure 16.4).

Figure 16.4

Share in All-India Total Stamp Duties and Registration Revenue in 2009

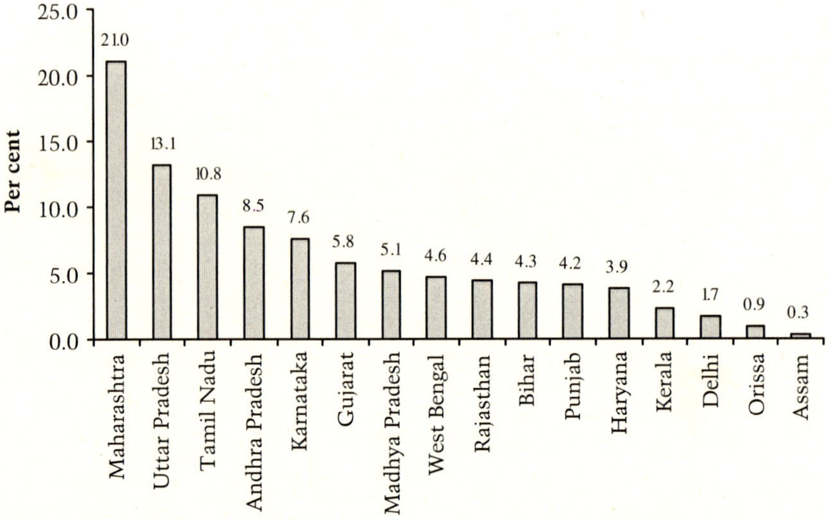

Source: RBI.

The differences in the rate of stamp duties and registration fees across the states may not be a significant factor in outlining the trends in the business activity in this sector as all the dealings in real estate are required to get officially registered for legal ownership of the assets irrespective of the rates prevailing in the states. In other words, it may be inferred that the revenue generation in terms of stamp duties and registration in the states to an extent reflects the underlying spurt in the demand situation in the realty sector across the regional level though there are limitations in analysing the revenue data due to the possibilities of understatement of values of assets and differences in rates in stamp duties and registration fees (Figure 16.5).

Realty Sector and Revenue Buoyancy

It is observed that the top major states recorded high growth in revenue from stamp duties and registration, particularly, Haryana, Karnataka, Tamil Nadu, Andhra Pradesh which witnessed increased investments either in services or industrial sectors and were changing themselves as centres of economic growth during the period (Figure 16.5).

Figure 16.5

Average Growth in State Revenue from Realty Sector

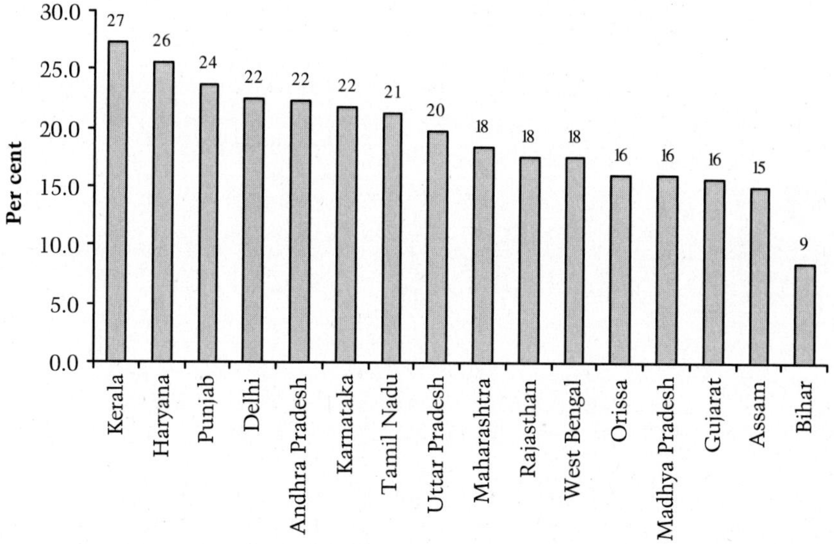

Source: RBI.

For analytical purpose, it may be useful to analyse revenue buoyancy that exists across the states which may help in identifying the concentration of real estate activity among the states relative to the changes in income. The states witnessed high revenue buoyancy measured as percentage change in revenue in the form of stamp duties and registration with respect to percentage changes in the income during the period 1999-2000 to 2009-10, ranging from 3.2 per cent in the case of Assam to 0.3 per cent in Bihar. This highlights that business activities in the realty sector in India is more or less broad-based as it is reflected in increased revenue generation in those states which are not traditionally known as realty heavy weights (Figure 16.6).

The increased revenue buoyancy across the states despite variations in tax rate across the states, reinstates the fact that realty sector developments were reflective of the growth observed and implies enhanced asset creation in the realty sector across the states during the high economic growth period of the Indian economy. The high revenue buoyancy across the states particularly in the low income category states may also underscore the level of convergence of realty sector growth achieved by the states during the period. The demand for housing in particular among high income group of population may be largely driven by speculative investment motive while the demand for housing among the low income group would be basically for direct consumption. In both the cases, the demand for housing is conditioned by the existing credit condition which plays a major determining role in fostering the realty sector in the country.

Figure 16.6

Stamp Duties and Registration: Revenue Buoyancy of States

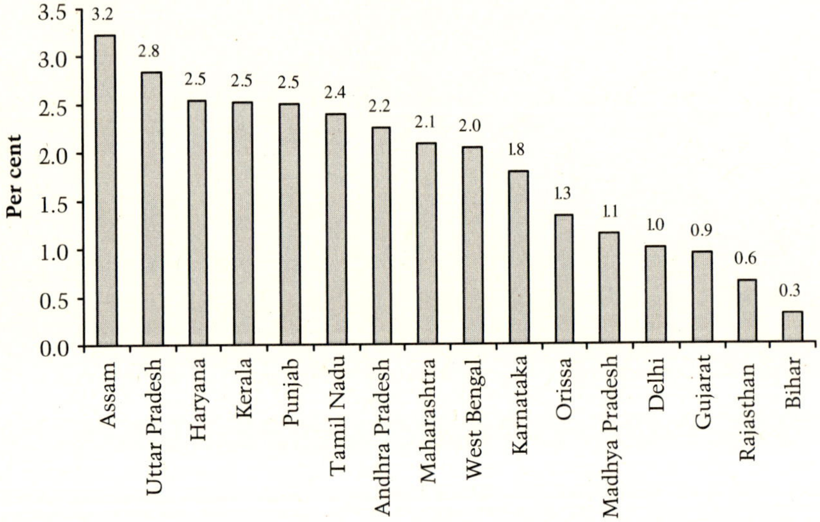

Source: RBI.

V

Regional Dimensions of Bank Credit Growth

The potential growth of credit could also influence the demand in the realty sector which may be for the purpose of investment in physical assets or for real housing consumption. The role of money and credit plays a major role in the determination of assets prices (Kindleberger, 1978). Many studies reinstated the role of credit on assets price bubbles in the backdrop of the burst of such bubbles unstabilising many economies at different periods of their economic history. India's high growth period during the second decade of reforms witnessed substantial growth in credit across the states. In the backdrop of the high level of real estate activity witnessed across the states, it would be appropriate to examine the trends in the flow of credit to this sector. Though per capita credit level does not provide much light on the real situation of the distribution of credit across the population but would reflect on the level of credit demand existing across the states. It is observed that the per capita income and bank credit growth witnessed sharp increase across the states during the period. However, the per capita credit distribution across the states is found to be skewed reflecting the variations in the level of credit absorptive capacity existing across the states. It is also observed that the growth of per capita bank credit outpaced the growth in the per capita income highlighting the role of bank credit in driving the demand conditions across the states (Figure 16.7).

Figure 16.7

Average Annual Growth: Per Capita Income and Credit

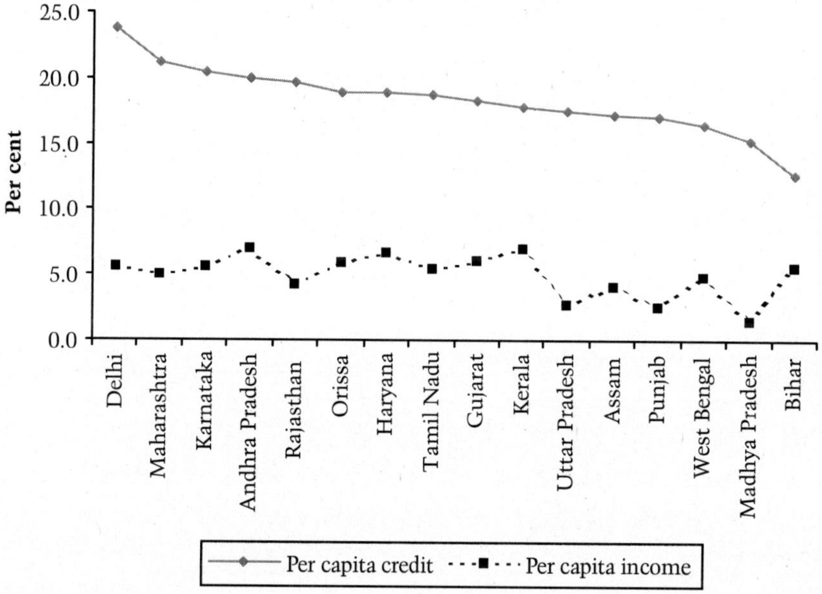

Source: CSO and RBI.

The growth in bank credit witnessed across the states prompts to examine the flow of credit towards the realty sector. The information on bank credit towards realty sector is available from the banking source in two forms, *viz.*, credit towards construction (wholesale credit) and the retail loans as personal loans for housing. The movements in both the credit flows could be viewed as response to the supply and demand conditions prevailing in various states owing to their characteristic end-use.

The emerging trends in the wholesale and retail bank credit and its geographical distribution reveals that most of the states apparently represent the pockets of increased realty sector activity driven by the growth in their industrial as well as services sector. In a regulatory perspective, the data also reveals the extent of concentration of wholesale and retail bank credit towards the realty sector. The pace of growth in the share of wholesale *vis-à-vis* retail bank credit highlights the underlying level of mobilisation of non-bank finance in the realty sector across the states. The recent trends in per capita income, housing credit as well as bank credit and the increased share of revenue generation from registration and stamp duties across the states reflect the accelerated real estate business activity across the states. Concomitantly, the share of realty sector to GSDP also showed a rise in the regional economic growth. It is observed that Kerala, Delhi, Karnataka, Haryana and West Bengal, respectively are

Table 16.3

Relative Growth in Credit and Realty Sector

	Shares							
	CC/BC		*HC/BC*		*BC/GSDP*		*REALTYGSDP/ GSDP*	
	2000	*2008*	*2000*	*2008*	*2000*	*2008*	*2000*	*2008*
Andhra Pradesh	0.9	11.6	6.2	12.3	25.3	91.1	13.6	17.3
Assam	2.4	3.0	6.5	12.5	10.5	30.6	8.4	7.6
Bihar	0.6	1.5	8.9	14.5	11.1	25.8	7.1	15.5
Delhi	2.4	8.7	2.4	6.9	135.0	351.3	20.5	22.3
Gujarat	1.6	6.8	4.2	8.5	26.8	62.2	12.0	11.3
Haryana	0.3	5.2	5.4	10.9	19.3	57.8	13.0	21.1
Karnataka	1.0	8.8	7.2	15.7	33.0	117.0	18.3	21.6
Kerala	1.3	2.8	10.4	22.4	26.1	61.7	17.4	25.3
Madhya Pradesh	0.7	3.1	6.5	11.1	20.5	51.8	14.3	15.9
Maharashtra	1.7	9.4	3.0	7.2	59.4	177.6	14.9	15.2
Orissa	0.5	3.5	8.6	12.8	14.8	46.9	13.1	11.5
Punjab	2.4	2.3	4.6	8.5	26.8	75.9	9.0	10.0
Rajasthan	0.4	4.0	8.0	10.8	16.9	55.5	15.7	18.6
Tamil Nadu	0.8	4.4	5.2	10.5	40.2	123.8	13.6	15.7
Uttar Pradesh	0.3	3.6	5.1	12.5	15.5	48.1	12.0	16.1
West Bengal	0.9	4.3	4.6	9.9	21.0	60.0	13.0	19.2

Notes: CC: Construction Credit, HC: Housing Credit, BC: Total Bank Credit, REALTYGSDP includes GSDP of construction industry and real estate services, GSDP: Gross State Domestic Product.

Source: Reserve Bank of India and CSO.

the top five states having large share of realty sector in their GSDP. However, the leading share of bank credit in their growth (GSDP) was attributed to Delhi, Maharashtra, Karnataka, Tamil Nadu and Andhra Pradesh. In terms of the share of construction credit to the total bank credit, Andhra Pradesh, Maharahstra, Karnataka, Delhi and Gujarat respectively are the leading states while accounting highest growth in whole sale credit to realty sector. The top states with highest share of retail housing loans in total bank credit are Kerala, Karnataka, Bihar, Orissa, Assam and Uttar Pradesh (Table 16.3).

The retail housing loans for the prospective buyers, in effect, may represent the underlying demand for credit for housing across the states. The commercial banks are one of the major institutions engaging in providing retail housing credit on a large scale basis. Its retail housing credit share is much higher than its share of wholesale credit in their total credit portfolio. The retail credit for housing which outpaced the bank credit growth across the states reflect the growing share of housing credit in total bank credit and the underlying the demand for housing across the states (Figure 16.8).

Figure 16.8

Outpace of Housing Credit and Increasing Housing Share

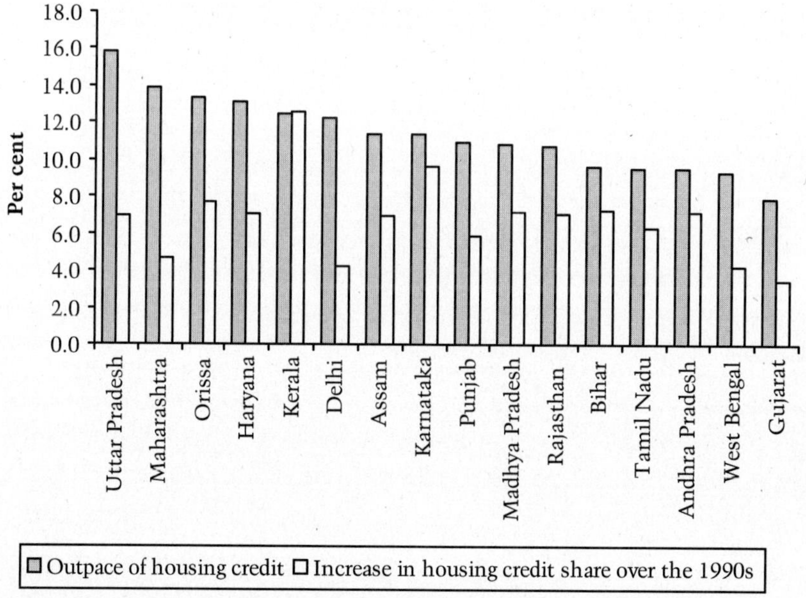

Source: RBI.

An Empirical Analysis on Housing Credit

Since the growth of retail credit for housing which outpaced the bank credit growth of the scheduled commercial banks across the states reflects the increase in share of housing credit in total bank credit across the states, it is imperative to understand the response of housing credit demand to relative changes in overall growth of bank credit, changes in income, prices and interest rate across the states. The study adopted a pooled regressive methodology to identify the relative significance of explanatory variables across the states during the period 1990 to 2008 which witnessed high growth in the Indian economy. The pooled regression model with explanatory variables could be given as follows:

$$Y_{it} = \alpha + \beta_1(pci_{it}) + \beta_2(sr_{it}) + \beta_3(r_t) + \beta_4(bca_{it}) + e_{it} \qquad ...(4)$$

where, Y is the independent variable housing credit of commercial banks represents housing credit demand, while the explanatory variables are (pci) the per capita income, (sr) state revenue from stamp duties and registration proxied for capturing price trends of real estate properties, (bca) credit availability indicated in terms of total scheduled commercial banks' credit normalised with respective net state domestic products of the states, (r) interest rate is the advance rate of State Bank of India, the largest commercial bank.

Regarding the testing of unit root hypothesis in a pooled cross-section time series, the power of the panel-based unit root test is higher compared to performing a separate unit root test for each individual time series (Levin *et al.*, 2002). The unit root tests statistics of tests Levin, Lin and Chu; Im, Pesaran and Shin W-stat; ADF and PP indicate that the null hypothesis is rejected, meaning that the 'residuals of the cross-sectional group' is stationary (Table 16.4).

As the growth and development characteristics of regional economies are highly diversified particularly under varied socioeconommic situations, exploring a linear relationship among the states in terms of the growth in realty sector, income and credit is quite cumbersome and subjected to limitations. In the panel data analysis in which the cross-sectional data is heterogeneous—of different states, a pooled OLS regression would not be sufficient to expalin whether all the states have a common intercept for the

Table 16.4

Pool Unit Root Test: Summary

Method	*Statistic*	*Prob.***	*Cross-Sections*	*Obs*
Null: Unit root (assumes common unit root process)				
Levin, Lin and Chu t*	-9.77904	0.0000	16	208
Null: Unit root (assumes individual unit root process)				
Im, Pesaran and Shin W-stat	-7.49685	0.0000	16	208
ADF - Fisher Chi-square	109.725	0.0000	16	208
PP - Fisher Chi-square	112.928	0.0000	16	208

Note: ** Probabilities for Fisher tests are computed using an asymptotic Chi-square distribution. All other tests assume asymptotic normality.

relationship among the regressors. Therefore, it is highly recommandable to go for fixed-effects or random effects model. Since the panel data under consideration is a balanced panel, model appropriate is with fixed-effects. However, the most common way to choose fixed *versus* random effects model would be to perform the Hausman test. However, the variance difference of the estimated coefficients provided by the Hausman test is set to zero. In this context, as the selection of states for the analysis is not based on random sampling and also the major share of the effects are idiosyncratic as provided by the Swamy and Arora (1972) estimator of component variances, the study followed the fixed-effects model. As compared to random effects model where the unobserved individual/time effects are attached to the common error; in the fixed-effects model, the effects are attached to the common intercept. The fixed-effects take the following functional form factoring the time invariant individual-specific effects of the unobserved variables to the dependent variable while it is constant across the states.

$$Y_{it} = \alpha + \beta_1(pci_{it}) + \beta_2(sr_{it}) + \beta_3(r_t) + \beta_4(bca_{it}) + \mu_i D1_{i+} \mu_i D2_i + ... + \mu_I DN_I + e_{it} \qquad ...(5)$$

The fixed-effects of the analysis shows whether the intercepts varies across the states as the individual-specific effects are attached to the common constant α highlighting the diversity in the growth process of realty sector across the states. This could be due to the fact that the heterogeneity in the attributes driving housing demand is strong particularly the taste and preferences of potential buyers governred by the different local socioeconomic situations existing across the states. However, the redundant tests fails to validate the presense of fixed-effects. This may be due to fact that the independent variable interest rate used in the model is common among cross-sections across the time periods nullifying both the effects. Therefore, the relationships among the variables in the model are illustrated by using the pooled least square method to make the analysis parsimonious despite its limitations.

It is observed from the pooled least square regressor coefficients that all the factors—income, prices, interest rate and credit availability are significantly affecting the demand for housing credit across the states. However, the most significant factor determing the demand for housing credit is the availability of credit as compared with the income, interest rate and price factors. Regarding the income effects, the relationship is found positive and significant but less than unity similar to the findings by Bandopadhyay *et al.*, 2008. As envisaged by theories, the interest rate relationship with the demand for housing credit is found negative and significant, while the relationship with price proxied variable remained significantly positive since housing is being considered as luxury good. In general, the regression estimate implies that one per cent change in bank credit availability, as defined in terms of share of bank credit in growth, induces 0.94 per cent increase in the demand for housing bank credit (Table 16.5).

Table 16.5

Demand for Housing Bank Credit

Variable	*Coefficient*	*Std. Error*	*t-Statistic*	*Prob.*
DLOG(HC?)				
C	0.101837	0.038320	2.657552	0.0085
DLOG(PCI?)	0.696457	0.324828	2.144077	0.0331
DLOG(SR?)	0.174130	0.096980	1.795518	0.0739
D(R?)	-0.039334	0.018765	-2.096119	0.0372
DLOG(BCA?)	0.947578	0.211935	4.471072	0.0000
R-squared 0.306791	Adjusted R-squared 0.294129		S.E. of regression 0.182779	
F-statistic 24.23049	Prob (F-statistic) 0.000000		Durbin-Watson stat 2.031035	

The empirical results show that during high income growth period which also witnessed enhanced asset creation in the realty sector across the states, among the factors affecting demand for housing credit, credit availability in terms of credit's share in growth, with positive relationship plays a major and significant role among the factors across the states and the findings are in line with the views expressed by many studies on role of credit in this regard. Further, the cross-section of credit coefficients indicates the role of credit is significant across the states implying that any excess growth in credit can accelerate the demand for housing credit. Therefore, any excess credit growth dispropotionate to the growth of the regional economies can inflate asset prices as well across the states (Table 16.6).

Supply Response: Emerging House Price Trends

The supply response to the increasing demand for housing may be traced from the movements in the housing prices as in the case of any other commodities. The RESIDEX was first launched in 2007 by the National Housing Bank (NHB) to provide an index of residential prices in India across cities and over time. RESIDEX is now being updated on a quarterly basis with 2007 as base year covering 15 cities. The movement in prices of residential properties showed a mixed trend among these 15 cities. Residential housing prices in 10 cities, *viz.*, Surat, Mumbai, Lucknow, Ahmedabad, Chennai, Pune, Kolkata, Patna, Faridabad and Bhopal showed an increasing trend while five cities , *viz.*, Jaipur, Bengaluru, Kochi, Delhi and Hyderabad witnessed some correction in prices in first half of 2010. (Figure 16.9).

Figure 16.9

Growth in House Price Index: 2008-2010

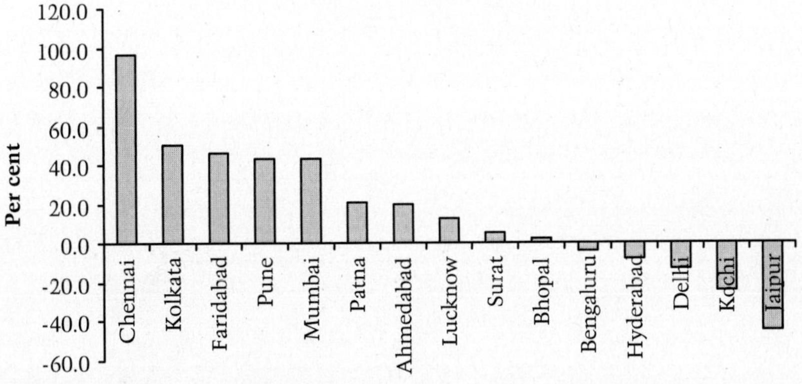

Source: National Housing Bank (NHB).

Table 16.6

The Cross-Section Effects of Demand for Housing Bank Credit: A Pooled Least Square Estimation

		Coefficient with Cross-Section Weights	*t-Statistic*	*Prob.*	*Coefficient with Time Period Weights*	*t-Statistic*	*Prob.*
	DLOG(HC?)						
	C	0.109759	3.033999	0.0027	0.079207	2.193309	0.0294
	DLOG(PCI?)	0.608922	1.643318	0.1019	0.730032	2.946577	0.0036
	DLOG(SR?)	0.122346	1.423517	0.1561	0.110440	1.354150	0.1772
	D(R?)	-0.040962	-2.153723	0.0324	-0.039111	-2.819750	0.0053
Andhra Pradesh	DLOG(BCA)	0.836653	4.566760	0.0000	1.059243	6.441733	0.0000
Assam	DLOG(BCA)	0.483592	2.525696	0.0123	0.580135	2.443301	0.0154
Bihar	DLOG(BCA)	1.005590	2.330957	0.0207	0.991897	2.847640	0.0049
Delhi	DLOG(BCA)	1.664547	4.802328	0.0000	1.632852	5.351586	0.0000
Gujarat	DLOG(BCA)	0.691116	2.490402	0.0136	0.974004	3.551171	0.0005
Haryana	DLOG(BCA)	1.230965	2.902868	0.0041	1.540224	3.707127	0.0003
Karnataka	DLOG(BCA)	1.063036	6.584802	0.0000	1.073201	7.641728	0.0000
Kerala	DLOG(BCA)	1.147516	4.350616	0.0000	1.304577	4.370455	0.0000
Madhya Pradesh	DLOG(BCA)	0.670111	3.622243	0.0004	0.873836	5.615314	0.0000
Maharashtra	DLOG(BCA)	1.323857	2.773968	0.0061	1.358712	4.146505	0.0000
Orissa	DLOG(BCA)	0.938751	1.851170	0.0656	1.241687	3.652838	0.0003
Punjab	DLOG(BCA)	0.328587	0.930795	0.3531	0.594574	1.794736	0.0742
Rajasthan	DLOG(BCA)	0.766958	3.428495	0.0007	0.984789	4.250525	0.0000
Tamil Nadu	DLOG(BCA)	0.781613	4.658642	0.0000	0.914131	4.874752	0.0000
Uttar Pradesh	DLOG(BCA)	1.516635	10.06714	0.0000	1.584948	11.41094	0.0000
West Bengal	DLOG(BCA)	1.017054	2.876735	0.0044	1.311860	4.439025	0.0000
		R-squared 0.393986 Adjusted R-squared 0.337544 S.E. of regression 0.176767 F-statistic 6.980315 Prob(F-statistic) 0.000000 Durbin-Watson stat 1.8027			R-squared 0.508480 Adjusted R-squared 0.462701 S.E. of regression 0.174956 F-statistic 11.10733 Prob(F-statistic) 0.000000 Durbin-Watson stat 1.925		

VI

Conclusion and Summary

The sharp and rapid movements of asset prices especially the realty prices poses systemic risks to financial as well as the economic system. As one of the fast-growing emerging economy, the asset price movement is bound to drive the growth momentum in various ways affecting the overall demand conditions. Therefore, it is imperative to monitor the asset price movement for the monetary policy deliberations. The asset price bubble is a serious monetary concern of the central banks across the globe in the post-global financial crisis scenario. In India, the policy developments during the post-reform period characterised by changes in structural composition and high income growth encouraged the realty sector activities though the factors stimulating the demand in realty sector may vary across the states. It is observed that the changes in the growth process witnessed across the states enabled substantial growth of the regional economies reflecting higher per capita income growth stimulating the demand conditions prevailing in the regional economies, and the changes in the level of per capita income was more broad-based reflecting the convergence of the regional growth in India.

The high income growth and the increased revenue generation from the realty sector observed across the states implies enhanced asset creation in the realty sector during the high economic growth period of Indian economy and underscores the convergence of growth in realty sector. The geographical distribution of the wholesale bank credit to the realty sector reveals that the top 10 states apparently represent pockets of increased realty sector activity driven by the growth in industrial sector as well as services sector especially information technology related growth witnessed by these states. The trends in house price index of major cities indicate low pace of supply response to the increasing demand for housing in India highlighting the critical role of realty sector in urban growth in India. It may be perceived that credit growth is reflective of underlying growth dynamics of Indian economy and may not be a cause for concern as long as asset prices do not contribute to inflation growth dynamics. The empirical results support the increased role of bank credit growth across the states underlining the outpace of housing credit witnessed across the states. This implies underlying extent of asset creation potential across the states due to the excess credit growth, disproportionate to growth of the respective regional economy. The outpace of housing credit across the states indeed warrants intense regulatory and supervisory surveillance in order to contain the effects of any plausible asset price distortions across the business cycles of the economy. Therefore, the policy implication is to curtail excess credit growth which distorts asset prices and whether to have threshold level of credit growth proportionate to the growth of regional economy across the states.

References

Allen, Franklin and Douglas Gale (2000). *Asset Price Bubbles and Monetary Policy*. The Wharton Financial Institutions Center, May.

Asian Development Bank (2008). *India: Housing Finance II Project*. Project Number IND 30204Loan Number: 1759-IND and 1761-IND,October 2008.

Bandopadhyay, Arindam, S.V. Kuvalekar, Sanjay Basu, Shilpa Baid and Ashish Saha (2008). "A Study of Residential Housing Demand in India; Munich Personal RepEc Archive", *MRPA Paper* No. 9339, June.

Bernanke, B. (2010). "Monetary Policy and the Housing Bubble", At the Annual Meeting of the American Economic Association, Atlanta, Georgia, January 3.

Cecchetti, S.G., H. Genberg, J. Lipsky and S. Wadhwani (2000). "Asset Prices and Central Bank Policy", *Geneva Report on the World Economy* 2, CEPR and ICMB.

Cecchetti, S.G., H. Genberg and S. Wadhwani (2002). "Asset Prices in a Flexible Inflation Targeting Framework", in W.C. Hunter, G.G. Kaufman and M. Pomerleano (eds.), *Asset Price Bubbles: The Implications for Monetary, Regulatory and International Policies*. MIT Press. pp. 427-44.

Cushman and Wakefield (2010). *Cushman and Wakefield India Real Estate Investment Report 2010: Riding the Wave—Re-emergence of Indian Realty Sector*. October.

European Central Bank (2008). "European Central Bank—House Prices, Money, Credit and the Macroeconomy", Charles Goodhart and Boris Hofmann *Working Paper Series*, No. 888/April 2008. *http://www.ecb.europa.eu or from the Social Science Research Network*

———. (2005). "Asset Prices Bubbles and Monetary Policy", *Monthly Bulletin*, April.

Gelfand, Jack E. (1970). "Mortgage Credit and Lower-Middle Income Housing Demand", *Land Economics* 46(2), May, University of Wisconsin Press. Available at *http://www.jstor.org/stable/3145174*

Joshi, H. (2006). "Identifying Asset Price Bubbles in the Housing Market in India: Preliminary Evidence", *Reserve Bank of India Occassional Papers* 27(1 & 2), Summer-Monsoon.

Kindleberger, C. (1978). *Manias, Panics, and Crashes: A History of Financial Crises*. New York, NY: Basic Books.

Levin, Andrew, Chien-Fu Lin, Chia-Shang James Chu (2002). "Unit Root Tests in Panel Data: Asymptotic and 'Finite-Sample Properties'", *Journal of Econometrics* 108 (2002): 1-24, *http://www.elsevier.com/locate/econbase*

Mahalik, Mantu Kumar and Hrushikesh Mallick (2009). "What Causes Asset Price Bubble in an Emerging Economy? Some Empirical Evidence in the Housing Sector of India", Annual Money and Finance Conference, Indira Gandhi Institute of Development Research, Mumbai, January 23-24. *http://www.igidr.ac.in/conf/money/mfc-11/index11.html*

Malpezzi, Stephen and Stephen K. Mayo (1998). "The Demand for Housing in Developing Countries: Empirical Estimates from Household Data", *Economic Development and Cultural Change* 35(4): 687-721. (July 1987).

Reserve Bank of India (2010). *Report of the Expert Group on Asset Price Monitoring System*. Reserve Bank of India, January.

Sahu, Basanta K. (2010). "Microfinance for Housing in India", Centre for Microfinance Research, (Main Centre), Bankers Institute of Rural Development (BIRD).

Swamy, P. and S. Arora (1972). "The Exact Finite Sample Properties of the Estimators of Coefficients in the Error Components Regression Models", *Econometrica* 40:261-75.

Tiwari, Piyush and Jyoti Parikh (1998). "Affordability, Housing Demand and Housing Policy in Urban India", *Urban Studies* 35(11): 2111-2129.

17 Debt Management Strategies in Uttar Pradesh and Uttarakhand

VINEET KUMAR SRIVASTAVA[1]

Introduction

The decade of 1990s witnessed the transition in the management of domestic debt towards market orientation and transparent practices both at the Central and state levels. The abolition of automatic monetisation through ad hoc Treasury Bills and system of Ways and Means Advances (WMA) to the Centre not only provided the operational autonomy to the Reserve Bank but also helped in the development of Government securities market. Based on the experience and market conditions, innovative strategies to place the state government debt also evolved. Management of domestic debt forms an integral part of fiscal discipline of the state governments. Debt sustainability assumes an intertemporal dimension in the context of the states, i.e., movements in the debt/GDP ratio, the primary deficit and the interest rate on the debt stock have to be monitored in terms of a sustainable path. Sustainability also depends on the extent of the development of the financial markets, which determines the absorptive capacity of the markets. The Twelfth Finance Commission (TFC) emphasised the need for fiscal discipline on the part of the states and suggested that the overall borrowing programme of a state should be within the prescribed limit, determined annually, taking into account borrowings from all sources. State governments have been gradually putting in place institutional mechanisms to contain the level of debt, also to bring it to a sustainable level by way of the enactment of Fiscal Responsibility Legislations (FRLs), setting up of Consolidated Sinking Fund (CSF),

1. Views expressed in the study are of the author and not of the institution to which he belongs.

Guarantee Redemption Fund (GRF) and placing ceilings on guarantees. The aggregate outstanding liabilities of the state governments as a percentage of GDP showed a persistent decline from the peak of 32.8 per cent in 2003-04 to 26.6 per cent in 2007-08. Notwithstanding the deterioration in key deficit indicators during the years 2008-09 and 2009-10, the debt-GDP ratio continued to decline and was placed at 23.1 per cent in 2010-11 (BE) as GDP grew faster than the debt. State governments of Uttar Pradesh and Uttarakhand also saw a gradual decline in their debt-GSDP ratio from 46.8 per cent and 42.8 per cent in 2008-09 to 43.5 per cent and 41.1 per cent in 2009-10, respectively.

Over the years, the state governments have taken various measures towards debt management *viz.*, market based market borrowings, setting up of CSFs, GRFs, imposing ceiling on guarantees and introduction of guarantee fees, Calamity Relief Fund (CRF), introduction of non-competitive bidding in the auctions of state development loans (SDLs), rationalisation of market borrowing schedule for raising resources in a planned manner, etc. Further, enactment of Fiscal Responsibility and Budget Management (FRBM) Act has also facilitated fiscal consolidation and more effective debt management. Besides, state governments have taken various measures to accelerate the fiscal consolidation through revenue augmentation and reduction of non-Plan expenditure. The period up to 2007-08 witnessed a considerable improvement in the consolidated fiscal position of state governments. States were given incentives by the Twelfth Finance Commission (TFC) to implement their own FRL in the form of conditional debt restructuring and interest rate relief. However, the economic slowdown following the knock-on effects of the global financial crisis and the accompanying moderation in the pace of revenue growth adversely affected the finances of the states during the last couple of years.

The composition of states' outstanding liabilities has witnessed a noticeable change in recent years. With the increasing emphasis on financing Gross Fiscal Deficit (GFD) through market borrowings, its share in outstanding liabilities of state governments has increased gradually, while the dependence on loans from the Centre declined sharply from 1999-2000 onwards. Besides market borrowing, National Small Savings Fund (NSSF) has also emerged as a predominant source of GFD financing. The gradual evolution of strategies adopted under the market borrowing programme of Uttar Pradesh and Uttarakhand reflects not only fiscal consolidation processes but also affirms the proactive approach of state governments towards debt sustainability.

The study attempts to evaluate the debt management strategies adopted by the states of Uttar Pradesh and Uttarakhand in the recent years. The effectiveness of the debt management strategies of these states have been analysed based on the recent performance in raising the resources under the market borrowing programme as well as a comparative analysis in respect of performance of major fiscal indicators in respect of the target set out by the TFC. Section I of the study highlights the conceptual issues relating to the debt management. A review of debt management policies of the state Governments in India highlighting the developments that took place during the last decade is presented in Section II. It will also account the findings and recommendations of the various committees/working groups set up by the Reserve Bank and the Government of India. The debt management strategies particularly in respect of market borrowings of the states of Uttar Pradesh and Uttarakhand is analysed in Section III. Finally, the concluding observations and recommendations are presented in Section IV.

I

Debt Management: Concepts and Evolving Strategies

Public debt management is the process of establishing and executing a strategy for managing the government's debt in order to raise the required amount of funding, achieve its risk and cost objectives and to meet any other sovereign debt management goals the government may have set, such as developing and maintaining an efficient market for government securities. In a broader macroeconomic context for public policy, governments should seek to ensure that both the level and rate of growth in their public debt is fundamentally sustainable, and can be serviced under a wide range of circumstances while meeting cost and risk objectives.

The Government securities market has generally increased in size across countries in tandem with the growing financing requirements of Government over the years. Notwithstanding the onset of fiscal consolidation processes and the consequent shrinking supply of issuances in the primary market in some countries in recent years, public debt managers have honed the development of government securities market through various measures. Several governments now raise funds through market-based mechanism in the transparent and predictable fashion. They have also strived to broaden the investor base for the issuances of government securities. The governments and central banks have adopted a strategy of jointly working with market participants to promote the development of the secondary market for government securities as also to establish sound clearing and settlement systems to handle transactions in government securities. While an abiding objective of public debt management in various countries has continued to be minimising the cost of government borrowings, a striking feature in the last two decades has been to pursue this objective with a focus particularly on managing risks inherent in the debt portfolio (IMF-World Bank, 2002).

The sizable subnational debt markets have begun to emerge in countries such as Argentina and Brazil (accounting for about 5 per cent of GDP); however, it remained embryonic in the vast majority of developing and transition countries. The contrast is especially striking in advance transition countries of Central Europe, where subnational debt markets typically remain below 0.5 per cent of GDP, despite considerable progress achieved in financial sector restructuring and privatisation and in capital market depending and diversification, and despite the growing demand for local infrastructure investment finance. Among developing and transition countries, Latvia provides an interesting example of a country that chose to virtually close down an emerging subnational debt market and revert to a centralised system of credit allocation to municipalities. Until the second half of the 1990s, local governments in Latvia had wide powers to borrow from domestic and foreign sources, under a well-structured prudential framework that supported the development of local government borrowings from private banks by providing a significant degree of regulatory clarity. There were no reported cases of defaults or litigations. However, tight fiscal policies, accompanied by a general distrust of the banking sector and an inclination towards a simple and direct control over local government finances, led to an effective ban on commercial borrowing from domestic banks in 1997. The new legislation required the municipalities to borrow from the Treasury and also subjected local borrowings from international banks and international financial institutions (IFIs) to the approval and sovereign guarantee from the Ministry of Finance. As a result, private lending to local governments virtually disappeared, and Treasury lending to local governments, mostly short-term, increased rapidly. In developing countries, there is a pending development clash between the rapidly increasing investment financing needs of subnational entities and the limited development of the domestic subnational debt market.

II

The financial sector reforms initiated in 1991 led to the introduction of auction system for market borrowings of the Central government. The auction system for the sale of Government of India medium and long-term securities was introduced from June 3, 1992. Since then, the Reserve Bank and the Government of India has undertaken series of measures to widen and deepen the government securities market. However, market oriented borrowings of state governments under the market borrowing programme started only in 2001-02 and complete shift to the market based borrowings took place in 2006-07. During the last decade, there has been a remarkable shift in the debt management strategies of the state governments.

Debt Management of State Governments

In terms of the Section 20 of the Reserve Bank of India Act, 1934, management of the public debt of the Government of India is vested with the Reserve Bank of India. Further, Section 21 A of the RBI Act provides that the bank may undertake the management of the public debt of the state governments by agreement with the government of any state. The matters relating to issuance, servicing, redemption of the government debt are governed effective from December 1, 2007 by the Government Securities Act, 2006 and Government Securities Regulations, 2007 framed thereunder (replacing the Public Debt Act, 1944 (PD Act) and the Public Debt Rules framed thereunder). In view of the sharp increase in the volume of the public debt and the changes in the external environment, some of the provisions of the Public Debt Act and the Rules thereunder were found to be onerous and, at times, impeded the further development of the debt market. Accordingly, the Government Securities Act, 2006 was enacted to replace the Public Debt Act, 1944 and repeal the Indian Securities Act,

1920. The Act proposes to consolidate and amend the law relating to issue and management of Government securities by the RBI. The Reserve Bank manages the debt of all the 28 state governments and union territory of Puducherry. Government of Puducherry entered into an agreement with the Reserve Bank on December 3, 2007 under Section 21A of the Reserve Bank of India Act that enabled the Reserve Bank to act as bankers to the Government of Puducherry and also their debt managers.

During the 1990s, the Reserve Bank used to complete the combined borrowing programme of all the states generally in two or more tranches through issue of bonds with a predetermined coupon and pre-notified amounts for each state (traditional tranche method). High statutory pre-emption in the form of Statutory Liquidity Ratio (SLR) and the small size of state government borrowings ensured the success of these primary issues. However, progressive reduction in SLR requirements which resulted in most banks having excess SLR securities in their investment portfolio and differing perceptions of individual states by the investor community required a move away from marketing state government loans using this method. This mechanism was reviewed in the context of financial sector reforms and to provide scope to better managed states to access funds at market rates. Accordingly, an option was made available to the state governments to enter the market individually to raise resources using the auction method or tap method (auction between 5 to 35 per cent of the allocated market borrowings, at the discretion of the state) in 1997. The first state to avail of the option of using the auction method was Punjab in January 1999. In February 1999, Andhra Pradesh, Goa and Uttar Pradesh mobilised resources through the Tap method (without notified amount).

Of the states that used the auction method, some were able to mobilise loans at competitive rates (at relatively lower spreads from the secondary market yield as compared with securities of the Central Government of similar residual maturity), whereas other states had to pay higher rates (about 30-68 basis points over comparable Central government securities). The major determinants of the spreads, apart from size and timing of issues are: (i) overall economic strength and prospects of the state; (ii) fiscal position and the overall indebtedness profile, including off-budget borrowings and contingent liabilities like guarantees of state governments; (iii) efforts to control indebtedness and (iv) the track record in honouring guaranteed commitments.

Some of the states preferred not to adopt the flexible auction method. For such states, borrowing through the traditional tranche method has been perceived as both preferable and cost-efficient. However, it was becoming difficult to complete the borrowing programme for the notified amounts. First, banks and financial institutions are increasingly linking their allocations to individual states depending on the track record of states in making payments in respect of their guaranteed bonds, servicing of loans taken by state-owned enterprises, etc. Second, most banks have exceeded their SLR requirement; and third, the choice of investing in government securities is increasingly based on factors such as liquidity, among others. To avoid the risk of under-subscription, the Tap Tranche method was introduced during 2001-02. Under this method, borrowings for all states together are raised, indicating a total targetted amount at a predetermined coupon but without notifying the amounts for individual states. The tap was normally kept open for 1-3 days and was closed as soon as the targetted amount was mobilised, or depending upon the decision taken by the state to close the tap. Under the traditional tranche method, pre-announced coupon was fixed at around 25 basis points over Central government securities of corresponding maturity. However, as interest rates fell sharply in 2000-01, and yield differences started emerging between liquid and illiquid Central government papers, it became difficult to complete the market borrowing programme of the states at these spreads. Since 2001, such spreads increased to around 50 basis points. Since 2006-07, the market borrowings of state governments have been raised entirely through the auction method.

In terms of Article 293(1) of the Constitution of India, the state governments can give guarantees within such limits as fixed by the legislature of the concerned state. While guarantees do not form part of debt, as conventionally measured, these have, in the eventuality of default, the potential of exacerbating an apparently sound fiscal system. Till 1993-1994, the public sector enterprises (PSEs) were getting a separate share of market borrowing (SLR linked). Since 1994-95, a separate allocation of market borrowing for PSEs were discontinued but allocation under approved market borrowing programme was continued to State Financial

Corporations (SFCs) and State Cooperative Agricultural and Rural Development Banks (SCARDBs) only. In continuation of the Government of India's policy to restrict the issuance of SLR securities under the market borrowing programme (MBP) only to the Central and the state governments through RBI, the market borrowing for the SFCs and SCARDBs were discontinued from the year 2003-04.

Based on the Ahluwalia Committee (2001),[2] a scheme for one-time settlement of outstanding dues of the State Electricity Board (SEBs) to Central Power Sector Undertakings (CPSUs) was finalised. Under the scheme, the state governments would issue 15-year Power bonds worth about Rs 32,000 crore to the CPSUs for the outstanding dues at a nominal tax-free interest rate of 8.5 per cent per annum repayable over 10 years after a moratorium period of five years. Subject to approval of RBI, 10 per cent of the bonds can be offloaded in the market each year for trading. The Tripartite Agreements (TPA), in this regard, were signed among the Government of India, the Reserve Bank of India and all the 28 state governments. The aggregate amount issued by 27 state governments (except Goa) amounted to Rs 31,581 crore. The repayment of these Power bonds started from the year 2006-07. Besides, state governments also borrowed in the past under the Debt Swap Scheme (DSS), Government of India permitted the state governments to prepay high cost debt exceeding Rs 1,00,000 crore (contracted at interest rates of 13 per cent or more) from the Centre between the financial year 2002-03 to 2004-05, partly out of fresh allocations under small savings collections and partly through fresh market borrowings. During 2004-05, as a one time measure, state governments also raised Rs 1,387 crore for the prepayment of Rural Infrastructure Development Fund (RIDF) loans to National Bank for Agriculture and Rural Development (NABARD). In order to meet the NSSF shortfall under the market borrowing programme, the state governments also raised large resources under the market borrowing programme in the recent past.

2. Report of the Expert Group on Settlement of SEB Dues (Chairman: M.S. Ahluwalia) submitted to the Ministry of Power on May 11, 2001 proposed for one time settlement linked with an arrangement to ensure payment of current SEB dues in future.

The reforms undertaken to develop the government securities market necessitated having a continuous dialogue between the issuer (Central and state governments) and the debt manager (Reserve Bank of India). The Reserve Bank of India started a biannual conference of State Finance Secretaries in November 1997. These biannual conferences, over the years, have become a useful forum for interaction among finance secretaries of the states and senior officials of the Ministry of Finance, Government of India, Planning Commission and the Reserve Bank of India. In the current context of reforms in the financial sector, the importance of interaction between the debt and cash manager and the state governments assumes critical importance. The ongoing process of development of institutions, markets, instruments and technology and the integration among the market segments have several ramifications. This has facilitated a quick transmission of monetary policy signals across the various segments of the market and maturity spectrum and in lowering the transactions costs of resource mobilisation. Further, the process of integration of market segments also accelerated the pace of contagion from one segment to the other with implications on financial stability. Over the period, the Conference has witnessed a host of reform measures recommended towards effective debt management through a process of constant dialogue. The important measures undertaken during the last decade are set out below:

Market Borrowings of State Governments

Since 1998-99, the state governments have the flexibility of raising 5 to 35 per cent of their market borrowings through the auction route. In 2001, a decision was taken to raise resources for all the states put together without notifying state-wise targetted amount. However, states could also go to the market individually for 'tap issue'. In 2003, the tenure of the loans was elongated up to 13 years in order to space out the redemption pressure. The Reserve Bank, in its *Annual Policy Statement* for the year 2006-2007, proposed that the 'state governments may be encouraged to progressively increase the share of market borrowings under auction route with a view to covering the entire market borrowings through auctions as early as possible.' Accordingly, since the financial year 2006-07, the market borrowings of state governments have been raised entirely through the auction method.

Consolidated Sinking Fund (CSF)

In the first conference held on November 8, 1997 the need for creation of CSF at state level to facilitate smooth and timely repayments of their market borrowings and also to strengthen the confidence of investors in state loans was discussed. The decision of setting up of the CSF was made optional for the state governments with contribution of 1 to 3 per cent of the outstanding open market borrowings as at the end of previous year. Twenty states have set up the fund so far.

Guarantees by the State Governments

Recognising the growing magnitude of guarantees issued by state governments and their potential impact on the future fiscal position of the states, the need to have a policy on guarantees was felt in the interest of prudent financial management and the credibility of the guarantees issued. Based on decision taken in the first conference of State Finance Secretaries held on November 8, 1997, a Technical Committee of the Finance Secretaries to examine the issue of state government guarantees was constituted. The recommendations made by the Committee (February 1999) related to, *inter alia*, (i) imposition of ceiling on guarantees, (ii) selectivity in calling for and providing of guarantees, (iii) greater transparency in the reporting of guarantees and standardisation of documentation, (iv) rationalisation of guarantee fees and constitution of a contingency fund for guarantees, (v) avoidance of automatic debit mechanism and (vi) monitoring and honouring of guarantees.

The Reserve Bank also constituted a Group to assess the fiscal risk of state government guarantees in 2001. The Group recommended, among others, that: (i) guarantees to be met out of budgetary resources should be identified and treated as equivalent to debt, (ii) for other guarantees, projects/activities need to be classified and assigned appropriate risk weights, accordingly guarantees should be mapped and classified into very low, low, medium and high risk categories to assess the devolvement probability, (iii) Central financial institutions should amend their Acts/ policies and do away with the practice of insisting on guarantees, (iv) there should be regular publication of data regarding guarantees in budget documents, (v) state level tracking unit for guarantees should be set up and

(vi) at least one per cent of outstanding guarantees to be transferred to the GRF each year specifically to meet the additional fiscal risk. Technical assistance has been given by RBI to states in setting up GRF and managing these funds on behalf of the states. So far, the GRF has been set up in 14 states.

Indicative Calendar for Market Borrowings of State Governments

The *Annual Policy Statement* for the year 2006-07 proposed, *inter-alia*, that 'states, at their discretion and initiative, would be encouraged to develop an advance indicative open market borrowing calendar'. In order to initiate a step towards greater transparency in market borrowings of state governments in a progressive manner, the Reserve Bank has been issuing a Press Release on Market Borrowings of state Governments detailing net allocation, maturities, amount raised and the amount that could be raised during the remaining period of the financial year since 2007-08, in consultation with Government of India.

Re-Issuance of State Development Loans (SDLs)

Reserve Bank, in its *Annual Policy Statement* for the year 2007-08, proposed that the Reserve Bank, in consultation with the state governments, would introduce a system of re-issuance. The re-issuing of SDLs may be introduced in case a request from the state Governments is received.

Scheme of Non-Competitive Bidding Facility in the Auctions of SDLs

A scheme for Non-Competitive Bidding Facility was introduced since the auction of SDLs held on August 25, 2009 in order to widen the participation of retail investors. Under the scheme, up to 10 per cent of the notified amount of SDLs is allotted to individuals and institutions, subject to a maximum of one per cent of the notified amount for a single bid per stock.

III

An Analysis of Debt Management Strategies of Uttar Pradesh and Uttarakhand

With the implementation of recommendations of Twelfth Finance Commission, the year 2005-06 marked a watershed in the evolution of state finances and debt management. During 2005-06, 48.5 per cent of the total market borrowings were raised through the auction route as compared to 2.3 per cent in 2004-05. The moderation in fiscal imbalances and enactment of FRL facilitated the smooth transition to the conduct of entire open market borrowings by the auction route since 2006-07. The borrowings of the state governments have been by way of plain vanilla fixed coupon securities. The tenure of the bond is usually 10 years though securities with tenure of 11-13 years also issued in the past. The longish maturity of the state governments has protected the state government balance sheet from the refinance risk. Since the 10-year segment is the most liquid segment of the yield curve reflecting the good demand from the market and thus the illiquidity premium is minimised.

The market borrowings of Uttar Pradesh and Uttarakhand reflect higher borrowings during 2002-03 to 2004-05 due to Debt Swap Scheme (DSS) (Table 17.1). The higher level of market borrowings since 2008-09 onwards is reflective of stimulus push during the financial crisis.

The outstanding SDLs of Uttar Pradesh increased significantly from Rs 13,449 crore at end-March 2001 to Rs 68,013 crore at end-March 2011 (Table 17.2). The share of outstanding SDLs of Uttar Pradesh, however, declined from 15.5 per cent in 2000-01 to 11.2 per cent in 2010-11. The share of outstanding SDLs of Uttarakhand increased from 0.74 per cent to 1.34 per cent during the period.

Table 17.1

Market Borrowings of Uttar Pradesh and Uttarakhand

(Rs crore)

Year	*Uttar Pradesh*			*Uttarakhand*		
	Gross	*Repayment*	*Net*	*Gross*	*Repayment*	*Net*
2000-01	1490		1490	79		79
2001-02	2449	264	2185	212	14	198
2002-03	3237	299	2938	950	16	934
2003-04	5729	300	5429	1366	41	1325
2004-05	4060	748	3312	309	40	269
2005-06	3096	1034	2062	568	55	513
2006-07	3248	979	2269	369	52	317
2007-08	4422	1791	2631	830	95	735
2008-09	12693	2397	10296	1011	127	884
2009-10	13877	2634	11243	600	140	460
2010-11	12000	2011	9989	992	16	976

Source: Reserve Bank of India.

Table 17.2

Outstanding State Development Loans: End-March 2011

(Rs crore)

Year	*Uttar Pradesh*	*Uttarakhand*	*All States*
2000-01	13,449	646	86,767
2001-02	15,620	858	1,04,027
2002-03	18,518	1,808	1,33,066
2003-04	23,123	3,208	1,79,917
2004-05	26,435	3,443	2,13,480
2005-06	28,498	3,949	2,28,925
2006-07	30,759	4,266	2,42,777
2007-08	33,389	5,001	2,98,508
2008-09	43,686	5,885	4,01,924
2009-10	52,992	6,952	5,17,408
2010-11	68,013	8,112	6,05,806

Source: Reserve Bank of India.

The maturity profile of State Development Loans (SDLs) reflects higher redemption load towards long-term bucket (Table 17.3). In respect of Uttar Pradesh and Uttarakhand, the share of SDLs with more than seven years residual maturity amounted to 56.4 per cent and 39.5 per cent, respectively, at end-March 2010. This is mainly due to large market borrowings on account of debt swap scheme and NSSF shortfall in the last 6-7 years through the issuances of mostly 10-year bonds.

Table 17.3

Maturity Profile of SDLs of Uttar Pradesh and Uttarakhand

(Per cent)

Profile/Years	*Uttar Pradesh*	*Uttarakhand*	*All States*
0-1 Years	3.51	1.61	3.03
1-3 Years	11.35	18.76	10.20
3-5 Years	12.62	16.91	12.69
5-7 Years	16.10	24.26	12.93
Above 7 Years	56.42	39.46	61.14

Source: Reserve Bank of India.

The redemption profile of SDLs of Uttar Pradesh and Uttarakhand in the next six years will be comparatively higher due to the repayment of bonds issued under debt swap scheme during 2002-03 to 2005-06 (Table 17.4). Besides, the redemption of Power bonds will continue till 2016-17.

Table 17.4

Redemption Profile of State Government Securities

(Rs crore)

Year	*Uttar Pradesh*	*Uttarakhand*	*All States*
2011-12	3,025	212	21,989
2012-13	3,237	950	30,628
2013-14	2,946	764	32,079
2014-15	3,988	309	33,384
2015-16	4,699	1,170	35,191
2016-17	4,146	369	31,522

Source: Reserve Bank of India.

The cost of borrowings of state government securities is determined by various factors *viz.*, fiscal discipline, sustainability indicators of indebtedness and overall economic strength of the state. In the traditional tranche method, the coupon of SDLs used to be fixed at 25 basis points (later raised to 50 basis points) higher than the secondary market yield of comparative Central government securities. However, with the gradual shift towards the auction route for raising resources under the market borrowing programme, the spread has a tendency to decline reflecting the better price discovery due to ongoing development in the government securities market and also improvement in the state government liquidity in the secondary market. The higher spread between the average cut-off rate and the weighted average yield of 10-year government securities in the secondary market during 2009-10 and 2010-11 was mainly due to very high market borrowings by the state governments (Table 17.5).

Table 17.5

Weighted Average Cut-Off in the Auctions of SDLs of Uttar Pradesh and Uttarakhand

(Per cent)

Year	*Weighted Average Cut-off Yield*		*10-Year G–Sec. Yield (Weighted Average)*	*Spread for Uttar Pradesh (2)-(4)*	*Spread for Uttarakhand (3)-(4)*
	Uttar Pradesh	*Uttarakhand*			
2001-02	9.25	9.39	8.69	0.56	0.70
2002-03	7.22	6.51	6.89	0.33	-0.38
2003-04	6.12	6.18	5.47	0.65	0.71
2004-05	6.47	6.16	6.29	0.18	-0.13
2005-06	7.67	7.72	7.16	0.51	0.56
2006-07	8.17	8.18	7.78	0.39	0.40
2007-08	8.18	8.18	7.88	0.30	0.30
2008-09	8.43	7.90	7.59	0.84	0.31
2009-10	8.19	7.79	7.32	0.87	0.47
2010-11	8.37	8.48	7.91	0.46	0.57

Source: Reserve Bank of India.

In the last decade, there has been a remarkable shift in composition of outstanding liabilities of Uttar Pradesh and Uttarakhand. The share of market borrowings increased considerably while loans and advances from the Centre has declined. The share of market borrowings in financing of the fiscal deficit of the states increased significantly from 15.1 per cent of total outstanding at end-March 2002 to 31.6 per cent at end-March 2010. In Uttar Pradesh and Uttarakhand, it increased from 16.3 per cent and 17.1 per cent at end-March 2002 to 24.0 and 38.2 per cent at end-March 2010, respectively (Table 17.6).

Table 17.6

Comparative Shift in the Composition of Outstanding Liabilities of Uttar Pradesh and Uttarakhand

(Rs crore)

Items	2001-02			2009-10		
	Uttar Pradesh	Uttarakhand	All States	Uttar Pradesh	Uttarakhand	All States
SDLs	15,620	858	1,04,027	52,992	6,952	5,17,408
Compensation and other bonds	-6	0	59	3,817	372	18,784
NSSF	10,804	592	90,226	40	2	80
WMA from RBI	777	0	9,419	45,979	4,767	4,40,942
Loan from LIC	18	2	5,085	-31	202	1,685
Loan from GIC	0	0	0	-37	1	10,096
Loan from NABARD	857	24	8,969	71	5	927
Loan from SBI and other banks	1,352	31	7,139	2,910	846	40,347
Loan from NCDC	13	1	1,622	2,811	36	8,127
Loan from other institutions	0	0	0	-22	44	1,907
Other loans	177	-13	18,078	4,393	458	24,664
Loan from banks and FIs	2,417	46	40,894	10,126	1,390	86,068
Total internal debt	29,612	1,496	2,44,625	1,12,923	13,685	10,64,965
Loan and advances from Centre	36,044	1,850	24,9551	20,246	495	1,56,311
Provident fund etc	9,816	585	1,03,815	33,749	2,245	1,98,190
Reserve funds	9500	372	27,389	29,977	223	82,846
Deposit and balances (net balances)	11,642	714	64,325	23,866	1,468	1,31,610
Contingency funds	-793	1	1,042	346	100	2,480
Outstanding liabilities	95,822	5,018	6,90,747	2,21,106	18,216	16,36,403

Source: Reserve Bank of India, *State Finances: A Study of Budgets*, various issues.

The share of market borrowings as a percentage of GSDP for Uttar Pradesh increased from 8.2 per cent in 2001-02 to 12.9 per cent in 2010-2011. The share of loans from the Centre, however, declined from 10.0 per cent to 3.9 per cent during the period. The total liabilities of Uttar Pradesh as a percentage of GSDP declined from 43.6 per cent in 2001-02 to 38.7 per cent in 2010-11 (Table 17.7 and Figure 17.1). The share of small savings as a percentage of GSDP showed a decline in the recent past and ranged between 10-11 per cent, the share of provident and pension fund increased consistently from 6.6 per cent in 2008-09 to 7.9 per cent in 2010-11.

Table 17.7

Outstanding Liabilities of Uttar Pradesh
(As Percentage of GSDP)

Year	*Market Borrowings*	*Small Savings*	*Loans from FIs*	*Power Bonds*	*Loans from Centre*	*Provident and Pension Fund*	*Deposit and Advances*	*Other Liabilities*	*Total Liabilities*
2001-02	8.2	12.5	1.4		10.0	8.6	2.9	0.004	43.6
2002-03	9.0	12.8	1.1		10.3	8.5	2.7	0.003	44.1
2003-04	10.5	11.8	3.6		10.09	8.1	2.7	0.003	46.9
2004-05	10.0	11.8	3.4	2.4	10.35	8.4	2.4	0.003	48.7
2005-06	10.3	13.2	1.4	2.1	8.57	7.6	3.4	0.01	46.6
2006-07	9.9	14.1	1.3	1.8	7.50	7.6	2.3	0.01	44.5
2007-08	9.7	12.7	1.4	1.4	6.14	7.0	4.4	0.02	42.7
2008-09	10.9	11.0	1.3	1.0	5.08	6.6	3.3	0.01	39.2
2009-10	12.1	10.5	1.2	0.8	4.51	7.3	3.5	0.01	40.0
2010-11	12.9	9.6	1.2	0.6	3.99	7.9	2.5	0.01	38.7

Source: Budget Documents of Government of Uttar Pradesh.

Figure 17.1

Composition of Outstanding Liabilities of Uttar Pradesh (End-March 2011)

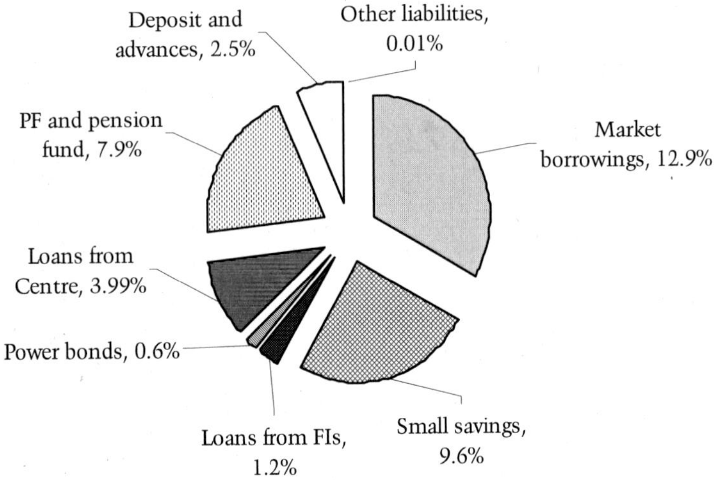

Keeping in view the sustainability of growing outstanding liabilities, the Twelfth Finance Commission had recommended following targets to be achieved by the states in a short-term period:

(i) Debt–GDP ratio of 30.8 per cent to be achieved by the states at end-March 2010.

(ii) Overall caps on the borrowing at 3.0 per cent of GSDP to be achieved by the state governments by end of 2009-10.

(iii) Ratio of interest payments to revenue receipts at 15 per cent to be achieved by 2009-10.

The debt relief mechanism prescribed by Twelfth Finance Commission, incentivised by the adherence to the rule based fiscal regime by the states has helped in containing the magnitude of outstanding liabilities. The outstanding liabilities of Uttarakhand increased significantly immediately after the formation of the state in 2000. The share of total liabilities as a percentage of GSDP increased from 2.7 per cent in 2001-02 to 35.6 per cent in 2010-11 (Figure 17.2).

Figure 17.2

Outstanding Liabilities as Percentage of GSDP

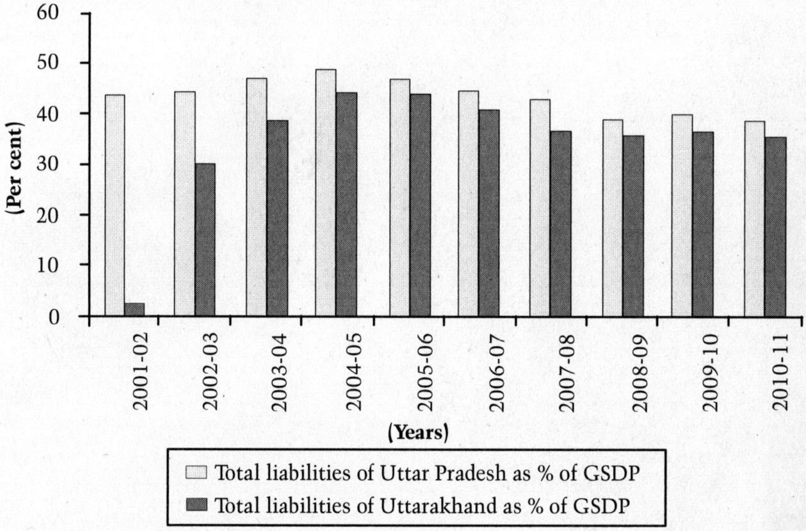

However, the debt-GSDP ratio of both states continued to be above the prescribed ceiling of 30.8 per cent set by the Twelfth Finance Commission (Table 17.8). In Uttar Pradesh, the interest payment as percentage of revenue receipts declined in the recent years while in Uttarakhand it continued to be around 13.0 per cent. In both the States, the interest payment as a percentage of revenue receipts is well within the prescribed target by the TFC. Since the market borrowings constitute the major share in the total borrowings of the state governments, the overall cap of 3 per cent of GSDP on borrowings, as recommended by TFC, is considered here only for the market borrowings. In Uttar Pradesh, market borrowings as a percentage of GSDP declined consecutively over the last three years and stood at 2.3 per cent at end-March 2011 as against 3.2 per cent at end-March 2009. In case of Uttarakhand, the share of market borrowings declined from 1.9 per cent as at end-March 2009 to 0.9 per cent at end-March 2010 but increased to 1.4 per cent at end-March 2011. The share of market borrowings of both the states as a percentage of GSDP are within the prescribed ceiling set out by the TFC.

Table 17.8

Select Indicators of Debt Sustainability

(Per cent)

Year	Total Liabilities as % of GSDP		Interest Payment as % of Revenue Receipts		Market Borrowings as % of GSDP	
	Uttar Pradesh	Uttarakhand	Uttar Pradesh	Uttarakhand	Uttar Pradesh	Uttarakhand
2008-09	39.2	36.0	13.4	13.0	3.2	1.9
2009-10	40.0	36.7	11.5	13.3	3.1	0.9
2010-11	38.7	35.6	11.1	13.0	2.3	1.4

Source: Budget Documents of Government of Uttar Pradesh and Uttarakhand.

IV

Conclusion

There has been remarkable improvement in the debt management of state governments over the last decade. With the implementation of the recommendations of TFC and RBI's consistent efforts in sensitising state governments, the market borrowings have been done through the auction system since 2006-07. As a result, the practice of providing commission to the banks/other investors in the SDLs raised through 'tap method' was discontinued since July 2008. Further, with a view to widen the participation, the scheme of non-competitive bidding in the auction of SDLs was also introduced in the 2009-10. The process of planning the market borrowings of state governments in pre-decided phase has reduced the number of tranche of market borrowings so that the lot size of scrip will increase for improving the liquidity in the secondary market. However, there are certain issues that need to be considered.

SDLs are usually issued for tenure of 10 years. This is in contrast to the maturity profile of Central government securities. The tenure of Central government securities extends up to 30 years. The SDLs are held primarily by the commercial banks, pension/provident funds and insurance companies. Pension/provident funds and insurance companies prefer to hold securities of longer tenure as their liabilities are long-term in nature.

Progressive elongation of tenure of SDLs would attract larger investments from pension/provident funds and insurance companies.

There is a gap in the yields on state government securities relative to the Central government securities of similar maturities. Further, there are even differences in yields across the state governments which mainly reflects the perspective of investors about the financial health of the respective states. Credit rating on state government securities would work as an indirect measure of market discipline and would also promote transparency. It would also help investors in taking appropriate pricing decisions. State governments may explore the feasibility for credit rating of their SDLs, which would enable them to raise the borrowings at competitive rates.

Lack of liquidity in secondary market for SDLs with the dominance of traditional buy-and-hold investors is an important issue. Liquidity of SDLs would provide an avenue for easy entry and exit for the market players that would not only attract new classes of investors thereby contributing to the primary market absorption of larger volumes of SDLs, but also lower the relatively high liquidity premium resulting in the improved pricing of SDLs. The Working Group on Liquidity of State Government Securities (2005) suggested various measures to improve liquidity in state government securities. In order to address the issue of fragmentation of SDLs across the states and maturities by building up volumes to ensure a critical minimum mass for secondary market liquidity, the Group suggested the following options: (i) increasing issue size, (ii) consolidation of securities, (iii) increasing the share of market borrowings and (iv) securitisation of SDLs. Development of secondary market for state government securities are critical to the size of the securities. State governments may introducc re-issuances of SDLs for consolidation. Further, in order to help the market participants to plan the market borrowings in advance, an auction calendar of state government securities, in lines of Central government, could help better price discovery.

References

Ahluwalia, M.S. (2000). "Economic Performance of States in Post Reforms Period", *Economic and Political Weekly* 35(19): 1637-1648.

Annual Report of RBI (various issues).

Fardoust, S. and A.K. Lahiri (2003). "Indian States the Road to Reform", in S. Howes, A.K. Lahiri and N. Stern (eds.), *State Level Reforms in India: Towards More Effective Government*. New Delhi: Macmillan.

IMF-World Bank (2002). *Guidelines for Public Debt Management.*

Ma, J. (2002). "Monitoring Fiscal Risks of Sub national Governments: Selected Country Experiences", in P.H. Brixi and A. Schick (eds.), *Government at Risk: Contingent Liabilities and Fiscal Risk*. Washington, DC: The World Bank. pp. 393-418.

Ministry of Power (2001). *Report of the Expert Group on Settlement of SEB Dues.* (Chairman: M.S. Ahluwalia). Government of India.

Noel, M. (2000). "Building Sub national Debt Markets in Developing and Transition Economies", *Policy Research Working Paper* 2339, The World Bank.

Petersen, J.E. (2001). "Sub national Debt, Borrowing Process, and Creditworthiness", *mimeo*, World Bank Institute.

Prasad, A., R. Goyal and A. Prakash (2004). "States Debt and Debt Relief", *Economic and Political Weekly* 39(26): 2726-37.

Reddy, Y.V. (2001). "Primary Dealers, Debt Markets and State Finances: Challenges and Responses", Speech at a seminar organised by Primary Dealers Association of India at Bangalore, September.

RBI (1999). *Report of the Technical Committee on State Government Guarantees.* Reserve Bank of India. February.

———. (2001), *Report of the Group to Assess the Fiscal Risk of State Government Guarantees.* July.

———. (2005). *Working Group on Liquidity of State Government Securities.* (Chairman: V. K. Sharma). September.

———. *State Finances: A Study of Budgets* (various issues).

Shah, A. (2004). *Fiscal Decentralisation in Developing and Transition Economies: Progress, Problems and Promise.*

World Bank (2005). *State Fiscal Reforms in India: Progress and Prospects.* New Delhi: Macmillan India Ltd.